Urban Exile

Urban Exile

Theories, Methods, Research Practices

EDITED BY

Burcu Dogramaci, Ekaterina Aygün, Mareike Hetschold, Laura Karp Lugo, Rachel Lee and Helene Roth

intellect

Bristol, UK / Chicago, USA

First published in the UK in 2023 by
Intellect, The Mill, Parnall Road, Fishponds, Bristol, BS16 3JG, UK

First published in the USA in 2023 by
Intellect, The University of Chicago Press, 1427 E. 60th Street,
Chicago, IL 60637, USA

A catalogue record for this book is available from
the British Library.

Copy editor: MPS Limited
Cover designer: Aleksander Szumlas
Cover image: Helene Roth, *18°55'17.9"N 72°49'59.8"E //
40°46'17.8"N 74°00'10.1"W*, 2019/2022 (© Helene Roth, 2022).
Production manager: Laura Christopher
Typesetter: MPS Limited
Translations and editing: Jennifer Leetsch
Editorial assistance: Maya-Sophie Lutz

Print ISBN (Hbk) 978-1-78938-712-4
Print ISBN (Pbk) 978-1-78938-767-4
ePDF ISBN 978-1-78938-713-1
ePUB ISBN 978-1-78938-714-8

To find out about all our publications, please visit our website.
There you can subscribe to our e-newsletter, browse or download our current
catalogue and buy any titles that are in print.

www.intellectbooks.com
This is a peer-reviewed publication.

This project has received funding from the European Research Council (ERC) under
the European Union's Horizon 2020 research and innovation programme (grant
agreement No. 724649).

Contents

Encountering Urban Exile: Theories, Methods, Research Practices – An Introduction

Burcu Dogramaci, Ekaterina Aygün, Mareike Hetschold, Laura Karp Lugo, Rachel Lee and Helene Roth

The German paperback edition of the book *Escape to Life* by Erika and Klaus Mann shows a photograph of Albert Einstein on its cover (Mann/Mann 1996, fig. I.1). The physicist is standing on top of the Rockefeller Center, the city of New York spreads out below him, he is leaning against the balustrade with his arm propped up, his white suit glowing in the sun, his right hand holding a cigar. Einstein's gaze is directed upwards towards the camera, and he looks as if he wants to say with his whole body: my city. Although the centre of Albert Einstein's life was in the university town of Princeton, this portrait is closely linked to the American metropolis on the Hudson River. The photo was taken in 1938 and bears a dedication to the authors of *Escape to Life*. Erika and Klaus Mann's book from 1939, published with Houghton Mifflin Press, was a who's who of German-speaking émigrés during the National Socialist era, and Einstein was only one of the many displaced intellectuals, scientists, writers and artists honoured in the book. While Einstein gave a face to this encyclopaedic overview, New York, the arrival city of many emigrants in the USA, provided further context for the topic. In their volume '*Escape to Life*' – a reference to the Manns' book – Sigrid Weigel and Eckart Goebel described New York as intrinsically connected to the émigrés fleeing National Socialist Germany:

> So much more than other American cities, New York with its promising Statue functions not only as a shimmering metonymy for immigration from all over the world, but also specifically, indeed dramatically and painfully, as an emblem for German and German-Jewish exile after 1933.
>
> (Goebel/Weigel 2013, 1ff.)

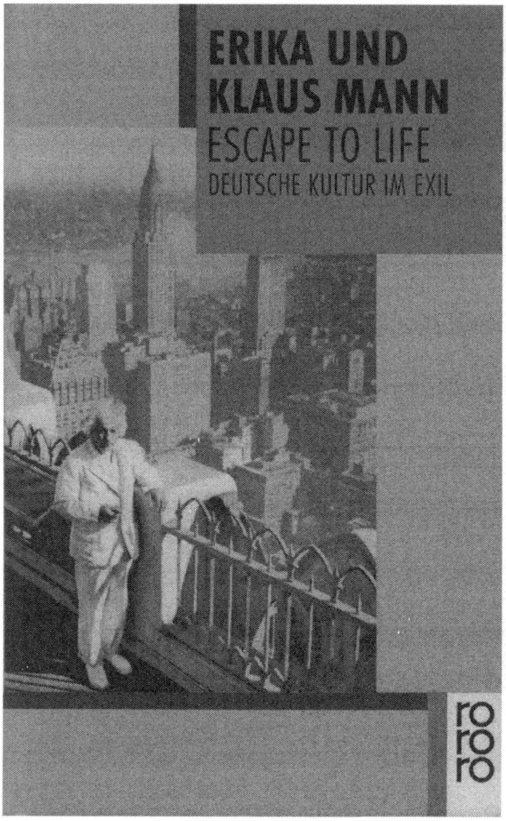

FIGURE I.1: Erika Mann and Klaus Mann. *Escape to Life: Deutsche Kultur im Exil*. Rowohlt, 1996, book cover with Albert Einstein on top of the Rockefeller Center in New York City (with permission of Rowohlt Verlag).

Goebel and Weigel connect the history of emigration to the USA with the brain drain from Germany in the 1930s and 1940s. The book by the siblings Erika and Klaus Mann, who were also exiled, and Einstein's photograph, which he dedicated to the two writers, leads to the question how city and emigration can be thought together in the early 20th century? New York, like many other metropolises of that decade – from Buenos Aires to Bombay to Shanghai – was a city constituted by migratory movements. It is widely accepted in sociology that migration shapes cities – Gerd Baumann speaks of city and migration as "heart and blood circulation" ("*Herz und Kreislauf*", Baumann 2009, 8) and Saskia Sassen not only posits immigration as "one of the constitutive processes of globalization today" but also defines the city as "one of the key sites for the empirical study of these transnational flows" (Sassen 2007, 106).

Nevertheless, until now, exile research has rarely been conceptualized from an urban perspective. One of the exceptions is the book *Metropolen des Exils*, in which Claus-Dieter Krohn described German émigrés during the Nazi period as a 'metropolitan population':

> Berlin, Frankfurt, Cologne, Breslau were the departure stations for an escape that led them in turn to mainly foreign metropolises: to Paris, Prague and London, to New York and Los Angeles, to Mexico City and Buenos Aires, to Jerusalem and Shanghai.
> (Krohn/Winckler 2002, 7)

Taking up this thought, this edited volume will make a significant contribution to the theory and methodology of research on exile in cities and modernities – in regard to artistic, photographic and architectural contributions. 'Modernities' does not only imply a certain period of art and cultural history from the late 19th century to the mid 20th century. It also includes 'modernisms' in the way the art historian Kobena Mercer defined the term in his book *Cosmopolitan Modernisms* in that it

> revisits the broad historical period in which modernist attitudes took shape in different national and cultural environments. Travelling through moments of crisis and innovation, it reveals the dynamic interplay between different cultures as a constant thread that weaves in and out of the story of modern art as a whole.
> (Mercer 2005, 7)

Urban Exile interweaves histories of modernism and exile in different urban environments and focuses on historical dislocations in the first half of the 20th century, when artistic and urban movements constituted themselves in global exchange. Although this book takes a historical perspective, it was written with an awareness of current flight movements. In recent years, numerous refugees have fled to Europe from Syria, North African states and the Balkans; the Rohingya people were forced to flee Myanmar; and, as we write, thousands of people are attempting to leave Afghanistan.[1] The knowledge of previous historical exile experiences is important for the understanding of contemporary flight movements: after all, these are not singular phenomena. For migration movements in the first half of the 20th century and for those of today, it is equally possible to speak of urban centres of attraction for refugees: today, Berlin is a European metropolis of exile; in the 1930s and 1940s, Paris, Prague, London, New York, Istanbul and Shanghai were destinations for refugees.

While there is already extensive research on the connection between the city and migration in the present (see among others Ottersbach/Yildiz 2004; Dika et al. 2011; Campkin/Duijzings 2016), there is only limited literature on historical dislocations in an urban context. Methodologically and theoretically oriented research on this topic is still a desideratum. Although there are obvious parallels between contemporary migration issues and historical phenomena in this field, this book voluntarily focuses on the first half of the 20th century. We hope that through this focus, our book will make steps towards closing the current gap that exists in historical urban exile research, particularly in terms of methods and theories. This volume will make a systematic contribution to the study of historical urban exiles that can be adapted by future research.

Employing an interdisciplinary approach and a historical perspective, the contributions to this volume formulate various theoretical and methodological approaches, and expound upon research practices, as they investigate how exile and urbanity are intertwined. Drawing on examples from a wide range of urban centres around the world, contributors from various disciplines share their thoughts, experiences and concepts relating to the challenges and benefits in building knowledge through interrogating the nexus of exile and urban research. By centring 'exile' as a category for methodological and theoretical investigations of urban culture, we rethink its application in a transnational, global context, thereby considering the varying concepts, historical usages and trajectories behind it. Through presenting case studies from a diversity of urban environments, we seek to form a basis for comparison of exilic experiences across cities (Robinson 2015) and to counter the still prevalent focus on cities of the global North (Robinson/Roy 2015).

In cities around the world, migration contributed significantly to the transformation of urban spaces by generating new communities, neighbourhoods and artists' quarters. Experiences of exile by locals and migrants alike formed the basis for a new and different perception of the urban spaces in which they lived and worked. When we examine artistic practices, for example, we find evidence of migrants capturing their new surroundings in photographs, drawings and writings. Taking different practices in the urban environment as a starting point, our volume activates acts of walking and strolling, mapping or reading and writing the city, orientation and notation. At the same time, objects such as address books, notebooks, city maps or photographs, and places of memory and research including databases, digital mappings and archives are mined as sources. Topics such as queerness, gender and sexuality, social life, social space and segregation, and methods such as oral history or artistic research are investigated in the five parts.

Part I: Sourcing traces

"But man is not a tree, [...] he will get on his feet and walk away" (Goytisolo 1992, 11, translation from Turkish by the authors). This is what writer Juan

Goytisolo, who himself once had to leave his home country Spain, thought about exiles. However, 'man' not only moves but also leaves his traces while moving. These traces may take the shape of works produced by exiles, be it books, paintings, sculptures, murals, buildings or a musical piece. These processes proliferate in metropolises which, as 'lands of opportunities', have always been attractive for exiles. Nevertheless, with time passing, it is growing more and more difficult to find these traces and to reconstruct interrelations between exiles and cities as personal possessions and artistic works are lost or sold, and as these fast-lived metropolises swiftly transform.

For researchers, this means that sometimes we must dig deep for traces. In other words, when there is a lack of written sources, non-written ones can help and vice versa. In this sense, archival records, published material such as magazines, newspapers, poems and novels, or autobiographical documents such as letters, diaries and memoirs, as well as non-written sources such as paintings, photographs, posters, films or musical recordings grow increasingly important. We might also find a ship ticket, a door sign or a suitcase like that of German-Jewish writer Walter Meckauer in which he kept his short stories (Deutsche Nationalbibliothek 2015). All these sources, albeit in different ways, provide us with information that helps find traces and to expand our knowledge on urban exile as a topic. With examples like this in mind, the *Sourcing traces* part emphasizes the importance of studying urban exile with the help of source-based research which can be productively combined with other methods and theories. Nevertheless, we need to link these sources to critical approaches: we need to bear in mind possible hidden meanings, and notions of accuracy, veracity or historical context. As David Hackett Fisher rightly states: "It is no easy matter to tell the truth, pure and simple, about past events; for historical truths are never pure, and rarely simple" (Fischer 1970, 40) (figs. I.2a and I.2b).

Sourcing traces contains six essays in different urban contexts including Paris, London and Istanbul. In the first chapter, "Expulsion from Exile: Tracking the Presence and Absence of German-speaking Dealers in Paris, 1910–1925", Maddalena Alvi focuses on the Parisian art market and its non-French art dealers with the help of archive material such as official art records and dealers' memoirs. Julia Eichenberg's contribution entitled "Taming the Polyp: Address Books and their Impact on Wartime Exile in London" emphasizes the way address books of London exiles have provided vital insights for her research. Ekaterina Aygün's "Close Reading Istanbul: Through the Lens of Two Almanacs by Russian-speaking Émigrés in the 1920s" explores the city of Istanbul by proposing a close reading of the almanacs produced by the 'first wave' of Russian-speaking émigrés as a method.

Nils Grosch's chapter "'Mobile Exile' and Urban Musical Theatre in the 1930s" discusses forms of theatrical mobility enacted by refugees fleeing the Nazi system,

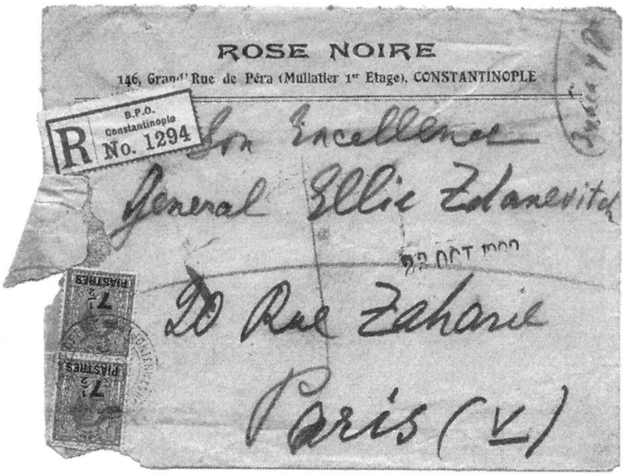

FIGURE I.2A: Front side of an envelope sent to the Georgian-born artist Ilia Zdanevitch who had settled in Paris after living in Constantinople. October 1922 (© The Ilia Zdanevitch Archives, Marseille, France).

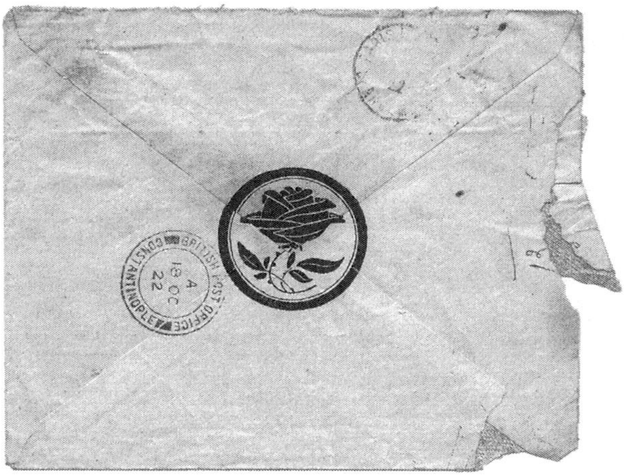

FIGURE I.2B: Back side of the envelope which shows a black rose, the emblem of the Rose Noire cabaret in Constantinople, sent to Ilia Zdanevitch by one of his friends. October 1922 (© The Ilia Zdanevitch Archives, Marseille, France).

and presents two related case studies with published and unpublished letters from archives. Shifting to oral history as a method, in her chapter “Oral History in Exile Studies – Potentials and Limitations”, Felicitas Söhner investigates this methodological approach within exile studies, particularly outlining biographical approaches. Finally, “*Movement* – A Conversation with Artist Michaela Melián” features Burcu Dogramaci's interview with Michaela Melián on her installation piece dedicated to the violinist Susanne Lachmann who had to flee from Hamburg to England in 1935. Two photographs and Lachmann's curriculum vitae in a lexicon, were used as sources for this visual and sonic artwork.

Part II: Practising the urban

When looking back to the 20th century, the urban street was a place where social, political, religious as well as cultural encounters and new artistic modes were negotiated (Starl 1988; Sonne 2014). The urban designer and theorist Donald Appleyard states in his book *Livable Street* that "the street has always been the scene of this conflict, between living and access, between resident and traveler, between street life and the threat of death" (Appleyard 1981, 1). Following recent developments in the field of urban and performance studies as well as art history, we can observe a shift from the city itself towards the dynamic practices and interventions of city dwellers and artists in urban space (see Nippe 2011; Whybrow 2011; Bürkle 2013; Holub/Hohenbüchler 2014; Laister et al. 2014; Whybrow 2014; Campkin/Duijzings 2016; Freudendal-Pedersen et al. 2018; Verloo/Bertolini 2020).

Based on these reflections on urban practice in the city, the question arises whether some of these theories can also be adapted to historical exile studies – to see artistic work in the context of the immediate urban environment as well as to perceive the artist as an active participant in and of the city. This perspective follows recent demands of contemporary exile and migration studies for the "specific urban skills" (Yildiz/Mattausch 2009, 14) of emigrants, while focusing on performative, artistic and aesthetic practices in and with the city (Davis 2011; Hess 2014). The notion of the city as a living body comes to the forefront, while the emigrants themselves also emerge as agential actors of the city (Whybrow 2011; Campkin/Duijzings 2016).

The aim of the part *Practising the urban* is to question how and via which artistic practices émigré artists appropriated the city. What methods did the émigré artists use to practice the urban in their works? And what methods, analytic tools and sources are necessary for us as researchers to analyze these historic urban practices? After their arrival, emigrants engaged with the city by employing various practices such as photographing, drawing, performing or writing. For example, depending on the camera type, the act of photographing could enable a variety of different encounters and practices in the urban environment, as can be seen in a portrait of the émigré photographer Fritz Henle (fig. I.3). Henle was photographed by his émigré colleague Herbert Matter in the city space of New York while holding a Rolleiflex camera in front of his body. As this type of middle format camera

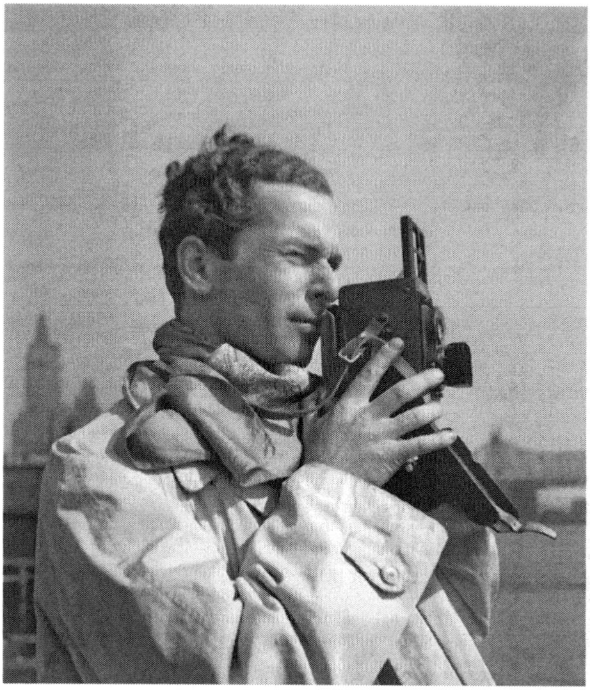

FIGURE I.3: Herbert Matter, *Portrait of Fritz Henle*, New York, 1937 (© Estate Fritz Henle).

had its viewer located on top of the apparatus, the act of photographing thus demanded a dynamic handling of the camera in the urban field. Therefore, this and other artistic practices can be re-thought as urban practices that define "the artistic action of all disciplines in relation to the city" (Vetter 2020).

The sociologist and philosopher Michel de Certeau states that walking through the city as an everyday practice is a mode of seeing that contributes to the emergence of urban forms, appropriation of topographical structures and involves a spatial realization and relationships with the environment (de Certeau 1984). This concept could be extended by asking whether émigré artists in their new urban environment developed new modes of working and seeing or whether they applied practices they had already established in their home countries before migrating. Creative urban practices follow a host of different methods and can – as the four essays with starting points in London, Tel Aviv, Bombay (Mumbai), Melbourne and New York show – be declared as a global phenomenon.

In the chapter "An Exile's Guide: Ernst Schaeffer's *Pictorial Bombay* and the Construction of Bombay's Touristscape", Margit Franz and Rachel Lee analyze the image of 1930s Bombay created in the guidebook by German émigré journalist and photographer Ernst Schaeffer. After his arrival, dissatisfied with the existing guidebook market, he published his own guidebook including his own images of the city, thereby contributing to the construction of Bombay's touristscape.

Pursuing a photographic approach, the chapter "Photographic Practices in Cities of Exile: Camera Views on Tel Aviv and New York" by Anna Sophia Messner and Helene Roth reflects on the practices with which émigré photographers such as Ellen Auerbach, Liselotte Grschebina, Fritz Henle and Rudy Burckhardt encountered cities with their cameras and from different perspectives. By considering these émigrés as actors of their images, the authors propose a close re-reading of their photographs in the context of photographic practices, such as the handling of the camera, and of the cities' individual architecture, topography and sociology.

The urban environment and social structures on the streets are also the topic of the Russian émigré painter Danila Vassilieff. Arriving in Australia in 1937, he painted his immediate living space, the streets of Fitzroy, Melbourne – a working class neighborhood. Robert Pascoe and Chris McConville contextualize Vassilieff's paintings using Kevin Lynch's urban typology in their visual essay "The Exilic Vision of a Once Fashionable Quarter: Danila Vassilieff in Interwar Fitzroy" to examine the exile's conception of the urban through both modernism and the vernacular.

Urban practices concern not only artistic practices but also the ways in which émigrés and specific gendered classes in particular were rendered (in)visible in the city. The chapter "Queering Exile London: Dislocations, Hidden Histories and Gendered Spaces" by Burcu Dogramaci reflects on the queer urban practices in London during the 1930s and 1940s. As this community remained almost hidden within urban spaces (their legacies therefore only recorded in fragmented ways), and has been largely invisible in exile studies, the text offers new materials and methods to give visibility to the topic of gender and sexuality in the context of the urban and exile.

Part III: Mapping/spatializing sites

While studying and mapping the transformation of urban space the researcher is confronted with a challenge: situated in time and space, urban transformations are driven by interacting complex, heterogenous and contingent processes and spatial practices.

Concepts of space as discussed in critical geography or sociology allow for a range of methodological and theoretical discourses that can be made fruitful for various disciplines, not least in the fields of architecture, urban planning, design and art (history) in postcolonial contexts. At the same time, the creation and the experience or use of space encompasses concrete physical or material processes. Concepts of space, therefore, touch on areas of the conceptual and ideological, as well as on material and empirical aspects, and embodied everyday practices (Lefebvre 1974; Harvey 1989; Soja 1989; Campkin/Duijzings 2016; Coomans et al. 2019). Spatial practices, theoretical, methodological, practical or representational, offer multifold perspectives to approach historical and contemporary urban geographies and involve a wide range of possible local and global agents. At the same time, these practices, with mapping being one of them, simultaneously produce and limit the spatial scope they render.

Mapping/spatializing sites is dedicated to methodological approaches regarding historical spatial (trans)formations of the urban environment and the migration of people, objects and ideas, in particular within exilic dynamics. This revolves around a broad understanding of mapping and spatial practices (Tolman 1948; Lefebvre 1974; Harvey 1989; Soja 1989; Shields 2003; Anderson 2016; Coomans et al. 2019). Mapping can be understood in many ways. As a spatial practice itself it deeply affects the formation of spatial concepts and hierarchies, such as the geo-body of a nationhood (Winichakul 1994). As an analytical tool it helps to identify relational actors and objects in their respective fields of reference, such as the spatio-temporal relation of actors informing urban processes.

Mapping/spatializing sites assembles five approaches in different historical and contemporary urban settings in Chile, China, Turkey and Serbia. The first chapter, Valentina Pino Reyes' artistic visual essay "Theatre After the End of Theatre: Abandoned Theatres in Chile" is part of an ongoing research project that is dedicated to the history of Chile's abandoned theatres. Scattered over vast landscapes in (former) urban centres, their history is closely interwoven with Chile's history of migration, its geology, climate, socio economic development and political events. The contemporary remains of the theatres begin to reveal their multifaceted histories through her artistic photographic documentation.

In her chapter "Redeveloping the Heritage of Migration: The Shanghai Jewish Refugees Museum in Urban Transformation", Xin Tong investigates the entwinements between exile and urbanity, global migration history and local memory practices in Shanghai. By mapping the 'media milieu' of the Jewish Museum site as a 'memory work' she traces the course of the development of the Shanghai Jewish Refugees Museum, along with the process of Shanghai's urbanization.

By locating historical photographic evidence of various kinds and functions, including journalistic images, staged studio photography and commercial or private photographs on historical maps, Katya Knyazeva's visual essay "Mapping the Russian Diaspora in Shanghai" traces the manifold ways of communication between the diaspora, the host culture and other foreign groups and in particular the engagement of Shanghai's Russian-speaking émigrés with the city.

A similar approach is proposed by Merve Köksal and Seza Sinanlar Uslu. Their study "Mapping Istanbul's Pera District between Arrivals and Departures" renders artists' studios and contact zones visible to reveal the multifaceted relations and networks cultivated by traveling, local (Muslim and non-Muslim), and migrant artists from the 1840s to 1960s.

In "Russian Belgrade: In-between Alive and Dead" Marina Sorokina centres her research around the New Cemetery (*Novo Groble*) in Belgrade – a place where collective historical memories and artistic practices of Russian-speaking migrants met with the challenges posed by a new environment and its urban agendas in the former Kingdom of Yugoslavia. Her methods are based on extensive archival research and fieldwork, including photographing the monuments, cleaning and reading the epitaphs to attribute the tombs to Russian émigrés.

Part IV: Situating experience

"Bombay [now Mumbai] is situate [*sic*] in lat. 18° 57' long. 72° 52'", explained the English orientalist, diplomat and politician Edward Eastwick in 1859, as he began introducing the city to potential visitors in his *Handbook* (Eastwick 1859, 271, emphasis added). Having described the colonially administered region of Bombay Presidency, he was now zooming in on its capital city. Anchoring it to the geographic coordinate system, he dropped a pin onto the British imperial map. Although the latitudinal and longitudinal numerical values situated the city relationally, within a global spatiality of measurable locations, they did little to evoke the experience of the place.

In the parts that follow, Eastwick takes the reader through a range of dry enumerations, stating distances between landing sites and hotels, noting prices of first-class train tickets and listing Bombay's principal sights from "1. The Fort, including the Town Hall" through to "5. The Elphinstone Institution and Grant Medical College" (Eastwick 1859, 273). With his sight-seeing itinerary, Eastwick steers the "European visitors", the imagined users of the book (ibid., 283), through landmark colonial institutions, as well as religious buildings and the mansions of the city's richest residents, remarking on their costs and defining features (ibid., 271–285).

Provoked by what he sees at Bhendi Bazaar, en route between the sights of Lowji Castle and Byculla Church, Eastwick adopts a more expressive tone, taking the reader on a short detour through the city's bazaars. Here the buildings and spaces take a back seat to the descriptions of the people and objects that Eastwick inhabits them with:

> women of the Nách girl caste, but of the very lowest description [...] Arabs with ponderous turbans [...] Persians in silken vests [...] Banians, dirty and bustling [...] Bangies with suspended bales [...] Jains in their snowy vests [...] Padres with round black hats [...] Fakírs from all over India [...] Jews of the tribe of Bene Israel [...] a Parsee, dashing onwards in his gaily painted buggy.
>
> (ibid., 283)

Marking difference through descriptors of caste, gender, religion, clothing, profession, geographical origin and hygiene, Eastwick conspicuously excludes colonial figures from this urban scene of locals and migrants (and those in-between) noting only, in another instance of othering, that Bhendi Bazaar is also frequented by "English sailors" (ibid., 282).

Eastwick's way of seeing life in Bombay corresponds with Donna Haraway's critique of Western cultural narratives of objectivity that squash "multiplicities into isomorphic slots or cumulative lists" (Haraway 1988, 586). His reductive, Orientalist figuring of people in Bombay produces, orders and appropriates difference (ibid., 587). Countering this approach, Haraway proposed an alternative epistemology of situated, embodied knowledge that can repair ruptured subject–object relations. By honouring the agency of objects, situated knowledge can be co-created through conversations. These dialogues are informed by their locations and mobilities, which delineate the field of vision through which the world is seen, and generate partial perspectives.

Exile accumulates partial perspectives that are shaped, among other contributing factors, by environments. The embodied experiences of exile environments inflect the way people in exile perceive and express themselves. As Fincher and Jacobs state, "people's relationships with places construct their identities" (Fincher/Jacobs 1998, 20). Just as the environment informs exilic experience and knowledge, exilic experience and knowledge in turn reform environments, creating a shifting, expanding web of spatial interactions. Characterized by difference and often marginality, exile profoundly re-situates the subjects who are experiencing it, as well as the places they encounter.

Thinking with Haraway, *Situating experience* works towards situating experiences of exile within urban fabrics. Focusing an exile lens on cities that have historically been shaped and reshaped by migration, the authors sharpen their gazes through applying a diverse selection of methods. Engaging domestic interiors, furniture and books, as well as apartments and neighbourhoods, they interrogate how urban environments and habitats interface with exile. These local reconstructions, built on close readings of documents and other materials produced in exile, enable the authors to render exilic life-worlds as partial perspectives. Situating exile experiences in spaces could be a way to see more clearly with those that inhabited them.

A specific urban exilic spatial typology forms the basis of Alexis Nouss' investigation, "Urban Exile: The Case of the Nazi Ghetto". Situating exilic experience in Nazi ghettos, Nouss theorizes how they restructure urban space and the people they confine: without allowing their inmates the possibility to settle, ghettos determine their identities. Invaginating public and private urban space, exile in the all-pervasive ghetto is exposed and anachronistic. Homogenous and opaque, it is a place of waking night that is embodied and dehumanizing.

Louis Kaplan argues that the exile experiences of the art historian Leo Steinberg, which took place in a series of different urban contexts, can be situated within his relationships to books. As social actors and sources of community, books provided continuity and refuge to Steinberg. "Booked for Exile: Leo Steinberg's Urban Passages and Textual Homelands" also foregrounds the ways in which cities' attitudes towards books resonated with Steinberg's sense of home, whether through witnessing book burnings or engaging with urban infrastructure such as public libraries.

Diana Wechsler also engages interior urban space in her chapter "Between Europe and America: Metropolitan Exchanges in the Context of International Antifascism". In Buenos Aires, a bookcase and the books and magazines it contains situate the experience of exiled and migratory artists, shifting between Europe and Latin America. Forging solidarities through exchange and local translations, migrant artistic networks supported movements of social and political activism.

In "Urban Exile: Bogotá in the First Half of the 20th Century", Claudia Cendales Paredes explores experiences of mid 20th century exiles in Colombia's capital. Situating them temporarily in hostels and hotels, and more permanently in apartments and houses in different neighbourhoods of Bogotá, she examines where and how they lived and worked. Through examples, including a menu created by an exiled translator couple to celebrate 10 years of exile in the city, Cendales Paredes interprets modes of self-expression, community and conviviality.

In "(Re)routing and (Re)rooting in Urban Exile: Exploring Villa Ocampo in Buenos Aires and Jassim House in Bombay with Actor-Network-Theory", Mareike Schwarz utilizes Actor-Network-Theory to examine two domestic urban settings that became hubs for local and exile intellectual communities alike. Exploring their spatiality in terms of the 'third space' proposed by Homi Bhabha, she analyses architectural forms and interior furnishings, such as arm chairs and mattresses, assessing how they may have contributed to the homes' potential for sociability.

She situates the exilic experiences of networking, collaboration and dialogue through reconstructions of relationships between subjects, objects and spaces.

Part V: Place-making/belonging

While studying networks and artistic production in exile, place-making and belonging become two major concepts within a methodological perspective. Belonging is an essential aspect of exile studies. The migrant who arrives in a new city, often with a view to settling there permanently, has to construct a space of belonging among the many possibilities offered by the metropolis. This way, the permeable space of the city is ineluctably transformed by the experiences of migrants. The links which will determine the relationship of each individual to the city are multiple and complex. Some will seek to integrate quickly into the local networks by locating their homes in the city centre, others will take refuge in the neighbourhoods frequented by a population of the same origin or language. Painted, illustrated and written photographic production signify this phenomenon. The migrant who has left their original land for different reasons seeks to feel at home in the new environment.

As the French philosopher Simone Weil stated, "[r]ooting is perhaps the most important and most overlooked need of the human soul"[2] (Weil 1949, 36). Belonging to a place takes time, as the French ethnographer Sylvie Sagnes writes in her article "After all, isn't 'being from somewhere' essentially a matter of patience?"[3] (Sagnes 2004, 35). Speaking of exile necessarily refers to displacement, loss and instability, but can also mean something more positive, such as connection and hybridity, which enrich cultures across the globe. In city-migrant interactions, newcomers reinvent public space (physical or imagined), and the city in turn shapes the identities of the exiles. What kinds of links are created between people and their urban environment? How do the artists interact with the public space?

Place-making/belonging follows a place-based perspective in which creative production processes and behaviours are inscribed in profoundly spatial logics of the exile, a real space physically experienced (Kwaterko 1981, 39; Cresswell 2015, 16). It examines artistic experiences linked to place-making in order to better understand exiles' material and embodied experiences of exile, sometimes by mapping the exiles' movements and dwellings or by studying the artistic work through which they affirmed their belonging to a particular space (fig. I.4).

This part contains five essays that address these issues. The first one, "From Hamburg to Cape Town: The Denizen Photography of Else and Helmuth Hausmann" by Jessica Williams Stark, explores the exile experience of this German

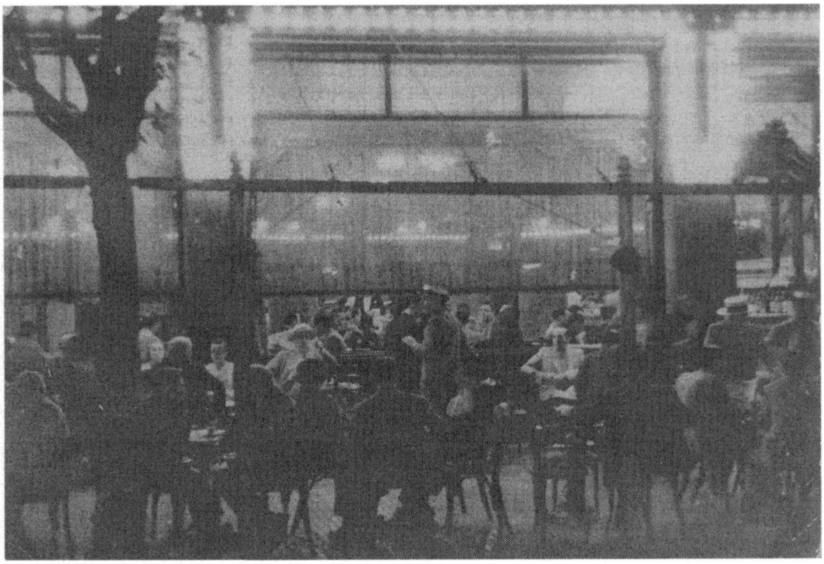

FIGURE I.4: Unknown photographer, *Café on Avenida de Mayo*, Buenos Aires, 1935 (© Archivo General de la Nación, Buenos Aires).

photographer couple in a colonial context. The author critically examines their work undertaken in South Africa and the way in which the two photographers *produced* the particular world they photographed through their cameras.

Mareike Hetschold in her contribution "Suzhou River and Garden Bridge: Reading Images of Exile in Shanghai" works on the trajectories and the artistic production of exiles in Shanghai through a conceptual historical perspective. Federico Martín Vitelli studies the spatial experience of Spanish Republican exiles in La Plata and Bahía Blanca between 1936 and 1975 in his chapter "The Territorial Dimension of Spanish Republican Exile in the Cities of Argentina". In doing so, he aims to reconstruct the urban spaces of the academic, cultural, associative and political networks the exiles integrated into.

Valeria Sánchez Michel provides a fascinating case study of a single street in the centre of the metropolis of Mexico City in an chapter entitled "Calle de López or Spain in Mexico". From a micro-scale perspective, Calle de López has for years constituted a place of arrival and settlement for Spanish exiles, who have opened shops there and who appropriated the space, creating communal networks of sociability.

The final contribution of this part is Laura Karp Lugo and Marine Schütz's chapter, entitled "Reinhabiting the City as an Artistic Open Space: Urban Imprints of Exile Artists in Buenos Aires and Marseille in the 20th Century", which proposes a methodological approach based on the comparative reading of two cities, geographically distant but linked by transatlantic travel and their cosmopolitan natures.

Urban Exile: Theories, Methods, Research Practices is the second volume of the ERC Consolidator Grant research project "Relocating Modernism: Global Metropolises, Modern Art and Exile (METROMOD)", which was established in 2017 at the Ludwig-Maximilians-Universität in Munich. This volume opens new paths for studying historical exile and migratory movements from an urban perspective, inquiring how artists, architects and photographers worked in interaction with their metropolitan environments. Although the chapters deal with exiles in a range of geographies, including Latin America, China, South Asia and Australia, the majority of the exiled actors in this volume fled from Europe.[4] This is partly due to METROMOD's aim to focus on six metropolitan destinations for refugee European artists between 1900 and 1950. At the same time, this book discusses methods and theories for researching urban exile constellations from various perspectives. Some of our contributors presented their first thoughts in a series of online panels which were organized in December 2020 and January 2021 by METROMOD.[5]

We are deeply grateful to the European Research Council for funding our research and this book. Our gratitude goes to our copy-editor Jennifer Leetsch and the project's student assistant, Maya-Sophie Lutz, who was responsible for the correction process and the index. *Urban Exile* would not have been possible without the valuable contributions of the authors. We are thankful to Intellect for accepting our book and for making our research more visible and accessible.

NOTES

1. See Kermani (2016), Kingsley (2016), Galache (2020); www.bbc.com/news/world-asia-58283177. Accessed 1 April 2022.
2. "L'enracinement est peut-être le besoin le plus important et le plus méconnu de l'âme humaine." Author's translation.
3. "Après tout, 'être de quelque part', n'est-ce pas essentiellement une affaire de patience?" Author's translation.
4. Russian-speaking artists, architects and intellectuals are also presented in the volume. It is worth noting that many of them adopted a European way of life and identified themselves with Europeans/or were of European origin but this isn't applicable to all of them.
5. The recorded session can be accessed through the METROMOD's homepage: https://metromod.net.

REFERENCES

Anderson, Benedict. *Imagined Communities: Reflections on the Origin and Spread of Nationalism*. Verso, 2016.

Appleyard, Donald. *Livable Streets*. University of California Press, 1981.

Baumann, Gerd. "Stadt und Migration: Herz und Kreislauf. Statt eines Vorworts." *Urban Recycling. Migration als Großstadt-Ressource* (Bauwelt Fundamente, vol. 140: Stadtforschung/Stadtpolitik), edited by Erol Yildiz and Birgit Mattausch, Birkhäuser, 2009, pp. 8ff.

Bürkle, Stefanie, editor. *Kunst Raum Stadt/Art Space City*. Deutscher Kunstverlag, 2013.

Campkin, Ben, and Ger Duijzings, editors. *Engaged Urbanism. Cities & Methodologies*. I.B. Tauris, 2016.

Coomans, Thomas, et al., editors. *Mapping Landscapes in Transformation: Multidisciplinary Methods for Historical Analysis*. Leuven University Press, 2019.

Cresswell, Tim. *Place: An Introduction*. Blackwell, 2015.

Davis, Rocío G., et al., editors. *Aesthetic Practices and Politics in Media, Music and Art. Performing Migration*. Routledge, 2011.

de Certeau, Michel. *The Practice of Everyday Life*. Translated by Steven Rendall, University of California Press, 1984.

Deutsche Nationalbibliothek. "Testimony of Exile History – Suitcase of Author Walter Meckauer (1889–1966) to be preserved." 2 September 2015, *dnb.de*, www.dnb.de/EN/Ueber-uns/Presse/ArchivPM2015/meckauerKoffer.html. Accessed 5 July 2021.

Dika, Antonia, et al. *Balkanmeile. 24 Stunden Ottakringer Straße. Lokale Identitäten und globale Transformationsprozesse. Ein Reiseführer aus Wien*. Turia + Kant, 2011.

Eastwick, Edward B. *A Handbook for India; Being an Account of the Three Presidencies and of the Overland Route, Intended as a Guide for Travellers, Officers and Civilians, with Vocabularies and Dialogues of the Spoken Languages of India: With Travelling Map and Plans of Towns. II*. John Murray, 1859.

Fincher, Ruth, and Jane M. Jacobs. *Cities of Difference*. Guilford Press, 1998.

Fischer, David Hackett. *Historians' Fallacies: Toward a Logic of Historical Thought*. Harper & Row, 1970.

Freudendal-Pedersen, Malene, et al., editors. *Experiencing Networked Urban Mobilities: Practices, Flows and Methods* (Networked Urban Mobilities Series, 2). Routledge, 2018.

Galache, Carlos Sardiña. *The Burmese Labyrinth: A History of the Rohingya Tragedy*. Verso, 2020.

Goebel, Eckart, and Sigrid Weigel. "Introduction." *'Escape to Life': German Intellectuals in New York: A Compendium on Exile after 1933*, edited by Eckart Goebel and Sigrid Weigel, De Gruyter, 2013, pp. 1–8.

Goytisolo, Juan. *Yeryüzünde Bir Sürgün*. Metis Yayınları, 1992.

Haraway, Donna. "Situated Knowledges: The Science Question in Feminism and the Privilege of Partial Perspective." *Feminist Studies*, vol. 14, no. 3, 1988, pp. 575–599. *JSTOR*, doi: 10.2307/3178066. Accessed 14 July 2021.

Harvey, Davis. *The Condition of Postmodernity*. Basil Blackwell, 1989.

Hess, Sabine. "The City is Migration. Ethnographie-Genealogical Perspectives on Urban Space." *The Art of the Urban Intervention / Die Kunst des urbanen Handelns*, publication of the international conference *Urban Neighbourhood Cultures – Diversity, Participation, Spaces of Negotiation* at the Theater im Bahnhof Graz 2011, edited by Judith Laister et al., Löcker, 2014, pp. 236–249.

Holub, Barbara, and Christine Hohenbüchler, editors. *Planning Unplanned – towards a New Positioning of Art in the Context of Urban Development*. Verlag für moderne Kunst, 2014.

Kermani, Navid. *Einbruch der Wirklichkeit: Auf dem Flüchtlingstreck durch Europa*. C.H. Beck, 2016.

Kingsley, Patrick. *The New Odyssey: The Story of Europe's Refugee Crisis*. Faber & Faber, 2016.

Krohn, Claus-Dieter, and Lutz Winckler. Vorwort. *Metropolen des Exils (Exilforschung. Ein internationales Jahrbuch*, vol. 20), edited by Claus-Dieter Krohn et al., edition text + kritik, 2002, pp. 7–13.

Kwaterko, Jozef. "Milosz: l'exil et l'appartenance." *Liberté*, vol. 23, no. 3, May–June 1981, pp. 38–42. *érudit*, https://id.erudit.org/iderudit/60279ac. Accessed 14 July 2021.

Laister, Judith, et al., editors. *The Art of the Urban Intervention/Die Kunst des urbanen Handelns*, publication of the international conference *Urban Neighbourhood Cultures – Diversity*, Participation, Spaces of Negotiation at the Theater im Bahnhof Graz 2011, Löcker, 2014.

Lefebvre, Henri. *La production de l'espace*. Edition Anthropos, 1974.

Mann, Erika, and Klaus Mann. *Escape to Life: Deutsche Kultur im Exil*. Rowohlt, 1996.

Mercer, Kobena. "Introduction." *Cosmopolitan Modernisms (Annotating art's histories*, 1), edited by Kobena Mercer, inIVA, 2005, pp. 6–23.

Nippe, Christine. *Kunst baut Stadt: Künstler und ihre Metropolenbilder in Berlin und New York* (Image, 20). transcript, 2011.

Ottersbach, Markus, and Erol Yildiz, editors. *Migration in der metropolitanen Gesellschaft: Zwischen Ethnisierung und globaler Neuorientierung*. LIT, 2004.

Robinson, Jennifer. "Comparative urbanism: new geographies and cultures of theorizing the urban." *International Journal of Urban and Regional Research*, vol. 40, no.1, 2015, pp. 187–199, doi: 10.1111/1468-2427.12273. Accessed 15 November 2021.

Robinson, Jennifer, and Ananya Roy. "Debate on global urbanisms and the nature of urban theory." *International Journal of Urban and Regional Research*, vol. 40, no.1, 2015, pp. 181–186, doi: 10.1111/1468-2427.12272. Accessed 15 November 2021.

Sagnes, Sylvie. "Cultiver ses racines. Mémoire généalogique et sentiment d'autochtonie." *Ethnologie française*, vol. 34, no. 1, 2004, pp. 31–40, *cairn.info*, doi: 10.3917ethn.0031. Accessed 10 June 2021.

Sassen, Saskia. *A Sociology of Globalization*. W.W. Norton & Company, 2007.

Shields, Rob. *The Virtual*. Routledge, 2003.

Soja, Edward W. *Postmodern Geographies: The Reassertion of Space in Critical Social Theory*. Verso, 1989.

Sonne, Wolfgang. *Urbanität und Dichte im Städtebau des 20. Jahrhunderts*. DOM Publishers, 2014.

Starl, Timm. *Ein Blick auf die Straße: Die fotografische Sicht auf ein städtisches Motiv* (Stationen der Fotografie, 1). Verlag Dirk Nishen, 1988.

Tolman, Edward Chace. "Cognitive Maps in Rats and Men." *The Psychological Review*, vol. 55, no. 4, 1948, pp. 189–208.

Verloo, Nanke, and Luca Bertolini, editors. *Seeing the City: Interdisciplinary Perspectives on the Study of the Urban* (Perspectives on Interdisciplinarity, vol. 6). Amsterdam University Press, 2020.

Vetter, Danilo. "Urbane Praxis als zukunftsweisender Ansatz." 8 September 2020, *Rat für die Künste*, www.rat-fuer-die-kuenste.de/urbane-praxis-als-zukunftsweisender-ansatz/. Accessed 21 June 2021.

Weil, Simone. *L'Enracinement : prélude à une déclaration des devoirs envers l'être humain*. Gallimard, 1949.

Winichakul, Thongchai. *Siam Mapped: A History of the Geo-Body of a Nation*. University of Hawaii Press, 1994.

Whybrow, Nicolas. *Art and the City*. I.B. Tauris, 2011.

Whybrow, Nicloas, editor. *Performing Cities*. Palgrave Macmillan, 2014.

Yildiz, Erol, and Birgit Mattausch, editors. *Urban Recycling. Migration als Großstadt-Ressource* (Bauwelt Fundamente, vol. 140: Stadtforschung/Stadtpolitik). Birkhäuser, 2009.

PART I

SOURCING TRACES

1

Expulsion from Exile: Tracking the Presence and Absence of German-speaking Dealers in Paris, 1910–1925

Maddalena Alvi

It is difficult to capture what the literary scholar John Attridge has called "the endogamous family tree of côteries and cénacles, of intellectual friendship, patronage, collaboration and, above all, 'movements' overarching the geography of Paris" (2009, 167). At the end of the 19th century, these networks shaped the city perhaps less visibly, yet just as strongly as the Hausmannian renovation of Parisian boulevards, the background for its thriving business activities. During these decades, Paris experienced a boom in the real estate market and in commercial culture (Yates 2012). Starting in the 1880s, the upper classes and the bourgeoisie discovered new objects of luxury associated with modernity (Daumas 2018, 232). One of the branches of business that expanded in the "new" capital was the trade with art. The last decades of the 19th century were so dominated by French cultural influences that they have become universally known as the *fin de siècle*, a term meant to encompass the atmosphere of this period. Paris was the thriving cosmopolitan centre, from which the spirit of a dying century and a new era seemed to radiate. Yet, the cultural life of Paris was shaped by foreign influences and influxes. Few communities were as present both in the artistic and business life of Paris before the First World War as German-speaking art dealers. Names such as Jacques Seligmann and Daniel-Henry Kahnweiler have become the epitome of French art dealing. They belonged to two generations of Germanophone cosmopolitans who changed the French art market before 1914.

The outbreak of the First World War as the legitimate end of the long 19th century destroyed the transnational market and forced German and

Austro-Hungarian nationals to leave the country, while the French state confiscated all their possessions. Unlike artists, German-speaking dealers in Paris have never been the subject of a collective biography (Gautherie-Kampka 1995). Consequently, neither the disruption of the lives of an entire community which became an explicit enemy in the Summer of 1914 has ever been thematized, even though prominent dealers like Wilhelm Uhde and Daniel-Henry Kahnweiler wrote about their First World War experiences in their autobiographies (Kahnweiler/Crémieux 1971; Uhde 2010).

This paper discusses how historians and art historians can use the expulsion of these dealers to reflect on the nexus between foreign money and urban space. The war measures allowed the French state to appropriate the dealers' capital and disperse it in a series of auctions held mainly after 1918, a time of financial need. Yet, the fact that many of these dealers would never come back to Paris was a substantial blow to the French art market, as a study of sale records shows. This paper offers an interdisciplinary perspective on how much the presence and absence of this community shaped Paris, by quantifying the price of its disappearance. As a case study, it analyses the consequences that exile and expulsion had on the business spaces of a European capital by pointing at the disintegration of different types of networks. It also shows how sources such as sale records and commercial address books can be used to construct a history of exile and expulsion.

Tracking exile and expulsion

The official Bulletin of the chamber of art dealers in Paris shows that before 1914, the majority of non-Francophone dealers in the French capital stemmed from the German-speaking world (Bulletin 1903). The pre-war biographies of these dealers represent a collective success story of highly skilled individuals who established themselves as businessmen in Paris. During the second half of the 19th century, French cities witnessed an increase in human mobility. In large cities, social exclusion was related to cultural differences between internal migrants and natives; in this context, economic capital was not an antidote to marginalization (Puschmann et al. 2015). Despite cultural differences, German-speaking dealers managed to carve out successful careers in a society that worried about cultural differences and the "immigrant threat" represented by other foreign communities (Lucassen 2005). When referring to the generation that had emigrated to France after 1870, a clarification concerning the notion of exile appears important. A striking similarity between the biographies of dealers as different as Jacques Seligmann and Wilhelm Uhde was their problematic relationship to the newly unified "Prussian" Germany (Seligman 1961, 3; Uhde 2010, 298). Their existence in France was the result of a voluntary exile from German society, which they perceived as illiberal and reactionary. However, their voluntary exile did not always encounter amiable feelings in Paris. While the French art world was undeniably the playground of their success, it was also drenched in antisemitism and anti-German feelings (Stammers 2014, 85). With the outbreak of war in 1914, a generation that had already exiled itself from German society was expelled from its new home.

Measures against art dealers from Germany and Austria–Hungary were announced in a decree on 27 September 1914, while further details on the confiscations of the movable and immovable properties of German, Austrian and Hungarian businesses were published at the beginning of November (République Française 1914, 8541f., 9063f.). In the context of these measures, works of art were put on sale in a series of auctions held at the public auction house *Hôtel Drouot* between 1918 and 1924.

In 1914, a constituent part of the French art world was suddenly expelled from France. The majority of the names associated with these expropriations are now completely forgotten, as they left no written records about their expulsion. One of the exceptions is Wilhelm Uhde, who gave an account of his experience in his memoirs: at the outbreak of war, he left France and went to Germany to train for the trenches he would never fight in (Uhde 2010, 177–185). Daniel-Henry Kahnweiler's memoirs focussed instead on the fate that lay in store for his Cubist art as it was auctioned off at the Drouot once the war ended (Kahnweiler/Crémieux 1971, 68).

In the first two postwar years, the auction market in France would be kept alive by the sales of auctions postponed in 1914 and by the sales of confiscated material. In 1919, the Drouot had an enormous stock of pending successions, voluntary sales and a great quantity of confiscations to deal with (Anonymous 1925). Thirty-eight dealers were expropriated. The sales of confiscated material would start properly after 1918 and would continue up until 1924. To retrace these proceedings, I constructed a database of auctions held at the main Parisian auction house *Hôtel Drouot* between 1910 and 1925, based on the results published in the auction journal *La Gazette de l'Hôtel Drouot*. This database allows us to understand how much revenue the French state gained from the appropriation of foreign art. Such records are not simply interesting from a business history perspective, they also represent the only remnant source of information on mid-brow dealers, whose names would otherwise be completely forgotten.

While economists since William Baumol have mostly used art market prices to reflect on investments in art (Baumol 1986), historians can combine sale records with qualitative sources to make historical observations about cultural and social developments (Alvi 2020). In this specific case, the records allow for quantifying the economic importance of expropriated dealers. The records for 1921, for example, show that roughly 10 per cent of a yearly revenue of roughly sixteen million Francs came from confiscated material. Even more interesting, however, is the fact that the auctions of art properties confiscated from 'enemy dealers' brought twice as much revenue as French material on an average. In other words, bidders were likely to bid higher for these works of art than for other objects sold on the French market.

The money that the French state gained from these auctions in the short term was lost in the long term: what was sold was the capital that these individuals had accumulated over the years and this capital was a measure of their talent as businessmen. While the French state was in desperate need of cash after the war and certainly benefited from appropriating 'German-speaking capital', it damaged its economy in the long term by losing some of the most important foundations of its art market. The disappearance of these businessmen from the French capital was a loss that could never be replaced after 1919.

One possible way to map the disappearance of German-speaking dealers from Paris is to examine seemingly marginal sources, such as address books and commercial registers. In 1920, for example, the *Annuaire* of dealers shows that the list of addresses of Parisian dealers had lost 39 per cent of the German names that started with the letter 'W' compared to 1914 (the initial letter W is rare in French names) (Annuaire 1914; Annuaire 1920). Much like sale records, such commercial address books testify to the presence of individuals who would be otherwise forgotten.

Disintegrated spaces

Through French policies of expropriation and expulsion, Paris did not simply lose good businessmen, it also lost important agents that linked Paris with other business capitals. The disappearance of each German name from a commercial address book signified the erasure of an agent in a trade network. Ultimately, this is a story about market disintegration and forceful nationalization: Paris, in other words, became less cosmopolitan.

In my interpretation of this term, cosmopolitanism is not only measured through the fleeting presence of 'foreigners' in a country but also through their permanence. The expropriation of German-speaking dealers thus illustrates the breakdown of personal connections and international networks following the outbreak of the First World War. The war was a profound disruption to world trade in an increasingly globalized economy (Strikwerda 2016, 112f.). Economic historians have remarked that 1914 represented the end of a first wave of globalization (O'Rourke/Williamson 2001). For an integrated market like the art market, the consequences were serious (Alvi 2020, 602; Bayer/Page 2011, 203–206). Interactions with high-quality goods were often based on personal connections and different forms of reciprocal exchange, which the economic historian Avner Offer has defined as an 'economy of regard' (Offer 1997). This meant that external disruptions of such networks had particularly long-lasting effects.

Art market scholars have also pointed at the importance of the specialized, circumscribed and exclusive networks that the sociologist Viviana Zelizer called 'circuits of commerce' (Zelizer 2006; Velthuis 2007; Pezzini 2017). Embeddedness in such networks was a prerequisite for the success of dealers, as both qualitative micro-historical and economic studies on networks have highlighted (De Silva et al. 2017; Catterson 2020). Networks are part of what has been defined as the "negotiated space of market culture" (Horowitz et al. 2004, 1056): the abstract space between makers and users of goods and among those who sell and design the material culture of their society.

What measuring the price of expropriations ultimately tells us about Paris is that the market culture of the city became more provincial. This observation fits into studies questioning the internationality of the French art world in the first half of the 20th century. The art historian Béatrice Joyeux-Prunel showed how the Parisian art world became less cosmopolitan after 1914 by analyzing the lists of the contributors to art journals and newspapers and noticing that they worked within cliques that were not open to foreign influences (Joyeux-Prunel 2015). While the dealers who never came back shaped the city through their absence, those foreigners who did manage to return found a profoundly altered terrain.

The disruption of trade networks also changed urban space. Buildings, for that matter, are also social objects in that they are invested with social meaning and shape social relations (Marcus/King 1999). Works of art were sold and housed on premises that served as exhibition rooms, storage facilities and business rooms. As in every city, Paris's luxury streets reflected the location of the premises where precious objects were housed and sold, as much as they epitomized where the capital able to afford them was located.

An article published in 1913 in the *Gazette de l'Hôtel Drouot* retraced a geographical history of the Parisian art trade. First the antiquarians were grouped close to the *Hôtel Drouot*, then on the rive gauche in Saint-Germain, and in the Marais. Successively, the epicentre moved towards the Boulevard Haussmann, the Boulevard Malesherbes and then conquered the Champs-Élysées and the Faubourg Saint-Honoré (Anonymous 1913). The hesitant completion of the renovation project of Paris inaugurated by Napoleon III was interrupted by the First World War. By 1918, the geography of the city had been irreversibly modified by physical destruction. In Paris, the traditional art world arrondissements (the ninth, tenth and eighteenth) were defaced. Archival documents list the damages done to the

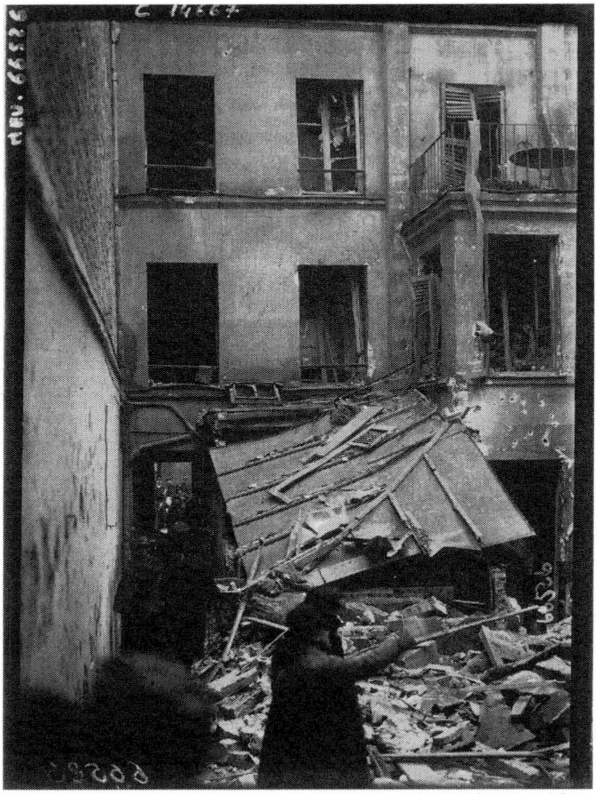

FIGURE 1.1: Agence de Presse Meurrisse, *Raid des Gothas le 8 mars, rue Geoffroy Marie*, 1918, Bibliothèque Nationale de France (Recueil. Actualités 1916-09-07**1918-03-13. Agence Meurisse MEU 61540-66561 © BnF).

ninth arrondissement and to the Rue Drouot (*Dommages de guerre* 2003, 39). A photograph dated to 1918 pictured the ruins of bombed buildings on Rue Geoffroy Marie, one of the streets that led to the *Hôtel Drouot* (fig. 1.1). Neighbours who had been intimately linked by a network of streets and commercial connections prior to 1914, became enemies after a war that completely changed the urban dynamics of the city. Wilhelm Uhde had feared going back to Paris, a city where he had been successful to start again at the age of 50 (Uhde 2010, 235). Gathering information on how the market had changed during his absence was not easy because hundreds of galleries had appeared and more were opening daily. Some of the old dealers still worked but they were not in Rue Laffitte anymore, they had moved to the eighth arrondissement: to Rue de la Boétie and Faubourg Saint-Honoré (ibid., 240). Kahnweiler came back to Paris right after the First World War and set up a new enterprise called Galerie Simon, named after the name of his partner André Simon (Hook 2018, 151). The gallery was located at 29 bis Rue d'Astorg in the eighth arrondissement.

While it is not within the scope of this paper to reconstruct the spatial dislocation of German-speaking dealerships before and after 1914, this endeavour could certainly fit into new studies on the geography of the Parisian art trade. Based on the *Bottin du Commerce*, the official trade bulletin containing information on different branches of business, Léa Saint-Raymond constructed a ground-breaking database on the streets of Parisian art dealers and the geography of the art market between 1815 and 1955. Her cartographic analysis has proven that the development of the market can be geographically resumed in three stages: a grouping of galleries around Rue Laffitte in the 1870s, then a movement to the eighth arrondissement (testified to also by the anecdotal evidence provided in this paper), followed by the emergence of the Left Bank as a hotspot in the 1920s (Saint-Raymond et al. 2016, 120).

The data analyzed by Saint-Raymond was based on a geocoding system in a study of the Parisian art market, which mapped the spatial evolution of art dealerships over 140 years. In general, the benefits of charting the geography of the art market in Paris lie in providing a valuable historical reconstruction of the spaces in which business was done, and consequently also on where capital moved and was situated within the city. Tracking the movements of foreign dealers in Paris could provide a new understanding of how businesses set up by non-French dealers developed. This would allow historians to track a geography of non-French dealerships in the first decades of the 20th century and thus understand how foreign money shaped the streets of Paris before and after the Great War.

Final remarks

Jacques Derrida argued that it is the city, rather than the state, which offers the greatest potential of hospitality required in the age of migration (Derrida 2004). However, the confiscation and auction campaign of German art holdings dated to 1914–1924 demonstrates how quickly an allegedly cosmopolitan city can change, illustrating how fragile cosmopolitanism has historically always been in urban contexts. This paper has shown how the presence and absence of a community of foreign dealers shaped the art market of Paris and its culture by quantifying the gains and costs of the appropriation of foreign capital through the French state and placing this episode within the wider context of nationalization of the French art market after 1914. It also sketched major changes in the geography of the Parisian art market and proposed strategies to track how foreign capital shaped the streets of the French capital.

Studying the expropriation of German-speaking dealers is facilitated by their former embeddedness in a network of streets and commercial relations. By using the documents that recorded these networks, this paper has sketched how to quantify the consequences of the expulsion of a community for a space. While these sources provide the material for a less 'personal' history than, for instance, memoirs or diaries, they also offer opportunities to look at expulsion and exile from a different, more interdisciplinary perspective. Moreover, they also allow scholars to account for the existence of individuals who would otherwise be forgotten in wider historical narratives, proving that belonging to a network means becoming historically visible.

This paper considered the physical space occupied by business premises and the abstract negotiated space regulating trade interactions. Businessmen in the early 20th century were both embedded in transnational trade networks and anchored to urban street networks. By combining the existing memoirs of expropriated dealers with documents such as sale and confiscation records and commercial address books, this paper has highlighted the importance of this community of enterpreneurs. More significantly, however, it has also outlined new methodological avenues for a study of how both voluntary and forced migration shaped the geography of a vibrant European capital.

REFERENCES

Alvi, Maddalena. "The Land of Cockaigne: The German Art Market and the First World War." *German History*, vol. 38, no. 4, 2020, pp. 594–615, doi: 10.1093/gerhis/ghaa038. Accessed 22 April 2021.

Annuaire de la curiosité et des beaux-arts. Paris-Départements- Étranger 4. Lib. Imp. Réunies, 1914.

Annuaire de la curiosité et des beaux-arts. Paris-Départements- Étranger 10. Lib. Imp. Réunies, 1920.

Anonymous. "Les Ventes de la Saison." *La Gazette de l'Hôtel Drouot*, vol. 33, no. 20, 1925, n.p.

Anonymous. "Un nouvel antiquaire s'installe Place Vendôme." *La Gazette de l'Hôtel Drouot*, vol. 22, no. 75, 1913.

Attridge, John. "Paris, Capital of the Nineteenth-Century Novel?" *Modernism/modernity*, vol. 16, no. 1, 2009, pp. 167–171. *Project MUSE*, doi: 10.1353/mod.0.0055. Accessed 7 May 2021.

Baumol, William J. "Unnatural Value: Or Art Investment as Floating Crap Game." *The American Economic Review*, vol. 76, no. 2, 1986, pp. 10–14.

Bayer, Thomas, and John R. Page. *The Development of the Art Market: Money as Muse 1730–1900*. Routledge, 2011.

Bulletin de la chambre syndicale des négociants en objets d'art, tableaux & curiosités, vol. 1, no. 1, 1903.

Catterson, Lynn, editor. *Florence, Berlin and Beyond: Late Nineteenth-Century Art Markets and Their Social Networks*. Brill, 2020.

Daumas, Jean-Claude. *La révolution matérielle: une histoire de la consommation; France, XIXe-XXIe siècle*. Flammarion, 2018.

De Silva, Dakshina G., et al. "Market Evolution of Art Dealers." 28 August 2017. *Social Science Research Network*, doi: 10.2139/ssrn.2866949. Accessed 22 April 2021.

Derrida, Jacques. "On Cosmopolitanism." *Drifting: Architecture and Migrancy*, edited by Stephen Cairns, Routledge, 2004, pp. 48–61.

Gautherie-Kampka, Annette. *Les Allemands du Dôme: La colonie allemande de Montparnasse dans les années 1903–1914*. Peter Lang, 1995.

Hook, Philip. *Rogues' Gallery: A History of Art and its Dealers*. Profile Books, 2018.

Horowitz, Roger, et al. "Meat for the Multitudes: Market Culture in Paris, New York City, and Mexico City over the Long Nineteenth Century." *The American Historical Review*, vol. 109, no. 4, 2004, pp. 1055–1083.

Joyeux-Prunel, Béatrice. "Provincializing Paris. The Center-Periphery Narrative of Modern Art in Light of Quantitative and Transnational Approaches." *Artl@s Bulletin*, vol. 4, no. 1, 2015, pp. 40–64, compttps://docs.lib.purdue.edu/artlas/vol4/iss1/4. Accessed 25 May 2021.

Kahnweiler, Daniel-Henry, and Francis Crémieux. *My Galleries and Painters* (The Documents of 20th-Century Art). Thames & Hudson, 1971.

Lucassen, Leo. *The Immigrant Threat: The Integration of Old and New Migrants in Western Europe since 1850* (Studies of World Migrations). University of Illinois Press, 2005.

Markus, Thomas A., and Anthony D. King. "Foreword." *Gender Space Architecture: An Interdisciplinary Introduction* (The Archi*text* Series, edited by Markus and King). 1st ed., edited by Iain Borden et al., Routledge, 1999, p. i.

Offer, Avner. "Between the Gift and the Market: The Economy of Regard." *The Economic History Review*, vol. 50, no. 3, 1997, pp. 450–476.

O'Rourke, Kevin, and Jeffrey Williamson. *Globalization and History: The Evolution of a Nineteenth-Century Atlantic Economy*. MIT University Press, 2001.

Pezzini, Barbara. *Making a Market for Art: Agnew's and the National Gallery, 1855–1928*. Dissertation, University of Manchester, 2017.

Puschmann, Paul, et al. "From Outsiders to Insiders? Partner Choice and Marriage among Internal Migrants in Antwerp, Rotterdam & Stockholm, 1850–1930." *Climate and Beyond: The Production of Knowledge about the Earth as a Signpost of Social Change*, special issue of *Historical Social Research/Historische Sozialforschung*, vol. 40, no. 2 (152), 2015, pp. 319–358.

République Française. "Circulaire relative aux conditions du fonctionnement du séquestre des maisons c autrichiennes et hongroises." *Journal Officiel de la République Française*, vol. 46, no. 303, 1914, pp. 8541f.

Saint-Raymond, Léa, et al. "Les rues des tableaux: The Geography of the Parisian Art Market 1815–1955." *Artl@s Bulletin*, vol. 5, no. 1, 2016, pp. 120–159, www.docs.lib.purdue.edu/artlas/vol5/iss1/10. Accessed 26 May 2021.

Seligman, Germain. *Merchants of Art: 1880–1960: Eighty Years of Professional Collecting*. Appleton-Century-Crofts, 1961.

Stammers, Tom. "Collectors, Catholics, and the Commune: Heritage and Counterrevolution, 1860–1890." *French Historical Studies*, vol. 37, no. 1, 2014, pp. 53–87. doi: 10.1215/00161071-2376519. Accessed 22 April 2021.

Strikwerda, Carl. "World War I in the History of Globalization." *Historical Reflections/Réflexions Historiques*, vol. 42, no. 3, 2016, pp. 112–132.

Uhde, Wilhelm. *Von Bismarck bis Picasso: Erinnerungen und Bekenntnisse*. Römerhof Verlag, 2010.

Velthuis, Olav. *Talking Prices: Symbolic Meanings of Prices on the Market for Contemporary Art*. Princeton University Press, 2007.

Yates, Alexia. "Selling Paris: The Real Estate Market and Commercial Culture in the Fin-de-siècle Capital." *Enterprise & Society*, vol. 13, no. 4, 2012, pp. 773–789. doi: 10.1017/S1467222700011460. Accessed 22 April 2021.

Zelizer, Viviana. "Circuits in Economic Life." *Economic Sociology_The European Electronic Newsletter* (MPIfG), vol. 8, no. 1, 2006, pp. 30–35. *Econstor*, www.econstor.eu/handle/10419/155879. Accessed 22 April 2021.

2

Taming the Polyp: Address Books and Their Impact on Wartime Exile in London

Julia Eichenberg

"The most unexpected thing about coming to Britain was the sheer size of London, then still by far the largest city in the western world, a vast shapeless polyp of streets and buildings stretching its tentacles into the countryside" (Hobsbawm 2002, 78). This is how historian Eric Hobsbawm describes his first encounter with London after moving to Great Britain in 1933. He was by far not the only one to newly arrive in London. During the 1930s, many members of the political opposition as well as artists and others fled from Nazi Germany to British shores. From 1940 onward, after the rapid conquest by the German *Wehrmacht* had left the European continent under a suppressive occupation regime, exiles from the occupied countries followed to the last remaining free allied country in reachable distance. Just as Hobsbawm, they needed to adjust to exiled life as such, but also to the urban space of London in particular.

Address books enabled the émigrés to connect with old acquaintances in the new country and helped them establish new contacts and networks (Atze/Waldner 2001; Fischer-Defoy 2006a, 2006b, 2007). "Every contact was useful. For those furnished with the right addresses and phone numbers, [...] there were succulent fruits to pick" is how Daniel Snowman describes these address books' importance for artist émigrés in Great Britain (2002, 101). This was particularly true for European exiles during the Second World War in London. The following chapter will introduce address books as a crucial link in the historical analysis of political, diplomatic and academic networks. In a first step, the chapter will discuss address books as a primary source for historical studies. Offering a case study of European exiles in London during the Second World War, I will analyze two examples of address books used in London during the time: one directory and two private address books. The aim is to show that address books were, first, necessary material carriers of knowledge (i.e. of addresses and contacts) which then, second, enabled the construction of networks in an unfamiliar urban space. Analyzing address books as archival material for historical research thus helps us to source traces of exile, to discover connections and networks build by exiles, but also to discover how exiles proceeded to make this foreign city their own. Accordingly, the chapter encourages further inclusion of address books not only in historical analysis but also in other disciplines engaging with exiles and/or the appropriation of urban space.

Using address books as primary sources

Contacts and networks were vital for survival in exile, for politicians as well as for artists and intellectuals. Their new situation meant that they needed to gather and store knowledge about people formerly unknown to them, people from possibly different educational backgrounds, different social hierarchies, different professional environments and different systems of government. At the same time, it was necessary for the exiles to publicize themselves, their education and qualifications. Contact addresses are to be seen as active agents in this new environment. Data were moving fast in exile. Despite all consolidation and improvement of their status, these people were still refugees: many had moved quickly, changed address, city or even country, even more so once the Blitz came to London. When arriving in a new city, it is of vital importance to discover, structure, memorize one's urban environment (for an insightful analysis of the process, see Pooley 2004). Address books were needed to keep track of this process, to build up and maintain networks.

Address books are particularly essential to exiles, their material existence helps them to organize their networks and to remember contacts and connections. They contain datasets which are far more difficult to coordinate mentally – in particular when dealing with notoriously dry and repetitive information like phone numbers and addresses. Writing down administers and assists our memory. As material objects, address books serve the delegation of knowledge. As material objects, they also acted as temporal carriers of an immaterial function for their users: they structure the present and are connections to both past and future; they are part of a portable connection back home and proof of the process of integration. With these two functions, address books contributed to increased transnational collaboration in London during the war years. They helped exiles to navigate the new city with its many new inhabitants and enabled the establishment and maintenance of networks, which again enabled further collaboration, or, as Latour phrased it: "[e]very time you want to know what a nonhuman does, simply imagine what other humans or other nonhumans would have to do were this character not present" (Latour 1992, 155).

Address books and agendas offer an insight into life in London as the quasi capital of Europe with its unique social life. They serve as "[i]nventories of Social history, navigation books through the networks of individual relations", as Karl Schlögel writes, the renowned historian of Eastern Europe who (re)introduced space into German historiography and feuilleton debates (Schlögel 2003, 344, for his impact see Döring/Thielmann 2008, 19–24). By following listed addresses and penned meeting places, we can reconstruct who met whom when and where and we can discover the everyday life and social conditions of intellectual and political collaboration. Linking daily logistics, social life and memory, address books are both a tool and a cultural technique (Pethes 2013; Atze/Waldner 2001). Address books thus become a material part of networks, which could not be maintained without them (Latour 2007; Appadurai 1986; Dölemeyer 2005). Unfortunately, not many of these books have survived, perhaps because they were considered common household objects, or because the quality of paper in wartime meant they were not durable. Maybe their owners, when returning from exile, decided that luggage space could be used in a better way than by transporting now out-of-date addresses, as small as the books might have been. Additionally, families, heirs and archivists often regarded address books as less important to keep for posterity or for their historical research than letters or diaries. However, social and cultural history increasingly use address books as sources; social history with a focus on address books of certain cities and parishes, cultural history with a focus on the personal.

Directories of the 'London Moment'

During the war, political representatives from occupied European countries fled to Britain, among them monarchs, heads of states, cabinets and others. This created a historically extraordinary situation and turned London into the seat of most European governments, making it a sort of capital of free Europe. This moment of geographical vicinity during wartime made politicians, diplomats and lawyers of neighbouring states actual neighbours and provided a greenhouse for possible post-war partnerships. Most Allies amongst them were recognized as governments-in-exile, namely, Belgium, Czechoslovakia, Greece, Luxembourg, the Netherlands, Norway, Poland and Yugoslavia. Free France was recognized as a National Committee. These European exiles in London were far from their German-occupied home countries, in a city unknown to most of them, speaking a different (and to many a new) language. They had left their old lives behind, including family, friends and former work environments. Most refugees arrived in London stripped of their belongings, their former networks and social status. Even a privileged figure like Dutch Queen Wilhelmina allegedly arrived without luggage, dressed in a trench coat worn over her nightgown (Wilhelmina 1961, 247).

Address books, formerly things of daily routine, became an essential accessory to help build up political and juridical networks in London. Establishing new contacts was central to the exiles' new lives: They needed links to compatriots to strengthen national committees, maintain communication to their home country and ensure efficient representation. They needed contacts to the British Government and British ministries to secure their own status, to lobby for privileges for themselves, their national representations and their agendas. Not least, they needed contacts to other Europeans in London (and the UK) to discuss shared experiences of exile with kindred spirits, get advice, forge alliances and plan a new European post-war future.

Address books were an important device during the 'London Moment' and increased its characteristic informal diplomacy. While they cannot be categorized as official diplomatic documents, address books were certainly an essential material tool to the modern diplomat (compare Rudolph 2016, 1–28). The 'London Moment', defined as a microcosm created by the presence of the European exiles and the willingness of the British to embrace (at least temporarily) London's new role as a place of refuge that allowed close political communication under circumstances condensed in time and space, highly depended on informal contacts and diplomacy (Eichenberg 2018, 471ff., compare Manela 2007; Conrad/Sachsenmaier 2007).

Besides many private address books, an allied directory, *The Who's Who of the Allied Governments in Great Britain*, catered to this niche. In 1941, the publishing house Allied Publications Company published the first edition of *The Who's Who of the Allied Governments in Great Britain* in London (Cang 1941, fig. 2.1). Edited by the Polish-born journalist Joel Cang, its subtitle advertised: "A Handy Reference Book with Information about the Allied Governments, Their Forces and Institutions". It contained 80 pages of information on all governments who had arrived in London in 1940: Poland, Czechoslovakia, Norway, the Netherlands, Belgium and Free France. It aimed to inform the British public about these allied governments in London and served as a reference book for the governments in question to facilitate transnational cooperation. The increasing number not only of refugees but also of allied governments, committees and other institutions in London had created a market for such a special directory. Previously, other migrants had profited from non-governmental refugee organizations collecting and distributing addresses to them, as was the case, for example, for Russian refugees arriving in Berlin in the 1920s (Schlögel 2007, 109–113). The *Who's Who*

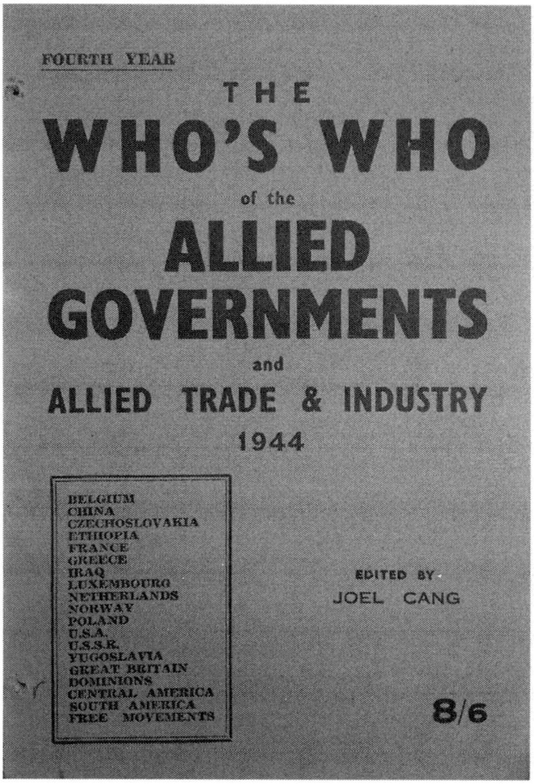

FIGURE 2.1: Joel Cang, editor. *The Who's Who of the Allied Governments and Allied Trade & Industry*. Fourth Year. Allied Publications Company (London), 1944, cover page (Photo: Archive of the author).

directory, presenting important addresses for the European governments-in-exile as well as for their editing houses, associations and enterprises, followed a British tradition of privately published directories catering to local, political and business affairs, established in the late 17th century (Sasse 2021).

The *Who's Who* was published annually during the war (1940–1944), but did not change much in appearance over the years: it was a small paperback brochure, printed on poor quality paper as was characteristic for wartime publications due to paper shortages. Clad in an orange coloured cover, its pages were filled with small print – clearly designed as ephemera rather than something to last for eternity. The lack of a price and the amount of advertisements included in it indicate that it was probably distributed without a fee and financed by ad revenue.

All volumes included addresses and phone numbers for each government (and some other institutions) as well as lists of cabinet members and extensive biographical sections: members of the allied governments, committees and political movements were introduced by name and with a short biography. These biographical sections, not usually part of address books, were an extremely helpful tool for London's microcosm of exiles. Due to different national educational systems and uprooted vitas, it was not easy to identify the right addressee amongst other exiles. The *Who's Who* thus served as the white pages and yellow pages of exile, simultaneously providing a list of the merits and qualifications of allied curricula vitae. This directory had the added advantage of being potentially available to everyone, not just the exiles, thus broadening the visibility and accessibility of people and addresses. The *Who's Who* (fig. 2.2) served three functions: first, it materialized contacts by containing

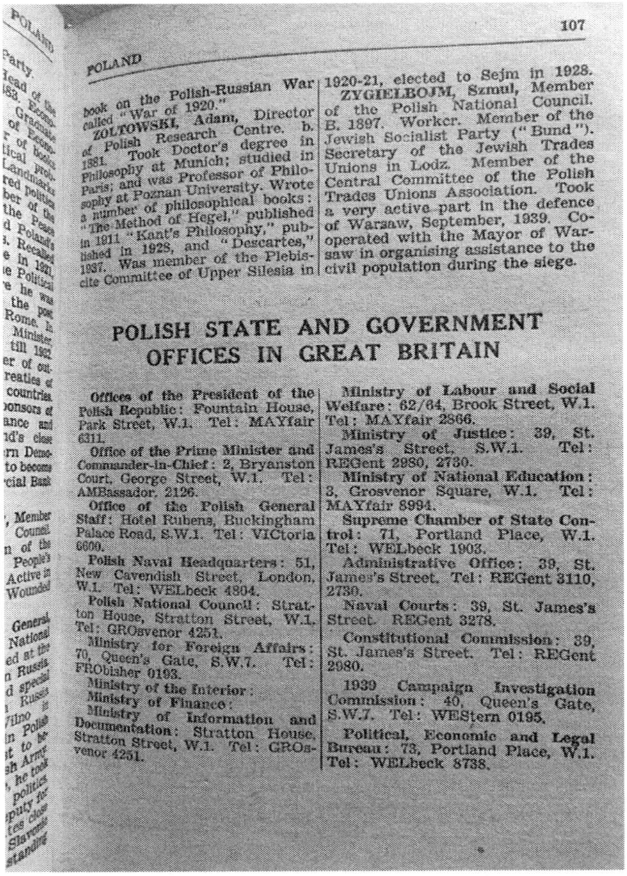

POLAND 107

book on the Polish-Russian War called "War of 1920."

ZOLTOWSKI, Adam, Director of Polish Research Centre. b. 1881. Took Doctor's degree in Philosophy at Munich; studied in Paris; and was Professor of Philosophy at Poznan University. Wrote a number of philosophical books: "The Method of Hegel," published in 1911 "Kant's Philosophy," published in 1928, and "Descartes," 1937. Was member of the Plebiscite Committee of Upper Silesia in 1920-21, elected to Sejm in 1928.

ZYGIELBOJM, Szmul, Member of the Polish National Council. B. 1897. Worker. Member of the Jewish Socialist Party ("Bund"). Secretary of the Jewish Trades Unions in Lodz. Member of the Central Committee of the Polish Trades Unions Association. Took a very active part in the defence of Warsaw, September, 1939. Co-operated with the Mayor of Warsaw in organising assistance to the civil population during the siege.

POLISH STATE AND GOVERNMENT OFFICES IN GREAT BRITAIN

Offices of the President of the Polish Republic: Fountain House, Park Street, W.1. Tel: MAYfair 6311.

Office of the Prime Minister and Commander-in-Chief: 2, Bryanston Court, George Street, W.1. Tel: AMBassador. 2126.

Office of the Polish General Staff: Hotel Rubens, Buckingham Palace Road, S.W.1. Tel: VICtoria 6600.

Polish Naval Headquarters: 51, New Cavendish Street, London, W.1. Tel: WELbeck 4804.

Polish National Council: Stratton House, Stratton Street, W.1. Tel: GROsvenor 4251.

Ministry for Foreign Affairs: 70, Queen's Gate, S.W.7. Tel: FRObisher 0193.

Ministry of the Interior:

Ministry of Finance:

Ministry of Information and Documentation: Stratton House, Stratton Street, W.1. Tel: GROsvenor 4251.

Ministry of Labour and Social Welfare: 62/64, Brook Street, W.1. Tel: MAYfair 2866.

Ministry of Justice: 39, St. James's Street, S.W.1. Tel: REGent 2980, 2730.

Ministry of National Education: 3, Grosvenor Square, W.1. Tel: MAYfair 8994.

Supreme Chamber of State Control: 71, Portland Place, W.1. Tel: WELbeck 1903.

Administrative Office: 39, St. James's Street. Tel: REGent 3110, 2730.

Naval Courts: 39, St. James's Street. REGent 3278.

Constitutional Commission: 39, St. James's Street. Tel: REGent 2980.

1939 Campaign Investigation Commission: 40, Queen's Gate, S.W.7. Tel: WEStern 0195.

Political, Economic and Legal Bureau: 73, Portland Place, W.1. Tel: WELbeck 8738.

FIGURE 2.2: "Addresses and Phone Numbers for Polish State and Government Offices in Great Britain." *The Who's Who of the Allied Governments in Great Britain*, edited by Joel Cang. Allied Publications Company (London), 1942, p. 107 (photo: archive of the author).

knowledge in a material brochure. Second, it became integral to allied networks, which could only be maintained with the information contained within it. Third, it was also instrumental in structuring the networks: it determined the exiles' visibility and approachability within the network by setting out what section, order and biographical details were ascribed to them. The directory thus fundamentally impacted urban network structures, further proving the interconnection between material things and the social sphere (compare Derix et al. 2016, 392).

Private address books and informal networks

There are few remaining private address books of the London Moment. However, some did survive, amongst them those belonging to René Cassin and Edward Raczyński. They offer vital insight into these men's roles and networking activities within the 'London Moment'.[1] René Cassin, who until his emigration was a professor of law in Paris and a former French representative to the League of Nations, was Free France's Commissary of Justice and Public Education and an active networker in allied London. Central to the networks of legal experts, he became a permanent member of the commission on the Trial of War Criminals (predecessor of the United Nations War Crimes Commission). After the war, he continued his internationalist commitment in international law and would later receive the Nobel Peace Prize for his co-authorship of the Human Rights Declaration. There were few figures as central to the networking of the 'London Moment' as Cassin, but Edward Raczyński was surely one of them. The Polish ambassador Count Edward Raczyński had arrived in London as early as 1934 and went on to serve until 1945, a rare extensive time of service as an ambassador. He was essential to prepare the ground and ease the transition of the exiled Polish government to the British capital. Through his experience, and his (in exiled circles rarely matched) knowledge of London's political microcosm as well as of the English language, he was an important mediator in political affairs far beyond the typical obligations of an ambassador. This is underlined by his additional promotion to Minister for Foreign Affairs from 1941 to 1943. Together with his wife, Rogalinie Cecylia Raczyńska, he hosted many embassy receptions, serving as a social mediator. According to their central position within London and exiled networks, keeping track of addresses was all the more important to their influence (Raczyński 1962).

Cassin's London address book contains telephone numbers and addresses, though not every entry has both. Strictly speaking, it was a small, chequered writing pad with spiral binding which had been transformed into an address book by adding small alphabetical register stickers (which might have been added by himself, or his secretary). That the pad was used regularly is clearly visible: entries are made with different pens and even in different handwriting (maybe they feature Cassin's alternating script and print handwriting, perhaps others wrote in it). Several entries have been changed or corrected. Many names one would assume to have been important for Cassin are missing – we do not know why. Were members of the Free French not included because daily contact made it unnecessary and telephone numbers were known by heart? René Pleven, French exiled commissioner of finance, colonies and foreign affairs, is listed, as are multiple entries for "Cabinet du Général" (de Gaulle). Many entries speak of Cassin's commitment for human rights and post-war justice.[2] A number of addresses in Algiers indicate the division of the French national committee: while de Gaulle often resided in Algiers, Cassin remained his representative in London, commuting regularly. Juggling networks in two cities at once was only feasible with the help of his address books. While surprisingly many members of European exile governments do not feature in the address books that still exist, Cassin's centrality for European networks in London is undisputed and clearly displayed by his activities and correspondences (fig. 2.3).

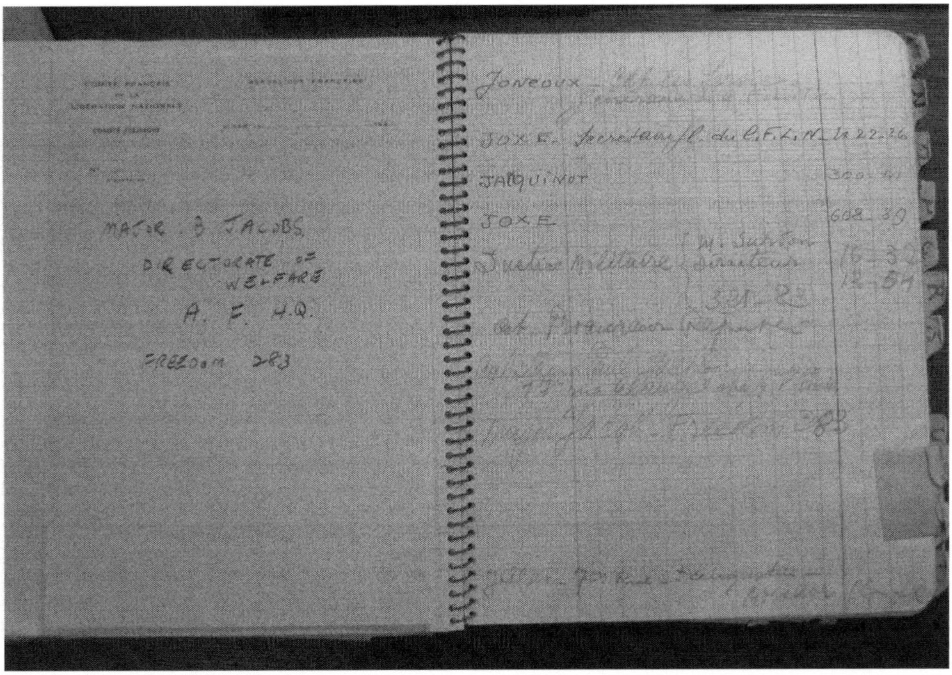

FIGURE 2.3: Page from René Cassin's address book (Archives Nationales [AN] Paris, Fonds René Cassin. 382 AP 27 Papiers personnels 1940–1945, Doss. 4, Portfolio "Reliske et calepins d'Adresses [s.d.] et cahier d'enregistrement du courier reçu du 30 août 1941 au 27 février 1943 et adressé du 2 septembre 1941 au 26 février 1943 [3 pièces]").

Raczyński's address books were more formal; two small books with a brown, fake-leather binding. The first one seems to cover the pre-war and war years as it contains London addresses but also lists addresses from the continent in Paris, Warsaw, Geneva and Berlin. The second one seems to expand into post-war exile, as some notes are dated in the 1960s, though it still includes war-time addresses. Some of the entries have telephone numbers (e.g. Winston Churchill, the Foreign Office, several clubs and hotels, among them Claridge's, The Kennel Club, Queen's Club), some list postal addresses (e.g. W.R. Litte, Director of European Emigration). Most interestingly, Raczyński also used his address book to make notes about where he met someone or what they could be of help with: who to contact about passports in the French Consulate, the director of intelligence in the Reuters Office, *The Times* correspondents for several cities, who came over for dinner, as well as who introduced him to whom. Owen O'Malley, former Minister to Hungary and later British Ambassador to the Polish government in exile, is listed both as a contact in the Foreign Office's Northern Department as well as with a personal home address in the English countryside (*'na wsi'*/in the country).[3]

During the war, Raczyński must have changed to the new address book, probably because all those continental addresses were no longer of use while the expanding network of the European political elite in Britain created a new allied microcosm with countless new addresses. The new book holds numbers of London hotels and clubs, essential contact points for meetings, lunches, dinners or to arrange stays for travelling members of the Polish government and military. In his position as the ambassador, and responsible for all contacts with the British government, Raczyński's address book holds phone numbers for Buckingham Palace, the Foreign Office, the Home Office, the House of Lords, the Stationery Office (in charge of publications) and the Treasury, but also for central British contacts within the exile microcosm, such as Owen O'Malley (Ambassador to the Polish government-in-exile, 1943–1945), Sir Alexander Cadogan (Permanent Under-Secretary of State for Foreign Affairs 1938–1946), Victor Cazalet (MP and liaison officer with General Sikorski of the Polish government-in-exile, 1940 until his sudden death in 1943) and Sir Lancelot Oliphant (Ambassador to Belgium since 1939 and to the Belgian and Luxembourg governments-in-exile, 1941–1944). The BBC is listed with its Bush House address and number, the location of the BBC world service and, from 1940s on, the headquarters of the European service. Raczyński's address books display his immense networking abilities in what was a new urban environment: the members of the Polish circle were obviously present, such as diplomat Jan Ciechanowski, jurist Stefan Glaser, General Sosnkowski (post-war), but we can also find Czechoslovakian names like president Edvard Beneš, the head of the chancellery Jaromír Smutný, and the political adviser Hubert Ripka, as well as a (post-war) address for the Belgian politician Paul-Henri Spaak (the later prime minister and supporter of European unification, who was the wartime minister of foreign affairs for the Belgian government-in-exile during the war). Several embassies are included, and so, too, is a selection of bilateral and transnational circles of cooperation: The Anglo-Polish Society (52 Argyll Rd., W 8), the Allied Club (148 Piccadilly), the Allied Circle (46 Green Street, W1) and the Central European Federal Club (Sfo 2199).[4] Just as Raczyński later entitled his memoirs *In Allied London*, his address books are material proof of this allied microcosm (Raczyński 1962, compare Beardon 2013), which in many ways compares to other exiled microcosms, such as Schlögel's description of the 'Global Village Komintern' in Berlin (Schlögel 2007, 179–208).

Conclusions: Address books and knowledge

While Cassin's and Raczyński's private address books speak of their ability as networkers and 'brokers' in London, the print edition of *Who's Who of the Allied Governments in Great Britain* democratized insider knowledge. The biographical information included in the *Who's Who* added further valuable information to the reader while at the same time structuring and influencing newly-developing trans-European networks: it offered a means of researching people, functions and addresses amongst recently constructed community of exiles. At the same time, editorial decisions on the directory's structure could be exclusive: whoever was not represented in the brochure was less visible and was not part of the network to the same extent as those included in its pages. Because a personal address book only contains the contacts established by its owner, who also structures and orders its contents, it is not necessarily of use to others. Some entries are hardly legible, others contain only last names without further explanation – a memory aid for whoever took the note, but not very useful for outsiders. They had to be decoded by their owner, which in turn symbolized the owner's knowledge and control over their network. This turned the storage of facts, of individual addresses, into an important part of a broader migrant knowledge (Lässig/Steinberg 2017). The *Who's Who*, on the other hand, worked like a public directory and thus democratized contacts in exile.

Analyzing address books thus enables us to reconstruct exiled lives: contacts, the distances between meetings, venues of accommodation and work. At the same time, it offers insight into exiles' techniques to gather, administer and transfer knowledge which then enabled them to adapt to exiled life. Managing your addresses in exile was essential for exiles and refugees to structure their new life, to take possession of the new city, to tame the polyp. These address books can be considered just as essential as a historical source for all who research the lives, networks and collaborations of exiles, to trace the way they explored, structured and adapted to new and unfamiliar urban spaces.

NOTES

1. The Cassin collection contains two address books, the more substantial one, which is largely focussed on London, is discussed here. AN Paris, Fonds Cassin, 382 AP 27 Papiers personnels 1940–1945, Doss. 4, Portfolio Reliske et calepins d'adresses (s.d.) et cahier d'enregistrement du courier reçu du 30 août 1941 au 27 février 1943 et adressé du 2 septembre 1941 au 26 février 1943 (3 pièces).
2. E.g. 'Bazat (Liason Crimes de Guerres)'; 'Dejan – délégué du C.F.L.N. auprès des courts alliés replis à Londres'; 'United Nations Commission for the Investigation of War Crimes, Room 201, Royal Courts of Justice, Strand, London W.C. 2'.
3. Raczyński, Edward. First address book. Kolekcja *Raczyński*/Personal Papers (Polish Institute and Sikorski Museum (PISM), London, KOL 23H/364 Książki adresowe 1942–1945.
4. Raczyński, Edward. Second address book. Kolekcja *Raczyński*/Personal Papers, PISM, KOL 23H/364 Książki adresowe 1942–1945.

REFERENCES

Appadurai, Arjun, editor. *The Social Life of Things: Commodities in Cultural Perspective*. Cambridge University Press, 1986.

Atze, Marcel, and Kyra Waldner. *Andere Seiten: Private Adreßbücher prominenter Zeitgenossen aus zwei Jahrhunderten Kunst, Literatur und Musik*. With an essay by Christine Fischer-Defoy. Metro Verlag, 2001.

Beardon, James. *The Spellmount Guide to London in the Second World War*. Spellmount, 2013.

Cang, Joel, editor. *The Who's Who of the Allied Governments in Great Britain: A Handy Reference Book with information about the Allied Governments, Their Forces and Institutions*. Allied Publication Company, 1941 (1942, 1943, 1944).

Conrad, Sebastian, and Dominic Sachsenmaier, editors. *Competing Visions of World Order: Global Moments and Movements, 1880s–1930s*. Palgrave Macmillan, 2007.

Derix, Simone, et al. "Der Wert der Dinge. Zur Wirtschafts- und Sozialgeschichte der Materialitäten." *Der Wert der Dinge*, special issue of *Zeithistorische Forschungen/Studies in Contemporary History*, vol. 13, no. 3, 2016, pp. 387–403, doi: 10.14765/zzf.dok-1381. Accessed 3 June 2021.

Dölemeyer, Barbara. "Dinge als Zeichen des Rechts – Zur Rechtsikonographie und Rechtsarchäologie." *Die Dinge als Zeichen. Kulturelles Wissen und materielle Kultur*, edited by Tobias L. Kienlin, Habelt, 2005, pp. 221–230.

Döring, Jörg, and Tristan Thielmann, editors. *Spatial Turn: Das Raumparadigma in den Kultur- und Sozialwissenschaften*. transcript, 2008.

Eichenberg, Julia. "Macht auf der Flucht. Europäische Regierungen in London (1940–1944)." *Flucht als Handlungszusammenhang*, special issue of *Zeithistorische Forschungen/Studies in Contemporary History*, vol. 15, no. 3, 2018, pp. 452–473, doi: 10.14765/zzf.dok.4.1291. Accessed 3 June 2021.

Fischer-Defoy, Christine, editor. *Walter Benjamin. Das Adressbuch des Exils 1933–1940. '... wie überall hin die Leute verstreut sind ...'*. Koehler & Amelang, 2006a.

Fischer-Defoy, Christine, editor. *Heinrich Mann. Das private Adressbuch 1926–1940. 'Auch ich kam aus Deutschland ...'*. Koehler & Amelang, 2006b.

Fischer-Defoy, Christine, editor. *Hannah Arendt. Das private Adressbuch 1951–1975. 'Mir ist, als müsste ich mich selbst suchen gehen'*. Koehler & Amelang, 2007.

Hobsbawm, Eric. *Interesting Times: A Twentieth-Century Life*. Pantheon, 2002.

Lässig, Simone, and Swen Steinberg, editors. *Knowledge and Migration*, special issue of *Geschichte und Gesellschaft*, vol. 43, no. 1, 2017.

Latour, Bruno. *Eine neue Soziologie für eine neue Gesellschaft: Einführung in die Akteur-Netzwerk-Theorie*. Translated by Gustav Roßler, Suhrkamp, 2007.

Latour, Bruno. "Where are the Missing Masses? Sociology of a Few Mundane Artifacts." *Technology and Society: Building Our Sociotechnical Future*, edited by Deborah G. Johnson and Jameson M. Wetmore, MIT Press, 1992, pp. 151–180.

Manela, Erez. *The Wilsonian Moment: Self-Determination and the International Origins of Anticolonial Nationalism*. Oxford University Press, 2007.

Pethes. Nicolas. *Kulturwissenschaftliche Gedächtnistheorien* (Zur Einführung, 356), 2nd ed., Junius Verlag, 2013.

Pooley, Colin G. "Getting to Know the City: The Construction of Spatial Knowledge in London in the 1930s." *Urban History*, vol. 31, no. 2, 2004, pp. 210–228. *ResearchGate*, doi: 10.1017/S0963926804002111. Accessed 5 June 2021.

Raczyński, Edward. *In Allied London*. Weidenfeld & Nicolson, 1962.

Rudolph, Harriet. "Entangled Objects and Hybrid Practices? Material Cultures as a new approach to the History of Diplomacy." *Material Culture in Modern Diplomacy from the 15th to the 20th Century* (Jahrbuch für europäische Geschichte/European History Yearbook, vol. 17), edited Harriet Rudolph and Gregor Metzig, De Gruyter Oldenbourg, 2016, pp. 1–28.

Sasse, Cristina. *Die Stadt lesen. Englische "Directories" als Wissens- und Orientierungsmedien, 1760–1830* (Veröffentlichungen des Deutschen Historischen Instituts London/Publications of the German Historical Institute London, 85). De Gruyter Oldenbourg, 2021.

Schlögel, Karl. *Im Raume lesen wir die Zeit: Über Zivilisationsgeschichte und Geopolitik*, Hanser, 2003.

Schlögel, Karl. *Das Russische Berlin: Ostbahnhof Europas*. Siedler, 2007.

Snowman, Daniel. *The Hitler Émigrés: The Cultural Impact on Britain of Refugees from Nazism*, Pimlico, 2002.

Wilhelmina. *Einsam und doch nicht allein*. Evangelisches Werk, 1961.

3

Close Reading Istanbul: Through the Lens of Two Almanacs by Russian-speaking Émigrés in the 1920s

Ekaterina Aygün

While the etymology of the word *almanac* is unclear, one of its meanings as described in the Cambridge Dictionary is that of "a book published every year that contains facts and information about a particular subject or activity" (Anonymous 2013, n.p.). From this explanation, it is evident that 'books' of this type can address a wide range of topics. The peculiarity of almanacs in the Russian language is that they cannot be defined as periodicals: they were not published on a daily or monthly basis but as the material accumulated. However, they were not considered non-periodical publications either.[1] This chapter offers to look for 'traces' by exploring the nexus between Russian-speaking émigrés in Istanbul in the 1920s and urban space with the help of a specific form of Russian almanacs: non-periodic documentary miscellanies of the 'First Wave' of Russian emigration which were created by the émigrés themselves, thus allowing us to hear their voices.

Russian-speaking refugees[2] who were forced to flee from the consequences of the revolution and civil war in the former Russian Empire and settled in Istanbul in the early 1920s, published many books and newspapers in the city. All of them are useful sources for exile studies, but the almanacs *Farewell* and *Les Russes sur le Bosphore* (Russians on the Bosphorus) occupy a special place in this list, primarily because of their contents. As what could be termed 'encyclopaedias of the life of Russian émigrés in Istanbul' they provide detailed information about the protagonists and events of the time. Another important aspect is that both almanacs were published at turning points in the life of Russian émigrés in Istanbul: that is, in 1923, when some refugees decided to move to other countries due to changes in the rules for refugees after the formation of the Turkish Republic, and in 1928, after the rules for refugees were significantly tightened.

Both almanacs can be described as collaborative works compiled by Russian émigré journalists, writers, painters and photographers in Istanbul.[3] *Farewell* was published to express "the Russian public opinion of gratitude in all sincerity for the moral and material help lavished upon Russian Refugees by those of all Creeds and Nations in Constantinople" (Bournakine/Valery 1923, n.p.), whilst *Les Russes sur le Bosphore* wanted to inform readers about the achievements of Russian émigrés during their presence in the city and express "Russian gratitude to Turkey for its hospitality and Russian sympathy for the Turkish people" (Anonymous 1927, n.p.). Taking into consideration the purposes for creating such almanacs and the fact that they are neither political, military nor wholly literary texts, it appears that the principal difficulty in dealing with them lies not in hidden hazards but in the incompleteness of the information conveyed and its insufficient systematization due to the "forced haste of work", as explained by the authors themselves (Bournakine/Valery 1923, n.p.).[4] In order to examine and mine locations, addresses and other important places for the exile community in Istanbul, in the following, I will implement a close reading of these almanacs, that is to say, I will engage in a thoughtful and critical analysis of both book objects. Verbs such as 'to trace', 'to dive' and 'to dig' most fully reveal the essence of this process, since it is always about paying attention and focusing on key details, just as if these objects (in this particular case almanacs) were put under a microscope. According to Jane Gallop, close reading is a widely applicable skill which is of value to a wide range of scholars in different disciplines: "Students trained in close reading have been known to apply it to diverse sorts of texts – newspaper articles, textbooks in other disciplines, political speeches – and thus to discover things they would not otherwise have noticed" (2007, 183). Yet, perhaps the most important issue in working with this method is the presence of an appropriate background knowledge which is often neglected[5]: in many cases, it is only an understanding of historical and/or cultural context that makes close reading meaningful[6] by allowing "to engage in an active process of connecting things in a pattern" (Wineburg 2001, 21). As Neil McCaw (quoting Julian Wolfreys in *Readings: Acts of Close Reading in Literary Theory*) rightly notes, "reading closely can still (if carried out in the right way) be a dynamic process in which texts and knowledges are thrown together, with the readers opening themselves up 'to receiving numerous significations, a complex web of possible meanings, a skein of traces and inscriptions within the single – and singular word'" (2011, 31; Wolfreys 2000, vii). Because I myself have the appropriate background knowledge regarding the topic of this chapter, my first steps were to read the almanacs and then to re-read them, in order to dive into the texts by focusing on the topic of urban exile, noting all significant places and trying to parse as much as I could whilst not disregarding possible subtexts. The next step was to analyze and synthesize the information by way of drawing connections and by combining several patterns; or, in other words, by moving from the observation of particular details to an act of interpretation while also considering how the contents of these almanacs connect with other texts on the topic that I have encountered.[7]

Reading 'Russian Istanbul' through the Farewell *Almanac (1923)*

This part of the chapter focuses on reconstructing important exile places in Istanbul with the help of the almanac *Farewell*. Since this almanac was created and published almost immediately following the first, and perhaps most difficult, period for Russian refugees in Istanbul (1919–1921), it mostly references places of the city that helped them survive in those years in Istanbul, years of hopelessness and despair. As the city was overcrowded with refugees, its life (especially in Péra, today's Beyoğlu) had to be organized in accordance with the needs and requirements of the newcomers. Charles King mentions around 185,000 civil war refugees from the former Russian Empire who came with Wrangel's fleet, raising the total population by 20 per cent (2019, 97). Thus, it was imperative to provide suitable living conditions in the city so that those left without means of subsistence were not forced to die of diseases right on the streets or rob residents for a piece of bread. Nevertheless, the situation was far from perfect: pickpockets and burglars were operating, drunken soldiers fought in the streets, prostitution flourished and there were about 10,000 cocaine addicts in the city (Alexandrov 2017, 235f.; Litvine 1921). This situation, of course, discouraged residents from leaving their homes at nightfall, and when they had to, they tried to walk carefully and quickly along the streets of Péra (today's Beyoğlu) and Galata, which was considered especially insecure (ibid.) (fig. 3.1).

Judging by the information given in the almanac, among the first to open their doors to refugees were 'Russian' places that already existed in Istanbul, such as the Russian embassy, the Russian consulate, Russian churches in Karaköy and the Church of St Nicholas in Harbiye. Russian consular establishments at that time were located in Narmanlı Han, "one of the most important iconic historic structure [*sic*] with its intangible dimensions in the memory of the city", originally built to house the Russian Embassy sometime after 1831 (Sav 2018, 652–659). In close vicinity to it, on Grande Rue de Péra, you could find the new neo-Renaissance building of the Russian Embassy – the exact spot where Russian refugees gathered in the early morning hours in the 1920s: some looking

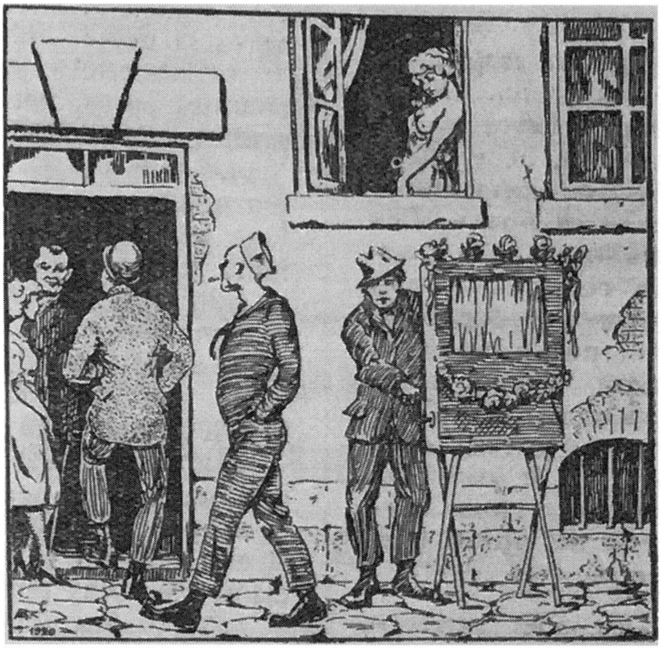

FIGURE 3.1: Illustration of Galata neighbourhood, 1920, in the *Nashi Dni* Periodical, January 1921, no. 1, p. 15 (Slavonic Library/Slovanská knihovna, Prague).

for someone, some trying to get information about the progression of the civil war in Russia, while others simply needed help (Chebyshev 1933, n.p.). At the time, the Russian Embassy was extremely multifunctional: it served as an enquiry office, a church, a shelter, a canteen and even a place where auctions were held. As for the churches in Karaköy, they were and still are located at Athos courtyards, on the upper floors of low residential buildings. Once, they served as hotels for Orthodox pilgrims on their way to Jerusalem and Athos, but in the 1920s, Russian refugees lived there. This is how writer and poet Ivan Korvatsky described it: "The monastery courtyard, where 2–3 families huddled in each room, the inevitable primus stove made noise and smelled, the beds were partitioned off with torn sheets, and a cry of a child monotonously sounded in the air" (qtd. in Sığırcı 2018, 49). Another important place was the Church of St Nicholas in Harbiye, and the Russian Nikolayevskiy Hospital next to it. It was built in 1875 under the guidance of the Russian ambassador to the Ottoman Empire, Nikolay Ignatyev, and offered free health assistance to Russians and Orthodox Christians in need living in Istanbul until the first years of the Turkish Republic (Ünal 2018, 235–239).

Considering that "Istanbul's 'Russian' moment",[8] or, in other words, the arrival of Russian refugees in Istanbul, happened at a time when the city was occupied by Allied forces after the defeat of the Ottoman Empire in the First World War (1918–1923), all kinds of assistance was also provided by non-local communities in Istanbul. All of the Istanbul Red Cross branches and hospitals played, without any doubt, a vital role in this regard. According to the almanac, if not 70 per cent, then at least 50 per cent of the Russian refugee masses "breathed" owing to the help of the American Red Cross, which was headed by Admiral Bristol: "This is where the Russian refugee goes first of all with all his needs and sorrows. Whether there is a need for financial support for departure, the only dress has come to complete disrepair, someone needs urgent medical assistance, or simply cannot find any job" (Bournakine/Valery 1923, XVII–XXI). Among the hospitals mentioned in the almanac is the American Hospital established in 1920, Jeanne D'Arc Hospital, known among the Russian refugees as the "asylum for motherhood" (ibid., XXII), the Bulgarian hospital in Şişli, where they not only recovered but also could "feel refreshment of mind and body" (ibid., XXXIX), and the Jewish Or-Ahayim hospital in Balat, which provided medical care to Jews and non-Jews who asked for help. No less important were free meal sites. One of these canteens was opened at Sirkeci Railway Station, "in the train yard under ship's awnings", by Madame Bristol, wife of Admiral Bristol (ibid., XI). This place was very convenient because here many refugees embarked from ships and were distributed to camps. Another canteen, for 600–700 people, was opened at the school of Sainte Pulchérie by the French Ladies' Committee, whose representatives were mainly spouses of the leaders of non-local communities (ibid., XIX). Concerning housing, some 7000 Russian refugees were lucky enough to obtain residence through the Russian Embassy, but far more lived in wooden barracks and tents (Near East Foundation 2016, n.p.). The Russian overnight shelter in Dolmabahçe was quite famous, although the almanac also mentions barracks for refugees in the headquarters of Near East Relief, Miss Cox's rest house for convalescents in Büyükada, and private houses, villas and hotels that were transformed into shelters in Burgazada by the Italian colony. There was also a YWCA place for young Russian girls in Péra (Beyoğlu) that served not only as a hostel but also as a place where girls were able to learn crafts which could provide them with a livelihood, for example hat-making (Bournakine/Valery 1923, XLII–XLIII). Additionally, several schools were opened, among them a free Russian school financed by American sailors, and a Russian school in Büyükdere which was maintained by representatives of the British colony. American 'spiritual institutions', as Russian refugees called them, also operated throughout the city. The most famous ones were the Christian Science Relief Committee and The

Russian Lighthouse (known as Mayak). The Christian Science Relief Committee was located on Sıraselvi Street, at a small house with an inscription that read "Christian Science". Here, refugees were provided not only with moral support but also very often with pecuniary assistance: "Russian refugees familiar with the humiliating treatment they received in Constantinople and of being always looked down upon, have always found here an exceptional kindheartedness and lively interest" (Bournakine/Valery 1923, XXIV). Mayak deserves special attention because it hosted a YMCA center, where refugees from the (former) Russian Empire were served food in the dining room, were gifted clothes and where they could arrange visits to the dispensary and employment bureau. The authors of the almanac also mention splendid concerts by Russian-speaking artists and good parties, lectures and discussions, scholarly conferences led by Russian-speaking priests, cinema shows, Christmas and Easter celebrations for poor children, as well as many other activities which took place at Mayak (ibid., XXIII–XXIV). From the point of view of architectural history research, it is very important to understand that all these places, including hospitals, canteens, shelters and many others, were located at either already existing buildings or functionally transformed available buildings (Ar 2019, 101–122). As Bilge Ar rightly points out, despite an enormous need for new spaces to serve Allied forces as well as refugees, 'the city' failed in providing new housing (ibid., 101).

Meanwhile, small photographs, used by the creators of the almanac to illustrate their texts, remind us that the process of creating acceptable living conditions for refugees and transforming existing premises with regards to their needs took place on the shores of the Bosphorus. Unfortunately, the authors and sources of these images are not indicated. There are more than thirty images in the almanac: among them are pictures of the Hagia Sophia, Rumeli Fortress, Dolmabahçe Palace, the Bulgarian St. Stephen Church, Galata Mevlevi House, the Ortaköy district and other well-known ancient monuments and urban locations. It is worth noting that this selection is not surprising: Russian émigrés were quite familiar with local attractions, not only because many of them are mentioned in the *Le Russe à Constantinople* (Russian in Constantinople) guide published in 1921 but also because they regularly attended city tours arranged by Russian-speaking intellectuals in Istanbul (Anonymous 1923, 3; fig. 3.2). In *Farewell*, we can also observe a series of images that feature leitmotifs of water and ships. This is due not only to the fact that water has always played an important role in the life of Istanbul but also due to the fact that refugees arrived in the city by water and left it by water. Another indication of this is the advertisements of numerous maritime companies published in *Farewell*.

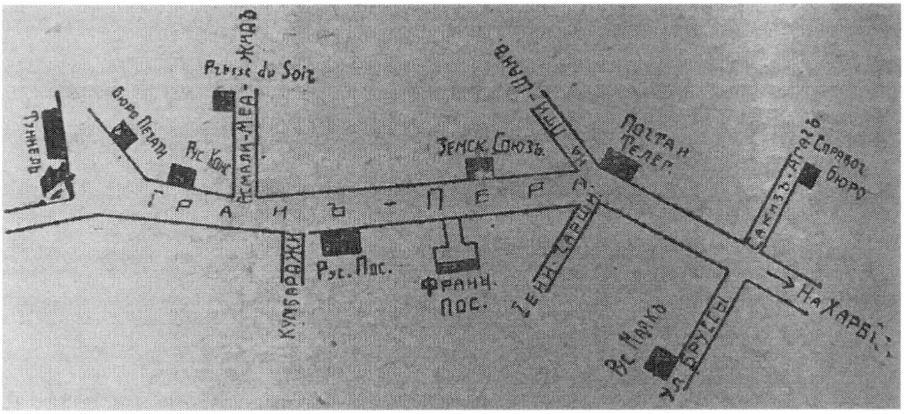

FIGURE 3.2: Grand Rue de Péra (Istiklal Avenue) and its surroundings in the Istanbul guide for Russian refugees *Russkiy v Konstantinopole. Le Russe à Constantinople*. Konstantinopol': Tipografiya "Pressa", 1921, p. 6, in Russian language (Slavonic Library/Slovanská knihovna, Prague).

Reading 'Russian Istanbul' through the Les Russes sur le Bosphore *Almanac (1928)*

This part of the chapter reconstructs important exile places in Istanbul with the help of the almanac *Les Russes sur le Bosphore*. Published approximately five years after the Turkish Republic came into being and Ankara was transformed into the new capital, it was an almanac of a completely different type. With minor exceptions, there is no mention of occupied Istanbul and the arrangement of housing or social amenities for refugees, but there are quite a few references to Istanbul's cultural sights and entertainment venues, focusing especially on the Beyoğlu district. With the arrival of Russian immigrants, the 'entertainment program' of the city underwent serious changes: "Thanks to the asylum seekers from Russia, things suddenly picked up speed. The city was introduced to the pleasures of nightlife, sunbathing on public beaches by the sea, gracefulness of classical ballet, American-style jazz and many other innovations" (Dumont 2015, 216). It is also interesting that the almanac mentions only those locations that retained their popularity until 1927: among them hotels, cafes, cinemas, theatres and clubs. Famous deluxe hotels, like Pera Palace and Tokatlıyan, not only hosted guests of the city but also provided them with entertainment. These were the places where Russian bazaars were held, where one could listen to a concert of a Russian salon orchestra, or purchase paintings by Russian-speaking artists at one of the exhibitions (Anonymous 1921, 23; Deleon 1995, 57, 64). Another place where one could enjoy music performed by a Russian orchestra was the Theatre des Petits Champs, where Russian-speaking émigré artists created decorations and costumes in the early 1920s. Subsequently, the number of Russian stage designers noticeably decreased, but well-known Russian ballet dancers from time to time still gave performances in the theatre. In addition, a "dance restaurant", where one could eat delicious food, dance and listen to chosen artists, was opened in the theatre garden in 1925, a location very well-liked by locals and guests of the city (Anonymous 1925, n.p.). In Cine Magic (Majik), visitors were presented with a musical interpretation of the cinematic plot, which "often saved plays from failure" (Anonymous 1924, 15). According to a newspaper note from 1924, some visitors came only for the sake of music performed by famous Russian-speaking musicians who had to make extra money on the side because of their desperate financial situation. The note also says that there were always long lines of cars at the entrance to Istanbul cinemas since women usually came to such events bejewelled and dressed up to the nines (ibid.). Some of the specific urban locations mentioned in the almanac make visible "how specific migrant groups create their own urban spaces to exchange information, trade goods, gather and communicate" (Wildner 2008, 212). For instance, social interactions between Russian-speaking émigrés took place at café-cabaret Rose Noire and Club Maxim, famous for their jazz bands and what was at the time called 'gypsy' repertoire. The Rose Noire was known to many people primarily because it advertised its programme in the form of a black cardboard giant with a red nose, wearing a top hat (fig. 3.3). Another factor that drew crowds to the cabaret was Alexander Vertinsky, who, when performing songs there, intentionally opened the windows wide, because he knew that fans would gather outside (Sığırcı 2018, 107). According to some journalists of the time, everything in this cabaret was à la Vertinsky, including the programme and waitresses who were dressed in modest black clothes with hairpins on their heads and gold roses embroidered on them (Slobodskoy 1925, n.p.). Club Maxim opened in late 1921 on Taksim Square (today's Beyoğlu): its owner was Fyodor Tomas (real name – Frederick Bruce Thomas), an African American from Mississippi with Russian citizenship.[9] The spacious club had a stage and a dance floor, an American bar and a terrace overlooking the Bosphorus (Sığırcı 2018, 114). In addition, it was here that many locals first heard jazz and learned how to dance the Foxtrot, Shimmy and Charleston (ibid., 115). The cafe-confectionery Petrograd on the corner of Istiklal and Bursa (today's Sadri Alışık) Streets was so popular that over time it became crowded even in its expanded two-story building. This cafe was a meeting and resting place where everything was à la russe: coffee, chocolate, cakes, pies, Easter desserts. The Russians in Istanbul compared it to the iconic Filippov café-bakeries in Moscow and St. Petersburg. It was famous not only for good service and sweet buns but also because it welcomed guests around the clock.

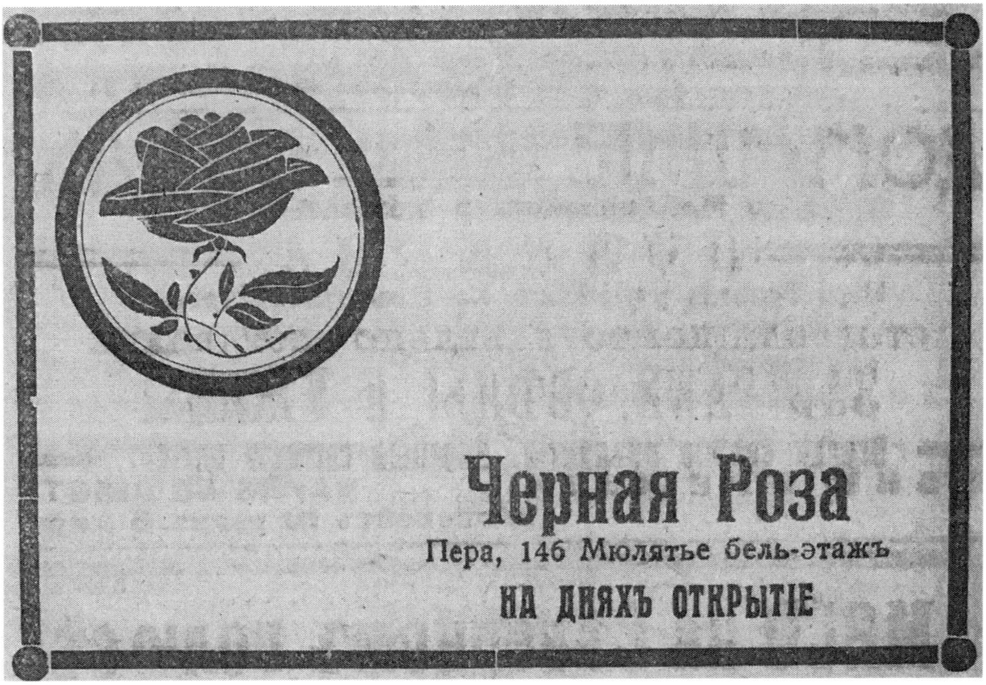

FIGURE 3.3: Announcement concerning Rose Noire's opening in the Russian newspaper *Presse du Soir*, 21 August 1922, n.p. (Slavonic Library/Slovanská knihovna, Prague).

Those who were late for the last ferry, going to the Asian part of Istanbul, often whiled away the night here (Uturgauri 2013, 174). It also became the subject of numerous jokes: for example, in any other restaurant a client could be kiddingly told "This is not Petrograd to sit here all night long" (ibid.). As an addition to this panorama of the 'Russian Beyoğlu', the almanac mentions the Russian section of the Turkish auto club, the cars of which were parked on the corner of Grand Rue de Péra and Asmalı Mescit Street, and on the corner of Grand Rue de Péra and Ada Street. It is known that Russian-speaking drivers not only had a good sense of direction in the city and drove competently but also that they always helped fellow-countrymen by taking them to hospitals, organizing funerals or distributing tickets for charity evenings (Bournakine 1928, n.p.; fig. 3.4).

But does the almanac only refer to the Beyoğlu district? As is the case with the *Farewell* almanac, the silhouettes of the historic peninsula are visible only 'between the lines'. If one looks, for example, at the poems of Russian émigré poets published in the almanac, one can glimpse the daily life of Istanbul with its mosques and cypresses, laurels and roses, the Golden Horn and seagulls as described by Ivan Korvatsky, or the dreamlike version of Istanbul as a city with "chiseled palaces",

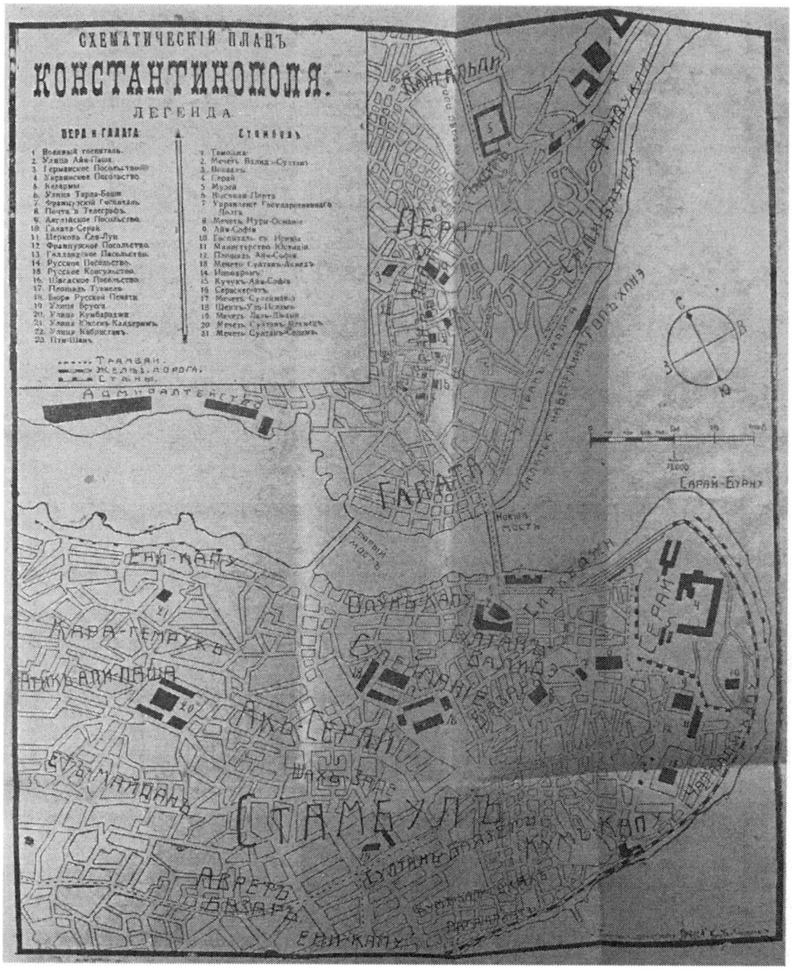

FIGURE 3.4: Schematic plan of Constantinople for Russian refugees in the guide *Russkiy v Konstantinopole: Le Russe à Constantinople*. Konstantinopol': Tipografiya "Pressa", 1921, n.p. (Slavonic Library/Slovanská knihovna, Prague).

"tropical gardens", "white mosques" and "spicy flavor of the East" imagined by Elena Bokard (Bournakine 1928, n.p.). In addition, rather detailed information about the Russian-speaking émigré artists of Istanbul and their works makes it possible to conclude that their main themes were Byzantine architecture (not only due to commissions by foreign clients but also due to personal interest), as well as mosques, palaces, cemeteries and ancient ruins of the old town that also often appeared on their canvases. Numerous symbolic structures of this kind are also presented in vignettes and illustrations, and on the cover made by Nikolai Saraphanoff. All this allows us to conclude that although many of the refugees lived, worked and opened their businesses in the 'European' Beyoğlu, in most cases they were inspired not by this slice of the city but by Istanbul's historical peninsula, the old city with its fascinating past.

Conclusion

Even though at first glance both almanacs have almost nothing in common with illustrated city guides, on closer examination it becomes clear that they do reveal parts of Istanbul's urban texture at the time. Because they were published five years apart, the almanacs allow us to look at 1920s city life from two angles: one encompasses the arrangement of housing and social amenities for refugees in the occupied city between 1919 and 1923, and the other illuminates the city's cultural life, its public spaces teeming with social interactions between displaced persons and others until at least 1928. These two angles quite tellingly show that Russian-speaking refugees succeeded in taking their place on the Istanbul 'stage', even though they arrived empty-handed and with no idea of how to survive in this "nobody's"[10] city. At the same time, their engagement with the city highlights and mediates the considerable changes that Istanbul underwent, transitioning from a city in crisis (an occupied capital with a constant, overwhelming influx of refugees) to a free city that, even though it lost its function as the country's capital, remained its cultural centre. The details provided by the almanacs' designs are a major asset since they enable us to see the city through the eyes of the creative stratum of émigrés from the Russian Empire and to understand, at least in some ways, how the local cultural contexts influenced their perception of Istanbul.

Throughout this chapter, I have hoped to stress the importance of close reading the almanacs conceived during the 'First Wave' of the Russian emigration, while also highlighting the importance of urban exile as a topic. I set out to show this method, while also taking into account an in-depth knowledge of historical and/or cultural contexts, is a useful tool for the study of urban exile. This is particularly important in the case of Istanbul, since many other sources such as émigré letters, diaries and photographs were lost in the process of moving from one city to another or are held in private archives, often unavailable to researchers. A close reading of these almanacs gives fruitful results because they were created by the émigrés themselves and can be defined as inherently collective works, folding together writers, journalists, photographers and painters based in emigration hubs such as Istanbul, Shanghai, Berlin, Paris and others.[11] References to local addresses, advertisements for various establishments, prose and poetry devoted to an exile place, as well as images and other details published in these almanacs, offer the opportunity to examine Russian-speaking émigrés' engagement with cities. One should not disregard, of course, possible drawbacks such as intentional omissions of certain places due to political or other reasons, the fact that the city is rendered from an ultimately subjective perspective, or, as was the case with the two almanacs I examined, the incompleteness of the information and its insufficient systematization due to the hurry with which they were produced. The authors did not have enough time to create thorough and well-corrected editions, since the Allied forces to whom (among others) their gratitude was addressed were about to leave Turkey in 1923, and in 1927 many of the émigrés, including some of the authors of the two almanacs, had to literally pack up and wait for the moment of departure. Ready to sail towards more hopeful shores, and a home where their existence would be more stable in legal terms, they still wanted to leave their trace behind, in the form of a memento speaking of a tremendous sense of creative mission – so, they left us *Farewell* and *Les Russes sur le Bosphore* which, despite their shortcomings, remain valuable sources on the subject.

NOTES

1. On almanacs in Russian and their different forms throughout history, see Balashova 2011.
2. It is important to note that not all refugees were Russian, but all of them came from the Russian Empire.
3. The Almanac *Farewell* is a collaborative work of Russian-speaking (A. Bournakine, B. Ratimoff and others) and local journalists and writers in Istanbul (Pierre Le Goff, Gilberto Primi, Grati Bey and others). Needless to say, designers also made contributions to the almanac, but, unfortunately, their names are not indicated. As for *Les Russes sur le Bosphore*, its elegant cover was created by Nikolai Saraphanoff, headpieces were made by V. Lyubomirsky, and portraits for biographies, groups, interiors and views were provided by the painter and photographer Jules Kanzler. Furthermore, photographs of some of the artworks were taken by Russian-speaking émigré painters in Istanbul (Boris Eguize, Nikolai Peroff, Nikolai Saraphanoff, Dimitri Ismailovitch, V.P.-Tch.) and the architect I.W. Pitlenko: that is to say they photographed their own works as well as works of their colleagues.
4. The *Farewell* almanac, for instance, was written in three languages at once (Russian, French and English), but not all the texts in French and English are translations of the ones in Russian – they differ in content and complement each other. For the same reason, this almanac is composed of three parts: the first one in Russian "Na Proshchanie", the second one in French "Nos Adieux", and the third one in English "Farewell". As the parts have identical enumeration, some of the almanac's page numbers are used two and sometimes even three times. In addition, an insufficient systematization and the absence of some artists' full names in both almanacs lead to the fact that in studies on Russian-speaking émigrés in

Istanbul artists who were not members of the Union of Russian Painters in Constantinople have been wrongly indicated as such. For the same reasons, Vasily Ivanov was named as the chairman of the Union, while in fact, it was Vladimir/Wladimir Ivanoff.

As for the almanac *Les Russes sur le Bosphore*, initially, it was a 150-page luxurious edition on enamel paper, of large format and with 300 illustrations. Judging by the fact that the libraries in the Czech Republic and Turkey possess copies of this almanac that differ from each other in appearance and content, the almanac either underwent changes during the publication process or was subsequently distributed and sold as copies of the original (which, again, differ in appearance and content). Further evidence to that is the fact that some of the private archives contain pages from *Les Russes sur le Bosphore* that are presented neither in the copy in Prague nor in the copy in Istanbul.

5. Certain 20th-century schools of literary study, such as Formalism or New Criticism, chose to ignore socio-political contexts, and focused instead purely on text-oriented approaches.
6. New historicism and cultural materialism suggested to understand literary texts historically.
7. On strategies and techniques of close reading and comprehension of informational text, see Oczkus 2014.
8. This term was used for the lecture and talks on Russian-speaking refugees in Constantinople/Istanbul which were organized by the Sakıp Sabancı Center for Turkish Studies of Columbia University (9 December 2019, www.sakipsabancicenter.columbia.edu/events/iraida-barry-thomas-whittemore-istanbuls-russian-moment. Accessed 2 February 2021; 7 December 2020, www.sakipsabancicenter.columbia.edu/events/istanbuls-russian-moment-1919-1923. Accessed 2 February 2021). Prior to that, and in the French context, the term was used by Katherine Foshko (2008) in her dissertation (cf. *France's Russian Moment: Russian Émigrés in Interwar Paris and French Society*).
9. On Frederick Bruce Thomas and his life story, see Alexandrov 2017.
10. Journalist Chebyshev Nikolai: "Constantinople at that time had one advantage for refugees. There were no masters in Constantinople at that time. All of us were guests, including the Turks themselves. The Allied command could be considered as a master. But it was in this position only by the right of force and capture, and therefore, morally, it also could not be recognized as a real master. As for the Turks, their moral rights to the position of the master were fiercely contested by the Greeks. The Greeks were intensely, passionately rejected by the Turks, who hated them more than the 'Allies'. Thus, the Russians, having arrived from Crimea, felt at home. I think it can be argued without exaggeration that never again during emigration, even in the hospitable Slavic countries, did the Russians feel themselves to be 'so at home' as they did in 1921 and 1922 in Constantinople" (Chebyshev 1933, n.p., my own translation).
11. The www.emigrantica.ru/ website could be useful for future studies on urban exile with the help of close reading of the almanacs and other sources published by Russian émigrés all over the world.

REFERENCES

Alexandrov, Vladimir. *Chernyi Russkiy: istoriya odnoy sud'by*. Novoye literaturnoe obozrenie, 2017.

Anonymous. *Russkiy v Konstantinopole. Le Russe à Constantinople*. Konstantinopol': Tipografiya "Pressa", 1921.

Anonymous. "Bazar kn. M.V. Baryatinskoy." *Zarnitsy*, 20 March 1921, p. 23.

Anonymous. "Ekskursii." *Konstantinopol'skiy Kommercheskiy Kur'yer*, 18 June 1923, p. 3.

Anonymous. "Al'gambra." *Put'*, 19 October 1924, p. 15.

Anonymous. "Garden Petits Champs." *Vecherniaia Gazeta*, 7 December 1925, n.p.

Anonymous. "Russkiye na Bosfore. Les Russes sur le Bosphore." *Radio*, 22 May 1927, n.p.

Anonymous. "Almanac." *Cambridge Advanced Learner's Dictionary*. 4th ed., Cambridge University Press, 2013, www.dictionary.cambridge.org/dictionary/english/almanac. Accessed 2 Feb 2021.

Ar, Bilge. "İşgal İstanbul'unun Kentsel Dönüşümünü Beyaz Ruslar Üzerinden Okumak." *YILLIK: Annual of Istanbul Studies*, vol. 1, no. 1, 2019, pp. 101–122. *DergiPark*, www.dergipark.org.tr/en/download/article-file/904824. Accessed 17 May 2021.

Balashova, Yulia. *Evolutsiya i Poetika Rossiyskogo Literaturnogo Almanaha kak Tipa Izdaniya*. Dissertation, Saint Petersburg State University, 2011.

Bournakine, Anatoliy, editor. *Russkiye na Bosfore. Les Russes sur le Bosphore*. Imp. L. Babok & fils, 1928.

Bournakine, Anatoliy, and Dominic Valery, editors. *Al'manah Na Proschaniye: The Farewell Almanac. L'Almanach Nos Adieux (1920–1923)*. Imp. L. Babok & fils, 1923.

Chebyshev, Nikolai. *Blizkaya Dal': Vospominaniya*. Imp. de Navarre, 1933.

Deleon, Jak. *The White Russians in Istanbul*. Remzi Kitabevi, 1995.

Dumont, Paul. "Beyaz Yıllar." *Istanbul 1914–1923*, edited by Stefanos Yerasimos, İletişim, 2015, pp. 215–239.

Foshko, Katherine. *France's Russian Moment: Russian Émigrés in Interwar Paris and French Society*. Dissertation, Yale University, 2008.

Gallop, Jane. "The Historicization of Literary Studies and the Fate of Close Reading." *Profession*, 2007, pp. 181–186. *JSTOR*, www.jstor.org/stable/25595865?seq=1. Accessed 11 Feb 2021.

King, Charles. *Pera Palas'ta Geceyarısı: Modern Istanbul'un Doğuşu*. Translated by Ayşen Anadol, ALFA Tarih, 2019.

Litvine, Nikolai. "Celles de Galata." *Nashi Dni*, 1 January 1921, pp. 13ff.

McCaw, Neil. "Close Reading, Writing and Culture." *International Journal for the Practice and Theory of Creative Writing*, vol. 8, no. 1, 2011, pp. 25–34. *ResearchGate*, www.researchgate.net/publication/233319599_Close_Reading_Writing_and_Culture. Accessed 11 February 2021.

Near East Foundation. "Constantinople, Part 2: Refugees in Peril." 14 July 2016, *neareastmuseum.com*, neareastmuseum.com/2016/07/14/constantinople-part-2/. Accessed 20 November 2020.

Oczkus, Lori. *Just the Facts: Close Reading and Comprehension of Informational Text*. Shell Education, 2014.

Sav, Sedef. "The Change of Cultural Memory on an Iconic Historic Structure: Narmanlı Han." *BEYOND ALL LIMITS 2018: International Congress on Sustainability in Architecture, Planning*, and Design/Proceedings Book of The Extended Abstracts, Çankaya University Press, 2018, pp. 652–659, www.beyondalllimits.cankaya.edu.tr/. Accessed 18 May 2021.

Sığırcı, Marina. *Spasibo, Konstantinopol'! Po sledam beloemigrantov v Turtsii*. "Yevropeyskiy Dom," 2018.

Slobodskoy, A. *Sredi Emigratsii: Moi Vospominaniya*. Izdatel'stvo "Proletariy," 1925.

Ünal, Fatih. "Osmanlı İstanbul'unda Bir Rus Misyoner Hastanesi: Pangaltı Nikolayev Hastanesi." *Marmara Türkiyat Araştırmaları Dergisi*, vol. 5, no. 2, 2018, pp. 235–258. *Academia*, www.academia.edu/37962885/Osmanli_Istanbulunda_Bir_Rus_Misyoner_Hastanesi_Pangalti_Nikolayev_Hastanesi. Accessed 18 May 2021.

Uturgauri, Svetlana. *Belye russkie na Bosfore 1919–1929*. Institut vostokovedeniya RAN, 2013.

Wildner, Kathrin. "Introduction: Spaces of Everyday Life." *Public Istanbul: Spaces and Spheres of the Urban*, edited by Frank Eckardt and Kathrin Wildner, transcript, 2008, pp. 209–214.

Wineburg, Sam. *Historical Thinking and Other Unnatural Acts: Charting the Future of Teaching the Past* (Critical Perspectives of the Past). Temple University Press, 2001.

Wolfreys, Julian. *Readings: Acts of Close Reading in Literary Theory*. Edinburgh University Press, 2000.

4

'Mobile Exile' and Urban Musical Theatre in the 1930s

Nils Grosch

Mobility, musical theatre and the city in the early 20th century

Urban cultural life in Europe in the early 20th century was substantially characterized by a wide range of musical theatre events – ranging from first-class opera performances, lavish and ambitious revue and operetta productions and mixed stage performances in *café concerts,* music halls and *cabarets* to a dynamic multitude of new hybrid forms that reconfigured elements of other performative genres. In this period, musical theatre in Germany and Austria had developed a binary system of production, including state-subsidized stage productions (predominantly operas) in metropoles and smaller cities, on the one hand, and commercial productions of operettas, revues and musicals in privately managed metropolitan theatres, on the other hand. It is especially the latter which made its mark on the musical theatre culture of European capitals, with gigantic auditoriums with up to 3400 seats, such as in Berlin's Großes Schauspielhaus but also with opera houses in big cities that allowed several thousands of spectators to experience extravagantly produced performances, such as the city opera in Berlin-Charlottenburg with its 2224 seats (Grosch 2012, 239–242).

Whereas the audience – regional or travelling – often perceived this combination of forms and styles as regionally specific to the culture of a certain city, many developments, invisible to the public, were based on well-calculated networks of transnational cooperation, transcultural exchange and interurban mobility (Platt 2014, 25–40). Music theatre in itself is anything but a *musica mobilis.* Opera houses are strong markers of and architectural, cultural anchors within urban spaces and as such opposed to mobility. They are usually located in city centres and constitute an important night-on-the-town destination for both tourists and local audiences. Nevertheless, urban spaces enable mobility in theatrical production in many ways. Whereas opera has been a commuting genre since the 18th century (*Pendleroper,* in Reinhard Strohm's words), in the 20th century the oscillation of works, productions, creatives, conceptions of staging and production was and still is, sometimes covertly, a property, if not an enabling condition for the performance of both serious and popular genres of music theatre.

This mobility of musical theatre provides numerous pull factors for the transfer of works and genres, for the transcultural distribution and communication of theatrical music (Grosch/Stahrenberg 2014), the mobility of styles and routines of production, and of theatre creatives. From 1933 onwards, and intensifying around 1938 as well as during the war years, push factors such as racism, political ostracism and persecution by the Nazi regime led to the emigration of many theatre creatives. But already before Hitler's coming to power, the growing influence of national socialism's pressure on public cultural life caused artists to leave Germany, to expand their international networks and to increasingly contrive options for artistic activity abroad.

In those cases, the boundaries between exile or forced migration and voluntary mobility start to blur. Instead, we can observe a dynamic mélange of motives and obstacles, of push and pull factors that overlap and interweave in processes of decision making and the retention of creative agency by conceiving or imagining prospective routes of escape. Seeming perhaps initially paradoxical, we might name this emerging set of coordinates 'mobile exile'.

Traditional definitions of exile have tended to emphasize aspects of persecution or violence relating both to the process of migration itself as well as to the diasporic situation after having migrated (Grosch 2022). They have also tended to connect exile to the idea of not being at home or in the 'right' place. And as exile cannot exist without the idea of homeland, as Friedrich Geiger has pointed out (2014, 39), it presupposes an understanding of cultures "not as mobile or global or even mixed, but as local" (Greenblatt 2009a, 252). Thus, exile has traditionally been connected to concepts of fixity rather than mobility. In contrast, the concept of mobility offers an expansive field of forms and motives of movement (Adey 2017; Greenblatt 2009b); movement that also of course includes forced migration and escape. Thus, the concept of 'mobile exile' turns exile into a dynamic web of mobilities, options, opportunities for artistic activity, creativity and agency on the one hand, and push factors on the other hand – i.e. dynamic and changing circumstances that tend to constrict movement, especially as war approaches and scopes of activity start to shift or narrow down.

The creative, pulsating nature of big cities is largely shaped by mobility. As Erol Yildiz has shown, migration has crucially contributed to the openness and cosmopolitan attitudes of urban life since the period of industrialization (2011, 72 f.) – an observation that can be traced back to histories of migration pre-dating the Industrial Revolution (for example in the British context, see: Olusoga 2017). The activity and creative input of immigrants play an essential role in this momentum. Regardless of the reasons for emigration, migrants imagine creative alternatives and implement them in their new-found cultural urban contexts. With respect to urban migration and music, Ruard Absaroka has reminded us of migrants' bottom-up contributions to the image of so-called 'global cities' and the narratives surrounding their 'creative and cultural industries' (Absaroka 2021). This enables us to challenge the stereotypical passive image of the 'refugee', whose fate is shaped solely by the decisions of those who expelled them. We might rethink agency in mobility, a key aspect in migration debates, and reconsider the extent to which migrants from artistic backgrounds use their creativity to become agents of innovation. In his 1984/85 essay "Exile and Creativity" (Flusser 2003, 81–87), the philosopher Vilém Flusser depicts exile, "no matter the form", as an "incubator of creativity in the service of the new" (ibid., 87). Flusser's remarkable interpretation revolves around the relationship between expeller and expellee at the very moment when the expellee "discovers that a human being is not a tree. And that human dignity may consist precisely in not having roots" (ibid., 84). From here, Flusser sees the expellee as an active, creative participant in the migration process; history is made not just by those who expel but by those who are expelled. Nevertheless, we cannot forget about retrenchments and conditionality of activity in exile. Stephen Greenblatt, in his cultural mobility manifesto, encourages us to "account in new ways for the tension between individual agency and structural constraint" (2009a, 251). In emphasizing the importance of this tension, he states that "[m]obility studies should be interested, among other things, in the way in which seemingly fixed migration paths are disrupted by the strategic acts of individual agents and by unexpected, unplanned, entirely contingent encounters between different cultures" (ibid., 252). In situations of threat and persecution, agency is restricted and creative action is challenged by ever-changing dynamics of danger and opportunity. The notion of 'mobile exile' accounts for both sides of the coin but permits a focus on the creative plans and operations of artists as they react and operate in this field.

Musical theatre in the 1930s presents perhaps a special case of 'mobile exile'. The dynamic and decidedly transnational predisposition of the genre encouraged artists not only to conceive of paths into exile but also to frame this exile in a manner that emphasized their own agency. In the following two case studies, my interest lies in the reflections and discussions of a group of important representatives of musical theatre in the Weimar Republic. The following case studies document, first, the considerations at stake and the related dynamics in processes of decision-making embedded within 'mobile exile' and, second and more generally, the vast mobility present, real and imagined, in the field of musical theatre.

A case study in threefold mobility: Kurt Weill's and Erik Charell's unrealized bridge into exile

In 1932, the composer Kurt Weill and the musical theatre producer Erik Charell conceived a plan for a new, mobile theatre production: this was, at the same time, a well-calculated effort to extricate themselves from the cultural and political situation in Germany and to leave the country in favour of an international network of theatre productions. This plan would not come to fruition and both artists had to escape along very different routes than they had originally envisaged. Still, their undertaking is a fascinating example for an imagined, and ultimately imaginary, bridge into exile that was to maintain both artists' agency, despite the necessity to flee their home country: "The plan is to start the show in Vienna, then go to Paris and London and only finally to Berlin",[1] Weill reported on 29 June 1932, describing a new theatrical production he planned in collaboration with Charell (Weill 2002, 400). As can be traced in Weill's mid 1932 correspondence with the publishing house Universal Edition in Vienna, Weill and Charell were mulling over ideas of adapting, amongst others, William Shakespeare's *Romeo and Juliet* or Robert Wiene's *Das Cabinet des Dr. Caligari* (ibid., 392–406). But even before having agreed on the theme for their production, the two experienced theatre creatives were of one mind about the aim of making their new collaboration an international success, one that asserted their artistry beyond the state-controlled German national theatre system of opera and drama production, and one that would, in doing so, provide them with creative independence from that system (Grosch 2003, 283–288). To this end, they decided to both produce the work within the structures of commercial theatre and to launch the show in urban metropolises abroad. In order to establish it as a piece that could be adapted for any theatre, "it should be made in such a way that it can go across all stages" (Weill 2002, 397: 15 June 1932).

From the perspective of cultural mobility (Greenblatt 2009b), I find three aspects of this plan, although the plan itself went unfulfilled, intriguing: First, it conceptualizes musical theatre as an extremely mobile genre, resembling in this respect cinema more than any other theatrical production that either Charell or Weill had brought into the world throughout their respective careers. Weill's 1928 *Die Dreigroschenoper*, for example, although it "was to be translated into most of the world's major languages" and quickly achieved tremendous success on stages in German speaking countries and beyond (cf. Hinton 1990, 50f.), initially was moulded for and around its initial Berlin production in the Theater am Schiffbauerdamm, where it ran *en suite* for 250 performances. Similarly, *Erik Charells im Weißen Rößl* [*sic*], authored by Ralph Benatzky, Robert Gilbert et al., had been conceived for its original Berlin production in the Großes Schauspielhaus in 1930 (Grosch 2016, 40ff.), before it was successfully staged elsewhere in Germany and abroad in translated and adapted versions.

Second, it perfectly fulfils the criteria of what Greenblatt calls "theatrical mobility": the fluent form and adaptability with regard to questions of where, when and in which context a stage work could be performed, something which also applies to the textual structure of the work – representing "multiple states" instead of "definitive, [...] authorially approved versions" (Greenblatt 2009c, 76f.) which can be smoothly recontextualized, rewritten and adapted.

Third, this theatrical concept is inextricably tied to the artists' own fear of being endangered in terms of both artistic agency and physical integrity. In the correspondence regarding the project, we never read directly about the sensation of being persecuted, and neither are the terms 'escape' or 'exile' explicitly mentioned. Nevertheless, for Weill this plan arose out of and was strengthened by his recent experiences. His latest opera *Die Bürgschaft* had been rejected by many theatre directors who had already formally agreed to produce it, after the threat of possible Nazi attacks on theatre productions that collaborated with Jewish authors intensified in the early 1930s (cf. Grosch 2003, 279–283). *Die Bürgschaft* was based on a libretto that the author and stage designer Caspar Neher had developed in collaboration with Weill himself, and the composer judged it to be his hitherto most ambitious composition. The dependence upon a state-subsidized and state-controlled theatre production system in German speaking countries turned out to be a very real obstacle to the evolution of modern-minded Jewish creatives in the field of opera. As the composer asserted, "of course, the catastrophic conditions of the theatre, which actually neutralize a show like *Die Bürgschaft*, play a major role in all of my plans" (Weill 2002, 396).[2]

Thus, Weill's multi-layered attempt to internationalize his creative activities around 1932 by means of a turn to international, commercial theatre, must be seen as an impulse of cultural mobility (in Stephen Greenblatt's sense), an attempt to regain agency by side-stepping the array of German state-subsidized systems of cultural production which 'neutralized' not only his major works but also himself as an artist.

The experience of being severely hampered in their creativity boosted both Weill's and Charell's imagination and led them to utilize the mobility of an urban network of theatrical production, one they had had the chance to become acquainted with so well during the past decade, in order to envision routes for exile and artistic work at the same time. This form of 'mobile exile' can also be found in the careers of other émigrés, not only around 1933 but also in the late 1930s, when the power of the Nazi regime swelled across Europe. This was the case with opera stage director Carl Ebert, conductor Fritz Busch and opera manager Rudolf Bing, when they conceptualized routes of escape from England to New York City.

Carl Ebert's and Rudolf Bing's foray to New York

> *He feels mobile enough to steer his family even through these dangers, as long as he retains the opportunity to interconnect, establish and develop new connections. [...] the threat of war seemed to cut off this possibility and to restrain him and his family without any means of subsistence as if they were on a blockaded island.*
>
> (Ebert 2 October 1938, n.p.)

This statement about his own situation, taken from a letter written in the fall of 1938 by the opera director Carl Ebert, then artistic director of the Glyndebourne opera festival, to the same festival's General Manager Rudolf Bing, reveals the mobility of music theatre creatives during times of persecution and exile in the lead up to the war.

The Glyndebourne Festival Opera, set in a theatre built as an architectonical appendix to a country house in the south of England (East Sussex) and a prestigious annual event from the 1930s to the present day, had opened its doors in 1934 with productions of Wolfgang Amadé Mozart's *Così fan tutte* and *Le nozze de Figaro*. The productions of the first five years were marked by artistic collaborations between the artistic directors, conductor Fritz Busch and stage director Carl Ebert, and the festival's general manager Rudolf Bing, all of whom had emigrated from Nazi Germany in 1933. During those first five years, the festival's creative team had succeeded in establishing a reputation for Glyndebourne as a place of opera production on an international level and with an approach in opera production remarkably different from the production style British audiences had experienced up to then. After having been driven out of Germany by the Nazis, both artistic directors of the festival, Ebert and Busch, had first pitched their tent elsewhere on the continent: Busch in Copenhagen, Denmark, and Ebert in Cureglia in the Ticino department of Switzerland (for Ebert's biography cf. Dogramaci 2007b). From these locations they commuted all over Europe (necessarily avoiding Nazi-controlled territories) and beyond, to conduct musical events and to direct operas. As is documented in the extensive correspondence held by the festival's archive in Glyndebourne, and in Busch's and Ebert's personal archives in

Karlsruhe and Berlin respectively, the places to which those artists imagined going to work are varied and spread around the globe, from Scandinavia to Buenos Aires, from Lucerne to Ankara.

By focusing on the narrow period of the fall and winter of 1938 and on plans for a Glyndebourne guest appearance at the New York World's Fair of 1939, in the following, I will briefly trace the paths envisioned for Glyndebourne's operatic mobility. This was the period when war had not officially begun, but after the Austrian 'Anschluss' in March and Hitler's annexation of the Sudetenland during the summer. The threat of imminent war, in which England would be involved, threw its shadow across more than just Glyndebourne's plans for the festival of summer 1939. "Insane times", Ebert stated in a letter to Bing on 23 August 1938, as he continued to explain his plans: "It is likely that I will stay in Ankara" (Ebert 23 August 1938, n.p.). Ebert was assigned there by the Turkish state government to help in building a modern system of theatre education and performance following the German model (Dogramaci 2007a):

> until January 15th, because, even if old Europe will still be standing by then, there is no really interesting job that awaits me. [...] This situation is damn similar to the year 1933; that is to say, that Adolf's arm has grown longer in between, and now already reaches my radius of activities. Vienna and Italy (difficult to conquer at the best of times) are out of the question, and developing new projects is darn slow. My interest is increasingly concentrated on the USA.
>
> (Ebert 23 August 1938, n.p.).[3]

The option of a guest appearance of the Glyndebourne opera ensemble at the 1939/40 New York World's Fair entered the discussion, and Ebert repeatedly tried to convince Bing, stating that he considered "Glyndebourne's participation at the world's fair to be an opportunity for great global publicity and I am of the opinion that everything must be done in order to overcome any technical obstacles" (Ebert 9 September 1938, n.p.).[4] In their subsequent exchange it becomes clear that this option was indeed being considered by Bing, Ebert and Busch, not only as an institutional stepping stone into the field of global artistic activity but also as a possible personal path to live in exile in the United States. Bing did not feel "in the state of mind, to discuss festival plans [in Glyndebourne] for 1939 at all", as he feared "internment, in the case that the catastrophe will occur", and because he interpreted Chamberlain's quick return from the Munich conference, held by Hitler, Chamberlain, Mussolini and Daladier, as a bad omen. He already had requested an American visa and was "thinking more than seriously about leaving this hospitable country", as Bing confided to Ebert:

> From all the misery of the last few years you should at least have learned to recognize when it's time to leave; I think the time has come, if it's not already too late. It's an insane fight that I am fighting with myself and an outrageous responsibility to leave GLYNDEBOURNE behind in order to jump into nothing.

And he adds: "Couldn't we just pass right by America and proceed straight to the next country?" (Bing 23 September 1938, n.p.).[5] This proposition opens up an interesting and remarkable vision of artistic oscillation and mobility, driven by the need to flee deteriorating situations and characterized by a willingness to seize chances (not only on Ebert's and Busch's side but also for Bing). As we now know today, of the former Glyndebourne trio it was Bing who – albeit not earlier than 1950 – succeeded in starting a career in the United States, namely as long-term director of the Metropolitan Opera house.

In his response to Bing, Ebert made clear that he was ready to

> give up Europe and focus on the USA. And if in my last letters I pressed so hard for the Glyndebourne guest performance at the World's Fair, the driving thought was the chance to establish a life in North America using this as a business card, of course, for you and Busch as well as for me.
>
> (Ebert 26 September 1938, n.p.)

For him, it was crucial "to stand out from the group [of emigrants] by means of achievement",[6] thus migrating without any damage to his career status (Ebert 26 September 1938, n.p.).

On 12 January 1939, Bing and Ebert, armed with Busch's instructions, left for New York to undertake negotiations and preparations regarding the Glyndebourne performances at the World's Fair. However, due to economic problems and difficulties in adapting the sets and the mise-en-scène, developed for the small Glyndebourne stage, to the gigantic space at the Metropolitan Opera (Met) where the guest performance was designated to take place, as well as due to other circumstances which I cannot expound here, the negotiations eventually failed.

Subsequently, Ebert reported to Busch in detail in a long manuscript letter written on the ship back, outlining not only the reasons for the failure but also his vision of a future career for both, Busch and Ebert, in New York City. Despite the disappointment, Ebert concluded enthusiastically:

> this is the city for us, Fritz! My first impression: great, overwhelming. Also, when taking a closer, more sceptical look, you find out: the decisive factor is not the immense hype that jumps into the eye, but what's behind it, a great activity, real

> youth and power! It will take longer for real quality than it did in Berlin and even in London – but in 10 years this will be the center of the world, also in artistic terms.
> (Ebert n.d. [January 1939], n.p.)

Under the threat of war, these former protagonists of Austro-German opera production were able to reformulate their conditions of forced mobility to sound out global dynamics in their field and to detect and seize the best opportunities and chances in urban centres that could and would soon become hubs for the art world.

Concluding thoughts

Sending a letter from Paris to Ebert, then in Florence, in late April of 1933, Weill found himself intrigued by the idea to "now show the modern opera culture that we have created in the other countries" (Weill 1933). Even in those early days of exile, the enthusiasm for the internationalization of the genre and the simultaneous frustration about his exile were deeply entangled. The mobility of theatrical concepts, embodied by such different figures as Weill, Bing, Ebert and Charell, was expedited as a result of expulsion and escape. When Ebert and Bing, who in 1932s Berlin had become pioneers by producing and staging Weill's *Die Bürgschaft* against all odds, set their feet on American ground in 1939, Weill had already started what was to become a successful career as a composer of innovative Broadway musicals. Opera as it was performed in the Met he regarded as museal and disconcerting. He did not live to see the changes that Bing brought to the opera house, introducing all the modernist experience he had acquired throughout his activity in Germany and the UK: Bing only took over the Met in 1950, the year Weill died. What would have happened to American operatic culture, if the Met and World's Fair audiences had had the opportunity to experience the operatic style developed by Busch and Ebert in Germany and Glyndebourne? Ebert, however, who in 1939 had envisioned New York as a heterotopia for an ideal unfolding of modern art and for the continuation of his collaboration with Busch, then reoriented himself towards Turkey, an occasion that would become equally momentous for that country.

For refugees from the Nazi system in the 1930s, urban exile and theatrical mobility entangled into a mélange of push and pull factors, which I call 'mobile exile'. This denotes a matrix of imagined and sometimes actually realized routes of escape and creative activity. In the case of Weill, Ebert, Bing, Charell and Busch, the complexities of such 'mobile exile' were pivotal, not only for these artists' biographies but also for the development of theatrical concepts and aesthetics and for the condition and appearance of urban centres.

NOTES

1. "Es ist geplant [...], das Stück in Wien zu starten, dann nach Paris und London und zuletzt erst nach Berlin zu bringen."
2. "selbstverständlich spielen bei meinen ganzen Plänen die katastrophalen Theaterzustände, die tatsächlich ein Stück wie die *Bürgschaft* vorübergehend kaltstellen, eine grosse Rolle."
3. "diese irrsinnige Zeit [...] Voraussichtlich werde ich bis zum 15. Januar, – da mich ja selbst in dem Fall, dass dieses alte Europa dann noch stehen sollte, hier keine mich wirklich interessierende Arbeit erwartet. Ich könnte mich nach Zürich oder Basel als Regisseur oder Schauspieler verdingen, aber das lockt mich nicht übermässig, Dieser Zustand hat eine verdammte Ähnlichkeit mit dem Jahre 33; das macht, dass Adolfs Arm inzwischen länger geworden ist und mich in meinem heutigen Aktionsradius bereits erreicht, Wien und Italien (schwer genug erworben) fallen wieder weg, und der Ausbau 'neuer Stellungen' geht verflixt langsam vor sich. [...] Immer mehr konzentriert sich mein Interesse auf U.S.A."
4. "Ich wiederhole. Was ich Ihnen bereits schrieb: dass ich die Teilnahme Glyndebourne's auf der Weltausstellung für die Chance einer großen Weltpublicity halte und der Meinung bin, dass von uns alles daran gesetzt werden muss, um eventuelle technische Schwierigkeiten zu überwinden."
5. "Ich selbst habe – streng vertraulich – mein Amerikanisches Visum eingereicht und denke mehr als ernstlich daran, dieses gastliche Land zu verlassen. Aus all dem Elend der letzten Jahre sollte man sich wenigstens gelernt haben zu erkennen, wann's Zeit wird zu gehen; ich glaube, die Zeit ist gekommen, wenn es nicht schon zu spät ist. Es ist ein wahnsinniger Kampf, den ich mit mir selbst kämpfe und eine ungeheuerliche Verantwortung GLYNDEBOURNE aufzugeben, um in's Nichts zuspringen; falls ich mich dazu entschließen sollte, ist es durchaus nicht nur die Angst vor Gasbomben, sondern die Sorge vor dem offenbar unausbleiblichen Zusammenbruch Europas und der faschistischen Diktatur in England, die ja nahezu schon heute besteht. Ich will nicht wieder warten, bis man muss und es zu spät ist."
6. "Ob man Amerika nicht gleich überschlagen könnte und gleich in's nächste Land danach??? Sollte das dann vielleicht wieder Berlin sein?? && Should it then be Berlin again??"
7. "Ténor fast aller meiner Äusserungen seit Wien [...] Aufgabe Europas und Konzentration auf USA. Und wenn ich in meinen letzten Briefen so stark auf das Glyndebourne-Gastspiel bei der Weltausstellung drängte, so war natürlich der treibende Gedanke, mit dieser Visitenkarte eine Existenz in Nordamerika begründen zu können, für Sie und Busch ebenso wie für mich."

REFERENCES

Absaroka, Ruard. "Musik und Urbane Migration." *Musik und Migration: Ein Theorie- und Methodenhandbuch*, edited by Wolfgang Gratzer et al., Waxmann, 2021.

Adey, Peter. *Mobility (Key Ideas in Geography)*. 2nd ed., Routledge, 2017.

Bing, Rudolf. Letter to Carl Ebert. Bing Correspondence (Glyndebourne Festival Archives, Glyndebourne, East Sussex, UK, 23 September 1938).

Dogramaci, Burcu. "'Faust' für Ankara – Carl Ebert im türkischen Exil." *Musiktheater im Exil der NS-Zeit* (Musik im "Dritten Reich" und im Exil, 12), edited by Peter Petersen and Claudia Maurer Zenck, Von Bockel, 2007a, pp. 35–64.

Dogramaci, Burcu. "Carl Ebert." *Lexikon verfolgter Musiker und Musikerinnen der NS-Zeit*, edited by Claudia Maurer Zenck et al., Universität Hamburg, 2007b, www.lexm.uni-hamburg.de/object/lexm_lexmperson_00002560. Accessed 30 December 2020.

Ebert, Carl. *Letter to Fritz Busch* (Brüder-Busch-Archiv, Max Reger-Institut, Karlsruhe, Germany, n.d. [January 1939]), B 2904.

Ebert, Carl. *Letter to Rudolf Bing. Bing Correspondence* (Glyndebourne Festival Archives, Glyndebourne, East Sussex, UK, 23 August 1938).

Ebert, Carl. *Letter to Rudolf Bing. Bing Correspondence* (Glyndebourne Festival Archives, Glyndebourne, East Sussex, UK, 9 September 1938).

Ebert, Carl. *Letter to Rudolf Bing. Bing Correspondence* (Glyndebourne Festival Archives, Glyndebourne, East Sussex, UK, 26 September 1938).

Ebert, Carl. *Letter to Rudolf Bing. Bing Correspondence* (Glyndebourne Festival Archives, Glyndebourne, Sussex, UK, 2 October 1938).

Flusser, Vilém. *The Freedom of the Migrant: Objections to Nationalism*. Translated by Kenneth Kronenberg, edited by Anke K. Finger, University of Illinois Press, 2003.

Geiger, Friedrich. "'Eine Heimat muss man doch am Ende haben': Wagners Dresden." *Exil als Daseinsform. Die Schauplätze Richard Wagners* (Züricher Festspiel-Symposien, 5), edited by Laurenz Lütteken, Bärenreiter, 2014, pp. 37–47.

Greenblatt, Stephen. "A Mobility Studies Manifesto." *Cultural Mobility: A Manifesto*, edited by Stephen Greenblatt et al., Cambridge University Press, 2009a, pp. 250–253, doi: 10.1017/CBO9780511804663.008. Accessed 30 April 2021.

Greenblatt, Stephen. "Cultural Mobility: An Introduction." *Cultural Mobility: A Manifesto*, edited by Stephen Greenblatt et al., Cambridge University Press, 2009b, pp. 1–23, doi: 10.1017/CBO9780511804663.001. Accessed 30 April 2021.

Greenblatt, Stephen. "Theatrical Mobility." *Cultural Mobility: A Manifesto*, edited by Stephen Greenblatt et al., Cambridge University Press, 2009c, pp. 75–95, doi: 10.1017/CBO9780511804663.003. Accessed 30 April 2021.

Grosch, Nils. "Kurt Weill und das kommerzielle Musiktheater 1928–1933." *Jahrbuch des staatlichen Instituts für Musikforschung, Preußischer Kulturbesitz*, edited by Günther Wagner, Metzler, 2003, pp. 265–295.

Grosch, Nils. "Zur medialen Dramaturgie des populären Musiktheaters in der Weimarer Republik." *Populärkultur, Massenmedien, Avantgarde 1919–1933*, edited by Jessica Nitsche and Nadine Werner, Wilhelm Fink, 2012, pp. 239–250.

Grosch, Nils. "*Im weißen Rößl*. Gattungen und Subgattungen im populären Musiktheater." "*Im weißen Rößl*". *Kulturgeschichtliche Perspektiven* (Populäre Kultur und Musik, vol. 19), edited by Nils Grosch and Carolin Stahrenberg, Waxmann, 2016, pp. 25–42.

Grosch, Nils. "Exil." *Musik und Migration: Ein Theorie- und Methodenhandbuch*, edited by Wolfgang Gratzer et al., Waxmann, 2022.

Grosch, Nils, and Carolin Stahrenberg. "The Transculturality of Stage, Song and Other Media: Intermediality in Popular Musical Theatre." *Popular Musical Theatre in London and Berlin: 1890 to 1939*, edited by Tobias Becker et al., Cambridge University Press, 2014, pp. 187–200, doi: 10.1017/CBO9781107279681.014. Accessed 30 April 2021.

Hinton, Stephen. "The Première and After." *Kurt Weill. The Threepenny Opera* (Cambridge Opera Handbooks), edited by Stephen Hinton, Cambridge University Press, 1990, pp. 50–77.

Olusoga, David. *Black and British: A Forgotten History*. Pan Macmillan, 2017.

Platt, Len. "Berlin/London: London/Berlin – An Outline of Cultural Transfer 1890–1914." *Popular Musical Theatre in London and Berlin: 1890 to 1939*, edited by Tobias Becker et al., Cambridge University Press, 2014, pp. 25–43, doi: 10.1017/CBO9781107279681.004. Accessed 30 April 2021.

Weill, Kurt. Letter to Carl Ebert (Carl-Ebert-Archiv, Stiftung Archiv der Akademie der Künste, Berlin, 30 April 1933).

Weill, Kurt. *Musik und musikalisches Theater: Gesammelte Schriften*, edited by Stephen Hinton and Jürgen Schebera, Schott, 2000, pp. 186f.

Weill, Kurt. *Briefwechsel mit der Universal Edition*, edited by Nils Grosch, Metzler, 2002.

Yildiz, Erol. "Stadt ist Migration." *Eigensinnige Geographien: Städtische Raumaneignungen als Ausdruck gesellschaftlicher Teilhabe*, edited by Malte Bergmann and Bastian Lange, Verlag für Sozialwissenschaften 2011, pp. 71–80.

5

Oral History in Exile Studies – Potentials and Limitations

Felicitas Söhner

Remembrance is a form of meeting.

(Khalil Gibran 1926, 1)

Can an oral history approach to exile studies contribute to contemporary social and cultural issues? As exile researchers have pointed out, many narratives of emigrants possess an outstanding explanatory power (Dietze 2006; Hagemann 1998). In such narratives, processing the personal experiences of flight and expulsion is just as important as reflecting on the social processes in the host country and how one's own group deals with these processes, both for the emigrants themselves and for the society from which they came. Research on exile has made use of oral history as a method of investigation early on, as can be seen, for example, in the work of contemporary historians like Röder/Strauss (1983), Strauss/Rohrbaugh (1986) or Benz (1994). According to scholar of book science Ernst Fischer, this affinity can be attributed to several factors. On the one hand, research on and of exile is regarded as foremost biographical research, each individual destiny being part of a collective biography; on the other hand, with various methodical approaches, it has proven to be an ideal instrument for exile studies, since these techniques harmonize with the concerns of every exile researcher: to take up individual life stories and collective biographies, to present them and to bring them into the historical consciousness (Fischer 2008, 97).

Oral history is a retrospective, heuristic method in which data (people's memories) are generated and analyzed in a collaborative exchange (eyewitness conversation) (Leavy 2011, 4). For this purpose, oral narratives are recorded as audio or video documents, transcribed and then examined (Lücke/Zündorf 2018, 74). Oral history, explicated, means 'orally transmitted history'; an approach best described as 'oral tradition' or 'remembered history'. At the heart of oral history research is the desire to let a group speak for themselves, if possible, in order to capture their subjective viewpoint. The basic assumption here is that people are self-reflective subjects who act as experts on themselves and should be understood as such (Söhner 2017, 273f.). This aim to include eyewitness-based documents as a central source is shared by historical research within other disciplines working with eyewitnesses, especially sociological biographical research (life course analysis) (Fischer/Kohli 1987) and folkloristic narrative research (form, motive, performance and transmission of the narrative) (Leavy 2011, 4). Oral history is considered an effective instrument for investigating far-reaching questions and perspectives. Oral history interviews provide insights into the perception of the collective and individual consequences of exile experience. Ideals and norms, as well as perceptions of the Other and the Self, are discussed. In this way, the relationship between everyday practices and dynamic urban structures can be problematized. This approach makes it possible to approach history 'from below' or 'from within'. Historical contemporary witness work aims to investigate aspects of subjective histories of experience alongside narratives (collective memory) handed down in the respective subject cultures (Rosenthal/Bogner 2017).

This paper focuses on the potentials and limitations of the historical approach. To this end, experiences from past and current eyewitness projects are systematically examined and analyzed. In the course of this chapter, I will focus on the question of how spatial structures, biographically relevant patterns of action, processes of change and the interdependence of urbanity and exile can be examined from a historical perspective. One potential of oral history lies in "raising new questions that research has not yet asked and that arise from the answers of contemporary witnesses" (Obertreis 2012, 11). In this manner, I will analyze which gaps in knowledge can be closed by the methodological approach of oral history within exile studies and to what extent such a method can be seen as suitable to answer questions for future avenues of investigation.

Particular attention is paid to biographical approaches as a way of accessing the perception of alterity. First of all, the connections between intercultural education and intercultural culture of memory are explained. Subsequently, research interests and questions of biographical research are presented and discussed. This will shed light on the resulting potential and limitations of a methodological approach to exile experiences. The article concludes with a reflection on how oral history potentially adds value for more substantiated research on exile.

Oral history as a way to access perceptions of alterity

The central question is how spatial structures, biographically relevant patterns of action, processes of change and the interrelation between urbanity and exile can be examined from a historical perspective. The research interest of oral history focuses on continuities and ruptures in social processes and their related effects on institutional and individual biographies. The effects of traumatic experiences, such as persecution under National Socialism or the experience of violence in institutional contexts (Tych et al. 2008; Weyell 2011), are among the classic thematic focuses of oral history (Kuhlmann 2008; Arp 2017). Particularly in the case of complex topics such as social issues of migration and integration, the subjective perspectives of those experiencing and living within such social environments can contribute significantly to the coverage of the subject area. Due to its many points of contact, an educational research approach may offer an opportunity to examine the life-historical constitution of meaning and significance in past everyday life and its resulting subjective forms of processing (Herrmann 1991; Krüger 1993). A comparison to historical research shows that numerous thematic overlaps have existed and are developing further. A historical view perceives 'migration' as foundational to human history and at the same time as an everyday form of mobility in our contemporary society (Alavi/Henke-Bockschatz 2004, 34). Questions of emigration in general and exile movements in particular have always been the subject of social discourse, although the topics have changed over time and have been accentuated in different ways. At the same time, 'migration and exile' are politically charged issues, not least because discourse usually revolves around how and where a social space defines its symbolic boundaries and how to deal with differences and inequality within these boundaries (Mecheril et al. 2010).

In the encounter between one's own and the other's lived realities as different worlds of meaning, different patterns of perception and interpretation inevitably collide. This can lead to misunderstandings and conflicts. Oral history offers more than just an alternative historical approach to this question. It makes it possible to achieve "limited but rewarding progress in historical knowledge and communication in nameable areas in different ways" (Niethammer 1985, 394). A biographical approach can serve as a method for expanding, refining and questioning psychological concepts, correcting stereotypes and multiplying the repertoire of the thinkable.

Perspectives of biographical historiography

Based on the assumption that "the structures that enable biographical communication correspond to socio-cultural knowledge" (Drews-Sylla et al. 2010, 181), biographical research is interested in looking at the conventional, socio-culturally anchored structural patterns of biographical articulation of individual actions. Since narrated life stories are unconsciously bound to 'traditions of form' and 'orientation foils', biographical research can sensitize our understanding of different lived realities, perspectives, social discrepancies and distribution of power (Ecarius 2018, 163). According to Vorländer, a standardized biography and learned structural principles play just as effective a role here as an orientation to norms and expectations and knowledge of historical contexts, so that biographical reports provide a structure that is predetermined retrospectively (Vorländer 1990, 15). By applying methods that critically engage with such biographical sources, research may perhaps not gather historical facts, but instead could gain an understanding of retrospectively presented stories of experience, collective biographies or subjective personal histories. The aspect of negotiating affiliations to the norm as well as deviation from the norm as dynamic, reciprocal processes which affect, for example, questions of religion, language competence, everyday behaviour or naming, remains a determining factor in research on exile in particular. According to Drews-Sylla, it is yet to be examined to what extent an increasing normalization of those who deviate from certain societal norms is accompanied by an increasing denormalization of the dominant order (Drews-Sylla et al. 2010, 189). Biographical interviews could be used, for example, to examine the extent to which the interviewees centre the ways they had to assimilate in a new social environment. One possible approach could be to show which narrative strategies are used (consciously or unconsciously) to present and interpret negative or even traumatizing experiences. It should be noted that any researcher's interpretations of the life course of the biographical subject are always already influenced by the norms deeply inscribed in their own mainstream society, and consequently by definitions and imaginations of self and other as they circulate within that society. Thus, interview partners project hegemonic norms which they reproduce in their biographical reports, even if they critically question them (Drews-Sylla et al. 2010, 189).

Biographical research is therefore to be understood as a second-degree construction, an interpretation of an interpretation. According to Ackermann et al. (2012), a sustained reflection on the "contingent conditions of the interpretation of interpretation" (Mecheril/Rose 2012, 118) is particularly essential here – this means that it is vital to always reflect upon one's own methodological, ideological and epistemological preconditions.

In the author's view, historical research on biography can contribute to an understanding of identities. In the encounter between selfhood and alterity as different worlds of meaning, different patterns of perception and interpretation inevitably collide. This can lead to misunderstandings and conflicts with regards to factual content, beliefs, value convictions, value orientations, interests or claims. Here the question arises as to what is to be understood by alterity if this is to go beyond the understanding of the counterpart. Alterity here means an otherness that has a reciprocal relationship to identity (Schwibbe 2013, 59f.). According to Schwibbe, identity is constituted within the framework of socio-cultural practices, in dialogue, in interaction and in agreement with or differentiation from others (ibid., 57). In this process, according to Tajfel, the foreign is first determined by a majority society in processes of demarcation from the own; it is perceived as deviating from the familiar; that is, as something actually or supposedly different (cf. Tajfel 1978, 1982). On an institutional level, the construction of norms serves to explain, enhance and legitimize one's own patterns of action and interpretation. It can also serve the generalization of expectations and as a control mechanism in institutions.

According to Holzbrecher, 'the Other' is to be understood as more than just a counterpart on an individual, personal level, but as a counterpart that is perceived as a risk as well as an opportunity, as alienating or as fascinating, in a larger political and societal context. It tends to appear as a chaotic force (Holzbrecher 1995, 1), i.e. as something that challenges a familiar world view. 'The Other' is considered a counterpart that can appear as a risk as well as an opportunity. In this way, 'the Other' calls into question a previously familiar world view since it calls for a history of relationships with an open outcome (ibid.). Therein lies an opportunity for oral history, because contact with individual and collective pasts can create the basis for new relationalities in intercultural encounters. This approach has to be used to clarify what the strangeness of another person consists of, because the tense relationship between self and other confronts us, above all, with our own modes of perception and possibilities of experience (Schäffter 1991). By reflecting on the biographical narrative, patterns of interpretation of alterity can be revealed and exposed as politically effective subliminal achievements of order in their repressive nature, if their understanding as 'natural order' or their absolutization into a universal pattern of interpretation is recognized and critically discussed. A limiting factor here is that by understanding the other, by recognizing the differences, otherness can be reduced, yes, but never ultimately.

The biographical reports generated with the access to oral history can be understood as a reflection of cultural normativity (world production) as well as narrative constructions (self-production). In this tension between self- and world production, they offer fruitful avenues for exploring exile experiences. In this way, biographical categories can be analyzed as the results of institutional and social norms. Starting from the question of how biographical narratives are formulated, rather than what they contain, biographical interviews can be used to develop statements about processes of interpretation and appropriation (Mecheril/Rose 2012). The following section will focus on the question of the potentials and limits of the historical approach.

Potentials of oral history

Oral history offers access to the histories of both individuals and groups, often only poorly recorded in writing as a consequence of exile experiences and circumstances. Due to flight or emigration, missing documents, broken contacts and network structures may sometimes influence the transmission of narratives and perspectives. At the same time, the narratives are often lost in the media discourse in the new homeland as perspectives of a minority group. Official documents produced by authorities and other institutions, just as their collection and transmission in archives, often reflect the perspective and concerns of the issuing authorities in terms of content and composition. The experiences that are missing because they are not handed down or not received by the majority society can, however, be recorded through the approach of the biographical interview. At the same time, biographical interviews offer the chance to explore experiences of otherness from the perspective of the interviewee. By leaving it up to the interviewees to set the focus, oral history can provide a valuable supplement to hegemonic historical discourses.

One potential of oral history is to raise new questions from the answers given by the interviewees, questions that have not yet been asked. In research on urbanity and exile experience, an oral history method offers specific opportunities. Especially against the background of collective memories and their solidification into 'patterns' of memory, it is important and indispensable for our understanding of life histories, according to Miller-Kipp, "to stay on the track of individual experience, to see differences" (Miller-Kipp 2007, 15). As oral history focuses on individual experience, already known historical processes can be illustrated in an exemplary way and individual and general history can be linked. This often results in multi-layered, often contradictory atmospheric images and impressions in the depiction of what is remembered (Meynert 1988, 16). This is in line with the goal of exile studies to deal with the complex problems of emigration and exile from German-speaking Central Europe in an interdisciplinary manner: to communicate the political, scientific, cultural and artistic achievements of the exiled and the returnees and – under the aspect of memory work – to promote dialogue between researchers and those affected, with subsequent generations, interested parties, related institutions or organizations, as well as with the public (Künste im Exil 2021). The approach of oral historiography can also be used to record the many forms of forced migration and diaspora in contemporary history.

By shedding light on personal as well as broader historical lines of connection, the methodological approach of oral history constitutes a distinct epistemological value. A biographical approach makes it possible to identify lines of connection between social and historical developments and the lives of those involved. Especially by observing ruptures, contradictions, distortions and other conspicuous features in the self-testimonies of the interlocutors, oral history methods help us understand historical processes (Göpfert 1999, 29). Biographical interviews can further facilitate the decoding of unfamiliar cultural patterns, enable a change of perspective and thus trigger intercultural sensitization processes. Studies focusing on biographies that deal with exile experiences can be understood less as a mere intercultural comparison and more as a possibility for the reconstruction and reflection of innovative social practices: in other words, new ideas, approaches and services that can be used to tackle social problems in more fruitful ways than has been possible until now. The methodological approach of oral history can serve here to reconstruct both experienced losses and gained opportunities. It can focus not only on second- and third-generation migrants born in a new homeland but also on migrants of the first generation and the plethora of changes societies undergo.

A further potential of accessing history via auto/biography is that researchers can gain insight into the causes for educational challenges. Biographical interviews, for instance, can promote a better understanding between researchers and interviewees and show that intergroup relations should not be understood in reductive black-and-white terms but as extremely complex. Even the effort to gain a mutual understanding of each other's beliefs and fluctuating cultural influences can help to reduce conflict and tension. To be able to categorize and order biographical narratives concerned with historical processes, it is important to consider individuals as participants in their socio-political environments. Oral history gives researchers the chance to examine the restrictions and opportunities individuals have experienced and the stereotypes and discrimination they have been confronted with. As a qualitative approach, oral history opens up the possibility of recognizing the diversity of perspectives, all the while placing them in larger contexts and reflecting on related viewpoints. This is a good starting point for an interdisciplinary approach to researching exile. Based on different patterns of perception and interpretation, research on exile and migration traces historical, social and cultural perspectives as well as the specific cultural dislocating experiences undergone by interview interlocutors. In this way, oral history promotes a critical view of historical readings, provides a greater sensitivity for historical plurality and diversity and offers conclusions for personal understanding and individual action. Thus, oral history opens a pathway to get to know other perspectives and to understand the actions, values and morals of others (Berg 2010).

The specifics and limitations of oral history

Since biographical reports should be understood less as a representation of historical processes than as the interpretation of earlier experiences from memory, they provide insights into identity constructions and contemporary social discourses

(Jacobi 1999, 288). The so-called "*Erinnerungsinterviews*", interviews that focus on memory and remembrance processes, must not be misunderstood as the mere reproduction of stored facts; rather, they represent an "active, complex, symbolically mediated reconstruction process" (Wirtz 1988, 346), which is influenced by the conversation and which features diverse narrative strands, interwoven to form a coherent perspective on one's own life. Individual and social dimensions are to be understood in close connection. It should be borne in mind that biographical narratives as self-generated sources should be classified as the result of a reconstruction process that the interview partners perform in communicative exchange with the researchers (Du Bois-Reymond 2001, 220). In order not to limit the interpretation of one's oral sources to a mere mimetic representation of each interviewee's individual self-perception and to be able to present an objective portrait, this aspect can best be dealt with by means of a critical analysis of the sources and by supplementing them with further references (Söhner, 2020a–2020c).

I agree with Lamnek that "to experience the social actors in their view" (Lamnek 2005, 194) during the data collection process, openness and flexibility are among the central principles. An open and at the same time focussed form of interview is a suitable method here; this means that the interviewees have room to manoeuvre in their responses, while at the same time the interview is centred around a complex set of topics to which the interviewees keep coming back to (Mayring 2002, 67). In order to counter the difficulty of narrating in a non-native language, it makes sense to resort to guiding questions, thus navigating the course of the conversation (Rothfuß/Dörfler 2013).

In interview situations, it is always important to keep in mind whether the relationship between interviewer and respondent is asymmetrical. This can be the case, for example, due to differences in language competence and expressiveness, which could suggest an inequality between the interview partners or make one party appear more competent simply by using more sophisticated language (Vorländer 1990, 16). Asymmetrical relations also arise when the interview partners belong to different generations or have had different experiences with stigma or trauma. All in all, it is essential for researchers to deal with the overall topic in advance in order to place the narrative in a larger context and to identify patterns of behaviour and interpretation. For biographical research, this means to remain aware of and take into account these problems in the conception, implementation and evaluation phases of the project (Palenga-Möllenbeck 2018).

Conclusion

This paper discussed which gaps in knowledge can be closed by the methodological approach of oral history in exile studies and to what extent the method can be considered suitable to answer questions for future projects. In summary, the approach of oral history for exile studies can be classified as a useful methodological approach that can be profitably applied to social and cultural issues. By opening up to everyday history, oral history offers the opportunity to examine processes of participation and resistance when societies change. Furthermore, the active participation of the interlocutors in the research process enables them not only to perceive themselves as objects of research but also to take possession of the experience of their own history (Wirtz 1988, 345).

In research that revolves around exile or migration, an oral history approach offers the possibility to analyze categories of perception, consciousness and the validity of norms. The socio-economic anchoring, the conditionality of mental structures such as emotions, must always be considered in the analysis (ibid., 347).

Against the backdrop of the socio-political effects of academic knowledge production, the biographical–historical approach requires sensitivity. It should reflect on and question any claims to norms or 'normality' underlying the research process. A source-critical examination of one's methods can protect researchers from making hasty generalizations. The professional competence of researchers with regard to planning, conducting and evaluating interviews is of central importance here. Thus, the potential of oral history lies, above all, in enabling access to the subjective perception of social processes and how they change (Apel 2018). Against this background, oral history writing offers a fruitful instrument in the research of self-images and external images and exile experiences in intercultural contexts.

REFERENCES

Ackermann, Friedhelm, et al., editors. *Qualitatives Forschen in der Erziehungswissenschaft.* Springer VS, 2012.

Alavi, Bettina, and Gerhard Henke-Bockschatz, editors. Migration und Fremdverstehen. *Geschichtsunterricht und Geschichtskultur in der multiethnischen Gesellschaft (Schriften zur Geschichtsdidaktik, 16).* Schulz-Kirchner, 2004.

Apel, Linde. "Kommentar, Tagungsbericht: Oral History und die historische Forschung zur frühen Kindheit. Quellen, Methoden, interdisziplinäre Perspektiven." 2018. *H-Soz-Kult*, www.hsozkult.de/conferencereport/id/tagungsberichte-8215. Accessed 22 May 2020.

Arp, Agnès. "Annäherung an die Gewalterfahrungen ehemaliger Heimkinder aus DDR-Spezialheimen. Eine Oral History-Untersuchung." *BIOS – Zeitschrift für Biographieforschung, Oral History und Lebensverlaufsanalysen*, vol. 30, nos. 1–2, 2017, pp. 235–258, doi: 10.3224/bios.v30i1-2.15. Accessed 9 June 2021.

Benz, Wolfgang, editor. Das Exil der kleinen Leute. *Alltagserfahrung deutscher Juden in der Emigration.* Fischer, 1994.

Berg, Tanja. *Multiperspektivität und Interkulturelles Geschichtslernen in der Jugendgeschichtsarbeit*, edited by Landesjugendring Brandenburg and Landesjugendring Berlin, Berlin, 2010, www.ljrberlin.de/sites/default/files/2019-10/handreichung_multiperspektivitaet_1.pdf. Accessed 10 June 2021.

Dietze, Carola. *Nachgeholtes Leben. Helmuth Plessner 1892–1985*. Wallstein, 2006.

Drews-Sylla, Gesine, et al., editors. *Konstruierte Normalitäten – normale Abweichungen*. VS Verlag für Sozialwissenschaften, 2010.

Du Bois-Reymond, Manuela. "Die Oral-History-Methode. Königsweg oder Schleichpfad der historischen Kindheitsforschung." *Kinder, Kindheit, Lebensgeschichte. Ein Handbuch*, edited by Imbke Behnken and Jürgen Zinnecker, Seelze-Velber, 2001, pp. 218–232.

Ecarius, Jutta. "Erziehungswissenschaftliche Biographieforschung." *Handbuch Biographieforschung*, edited by Helma Lutz et al., Springer VS, 2018, pp. 163–173.

Fischer, Ernst. "Oral History als Methode der Exilforschung. Überlegungen zu Theorie und Praxis." *Preserving the Memory of Exile. Festschrift for John M. Spalek on the Occasion of his 80th Birthday*, edited by Wulf Köpke, Refugium, 2008, pp. 97–109.

Fischer, Wolfram, and Martin Kohli. "Biographieforschung." *Methoden der Biographie- und Lebenslaufforschung*, edited by Wolfgang Voges, Leske + Budrich, 1987, pp. 25–49.

Gibran, Kahlil. *Sand and Foam & A Tear and a Smile*. Knopf Doubleday Publishing Group, 1926.

Göpfert, Rebekka. *Der jüdische Kindertransport von Deutschland nach England 1938/39. Geschichte und Erinnerung*. Campus, 1999.

Hagemann, Harald. "Deutschsprachige Wirtschaftswissenschaftler im britischen Exil." *Keine Klage über England? Deutsche und österreichische Exilerfahrungen in Großbritannien 1933–1945* (Publications oft he Institute of Germanic Studies, University of London, 72), edited by Charmian Brinson et al., Iudicium, 1998, pp. 241–262.

Herrmann, Ulrich "'Innenansichten', Erinnerte Lebensgeschichte und geschichtliche Lebenserinnerung." *Kinderwelten*, edited by Christa Berg, Suhrkamp, 1991, pp. 41–67.

Holzbrecher, Alfred. "Interkulturelles Lernen: Die Wahrnehmung des Anderen als pädagogische Herausforderung." *Politisches Lernen*, vol. 17, nos. 3–4, 1995, pp. 47–60.

Jacobi, Juliane. "Zur Konstruktion und Rekonstruktion des Selbstentwurfes." "Sag mir wo die Mädchen sind…". *Beiträge zur Geschlechtergeschichte der Jugend*, edited by Christina Benninghaus and Kerstin Kohtz, Böhlau, 1999, pp. 275–290.

Krüger, Heinz-Hermann. "Theoretische und methodische Grundlagen der historischen Jugendforschung." *Handbuch der Jugendforschung*, edited by Heinz-HermannKrüger, Leske + Budrich, 1993, pp. 279–304.

Kuhlmann, Carola. *"So erzieht man keinen Menschen". Lebens- und Berufserinnerungen aus der Heimerziehung der 50er und 60er Jahre*. VS Verlag für Sozialwissenschaften, 2008.

Künste im Exil. "Gesellschaft für Exilforschung e.V." *Künste im Exil – Exil-Netzwerk*, www.kuenste-im-exil.de/KIE/Content/DE/Netzwerkpartner/gesellschaft-fuer-exilforschung.html. Accessed 1 May 2021.

Lamnek, Siegfried. *Qualitative Sozialforschung – Lehrbuch*. Beltz, 2005.

Leavy, Patricia. *Oral History*. Oxford University Press, 2011.

Lücke, Martin, and Irmgard Zündorf. *Einführung in die Public History*. Vandenhoeck & Ruprecht, 2018.

Mayring, Philipp. *Einführung in die Qualitative Sozialforschung. Eine Anleitung zu qualitativem Denken*. Beltz, 2002.

Mecheril, Paul, et al. *Migrationspädagogik*. Beltz, 2010.

Mecheril, Paul, and Nadine Rose. "Qualitative Migrationsforschung – Standortbestimmungen zwischen Politik, Reflexion und (Selbst-)Kritik." *Qualitatives Forschen in der Erziehungswissenschaft*, edited by Friedhelm Ackermann et al., Springer VS, 2012, pp. 115–134.

Meynert, Joachim. "Jüdische Jugend 1933–1938. Aspekte eines leidvollen Alltags." *Pädagogik Heute*, vol. 40, no. 10, 1988, pp. 15–23.

Miller-Kipp, Gisela. "Der Führer braucht mich." *Der Bund Deutscher Mädel (BDM): Lebenserinnerungen und Erinnerungsdiskurs* (Materialien zur Historischen Jugendforschung). Beltz, 2007.

Niethammer, Lutz. "Fragen – Antworten – Fragen. Methodische Erfahrungen und Erwägungen zur Oral History." "Wir kriegen jetzt andere Zeiten." Auf der Suche nach der Erfahrung des Volkes in nachfaschistischen Ländern (Lebensgeschichte und Sozialkultur im Ruhrgebiet 1930 bis 1960, 3), edited by Lutz Niethammer and Alexander von Plato, Dietz, 1985, pp. 382–445.

Obertreis, Julia, editor. *Oral History* (Basistexte Geschichte, vol. 8). Franz Steiner Verlag, 2012.

Palenga-Möllenbeck, Ewa. "'Unsichtbare ÜbersetzerInnen' in der Biographieforschung: Übersetzung als Methode." *Handbuch Biographieforschung*, edited by Helma Lutz et al., Springer VS, 2018, pp. 669–680.

Röder, Werner, and Strauss Herber, editors. *International Biographical Dictionary of Central European Emigrés 1933–1945*. Saur, 1983. 3 vols.

Rosenthal, Gabriele, and Artur Bogner, editors. Biographies in the Global South. *Life Stories Embedded in Figurations and Discourses*. Campus, 2017.

Rothfuß, Eberhard, and Thomas Dörfler, editors. *Raumbezogene qualitative Sozialforschung*. Springer VS, 2013.

Schäffter, Ortfried. "Modi des Fremderlebens. Deutungsmuster im Umgang mit Fremdheit." *Das Fremde. Erfahrungsmöglichkeiten zwischen Faszination und Bedrohung*, edited by Ortfried Schäffter, Westdeutscher Verlag, 1991, pp. 11–42.

Schwibbe, Gudrun. "'Schlimmer als auszusteigen ist langsam in der RAF zu zerbrechen.' Narrative Identitäts- und Alteritätskonstruktionen von ehemaligen Mitgliedern linksterroristischer Gruppierungen." *Zeitschrift für Volkskunde*, vol. 109, no. 1, May 2013, pp. 55–75.

Söhner, Felicitas. "Methodische Problemfelder und ethische Implikationen in der zeitzeugenbasierten Historiographie. Ein Erfahrungsbericht." *BIOS – Zeitschrift für Biographieforschung, Oral History und Lebensverlaufsanalysen*, vol. 30, nos. 1–2, 2017, pp. 273–289, doi: 10.3224/bios.v30i1-2.17. Accessed 10 June 2021.

Söhner, Felicitas. *Psychiatrie-Enquete: mit Zeitzeugen verstehen. Eine Oral History der Psychiatrie-Reform in der BRD*. Psychiatrie-Verlag, 2020a.

Söhner, Felicitas. "Umgang mit Identitätskonstruktion und Zeitwahrnehmung in der Oral History." *Frontiers in Time Research – Einführung in die interdisziplinäre Zeitforschung*, edited by Elisabeth Schilling and Maggie O'Neill, Springer VS, 2020b, pp. 11–28.

Söhner, Felicitas. "Zeitzeugenbasierter Blick auf frühkindliche Bildung – Potentiale und Limitationen der Oral History." *Frühkindliche Bildung und Entwicklung*, edited by Fabienne Becker-Stoll and Stepanka Kadera, special issue of *Bildungsforschung*, vol. 2, no. 18, 2020c, pp. 1–16, doi: 10.25539/bildungsforschun.v2i18.303. Accessed 11 June 2021.

Strauss, Herbert, and Dennis Rohrbaugh, editors. Jewish Immigrants of the Nazi Period in the USA, vol. 5: *The Individual and Collective Experience of German-Jewish Immigrants 1933–1984. An Oral History Record*. Saur, 1986.

Tajfel, Henri. "Social Categorization, Social Identity and Social Comparison." *Differentiation Between Social Groups. Studies in the Social Psychology of Intergroup Relations (European Monographs in Social Psychology, 14)*, edited by Henri Tajfel, Academic Press, 1978, pp. 61–76.

Tajfel, Henri, editor. *Social Identity and Intergroup Relations* (European Studies in Social Psychology). Cambridge University Press, 1982.

Tych, Feliks, et al., editors. Kinder über den Holocaust. Frühe Zeugnisse 1944–1948. *Interviewprotokolle der Zentralen Jüdischen Historischen Kommission in Polen*. Metropol, 2008.

Vorländer, Herwart. "Mündliches Erfragen von Geschichte." *Oral History. Mündlich erfragte Geschichte. Acht Beiträge*, edited by Herwart Vorländer, Vandenhoeck & Ruprecht, 1990, pp. 7–29.

Weyell, Dörte. Kindheitserinnerungen jüdischer Deportierter. *Strukturen der Erlebnisverarbeitung in qualitativer Analyse* (Berliner Arbeiten zur Erziehungs- und Kulturwissenschaft, 53). Logos, 2011.

Wirtz, Rainer. "Vergangenheit in mündlicher Überlieferung. Einige Aspekte der Neueren Geschichte." *Vergangenheit in mündlicher Überlieferung* (Colloquium Rauricum, 1), edited by Jürgen von Ungern-Sternberg and Hansjörg Reinau, De Gruyter, 1988, pp. 331–344.

6

Movement – A Conversation with Artist Michaela Melián

Burcu Dogramaci

With the installation piece *Movement,* dedicated to the life and work of the violinist Susanne Lachmann, the artist Michaela Melián contributed to the exhibition *The Futureless Memory* (2020) at the Kunsthaus Hamburg. Born in Frankfurt am Main in 1888, Lachmann studied violin in Frankfurt, Leipzig and Vienna. She later moved to Hamburg where she played the second violin in the Bandler Quartet from 1925 and made her debut in 1931 with the Schneider Quartet at the Kleine Musikhalle in Hamburg. At the same time, she taught at the Pädagogische Akademie in neighbouring Altona, among other places. Her daughter was born in 1926. Because she was Jewish, Susanne Lachmann could no longer practice her profession after 1933 and was only allowed to give smaller performances in the context of the Jewish Cultural Association. In 1935, she managed to flee to England with her daughter. Unable to make a living in England, Susanne Lachmann continued to Elgin, Scotland, where she taught music at the Gordonstoun School – initially on a room and board basis – and also founded the school orchestra and choir. She remained connected to the Pädagogische Akademie after the end of the war, but never returned to Hamburg. Susanne Lachmann died in Elgin in 1967.

We sat down with multimedia artist Michaela Melián, who divides her time between Hamburg and Munich, to discuss the concept and form of the installation *Movement,* conceived as a result of artistic research into the life of a forgotten musician and the mapping of her escape route.

Burcu Dogramaci (BD): Michaela, your installation *Movement* was created for the exhibition *The Futureless Memory*, which opened in 2020.[1] Can you tell us about the background and the story of its creation?

Michaela Melián (MM): The starting point for the exhibition was the question of how art can bring the forgotten back into the present. Initially, the director of the Kunsthaus Hamburg, Katja Schroeder, asked me to contribute a piece on the American composer Conlon Nancarrow. However, I really wanted to work on a Hamburg-related topic and dedicate myself to a female biography. I had an urge to explore a female musician who was productive at a time when radio really took off, after the arrival of the gramophone but still in its early days, when only a limited number of musicians were recorded. Also, a lot of the material is not available as it was not released on shellac records and so could not be digitized later on.

BD: How did you find out about Susanne Lachmann?

MM: While working on the research project "Lexikon verfolgter Musiker und Musikerinnen der NS-Zeit" (Encyclopaedia of persecuted musicians of the Nazi era) at the University of Hamburg, we found an entry on the musician Susanne Lachmann (fig. 6.1).[2] Her vita, despite the limited information available, immediately appealed to me because it contains a lot of what *The Futureless Memory* is about. From a global perspective, the

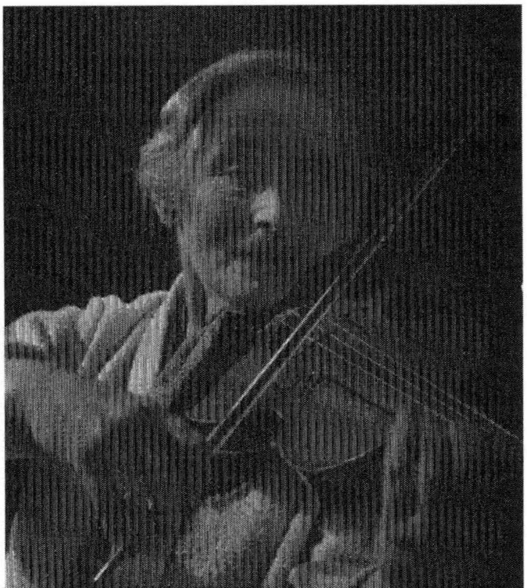

FIGURE 6.1: G.C.M. Gray, *Portrait of Susanne Lachmann*, published in *Gordonstoun Record*, no. 42, 1961, p. 105 (© Gordonstoun School Archives, see *Lexikon verfolgter Musiker und Musikerinnen der NS-Zeit*, University of Hamburg, www.lexm.uni-hamburg.de/object/lexm_lexmmedium00001334).

exhibition examines the importance of belonging, also in the context of flight and exile.[3] In the exhibition itself, I wanted to trace Susanne Lachmann's path, which was marked by exile and expulsion and make it physically tangible. I wanted to address the ephemeral nature of her biography. To me, Lachmann is representative of so many others who, in a sense, have escaped from our memory because they were driven into exile.

BD: What was it about Susanne Lachmann's life and work that appealed to you?

MM: First of all, I found it fascinating that, as a woman born in 1888, she had an exceptional career and played in well-known chamber music formations. She always played the second violin, which is quite extraordinary; almost all famous quartets in music history consisted exclusively of male musicians, something that has only changed in recent decades. Since I play a string instrument myself, this immediately stood out to me.

BD: For a long time, classical music was an exclusively male domain

MM: Many younger people aren't aware of this but: when I studied cello, before studying art, the Vienna Philharmonic and the Berlin Philharmonic didn't have a single female member. That's another reason why I was interested in Susanne Lachmann's life. The fact that she studied at famous music academies with important teachers and thus forged her own path – I found this remarkable.

BD: Susanne Lachmann's life was characterized by frequent displacement and is closely linked to big cities: from her birthplace Frankfurt am Main, she moved to Leipzig and Vienna where she pursued her studies, and finally ended up in Hamburg where she lived and worked until she emigrated.

MM: In Hamburg, she devoted herself to her career, performed on the radio and in the Musikhalle, played in quartets and likely played concerts all over Europe. In addition, Susanne Lachmann gave music lessons in reform-oriented socio-educational contexts at the Pädagogische Akademie Altona. She was committed to a certain social participation in the cultural asset of music.

BD: This intense musical life was abruptly curtailed when the Nazi Regime seized power, and Susanne Lachmann ultimately decided to emigrate to England. Unable to make a living there, she finally ended up in the Scottish province.

MM: This part of her life story was very important for my work. Susanne Lachmann hardly had any opportunity to perform in Germany, and in 1935 she fled to England – a single mother with her child – and got a job in the far north, at Gordonstoun School in Elgin, Scotland. There, she came full circle with Germany, since the founder of the school, Kurt Hahn, was a reform pedagogue who had also fled Germany and founded the Schloss Salem boarding school. At Hahn's British Salem School in Elgin, initially intended as a place for children and teachers who had fled from Germany, Susanne Lachmann (fig. 6.2) was offered a position; in the beginning without pay except for room and board. After the war, she stayed on and had to live in precarious conditions in Elgin. Only late in her life did she receive compensation from the city of Hamburg.

BD: In Susanne Lachmann's case, moving to the Scottish countryside can be interpreted as a metaphor for exile. Exile often means being relegated to the margins; including the margins of perception. Many exiles have permanently slipped out of public perception. How did you approach Susanne Lachmann's life, work and her path in exile, and what forms of artistic translation did you choose?

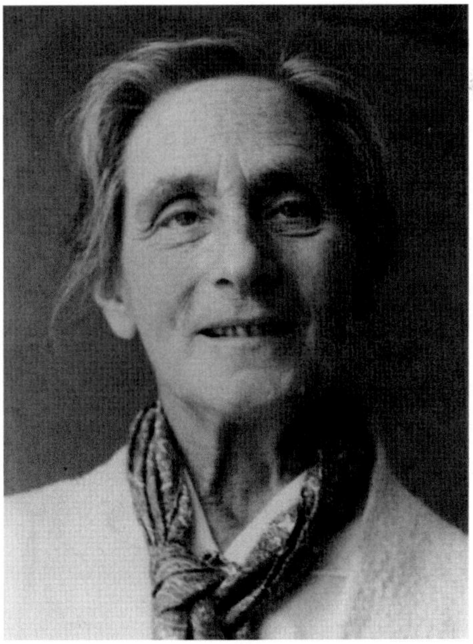

FIGURE 6.2: *Portrait of Susanne Lachmann*, no date and photographer indicated (Gordonstoun School Archives, Elgin, Moray, Scotland).

MM: It was important for me to trace her path from Central Europe, Frankfurt, the upper middle class environment, via Vienna and Berlin to Hamburg and, later, into exile in Scotland. The intention was to make this movement tangible in the exhibition space. However, I didn't want to simply trace the movement, and so I considered including a violin voice and let this sound, which has accompanied Susanne Lachmann her whole life, represent her path. What I did, then, was to transfer her stations in life onto a map in order to develop a notation from these points. This proved somewhat complicated since the movement goes back and forth in space between East and West while it continues through time.

BD: How did you solve the problem of changing directions to create a playable notation?

MM: I drew a simplified map of north-western Europe on a sheet of paper and mirrored it in Vienna, so that I could continue to draw the route from Vienna (fig. 6.3). Vienna then is the intersection and mirror point while Hamburg stands for the note H. Thus, the vertical distance to Hamburg gives the pitch of the other notes = locations. The duration of the notes then

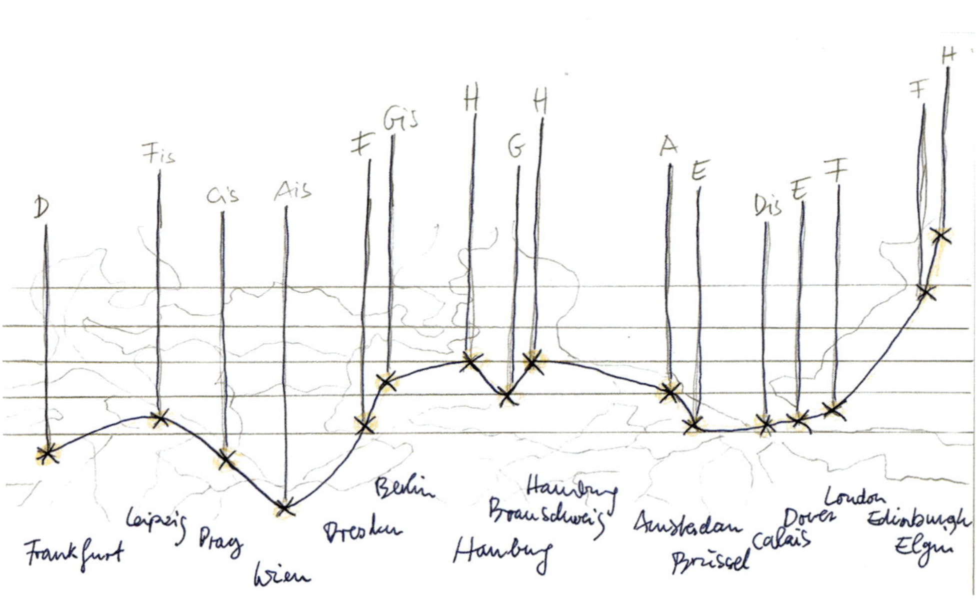

FIGURE 6.3: Michaela Melián, *Movement*, 2020, drawing, pencil, coloured pencil, ink on paper (© Michaela Melián).

depended on how long she lived in each place. The melody, which could be heard at regular intervals in the exhibition, was recorded for me in different versions by the Hamburg violinist Ruth May. The tempo is quite slow, about 80 bpm, which roughly corresponds to an *andante* (*andare* = to go), i.e. just slow or fast enough for the melody to remain playable and recognizable and not break up into individual notes.

BD: In your composition, the slowness and delays are striking. Nonetheless, flight is certainly associated with something abrupt and hurried.

MM: In the composition, all the stages of life formulate themselves selectively. Susanne Lachmann grew up in Frankfurt and continued her musical studies in Leipzig and Vienna. The time she spent in Frankfurt and Scotland, respectively would have taken up relatively long passages in the composition, since she lived there for longer periods of time. However, holding the two notes for too long would have made for a boring musical arc. Frankfurt sets the keynote; from there the melody swings up, first via Leipzig to Vienna, then Hamburg, Braunschweig, Hamburg again and then climbs up to Elgin. She lived in Hamburg, her child was born in Braunschweig. Why Braunschweig? We don't know. Perhaps she had given a concert and had her daughter there and then went back to Hamburg. The flight that followed later set the pace; I have adjusted the other places where Lachmann stayed much longer in proportion. So, here and there, I shortened or contracted the phases of stay so that the sounds combine to form a melody. You see, this should be heard as a fleeting movement that can be traced with the ear.

BD: In the exhibition, the recorded melody was visually linked to a series of light bulbs suspended on long cables at different levels, which then lit up in concert with the sounds.

MM: In addition to the translation of Susanne Lachmann's life path into a melody that can be audibly experienced in the room, the translation of the life journey comes as a fleeting light drawing across the room. For this, I implemented the notation via light bulbs hanging from the ceiling (fig. 6.4). The light bulbs are suspended at a height that corresponds to the respective pitch in front of an invisible tablature. The distance between the light bulbs corresponds to the length of the note value. As long as a certain violin note of the melody reverberates, the corresponding bulb lights up; as soon as it falls silent, the bulb goes out. Every three minutes, the short, one-minute melody was audible and visible via the movement of the light

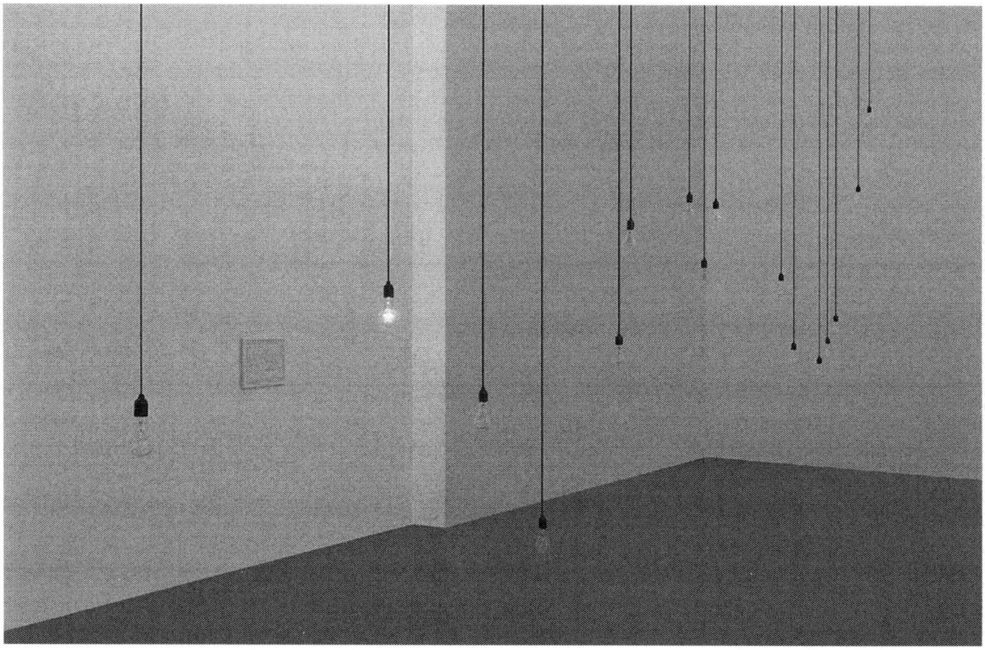

FIGURE 6.4: Michaela Melián, *Movement*, 2020, installation, 16 light bulbs, sound track, installation view *The Futureless Memory*, Kunsthaus Hamburg, 2020 (© Michaela Melián).

bulbs as they rose and fell. The work looked quite simple and minimalist, but behind it was a complex technical apparatus with four media players connected in series that controlled the light and sound. I enjoyed this; translating the complexity of the conceptual and constructively intricate into something simple, something that floats past in space – barely perceptible to the eyes and ears – and then disappears again. Or, in other words, like a short flash of memory. As I was able to observe on site at the Kunsthaus Hamburg, it was only after spending a while in the exhibition that visitors consciously perceived the melody and the light bulbs as belonging together as an installation.

BD: In the installation, your notation appears as an artistic mapping of a life. How important are these initial stages of artistic research and the search for traces which ultimately render possible what later becomes visible and audible in your work?

MM: Research is a starting point and thus an important part of my work. I am guided by the feeling that what concerns us today is not only a problem of the present but also has always accompanied human life, although perhaps in a different shape and appearance. The biography, the flight experience and the oblivion associated with it can be transferred to the present in the same way. In the case of Susanne Lachmann, it was important for me to give this person a new presence since so little material is available on her person. Only two photographs and her curriculum vitae are known to us, and we do not have any audio recordings of her.

BD: In this way, your work can also be understood as a commentary on the conditions of remembering.

MM: There are fundamental questions associated with such a project: Which musicians were recorded and which were not? Who was archived and who was not? Memory also has an element of deception to it. Archives reveal a certain perspective on history, others remain obscured. To what extent can art draw out what has been forgotten, and make it audible and visible?

BD: Nevertheless, knowledge gaps and empty spaces remain, and escape stories leave many questions unanswered. How do you deal with this missing information?

MM: Susanne Lachmann's frequent change of place is very unusual for a female existence at that time, even before the flight. For example, nothing is available about her concert activities, nor about her flight and departure, the route and means of travel or the departure from Germany and her arrival in England. I reconstructed the route from Hamburg via England to Elgin in Scotland by looking at several life stories of other exiles and using their route as a model. I figured if others took these routes into exile, then she may likely have done the same.

BD: Your artistic research and translation methods can be related to scientific methods of source work. As an artist, you can detach yourself from the objective and the factual position and shape your findings in a different way and make them your own. This is the case, for example, in your mappings or notations where a map of Europe is rotated so that a melody can emerge.

MM: Yes, that's right. I was a little helpless at first when I realized that Susanne Lachmann's life path is a back-and-forth, running first to the East and then to the West. How do I bring that into the room? It should be a continuous movement and not look like she is going backwards. And since the map and the globe are only aids to our spatial imagination anyway, I can also find other representations which correspond to my concept.

BD: In your work, the audible often meets the visual and vice versa. Are these simply two sides of the same coin, do they complement each other or do hearing and seeing require a life of their own?

MM: The note reaches visitors intuitively; the sound embraces them. In *Movement*, there is no defined position for the listener; one can stand in the middle of it or follow the sound. The eye, on the other hand, works quite differently, it focuses on what is inside the field of vision. You can approach the installation from all sides and walk around it, or, if you don't like it, you can turn around and walk away. The sound however is inescapable, as it can be heard throughout the exhibition space. And so, in the end, the sound of *Movement* flows around the viewers in the exhibition, leading them to the installation, even if they haven't seen my work yet.

BD: In doing so, you also challenge conventional perceptions of art.

MM: As exhibition visitors, we are trained to rely on sight as our main sense, and this sense is closely related to cognition. We want to immediately understand what we see, we want to read it, comprehend it and contextualize it. Listening, on the other hand, is very much about the physical experience, the body intuitively remembers sounds and melodies.

BD: How did you become interested in historical events, or rather: lesser-known history(ies)?

MM: During my studies, I was interested in marginalized female positions in the visual arts of the 20th century. At the time, I searched in vain for role models at the academy, because there were hardly any female professors at art colleges then. At the same time, I was always interested in old art and read a lot of art historical analyses of works of art. When I go to museums, I learn a lot about the respective work – about production conditions, and about historical and social contexts of earlier eras when recordings on film or photographs were not a possibility. Thus, in works of art, moments of history are condensed in specific contexts and from specific perspectives. In this way, the omissions of the official representations are marked again and again, often involuntarily, and raise doubt.

BD: And it is precisely this moment of doubt which intrigued you?

MM: Yes, I always found that interesting. Translating and updating the historical into the present with the use of today's media. This is, in the broadest sense, seizing histories or taking them as an opportunity. If you look closely, there are always different layers, narrative strands, shifts in meaning and perspectives. Naturally, it plays an important role which type of media I use and whether I work with sound, light or drawing, like in the work on Susanne Lachmann: Drawing as a means of cartography, sound or light as fleeting sensory stimuli. *Movement* thus, can be perceived as a contemporary composition or installation, as well as the recollection of a historical musician, of her life and work and her escape from Nazi Germany.

NOTES

1. Michaela Melián's installation *Movement* can be seen and heard in the film accompanying the exhibition *The Futureless Memory* (Kunsthaus Hamburg, 19 September–22 November 2020). www.kunsthaushamburg.de/film-zur-ausstellung-the-futureless-memory/. Accessed 10 June 2022.
2. Fetthauer, Sophie. "Susanne Lachmann." *Lexikon verfolgter Musiker und Musikerinnen der NS-Zeit*, edited by Claudia Maurer Zenck and Peter Petersen, University of Hamburg, 2010 (updated 15 January 2018), www.lexm.uni-hamburg.de/object/lexm_lexmperson_00004243. Accessed 28 May 2022.
3. www.kunsthaushamburg.de/en/the-futureless-memory/. Accessed 28 May 2022.

PART II

PRACTICING THE URBAN

7

An Exile's Guide: Ernst Schaeffer's *Pictorial Bombay* and the Construction of Bombay's Touristscape

Margit Franz and Rachel Lee

Our chapter explores the intersections of exile, urbanity and cultural production through the lens of a particular genre of publication: the guidebook. As a type of book that engages with the built environment, urban settings and cultural life, the guidebook offers a promising starting point for explorations of historical portrayals of urbanity.[1] Often written by outsiders, guidebooks offer specific views on places as they seek to be "helpful and tactful companions" (Parsons 2007, n.p.) to tourists and other visitors. The guidebook that we focus on here, *Pictorial Bombay*, was authored by the exiled German journalist Ernst Schäffer, later Ernest Norbert Schaeffer and Ernest N. (Norbert/Nathan) Shaffer (1892–1978),[2] and published in Bombay (now Mumbai) in 1936.[3] An unusual example of a guidebook written from an exilic perspective, *Pictorial Bombay* offers insights into both how Schaeffer grasped the colonial city and how he contributed to developing Bombay as a tourist destination.

Long before Bombay became a site of tourist spectacle and consumption, Schaeffer mapped out a landscape for visitors that encompassed colonial institutions and religious buildings, as well as daily life and labour. In doing so, he communicated his particular vision of a touristscape, which is still partially pertinent today. Through a close reading of the texts and images that constitute *Pictorial Bombay*, we examine how Schaeffer's approaches to sensing, experiencing and understanding the city contributed to the construction of Bombay's touristscape. We propose that his commitment to encountering the urban environment in a physical, embodied way inflected the media he produced and included in the guidebook. Working journalistically with anecdotes and photographs, he created narratives that, rather than reproduce 'objective' descriptions of sites and monuments, evoke the socio-cultural experiences of the city. Embracing his individual perspective and a partial point of view, he encourages, perhaps even emboldens, his readers to explore the city and engage with local culture at street level.

In our analysis, we consider Schaeffer's *Pictorial Bombay* in relation to the *Guide to Bombay* by the newspaper publisher *The Times of India* and *The Bombay Guide & Directory* by J. Contractor, which were published in 1926 and 1937, respectively.[4] While we posit that Schaeffer's guidebook is a key source for urban exile research, we also hope to establish guidebooks in general as important lenses for reading cities. With their listings, addresses, recommendations, maps, timetables, itineraries and prices, guidebooks hold immense potential for historical urban research. In the following, we reflect on *Pictorial Bombay* through its development, reception and cost, as well as its textual and visual content, suggesting that its hybrid form and particular perspective distinguished it from the other guidebooks, and impacted future guidebook production.

Ernst Schaeffer in exile in Bombay

Almost precisely three years before the publication of *Pictorial Bombay*, on 30 November 1933, the former Ullstein business editor and *Berliner Zeitung am Mittag*'s deputy editor-in-chief, Ernst Schaeffer, and his wife Welda Schaeffer, landed at Bombay's harbour. Following a five-week journey on an old cargo ship, the exiled journalist began his new professional life with a six-month contract as a correspondent for the German Ullstein publishing house. After the Nazis banned him from publishing in Germany, he worked as a freelance reporter for Swiss, Czech, Belgian and Dutch newspapers. However, as Europe was fighting rising fascism, the European media's interest in India decreased. The journalist was forced to diversify his activities, and shifted his focus to the local market. He became an English and German tour and travel guide for Thomas Cook, translated German film scripts to English for Bhavnani film studios, and, as a self-taught photographer, started his "Individual Photo Studio" (Shaffer 1971, 48; *The Times of India*, 4 April 1936, 2) in his Colaba living room. With the tagline "The Studio of the European AND Indian Society" (*The Times of India*, 4 April 1936, 2), he specialized in portrait photography. He also introduced the service of advertising photography to the city and became an associate of the Royal Photographic Society (A.R.P.S.) (Schaeffer 1936, first page with author's name).[5]

Continuing to draw on his international network, he combined journalism with photography to establish himself internationally as a photojournalist. With the support of his former Ullstein colleagues, in Bombay Schaeffer received assignments for the New York City-based Black Star photo agency[6] and *Life* magazine. His networks in India – including members of Indian and British Indian political and economic elites, leaders of the Indian independence movement, Indian royal families and members of Bombay's avant-garde art circles like Mulk Raj Anand and Anil de Silva – enabled him to present English-speaking, international audiences with images from India that they were unlikely to have seen before. Locally he engaged himself in Jewish exile and relief networks in Bombay, and became a founding member of the Jewish Relief Association. Internationally, he contributed to the New York City-based and worldwide distributed Jewish journal *Aufbau*, reporting about the Jewish exile community in India (see Schaeffer 1941).

The Second World War interrupted transcontinental transport, communication and the import of photography supplies.[7] Tourism vanished, as did Schaeffer's other businesses. Having just received British citizenship, career-wise Schaeffer survived as a print production manager for an American advertisement company for the next three and a half years. Welda Schaeffer's financial contributions supported the couple from the very beginning of their stay in Bombay and her salary enabled Schaeffer to establish his own businesses. She worked first as an assistant to the German emigrant ear, nose and throat doctor Hermann Lämmle, and later as a typist, supporting all of her husband's enterprises with her language, photographic, organizational and typing skills. In October 1943, Ernst Schaeffer became the assistant manager of Oxford University Press, eventually working there for twelve years before returning to freelance journalism. Schaeffer's connection to India remained long after he left the subcontinent in the early 1960s for Germany; he contributed, for example, substantially to setting up the Südasien (South Asia) department of Deutsche Welle (see Shaffer 1971).

During the mid 1930s, Schaeffer combined his photographic and journalistic skills with his experiences as a travel guide to produce *Pictorial Bombay*, an unusual illustrated guide to the city.

The guidebook market in Bombay and the development of Pictorial Bombay

Although they have existed in different forms for almost 2000 years, guidebooks established themselves as a recognizable, commercial genre in the 19th century (Parsons 2007). During the 1800s, the names of two men – Karl Baedeker, based in Germany, and John Murray of London – became synonymous with guidebooks, and their publishing houses dominated the growing market. This 19th-century flourishing in guidebooks accompanied Europe's burgeoning tourism industry. In the United Kingdom, the growth of a middle class and the defeat of Napoleon in 1815 had contributed to a consolidation of British power internationally, while new railways and shipping routes opened up lines of mobility, making other places accessible to more people (Epelde 2004, 13). International visitors took advantage of new passenger shipping lines, which started expanding towards Asia after the opening of the Suez Canal in 1869, and sinking travel costs, to explore more distant places. This new accessibility also applied to British colonies, as the rise of mass tourism coincided with Europe's colonial expansion (Fei 2010, 228).[8]

The first guidebook to India was published by John Murray in 1859.[9] Written by Edward Eastwick, *A Handbook for India* focused on the three Presidencies administered by the British East India Company – Madras, Bombay and Bengal. It presented its intended audience of "travellers, officers and civilians" (Epelde 2004, 56) with an unabashedly colonial perspective that proved popular enough to merit 22 editions, with the final edition published in 1975. The Bombay Presidency volume included a lengthy section on the city of Bombay. The 29 pages, which contain historical context, cultural observations, maps and tour routes, constitute the first guide to the port city on the Arabian Sea. As the economic motor of the British Empire, the closest major Indian port to the Suez Canal and the starting point for expanding rail networks, Bombay was a frequent stop on the itineraries of business and leisure visits to the sub-continent: by the late 19th century, Bombay was the portal for 90 per cent of travellers entering or exiting India (Maclean 1875, 141). Despite the city's prominence, Eastwick was not impressed with what awaited his readers there, writing: "The sights of Bombay, if the traveller confines himself to the island itself, are soon exhausted" (Eastwick 1859, 273).

John Murray's *Handbook* section was soon complemented by guides dedicated solely to the city, including James Maclean's (1875) *Guide to Bombay* and D.A. Pinder's *Visitors' Illustrated Guide to Bombay* from 1904. Around its publication in the late 1930s, Schaeffer's *Pictorial Bombay* was in competition with more recently published guides: J. Contractor's *The Bombay Guide & Directory* (1937), Ben Diqui's *A Visit to Bombay* (1927) and the second edition of *The Times of India*'s *Guide to Bombay* (1926). As both *The Bombay Guide & Directory* and the *Guide to Bombay* are illustrated with photographs, we refer mainly to those when analyzing the impact of Schaeffer's exilic perspective on Bombay's touristscape, which he constructed through both text and images.

Schaeffer was well-equipped to write a guidebook. In addition to his journalistic record in Germany, Schaeffer had already authored two books; one about flying and the other about aviators awarded the "Pour le Mérite" order of bravery in Prussia.[10] In Bombay, Schaeffer's experiences as a professional travel guide and passionate explorer of the city provided the necessary content to expand his writing skills to include the genre of travel literature in the creation of *Pictorial Bombay*.

His record as a photographer was perhaps less convincing. In Germany, Schaeffer had taken photos as an amateur photographer and as an aviator during the First World War.[11] His occasional work as a journalist for the *Berliner Illustrierte* had "refined" his view of photos, according to his own statements (Shaffer 1971, 45). In India, he "threw himself into the specialist literature and began to work systematically with the camera" (ibid., 45f.). After some practice he learned "to work with large cameras and with all kinds of lenses and lights" (ibid., 46).[12] By February 1936, he had developed his photographic skills to the point of being able to hold an exhibition: In collaboration with the Agfa Photo Company, he presented his photos in a *Rolleiflex Exhibition* in the Taj Mahal Hotel (*The Times of India*, 6 February 1936, 1), demonstrating "[t]he value of the small camera for taking pictures, which can be enlarged to almost any size within the bounds of what is reasonable" (*The Times of India*, 6 February 1936, 16).

After completing the manuscript of *Pictorial Bombay*, he presented it to one of the most famous book wholesalers in Bombay: the New Book Co. Pvt. Ltd. in the Kitab Mahal, owned by the Taraporevala family. D.B. Taraporevala & Sons, the "treasure house of books" (*The Times of India*, 19 November 1936, 3), was the first and leading bookstore and publisher in Bombay. It was a hub not only for international literature, foreign periodicals and newspapers, illustrated magazines and pictures, postcards and art publications, but also for artists themselves. They even offered temporary exhibition space when Bombay lacked gallery space (see Dalmia 2001, 53). The company was founded as a bookseller, newsagent and stationery dealer at 190 Hornby Road in 1864 (see Macmillan 1928, 232). In 1936, they ran the bookstore at 210 Hornby Road, with a branch in the Taj Mahal Hotel at Apollo Bunder to serve an elite Indian and high-class foreign clientele.

The owner of the publishing house, Phiroze Framroze D.B. Taraporevala, agreed to publish *Pictorial Bombay* for New Books & Co. as an album with 40 full-page black and white photographs and an accompanying independent text of a similar number of pages. Nine small black and white photos complete the texts' pages. D.D. Neroy prepared the blocks for publication, and F. Borton printed them for G. Claridge & Co. Ltd. in Frere Road in the Fort area (see Schaeffer 1936, 77). With the financial support of two German-Jewish emigrant businesspeople, Schaeffer was able to contribute a deductible of 2,000 rupees retention, which he quickly repaid after publication (see Shaffer 1971, 28).

Strategically launched in the pre-Christmas period of 1936, *Pictorial Bombay* was first advertised as an "album containing 40 unusual Photographs of the City's common sights" (*The Times of India*, 19 November 1936, 3). It was praised as "undoubtedly an ideal gift book" (*The Times of India*, 4 December 1936, 2):

"Exquisitely produced on art paper, it is an album that anybody would wish to possess. As a gift to one's friends and relations in the mofussil or abroad, there is nothing more expressive of life in Bombay" (*The Times of India*, 19 November 1936, 3). The December ads promoted "this little brochure" by focusing on the illustrations, but also added information about the text, describing it as "an intimate, chatty account of the highways and by-ways of the city and suburbs, containing a wealth of information, interestingly retained" (*The Times of India*, 3 December 1936, 3). The guide addressed an Indian audience outside of Bombay as well as foreign readers and lovers of photography. However, the November advertisement tried to draw the attention of the Bombay public by focusing on the overlooked elements of their city: "The well-known photographer here presents for the first time a collection of unique and beautiful photographs of the most common and typical scenes in Bombay which people pass un-noticed. A descriptive text, that offers interesting reading, runs alongside" (*The Times of India*, 19 November 1936, 3).

The sales were good enough for a second edition to be considered in 1939. However, these plans were shelved when the Second World War brought all tourism to a standstill. It was not until British and American soldiers and sailors came to Bombay for recreational leave or furlough from the South East Asian battlefields that a new type of tourism developed in the metropolis. In a travel guide for these soldiers, *Pictorial Bombay* was again named "An invaluable souvenir! An ideal gift!" (*Welcome to Bombay* n.d, n.p.).

Pictorial Bombay cost three rupees and twelve annas in 1936 (*The Times of India*, 19 November 1936, 3) and 1937 (*The Times of India*, 19 May 1937, 2).[13] Compared to other travel guides, which were co-financed by advertising and printed on less opaque, lower gauge paper, *Pictorial Bombay* was more expensive; the *Guide to Bombay* by *The Times of India* cost one rupee (Anonymous 1927, 14), and Diqui's *A Visit to Bombay* two rupees (Anonymous 1933, 1). At the other extreme, Murray's *Guide to India* cost eighteen rupees, almost double the cost of a more expensive book such as the ten rupees edition of *The Indian Who is Who* (*The Times of India*, 19 May 1937, 2). In terms of production quality, *Pictorial Bombay* could be compared with richly illustrated magazines such as *The Times of India Annual*, which was sold for two rupees in 1936 and also contained advertising.

With its almost square format and the high-quality photo reproductions, *Pictorial Bombay* also generated the impression of an artbook. Larger than a pocketbook or a more typical guidebook, it is a smaller, cheaper, more egalitarian version of a coffee table book: a coffee table guide booklet to Bombay. While Schaeffer compared *Pictorial Bombay* to other guidebooks, he also acknowledged that he had taken a different approach, using a different "recipe" (Schaeffer 1936, 1).

Schaeffer's exile experience as a mediator (see Reiter 2006) made it possible to create *Pictorial Bombay* as a kind of hybrid publication, in both form and content. It is a guidebook without maps or timetables; an artbook with restaurant recommendations and insider tips; a coffee table book with tour routes, excursions and a programme of evening entertainment. Its portrayal of the city includes photos from unusual angles, anecdotes and journalistic texts from the perspective of a stranger.

Pictorial Bombay*'s foreign view and a new touristscape for Bombay*

At the very beginning of *Pictorial Bombay*, Schaeffer is identified as a foreigner; the book's foreword presents it as a "graceful tribute from a stranger within our gates, who has made Bombay his home in the truest sense" (Taunton 1936, n.p.). Schaeffer himself underlines his position as an outsider:

> When you arrive in a city as a stranger, desirous of getting to know it, not merely of having a nodding acquaintance with it, but of making friend of its character, its peculiar quality, a part of your being, you endeavour to draw aside the veil which separates you from this entirely unknown environment. You listen with both your ears to unaccustomed sounds and noises, you strain every fibre of your being to grasp this new experience.
>
> (Schaeffer 1936, 1)

Schaeffer accustomed himself to this strange environment by walking through the lanes, streets and squares of Bombay and its surroundings, interacting with locals, tasting local food and drinking refreshing beverages. In slow strolls he takes possession of all these new places, habits, customs, smells and colours. Even 35 years later he compared his arrival in Bombay to "landing on a strange planet" (Shaffer 1971, 18). *Pictorial Bombay* seems to mirror his personal explorations and experiences during his first weeks and months. Like other migrant authors in Bombay, including Willy Haas or Ruth Prawer Jhabvala, Schaeffer recorded his impressions, using ethnography and writing as his personal psycho-analytical process of understanding the Self in this new environment by observing and describing the Other (see Krishnamoorthy 2003, 115–140).

In *Pictorial Bombay*, the author capitalizes on the foreigner's view, describing the unknown, the exotic, the unfamiliar to him. With admiration and an explorer's interest he observes everyday Indian habits, such as drinking water:

> The buyer who is just drinking does not put the goblet to his lips, but lets the water pour straight into his open throat. How hygienic! But you must learn how to perform this feat. We, the uninitiated, would clumsily spoil it or else get choked.
>
> (Schaeffer 1936, 9)

With a Western eye and a positive, open, interested and empathic attitude, Schaeffer views Indian culture. But despite his exuberant enthusiasm throughout his journeys, "he chooses to remain an observer" (Krishnamoorthy 2003, 126) of Indian life. He remains neutral, accepting the hierarchy between colonial power and colonized subject; he seems to be only biased in his favour for Bombay as a city and its surroundings: "But I must admit that I am biased, for I love this city! I love Bombay!" (Schaeffer 1936, 2) Schaeffer is unabashed about his partial perspective, and makes no claims to objectivity or scientific distance in *Pictorial Bombay*. "If this bias does not deter you, follow me!" (ibid.), he proclaims. Another winning feature of the book, which allows the reader to follow Schaeffer's text easily and on 'virtual' foot, is his way of addressing the audience directly: "Let us wander on" (ibid.) he implores. It feels like a friend is taking you by the hand through Bombay's sites, inviting you for a beer at VT station, and sharing a chat, letting you in on a secret and reminding you to drink again: "we are thirsty once more", he asserts (ibid., 20).

While most of the other emigrants and refugees who had fled from National Socialism to Bombay tried to assimilate with the British ruling class, whose status symbol was a private vehicle, Schaeffer explicitly neglects this comfort and prefers to go on strolls; owning a dog probably supported his initiative. Schaeffer's approach is individual, and can be seen as a precursor to "slow tourism" as he uses walking as his method of exploring. On the other hand, he presents himself as a world traveller by comparing his Bombay impressions with those of other major cities, like New York, London, Berlin and Paris. He constructs himself as a world citizen, always in favour of Bombay: "There is a saying which runs: 'See Naples and die.' I take it up and re-coin it. 'See Bombay and live!'" (ibid., 23), he announces. By suggesting modern improvements, like the illumination of the Municipal Office building (ibid., 19) or using the potential of window-shopping to advertise highlights of the city (ibid., 11), Schaeffer identifies himself as a present, engaged citizen of Bombay. He portrays himself as a man from the West with an open interest in the local. At the same time, he distinguishes himself from other Westerners without any local interest or knowledge, describing them in a pitying tone.

Schaeffer's in-between status and his interest for the local urban landscape, the inhabitants of Bombay, the surrounding districts with their rice-fields, beaches, coconut plantations and farms, enabled him to create this unique guidebook. The emigrant Schaeffer mediates between the different classes of Bombay. He creates virtual access to the Taj Mahal Hotel as well as to the Willingdon Club, the sugar-cane vendor at Null Bazar, the smokers in the Jogeshwari Caves or to sailors at their small boats. He even builds a bridge between the Municipal Commissioner and the *mali* (gardener) of the Prince of Wales Museum: After Schaeffer shares the insider tip of buying flowers from the *mali*, the civil servant wishes the gardener "continued prosperity" in his foreword (see Schaeffer 1936, 19f; Taunton 1936, n.p.) – usually, the *mali* was a person the dignitary would be unlikely to address because of the difference in their social positions.

Schaeffer's premier interest in the people of Bombay draws his attention away from the monuments, but towards the city's social life. With this self-generated knowledge of the by-lanes of Bombay and its inhabitants, he remaps Bombay as a tourist location. He recreates the social space of Bombay as a touristscape through text, photos and his individual perspective.

A partial perspective grounded in motion

> I led a Scottish woman to the table who greeted me with the words: "I already know you, sir." I could only reply: "That must be a mistake, because I've only been in Bombay for barely two weeks." She smiled at me: "Oh yes, I know you. You are the European who walks in Bombay." That, as the saying goes, struck me. All I could say was: "Madam, I am a journalist, and as such I have to walk to get to know the country and its people. Unfortunately, this is not possible from the window of the tram or the bus or from the car." "One doesn't drive the tram or bus here, one drives a car," she replied briefly.
>
> (Shaffer 1971, 18)[14]

As the above anecdote reveals, walking around the city was not an activity that Bombay's colonial community encouraged. It was not, as Schaeffer recalled, what 'one', as a member of the city's social and economic elite, did. Instead, in order to mark a separation between everyday life on the street and themselves, the elite travelled in private vehicles. As well as shielding them from the weather and unwanted interactions with locals, this isolation also recognized that streets and other public spaces were potentially volatile. An accumulation of violent encounters marked them as sites of protest and sometimes militarized confrontation between local groups and the colonial authorities (Metcalf 2013, 767). And following the *Dandi Satyagraha* (Salt March or Dandi March) led by Mahatma Gandhi in 1930, walking had also been acknowledged as an anti-colonial act.

Despite the friendly warning, Schaeffer continued walking. He walked in central Bombay, through the suburbs, and around more distant destinations, often with his camera. Walking, and documenting what he experienced, was vital to his practice as a journalist. In colonial Bombay, streets were central to the urban public culture that Schaeffer wished to communicate to readers within India and in other parts of the world (Kidambi 2007, 240). Although Schaeffer may not have expressed it as such, his urban rambling was also a creative act: from Walter Benjamin's *flânerie*, through the Situationists' unplanned *dérives* and Lucius Burckhardt's strollology, walking has consistently been connected with artistic practice.[15]

Reflecting Schaeffer's commitment to experiencing the city in an embodied way, throughout its pages *Pictorial Bombay* portrays the city from the pedestrian's perspective. The cover image illustrates this positioning. Standing at the busy junction of Hornby Road and Mahapalika Road, Schaeffer aimed his camera squarely at the Municipal Corporation building, the seat of Bombay's governing civic body since 1893 and an urban landmark. A key part of colonial administrative infrastructure, the Municipal Corporation underwent a series of reforms to render it more 'representative' of the enfranchised population (Kidambi 2007). Nonetheless, the building, designed by the English architectural engineer Frederick W. Stevens, who authored several of the city's other colonial institutions, was a marker of colonial power.

In the cover image, instead of representing the building iconically, Schaeffer used his street-level perspective to situate the Municipal Corporation within the urban fabric (fig. 7.1). He complicates the frontal perspective by introducing different elements into the picture plane. A cropped arcade of Victoria Terminus, a major rail hub in the city, juts into the image on the left, creating depth. It is obscured by the horse-drawn carriages that dominate the foreground and forge a dynamic diagonal space that emphasizes the focal point of the image. Here men walk on the road. One carries an umbrella that echoes the form of the building's domes. Heightening the sense of movement on the street, a man casually mounts a bicycle that appears to have already been pushed into motion. A tree, possibly a Burmese or Siamese cassia, frames the shot. Its blurred compound leaves interfere with the sharp lines of the building; the leaves' lack of definition perhaps suggest a breeze. Sharing Schaeffer's view through the proxy eye of his camera, the viewer is immersed in the scene that surrounds them. The colonial building forms a static backdrop to the bustling urban life unfolding around it. It is the angle of the bike, the drape of a man's hands joined loosely behind his back, and the lift in the horse's hoof that capture the viewer's attention, making them conscious of a dynamic urban environment.

Perhaps the cover image was chosen to appeal to I.H. Taunton, who endorsed the publication in his foreword. As the municipal commissioner, Taunton directed the work of the Municipal Corporation and worked in the building. In his foreword, Taunton highlighted the "unusual viewpoint[s]" from which Schaeffer took

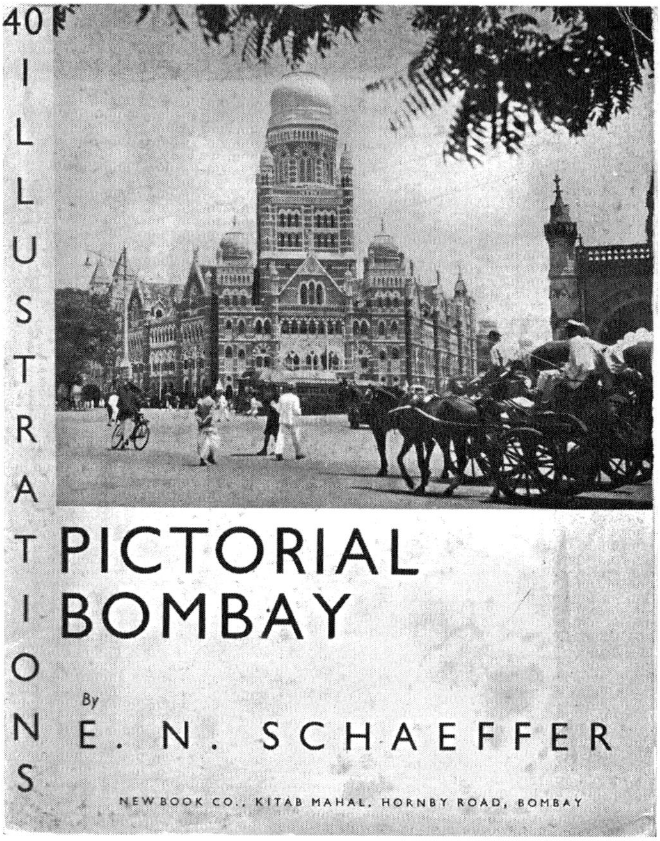

FIGURE 7.1: Ernst Schaeffer, Cover of *Pictorial Bombay* (Schaeffer 1936, cover).

his photographs, also recognizing the effects they had on the perception of the city, stating "his skill can invest a homely scene with unsuspected glory" (Taunton 1936, n.p.). His colonial stamp of approval likely added to *Pictorial Bombay*'s appeal to the English-speaking civic elite. While Schaeffer may have been committed to communicating everyday urban life, he was also aware of his potential market, aiming to please them without compromising his artistic vision. In *Pictorial Bombay*, Schaeffer imagines his readership as being European, aligning himself with that perspective when he writes "us in Europe" (Schaeffer 1936, 29).

Schaeffer carried his commitment to street-level photography through the book, as images such as the photograph of Victoria Terminus show (fig. 7.2). Here, in contrast to *The Times of India* and Contractor, both of whom present the Bombay Gothic station building from an elevated perspective (perhaps taken from the roof of a nearby building) and attempt to show as much of the enormous edifice as possible (figs. 7.3 and 7.4), Schaeffer focuses on the entrance. Taken from the road

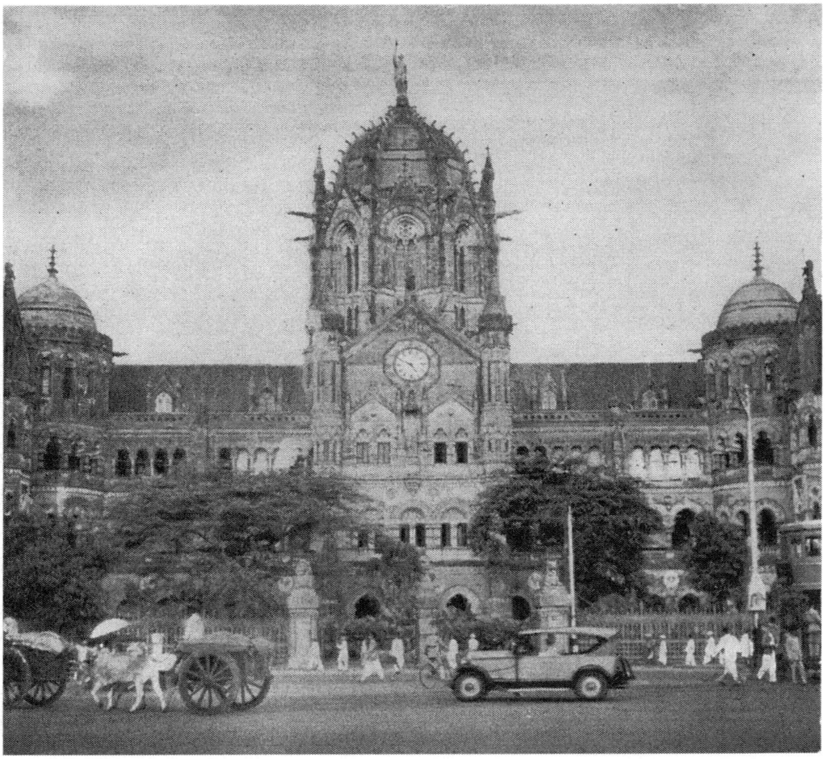

FIGURE 7.2: Ernst Schaeffer, *Victoria Terminus*, Bombay, n.d. (Schaeffer 1936, 18).

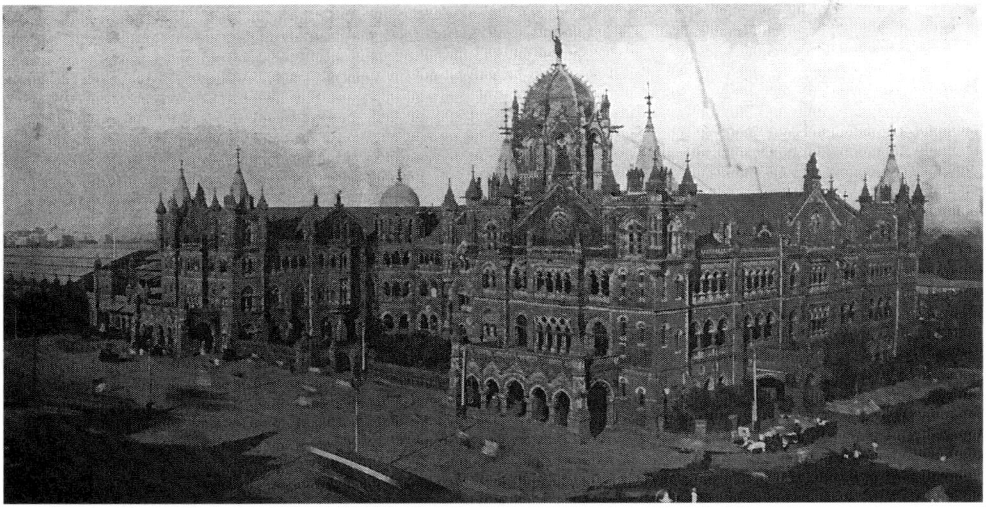

FIGURE 7.3: Unknown photographer, *Victoria Terminus*, Bombay, n.d. (*The Times of India* 1926, 3).

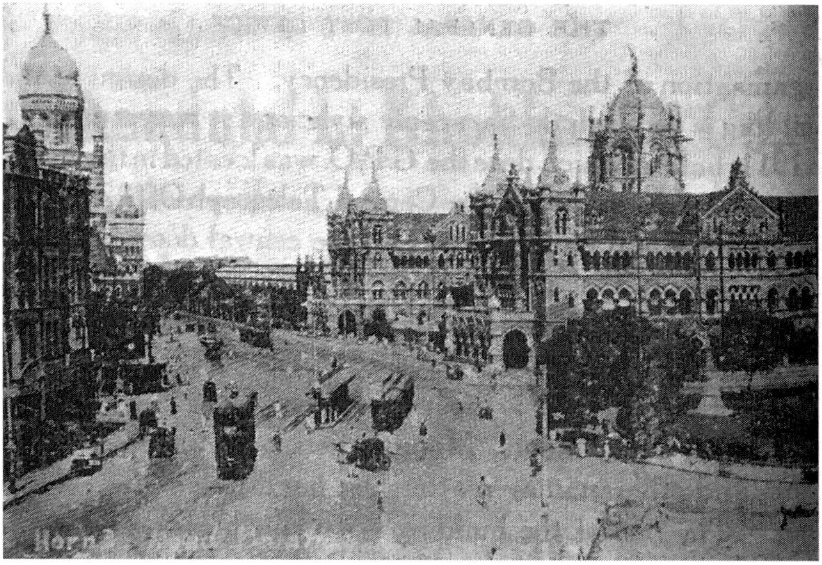

FIGURE 7.4: Unknown photographer, *Hornby Road* showing Victoria Terminus on the right, n.d. (Contractor 1938, 22).

outside, he again manages to capture the social life of Bombay. A *tonga* (a light horse-drawn two-wheeled vehicle) and a bullock cart move towards the left of the frame, a motor car and bicycle occupy the centre, and individuals and groups of people walk towards the right. While showcasing the station's clock tower, topped with a soaring octagonal masonry dome and a sculpted figure of *Progress*, Schaeffer also successfully draws the viewers' attention to the ground level and the lived experience of the city. Likewise, in his depictions of religious buildings – including Hindu and Parsi temples, churches and mosques[16] – the foregrounds are populated with unstaged local people, the vast majority of which are men, moving through their daily lives. His photograph *Jumma Masjid Entrance* (fig. 7.5) shows the mosque at the end of a narrow street, its domes illuminated by brilliant sunlight. Buildings on either side of the street both frame and obscure the view of the mosque, the canopies on their facades jut into the centre of the frame, bearing Urdu signage. Under the canopies are men wearing different types of head coverings. Some stand while others walk. In the foreground, a *dabbawalla* (a person who delivers lunch-boxes) is moving towards the mosque, carrying a tiffin box on his head and another in his hand. Schaeffer locates the mosque within a culturally diverse urban environment that, like him, is on the move.

Schaeffer's enthusiasm for discovering the city on foot permeates the whole book. Chapter titles, including "A Stroll Round the Town" or "Roaming through

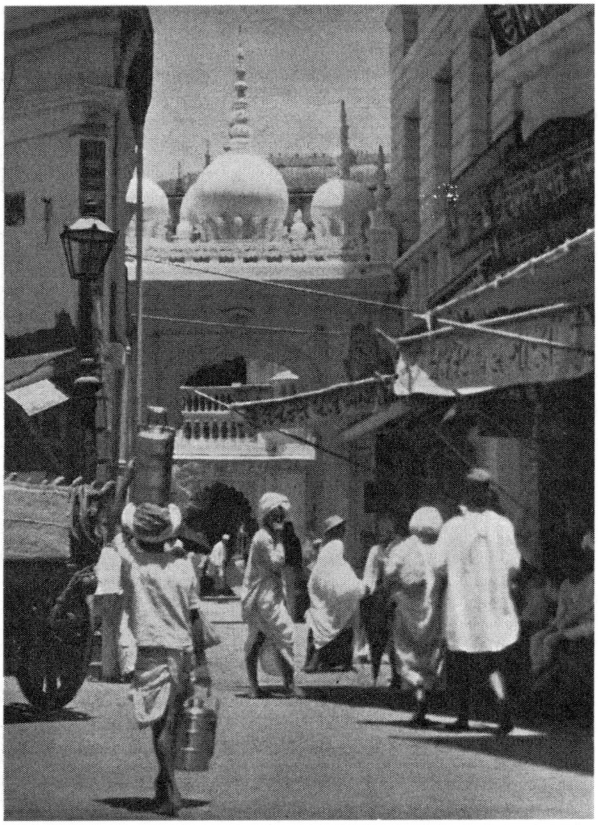

FIGURE 7.5: Ernst Schaeffer, *Jumma Masjid Entrance*, Bombay, n.d. (Schaeffer 1936, 32).

the Bazaar", underscore his pedestrian approach. He encourages his readers to take to their feet:

> We could, of course, make it a drive round the town, but a little exertion will not hurt us; it is worthwhile, for, as has already been remarked before, we get to know the town far better if we are on foot, letting the stream of other pedestrians flow past us, and looking at the shops and everything else pertaining to the life of a city. (Schaeffer 1936, 11)

For the cultural historian Rebecca Solnit, walking can be a "state in which the mind, the body, and the world are aligned" (Solnit 2014, 5). The rhythm of walking generates a "kind of rhythm of thinking, and the passage through a landscape echoes or stimulates the passage through a series of thoughts" (ibid., 5f.). The body's motoric and sensual responses to moving through the environment and engaging its kerbs and potholes, signboards, street foods and sounds, cohere to form a more profound attunement to the place. In Schaeffer's case, absorbing the rhythm of the city, or the "multifold melody" (Schaeffer 1936, 2), as he calls it, and thinking with it while he walked perhaps also induced him to reproduce it in his presentation of places in *Pictorial Bombay*.

Crawford Market, built in 1869, is mentioned in *The Bombay Guide & Directory* and the *Guide to Bombay* (on pages 38 and 18, respectively). Contractor describes it as "Bombay's largest Market for all types of household necessities" (Contractor 1938, 38) and includes a photograph, taken from the opposite side of the near-empty junction, showing the building's clock tower and pointed gables. Professing that there are no "architectural features worthy of mention",[17] *The Times of India* acknowledges dryly that "the management stock a wide selection of home and colonial food products" (*The Times of India* 1926, 18).

Schaeffer, in contrast, opens the chapter with a formula that centres Bombay's economic life – from cotton merchants to representatives of American firms, to housewives and medical doctors – within the "complexity" (Schaeffer 1936, 24) of the bazaar, of which Crawford Market is a part. He continues with a vivid description of the experience of shopping at Crawford Market, outlining the visiting times of different types of customers – cooks in the early morning, housewives later in the day – and guiding the reader on a tour through the wares, from "all possible and impossible kinds of fruits", flowers "of almost incredible colours", fish and meat (this section of the market has a "vile smell"), and "all manner of living creatures", including deer and monkeys (Schaeffer 1936, 24ff.). He peppers his tour with humorous anecdotes that connect the market to his acquaintances' experiences in Bombay, anchoring them to the spaces he describes.

The photograph that Schaeffer includes contrasts starkly with the image in Contractor's guidebook (fig. 7.6). Rather than squeezing the whole building into the frame as Contractor did, Schaeffer portrays the interior space (fig. 7.7). Observing a busy scene through one of the market's arches, Schaeffer captures the building's materiality: a metal drain cover, tarpaulins suspended across an external space to temper the bright sunlight, ornate ironwork and dressed stone. Rather than an abstract, static monolith, the architecture appears as a mediator and container of the daily activity that fills it. One man carries a large woven basket on his head, others sit behind their stalls engaged with their merchandise, a man in the centre of the frame walks towards the camera, casually putting something into his shirt pocket. Two people appear conscious of the camera's gaze and stare back at it. The majority, however, seems not to notice. Although he carefully frames the shot, Schaeffer seems uninterested in directing the figures he portrays. Schaeffer's photograph draws the reader into the experience of a spatial environment in flux, in which the actions of the people in the picture dictate its visual outcome. The

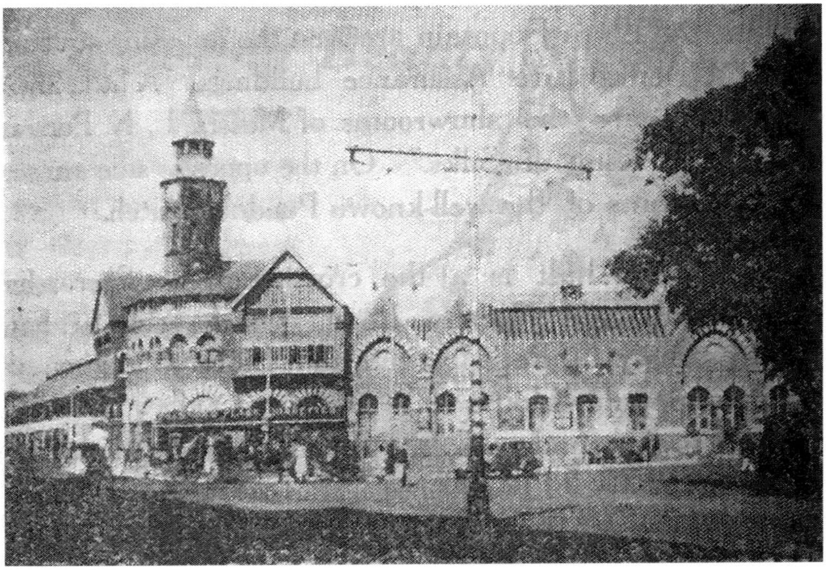

FIGURE 7.6: Unknown photographer, Crawford Market, Bombay, n.d. (Contractor 1938, 38).

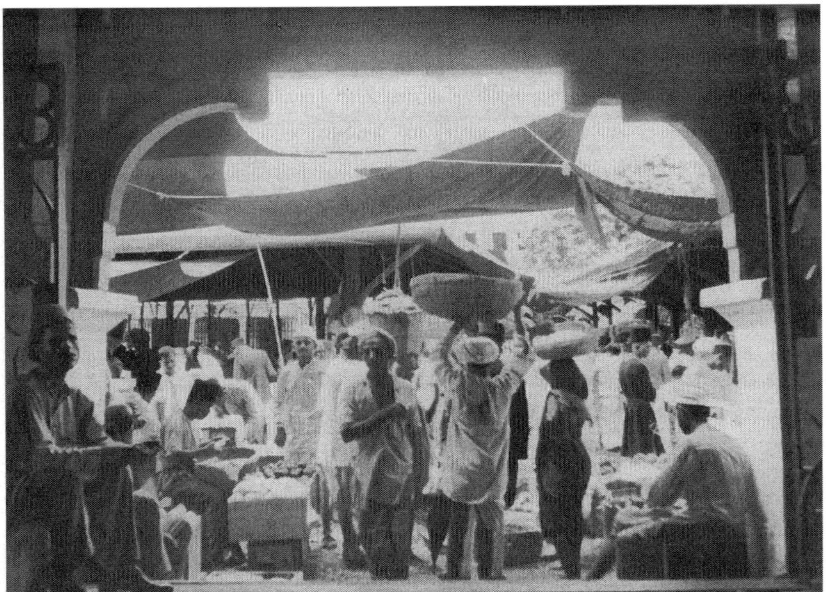

FIGURE 7.7: Ernst Schaeffer, *Crawford Market*, Bombay, n.d. (Schaeffer 1936, 25).

city's rhythms and Schaeffer's observations quicken to co-produce an image that immerses the reader in the belly of Crawford Market. Unlike Contractor's image, which places the viewer tens of metres away from the subject, Schaeffer dissolves the distance, locating the viewer within the space.

Schaeffer's interest in conveying Bombay's essence through observing and capturing interactions at street level can be read analogously with the work of other exiled photographers in other cities. Burcu Dogramaci and Helene Roth have proposed photography as the "diasporic medium *par excellence*" (Dogramaci/Roth 2019, 3) with several photographers, like Schaeffer, artistically documenting their new surroundings in photographic form shortly after arriving in the new environment.[18]

In *Pictorial Bombay*, beyond shooting street scenes, Schaeffer also depicted street life more individually, portraying people engaged in their professions. With an empathic, ethnographic eye, Schaeffer documented street vendors offering beverages, cleaning ears and shaving beards. In these images he strove for candid portrayals. The figures appear unposed. Some are conscious of the camera while others appear entirely unaware of its presence as they go about their daily business. Schaeffer probably used a Rolleiflex camera to take these images (*The Times of India*, 6 February 1936, 16). With the viewfinder located on top of the relatively compact middle format camera, the photographer did not have to hold the camera in front of their face when composing the shot. Held at waist or chest height, the Rolleiflex was perhaps less intrusive than other cameras, allowing the photographer to maintain eye contact and communicate better through body language with their subjects.

In a photo titled *Shoe Repairer* (fig. 7.8), sitting cross-legged on a low bench under a foldable, lightweight canopy, a cobbler seems engrossed in his work. Directly behind his repair shop, leaning her upper arm against the wall, a woman scrutinizes Schaeffer. On the ground, in the canopy's shade, sits a second man, possibly a customer or an apprentice. The three figures could be engaged in conversation. Schaeffer's photo of the local street-corner appears casual and unaffected, as if he had encountered the scene on one of his strolls through the city and spontaneously photographed it. Portraying local people 'authentically', and positioning snapshots of their lives and livelihoods as integral to Bombay's character, could be part of his attempt to "draw aside the veil" (Schaeffer 1936, 1) that separates him, as an outsider, from the new environment. On the other hand, there is an exoticizing element in these photos, as was the case with the pictures by the famous travel photographer Alice Schalek (see Manojlovic 2012) and the socially critical paintings by the Russian painter Magda Nachman, who was married to an Indian communist politician in Bombay.[19] They all created their portraits of local people with a Western eye, but empathic look.

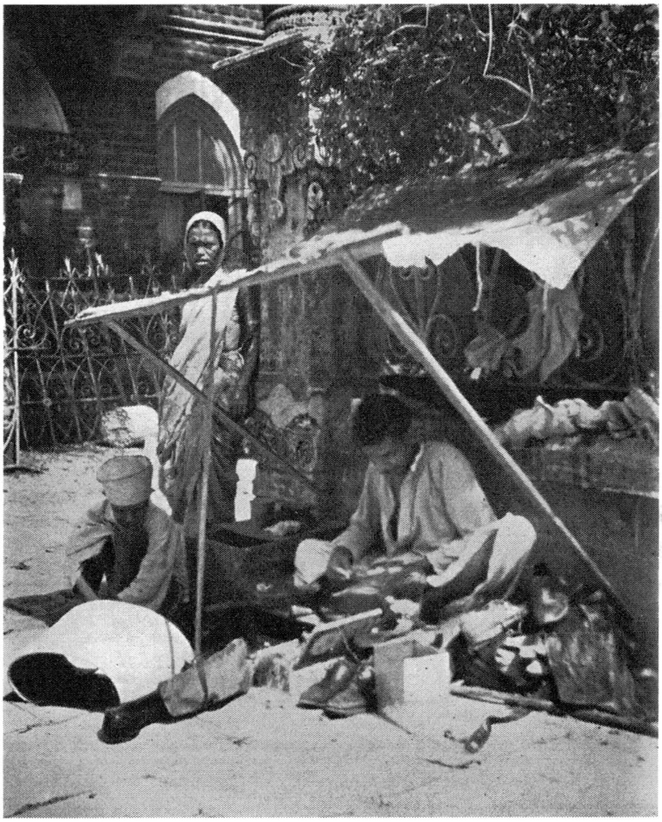

FIGURE 7.8: Ernst Schaeffer, *Shoe Repairer*, Bombay, n.d. (Schaeffer 1936, 28).

Periphery in central focus

The success of *Pictorial Bombay* generated income for Schaeffer and an increase in customers for his photo studio, in addition to general recognition. A short time later, in 1939, he also gained international appreciation through his photojournalistic work for the US magazine *Life*.[20] The individual chapters of *Pictorial Bombay* could be seen as a precursor to this work – as photojournalistic reports held together by the spine of the book.

Schaeffer developed his own style of street photography and created a unique coffee table guide booklet, which takes his readers along on his strolls through different parts of Bombay. His anecdotal writing combined with journalism gradually revealed individual parts of the sociocultural environment of Bombay, without ever turning too academic or falling into the familiar descriptive tropes of other guidebooks. With 40 full-page black-and-white photographs he visually documents the social environment of Bombay's famous sights and adds a few lesser-known sites, as well as places distant from the centres in Colaba and Fort, and portraits of people at work. In the nine small photographs that conclude his chapters, he mainly depicts the everyday life of local residents or creates photographic still lives in the urban landscape, adding faces to places and to his stories while documenting the diverse social fabric of the metropolis (fig. 7.9).

With his in-between status as a forced European emigrant in British India, a Westerner but without British colonial origins, equipped with a great interest in exploring his new place of refuge and its people, he put Bombay's side-lanes, outskirts and peripheries on the tourist map. His narratives create a new tourist map of Bombay that focuses on the local population and reflects the social complexity of the city. All of Bombay's social spaces become part of Schaeffer's interest and generate his unique touristscape, which he presents in *Pictorial Bombay*. He flips the colonial power structure by placing the local people at the centre of his attention, through his texts, his photos and his perspective. His street-level photography documents the vibrant daily movements of the residents of Bombay while placing the colonial architecture, as representative of imperial rule, in a static background.

Initial research suggests that Schaeffer's approach quickly impacted future Bombay guidebooks. A small travel guide for the armed forces, published by the Government of Bombay for visiting army members on recreational leave or furloughs during

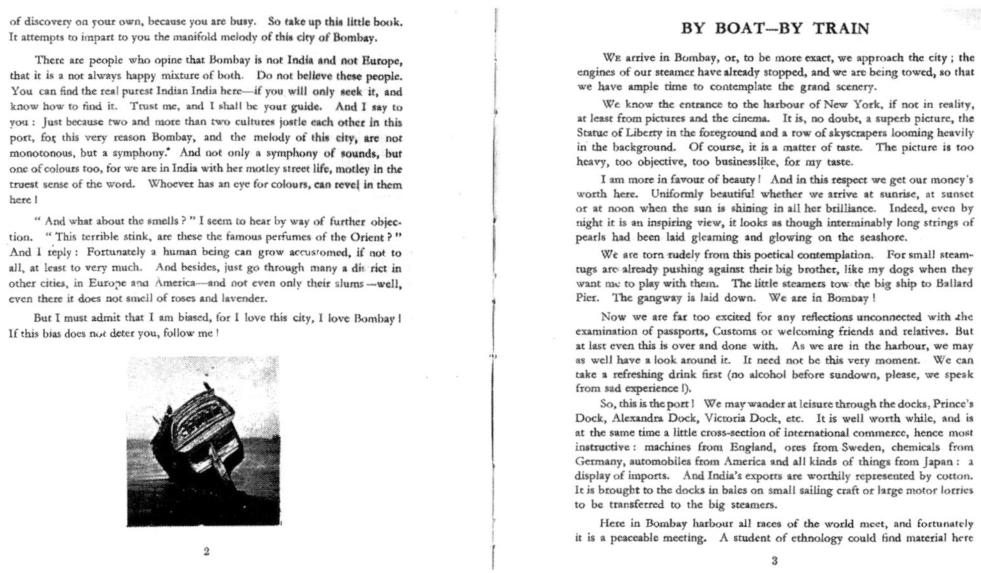

of discovery on your own, because you are busy. So take up this little book. It attempts to impart to you the manifold melody of this city of Bombay.

There are people who opine that Bombay is not India and not Europe, that it is a not always happy mixture of both. Do not believe these people. You can find the real purest Indian India here—if you will only seek it, and know how to find it. Trust me, and I shall be your guide. And I say to you: Just because two and more than two cultures jostle each other in this port, for this very reason Bombay, and the melody of this city, are not monotonous, but a symphony.* And not only a symphony of sounds, but one of colours too, for we are in India with her motley street life, motley in the truest sense of the word. Whoever has an eye for colours, can revel in them here!

"And what about the smells?" I seem to hear by way of further objection. "This terrible stink, are these the famous perfumes of the Orient?" And I reply: Fortunately a human being can grow accustomed, if not to all, at least to very much. And besides, just go through many a district in other cities, in Europe and America—and not even only their slums—well, even there it does not smell of roses and lavender.

But I must admit that I am biased, for I love this city, I love Bombay! If this bias does not deter you, follow me!

2

BY BOAT—BY TRAIN

We arrive in Bombay, or, to be more exact, we approach the city; the engines of our steamer have already stopped, and we are being towed, so that we have ample time to contemplate the grand scenery.

We know the entrance to the harbour of New York, if not in reality, at least from pictures and the cinema. It is, no doubt, a superb picture, the Statue of Liberty in the foreground and a row of skyscrapers looming heavily in the background. Of course, it is a matter of taste. The picture is too heavy, too objective, too businesslike, for my taste.

I am more in favour of beauty! And in this respect we get our money's worth here. Uniformly beautiful whether we arrive at sunrise, at sunset or at noon when the sun is shining in all her brilliance. Indeed, even by night it is an inspiring view, it looks as though interminably long strings of pearls had been laid gleaming and glowing on the seashore.

We are torn rudely from this poetical contemplation. For small steam-tugs are already pushing against their big brother, like my dogs when they want me to play with them. The little steamers tow the big ship to Ballard Pier. The gangway is laid down. We are in Bombay!

Now we are far too excited for any reflections unconnected with the examination of passports, Customs or welcoming friends and relatives. But at last even this is over and done with. As we are in the harbour, we may as well have a look around it. It need not be this very moment. We can take a refreshing drink first (no alcohol before sundown, please, we speak from sad experience!).

So, this is the port! We may wander at leisure through the docks, Prince's Dock, Alexandra Dock, Victoria Dock, etc. It is well worth while, and is at the same time a little cross-section of international commerce, hence most instructive: machines from England, ores from Sweden, chemicals from Germany, automobiles from America and all kinds of things from Japan: a display of imports. And India's exports are worthily represented by cotton. It is brought to the docks in bales on small sailing craft or large motor lorries to be transferred to the big steamers.

Here in Bombay harbour all races of the world meet, and fortunately it is a peaceable meeting. A student of ethnology could find material here

3

FIGURE 7.9: Ernst Schaeffer, Double-page spread of *Pictorial Bombay* (Schaeffer 1936, 2f.).

Second World War, shows a similar photographic style (see *Welcome to Bombay* n.d., n.p.). The photograph of the magnificent Taj Mahal Hotel (fig. 7.10), for example, was taken from the square in front of the Gateway of India. As with photographs in *The Bombay Guide & Directory* and *Guide to Bombay*, the photographer attempted to depict the immense size of the grand building while focusing on its main facade towards Apollo Bunder and the sea promenade. However, in the foreground of the image, the photographer shows two figures lying on their backs on the pavement, while another simply dressed man heads towards Apollo Bunder. A car is travelling in the same direction. More people are seen in the vicinity of the hotel. The photo appears like a snapshot in motion taken by a person standing in front of the arches of the Gateway of India. Unfortunately, we do not know anything about the photographer. But we can see that Schaeffer's approach of using street photography to centre the actions of local people while famous buildings merely provide the backdrop, was also adopted in the Bombay government's official wartime travel guide.

Beyond contributing to the construction of the local touristscape, *Pictorial Bombay* can also serve as an illustration of how an exile-authored guidebook can provide valuable insights into exilic experiences of urban environments. In terms of professional advancement and economic survival, it was a medium for generating

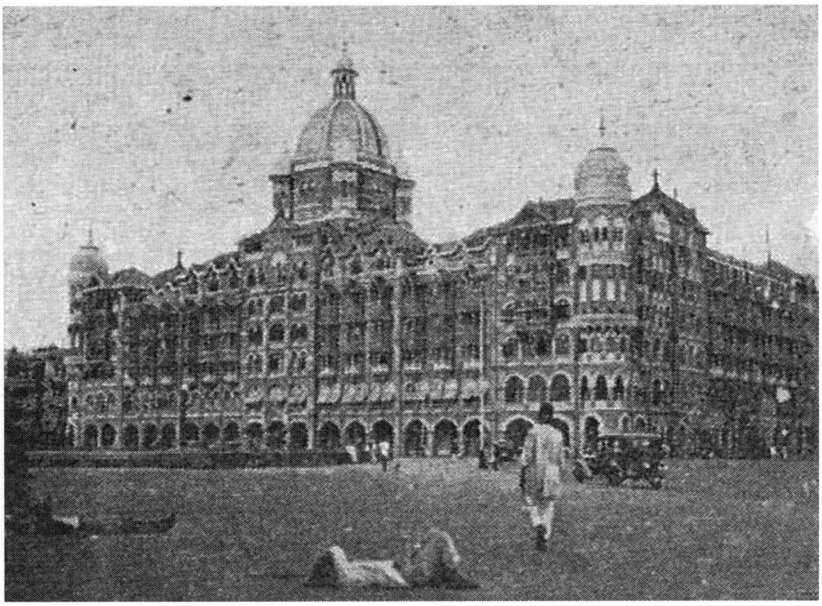

FIGURE 7.10: Unknown photographer, *Taj Mahal Hotel*, Bombay, n.d. (*Welcome to Bombay* n.d., 30).

income. As a kind of portfolio, it served as a reference for future commissions. It enabled Schaeffer to establish himself as a photographer in Bombay and as a photojournalist internationally. The making of the book allowed him to expand his networks and build relationships with central figures in Bombay's publishing scene. As a creative medium, *Pictorial Bombay* functions as a conduit for expressing Schaeffer's embodied experiences of the city in a self-imagined hybrid form. It documents how he determinedly met the city on foot, danced to its rhythms and developed an artistic method of practicing the urban. Perhaps it even opened a way to artistically process his initial impressions of his new home, allowing him to arrive fully. It could also be read as a love letter or a thank-you note to the city that provided him with refuge and gave new impulses to a career that had witnessed a massive rupture.

Schaeffer's texts and photographs are valuable witnesses to 1930s Bombay, providing information about the city's people and places, and mapping out fragmentary socio-cultural environments within the larger urban fabric. They form a kind of psycho-geographical interpretation of the city that also functions on a practical level. For those interested in urban exile in Bombay, *Pictorial Bombay* is a vital resource that uniquely bridges the intersection of urbanity, exile and artistic production. While there may not be many other guidebooks to cities authored by exiles, it can perhaps be compared to related media, such as photobooks and almanacs.[21] It may also signpost ways of exploring exile elsewhere, thereby continuing to serve as a guide.

NOTES

1. For a history of the guidebook see Parsons (2007). And for more on guidebooks in India, see subsection below.
2. Ernst Schaeffer changed his name several times during his lifetime. In the following, we refer to him as he chose to refer to himself during the period in which he authored *Pictorial Bombay*. For more about his names, see: Anonymous. "Schäffer (1892–1978)." *Kalliope-Verbund*, kalliope-verbund.info/gnd/117099600. Accessed 30 Jun 2021. In 1971, he published his autobiography: Shaffer (1971).
3. As the book does not contain a publication date, we used advertisements in *The Times of India* to locate its publication in November 1936.
4. For other guidebooks on Bombay from the same period, see: Contractor (1938), Diqui (1938), Newell (1920), *The Times of India* (1926) and *Welcome to Bombay* (n.d).
5. For biographical information, see: Shaffer (1971), Voigt (1991).
6. For more information on Black Star Agency, see the archive of the METROMOD research project, www.//archive.metromod.net/.
7. Photographic supplies were mainly imported from Germany.

8. It should be noted that before the establishment of guidebooks as a genre, there were other forms of travel writing, including reports, diaries and almanacs. These have been shown to have benefitted colonial expansion. See, for example: Bhatti (1997).
9. Thomas Cook followed, in 1889, with the publication of *Cook's Indian Tours*, and Baedeker's German-language guidebook was published 55 years later in 1914.
10. See Schäffer (1931a, 1931b).
11. Schaeffer was a First World War decorated aviator, see Vogel (1977, 188).
12. Translation by the authors. "Ich kniete mich in die Fachliteratur und began systematisch mit der Kamera zu arbeiten." Shaffer 1971, 45f.; "zu lernen, mit einer großen Kamera und mit allen möglichen Linsen und Lichtern zu arbeiten." Shaffer (1971, 46).
13. The price dropped to two rupees and eight annas during the Second World War.
14. Translation by the authors from original German:

    Ich führte eine Schottin zu Tisch, die mich mit den Worten begrüßte: 'Ich kenne Sie schon, mein Herr.' Erwidern konnte ich nur: 'Das dürfte wohl ein Irrtum sein, denn ich bin erst knapp zwei Wochen in Bombay.' Sie lächelte mich an: 'O doch, ich kenne Sie. Sie sind der Europäer, der in Bombay zu Fuß geht'. Das haute mich, wie man so schön sagt, hin. Mir blieb nur zu sagen übrig: 'Madam, ich bin Journalist, und als solcher muß ich zu Fuß gehen, um Land und Leute kennenzulernen. Vom Fenster der Straßenbahn oder des Autobuses oder vom Auto aus ist dies leider nicht möglich'. 'Man fährt hier nicht Straßenbahn oder Bus, man fährt Auto,' antwortete sie kurz.

15. See Benjamin (2002), Burckhardt (2015) and Debord (1956).
16. Interestingly, Schaeffer does not include photographs of either of Bombay's synagogues, although he mentions them in the text.
17. The building was designed by William Emerson in a 12th century Gothic style, and features large bas-reliefs by John Lockwood Kipling that depict scenes from everyday life in rural India (Chopra 2011, 39).
18. For examples of the work of exiled photographers in New York, see also Roth (2019, 2021) and the contribution by Anna Messner and Helene Roth in this volume.
19. For more on Magda Nachmann, see Bernstein (2020) as well as the METROMOD Archive and Bombay Walk on www.//metromod.net/.
20. See for example Schaeffer (19 June 1939).
21. See for example the chapter by Ekaterina Aygün in this volume.

REFERENCES

Anonymous. "Schäffer, Ernst (1892–1978)." *Kalliope-Verbund*, www.kalliope-verbund.info/gnd/117099600. Accessed 30 June 2021.

Anonymous. "Guide to Bombay: Price One Rupee." *The Times of India*, 25 April 1927, p. 14.

Anonymous. "Holiday Books, Guides and Maps." *The Times of India*, 5 May 1933, p. 1.

Benjamin, Walter, et al. *The Arcades Project*. Revised ed., Harvard University Press, 2002.

Bernstein, Lina. *Magda Nachman: An Artist in Exile*. Academic Studies Press, 2020.

Bhatti, Anil. "Europäische Erinnerungen am Indus: Carl von Hügel als Forschungsreisender in Indien." Übersetzung als Repräsentation fremder Kulturen, edited by Doris Bachmann-Medick, Erich Schmidt Verlag, 1997, pp. 98–112.

Burckhardt, Lucius. *Why Is Landscape Beautiful?: The Science of Strollology*. Translation by Jill Denton and edited by Markus Ritter and Martin Schmitz, Birkhäuser, 2015.

Chopra, Preeti. *A Joint Enterprise: Indian Elites and the Making of British Bombay*. University of Minnesota Press, 2011.

Contractor, J. *The Bombay Guide & Directory*. 2nd ed., Bombay Publishing Co., 1938.

Dalmia, Yashodhara. *The Making of Modern Indian Art: The Progressives*. Oxford University Press, 2001.

Debord, Guy. "Theory of the Dérive." *Les Lèvres Nues*, no. 9, 1956, www.cddc.vt.edu/sionline/si/theory.html. Accessed 6 April 2022.

Diqui, Ben. *A Visit to Bombay. [A guide book.]*. Watts & Co, 1927.

Dogramaci, Burcu, and Helene Roth, editors. Nomadic Camera. Fotografie, Exil und Migration, special issue of *Fotogeschichte. Beiträge zur Geschichte und Ästhetik der Fotografie*, vol. 39, no. 151, 2019.

Eastwick, Edward B. *A Handbook for India; Being an Account of the Three Presidencies and of the Overland Route, Intended as a Guide for Travellers, Officers and Civilians, with Vocabularies and Dialogues of the Spoken Languages of India: With Travelling Map and Plans of Towns. II*. John Murray, 1859.

Epelde, Kathleen R. *Travel Guidebooks to India: A Century and a Half of Orientalism*. Doctoral thesis, University of Wollongong, 2004, www//ro.uow.edu.au/cgi/viewcontent.cgi?article=1195&context=theses. Accessed 31 May 2021.

Fei, Siyen. "Ways of Looking: The Creation and Social Use of Urban Guidebooks in Sixteenth- and Seventeenth-Century China." *Urban History*, vol. 37, no. 2, 2010, pp. 226–248. doi: 10.1017/S0963926810000301. Accessed 31 May 2021.

Kidambi, Prashant. *The Making of an Indian Metropolis: Colonial Governance and Public Culture in Bombay, 1890–1920*. Routledge, 2007.

Krishnamoorthy, Kaushalya. *India and the Exile Experience as Mirrored in the Writings of Jewish Exiles and Indian Writers*. Doctoral thesis, Wayne State University, 2003. *ResearchGate*, www.researchgate.net/publication/34976696_India_and_the_Exile_Experience_as_Mirrored_in_the_Writings_of_Jewish_Exiles_and_Indian_Writers. Accessed 20 March 2021.

Maclean, James Mackenzie. *Maclean's Guide to Bombay*. Bombay Gazette Press, 1875.

Macmillan, Allister, editor. *Seaports of India & Ceylon: Historical and Descriptive, Commercial and Industrial, Facts, Figures, & Resources*. W.H. & L. Collingridge, 1928.

Manojlovic, Katharina. "Strolling through India: The Austrian Photographer and Journalist Alice Schalek." *Austrian Studies*, vol. 20, 2012, pp. 193–205. *JSTOR*, doi: 10.5699/austrianstudies.20.2012.0193. Accessed 30 June 2021.

Metcalf, Thomas R. "Colonial Cities." *The Oxford Handbook of Cities in World History*, edited by Peter Clark, Oxford University Press, 2013, pp. 753–769.

Newell, Herbert Andrews. *Bombay, The Gate of India: A Guide to Places of Interest, with Map*. 2nd ed., H. A. Newell, 1920.

Parsons, Nicholas T. *Worth the Detour: A History of the Guidebook*. The History Press, 2007.

Pinder, D.A. *Visitors' Illustrated Guide to Bombay*, G. Claridge & Co, Bombay, 1904.

Reiter, Andrea. "Diaspora und Hybridität: Der Exilant als Mittler." *Diaspora – Exil als Krisenerfahrung. Jüdische Bilanzen und Perspektiven (Zwischenwelt Jahrbuch, 10)*, edited by Armin Eidherr et al., Drava Verlag, 2006, pp. 36–51.

Roth, Helene. "First Pictures." *Nomadic Camera. Fotografie, Exil und Migration, special issue of Fotogeschichte*, edited by Burcu Dogramaci and Helene Roth, vol. 39, no. 151, 2019, pp. 17–26.

Roth, Helene "'First Pictures': New York through the Lens of Emigrated European Photographers in the 1930s and 1940s." *Contact Zones: Photography, Migration and Cultural Encounters in the United States*, edited by Justin Carville and Sigrid Lien, Leuven University Press, 2021, pp. 111–132.

Schäffer, Ernst. *Glück ab. Bahnbrecher der Lüfte*. Union Deutsche Verlagsgesellschaft, 1931a.

Schäffer, Ernst. *Pour le Mérite. Flieger im Feuer*. Union Deutsche Verlagsgesellschaft, 1931b.

Schaeffer, E.N. *Pictorial Bombay*. New Book Co., 1936.

Schaeffer, Ernst Nathan. "Feast in Bhopal. A Marriage Unites Two of India's Leading Muslims." *Life*, 19 June 1939, pp. 44–48.

Schaeffer, Ernest N. "Emigrantenleben in Indien." *Aufbau*, vol. 7, no. 18, 2 March 1941, p. 7.

Shaffer, Ernest N. *Ein Emigrant entdeckt Indien*. Verlag Information und Wissen, 1971.

Solnit, Rebecca. *Wanderlust: A History of Walking*. Granta Books, 2014.

Taunton, I. H. "Foreword." *Pictorial Bombay*, edited by E.N. Schaeffer, New Book Co., 1936.

The Times of India. *Guide to Bombay*. 2nd ed, Times Press, 1926.

The Times of India [Mumbai] *Archive on ProQuest, via Staatsbibliothek zu Berlin*, www.//staatsbibliothek-berlin.de/recherche/elektronische-ressourcen. Accessed 30 June 2021.

Vogel, Rolf. *Ein Stück von uns. Deutsche Juden in deutschen Armeen 1813–1976. Eine Dokumentation*. v. Hase & Koehler, 1977.

Voigt, Johannes H. "Die Emigration von Juden aus Mitteleuropa nach Indien während der Verfolgung durch das NS-Regime." *Wechselwirkungen, Jahrbuch aus Lehre und Forschung der Universität Stuttgart*, 1991, pp. 83–95.

Welcome to Bombay. V… for Victory. Government House Bombay, n.d. *ExploreHistory*, www.explorehistory.co.uk/wp-content/uploads/2015/11/Welcome-to-Bombay-V-for-Victory.pdf. Accessed 30 June 2021.

8

Photographic Practices in Cities of Exile: Camera Views on Tel Aviv and New York

Anna Sophia Messner and Helene Roth

Encountering the city in exile

Exile has specific temporal and spatial components, which in turn affect photographic practices.[1] On the one hand, émigré photographers attempt to re-establish the photographic methods and aesthetics they had already applied in their home countries; on the other hand, the new surroundings and cityscapes of their exile countries inspire them to experiment with new techniques and practices. Against this background, this paper argues that the act of photographing and encountering the city in exile can be understood as an urban practice and as a method that articulates a specific photographic language: in this chapter, we are consequently activating a double perspective to examine the transformations and implementations of style, techniques and aesthetics proliferating in exile photography.

By taking Ellen Auerbach's photographs of her two cities of exile, Tel Aviv and New York, as a point of departure, and by then moving towards other émigré photographers such as Rudy Burckhardt, Liselotte Grschebina and Fritz Henle, this paper analyses and discusses manifold perspectives on camera work in the two metropolises.[2] Trained in and shaped by the avant-garde photography movements of the Weimar Republic, such as 'New Vision' and 'New Objectivity', these photographers escaped the Nazi-Regime in the 1930s and 1940s and arrived in Tel Aviv and New York. With them, they brought their modes of artistic expression and photographic practices and translated them into their new surroundings. Through the perspectives of these photographers and by means of a close reading of exemplary photographs, the analyses in this chapter understand the photographers as (en)actors of urban practices: they used their camera as a tool and instrument to encounter, explore, appropriate and familiarize themselves with the city, their new and foreign home in exile.

In his book *Towards a Philosophy of Photography,* the philosopher Vilém Flusser proposes a new way of looking at photography by focusing on photographers as actors and by closely examining their handling of the camera. He considers the camera as an extension of the human eye and as "a tool whose intention is to produce photographs" and to make the world visible (Flusser 2000, 22). According to Flusser, photographers utilize their cameras and all its technical innovative possibilities not only to discover the world but also to create new modes of viewing and visualizing:

> They handle the camera, turn it this way and that, look into it and through it. If they look through the camera out into the world, this is not because the world interests them but because they are pursuing new possibilities of producing information and evaluating the photographic program. Their interest is concentrated on the camera; for them, the world is purely a pretext for the realization of camera possibilities. In short: They are not working, they do not want to change the world, but they are in search of information.
>
> (ibid., 26f.)

Working with Vilém Flusser's conceptualization of photographer/photography, the examples we have chosen for this chapter represent selected photographers' specific urban practices with regard to their interaction with the camera in their respective cities of exile. Such an interaction can be marked by a view from above onto the city, as is the case with Ellen Auerbach, it can evoke the view from below, as adopted by Liselotte Grschebina and Rudy Burckhardt, or it can express the way Ellen Auerbach and Fritz Henle encountered and engaged with socio-cultural urban spaces in Tel Aviv and New York. Often the act of photographing went hand in hand with a specific handling of the camera, such as the raising and lowering of the apparatus which then could also be differentiated depending on the camera type (such as miniature or middle format cameras). Ellen Auerbach and Liselotte Grschebina photographed with the miniature camera Leica, whereas Rudy Burckhardt and Fritz Henle used the middle format camera Rolleiflex for their images. While the viewfinder of the Rolleiflex is on the top of the camera and the camera must thus be held in front of the upper body, the viewfinder of the Leica camera is located on the back of the camera and can be placed directly before the eye. The two-camera models entered the German market around 1900 and developed quickly as a highly appreciated medium that enabled intimate photographic encounters in urban space. With the emigration movements of photographers, these new camera models began to circulate globally. New technologies accelerated the image-making process and the camera could thus be used as a mobile and portable medium to capture the many visual impressions of and in urban environments (*New York Photography* 2012; Dogramaci/Roth 2019; Hofmann-Johnson 2018, 136).

Despite the differences in the practical and technical use of cameras in urban space, it can be assumed that most émigré photographers walked through their new city as a creative practice. We, therefore, propose a triangulated approach to mine the critical potential of exile photography: how and in how far do (1) the exile situation of the emigrated photographers, (2) the practice of walking through the city and (3) the act of photographing (in) the city interrelate and depend on one another? Strolling the streets of a new exile city can be understood as a method and practice to render urban structures and relations not only experienceable in their specific spatial and temporal conditions but also to accentuate the experience itself visually – via the mobile medium of the camera. Contrary to the figure of the *flâneur* who is portrayed (and in the 19th century saw himself) as the observer of the industrialized and modern life of European cities, we argue that the practice of walking through the city is closely linked to the social and historical developments of global cities during the 19th and 20th centuries.[3] Thus, strolling through the city can be understood as an active method of visually perceiving one's urban environment (Certeau 1984; Neumeyer 1999; Solnit 2001; Adolphs 2018). In his book *Spazieren in Berlin. Ein Lehrbuch der Kunst in Berlin spazieren zu gehen* (Walking in Berlin. A textbook of the art of walking in Berlin, translation by the authors), 1929, the German writer Franz Hessel, who was a contemporary of the photographers discussed in this chapter, declared the need for historical and social awareness while walking through the city (Hessel 1929, 13). He thought of walking through the city as "a lecture of the street" (ibid., 274, translation by the authors). This is also the focus of Annemarie and Lucius Burckhardt, who founded the research field 'Strollology' in the 1980s in order to re-experience the conscious perception of the environment through walking:

> Strollology's task, therefore, is to gather impressions and string them together, to create impressive image sequences without renouncing traditional metaphors [...]. Strollology is hence a tool with which previously unseen parts of the environment can be made visible as well as an effective means of criticizing conventional perception itself.
>
> (Burckhardt 2015, 238)

Contrary to Franz Hessel or Annemarie and Lucius Burckhardt who focus on re-experiencing an already familiar city space, most of the émigré photographers experienced their cities of arrival for the first time. And the artists came to use walking as a specific photographic research method and photographic practice: it enabled them to find spaces and places which corresponded to their respective artistic and aesthetic visual languages, and it helped them visualize the temporal, spatial, social and cultural dimensions and dynamics of their new city of exile (Hesse/Weisshaar 2013, 205). By strolling through the city with their cameras, the émigré photographers also engaged with different methods, concepts and urban practices themselves, instead of merely capturing them within their work. If we understand photographers as actors of their own image, it is important for us as photo-researchers to find and discuss methods to analyze these images as urban practice. Through close re-reading and reconstruction of how and where the images were taken by the émigré photographers in their exilic city, we will activate different categories and layers of urban photographic practice. In addition to analyzing walking as an urban practice and method, and next to our interest in how photographers actively employed their camera apparatuses in the city, we also took recourse to Tel Aviv and New York city maps, city guides and different historical and cultural urban patterns to reconstruct the creation of the photographs.

The city from above: Overviews of Tel Aviv and New York

Taken from an elevated standpoint, a photograph by Ellen Auerbach shows a scenery of the cityscape of Tel Aviv (*c.*1934) (fig. 8.1). By standing on the rooftop of one of the houses of Ahuzat Bayit, one of the first Jewish settlements established in Tel Aviv from 1909 on, Ellen Auerbach directs her gaze through her Leica camera over the roofs of the historical buildings of the city's old part, towards the horizon where the white international Bauhaus-style buildings of new modern neighbourhoods under construction rise up. Modulated in a play of glaring sunlight and shadows, the houses appear like architectural sculptures. They form an almost abstract cityscape in which architectural structures and urban patterns disperse in geometrical forms. Besides these experimental and aesthetic elements of the visual language of 'New Vision', Ellen Auerbach also creates and follows a specific narrative structure. As a German-Jewish emigrant, she escaped Nazi-Germany in 1933 and arrived in Palestine the same year, where she settled in Tel Aviv (Graeve Ingelmann 2006, 49; Messner 2023, 178). In 1936, she left Palestine: she never felt at home there due to the harsh living conditions and due to the political and ideological circumstances which she could not identify with (Messner 2023, 204f.).

Her photographic work in Germany from 1929 to 1933 was dedicated to commercial and portrait photography. She ran the studio ringl+pit together with

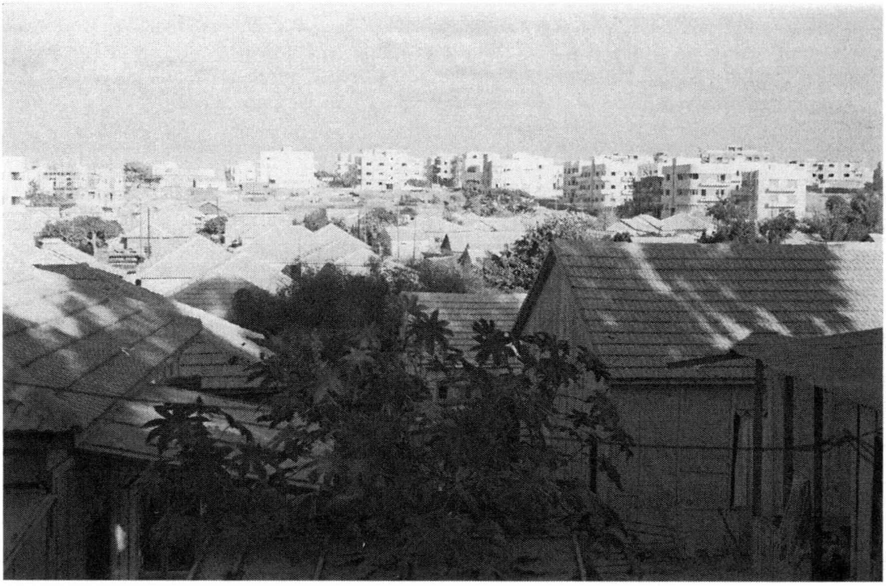

FIGURE 8.1: Ellen Auerbach, *View over Tel Aviv*, *c.*1934, KS-Auerbach 284, Akademie der Künste, Berlin (© VG Bild-Kunst, Bonn 2021).

her friend and colleague Grete Stern (Graeve Ingelmann 2006, 27–57; Messner 2023, 179). Her photographic practice during her stay in Palestine, the first station of her exilic journey, required new modes of expression. Ellen Auerbach used the miniature camera as an instrument to discover and familiarize herself with these new and foreign environments. Due to its flexible handling, the camera could easily be taken along on her explorations. This is why a large part of the photographic corpus created during her two-year stay in Palestine revolves around her new hometown Tel Aviv.[4] The view from above onto the cityscape of Tel Aviv allowed Ellen Auerbach to construct an overview of her new hometown and to familiarize herself with the structures and patterns of the city by using her camera as an instrument and mediator. Simultaneously, as an artist, she experimented with the medium with regards to modes of expressions and aesthetics which were both familiar and unfamiliar to her. By using the visual language of the Weimar Republic's avant-garde photography movements, which she had helped shape significantly during her time in Berlin, most of her photographic work in Palestine was created outside the studio on journeys through the country and on forays through Tel Aviv. During the latter, she focused on the inhabitants of the city, on the variety of cultural differences, on the burgeoning city life and on the newly developing construction sites of the city (Messner 2023, 202f.). The construction of Tel Aviv was in full swing at the time of Ellen Auerbach's arrival, not least because of the quickly increasing number of new emigrants from Europe who escaped Nazi-Germany and settled in Tel Aviv in the course of the 1930s and 1940s (Schlör 1996, 27). In the image mentioned above, Ellen Auerbach stands on the rooftop of a historic building in Tel Aviv, from where her gaze is directed towards the modern part of the city, still under construction. She familiarizes herself with the current history and the structure of her new hometown, by connecting familiar and new aesthetics and modes of expression.

The interest in and the photographic imagination of urban patterns and structures is a continuous topic also in Ellen Auerbach's third exile in New York City. Leaving Palestine for London in 1936, Ellen and Walter Auerbach emigrated to New York in 1937. After a stay at the Hotel Latham (4 East 28th Street), they lived in Brooklyn on 211 Clermont Street during the summer of 1937, before moving to Elkins Park in Philadelphia (Graeve Ingelmann 2006, 59). One of her first photos in New York was taken from Brooklyn Bridge (fig. 8.2). The letters on the roof on the left side and on the house front in the middle of the image, "COAL CO Inc." and "Abeel Brothers IRON & STEEL", give clues about the location. Research on the company "Abeel Brothers" with the help of historic images allows a detailed reconstruction of Ellen Auerbach's position and the direction of her focus: the company building in the photograph was located on 190 South Street. Auerbach

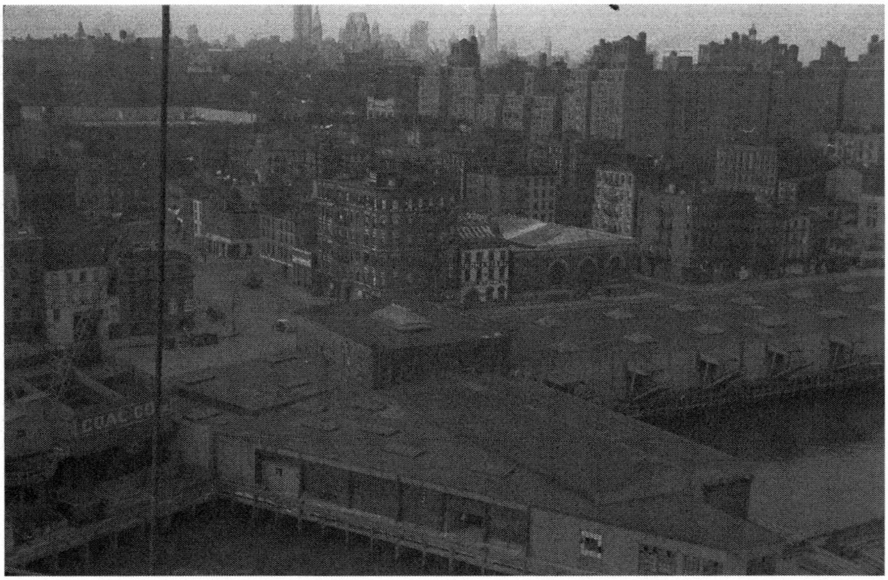

FIGURE 8.2: Ellen Auerbach, *Untitled* (view from the north side of Brooklyn Bridge towards the northwest), 1937, KS-Auerbach 652, Akademie der Künste, Berlin (© VG Bild-Kunst, Bonn 2021).

consequently must have positioned herself on the northside of Brooklyn Bridge and directed her camera towards the North-East of the Lower East Side.[5] This is the area where the East River landing docks of the coal and steel industry were located. Behind this industrial area, there were 19th-century brick buildings that formed the historic 'old' district of Manhattan. Towards the right, the buildings rise up to meet Tenement Houses, constructed due to the increasing population in the early 20th century. In the background, the skyscrapers of Midtown Manhattan gleam on the horizon. Auerbach chose a specific viewpoint, focussing on the staggering of the houses which become denser and rise up towards the background. The composition of the houses seems like a montage in which the houses merge into a large mosaic – it is no longer discernible where one house begins and another ends. Nevertheless, it is noticeable that Auerbach cut off the skyscrapers in the background: she was apparently more interested in the abundance and dense development of Brooklyn than in the landmark icons of contemporary New York.

Just like in the image taken of Tel Aviv described above (fig. 8.1), Ellen Auerbach chose a higher viewpoint to orientate herself in New York's cityscape, soon after her arrival. By using her camera as an instrument and mediator, she placed herself in a position from above to survey the city and to familiarize herself with its structure. In comparison to the photographs of other emigrated colleagues (like Andreas Feininger or Ilse Bing), she did not take her picture from the rooftops of newly erected skyscrapers in Midtown Manhattan, such as the Empire State Building or the RCA Building, but instead stood on Brooklyn Bridge. To view the city from New York's tallest buildings, you had to pay an admittance fee, but the bridges linking Brooklyn to Manhattan were not only a free and accessible urban space, available to everyone, but also an important connecting point between New York's disparate parts.[6] Since Ellen Auerbach had settled in Brooklyn, her photographs seem to narrate her first encounters with her new neighbourhood in the vicinity of her apartment.

The composition of the image follows a similar structure as her photograph of Tel Aviv, and we can read the city's history vis-à-vis the different architectural styles captured in the photograph. The older, more traditional housings in the foreground merge with the newer Tenement Houses until the gaze meets the super modern International Style high-rise buildings in the background (Stern 1987). Ellen Auerbach used her camera in New York with a similar artistic strategy in mind: she managed to obtain an overview of her new city by emphasizing the urban changes in a visual sequence. If we take another look at the industrial area in the foreground of the image, the street and the docks seem to be deserted. We do not know whether Auerbach deliberately chose a less frequented time for taking the photograph or whether the area was indeed more or less abandoned in 1937. During the 1930s the piers on South Street lost in importance as instead huge piers for bigger cargo ships were erected on the Hudson River (Federal Writers Project 1938, 331; Federal Writers' Project of the Works Progress Administration 1939, 81). Ellen Auerbach's image thus enables us to draw even further and more wide-ranging conclusions as to New York's industrial, architectural developments.

The view on the city from above was a common photographic and aesthetic practice of 'New Vision' avant-garde photography which took shape in the artistic upheaval of the Weimar Republic. The city in all its facets became a focus of artistic interest and a popular photographic motif (Breuer 2010). As an important representative of avant-garde photography in Berlin, Ellen Auerbach was familiar with these aesthetic conventions. In 1929, Ellen Auerbach begun her studies at Walter Peterhans' studio in Berlin and was an integral part of the new aesthetics photographic movements of the 1920s (Graeve Ingelmann 2006, 26). In the same year, Peterhans was appointed professor at the newly founded department of photography at the Bauhaus in Dessau, where teachers and students trained their eyes by experimenting with new photographic perspectives. Here, a novel avant-garde way of photographing and filming the city was developed, using the possibilities of the photographic apparatus in a creative way (*Bauhaus und die Fotografie* 2019; Rössler/Otto 2019; Herzogenrath 2020). It is during this time and in this context that Ellen Auerbach trained her photographic imagination and eye. Her photographic practices in exile in Tel Aviv and New York show a dynamic transfer of these artistic and aesthetic modes of expression when encountering, exploring and familiarizing herself with her new hometowns. Her innovations in form and medium illustrate a translation to and appropriation of the urban, social, cultural, political and historical conditions of new and foreign environments, especially in the cities Tel Aviv and New York.

Looking from below: Experiments on pavements

While the camera was used by the émigré photographers to obtain an overview of the city, it was also a tool to highlight the different architectural styles in close-up and more detailed shots of certain buildings. Returning to Tel Aviv and New York, examples by Liselotte Grschebina and Rudy Burckhardt further exemplify how exiled photographers experimented with their cameras and how they focussed on architectural fragments in the context of the city's historical layers. Taken from a view from below and in an oblique perspective, a photograph by Liselotte Grschebina, who escaped the threat of the Nazi-Regime in 1934 and settled in Tel Aviv (*Woman with a Camera* 2008, 151; Messner 2023, 253), shows the cut out of a Tel Aviv Bauhaus building (fig. 8.3). The curves of the round balconies are staged and modulated as

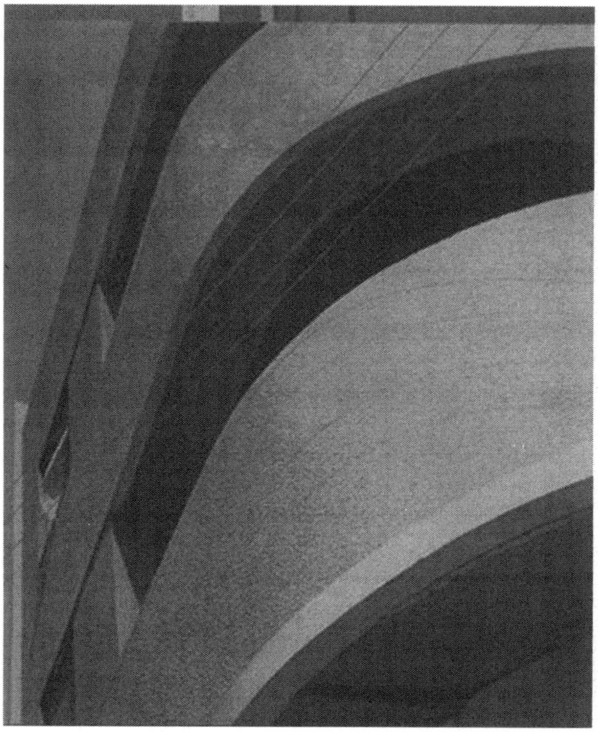

FIGURE. 8.3: Liselotte Grschebina, *Tel Aviv II*, 1940, The Israel Museum Jerusalem (© The Israel Museum Jerusalem).

architectural sculptural fragments through a play of light and shadow. The power lines which build diagonals in opposition to the curves of the balconies support the aesthetic claim of the image composition with its clear and sharp lines and its stark light-dark contrast. The flexible handling of the camera, the exceptional perspectives, the cut outs as well as the avant-garde and experimental visual language of her photographs, suggest that Grschebina was probably working with a Leica camera, as did her close friend and colleague Ellen Auerbach. The former student friends from the Art Academy in Karlsruhe met again in Tel Aviv and opened the studio Ishon where they worked together (Messner 2023, 253ff.).

Besides the artistic and experimental strategies evident in the image and its references to the photography of the Weimar Republic's 'New Objectivity', the Bauhaus architecture as well as the power lines present in Grschebina's photograph can also be read as ideological symbols of modernity with regard to its context, the city of Tel Aviv and its construction within the Zionist nation-building process. Tel Aviv was built in 1909 by Jewish emigrants from Eastern Europe and supposed to be the 'first Jewish city'. In the course of its construction, emigrants, mainly from Europe, brought different architectural styles from their home countries to Tel Aviv. This architectural eclecticism is reflected in the urban pattern of the city. Thus, in the course of the 1930s, the architectural style of Tel Aviv was dominated by International Style and Bauhaus architecture, imported to the city mainly by emigrants who had escaped Nazi-Germany. Consequently, this modern architectural style was adapted and appropriated by ideological Zionist claims in the context of the nation-building process: modern and new buildings for 'new people' should arise in a new country, and in this 'first Jewish city' of Tel Aviv (Levin 1984; Schlör 1996; Heinze-Greenberg 2003, 87–100; Rotbard 2015; Klei 2019). Grschebina's photograph of the architecture of the Bauhaus buildings reflects this ideological and aesthetic narrative. It shows a cut out, a snapshot of a certain moment in time and in history: the moment of a break with the past and a new beginning in a new and modern homestead for 'new people'. Liselotte Grschebina used the modern and avant-garde aesthetic language available to her in order to underline these ideological claims. But the photograph can be also read as an artistic experimentation with familiar modes of expression and as an approach to the novel conditions and architectural pattern of her new hometown Tel Aviv.

Instead of focussing on the construction of new buildings, as was the case with émigré photographers in Tel Aviv, emigrated photographers in New York paid attention to the many different architectural styles that could be discovered throughout the city. The exaggeration of urban eclecticism and simultaneous experiments in unusual perspectives and radical close-ups can be exemplarily seen in an image by Rudy Burckhardt (fig. 8.4). He had arrived in New York in 1935 and initially approached his new environment via film. In the years 1938 and 1939, however, he explored his Chelsea neighbourhood by photographing house facades and entrances on foot (Burckhardt 2008; Eklund 2008). He placed a 9 × 12 cm view camera on a tripod and took plain, direct photos of walls, building entrances, ornaments, drain pipes, advertisement signs and shop windows (Burckhardt 1998, 194). The intense and intimate focus on details, for example a house entrance, turns strange this everyday motif and offers unexpected perspectives and insights. By focussing on a close-up detail, Burckhardt could highlight the juxtaposition of different styles that he had discovered in only one architectural fragment of a house facade. The architect and photographer Erich Mendelsohn had already traced New York's architectural eclecticism on 5th Avenue in a series of four printed photographs in his 1926 photobook *Amerika. Bilderbuch eines Architekten* (*Picture Book of an Architect*, translation by the authors). He had added the description: "All styles of history close together: castle romanticism, church gothic, renaissance palace and skyscraper. Disorderly, wild growth, in just 100 years pumped up from the immigration port to the business centre of the world" (Mendelsohn 1926, 6).[7] Contrary to Mendelsohn's images, Burckhardt comprised the parallel existence of different architectural styles into one image, while

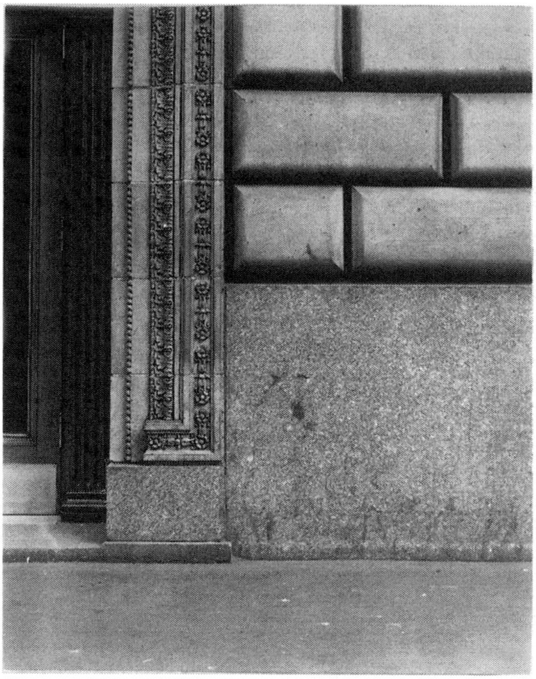

FIGURE 8.4: Rudy Burckhardt, *Building Front Detail with Acanthus Molding in Doorway*, New York City, 1938 (© VG Bild-Kunst, Bonn 2021).

also abstracting the house facade as an entity of different structures and surfaces. In contrast to the idealistic and modern visions of New York's buildings cultivated by US-American and European photographers in the 1920s and early 1930s, Burckhardt photographed the everyday life on the streets in response to new urban developments. He did not use an external perspective, but focused his gaze directly on everyday urban infrastructures as well as on inhabitants on the streets. Other US-American photographers such as Walker Evans and Helen Levit, as well as the German emigrant Lisette Model, followed this approach in their photographs during the late 1930s (Kozloff 2002; Lopate 2004; *New York Photography 1890–1950* 2012; Bajac 2016). This photographic and urban practice significantly differs from Liselotte Grschebina's. Grschebina took her photographs with a flexible Leica camera, which allowed exceptional perspectives – for example by pointing the camera steeply upwards and by aesthetically producing architectural cut outs and fragments. Nevertheless, both emigrants tried to envision the architectural styles of their exile cities by experimenting with their cameras in urban space and by referring to the different historic, ideological and aesthetic narratives of both Tel Aviv and New York.

The active and dynamic handling of the camera in urban space shows that the photographers – as actors of the city – engaged in high degrees of experimentation. Certain aesthetic practices, such as the raising and lowering of the camera to unusual perspectives, the cropping out and focussing on urban patterns and forms, were transferred and translated to the new environments in exile or adapted to photographic developments in these cities of exile. The photographs discussed here thus not only serve as historic sources but also can be read as aesthetic photo-objects which illustrate artistic strategies, creative principles and photographic practices in urban space. By focussing on detailed architectural fragments, the photographers were able to emphasize specific architectural developments and styles and to bring to light formerly hidden urban narratives. Paying close attention to the physical changes of a city and the process of visually discovering a new urban environment takes on particular valence and significance in exile. Émigré photographers, then, are uniquely positioned to engage with and highlight the urban and architectural specificities of their new hometowns.

Living in the city: Discovering socio-cultural urban spaces

Following Rudy Burckhardt, who stood on the streets with his camera and who captured the small architectural fragments that surround everyday life in the city, or adopting Liselotte Grschebina's practices, who aesthetically modulated architectural sculptural fragments through a play of light and shadow, other émigré photographers similarly used their cameras to draw attention to the variety of socio-cultural urban spaces in Tel Aviv and New York. By strolling through the city, Auerbach and Henle encountered and visually perceived the cultural differences and diversity of the inhabitants of their cities of exile with their cameras. In her article, "Looking at Photographs: Between Contemplation, Curiosity and Gaze", Elizabeth Edwards suggests the concept of curiosity as an alternative form of the gaze; she defines it as a "world-openness, even wonderment, a form of epistemic and conceptual inquisitiveness which opens up multiple meanings that stem from a consciousness of ignorance and the capacity for interest" (2013, 49). The concept of curiosity allows a more open space with regards to the visual representation of cultural difference and power relations, as it grants an active agency to the subject (ibid., 48–54).

Against this background, both Auerbach's and Henle's interest in the diverse socio-cultural urban environments and inhabitants of their new homes can be understood in the context of their curiosity: a curiosity expressed by interacting and familiarizing themselves with their novel surroundings. This curiosity can also be found in their photographs and in the way they handled their cameras, which contradicts colonial power relations, all too often expressed by asymmetries, hierarchies of gazes and the objectification of the 'other'. The way the photographers employ their cameras and meet the photographed subject on eye level, we argue, enables these subjects to gain active agency: they often return the photographic gaze and thus draw the exiled photographer into their world.

Ellen Auerbach's photograph *Tel Aviv* portrays two Arab boys playing together near a swing in a sandy environment in Jaffa (*c.*1935) (fig. 8.5). Taken from a perspective from slightly above, the narrow picture section is focused on the two boys at the swing, wearing traditional clothes with their bare feet in the sand. Their gazes are directed towards the camera and they smile at the photographer. The scenery is visually and aesthetically composed and arranged through elements such as the diagonals created by the ropes of the swing and the play of light and shadow. The slightly oblique perspective from above and the smiling gazes of the boys, who return the photographer's curiosity, convey the impression of a spontaneous image that the photographer might have taken in passing. Ellen Auerbach must have bent her knees to meet the boys with her camera at eye level. The photograph, which was probably taken on a foray through her new hometown Tel Aviv and the neighbouring Arab town Jaffa, illustrates Ellen Auerbach's interest in the levels of cultural difference and the different social structures and urban spaces of her place of exile. Furthermore, it shows her handling of the camera as an instrument of artistic experimentation which enabled and influences the way she took in her new surroundings in all their facets.

In New York, too, émigré photographers such as Fritz Henle understood the camera as a medium to visualize the everyday cultural and ethnic diversity on the

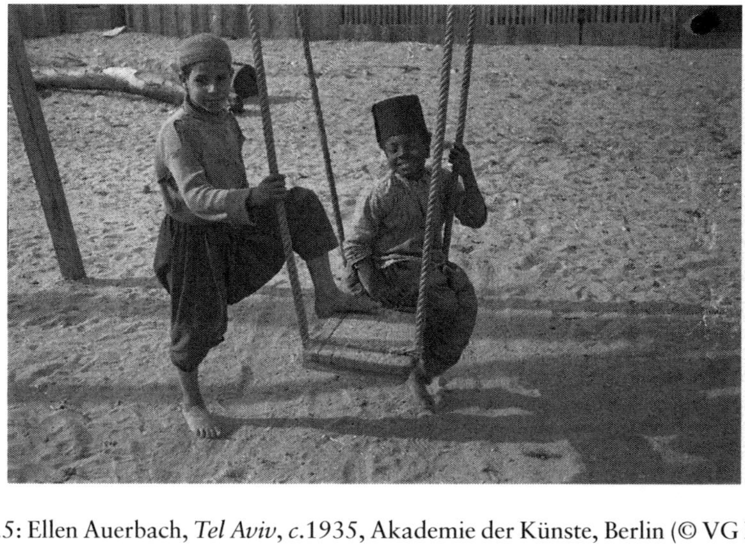

FIGURE 8.5: Ellen Auerbach, *Tel Aviv*, *c.*1935, Akademie der Künste, Berlin (© VG Bild-Kunst, Bonn 2021).

streets. In a series of 40 pictures, Fritz Henle captured the diverse cultural and ethnic life on 52nd Street. The photo series was published in the *Life* magazine as a response to the film *52nd Street* which was produced by Walter Wagner in 1937 (Anonymous 1937, 64–67) (fig. 8.6). The article clarifies that even though the movie is called *52nd Street* it only focused on one block – between the 5th and the 6th Avenue – as this was where the night clubs were: the film, therefore, provides only a one-dimensional, one-sided portrait of the neighbourhood. The street, which is about three kilometres long, reaches from the East River across Manhattan to the Hudson River and therefore crosses different neighbourhoods and areas of the city.

> At the East River end it is very, very toney, a little island of fashionability set in a sera of slums. […] When you cross First Avenue, going west, you run right into a tenement district. Block by block, the street changes, like a fancy layer cake, from luxury to tenements to smart shops to night clubs and back to tenements.
>
> (Anonymous 1937, 64)

In capturing not only the bars and the night clubs but also the entire character of the street in all its cultural and ethnic diversity, Fritz Henle put himself on an equal footing. When we analyze Fritz Henle's position from which he photographed the citizens living on the street, we can see that he put himself, and his Rolleiflex camera, on the same level as his protagonists. Instead of judging what was happening, he observed 52nd Street from a neutral perspective. In close-ups of people, as for example in figs. 20 or 22, we can see that he directed his camera upwards at the people: to do so, he would have had to squat down. In very dynamic movements, he wanted to reproduce an equal and versatile image of the residents and protagonists on the street, who actively participated in and shaped the life of the city. This photo series can thus be read as a sequence of images with a filmic character. In comparison to the *52nd Street* movie, however, Fritz Henle's sequences show a completely different view of this street. Transferred from this micro perspective on the street level to a macro perspective of the whole city, the photo series of 52nd Street can be regarded as a symbol for New York's cultural and ethnic diversity, shaping and forming the metropolis. This is a dynamic we can, in turn, transfer to Tel Aviv. As German emigrants, both Fritz Henle and Ellen Auerbach were part of diverse socio-cultural atmospheres and urban spaces in their cities of exile New York and Tel Aviv which they – as active agents and participants – likewise shaped with their cameras. They perceived themselves, the cultural and ethnic diversity of the other city dwellers and their socio-cultural environments as creative and living parts of the city. This understanding is visually expressed in their photographs and in the manifold ways they operated their cameras.

Page 64

MEMO TO: Walter Wanger
SUBJECT: 52nd Street

Photographs for LIFE by Fritz Henle

Your studio, Mr. Wanger, has made a movie called *52nd Street*. It is all about a New York street and its fine old houses, now turned into night clubs, and the daughter of an old family who becomes a hot-cha singer. The critics didn't like it at all and frankly, Mr. Wanger, they were right.

You're a big, important producer and we wouldn't try to tell you how to make movies, but there are a few things about 52nd Street that you ought to know. Your movie covered only one block—between 5th and 6th Avenues, where the night clubs are. "Swing Alley" they call it, on account of the hot swing bands at places like the Onyx Club and Leon & Eddie's. Visiting firemen go to Broadway for night life but 52nd Street between 5th and 6th is where native New Yorkers spend their big evenings.

Maybe you had a good idea in doing a movie about this one block. But maybe you could do a better movie on the whole street. It's only two miles long but worth $50,000,000, which is more than you could get for, say, the city of Galveston. You can do almost anything you think of on 52nd Street; eat, drink (in 64 bars), get a beauty treatment, shop, swim, go to school, get Federal relief or sail for Europe.

Nowhere else in the world will you find the amazing stratification that exists on a New York crosstown street. Fifty-second begins in one river (the East) and ends in another (the Hudson). At the East River end it is very, very toney, a little island of fashionability set in a sea of slums. You must know about this district because *Dead End* was laid there. When you cross First Avenue, going west, you run right into a tenement district. Block by block, the street changes, like a fancy layer cake, from luxury to tenements to smart shops to night clubs and back to tenements. We've taken pictures all along the way, so that you can see what you missed.

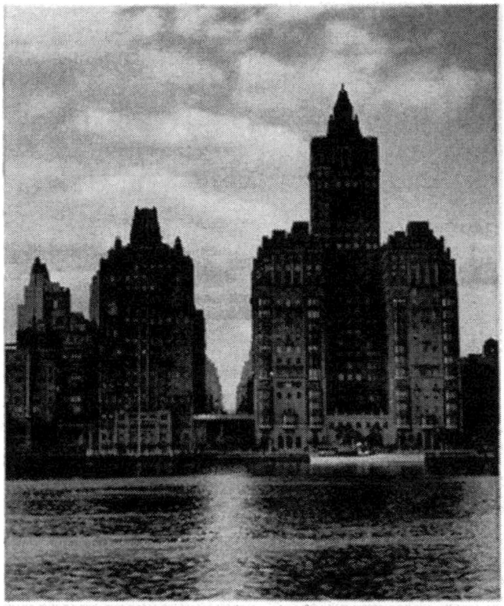

1 52nd Street begins snobbishly on a platform above the East River. On its right, snobbish River House with private dock. To right of River House, the *Dead End* slums.

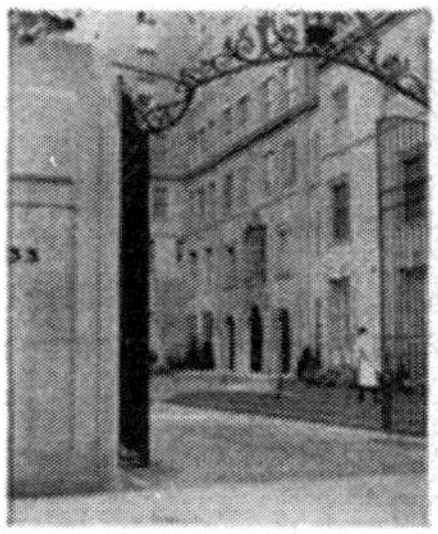

2 River House courtyard. A three-room apartment here costs $3,000 a year.

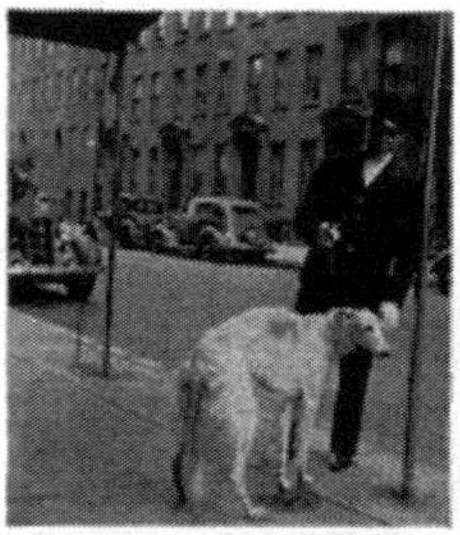

3 Dogs east of 1st Ave. are aired by doormen. Mrs. E. L. Cashman's wolfhound.

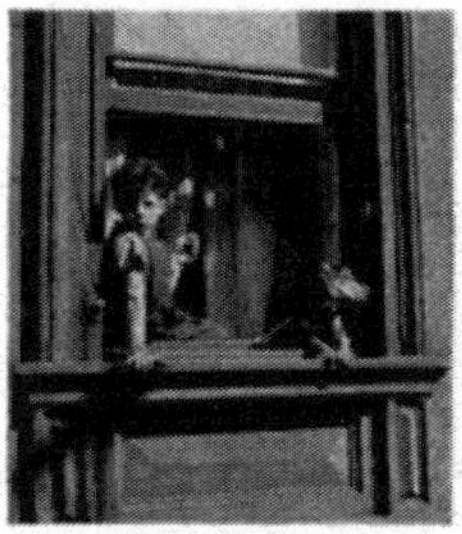

4 Dogs between 1st and 2nd Aves. see life from tenements with their masters.

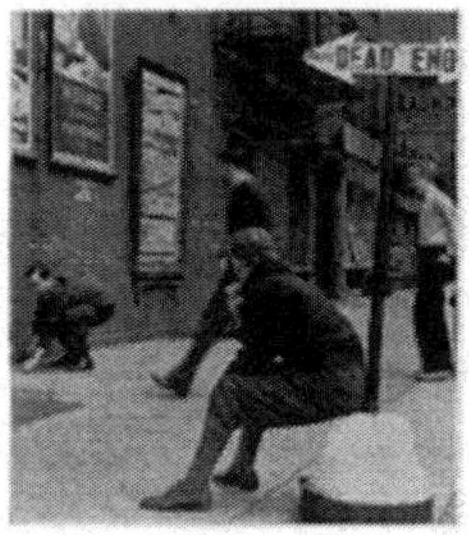

5 Boys pitch pennies on the corner of 1st Ave. 52nd Street is a dead end.

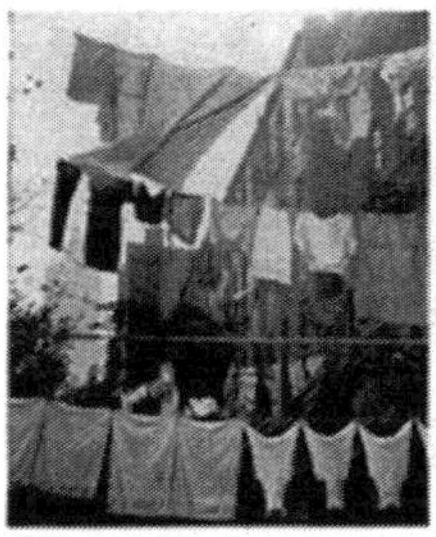

6 This is the view from a rear window of No 301, looking toward 1st Ave.

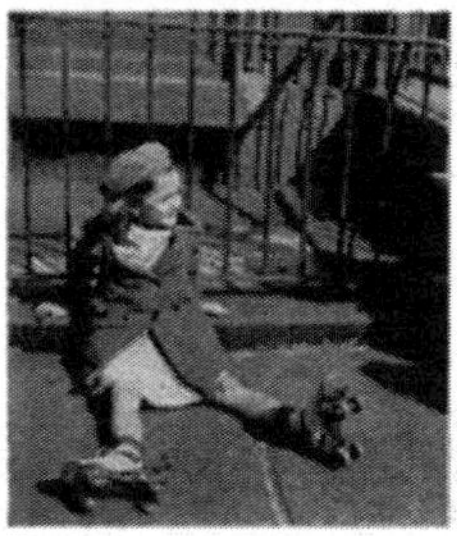

7 Sidewalks and streets are the playgrounds for children of the tenements.

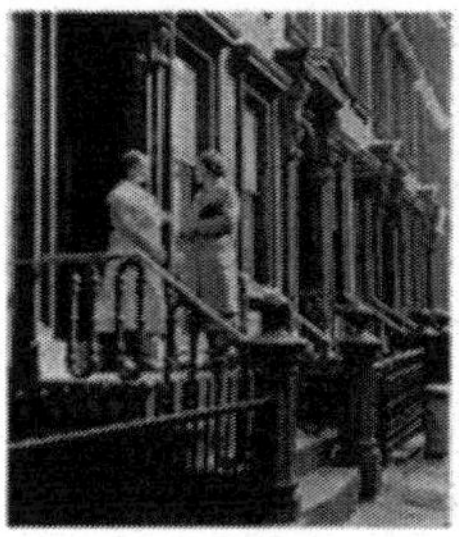

8 Mrs. Smith and Mrs. Jones gossip on brownstone stoops between 2nd & 3rd.

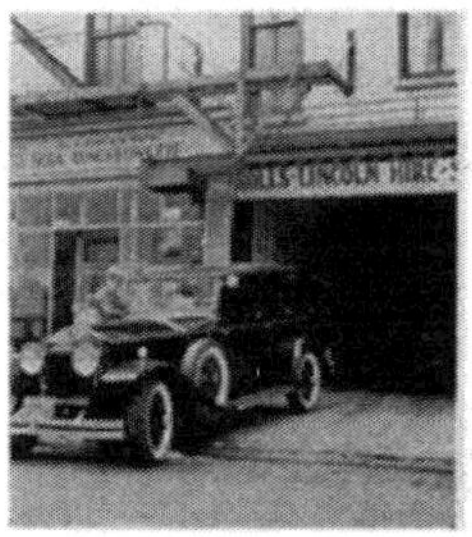

9 Around 3rd Ave., garages. A Rolls Royce with driver rents for $25 a day

FIGURE 8.6: Reportage "Memo to: Walter Wanger, Subject: 52nd Street". Photographs by Fritz Henle. *Life*, 1937, vol. 3, no. 22, pp. 64–67.

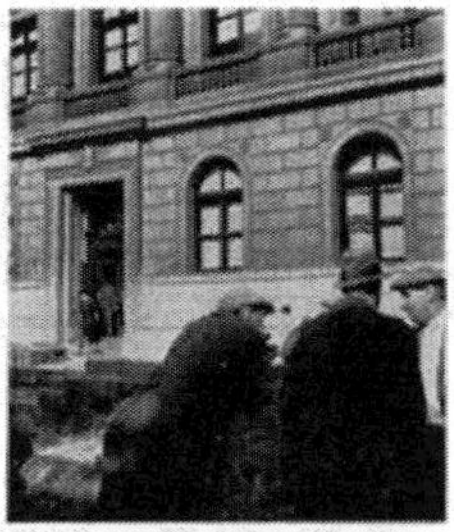

10 Corner of Lexington: Mrs. Wanger could swim at YWCA; you couldn't.

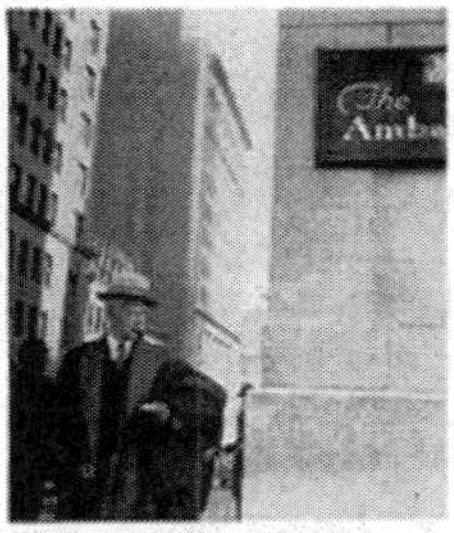

11 Corner of Park: Hotel Ambassador (good room: $8) and sleek businessmen.

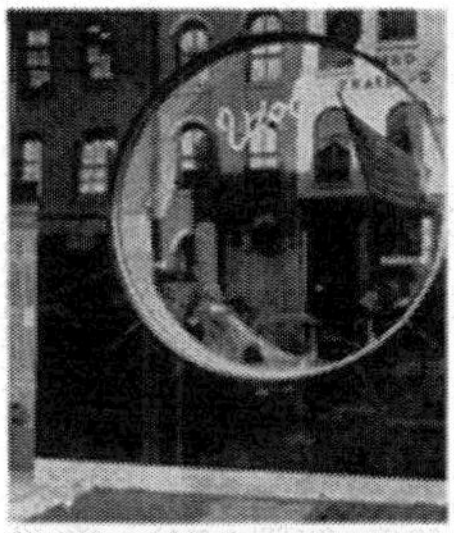

12 Between Park and Madison, Viola's sells "chapeaux." One good hat: $40.

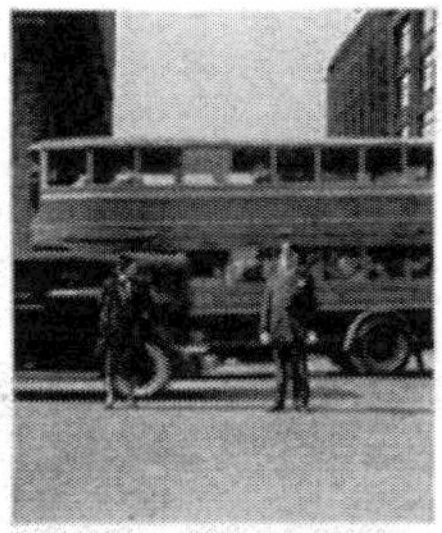

13 Fifth Ave: traffic, two-deck busses, Officer "Good-boy Dan" Sullivan.

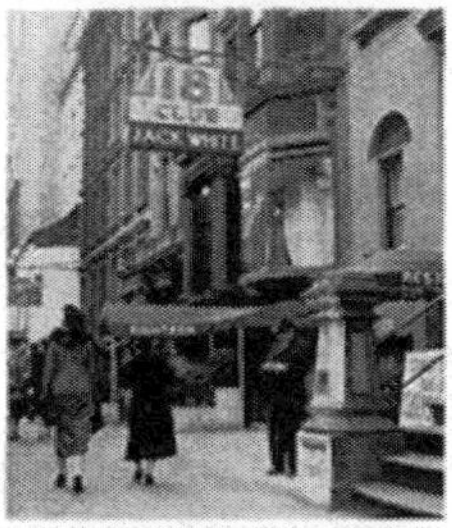

14 West of 5th, the night clubs begin. Jack White's has a $2.50 minimum.

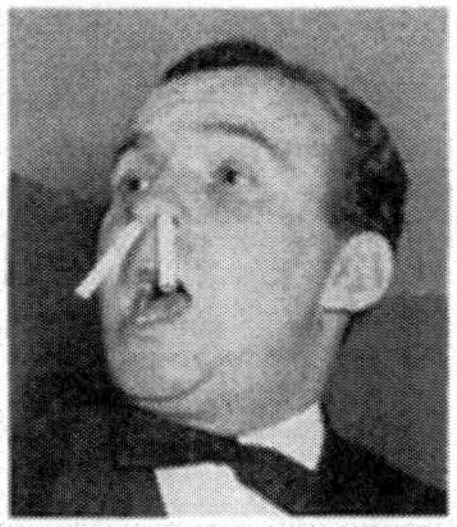

15 One attraction at Jack White's "18" is Pat Harrington, funny drummer.

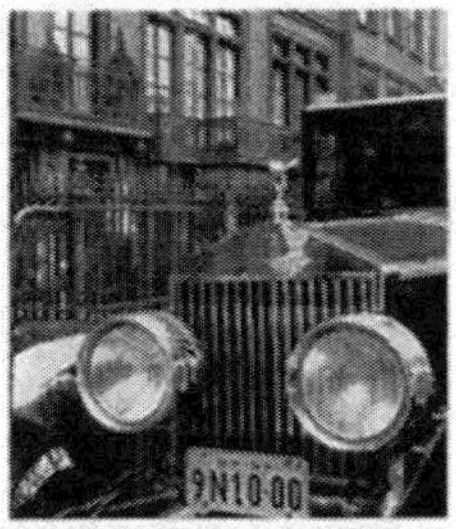

16 A Rolls Royce's radiator insolently reflects the "No Parking" sign.

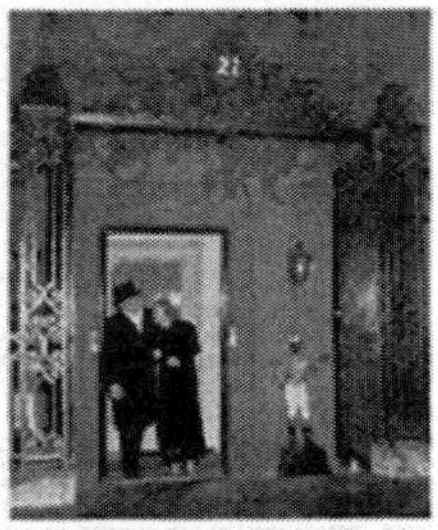

17 "21" is the most fashionable. You get in only if they like your looks.

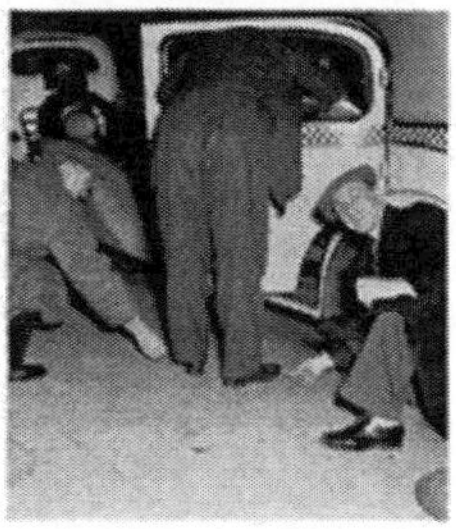

18 Taxi drivers playing hot-foot (lighting matches in victims' shoe-soles).

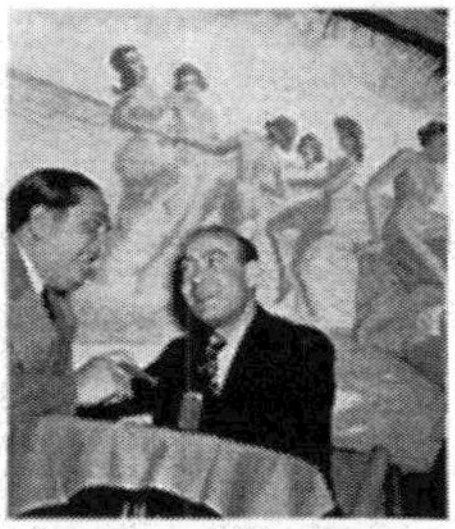

19 Leon Enken (*left*) is the co-proprietor of Leon & Eddie's at No. 33.

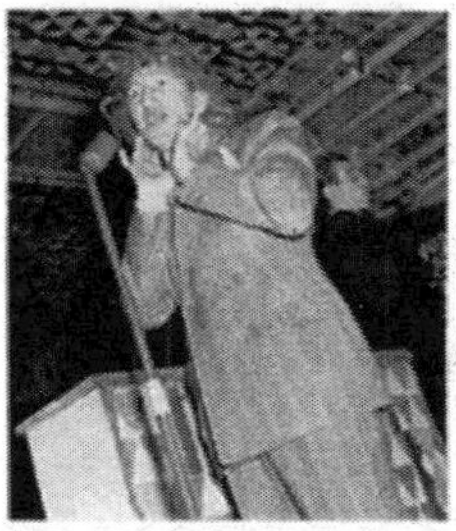

20 Eddie Davis, the other half of Leon & Eddie's, entertains with dirty songs.

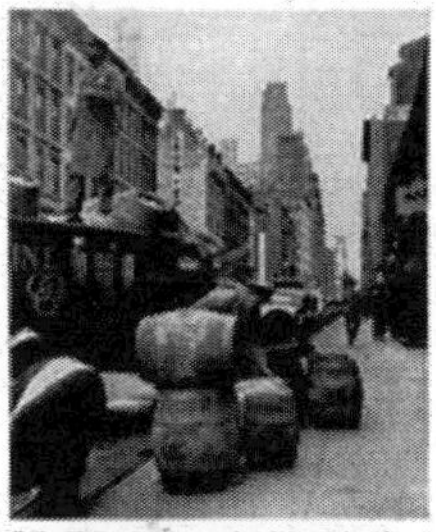

21 Unloading barrels of beer for Onyx Club, "Home of Swing" at No. 62.

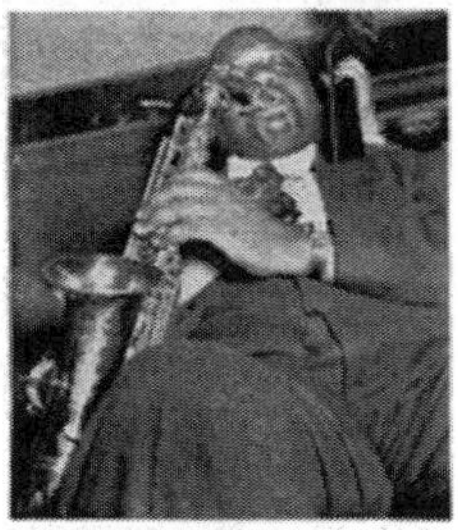

22 Pete Brown, Onyx saxophonist, belongs to the street's hottest band.

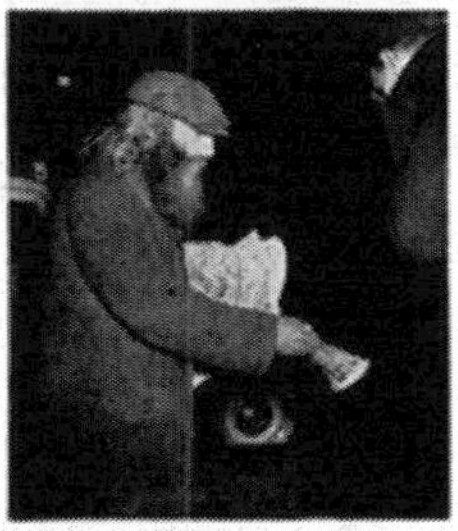

23 This old fellow sells morning papers to late travelers in "Swing Alley."

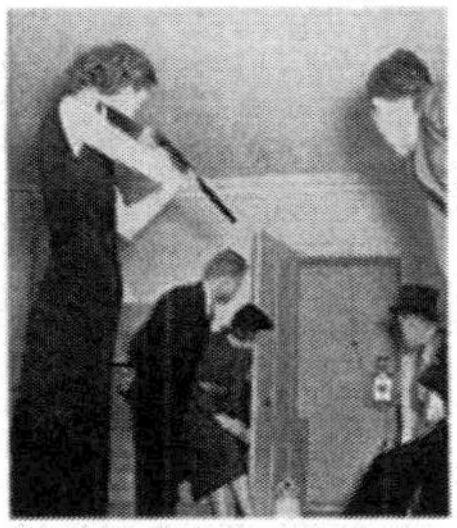

24 Above the night clubs are apartments. One has an illegal rifle range.

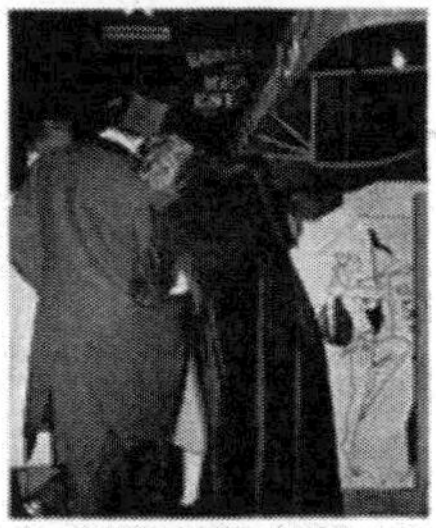

25 Outside the Club 52nd St., as the night gets old, tired heads find rest.

CONTINUED ON NEXT PAGE

FIGURE 8.6: (*Continued*)

Conclusion

By encountering the city with their cameras, émigré photographers discovered, visualized, appropriated and familiarized themselves with the different urban, social, cultural, ethnical and architectural patterns of their new hometowns. As illustrated by analyzing the works of Ellen Auerbach, Liselotte Grschebina, Rudy Burckhardt and Fritz Henle, who all emigrated from Nazi-Germany to New York and Tel Aviv during the 1930s and 1940s, the photographers applied a wide range of photographic urban practices: practices that enabled them to survey their new hometowns through the camera lens from below or above, to experiment with new artistic and aesthetic formats in urban space and to visualize the cultural and ethnic diversities of these cities of exile. As has become clear, the émigré photographers walked, or strolled, through the city in order to articulate the temporal, social and cultural dimensions and dynamics of the surrounding urban space. This could take form in either one single photograph, taken as a first step of orientation in a city (figs. 8.1 and 8.2), in experiments on the street with new camera views (figs. 8.3 and 8.4), in expressing a sense of the fugitive or passing-by (fig. 8.5), in a series of photographs visually internalizing the walk through the city or, as with Fritz Henle, portraying a street (fig. 8.6).

According to Vilém Flusser, the camera can be understood as an instrument and a medium to articulate new and creative urban visions. The émigré photographers can thus be regarded as actors of their images behind the camera, developing specific aesthetic practices and methods to photograph and visualize the city in exile. As demonstrated in the course of this chapter, these photographers referred to artistic languages and methods of avant-garde photography they were already familiar with and had practiced in Germany pre-exile. In Tel Aviv and New York, they translated and implemented these aesthetics and techniques into their new surroundings. They familiarized themselves with and appropriated the specific urban, architectural, historical, social, cultural and ethnical patterns of their exile cities and created new ways of visual expressions. Against this background, the handling of the camera and the act of photographing can be read as an urban practice of encountering the city in exile, articulating and developing a new and specific photographic and aesthetic language.

NOTES

1. Recent publications have shed light on the interdependencies between exile/migration and photography. See for example Perez (2013), Umbach/Sulzener (2018), Dogramaci/Roth (2019), Ashkenazi (2019), Troelenberg et al. (2020), Messner (2023).
2. Blog and archive entries in the digital database and the virtual walking tour on the homepage of the METROMOD project allow further insights into the work of Ellen Auerbach,

Rudy Burckhardt, Fritz Henle and many other émigré photographers living and working in New York. See more on: metromod.net.

3. This also links to recent work in the field of gender and urban studies regarding possible reconfigurations of the *flâneur*: such studies have focussed on feminist/female city walking (as expressed in and through the figure of the *flâneuse*), and on contested urban spatiality and questions on mobility in this context. See, for example: D'Souza/McDonough (2006), Dreyer/McDowall (2012), Elkin (2016).
4. In 1934, together with her partner Walter Auerbach, Ellen Auerbach made a film about Tel Aviv which promoted the Zionist project on behalf of the Keren Kayemeth LeIsrael (KKL). By using the aesthetic and visual language of 'New Vision' and referring to Zionist iconographies, the film visualizes Tel Aviv as a modern Jewish city in the context of the Zionist nation-building process. On *Tel Aviv* by Ellen Auerbach, see Messner 2023, 191–200.
5. With the help of historic images and city maps, it was possible to reconstruct that the description on the photograph in the archive of the Akademie der Künste Berlin does not correspond to Ellen Auerbach's position. She looked towards North-East and not towards North-West.
6. According to the WPA Guide Book, admission to the Empire State platform in 1939 cost $ 1.10 (corresponding to about $ 20 in 2021) and 40 ¢ for the RCA Building (corresponding to about $ 7.57 in 2021). In comparison, the entry fee for the Museum of Modern Art or the New York Zoo was 25 ¢ (Federal Writers' Project of the Works Progress Administration 1939, 319, 333, 347).
7. "Alle Stile der Geschichte dicht nebeneinander: Schloßromantik, Kirchengotik, Renaissancepalast und Wolkenkratzer. Ungeordnetes, wildes Wachstum, in eben 100 Jahren aufgepumpt vom Einwanderhafen zum Geschäftszentrum der Welt" (English translation by the authors).

REFERENCES

Adolphs, Volker. "Das Auge der Stadt / The Eye of the City." *Der Flaneur – vom Impressionismus bis zur Gegenwart / The Flâneur – from Impressionism to the Present*, edited by Volker Adolphs and Stephan Berg, exh. cat. Kunstmuseum Bonn, Bonn, 2018, pp. 9–30.

Anonymus. "Memo to: Walter Wanger, Subject: 52nd Street." Photographs by Fritz Henle. *Life*, 1937, vol. 3, no. 22, pp. 64–67.

Ashkenazi, Ofer, editor. "Exile Photography." Issue section in the *Leo Baeck Institute Yearbook. The Journal for German-Jewish History and Culture*, edited by Cathy S. Gelbin et al., vol. 64, no. 1, 2019, pp. 3–140.

Bajac, Quentin, et al. *Photography at MoMA: 1920 to 1960*. Museum of Modern Art, 2016.

Bauhaus und die Fotografie: zum Neuen Sehen in der Gegenwartskunst, edited by Corina Gertz et al., exh. cat. NRW Forum Düsseldorf, Düsseldorf, 2019.

Breuer, Gerda. "Großstadt und Signaletik. Gestalten des städtischen Raums in den 1920er Jahren." *Großstadt. Motor der Künste in der Moderne*, edited by Burcu Dogramaci, Gebr. Mann Verlag, 2010, pp. 189–204.

Burckhardt, Lucius. "The Science of Strollology (1995)." Idem. *Why Is Landscape Beautiful?: The Science of Strollology*, edited by Markus Ritter and Martin Schmitz, translated by Jill Denton, Walter de Gruyter, 2015, pp. 231–266.

Burckhardt, Rudy. "How I think I made some of my photos and paintings." Rudy Burckhardt, edited by Vincent Katz, exh. cat. IVAM Centre Julio González, Valencia, 1998, pp. 194f.

Burckhardt, Rudy. *New York, N. Why? Photographs by Rudolf Burckhardt, Poems by Edwin Denby*. Reproduction of 1938. Nazraeli Press, 2008.

de Certeau, Michel. *The Practice of Everyday Life*. Translated by Steven Rendall, University of California Press, 1984.

Dogramaci, Burcu, and Helene Roth, editors. *Nomadic Camera. Fotografie, Exil und Migration*, special issue of *Fotogeschichte. Beiträge zur Geschichte und Ästhetik der Fotografie*, vol. 39, no. 151, 2019.

Dreyer, Elfriede, and Estelle McDowall. "Imagining the *Flâneur* as a Woman." *Communicatio. South African Journal for Communication Theory and Research*, vol. 38, no. 1, 2012, pp. 30–44.

D'Souza, Aruna, and Tom McDonough, editors. *The Invisible Flâneuse?: Gender, Public Space, and Visual Culture in Nineteenth-Century Paris* (Critical Perspectives in Art History). Manchester University Press, 2006.

Edwards, Elizabeth. "Looking at Photographs: Between Contemplation, Curiosity, and Gaze." *Distance and Desire: Encounters with the African Archive* (African Photography from the Walther Collection, 2), edited by Tamar Garb and Awam Ampka, Steidl, 2013, pp. 48–54.

Eklund, Dough. "The Pursuit of Happiness: Rudy Burckhardt's New York, 1935–1940." edited by Rudy Burckhardt. *New York, N. Why? Photographs by Rudolf Burckhardt, Poems by Edwin Denby*. Reproduction of 1938. Nazraeli Press, 2008, n.p.

Elkin, Lauren. *Flâneuse: Women Walk the City in Paris, New York, Tokyo, Venice and London*. Vintage, 2016.

Federal Writers' Project. *New York Panorama: A Companion to the WPA Guide to New York City*. Pantheon Books, 1938.

Federal Writers' Project of the Works Progress Administration. *The WPA guide to New York City: The Federal Writers' Project guide to 1930s New York. A comprehensive guide to the five boroughs of the Metropolis – Manhattan, Brooklyn, the Bronx, Queens, and Richmond*. Random House, 1939.

Flusser, Vilém. *Towards a Philosophy of Photography*. Originally published in German as *Für eine Philosophie der Fotografie*. 1983. Translated by Anthony Mathews, Reaktion Books, 2000.

Heinze-Greenberg, Ita. "Zionistische Architektur in Palästina. Bauen in einer unbekannten Heimat." *Architektur und Exil. Kulturtransfer und architektonische Emigration 1930 bis 1950*, edited by Bernd Nicolai, Porta Alba, 2003, pp. 87–100.

Herzogenrath, Wulf. *Das bauhaus gibt es nicht*. Wewerka Archiv/Forum, 2020.

Hessel, Franz. *Spazieren in Berlin. Ein Lehrbuch der Kunst in Berlin spazieren zu gehen*. Verlag Dr. Hans Epstein, 1929.

Hesse, Kai-Olaf, and Betram Weisshaar. "Sind Fotografen eigentlich Spaziergangsforscher?" *Spaziergangswissenschaft in Praxis. Formate in Fortbewegung*, edited by Betram Weisshaar, Jovis Verlag, 2013, pp. 204–216.

Hofmann-Johnson, Barbara. "Perspektivwechsel. Die Stadt in den Bildern der Kamera / A Shift in Perspective. The City in the Images of the Camera." *Der Flaneur – vom Impressionismus bis zur Gegenwart / The Flâneur from Impressionism to the Present*, edited by Volker Adolphs and Stephan Berg, exh. cat. Kunstmuseum Bonn, Bonn, 2018, pp. 133–154.

Ingelmann, Graeve. Inka. Ellen Auerbach. *Das dritte Auge. Leben und Werk*. Schirmer Mosel, 2006.

Klei, Alexandra. *Wie das Bauhaus nach Tel Aviv kam. Re-Konstruktion einer Idee in Text, Bild und Architektur*. Neofelis Verlag, 2019.

Kozloff, Max. *New York. Capital of Photography*, exh. cat. The Jewish Museum, New York, 2002.

Levin, Michael. *White City: International Style Architecture in Israel: A Portrait of an Era*, exh. cat. Tel Aviv Museum, Tel Aviv, 1984.

Lopate, Phillip. *Rudy Burckhardt*. Harry N. Abrams, 2004.

Mendelsohn, Erich. *Amerika. Bilderbuch eines Architekten mit 77 photographischen Aufnahmen des Verfassers*. Rudolph Mosse, 1926.

Messner, Anna Sophia. *Palästina/Israel im Blick. Bildgeographien deutsch-jüdischer Fotografinnen nach 1933*. Wallstein Verlag, 2023.

Neumeyer, Harald. *Der Flaneur. Konzeptionen der Moderne (Epistemata, 252)*. Königshausen & Neumann, 1999.

New York Photography 1890–1950. Von Stieglitz bis Man Ray, edited by Ortrud Westheider and Michael Philipp, exh. cat. Bucerius Kunst Forum, Hamburg, 2012.

Perez, Nissan. *Displaced Visions. Émigré Photographers of the 20th Century*, exh. cat. The Israel Museum, Jerusalem, 2013.

Rössler, Patrick, and Elizabeth Otto, editors. *Bauhaus Bodies. Gender, Sexuality and Body Culture in Modernim's Legendary Art School*. Bloomsbury Visual Arts, 2019.

Rotbard, Sharon. *White city, black city: architecture and war in Tel Aviv and Jaffa*. Translated by Orit Gat, Pluto Press, 2015.

Schlör, Joachim. *Tel Aviv. Vom Traum zur Stadt. Reise durch Kultur und Geschichte*. Bleicher, 1996.

Solnit, Rebecca. *Wanderlust. A History of Walking*. Granta, 2001.

Stern, Robert, et al. *New York 1930. Architecture and Urbanism between the Two World Wars*. Rizolli, 1987.

Troelenberg, Eva-Maria, et al. "Encounters: Handling, Placing and Looking at Photographs in Relation to Migration." *Photography and Migration, special issue of International Journal for History, Culture and Modernity*, vol. 8, no. 1, June 2020, pp. 1–12, doi: 10.1163/22130624-00801004. Accessed 10 May 2021.

Umbach, Maiken, and Scott Sulzener. *Photography, Migration and Identity. A German-Jewish-American Story (Palgrave Studies in Migration History)*. Palgrave Pivot, 2018.

Woman with a Camera. Liselotte Grschebina, Germany 1908 – Israel 1994/Eine Frau mit Kamera. Liselotte Grschebina, Deutschland 1908 – Israel 1994, edited by Yudit Caplan, exh. cat. Israel Museum, Jerusalem, 2008.

9

The Exilic Vision of a Once Fashionable Quarter: Danila Vassilieff in Interwar Fitzroy

Robert Pascoe and Chris McConville

Danila Vassilieff fled Soviet Russia, sojourned the globe and worked in the Australian outback, before settling, briefly, (1937–1938) in industrial Fitzroy, Melbourne (fig. 9.1)(Moore, 2013). Living amongst unemployed factory-hands, single mothers, widows and Aboriginal families, he painted their working-class neighbourhood, winning almost no interest. One critic, Basil Burdett, was intrigued though, certain that Vassilieff had uncovered "the profounder spirit of the place [Fitzroy], of its real life, in these studies of children, at play or sitting and in these vivid glimpses of streets and alleys in this once fashionable and now faded quarter" (Burdett 1938, 8).

Vassilieff explores this "spirit of the place", often by painting on whitened plywood cut from tea-chests, material used as furnishings by the local poor. Consistently, he foregrounds children and women. Painting at street corners, he fills picture planes with scurrying pedestrians, ambling dogs and fragmented advertising text on walls, striking a rare optimistic note in a corner of Melbourne typically presented as monotone and bleak.

In *Fitzroy Street Scene* (fig. 9.2), our eye is drawn to a knot of children playing in the lower foreground. Confident, alert and inquiring, Vassilieff has sharpened their faces through linear reds and yellows on his whitened base. Vassilieff uses the sloping street to direct our gaze from the children towards a distant Collingwood Post Office tower. A red toy car glides across Fitzroy's Charles St, suggesting an enveloping 'kinetic' streetscape. His other street scenes typically play on such connectivities. *Little Sisters, Fitzroy Girls 1937* and *Valerie and Betty* all locate children in the foreground with tapering lines leading us down gritty streets. In this way, his "figures and objects are visually linked for a fluid spatial reading"

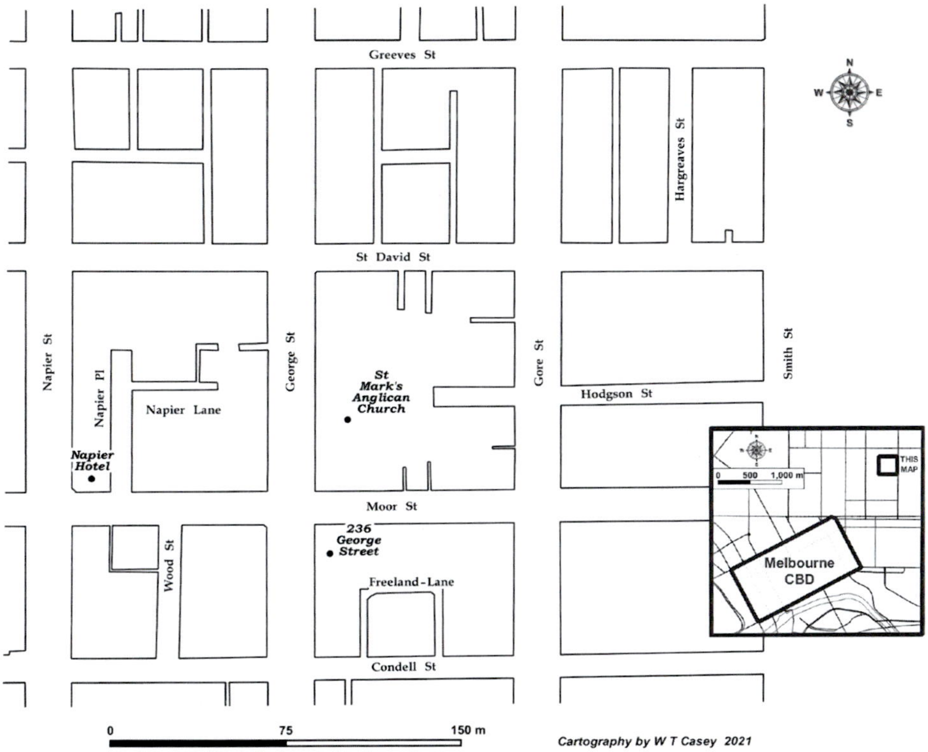

FIGURE 9.1: W.T. Casey, *Map of Fitzroy*, 1930s.

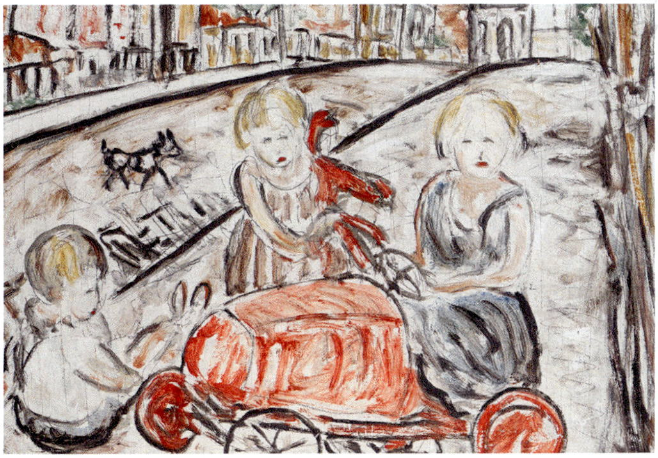

FIGURE 9.2: Danila Vassilieff, *Fitzroy Street Scene,* 1937, On board, 43.2 h × 47.0 w cm (OA 17.1965, Art Gallery of New South Wales, Copyright Heide Museum, Melbourne).

(Moore 2013, 58). Similarly, in *George Street, Fitzroy, 1938* (fig. 9.3) a boy in a toy car rolls in from the left. Girls chat in a circled group, St Mark's church spire glimpsed between them. *Children Playing, Collingwood* (fig. 9.4) takes the perspective upwards to shops, in Smith St, Fitzroy. A boy rolls a wheel; a girl is stepping energetically away, hinting again at youthful agency beyond the frame.

These paintings prefigure that imageability captured in Kevin Lynch's classic urban elements: landmark/edge/pathway/district/node (Lynch 1960; Götz/Holmén 2018). Vassilieff positions church spires and clock-towers as landmarks. Pathways connect people to place. His is a tightly edged district, the streets around his home. His eye is drawn almost magnetically to the node of Smith's grocery, Gore and Moor Sts.

Bill Hillier's spatial syntax updates Lynch's typology, such that axial lines and isovists can be identified in Vassilieff's streets (Dalton/Bafna 2003, 59.5, 59.9). Repeatedly, axial lines connect hands or shoulders of his subjects to alleyway entrances, or to passers-by centred in picture planes. His isovists avoid pubs, factories or sportsgrounds; the masculine nodes of Fitzroy. Instead, he explores the neighbourhood of woman and children, the corner store where they gathered, their role-playing in the street and the canine companions to their sociability.

Vassilieff sensed, as our 1938 critic suggested, a neglected "spirit of the place". Otherwise marginalized women and children are, through Vassilieff's scenes, in command of their streetspace. Because he is an exile, as so many in Fitzroy after the

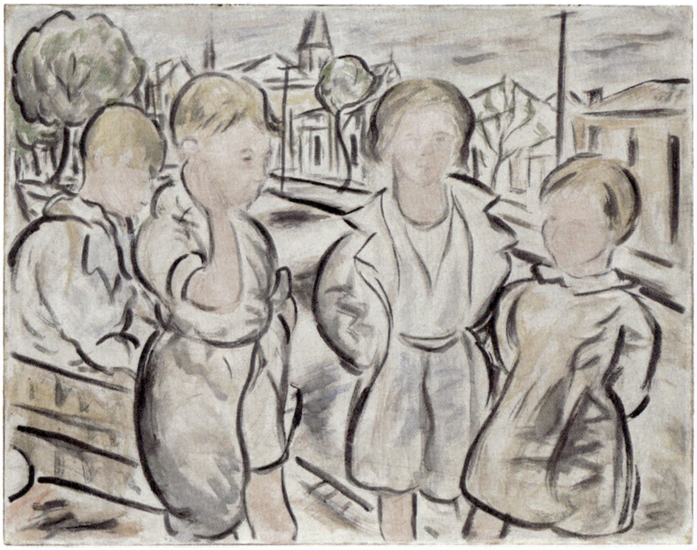

FIGURE 9.3: Danila Vassilieff, *George Street Fitzroy, 1938*, 1938, oil, canvas on board, 106.9 h × 84.7 w cm (NGA 76.268, National Gallery of Australia).

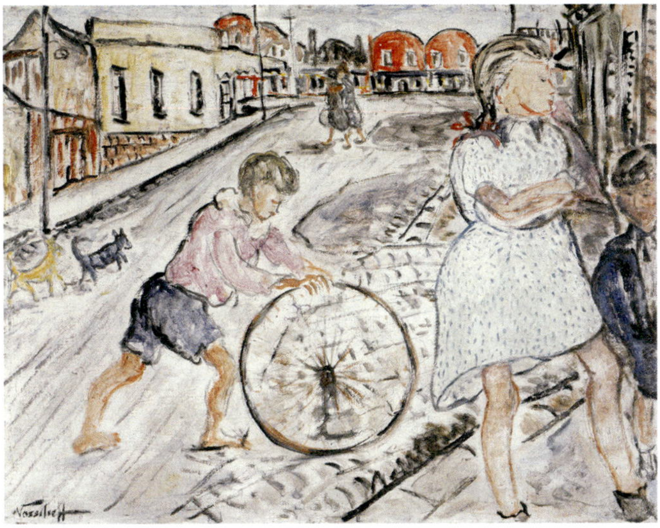

FIGURE 9.4: Danila Vassilieff, *Children Playing, Collingwood,* 1937, oil and pencil on canvas, 49.1 h × 60.0 w cm (1979.26, Geelong Art Gallery, purchase assisted by Caltex-Victoria Government Art Fund).

Great Depression were themselves, his perspective resonates as authentic. Vassilieff understood Russian modernism, through his London studies with Vladimir Polunin. No doubt a cultural memory colours his Fitzroy scenes (Bojić 2020). And yet, Vassilieff has little patience for 'academicians'. Rather, he embraces his neighbours' vitality, and so, uncannily, anticipates Lynch's legible city.

Social reformers descended on Fitzroy as the aftershocks of interwar Depression ravaged working-class lives. Intent on modernizing Fitzroy's urban fabric and thus reforming Vassilieff's neighbours, they frequently operated from St Mark's Social Settlement House, two doors from Vassilieff's boarding house. Tony Birch noted their use of text and photograph to "demonise women in particular" (2004, 8). On the whole, however, children remained their favoured precursors to reform. Their continuously circulated photograph *Entrance to a Slum Pocket* (fig. 9.5) shows two children, whom the camera isolates in the void of an empty laneway. In this hostile locale, devoid of passers-by, dogs, flowers or trees, Billy and Milly are not playing with carts, prams or dolls as children do in Vassilieff's scenes. Instead the reformer's camera reduces them to poking a stick at a mud puddle.

Propagandizing child-victims eventually enabled reformers to modernize Vassilieff's "once fashionable now faded quarter", through spartan, functionalist apartments. Although Vassilieff sold few of his Fitzroy paintings, his later Expressionist works did win respect, as inspirations for Australia's modernist art (Vassilieff, 1952). Interestingly, in 21st century Fitzroy, Vassilieff's "spirit of the place" rather

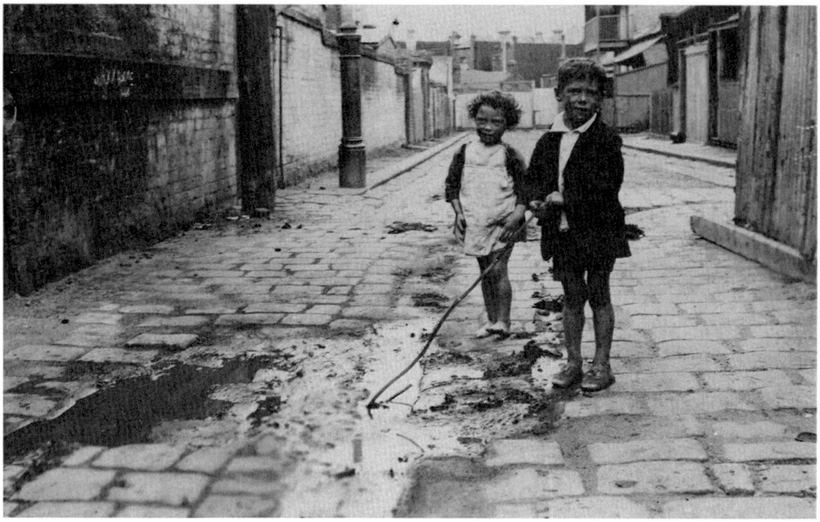

FIGURE 9.5: Oswald Barnett, *Entrance to a Slum Pocket*, *c.*1935, Photograph gelatin silver, 6.7 h × 9.7 w cm, Oswald Barnett Collection (H2001.291/12, State Library of Victoria).

than the reformers' modernist legacy has proven "the profounder", in Burdett's phrase. Austere, modernist apartments are reviled, the corner store revived, Vassilieff's vernacular romanticized. The Russian exile might have found in this thoroughly gentrified neighbourhood, a place to feel at home.

Acknowledgements

Art Gallery of New South Wales; Rosemary Clerehan; Geelong Art Gallery; Heide Museum; Felicity St John Moore; National Gallery of Australia; Norman Rosenblatt, State Library of Victoria; Victoria University colleagues in a seminar, 12 November 2020; Victoria University students in walking tour subjects.

REFERENCES

Birch, Tony. "'These Children have been Born in an Abyss': Slum Photography in a Melbourne Suburb." *Australian Historical Studies*, vol. 35, no. 123, 2004, pp. 1–15.

Bojić, Zoja. "Slav Cultural Memory, Nostalgia and Humour in the Oeuvre of Danila Vassilieff (1897–1958), Russian émigré artist in Australia." *Between Trauma and Exile, Nostalgia and Return, Special Issue of Philological Studies*, vol. 18, no. 1, 2020, pp. 18–44, www.journals.ukim.mk/index.php/philologicalstudies/article/view/1428. Accessed 7 June 2021.

Burdett, Basil. "An Artist in Fitzroy." *Herald [Melbourne]*, 1938, p. 8.

Dalton, Ruth Conroy, and Sonit Bafna. "The Syntactical Image of the City. A Reciprocal Definition of Spatial Elements and Spatial Syntax." *Proceedings – 4th International Space Syntax Symposium, London*, 2003, pp. 59.1–59.22, www.spacesyntax.net/symposia-archive/SSS4/fullpapers/59Dalton-Bafnapaper.pdf. Accessed 8 June 2021.

Götz, Norbert, and Janne Holmén, editors. "Mental Maps: Geographical and Historical Perspectives," *special issue of Journal of Cultural Geography*, vol. 38, no. 2, 2018.

Lynch, Kevin. *The Image of the City*. MIT Press, 1960.

Moore, Felicity St John, *Vassilieff and His Art, McMillan Art, Melbourne*, 2013.

Vassilieff, Elizabeth, 'Vassilieff's street scenes', *Meanjin*, vol. 8, no. 3, 1952, pp. 174–177.

10

Queering Exile London: Dislocations, Hidden Histories and Gendered Spaces

Burcu Dogramaci

Rodney Garland published his novel *The Heart in Exile* with the publishing house W.H. Allen in 1953. The book follows the quest of the first-person narrator and Oxford psychiatrist Anthony Page as he investigates the death of a former lover. His research takes him to London gay bars, clubs and cruising areas, all of them queer contact zones. The fictional story thus maps the British metropolis as a queer hidden city, creating an urban narrative of its own that develops parallel to London the tourist centre and parallel to London as the city of art or exile. *The Heart in Exile* significantly contributed to the visibility of gay urban infrastructure, with more than 10,000 copies sold by 1956 (Houlbrook/Waters 2006, 142).

Using Rodney Garland's novel as a starting point, the following reflections address the connections between exile and queerness in the 1930s and 1940s London – Garland himself was an emigrant and was one of the many exiles who came to the British capital from the European continent after 1933. While extensive attention has been paid to artistic and literary emigrations to Great Britain so far,[1] there have been no studies of queer emigrants to London or of London as a queer exile city to date.

This chapter is intended to be a preliminary step for such a study, and the challenges and possibilities of queer urban exile research that it deals with reach beyond London. Initial reflections on queer practices of urban experience are followed by observations on the fragmented record of queer exile stories, which leads to particular difficulties for researchers. Finally, this chapter will address the work of exiled photographer Edith Tudor-Hart who visualized the city's gendered spaces, thus discussing possible ways of accessing the topic of gender and exile.

In this text, the adjective queer does not primarily denote sexual orientation, but rather designates difference beyond normative binary assignments (Ackroyd 2017, 5). Queer is not only used as an adjective but also employed as a verb. The verb queer and particularly the active form of the present progressive, queering, refer to the scholarly practice of a resistant re-reading (Kumbier 2014, 3). Queering as a 'queer reading' of texts, films or – as in this case – a city, emphasizes less visible aspects of gender, sexuality and identity and calls into question heteronormative assignments.

Queer practices in the exile city

The novel *The Heart in Exile* is devoted to the homosexual infrastructure of London, *the* queer centre of Great Britain in the pre-, inter- and post-war period (Houlbrook 2005, 3; Cook 2003). Publications have increasingly given attention to the historic queer and/or homosexual city and thus contributed to an alternative (urban) history of the modern era (for example, Chauncey 1994; Abraham 2009). Such studies not only investigate somewhat overlooked or neglected social and sexual urban contact zones like clubs, bars, baths, streets or parks for the 19th and early 20th centuries. They also evaluate new practices of perceiving the city in the modern era, such as cruising as a queer visual confrontation in the city, which has been overshadowed by the more powerful *flânerie* (strolling). Cruising in the urban environment – "men looking at other men on the streets of modernity" (Turner 2003, 8) – may mean visual bonding (connection), a conversation or sexual contacts that occur in specific urban spaces: Preferred cruising areas in early 20th century London were Jermyn Street with its shirtmakers, cigar and wine shops that catered to a male clientele, or a Turkish bath for "men only" (ibid., 73–77). The urinals and public toilets in Jermyn Street, Waterloo Station or Hill Place, too, were popular sexual contact zones for men (Ackroyd 2017, 201f.).[2] In his book *Queer London* Matt Houlbrook describes historical informal places in the city, such as parks or urinals, where – mostly at night – homosexual acts took place and/or sex work was offered, as "geographies of public sex" (2005, 43–67; see also Trumbach 1999, 107).

The 19th century *flâneur*, as exemplified by the writer Charles Baudelaire or the painter Constantin Guys, is closely linked to literary or artistic productions in the urban space (in this case, Paris); *flânerie* is connoted as a creative action – mostly carried out by men – of walking, seeing and literary or else artistic appropriation (Baudelaire 1994, 290–320; Balducci 2017).[3] Cruising has a decidedly physical or sexual connotation, although movement and observation can be found in artistic *flânerie* as well. Turner defines "cruising" as the "process of walking, gazing, and engaging another (or others), and it is not necessarily about sexual contact. Sex may be the point of cruising for some, but cruising and having sex are different interactions" (Turner 2003, 60). Although cruising is a reference for contemporary artistic procedures and a subject for exhibitions,[4] a comprehensive study of cruising as a historical artistic practice in urban space still remains to be written.

The novel *The Heart in Exile* describes cruising from a double perspective: The main character moves through urban places where sexual contact is made, which he knows from memory (and which the author, too, can address based on his own experience or on experience communicated to him), and at the same time the readers follow the story through its queer urban topographies. Beyond this, *The Heart in Exile* also articulates queer life strategies that are necessary in a heteronormative society:

> The majority of the underground do not go to the queer pubs, clubs or even parties, do not linger around public lavatories, railway stations or other recognised or obvious places. There are thousands of young inverts among the millions of normal young men who live with their friends in boarding-houses, small flats, hostels, clubs, associations, sometimes under the roof of the parents of one of them. Secrecy is complete and scandals rare.
>
> (Garland 1953/1995, 105)

Garland describes how homosexual men, behaving discreetly and living in secrecy, lead as inconspicuous a life as possible in a restrictive environment. What is more, the author himself, and his experience of exile, is rendered invisible, too. The pseudonym Rodney Garland conceals the identity of the Hungarian emigrant Adam de Hegedus (1906–1958), who emigrated to London in 1939 (Burton 1995; Simmons 1995, 297) and published specialized political books and novels under his real name.[5] But his greatest success, *The Heart in Exile*, was written under a pseudonym. The "exile" in the book's title can thus be read in two ways – as an existence outside heteronormativity and as dislocation referring to the protagonist's and the author's origin.

Presumably, Hegedus used the name Rodney Garland to protect himself because gay men in the 1950s still had to fear ostracism and criminal prosecution. Homosexual acts in the public *and* private spaces were punishable until the Sexual Offences Act of 1967 (Ackroyd 2017, 217). Describing the surveillance and persecution of homosexuals in interwar London, Matt Houlbrook writes:

> If they [queer men] looked for partners in the street or park or simply had sex in their own home, they could be arrested, prosecuted, imprisoned for up to ten years, and – in certain cases – whipped. If they met friends in a café they could be caught

> up in a police raid, their names taken, and the venue closed. The formal technology of surveillance institutionalized and embodied by the law suggested that the British state was unwilling to tolerate any expressions of male same-sex desire, physical contact, or social encounter.
>
> (2005, 20)[6]

We may assume that the threat of prosecution forced homosexual emigrants in particular to live out their sexuality in secrecy or even to suppress it completely. Their fragile status as emigrants could not be jeopardized. Presumably, as a result of this, the record of gay or lesbian experiences of emigrants in England is fragmentary and has so far only rarely been the focus of research. Within the German-speaking migrant community in London, it is possible to identify queer actors, though we do not know whether and in how far they were active members of the city's homosexual scene. Another issue is that queer practices of appropriating the city during periods of rigid police control and criminal prosecution are designed precisely with an eye on transitoriness and invisibility (Turner 2003, 10). That is why later reconstructions are often fragmented and incomplete. Claudia Schoppmann, for example, ascribes the absence of relevant lesbian eye-witness accounts, diaries or autobiographies to discrimination. Often it was the women themselves who either 'cleansed' their literary estates before they were placed in an archive in order to eliminate compromising material, or who had these testimonies blocked all together (Schoppmann 1999, 140f.). Due to this lack of sources, there is no scholarship on case studies that could open up a different perspective on exile.

Hidden traces of queer exile

The challenges faced when researching queer exile are illustrated by Berlin writer and pacifist Kurt Hiller's exile; Hiller fought for gay rights in the 1920s and had close ties to Magnus Hirschfeld's Institute for Sexual Science. After spending the first phase of his exile in Prague, he travelled to London in 1938. During his exile and after his remigration to Germany (BRD), the writer was able to count on social democratic political contacts, but his homosexual networks were equally significant (Münzner 2015, 243). His relationship with the British musician Kenneth Dean was of vital importance for Hiller's immigration to Great Britain: Dean had contacted Hiller as early as 1934, since he wanted to acquire Hiller's book *§175. Die Schmach des Jahrhunderts* (Steegemann 1922); the two remained in contact. Later Dean vouched for the writer's political reliability to the British Home Office so that Hiller could be successfully evacuated from Prague (Münzner 2015, 244f). After his arrival in London, he spent several weeks at Kenneth Dean's home in

Hampstead (53 Fitzjohns Avenue, see Lützenkirchen 2006, 11). Although there are references to homosexual networks of contacts, Hiller barely touches upon his London exile in his posthumously published autobiography *Eros*. In it, he merely writes that he sought no contact with male sex workers in those years, for reasons of age – Hiller was 50 years old when he immigrated (Hiller 1973, 154). Moreover, it can be confirmed that Hiller did not advocate for gay rights or the liberalization of the law governing sexual offences as an activist while he was staying in London, as he had done before 1933 and after 1945. Instead, Hiller took part in cultural and political initiatives such as the founding of the Gruppe Unabhängiger Deutscher Autoren (Group of Independent German Authors) and the Freiheitsbund Deutscher Sozialisten (Free League of German Socialists).[7] It was not until the late 1940s and particularly after his re-migration to Hamburg that Hiller once more devoted his energies to the decriminalization of homosexuality and to gay rights (Münzner 2015, 320–345). The fact that Hiller backed away from his commitment to gay rights during his London exile could be an indication that the political conditions and his status as an exile in a foreign country were the reason for his restraint.

Although lesbians in England were not directly affected by criminal prosecution (in the laws in question, women are not mentioned), to say that queer lives were invisible is presumably truer for émigré women than for men.[8] Another reason for this invisibility of lesbian life stories is the widespread belief, reaching back to the 18th century, that sex cannot take place without a penis and that, consequently, no sexual love between women could exist (Horsley 2010, 10). It was primarily the women's movement in the second half of the 20th century that significantly contributed to making the stories of women and their same-sex relationships more visible (ibid., 9). This also pertains to gender-specific spaces and access to places and institutions, moral and/or societal conventions that restricted women more than men.[9] Despite this, there were secluded and protected safe spaces for the lesbian community, such as the club Gateways (239 King's Road, corner of Bramerton Street, Chelsea) which had acted, since the 1940s, as a meeting place of the Chelsea Art Club, a queer night club and a favourite gathering place for Black Caribbean people (Gardiner 2003). This shows how clubs functioned as places where marginalized people or social outsiders from various different communities were able to come together.

For queer women sporadic retreats from the city were an additional option: Just as she had in Vienna, the émigré psychoanalyst Anna Freud lived in a personal and professional relationship with the American Dorothy Tiffany Burlingham in London, although the two women never openly admitted they were in a relationship.[10] In Austria, from the 1930s onwards, Anna Freud and Dorothy Burlingham had owned a country retreat in Hochrotherd, which was located 30 kilometres from Vienna and could easily be reached by car.

In England too, Anna Freud and Burlingham had a country summer cottage in Walberswick, Suffolk. It is interesting to note that a suite of antique furniture of rural alpine origin, which the two women had installed in Hochrotherd, finally found a home in the British weekend cottage after a long detour by way of theUnited States. Later the furniture was shipped to 20 Maresfield Gardens, Anna Freud's London residence (Johler 2015, 11). The furniture thus connects the two weekend houses in Austria and England. Their weekend getaways made it possible for the couple to lead a discreet life as a twosome – after all, as a well-known psychotherapist and the daughter of Sigmund Freud, Anna was in the public eye in Vienna and presumably in London as well. This retreat to the country can be seen as an alternative strategy for women living and loving in a same-sex relationship. Their partnership was tacitly tolerated more than male homosexual relationships, both legally and socially. However, women could not frequent queer contact zones in the city and in the public space as freely as men.

The gender segregation of 'separate spheres' that was manifest in the 19th century (Cherry/Helland 2006), when women tended to be assigned to private family space and men to professional and public space, still prevailed, at least in part, in 1930s and 1940s London. Social codes of contact inevitably restricted spaces of movement and action, especially when where nightlife was concerned.

In general, however, Claudia Schoppmann argues that lesbians had greater resilience (*Widerständigkeit*) in exile. Frequently unmarried, they were accustomed to an independent and professional life even before emigration and thus "possibly somewhat better prepared for the struggle for survival in the extreme situation of exile than their married and hitherto nonworking counterparts, i.e., women who were dependent on a husband materially and in other respects" (Schoppmann 1999, 149f.). This argument seems to hold true for Anna Freud at least, as she not only continued the professional activities she had pursued in Vienna but also developed them further and made a name for herself with her research on child psychiatry. Together with Dorothy Burlingham (and partly financed by her), from 1937 on Anna Freud had run the Jackson Nursery, a psychoanalytically oriented research facility for infants from low-income families in Vienna. (Denker 1995, 26; fig. 10.1). Together, in December 1940, shaken by the bombing of London, Freud and Burlingham founded the research and child-care centre Hampstead Nurseries (Wedderburn Road and Netherhall Gardens).

During the Blitz, families had to seek shelter in underground bunkers or spend the night in the London Underground, where makeshift accommodations had been set up. Drawings by the artist Henry Moore from the year 1941 record the claustrophobic situation in an Underground tunnel.[11] The War Nursery offered children a temporary home during the war years. The nursery innovated the concept of "family groups", where three or four children were combined into family units

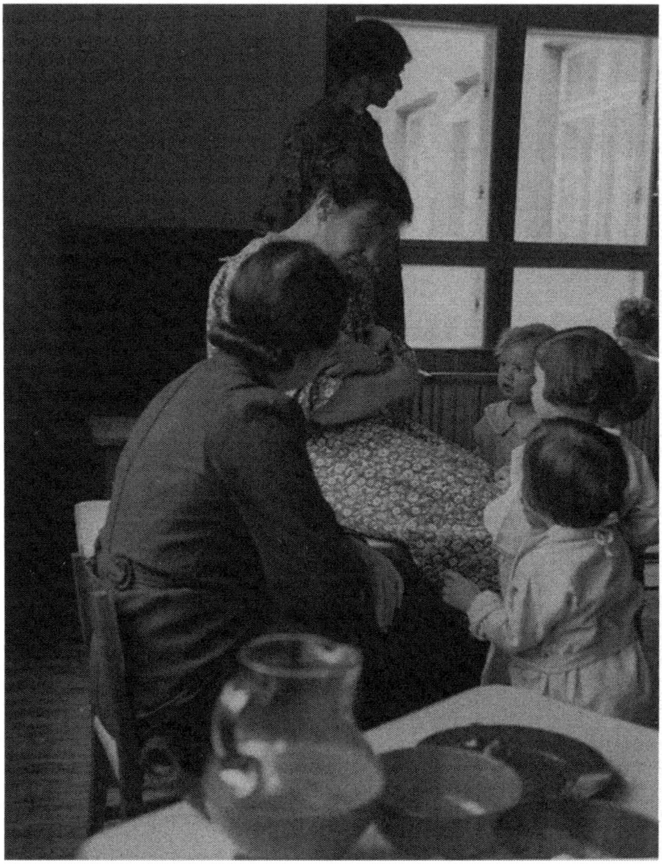

FIGURE 10.1: Anna Freud and Dorothy Burlingham, Jackson Nursery, 1937, unknown photographer (© Freud Museum London).

(Kennedy 2016, 314ff.). The War Nursery, which ran until November 1945, was not only a care centre in wartime, but also a laboratory in which Anna Freud und Dorothy Burlingham together with their team were able to make observations and test and carry out therapeutic interventions. Their work was reflected in the publications Freud and Burlingham wrote together – *Young Children in War-Time* (1942, German title *Kriegskinder*, 1949; fig. 10.2), *War and Children* (1943) or *Infants without Families* (1943).

Their exile offered the women an opportunity to continue their joint psychoanalytical work; the Hampstead neighbourhood where they lived and where their institution was located was an important frame of reference for them. As with other exiles, in Anna Freud's case emigration was possible, and feasible, only with the support of networks. For Anna Freud, female networks, in particular, offered her

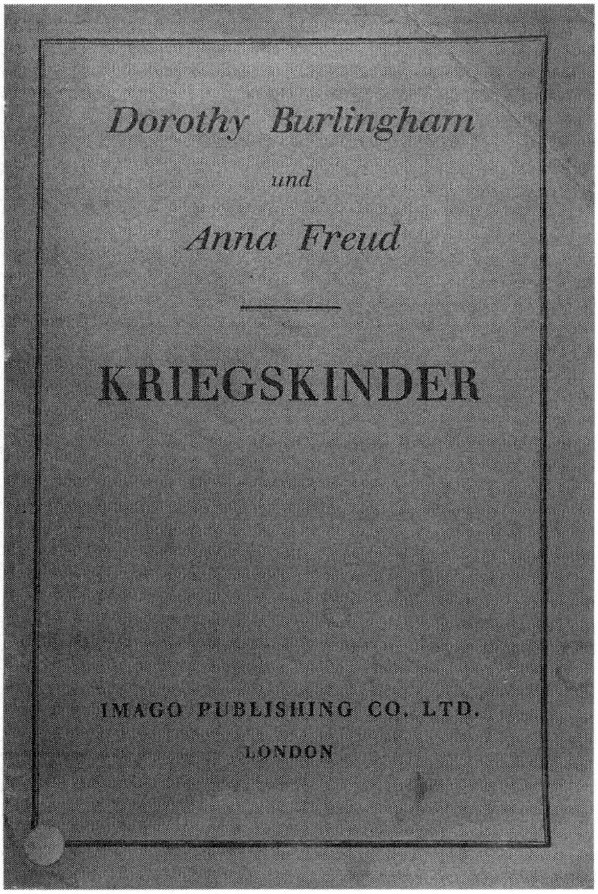

FIGURE 10.2: Dorothy Burlingham and Anna Freud. *Kriegskinder*: *Jahresbericht des Kriegskinderheims Hampstead Nurseries*. Imago Publishing, 1949, cover (METROMOD archive).

and her family economic and organizational help with their move from Vienna to London; her network included Princess Marie Bonaparte, who assisted the Freud family when they left Vienna (Eissler 1989, 34). But Dorothy Burlingham was able to help as well: As an American, Burlingham was not subject to the strict export regulations, and she could export moveable goods from Austria more easily, and without paying fees (Johler 2015, 20).

Gendered exile: Intersectionality and social contexts

It is impossible to address the topic of exile in London without covering gender-specific issues such as safe public spaces in the city or the struggle for survival in and with a partnership. It is important to develop a holistic perspective on exile situations that takes into account not only social (relationship) structures but also structural disadvantages – disadvantages that, for instance, arose due to a limited public presence.[12] Researching historiographies of exile, specifically pertaining to those fleeing National Socialism, Irene Messinger and Katharina Prager find that male heteronormative perspectives were predominant. Exile, they write, is defined primarily as an experience of loss, largely based on male biographies, often written by male historians, while the category 'woman' was neglected, especially in the early research on exile (Messinger/Prager 2019, 14). Exclusion and inclusion in exile are closely linked to gender, age, social class or ethnic origin. In this context "doing gender" means that sex assignments and gender identities within societal processes are constantly produced and reproduced (West/Zimmerman 1987; Fenstermaker/West 1995; Gildemeister 2010; Messinger/Prager 2019, 11). Helpful in this connection are recent studies on the intersectionality that see the relation of race, gender, sexuality, social class, nationality and reduced physical or psychic abilities in a holistic way, as they investigate multiple types of discrimination (Grosfuguel et al. 2017; Dietze 2017). The concept of 'intersectionality' goes back to the lawyer Kimberlé Crenshaw, who sees racism and sexuality as inherently interdependent; at their intersections, she claims, it becomes impossible to separate from one another acts of violence, injuries, stigmatization and marginalization (Crenshaw 1991). Crenshaw argues against a single-axis framework that "erases Black women in the conceptualization, identification and remediation of race and sex discrimination" (Crenshaw 1989, 140). In recent years, Carolin Küppers has taken up Crenshaw's claims by emphasizing that "intersectionality [means] the intertwining of different structural categories that generate inequality", referring to the intertwining and interaction of forms of oppression and discrimination (Küppers 2014).

At the same time, for the historical context examined here it is difficult to establish clear causal connections; rather, there is ambivalence and plurality: in British exile, it was not always *only* a disadvantage or *only* an advantage to belong to a certain gender. Exile could mean an opportunity or a new start, but could also create backlash (Messinger/Prager 2019, 10). Thus women sometimes found it easier to get work, even though the work did not correspond to their professional qualifications (ibid., 8). Immigration to Great Britain with a domestic permit was considerably easier because the restriction that no foreigner should be hired if British workers were also available for a certain position, stated in the "Aliens Order" (1920), was still in force (Bollauf 2011, 139). Potential immigrants required the authorization of the Ministry of Labour if they could not prove that they had independent means and intended to get a job (Hartig 2019, 97). In Britain, however, the demand for domestic servants and the shortage of qualified personnel was very high, so that women in particular used this opportunity to immigrate. By 1939,

20,000 German-speaking refugees had arrived in the country, with a residence permit for domestic workers in hand (Zwerger 2016, 221).

Among the immigrants with a permit to work as domestic helpers, there were numerous who had previously worked in other professions. Coming to Britain with a domestic permit were physicians and teachers (Bollauf 2011, 160f.), but also women in creative professions, such as writers, artists and photographers. One of them was Elly Niebuhr, who in February 1939 had fled to England together with her sister Ilse and who worked as a domestic and kitchen help in Cambridge and later in London, until she continued her journey to New York (Holzer 2009, 32). Some of the émigré women who worked as domestic servants were the main wage earners in the family and often had to provide for their partners and children since they could earn a living more easily than male refugees. But it was precisely the work as a domestic help and the caregiver tasks as a wife and mother that could mean regression to roles that many women believed they had left behind long ago (Messinger/Prager 2019, 8f.). As a result, they also quickly found themselves in a situation that kept them from doing their chosen work (as an artist).

The large number of female emigrants who entered the country with domestic permits demonstrates that women had an advantage when it came to emigrating since their labour was in demand. This was one of the reasons why targeted rescue operations focussed on bringing women who were at risk in Germany or Austria to England via a domestic permit. Worth mentioning here are the mediation efforts of the relief organization Council of German Jewry, which made it possible for thousands of female refugees to emigrate to England, but private initiatives have been documented as well (Holzer 2009, 31). Andrea Hammel describes how the entrepreneur and founder of the furniture company Isokon, Jack Pritchard, and his sister May Moncrieff went out of their way to bring two Viennese women – Margarethe Kohon and Emmy Epstein – to Great Britain as domestic servants. This is part of Pritchard's altruistic commitment to help persons at risk to emigrate from Germany and Austria (Hammel 2006, 28f.). Jack Pritchard continued to be an important source of support and a sponsor for those who had already immigrated, among them the Viennese photographer Edith Tudor-Hart.

Gendered spaces and the social eye of exile photography

In Edith Tudor-Hart's photographic oeuvre, gender-specific perspectives overlap with an enduring interest in social structures, mechanisms of social exclusion and the lives of marginalized people, the socially deprived, working-class families. At the same time, Edith Tudor-Hart's socio-critical observations were closely linked to urban spaces.

As early as 1931, even before she came to England, Tudor-Hart (née Suschitzky) photographed the hustle and bustle at the Caledonian Market in London and published the report under the headline "Der Markt des nackten Elends" (The marketplace of sheer misery) in the Social Democratic magazine *Der Kuckuck*. In her photographs she shows weary vendors sitting in front of the wares they had spread out on the ground, waiting for an equally precarious clientele – a "trading place for the poorest among the poor", a hub for the most wretched among the city's inhabitants (Suschitzky 1931, 15; see also Holzer 2009, 43).

Even after her emigration, Edith Tudor-Hart continued these photographic observations in urban neighbourhoods, paying special attention to the living conditions of children and women. Tudor-Hart's photos from the backyards of Gee Street in Finsbury/London are devoted to children between roughly one year of age and adolescence. They stand crowded together, among clothes lines and old pots, surrounded by high walls. The older girls take care of the youngest, carry them in their arms, and sometimes one cannot really tell whether these are young mothers or siblings. There is a closeup portrait of a little girl with a dirty face looking dreamily off into the distance while an older child smiles at her (fig. 10.3). The

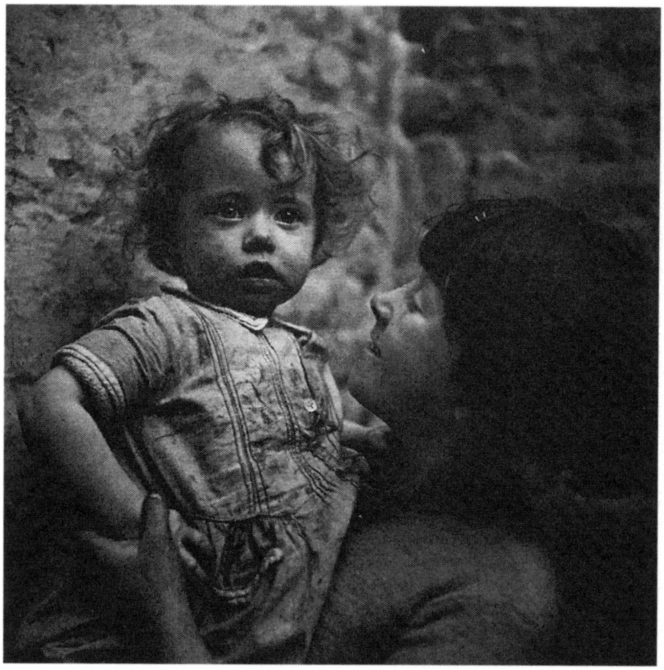

FIGURE 10.3: Edith Tudor-Hart, *Gee Street*, Finsbury, London, *c.*1936 (Tudor-Hart 1986, 78; © Estate of Wolfgang Suschitzky).

series of pictures shot in the backyard conveys a sense of relaxation that almost seems inappropriate in this dreary place and at the same time shows how natural the interaction of the photographer with her models was and how – conversely – those she photographed allowed her to come close to them.

Tudor-Hart published her photographs in various contexts that altered their meaning and interpretation: A photo in the series from Gee Street appeared in Wal Hannington's book *The Problem of the Distressed Areas*, which was published in 1937 in a Left Book Club Edition (fig. 10.4). Hannington was the founder of the Communist Party of Great Britain (CPGB) in 1920 and was part of the organization National Unemployed Workers' Movement, which wanted to raise awareness for the situation of the unemployed.[13] *The Problem of the Distressed Areas* intended to make visible the issues of the poor, underprivileged and unemployed by directing attention to housing conditions, slums and impending political radicalizations.[14] Before her emigration Tudor-Hart was a member of the Communist Party of Austria and presumably was put in touch with Wal Hannington through the Communist Party of Great Britain.[15] Moreover, Edith Tudor-Hart was already involved in working on a pamphlet, dated 1935, of the National Unemployed Workers Movement (Forbes 2013, 69).

The photograph reproduced in Hannington's book shows the backyard with the children from above, with the persons below looking, for the most part, into the camera (fig. 10.5). This photograph makes visible the living conditions in Gee Street, with few open spaces and little light and ventilation. Architecture and urban space stand for a precarious existence; urban life does not imply participation – rather, it is associated with segregation and exclusion. Tudor-Hart's photograph is subtitled "'Living' Conditions in 1937" and can be read as an accusation against living conditions that are hostile to life – that is why the word "Living" is put in quotation marks. It is precisely the tightly packed crowd of children and young women that is supposed to get to the heart of the problem and show that a precarious existence in the London slums has serious consequences for the younger generation. Admittedly, this empathetically photographed picture does not work as a pars pro toto; the children in their mutual harmony and with their cheerful expressions look remarkably stable in their otherwise dismal surroundings. Unlike what is suggested by the caption, they seem to have retained a fundamental trust in themselves and in the photographer.

The same photograph from the backyards of Gee Street was published in the magazine *Lilliput* along with another photo by Tudor-Hart (fig. 10.6) that shows a dog salon. In this beauty salon, a bulldog is in the process of being groomed by two women. As paired images, the two photographs juxtapose hedonistic lifestyle with bare survival in poverty and show them as existing side by side in the city. Rich and poor, man and beast, cosmetics and hunger

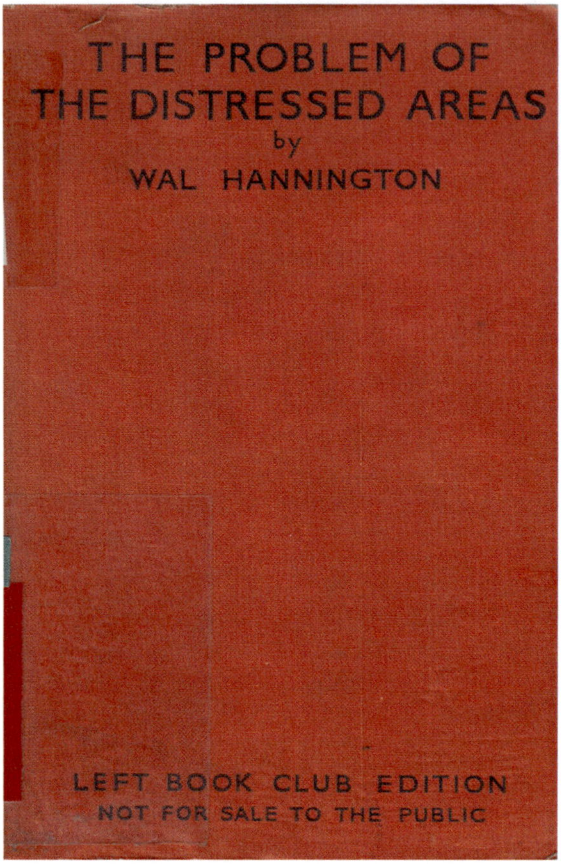

FIGURE 10.4: Wal Hannington. *The Problem of the Distressed Areas*. Left Book Club Edition, 1937, cover (METROMOD archive).

collide in *Lilliput*'s visual logic. The caption below the "beauty parlour for dogs" asks, "Should we have this?" and asks a similar question about the backyard photo from a "London slum": "Must we have this?". The readers are thus addressed and actively included in the "we"; each of them can join in deciding whether a beauty salon for dogs – in the sense of the photographic statement – is a necessity and whether a society should tolerate the existential hardship of children.

Tudor-Hart's interest in gender-specific themes is reflected in her contributions to the book *Working-Class Wives: Their Health and Conditions* (fig. 10.7) by the British social reformer Margery Spring Rice, which was distributed in 1939 as a cheap Pelican Books paperback by Penguin Press, accessible to

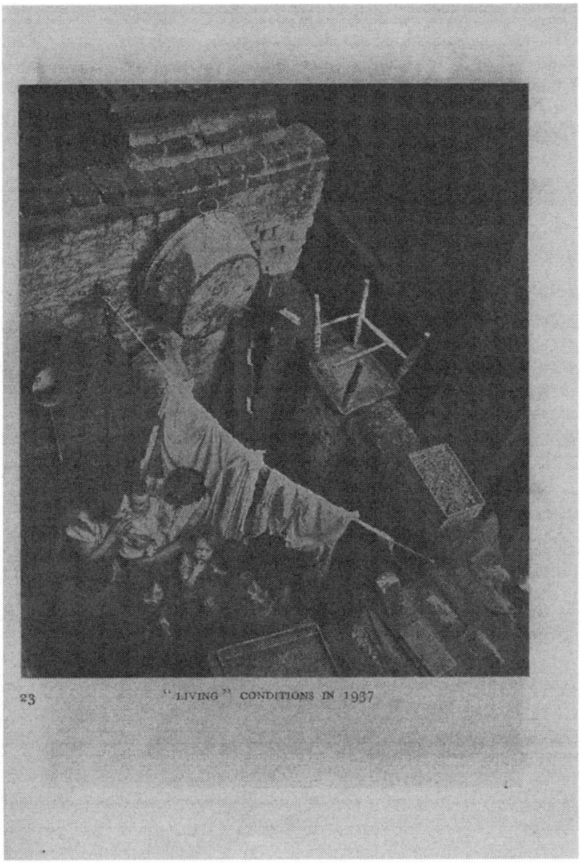

FIGURE 10.5: Edith Tudor-Hart, *Gee Street*, Finsbury, London, *c.*1936, in: Wal Hannington. *The Problem of the Distressed Areas*. Left Book Club Edition, 1937, pl. 23 (© Estate of Wolfgang Suschitzky).

a wide readership. Spring Rice's publication was based on a survey of 1200 working-class women examining their state of health and government relief measures, which in the book are described as being unsatisfactory and in need of improvement. However, Edith Tudor-Hart's photos are less accusatory, generalizing or homogenizing than the text in the book. Spring Rice's arguments concerning young working-class mothers are quite paternalistic, and, at the same time, she disregards gender-specific constellations, such as the position of the family fathers (Forbes 2013, 68).

Tudor-Hart's photographs develop an agenda of their own and pose a counter-narrative by emphasizing people's individuality: in close-up portraits, everyday

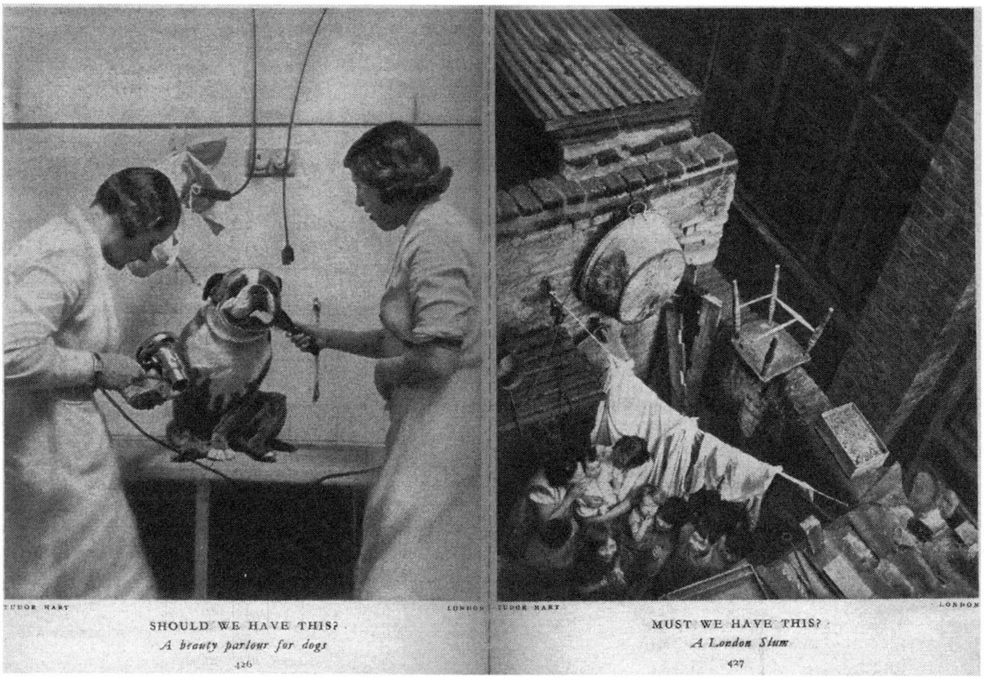

FIGURE 10.6: Edith Tudor-Hart, *Beauty parlour for dogs*, *c.*1937 (left) and *Gee Street*, Finsbury, London, *c.*1936 (right), in: *Lilliput*, April 1939, pp. 426f. (© The Estate of Wolfgang Suschitzky).

situations and through mutual affection. At the same time, things that are wrong are not ignored; rather, Tudor-Hart's photographs attribute autonomy and agency to the women and mothers in spite of (or precisely because of) their harsh living conditions. The captions of the pictures, which look for the general in the specific – "The abiding maternal personality" or "The typical afternoon 'rest'" –, barely capture what Edith Tudor-Hart is focusing on. Her photo of an afternoon break (fig. 10.8) showcases four generations at once, with the grandmother on the right, the middle-aged woman in the middle, the young mother on the left and the baby in a pram – taking a break outside in the sunshine and having a cup of tea. Accordingly, the message of this photograph could also be that no matter how adverse a precarious existence may be, interpersonal relationships between people of different ages have not fallen by the wayside.

All three publications mentioned here in which Tudor-Hart's socio-critical photos appeared addressed different audiences: *The Problem of the Distressed Areas* addressed a politically left-wing public, *Working-Class Wives: Their Health*

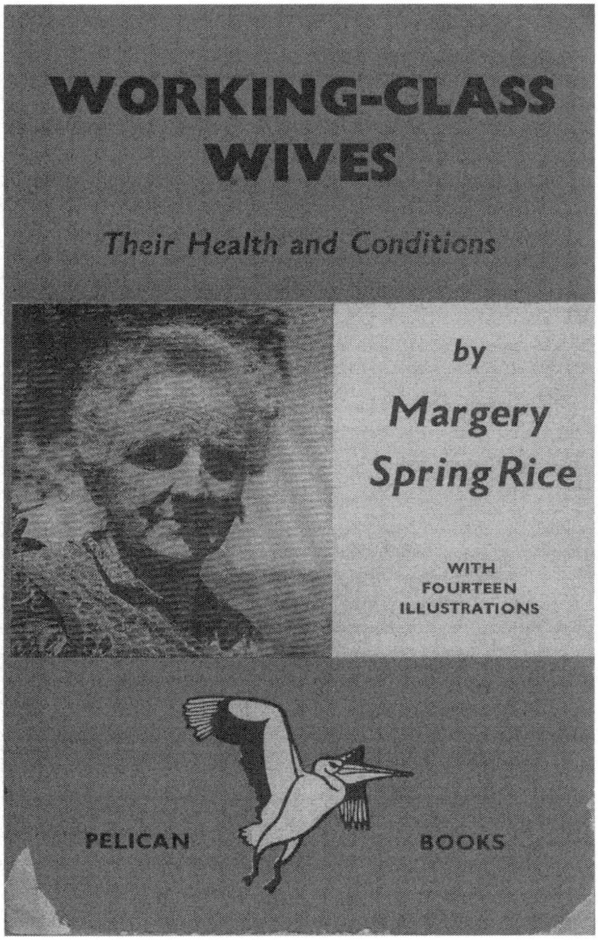

FIGURE 10.7: Margery Spring Rice. *Working-Class Wives: Their Health and Conditions*. Penguin Press, 1939, cover with photograph by Edith Tudor-Hart (© The Estate of Wolfgang Suschitzky).

and Conditions spoke to readers who at least were interested in (and perhaps also had sympathy for) the living conditions of socially marginalized people. But *Lilliput* reached a wide newspaper audience of different ages, genders and social origins. It was precisely in this spectrum of publications that Tudor-Hart's photographs were able to affect diverse social strata and sensitize them for the cause of disadvantaged people with a particular focus on gender-related issues (McGrath 2013, 123).

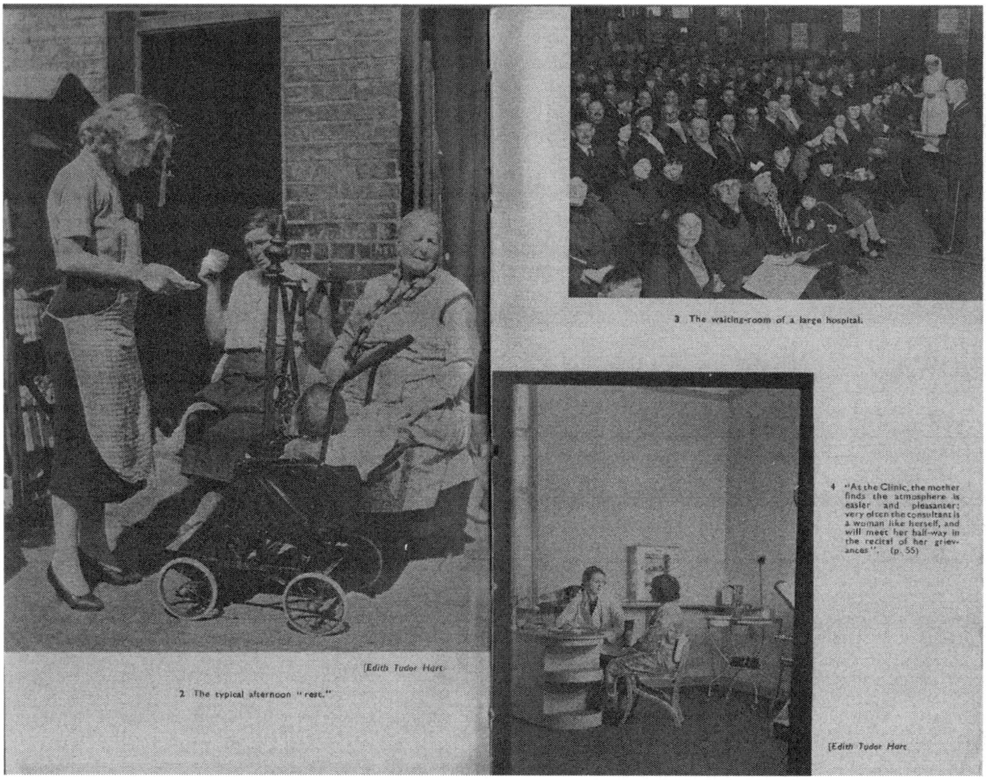

FIGURE 10.8: Margery Spring Rice. *Working-Class Wives: Their Health and Conditions*. Penguin Press, 1939, pl. 2–4, photographs by Edith Tudor-Hart (© The Estate of Wolfgang Suschitzky).

Queering exile studies – Challenges and perspectives

This chapter has put to the test various ways of accessing the topic of exile, urbanity, queerness and gender, while also pointing out some key challenges for future research on the topic. The very fact of exile is accompanied by loss: The exiles' personal property and artistic creations must often be left behind in their places of origin, for all too often flight means limiting oneself to what is necessary or essential for survival. As a result, parts of the emigrants' own history are lost. At the places of exile, the problem of preserving records and cultural heritage continues, for refugees in the 1930s and 1940s not only exchanged their home countries for but also frequently relocated within a city due to their uncertain economic situation. The exiles were also constantly haunted by the worry that compromising material could be discovered, for example by a potentially invading German army. The result was that often private documents were gotten rid of: a fact described, for instance, by Julia Eichenberg who refers to the private address books of emigrants; as everyday items, due to the scarcity of resources and size limits of luggage in emigration or remigration, address books were often discarded (Eichenberg 2019).[16]

The documentation of life in exile becomes even more fragmentary when it comes to queer emigrants: For here the need for an inconspicuous life that would not provoke the attention of authorities at the places of exile was particularly vital. Homosexuality was prosecuted, not only in London. Therefore it can be assumed that a homosexual life could take place only in secrecy, beyond heteronormative rules, and that any evidence of it had to be carefully eliminated. For there was undoubtedly serious concern that if an immigrant was arrested, their already uncertain residency status could be at greater risk. The challenge for research in exile studies is that hardly any source material is available. Naturally, there are exceptions: The preserved exile guestbook of German sexologist Magnus Hirschfeld is an important source delineating the routes and different stages of his emigration history. At the same time, the document offers valuable and rare insights into Hirschfeld's exilic networks, including queer networks (Bergemann et al. 2019).

Autobiographies such as by Kurt Hiller and Charlotte Wolff, both of them queer and exiled in London, provide an additional important point of access. Admittedly here, too, we need to stipulate that these should be read critically, including against the grain. After all, these are life stories that were meant for publication and which were probably carefully edited. An examination of the photographs of Edith Tudor-Hart has shown how important works or objects in particular are for a queer or gender-specific reading of creative work produced in exile. They point to continuities in the work of the photographer, who had already addressed social issues at a young age and continued to deal with them in emigration as well. At the same time, the photos also reveal a keen eye for London-specific themes and a familiarity with urban structures. Tudor-Hart's photos from London's East End backyards are full of empathy for the lives and living conditions of socially marginalized people. In them, Tudor-Hart primarily approaches young women, girls and children, whom – despite their adverse circumstances – she portrays as hopeful people who support each other.

Exile studies need to be more open to queer readings – a queering that not only critically questions conventional perspectives but one that also reveals gaps and absences which have hitherto not been the focus of research.

NOTES

1. Worth mentioning here is the *Insiders/Outsiders* Arts Festival, www. insidersoutsidersfestival.org. Accessed 1 April 2022, organized by Monica Bohm-Duchen, which is

representative for many additional and preceding research activities on artistic exile in Great Britain.

2. "Cottaging", i.e., sexual acts in public toilets, is discussed in the 1937 guidebook *For Your Convenience: A Learned Dialogue Instructive to all Londoners and London Visitors* (Pry 1937).
3. In this context, it is important to say that the flâneur also evokes sexual connotations: In feminist scholarship on the flâneur and female flâneuserie, the figure of the male flâneur is described "as the embodiment of the male gaze", who is able to observe and 'consume' women. See Elizabeth Wilson. "The Invisible Flâneur". *New Left Review*. 191, pp. 90–110, here p. 98. I would like to thank Jennifer Leetsch for this valuable information.
4. On the artistic or curatorial contemporary perspective see, for instance, www.thisisliveart.co.uk/opportunities/diy-15-2018-liz-rosenfeld-un-doing-cruising-practices/ and www.cruisingpavilion.com. Accessed 1 April 2022.
5. Adam de Hegedus published such books as *Hungarian Background* (1937), *The State of the World: Reflections on Peace and War in Our Time* (1946) or *Home and Away: Notes on England after the Second World War* (1951).
6. On police surveillance practices see also Ackroyd 2017, 213–217; Tamagne 2004, 392.
7. I would like to thank Harald Lützenkirchen of the Kurt Hiller Gesellschaft for this and additional information and for supporting my research on Kurt Hiller.
8. In 1921, there was an unsuccessful attempt to add a clause to the "Criminal Law Amendment Act 1885" that defined sexual relationships between women as a criminal offence. Cf. www.bl.uk/lgbtq-histories/lgbtq-timeline. Accessed 29 May 2020. To this day there has been no separate study on lesbians among the emigrants who came to London. However, Tamagne writes that many lesbians left National Socialist Germany and mentions, among others, the Jewish Berlin physician Charlotte Wolff, who came to London by way of Paris (Tamagne 2004, 395; see also Wolff 1982). There is an article on queer networks around Erica Anderson by Brunner 2019.
9. Matt Houlbrook argues that his gay history of "Queer London" cannot automatically be applied to lesbians (2005, 10). Turner, too, points out that "women's cruising", for instance, is a different matter (2003, 9).
10. Cf. Sibylle Duda. "Anna Freud." *FemBio*, www.fembio.org/biographie.php/frau/biographie/anna-freud/. Accessed 12 December 2020. On the relationship of Burlingham and Freud, see Burlingham 1989; Denker 1995, 44f.; Schmölzer 2009, 190–217.
11. www.tate.org.uk/art/artworks/moore-tube-shelter-perspective-n05709. Accessed 1 April 2022.
12. Jutta Vinzent points out that while women artists were certainly regularly represented in the group exhibitions of the Free German League of Culture, an emigrant association founded in London, they hardly ever had solo exhibitions (Vinzent 2006, 113). In recent years, the studies and publications of the working group Frauen im Exil (Women in Exile) in particular have been devoted to the life and work of émigré women. www.exilforschung.de. Accessed 1 April 2022. Jutta Vinzent's research was fundamental not only to the study

of the Free German League of Culture. Her passing in 2021 is a great loss for exile research. She will be greatly missed by all colleagues.

13. On Walter "Wal" Hannington, see www.spartacus-educational.com/TUhannington.htm. Accessed 1 April 2022.
14. The book was part of a series by the Left Book Club and was distributed to the members of the club by the London publishing house of Victor Gollancz Ltd.
15. It was not until later that it became known that Edith Tudor-Hart spied for the Soviet Union in England and played a key role in setting up a spy ring (Jungk 2015).
16. On address books as sources see Julia Eichenberg's article in this book.

REFERENCES

Abraham, Julie. *Metropolitan Lovers. The Homosexuality of Cities*. University of Minnesota Press, 2009.

Ackroyd, Peter. *Queer City. Gay London from the Romans to the Present Day*. Chatto & Windus, 2017.

Balducci, Temma. "Gender, Space, and the Gaze in Post-Haussmann Visual Culture." *Beyond the Flâneur*. Routledge, 2017.

Baudelaire, Charles. "Der Maler des modernen Lebens." 1863. Idem. *Der Künstler und das moderne Leben*, edited by Henry Schumann, Reclam, 1994, pp. 290–320.

Bergemann, Hans, et al., editors. *Magnus Hirschfelds Exil-Gästebuch 1933–1935*. Hentrich & Hentrich, 2019.

Bollauf, Traude. *Dienstmädchen-Emigration. Die Flucht jüdischer Frauen aus Österreich und Deutschland nach England 1938/39*. 2nd ed., Lit Verlag, 2011.

Brunner, Andreas. "Die queeren Netzwerke der Erica Anderson." *Doing Gender in Exile. Geschlechterverhältnisse, Konstruktionen und Netzwerke in Bewegung*, edited by Irene Messinger and Katharina Prager, Westfälisches Dampfboot, 2019, pp. 142–155.

Burlingham, Michael John. *The Last Tiffany. A Biography of Dorothy Tiffany Burlingham*. Antheneum/MacMillan, 1989.

Burton, Peter. "Biographical note." Rodney Garland. *The Heart in Exile. 1953*. Millivres Books, 1995, pp. 299f.

Chauncey, George. *Gay New York. Gender, Urban Culture, and the Making of the Gay Male World, 1890–1940*. Basic Books, 1994.

Cherry, Deborah, and Janice Helland, editors. *Local/Global: Women Artists in the Nineteenth Century*. Ashgate, 2006.

Cook, Matt. *London and the Culture of Homosexuality 1885–1914*. Cambridge University Press, 2003.

Crenshaw, Kimberlé. "Demarginalizing the Intersection of Race and Sex: A Black Feminist Critique of Antidiscrimination Doctrine, Feminist Theory and Antiracist Politics." *University of Chicago Legal Forum*, no. 1, 1989, pp. 139–167.

Crenshaw, Kimberlé. "Mapping the Margins: Intersectionality, Identity Politics, and Violence against Women of Color." *Stanford Law Review*, vol. 43, no. 6, 1991, pp. 1241–1299.

Denker, Rolf. *Anna Freud zur Einführung*, in collaboration with Friederike Denker, Junius, 1995.

Dietze, Gabriele. *Sexualpolitik. Verflechtungen von Race and Gender (Politik der Geschlechterverhältnisse, vol. 36)*. Campus, 2017.

Eichenberg, Julia. "London Calling. Adressbücher des britischen Exils im Zweiten Weltkrieg." *Zeithistorische Forschungen*, no. 2, 2019, www.zeithistorische-forschungen.de/2-2019/5734. Accessed 10 December 2020.

Eissler, K.R. "Eine biographische Skizze." *Sigmund Freud. Sein Leben in Bildern und Texten*. 1976, edited by Ernst L. Freud et al., Insel, 1989, pp. 10–39.

Fenstermaker, Sarah, and Candace West. "Doing Difference." *Gender and Society*, vol. 9, no. 1, 1995, pp. 8–37.

Forbes, Duncan. "Edith Tudor-Hart in London." *Edith Tudor-Hart. Im Schatten der Diktaturen*, edited by Duncan Forbes, exh. cat. National Galleries of Scotland, Edinburgh, Hatje Cantz, 2013, pp. 65–74.

Gardiner, Jill. *From the Closet to the Screen: Women at the Gateways Club 1945–85*. Pandora Press, 2003.

Garland, Rodney. *The Heart in Exile*. 1953. Millivres Books, 1995.

Gildemeister, Regine. "Doing Gender: Soziale Praktiken der Geschlechterunterscheidung." *Handbuch Frauen- und Geschlechterforschung: Theorie, Methoden, Empirie*. 3rd ed., edited by Ruth Becker and Beate Kortendiek, VS Verlag für Sozialwissenschaft, 2010, pp. 137–145.

Grosfuguel, Ramon, et al. "'Racism', Intersectionality and Migration Studies: Framing Some Theoretical Reflections." *Interrogating Intersectionalities, Gendering Mobilities, Racializing Transnationalism*, edited by Ramon Grofuguel et al., Routledge 2017, pp. 1–18.

Hammel, Andrea. "Jack Pritchard, Refugees from Nazism and Isokon Design." *Exile and Patronage: Cross-cultural Negotiations Beyond the Third Reich* (Mittel- und Ostmitteleuropastudien, 3), edited by Andrew Chandler et al., Lit Verlag, 2006, pp. 23–32.

Hannington, Wal. *The Problem of the Distressed Areas*. Left Book Club Edition, 1937.

Hartig, Christine. "Einwanderungsrecht und die Konstruktion von Geschlechterrollen. Die Situation von jüdischen Flüchtlingen in Großbritannien und den USA im Vergleich." *Doing Gender in Exile. Geschlechterverhältnisse, Konstruktionen und Netzwerke in Bewegung*, edited by Irene Messinger and Katharina Prager, Westfälisches Dampfboot, 2019, pp. 95–109.

Hiller, Kurt. *Leben gegen die Zeit*, vol. 2: *Eros*. Rowohlt, 1973.

Holzer, Anton. *Elly Niebuhr. Fotografin aus Wien. Alltag und Haute Couture*. Böhlau, 2009.

Horsley, Joey. "'Anders lieben ... andere Lust'. Nicht nur Männer haben Frauengeschichten. Vorwort." *Frauengeschichten. Berühmte Frauen und ihre Freundinnen*, edited by Joey Horsley and Luise F. Pusch, Wallstein, 2010, pp. 7–18.

Houlbrook, Matt. *Queer London. Perils and Pleasures in the Sexual Metropolis, 1918–1957*. The University of Chicago Press, 2005.

Houlbrook, Matt, and Chris Waters. "The Heart in Exile: Detachment and Desire in 1950s London." *History Workshop Journal*, no. 62, Autumn 2006, pp. 142–165.

Johler, Birgit. *Freud's Dining Room. Möbel bewegen Erinnerung. Furniture moves memory*, exh. cat. Österreichisches Museum für Volkskunde, Vienna, 2015.

Jungk, Peter Stephan. *Die Dunkelkammern der Edith Tudor-Hart. Geschichten eines Lebens*. S. Fischer, 2015.

Kennedy, Hansi. "Children in Conflict. Anna Freud and the War Nurseries." *The Psychoanalytic Study of the Child*, vol. 64, no. 1, 2016, pp. 306–319. *Taylor & Francis Online*, doi: 10.1080/00797308.2009.11800826. Accessed 4 June 2020.

Kumbier, Alana. *Ephemeral Material. Queering the Archive*. Litwin Books, 2014.

Küppers, Carolin. "Intersektionalität." *Gender Glossar*, 2014. www.gender-glossar.de/glossar/item/25-intersektionalitaet. Accessed 10 May 2021.

Lützenkirchen, Harald. "Auf Kurt Hillers Spuren in London." *Nachrichtenbrief der Kurt Hiller Gesellschaft e.V.*, no. 14, 2006, pp. 10–16.

McGrath, Roberta. "Pass Nummer 656336." *Edith Tudor-Hart. Im Schatten der Diktaturen*, edited by Duncan Forbes, exh. cat. National Galleries of Scotland, Edinburgh, 2013, pp. 119–125.

Messinger, Irene, and Katharina Prager. "Doing Gender, Doing Difference – Die interdependente Kategorie Geschlecht in der Exil- und Migrationsforschung." *Doing Gender in Exile. Geschlechterverhältnisse, Konstruktionen und Netzwerke in Bewegung*, edited by Irene Messinger and Katharina Prager, Westfälisches Dampfboot, 2019, pp. 7–28.

Münzner, Daniel. *Kurt Hiller. Der Intellektuelle als Außenseiter*. Wallstein Verlag, 2015.

Pry, Paul [Thomas Burke]. *For Your Convenience: A Learned Dialogue Instructive to all Londoners and London Visitors, Overheard at the Thélème Club and Taken Down Verbatim*. G. Routledge & Sons, 1937.

Schmölzer, Hilde. *Frauenliebe: Berühmte weibliche Liebespaare der Geschichte*. Promedia, 2009.

Schoppmann, Claudia. "'Das Exil war eine Wiedergeburt für mich.' Zur Situation lesbischer Frauen im Exil." *Sprache – Identität – Kultur: Frauen im Exil (Exilforschung. Ein internationales Jahrbuch*, vol. 17), edited by Claus-Dieter Krohn et al., edition text + kritik, 1999, pp. 140–151.

Simmons, Jeffrey. "Afterword." *The Heart in Exile*, edited by Rodney Garland, 1953, Millivres Books 1995, pp. 297f.

Spring Rice, Margery. *Working-Class Wives. Their Health and Conditions*. Penguin Press, 1939.

Suschitzky, Edith [Edith Tudor-Hart]. "Der Markt des nackten Elends." *Der Kuckuck*, 1931, p. 15.

Tamagne, Florence. *History of Homosexuality in Europe*, vols. 1 & 2: *Berlin, London, Paris 1919–1939*, Algora Publishing, 2004.

Trumbach, Randolph. "London." *Queer Sites. Gay Urban Histories Since 1600*, edited by David Higgs, Routledge 1999, pp. 89–111.

Tudor-Hart, Edith. *Das Auge des Gewissens* (Das Foto-Taschenbuch, 6). Dirk Nishen Verlag, 1986.

Turner, Mark W. *Backward Glances. Cruising the Queer Streets of New York and London.* Reaktion Books, 2003.

Vinzent, Jutta. *Identity and Image. Refugee Artists from Nazi Germany in Britain (1933–1945)* (Schriften der Guernica-Gesellschaft, 16). VDG, 2006.

West, Candace, and Don H. Zimmerman. "Doing Gender." *Gender and Society*, vol. 1, no. 2, June 1987, pp. 125–151.

Wolff, Charlotte. *Augenblicke verändern uns mehr als die Zeit. Eine Autobiographie*. Translated by Michaela Huber, Beltz, 1982.

Zwerger, Veronika. "Österreicherin im Haushalt: The Periodical of Austrian Domestics. Überlegungen zu den Arbeits- und Lebensbedingungen der österreichischen Hausgehilfinnen in England." *Exile and Gender I: Literature and the Press* (Yearbook of the Research Centre for German and Austrian Exile Studies, 17), edited by Charmian Brinson and Andrea Hammel, Brill Rodopi, 2016, pp. 220–236.

PART III

MAPPING/SPATIALIZING SITES

11

Theatre After the End of Theatre: Abandoned Theatres in Chile

Valentina Pino Reyes

I begin this text with a childhood memory – a memory of family trips to Valparaíso and visits to the traditional craft markets there.

Eighteen years later, when I visit again, there is not much left of the traditional handicraft that had once filled the market. When I look closely at the place with its exuberant decoration and the many cuddly animals on sale, I realize for the first time that I am in an old theatre. I begin to ask myself questions about the history and transformation of the place. The question of why and how the theatre space

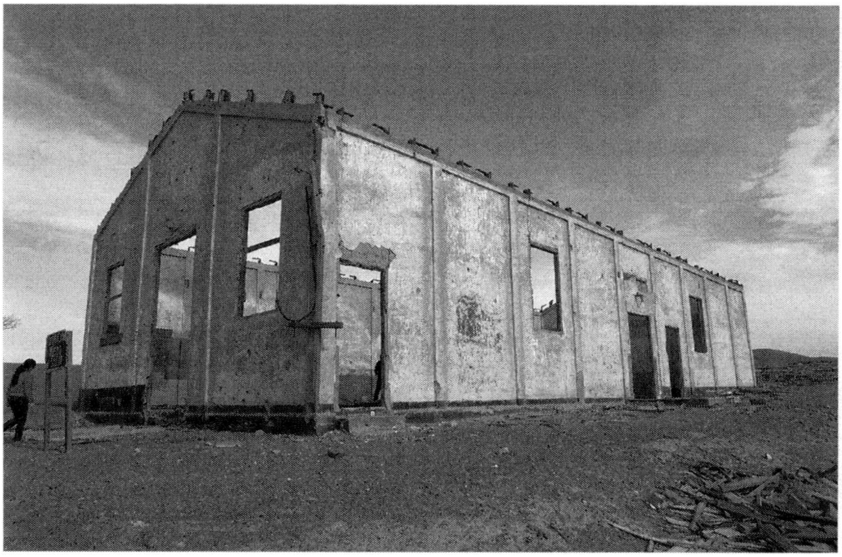

FIGURE 11.1: *Teatro Oficina Salitrera Peña Blanca*, Tarapaca, Pozo al Monte (© Valentina Pino Reyes).

had been transformed into a marketplace was the beginning of a long search for abandoned theatres all over Chile.[1]

European emigrants are considered the main founders of Chile's theatres. During the first decades of the 19th century and the colonization of large parts of the country, more and more theatres were built. This resulted in different, hybrid, peculiar architectures – the concepts the émigrés brought with them were adapted to the geography and the building practices they discovered in Chile.[2] This history has barely been dealt with so far. Therefore, I began a search for transformed venues, their photographic documentation and research into the history of these places. The medium of photography affords me the opportunity to capture specific architectures in different climates and their transformation, and to give these places a different, new artistic identity and visibility.

Along my travel route I meet different people, either spontaneously or preplanned, who share their knowledge with me. The numerous interviews and narratives, I collected and recorded along the way line up to form a heterogeneous collection of stories and have grown into a multi-layered, oral archive that, alongside the photographic exploration, forms the starting point of my narrative about (abandoned) theatre sites.[3]

Theatre and madness

The first known theatre in Santiago was probably built in 1896 as part of the first psychiatric institute: Teatro Grez is now part of the Jose Horwitz Barak Psychiatric Institute. Since that time, it has had different functions: as a place for the sick to stay and as a place for entertainment and theatre. Today, some of the theatre rooms are used as a laundry. Paintings inside the theatre refer to European theatre history.[4] Portraits of famous European playwrights, such as Molière, Goethe, Shakespeare, Homer, Dante, Vergil, Lope de Vega and Calderón de la Barca look down from the walls, joined by two allegories of muses. To get inside, the path leads through the gardens of the psychiatric institute, where the patients can walk around. The motif of "madness", of those who are segregated from society and the theatre, has received attention and research in many ways. Here, the spatial boundaries are fluid and tell a common story.

Transformation in the desert

North of Santiago, the Atacama Desert holds ruins and traces of about 217 saltpeter offices including settlements. It can be assumed that many settlements had a theatre. Today, about 60 theatres have been safely preserved.[5] Their fragments point to a brutal history. They bear witness to the atrocities of Pinochet's military dictatorship, which used the abandoned saltpeter settlements and out-of-sight ghost towns as remote concentration camps.[6] Today, the desert is reclaiming these places, indiscriminately covering the ruins under growing layers of sand. Many of these places and theatres have been destroyed, others lie in ruins or are buried under the surface. During my research, I meet Georgina Pastene. She works for the Saltpeter Museum Corporation and is the director of the saltpeter offices in Humberston and Santa Laura. Both are now open-air museums. She shows me the former venues and from her I learn about other places that are impossible to find without her knowledge.

She explains to me the 'golden rule' that can be used to find a former theatre: "Where there was a tennis court, we will find a theatre" (Pastene 2019). There are no financial resources for systematic archaeological excavations, so I become a spectator of Georgina's daily performance. She wears surgical gloves, digs in the sand and hopes to find traces of the former theatre life. Her stories are a treasure and tell of a lively past. Above all, she sensitizes me to another hitherto unexplored chapter in the history of abandoned theatres. She talks about the central role of women in the realization and staging of the plays performed in the saltpeter settlements.

Multifunctional theatre

As the saltpeter business dwindled, the towns and their theatres also began to disappear. But it was only after the military coup in 1973 and the beginning of Pinochet's dictatorship that the theatres and theatre life with their protagonists finally fully disappeared. Chilean researchers discuss this dictatorial strategy under the term 'Apagon Cultural'.[7] In the last 30 years, after the end of the dictatorship, the theatres underwent a transformation and are now used in many ways: As Protestant churches, discotheques, banks, restaurants, craft fairs, car dealerships, mechanical workshops or car parks. The legendary Teatro Huemul in Santiago's Barrio Franklin,[8] which played an important role during the NO political campaign in the late 1980s,[9] is now in the hands of the Archbishop of Santiago. Despite several letters and requests, I unfortunately did not receive permission to enter and photograph the theatre. Now, Sunday masses, commercial parties and wrestling matches take place there. Other formerly well-known theatres were severely damaged by earthquakes, such as the Teatro Enrique Molina in the coastal town of Concepción.[10] Built in neoclassical style, it suffered through two major earthquakes and tsunamis, including the 1960 earthquake, considered the strongest earthquake on record in the world as yet.

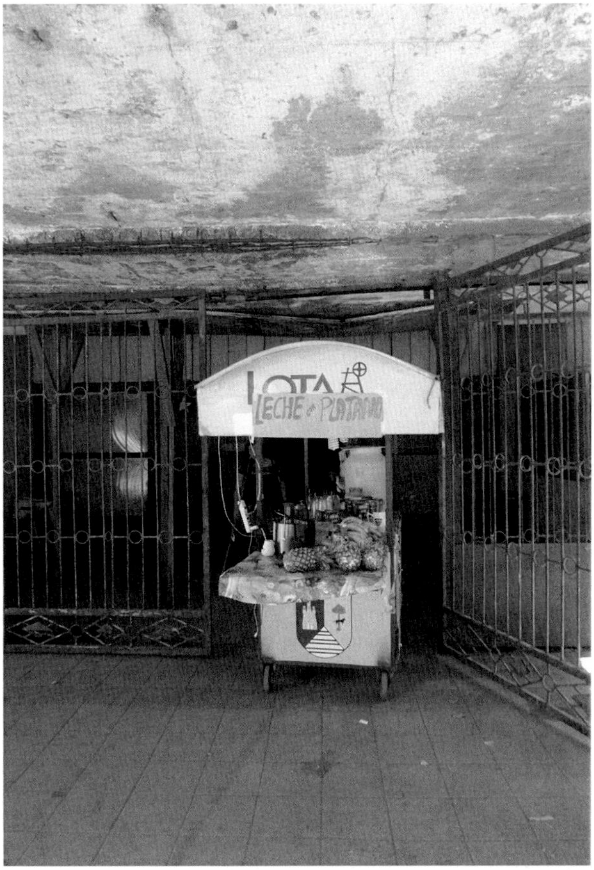

FIGURE 11.2: Teatros de los Mineros de Lota, Bio-Bio Lota (© Valentina Pino Reyes).

Industry and theatre – N6 Union Theatre of the Miners of Lota

The theatres had a special social and political function in the context of the trade unions. The former miners' theatre in Lota played a prominent role in the cultural life of Lota.

I meet José Carrillo,[11] who managed the last coal mines that were in operation until 1998. He shows me the badly damaged theatre, which looks more like a ruin. The decline of this institution began with the military coup in 1973: the theatre was occupied by the military regime and even years after the coup the miners had difficulties to recover their theatre. The former foyer is now a warehouse for street vending carts used in the old town. The planning of the theatre reflected working class ideals. In 1954, it was built for 1,400 spectators. Multipurpose rooms or workshops for the miners' families and children were important parameters of the

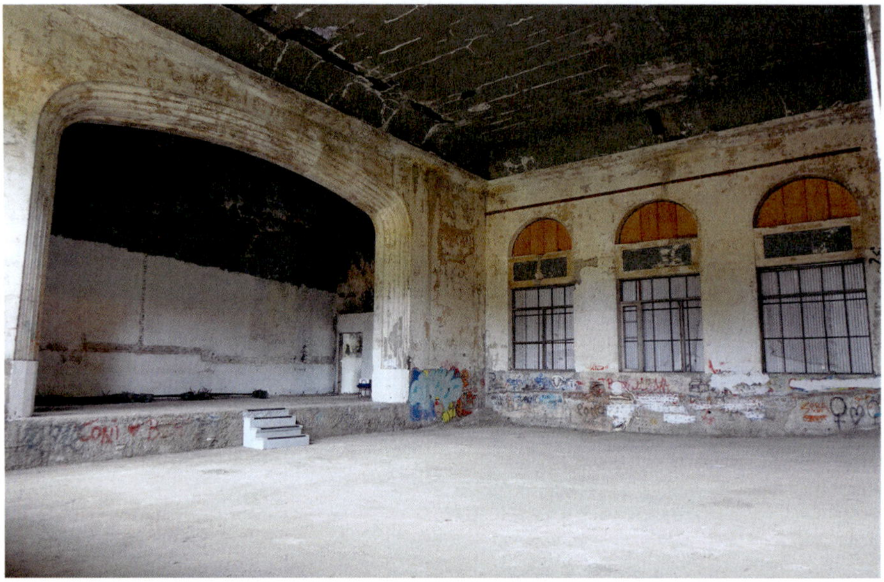

FIGURE 11.3: Teatro Enrique Molina, Concepción (© Valentina Pino Reyes).

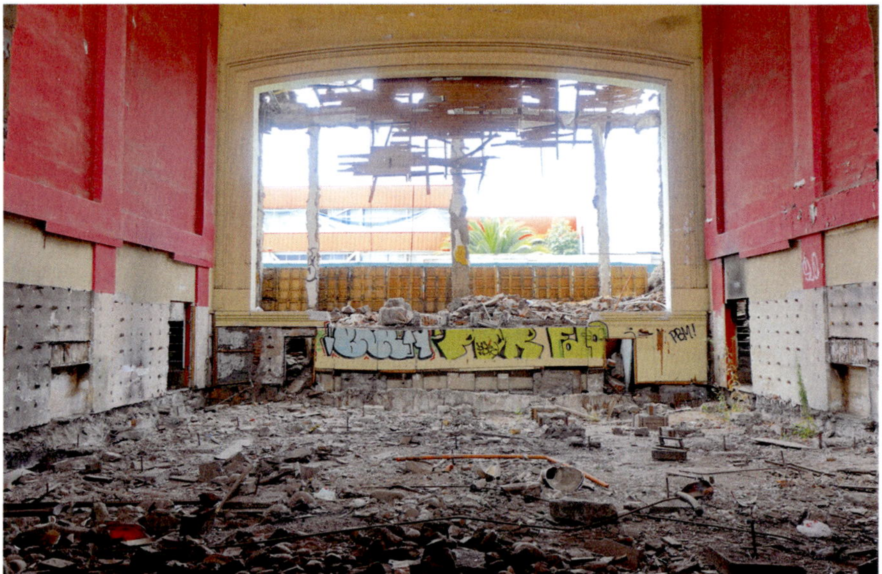

FIGURE 11.4: Teatro Victoria, Maule Cúrico (© Valentina Pino Reyes).

architectural concept. It was conceived and built by a group of Chilean-German architects as a cultural and community centre.[12] The current state of the miners' theatre can be understood as a symbol for structural and political change. The ruins of the theatre read like fading traces of former ideals and the cultural life of the miners.

Valparaíso, a jewel of the Pacific – From theatre to market

Between the 19th and the 20th century, Valparaíso was one of the most important port cities in South America. Declared a World Heritage Site by UNESCO in 2003, the city looks back on an eventful history. Each of its hills had its own theatre, of

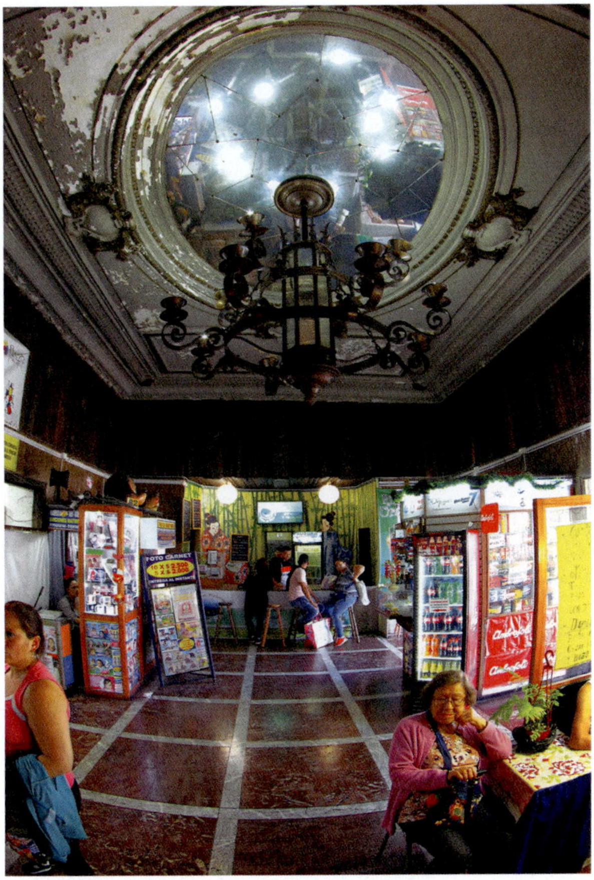

FIGURE 11.5: Teatro Imperio, Valparaiso, Valparaiso (© Valentina Pino Reyes).

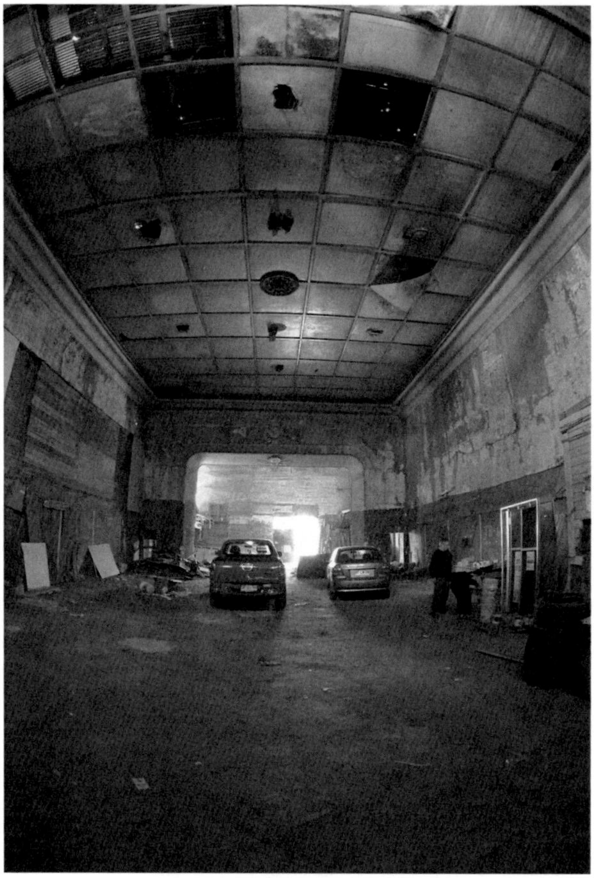

FIGURE 11.6: Teatro Odeon, Valparaiso, Playa Ancha (© Valentina Pino Reyes).

which only a few remain today. Many of the townspeople I ask, be it the fishermen of Caleta Portales or a primary school teacher, talk about the great general esteem in which the theatres were once held. Among them is the Teatro Imperio, which was built about a hundred years ago. Since then, it has reinvented itself for the third time – first as a cinema, then as a church and finally as a craft market. In 2012, a fire caused severe damage. I meet Ms Isabel, caretaker, landlord and sole cleaner of the Teatro Imperio's gents. She tells me she is proud to have worked at the Teatro for fifteen years and to be able to finance her children's university studies. She tells me about her special relationship with this place and recounts her memories when she visited the theatre as a spectator. She bought cheap tickets for seats she calls the *gallineros*. She recalls a lively place, best suited for eating, drinking, smoking and flirting.[13] After the fire, the theatre was restored by the traders, raffle organizers and hotdog vendors of the artisan market. Isabel spent over one month removing the layer of soot that permeated the foyer. Financial resources for restoration are lacking.

Se Vende

The maintenance and care or restoration of the many privately owned theatres is often beyond the financial means of the owners. Recognition as cultural heritage sites is not possible in their dilapidated condition. So, they are often sold, burnt or demolished. It is therefore not uncommon for theatres to be advertised for sale, such as the Teatro Odeon in Playa Ancha in the Valparaiso region.[14] The owners wish to remain anonymous and do not want to be interviewed. I am not allowed

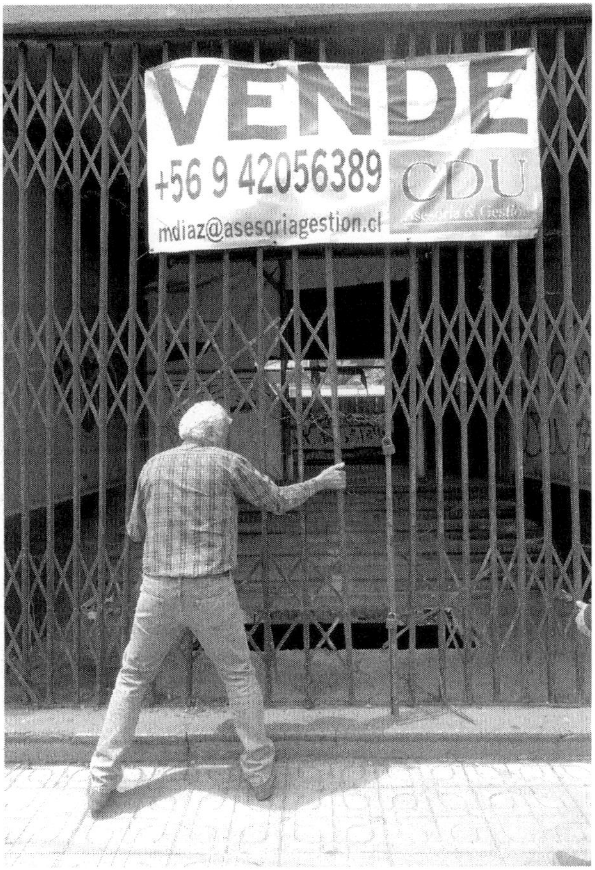

FIGURE 11.7: *Teatro Victoria and owner*, Maule, Curico (© Valentina Pino Reyes).

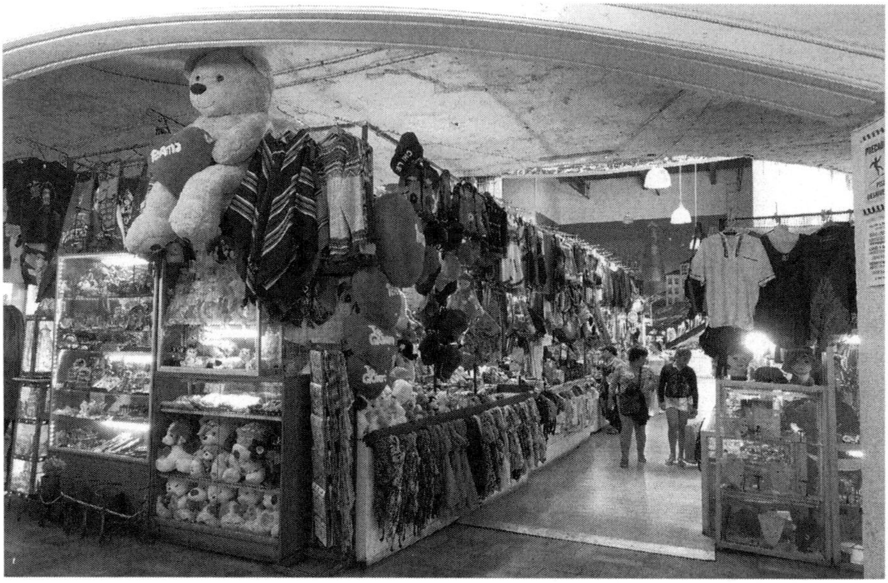

FIGURE 11.8: *Teatro Imperio*, Valparaiso, Valparaiso (© Valentina Pino Reyes).

to visit the theatre site, at least at first. Together with a friend, I pretend to be a prospective buyer and contacted the real estate agent. My friend plays the buyer, I act as his interpreter and an appointment on site is made.

The Teatro Odeon has undergone some transformations in recent years. For a long time, it was a workshop, today it is used as a car park. Part of the theatre is underground. The stalls with the original seats are buried, as is the former theatre culture. Nevertheless, in many places these people are fighting to preserve the theatres, including the community of Playa Ancha.[15] Almost a year after my trip the Playanchinxs have now organized a solidarity campaign and are collecting donations. The theatre is still for sale – for 300,000 Euros. So far, the Playanchinxs have received about 3,000 Euros in their first month and hope to raise the sum to buy the theatre at some point.

Overview

Chile has a lively and large theatre scene. The theatre festival *Teatro a mil* is one of the most important international theatre meetings. Every year, artists from Germany, among other countries, are invited. Lines of tradition from the time of colonization and the emergence of the many theatres, of which only a few have been presented here, are continued and are still present in this immaterial way. The transformations of the historical theatre sites were and still are largely politically and economically motivated. As theatre regains its status as an important cultural site of exchange, and as initiatives of individuals and communities and their relationship to the (abandoned) venues proliferate, it becomes crucial to visualize the history of theatre in Chile – its places and its people. The interrelationship between people or society and their theatres tells a common story. These places can reconnect people to their history. With my photographic work and research, I try to make this dynamic visible – to address loss and forgetting, but also to remind us of the beauty of these places, which is closely interwoven with the people and their history.

NOTES

1. Between December 2018 and early March 2019, I travelled across the 4,000 kilometres of Chile: a country of climate extremes and marked by great cultural and socio-economic differences.
2. The theatres that were built in the 19th century in the coastal areas and in the major ports were soon accepted by Chilean society of the time and created a boom in the world of theatre. Curiously, until 1950, it was not easy to distinguish between a theatre and a cinema building, as they were used for both artistic means (Courtois 1994).
3. A comprehensive registration and documentation of former venues built during the 19th century has not yet been done. The starting point for my search was the research of Alberto Prado Díaz (Prado Díaz 2012) and 21 theatres for which the Consejo de monumentos Nacionales de Chile (CMN) has information. Georgina Pastene, the museum director of the Saltpetre Museum Corporation in Humberstone and Santa Laura, estimates the number of theatres in the desert at 120. It is likely that there are far more in total.
4. Not much is known about the frescoes; I learned on site that they were painted in 1904.
5. This is known thanks to the research of Alberto Prado Díaz (Prado Díaz 2012).
6. Patricio Guzmán explored the desert as a place of memory in the documentary *Nostalgia de la Luz* (2010).
7. Read more: Richard (2011, 38). Or: Vásquez/Saavedra Utman (2015, 295).
8. Barrio Franklin is a neighbourhood in Santiago de Chile: the historic business district features 4,500 businesses, among them mainly workshops, small businesses, retail shops, factory and market halls. Life in the neighbourhood is linked to the construction of the slaughterhouse in 1847, which closed its doors during the 1979 crisis. In 1982, Santiago's city council gave the shack-like buildings to street vendors and the typical *persas* (bazaars) emerged, offering a wide variety of (antiquarian) products and services. Cf. "El Barrio Matadero-Franklin (1847–2007)." *Memoria Chilena, Biblioteca National de Chile*, www.memoriachilena.gob.cl. Accessed 15 December 2020.

9. 'NO' refers to a political advertising campaign against the Pinochet regime: The 1988 referendum in Chile was held on Wednesday, 5 October 1988, during the military dictatorship. The referendum was to decide on the continuation of the military dictatorship under Augusto Pinochet or on the admission of alternative presidential candidates. The 'NO' option chosen by the majority meant that Augusto Pinochet was not allowed to stand as the only candidate in the election. As a result, Pinochet was replaced as president by Patricio Aylwin on 11 March 1990. Cf. Valdés et al. (1989).
10. The theatre was built between 1929 and 1935 and was attached to the men's high school Enrique Molina Garmendia Gymnasium and later to Liceo de Concepción or Liceo de Hombres No. 1 de Concepción. The school was founded in 1823 and is considered the third oldest grammar school in Chile. See "Historia de Concepción: 1550–1970." *Memoria Chilena, Biblioteca National de Chile*, www.memoriachilena.gob.cl. Accessed 15 December 2020.
11. The president of the miners' union of Lota.
12. The architects involved in the construction of the theatre in 1954 were: Sergio Bravo Ramos, Javier "Maco" Gutiérrez, Betty Fischman Lohaus and Carlos Martner. The construction of the theatre was a project of the Faculty of Architecture of the University of Chile. Betty Fischman Lohaus and Sergio Bravo Ramos describe the project as follows: During the design, we set out to harmonise the main axes of the spaces for the interior with the environment of urban life: The privileged location facing the harbour square helped to highlight the symbolic character of the building. Thus, was born the system of external staircases, the double stage open to the square, the mural alluding to mining life on its main façade [...]. In the mid-1950s, amidst the euphoria caused by the unity of the Chilean trade union movement with the creation of the Central Unica de Trabajadores, the miners of Lota undertook to finance the construction of the theatre with their resources [...]. (Private Archive of Jose Carillo)
13. The term *gallinero* actually refers to a chicken coop and was used for cheap and therefore popular theatre seats.
14. It was built, it is said, by a family of German immigrants in 1875.
15. Through its website, the Odeon Theatre community collects donations and provides information: www.teatroodeon.cl/.

REFERENCES

Consejo de monumentos Nacionales de Chile (CMN).

Courtois, Juan Benavides, et al. *Ciudades y arquitectura portuaria: los puertos mayores del litoral chileno*. Editorial Universitaria, 1994.

Courtois, Juan Benavides , et al. "Arquitectura de los puertos mayores del litoral chileno." *De Arquitectura*, no. 6, 1995, pp. 2–7. *Repositoria Académico de la Universidad de Chile*, doi: 10.5354/0719-5427.1995.30506. Accessed 21 January 2020.

Diaz, Patricio. *Informe teatros y Filarmonicas Salitreras*. PhD dissertation, Universidad de Chile, 2014.

Fuentes Gonzalez, Alejandra, and Ximena Gallardo Saint-Jean. *Teatro Grez. Locura y Arte.* Consejo Nacional de la Cultura y de las Artes, 2014, pp. 7–81. *Academia*, www.academia.edu/20148682/TeatroGrezLocurayArte. Accessed 17 July 2021.

Pastene, Georgina. Personal Interview by Valentina Pino Reyes. Maria Elena, Antofagasta. January 2019.

Prado Díaz, Alberto. *Los Teatros del Desierto: producción del espacio durante el ciclo del salitre Chile 1830–1979*. Doctoral thesis, Universidad Politècnica de Catalunya, 2012, www.hdl.handle.net/2117/94687. Accessed 17 July 2021.

Private Archive.Jose Carillo, Lota.

Richard, Nelly. *Lo político y lo crítico en el arte Artistas mujeres bajo la dictadura en Chile* (IVAM documentos iberoamericanos, 2). IVAM Institut Valencià d'Art Modern, 2011.

Valdés, Juan Gabriel, et al., editors. *La Campaña del NO. Vista por sus creadores* [Conference publication, "La Campaña del NO. Análisis y Perspectivas", Santiago, 24–25 November 1988]. Editiones Melquiades, 1989. *Memoria Chilena, Biblioteca Nacional de Chile*, www.memoriachilena.gob.cl/602/w3-article-85817.html. Accessed 17 July 2021.

Vásquez, Mario Poblete, and Jorge Saavedra Utman. "Theatres in the Intimate Chile of the 20th Century. A Sociological Approach from a Local History." *Revista Atenea*, no. 512, 2015, pp. 285–302. *Scielo Chile*, www.scielo.conicyt.cl/pdf/atenea/n512/art16.pdf. Accessed 17 July 2021.

12

Redeveloping the Heritage of Migration: The Shanghai Jewish Refugees Museum and Urban Transformation

Xin Tong

Introduction

The exodus of European Jewish refugees to China, especially to the port city Shanghai during the Second World War, interwove various historical events, world regions and collective memories. For the past decades, the topic has drawn increasing academic and public attention in countries such as Germany, Austria, Israel, China, Japan and the USA (Kranzler 1976; Armbrüster et al. 2000; Zhuang 2015). Meanwhile, the history of Jewish exile in Shanghai has been widely reconstructed in various media – from scientific and literary publications to cinematic, exhibited or artistic representations as well as digital and online productions. In this transcultural process of remembrance and remediation, Jewish history in Shanghai has become a matter of active and functional memory (Assmann 2008) that is continuously kept alive and transmitted to future generations.

With the heterogeneous cultures of memory of Jewish exile in Shanghai in mind, this paper focusses on the case of the Shanghai Jewish Refugees Museum in China. The museum not only functions as a unique example of an exhibitionary institution's involvement in the commemoration of global migration and exile history but also raises a series of questions regarding the preservation, restoration and utilization of bygone Jewish presence in a contemporary Chinese metropolis. While topics like the museum's exhibition narratives, branding strategies and cultural policies have been addressed by different scholars (Zhang/Wang 2011; Pan 2014; Michaels 2017), the role and function of the museum itself as a medium and its specific mediatized memory work of Jewish exile, has not yet been fully explored.

By proposing a process-oriented media approach of cultural memory studies, or, to be more precise, by approaching the 'media milieu' of this museum as memory work, the following chapter traces the course of the development of the Shanghai Jewish Refugees Museum along with processes of Shanghai's urbanization (particularly in its former ghetto) and investigates the entwinements of exile and urbanity, global migration history and local memory practices.

Museums as mediatized memory works and their media milieus

Within the last decade, the discipline of cultural memory studies has increasingly perceived memory as an ongoing process and has shifted its focus towards the "dynamics of memory and its global remediation" (Brunow 2015, 2). Remembering the past, which is conceived of either as general historic knowledge or as specific collective experience and memory, necessitates certain media that document, store, represent and pass on historical events. Hence, despite the internal heterogeneity within scholarship, cultural memory studies can be understood as a field that focuses on questions of media and mediatization in the construction of the past (Erll 2017). As Jan Assmann puts it, "the history of memory is in this perspective the history of its media" (Assmann 2002, 414).

Based on the heightened awareness of the close relations between the "media boom" and the "memory boom" (Hoskins/O'Loughlin 2010), cultural memory research requires a broader understanding of media. When proposing a media–theoretical approach, it is therefore not primarily a question of "what" exactly a medium is, but rather "how" it functions at different times and in varying ways within specific social contexts and remembering processes (Pethes 2008, 15). This requires a theoretical and methodological shift away from traditional 'text analysis'[1] and conditional production or reception research[2] towards a process-oriented media approach. This alternative view should come from a broader, but not unlimited understanding of media that brings together technical–material dimensions with institutional and social dimensions. Meanwhile, such an alternative approach should also be able to describe the layering, diversification and interconnectivity of various media in the process of mediating cultural memory, without losing sight of each individual medium at the same time.

The starting point for such an approach is the concept of the "media milieu" (Weber 2017), which does not ask how a medium should be defined, but places emphasis on the interaction of actors (both human and non-human actors in the sense of Latour's Actor-Network-Theory, Latour 2002) within a media field. The term 'media milieu' does not refer to a static status, but to the processes and the dynamics of media:

> In the following, the term 'milieu' does not only refer to the members of a certain professional or activity group, but rather includes their networking with other industrial segments and in this respect not just a processing or a transformation in general, but rather the processuality of working processes, which should be understood as across several industrial segments.
>
> (Weber 2017, 13)

Here, Weber conceptually extends the category of media and takes into account the procedural character of mediatization, which includes "craft-technical forms of processing as well as forms of connectivity, cooperation and collaboration" (ibid., 16). As a result, the various actors, dimensions of media and their interplays are integrated into the term of 'media milieu'. Based on Weber's process-oriented view, we can further differentiate three general phases of communicative and cooperative working processes of a mediatized work: the production, the distribution and the reception process (fig. 12.1).

In each phase, actors – personnel, technical-material, institutional or social actors – and their interactions during the working processes should be taken into consideration. This does not mean lumping everything together and handling them simultaneously, but rather points to the weighting of crucial actors in the relevant media field and in each working process. The dynamics of a media milieu therefore do not just apply to the procedural nature of the working processes but also encompass the fact that these actors, processes and mediatized end products

	production	distribution	reception
actors			
working processes			
end products			

FIGURE 12.1: Media milieu of a mediatized work (Model and illustration: Xin Tong, 2020).

are dynamically intertwined, correlate with one another and can freely circulate within and beyond their media milieu.[3]

Thus, in the context of cultural memory and its remediation processes, mediatized memory works themselves – be they a novel, film, comic, painting, photograph, performance, exhibition, online portal or hologram (re-)presenting the past – can be regarded as dynamic media milieus instead of a static media 'text'. Through cross-milieu and cross-media networking, these seemingly incoherent and structureless memory works emerge as composed, constructed and connected: Only such a mediatized and socially communicative remembering process of selection, connection and reconstruction can make possible society's appropriation of cultural and functional memory.

With this perspective, museums that preserve, construct and exhibit the past can no longer be perceived as just as a static medium. In this sense, museums are mediatized memory works with procedural and dynamic character. They consist of their own distinctive media milieus, yet they are also able to correlate, intersect and overlap with the media milieus of other memory works, as long as there are shared actors and working processes such as archival documents and old photos as exhibits, historiographical books by researchers affiliated with museums or artistic projects sponsored by museums. Taking into account such milieu-concepts, the processuality of media can be traced back to their concrete actors, working processes and end products, and the mediatization process of memory can be illuminated by exploring the interplays and entanglements among those media milieus.

In the case of the Shanghai Jewish Refugees Museum, when examined through the lens of a process-oriented approach of media milieu, the focus lies not on the analysis of what has been 'said' and 'remembered' – that is, the aesthetics and contents at play within the museum's exhibitions –, but rather on investigating processes of 'saying' and 'remembering' (Köhr 2012). In the following, this chapter takes a closer look at some significant actors and working processes in the media milieu of the Shanghai Jewish Refugees Museum, in order to discuss how exile memory is restored in the working processes of the museum and how these actors shape Shanghai's modern urban space and cultural identity.

Jewish heritage in Shanghai's urban planning and development

Parry describes the media specifics of museums as following: "Museums, after all, are a medium – in their most common state a unique, three dimensional, multi-sensory, social medium in which knowledge is given spatial form" (Parry 2007, 11). One of the essential actors in the media milieu of the Shanghai Jewish Refugees

Museum are its infrastructures which provide archive, research, exhibition, interaction and resonance spaces for both its producers and spectators.

In the late 1990s, the museum was established at the Ohel Moshe Synagogue and further expanded in subsequent years. The synagogue is located in the former ghetto area in Shanghai's Hongkou district. In 2002, this area was officially listed as a heritage site, including the Ohel Moshe Synagogue and other historical buildings such as the American Jewish Joint Distribution Committee (JDC). As a consequence, the entire area gained exhibitionary character and can be seen as part of the Shanghai Jewish Refugees Museum. Visitors to the museum can tour the ghetto to get an idea of its historic location and spatiality (figs. 12.2 and 12.3). While the museum also consists of several exhibition halls and "is still developing its space and its collection" (Michaels 2017, 211), one of its key aspects has always been the historical architecture of the Ohel Moshe, which once acted as a spiritual centre for the European Jewish refugees living in this area and which nowadays serves to "highlight the importance of place as a rhetorical trope to forge links between the past and the present" (ibid.). The Ohel Moshe Synagogue is one of only two remaining Jewish synagogues in Shanghai today – the other is the Ohel Rachel Synagogue in the former French Concession in the city centre.

Questions of how to deal with Jewish heritage in the city, especially with concerning Jewish synagogues, were intractable problems for the local authorities

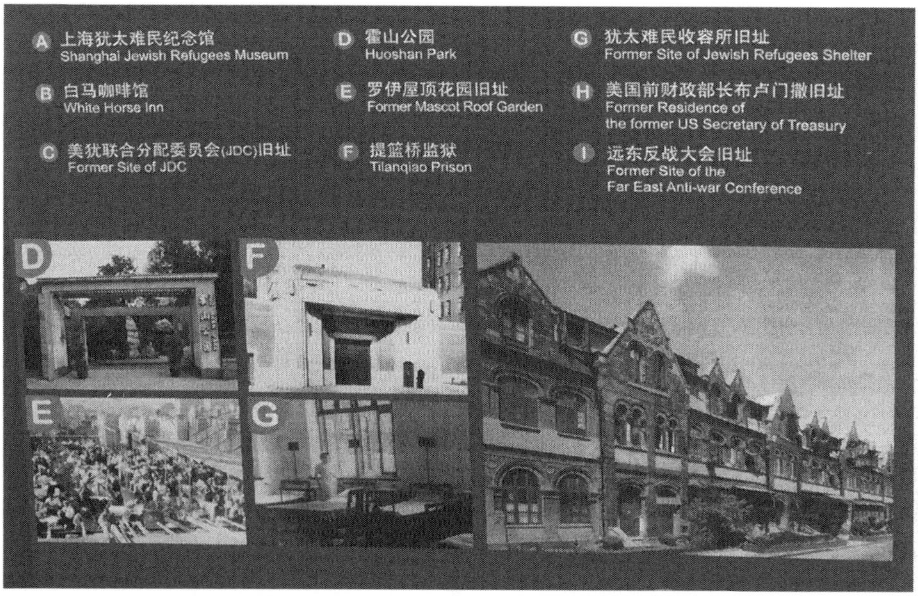

FIGURE 12.2: Shanghai Jewish refugees museum, *Tour Scenic Spots in the Surrounding*, first part, District Hongkou, Shanghai (Photo: Xin Tong, 2017).

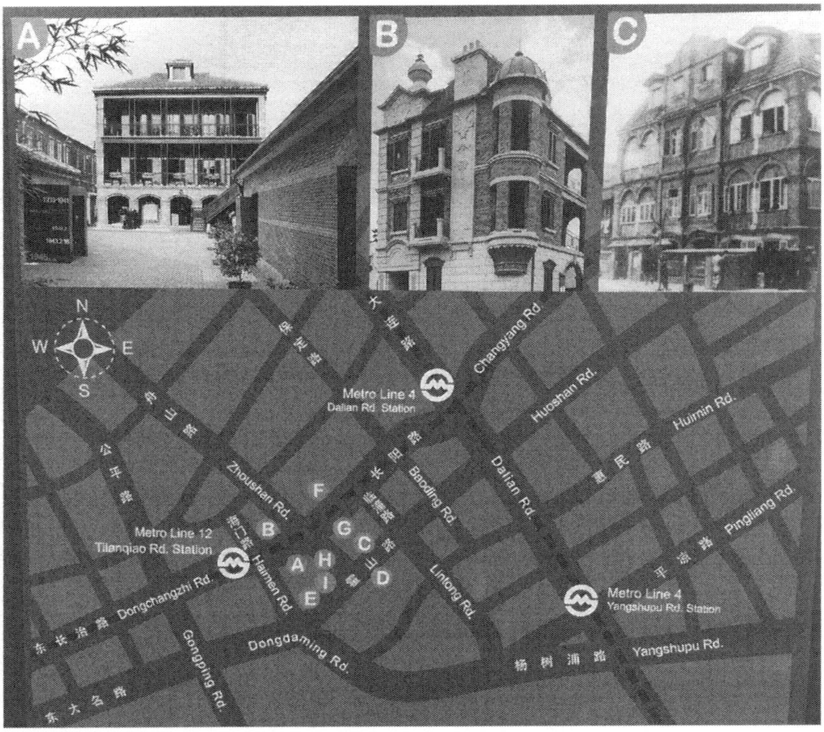

FIGURE 12.3: Shanghai Jewish refugees museum, *Tour Scenic Spots in the Surrounding*, second part, District Hongkou, Shanghai (Photo: Xin Tong, 2017).

in the beginning phase of the memory practices of the museum, as Jakubowicz summarizes:

> In the mid-1990s, the Shanghai authorities began to notice an increasing pressure to recognize the Jewish history of the city. They had to clean up the front and inside of the Ohel Rachel in expectation of a visit by President Bill Clinton – in actuality it was Hillary and Madeleine Albright who turned up, and the synagogue had become a matter of international diplomacy. The synagogue building remains an unresolved question – the Chabad want it to be returned to Jewish control and reopened as a working Orthodox synagogue; the Shanghai government does not want to lose control; the Shanghai Academy would quite like it as a museum and fundraiser, and for it to be made available occasionally for Jewish ceremonies. But as Judaism is not recognized, it is difficult for any government body to license a Jewish religious building.
>
> (Jakubowicz 2009, 165)

In comparison to the Ohel Rachel Synagogue, which was uninhabited and eventually became a cultural monument used for rare political and religious occasions, the preservation of the Ohel Moshe Synagogue along with the whole former ghetto area was imbued with much greater complexity.

After Shanghai's Jewish refugees either emigrated elsewhere or returned to Europe in the late 1940s, local Chinese residents moved into the former ghetto complex. Until the 1980s, the area was densely populated and the Ohel Moshe Synagogue was used successively as a barrack, factory, psychiatric clinic and government facility. Only with the institutionalization of Chinese exile research from the late 1980s on, and through visits of Jewish celebrities in the 1990s, including the former exile and American Finance Minister Michael Blumenthal and Israeli Prime Minister Yitzchak Rabin, has the ghetto area received greater attention. The establishment of the museum at the former Ohel Moshe and the historical area was thereby driven by multiple actors: an increasing global interest in migration and exile history, the systematization of Chinese exile studies, the need for appropriate remembrance for former Jewish refugees who came back to visit Shanghai, and the diplomatic agendas of western politicians. There was in this phase, as Michaels notes, a "recognition of the neighborhood's historical importance, its potential for tourism, and its value as soft diplomacy" (Michaels 2017, 205). Issues like how to involve these actors in the urban planning and development of Shanghai led to extensive discussions within Chinese society and to massive infrastructure projects in the District Hongkou.

The demolition of the old buildings in Hongkou and the renovation of the Ohel Moshe Synagogue began in the late 1990s, and in view of its historical and diplomatic importance, the ghetto area was also integrated into a big development project[3] in 2000. In the initial planning phase, however, the historical Jewish architectures were either ignored or marginalized in comparison to real estate and business units in the specific plan: "The project would remove the remnants of the old Jewish quarter, leaving perhaps only Ohel Moishe and the row houses of Houshan Lu (little Vienna)" (Jakubowicz 2009, 167). This demonstrates above all how the commercial exploitation of the historic ghetto area took precedence in the original plan, which was later revised through the initiatives and efforts of Chinese intellectuals and the Jewish and western public (Zhang and Wang 2011). The revised urban development plan emphasized the historical and cultural values of the area on the one hand, and the living environment for local residents on the other hand: The touristic and commercial aspects were to play a subordinate role in order to foster the vitality and sustainability of the area (ibid., 84).

As a result of legal regulations and municipal financing, several infrastructure projects have been carried out in this area since 2003; they preserved cultural monuments of Jewish heritage and modernized the living conditions of the locals. For example, the Ohel Moshe Synagogue has been restored to its original construction plan and architectural style, with the help of architectural drawings from the city archives (Zhang/Wang 2011; Michaels 2017, 211); public transportation including three metro stations are now in operation in this area; damaged streets, alleys and obsolete residential buildings have been completely renovated and refurbished inside and out. Such measures have significantly improved the living environment and the quality of life for local residents, while the expanded museum and other new units, located at the renovated Ohel Moshe, reopened officially in 2007.

Besides the productive results of infrastructural implementation and renewal, however, some questionable decisions were made during the development process of the museum, as the following example shows. In a construction project on Changyang Road, at that time one of the central streets in the ghetto, the architecture which had housed the historical café and hotel 'Zum weißen Rössl', was demolished in 2009 due to road expansion, although many of the former Jewish refugees and Chinese intellectuals opposed this project.[4] The name of the building came from the German Singspiel *Im Weißen Rößl*,[5] and this typical Austrian coffee house and hotel was run by an Austrian-Jewish family, the Mosbergs, from 1939 to 1949. As a popular place in the ghetto, Jewish refugees often met there, and events such as weddings were also held occasionally. This means that the building had not only functioned as a kind of 'cultural homeland' for Jewish refugees at the time, it also holds the memories and emotions of Jewish refugees and later its local Chinese residents. In this respect, historical buildings such as the 'Zum weißen Rössl' can therefore be thought of as "*lieux de mémoire*" in the sense of Nora (Nora 1996) – places of remembrance for a varied and complex history, which points to multi-layered cultural meanings and collective identities.

This historical value is known to the authorities as well, so that later in 2014, a new building was built opposite the Ohel Moshe Synagogue as a side wing of the Shanghai Jewish Refugees Museum. It was reconstructed according to the original plan with similar furnishings and decorations as the coffee house – in addition, it was named after 'Zum weißen Rössl' (or 'White Horse Inn' in English). Although the reconstruction was welcomed by the descendants of the Mosberg family, and the café offers a touristic incentive for the museum, certain questions arise as to the appropriateness of this demolition and rebuilding process. Because apart from problems related to the historical reality and authenticity in the reconstruction, the widening of streets – the main reason for the demolition – does not offer a once-for-all solution for the traffic problems in a modern metropolis such as Shanghai (Zhang/Wang 2011). In addition, the original building was only a few minutes' walk from the Ohel Moshe Synagogue, so that the reconstruction seems less meaningful in view of the museum-character of the entire area.

The Shanghai Jewish refugees museum: A commemorative urban space for whom?

When examining infrastructure as an important actor in the media milieu of the museum, along with relevant working processes of implementation and renewal in the area, its reception is also notable. On the one hand, the museum and its efforts in preserving exilic history are often appreciated and positively received in western countries, especially by Jewish visitors. Still, it seems that many Chinese, even local residents in the District Hongkou are largely unfamiliar with this past, or cannot identify themselves with it. Although locals are encouraged to visit the museum, which nowadays has become one of Shanghai's main tourist attractions and has turned into a quasi "compulsory program" for western politicians visiting the city (Kreissler 2012, 229), most visitors of the museum are not from China. The discrepancy between the desired appropriation of global exile history and the actual results in local practices indicates the tensions between different collective memories. This is demonstrated explicitly by some elderly residents, when they were invited to a local meeting in 2009 regarding planning and developing the area:

> At the moment there is already a certain amount of tourism, but there is neither multidimensional content nor depth of thought, so that it cannot attract a large number of tourists.
> (Mr Shen qtd. in Zhang/Wang 2011, 141)

> Actually, we the residents, didn't want Tilanqiao [name of the former ghetto area] to be listed as historical monument. In this way, the buildings here are not allowed to be demolished and the residents lose their right to resettlement and compensation.
> (Ms Chen qtd. in Zhang/Wang 2011, 143)

> A few years ago, it was said that Tilanqiao should be restored as an entirely Jewish neighborhood in order to keep its original ecology. I think this is unrealistic. Tilanqiao was an area where Chinese and Jews lived together. [...] it is not comparable with other memorial sites like the First or Second National Congress of the Communist Party of China, which are of great importance for our national development or revolution. It can only serve as an evidence that we Chinese once looked after the others when they were in trouble. This is the virtue of the Chinese. Apart from the lesson that one should help others in suffering, it has no didactic impact on the Chinese, but above all on the Jewish refugees.
> (Ms Qi qtd. in Zhang/Wang 2011, 144).

Such opinions indicate not only the complexities of preserving historical heritage sites in general and the potential conflict of interests during such processes but they also point to certain confrontations between Jewish and Chinese cultural identities in the area. The perception of the Jewish past in this way can be traced back to the memory politics in China, which functions as another key actor in the media milieu of the museum and profoundly shapes its historiographical narratives and memory practices.

The question of cultural memory politics in China has been addressed by several scholars. Michaels, for example, examines the cooperation between the Shanghai Jewish Refugees Museum and the Consulate General of Germany in Shanghai at the World Exhibition *Expo 2010* and argues that the museum's functions partly as a touristic strategy and partly as diplomatic agenda (Michaels 2017). This case emphasizes that the commemoration of Jewish history in Shanghai is inextricably linked to Chinese foreign policies and that it has been affected by outside actors. Pan criticizes further that in Chinese historiography and standard interpretations exile in Shanghai seems to be primarily, if not exclusively, a 'Jewish' story and that it foregrounds the cultural memory praxes of 'others', while the majority of the locals do not participate in the official commemorative culture (Pan 2014). The voices of Chinese individuals,[6] who lived together with European Jewish refugees in the ghetto, are indeed marginalized or absent in Chinese historiography, contrasting sharply with the extensively collected Jewish testimonies as oral history by Chinese historians. The Chinese people are often pictured as the collective 'good' who extended a helping hand to the Jews. Such historiographical views and exile discourses in China act as a "humanitarian fantasy", as Lee posits (Lee 2020, 142).

The museum's functionalization in the field of foreign policy, the instrumentalization of a moral self-image of the Chinese people, and the omission of the exile history of its own nation – such as the waves of Chinese refugees fleeing from mainland China to Hong Kong between the 1950s and 1980s, or today's Chinese exiles abroad – confirm the criticism expressed by those elderly local residents. However, exile discourse in China could evolve gradually once a generation change takes place, as Goldstein and Kreissler note: we can remain "cautiously optimistic" (Goldstein 2017, 244) as younger Chinese scholars take on archival research and source analysis more intensively and thereby gain distance from more orthodox Chinese historiography and memory politics (Kreissler 2012, 238).

In view of the dynamic development and perception processes the Shanghai Jewish Refugees Museum has been embroiled in throughout the last decades, especially with infrastructure and memory politics as essential actors in the media milieu of the museum, we can observe that the museum's memory practices are closely tied to a profound process of urbanization and social transformation of the city. Although the museum's mediatization of Jewish exile and migration history reflects certain problems, the museum itself as a memory work nevertheless plays a crucial role in ensuring that Jewish heritage is not entirely erased in contemporary Chinese society.

NOTES

1. Conventional 'text analysis' often focuses on media-specific contents, representations, technics and aesthetics dealing with the past, while neglecting other 'non-textual' social, economic, material and institutional aspects of the remembering process.
2. In view of the wide media spectrum in contemporary memory practice, approaches towards mediatized memory works differ substantially. For example, the analysis of a cinematic representation of the Holocaust may involve aspects such as its filmic distribution channels, relevant censorship and memory politics, while research on a novel about the Holocaust may not necessarily always be linked to its production and distribution process.
3. The so-called North Bund Project, which was begun in 2000, refers to an urban planning and development project in the riverside part of Hongkou. The design competition held in 2002 proposed a modern business and residential district (see Jakubowicz 2009; Zhang/Wang 2011).
4. See Lim (2009).
5. The Singspiel by the Austrian composer Ralph Benatzky premiered in Berlin in 1930. The venue in the music drama was the hotel 'Im Weissen Rössl' in Austria. The Singspiel has been adapted to film several times and enjoys international fame.
6. Apart from exceptional portrayed Chinese heroes, such as the 'Chinese Schindler', Dr Fengshan Ho, who was a diplomat at that time and saved Austrian Jews by issuing thousands of Chinese visas.

REFERENCES

Armbrüster, Georg, et al., editors. *Exil Shanghai 1938–1947. Jüdisches Leben in der Emigration.* Hentrich & Hentrich, 2000.

Assmann, Aleida. "Canon and Archive." *Cultural Memory Studies. An International and Interdisciplinary Handbook*, edited by Astrid Erll and Ansgar Nünning, Walter de Gruyter, 2008, pp. 97–108.

Assmann, Jan. Nachwort. *Soziales Vergessen. Formen und Medien des Gedächtnisses der Gesellschaft*, edited by Elena Esposito, Suhrkamp, 2002, pp. 400–414.

Brunow, Dagmar. *Remediating Transcultural Memory. Documentary Filmmaking as Archival Intervention* (Media and Cultural Memory / Medien und Kulturelle Erinnerung, vol. 23). Walter de Gruyter, 2015.

Erll, Astrid. *Kollektives Gedächtnis und Erinnerungskulturen. Eine Einführung.* 3rd ed., J.B. Metzler, 2017.

Goldstein, Jonathan. "Holocaust and Jewish Studies in Modern China: Functions of a Political Agenda." *Holocaust Memory in a Globalizing World* (Beiträge zur Geschichte des 20. Jahrhunderts, vol. 22), edited by Jacob S. Eder et al., Wallstein, 2017, pp. 228–244.

Hoskins, Andrew, and Ben O'Loughlin. *War and Media. The Emergence of Diffused War.* Polity, 2010.

Jakubowicz, Andrew. "Cosmopolitanism with Roots: The Jewish Presence in Shanghai before the Communist Revolution and as Brand in the New Metropolis." *Branding Cities. Cosmopolitanism, Parochialism, and Social Change*, edited by Stephanie Hemelryk Donald et al., Routledge, 2009, pp. 156–171.

Köhr, Katja. *Die vielen Gesichter des Holocaust. Museale Repräsentationen zwischen Individualisierung, Universalisierung und Nationalisierung*. V&R Unipress, 2012.

Kranzler, David. *Japanese, Nazis and Jews: The Jewish Refugee Community of Shanghai, 1938–1945*. Yeshiva University Press, 1976.

Kreissler, Françoise. "Europäische Emigranten (1933–1945) in der chinesischen Geschichtsschreibung. Zwischen Politik und Geschichte." *Exilforschungen im historischen Prozess* (Exilforschung. Ein internationales Jahrbuch, vol. 30), edited by Claus-Dieter Krohn et al., edition text + kritik, 2012, pp. 223–241.

Latour, Bruno. *Die Hoffnung der Pandora. Untersuchungen zur Wirklichkeit der Wissenschaft*. Translated by Gustav Roßler, Suhrkamp, 2002.

Lee, Haiyan. "A Sino-Jewish Encounter, a Humanitarian Fantasy." *Verge: Studies in Global Asias*, vol. 6, no. 1, 2020, pp. 142–167.

Lim, Louisa. "Historic Jewish Haven in Shanghai Faces Demolition." *National Public Radio*, 11 February 2009, www.npr.org/templates/story/story.php?storyId=100522156&t=1603832716469. Accessed 12 June 2021.

Michaels, Jennifer E. "Restoring and Utilizing the Past: The Shanghai Jewish Refugees Museum." *Global Mobilities: Refugees, Exiles, and Immigrants in Museums and Archives*, edited by Amy K. Levin, Routledge, 2017, pp. 205–222.

Nora, Pierre. *Realms of Memory. Rethinking the French Past*, vol. 1: *Conflicts and Divisions*. Translated by Arthur Goldhammer, Columbia University Press, 1996.

Pan, Lu. "Remembering the Pain of 'Others': Reflections on the Shanghai Jewish Refugees Museum and Beyond." 2014, *War Memoryscapes in Asia Project*, www.warinasia.com/iris-pan-lu. Accessed 10 May 2021 [Web site no longer accessible. Other option: PDF via Academia, www.academia.edu/6815615/Remembering_ the_ Pain_ of_ Others_ Reflections_ on_ the_ Shanghai_ Jewi sh_ Refugees_ Museum_ and_ Beyond.]

Parry, Ross. *Recoding the Museum. Digital Heritage and the Technologies of Change*. Routledge, 2007.

Pethes, Nicolas. *Kulturwissenschaftliche Gedächtnistheorien zur Einführung*. Junius, 2008.

Weber, Thomas. "Der dokumentarische Film und seine medialen Milieus." *Medienkulturen des Dokumentarischen*, edited by Carsten Heinze and Thomas Weber, Springer VS, 2017, pp. 3–26.

Zhang, Yanhua, and Jian Wang. *The Space, the Stories and Shanghai Jews – Hongkew Ghetto. Then and Now*. Yilin Press, 2011.

Zhuang, Wei. *Erinnerungskulturen des jüdischen Exils in Shanghai (1933–1950). Plurimedialität und Transkulturalität* (Memory Studies, vol. 1). LIT, 2015.

13

Mapping the Russian Diaspora in Shanghai

Katya Knyazeva

Introduction

For 30 years, between 1919 and 1949, Shanghai was home to a large community of ex-Russian subjects who came from the Far East, Siberia, Central Russia and the Western regions of the dissolved empire. Composed mostly of refugees from the 1917 revolution, the Shanghai Russian[1] diaspora eventually absorbed thousands of stateless compatriots from North China. Despite their different origins, legal status and religious affiliation, the Russians had in common their language and culture, as well as the shared experience of emigration. This chapter examines photographic and cartographic evidence of their presence in Shanghai and highlights the avenues of interaction with Chinese and international communities. By looking at visual and geographical data, we bring to the foreground the spatial dimensions of historical narrative, in line with spatial history's argument that the past exists in space, not in time, and that history is nothing but a map of places made by human action (Ethington 2007, 465).

A scrutiny of detailed city plans reveals the spatial distribution of Russian entrepreneurship throughout the city vis-à-vis non-Russian businesses. It showcases clusters of increased density of émigré businesses and helps identify their commercial profiles. The photographic evidence from the era, while not necessarily centered on the Russians, almost inevitably includes them and the aftereffects of their activities. There are journalistic images taken by visiting newspaper reporters, records of foreign brands' representation in the context of local commerce, staged portraiture created for private use and visual records of the émigrés' individual and collective achievements. We focus on those documents that put in high relief the manifold ways of communication between the diaspora, the host culture and

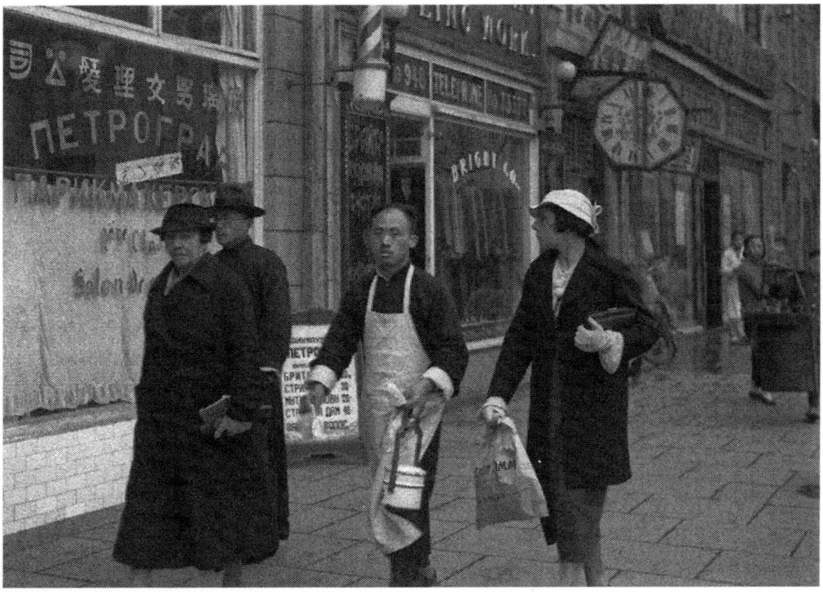

FIGURE 13.1: Harrison Forman, *Street scene in front of a restaurant*, Shanghai, 1937. Pedestrians on Avenue Joffre are shown walking past stores with Russian, Chinese, and English signage. (© American Geographical Society Library, University of Wisconsin-Milwaukee Libraries, digital image ID fr203002).

other foreign groups. This communication takes the form of multilingual store signage, distinct window dressing, the display of personal appearance and fashion, the insertion of national architecture into the city's skyline and the religious, social and consumer practices in the public place.

Characteristic urban landscape anchors Russian entrepreneurship in the French Concession

As the largest non-Asian group in the city, the Russian community counted more than 35,000 people by the end of the 1930s (Ristaino 2003, 5; Flamm et al. 2018, 61). They moved freely between Shanghai's three independently governed urban territories – Chinese City, International Settlement and French Concession. The latter offered the most opportunities for Russian residency and entrepreneurship, thanks to its growing pool of housing and easy paperwork and low taxes for businesses (Fedoulenko 1967, 82). It is in the French Concession that the diaspora built a dense and vibrant neighborhood with a European self-image that radiated throughout the city and gave this district a reputation for its goods, services and urban culture.

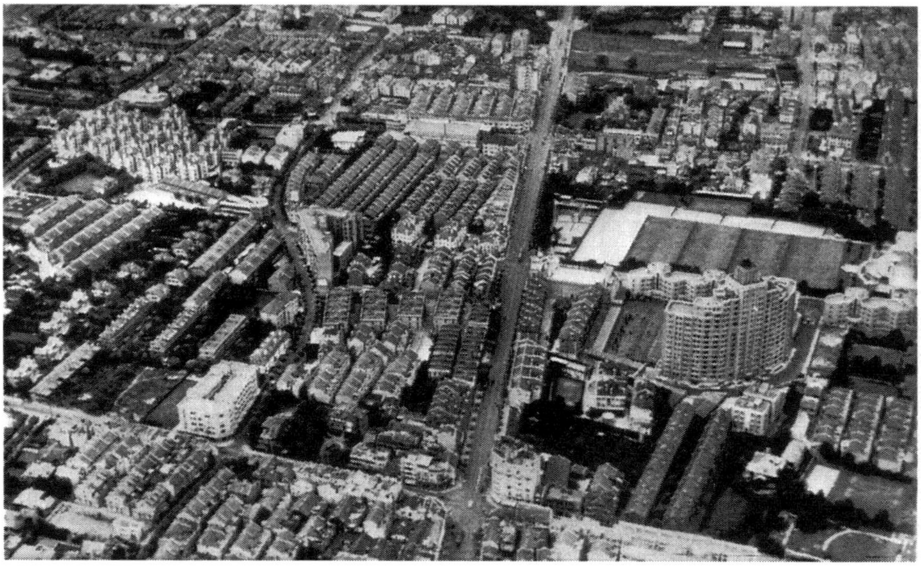

FIGURE 13.2: *Aerial view of the French Concession, with Avenue Joffre running in the center*, Shanghai, 1949 (© AP/Wide World).

The aerial image illustrates an element of the French Concession's urban layout that proved very conducive to the Russian diaspora's participation in the growth of this district – it shows the lively variation of street trajectories and sizes and shapes of city blocks which brought together high- and low-income residences and commerce and encouraged mutual awareness and cross-cultural influence.

Residences, organizations and commercial enterprises established by the Russian émigrés occupied a variety of buildings, including apartment blocks, terraced houses, individual structures and commercial strips. The latter, among the most common buildings on public promenades, were made up of two or three stories, with enterprises occupying the lower floors and the proprietors' private apartments located on the floors above. The Russian stores and service venues formed a continuous row along Avenue Joffre and adjacent streets. One of the oldest businesses – L.J. Baranovsky's store – had five large shop windows spread over Nos. 850 and 852, and remained in place for over seventeen years. A feature article about this store, with portraits of the personnel and images of shelves with textiles and accessories, was included in V.D. Jiganoff's 300-page volume *Russians in Shanghai* (1936) – a guidebook for and a chronicle of the diaspora. Jiganoff included exterior and interior photographs of 65 largest Russian enterprises to illustrate the émigrés' exceptional entrepreneurial zeal and their commitment to physical presence and visibility in the commercial landscape of Shanghai.

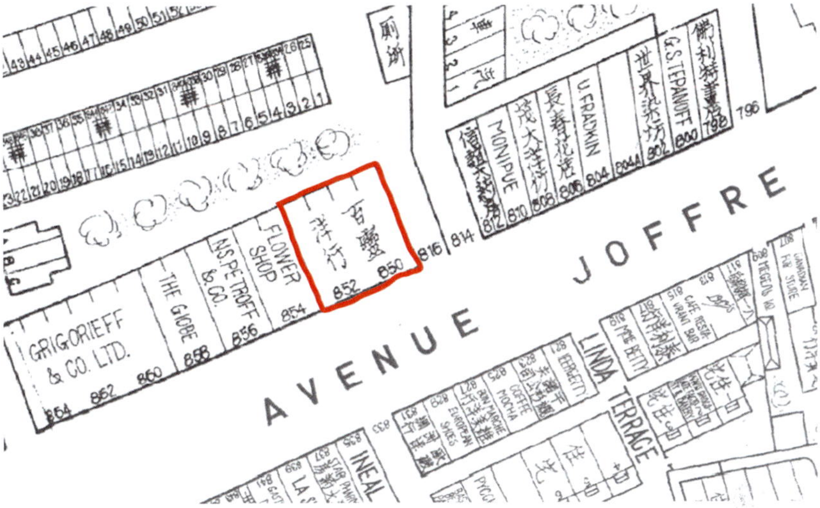

FIGURE 13.3: *Street map showing the predominance of the Russian enterprises on Avenue Joffre, including Baranovsky's store*, from *Shanghai Street Directory*, 1939, p. 66, Virtual Shanghai (© 2003–2021 IrAsia).

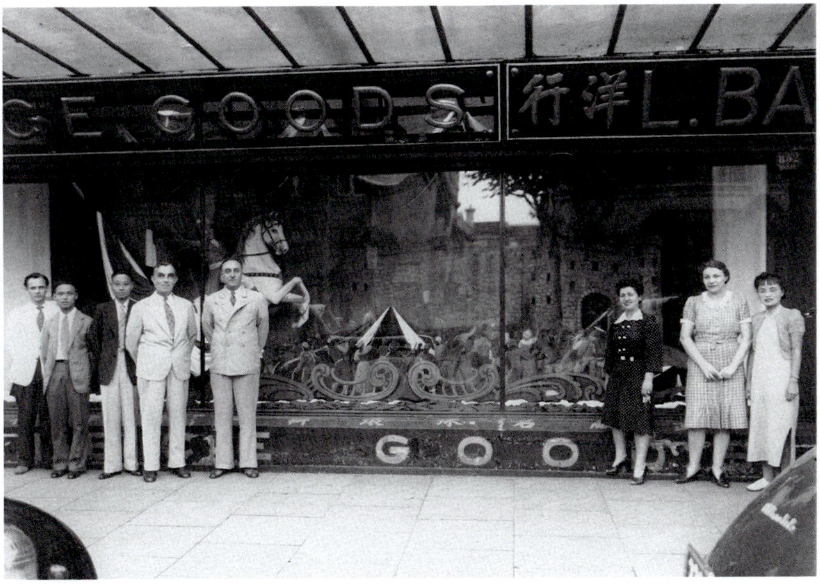

FIGURE 13.4: Family and employees outside Baranovsky's store on Avenue Joffre, Shanghai, *c.*1938 (© Antonina Baranovsky).

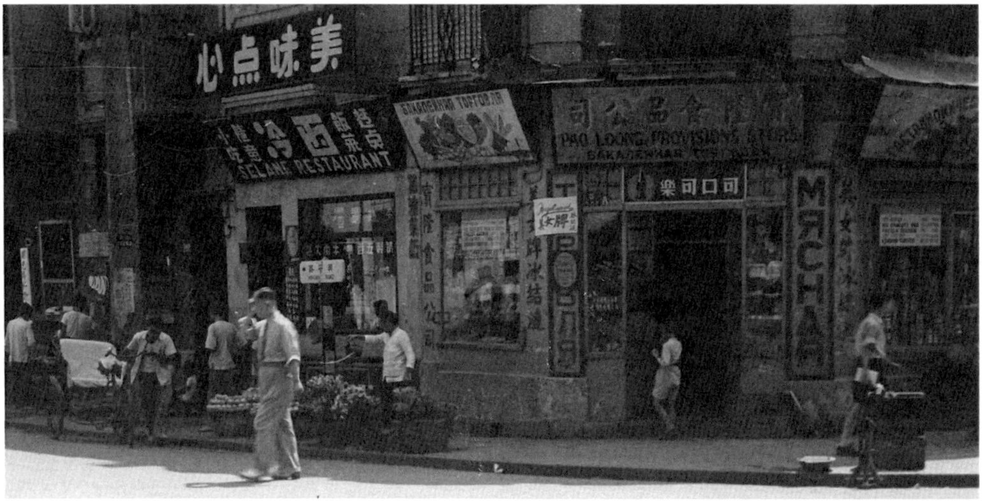

FIGURE 13.5: *Multilingual signage on the corner of Route Voyron and Rue Tillot*, Shanghai, 1940s (© Coca Cola Archives).

Entrepreneurship opens routes to diasporic women's self-realization

All sorts of food and hospitality businesses were especially prominent. The smaller and more specialized venues – delis, dairy stores and meal delivery services – targeted the compatriots by advertising in Russian and by mentioning low prices, familiar flavors and special products like the traditional Easter pastry. Larger cafés, restaurants, cabarets and tearooms appealed to all groups by advertising in the local English, French, Russian and Chinese newspapers. The multilingual signage and the décor offered a feeling of the familiar to members of the diaspora, and the promise of the exotic to other consumers. Russian women, firmly associated with the food, hospitality, décor and beauty industries, further strengthened their employability by attending vocational courses and study groups, such as the Women's Section of the *Shanghai Zaria* newspaper.

Commerce thrived inside semi-private residential blocks as much as on public promenades and at thoroughfares. Since its construction in 1924, Linda Terrace, at 833 Avenue Joffre (fig. 13.6), was populated almost exclusively by the Russians (The North-China Desk Hong List 1925–1941). Such terraced compounds, threaded by public alleys (*lilong*), were mostly comprised of commercial rentals. The primary lessees – often described as fairly wealthy and entrepreneurial women – turned individual units into boarding houses with in-house meals (Ilyina 1985, 223; Smolnikov 2001, 14; Slobodchikov 2005, 185). Rooms in boarding

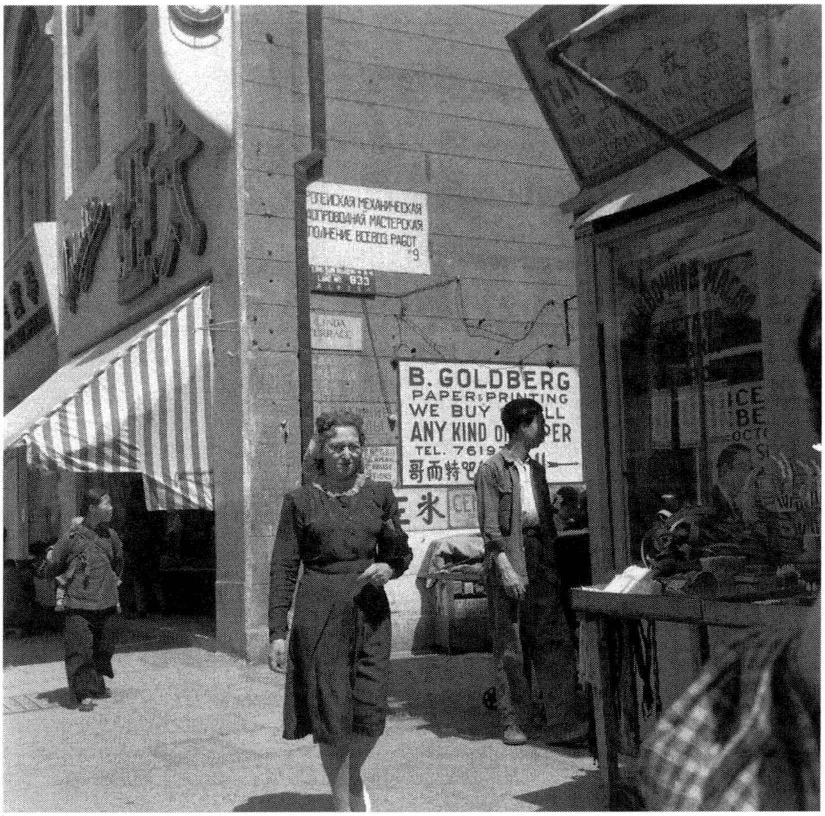

FIGURE 13.6: Jack Birns, *Entrance of the Linda Terrace, with Russian, Chinese and English signs for a mechanic, a plumber, a house-keeping agency, a typography and a food delivery service*, Shanghai, 1949 (© Life).

houses doubled as offices, studios and workshops for craftsmen, jewelers, doctors, teachers, interpreters, beauticians, tailors and fortunetellers.

Fashion industry was a well-developed area of Russian entrepreneurship, created by hundreds of refugee women in search of employment (Jiganoff 1936, 153; Paci Zaharoff 2005, 136). Engaged in the designing, tailoring, knitting, modeling, importing, marketing and selling of garments and accessories, these artisans essentially created and guided fashion consciousness in Shanghai. A combination of affordability with a prestigious European aesthetic ignited the interest of local and foreign clients who wanted to adhere to the 'Parisian' lifestyle. Images of trendy urbanites promenading along modern storefronts in the foreign settlements fed into the global perception of 1930s Shanghai as a fashionable and dynamic city, comparable to Paris and New York.

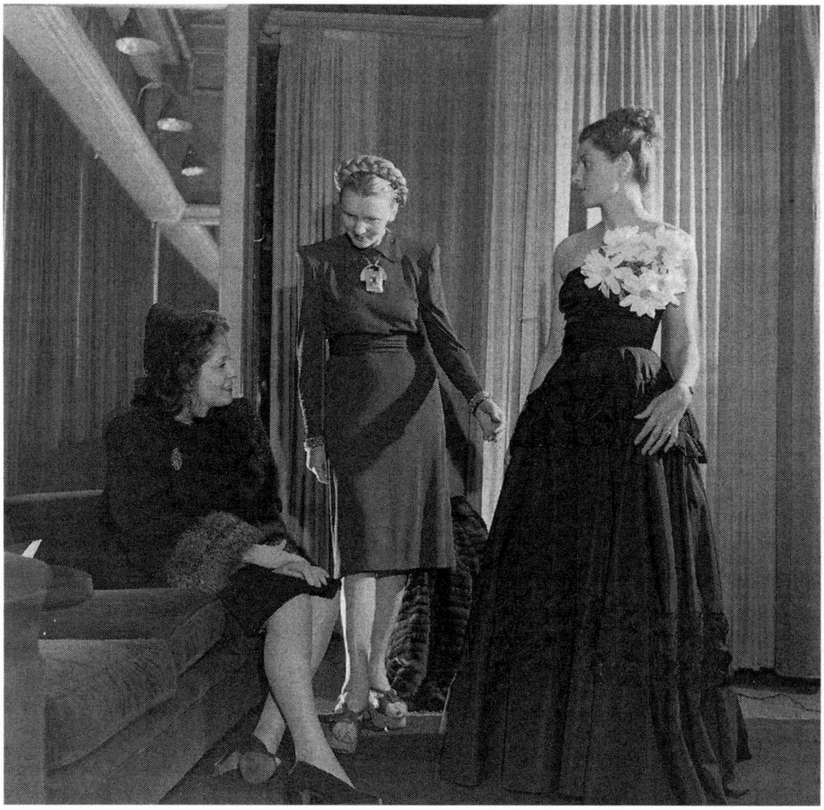

FIGURE 13.7: George Silk, *Dressmaker Eleonora Garnett (center) in her showroom, with a client and a model*, Shanghai, 1946 (© Life).

Russian architects contribute to the city's skyline and leave a tangible legacy

The diaspora's relationship with the city's built environment was not limited to inhabiting and using spaces created by others. Various Russian architects, engineers and decorators worked on construction sites in China, Hong Kong and Singapore. Over 70 of their architectural creations are still standing in Shanghai, like the works of Vladimir Kooklin (1903–77), who was active in the late 1930s and early 1940s. The image from the family archive shows Kooklin working on the construction of a luxury apartment building, the Hanray Mansions, designed by his compatriot Emmanuel Gran, for which Kooklin's construction firm was the general contractor. Close connections among the diaspora architects, engineers and builders led to professional alliances (Knyazeva 2020).

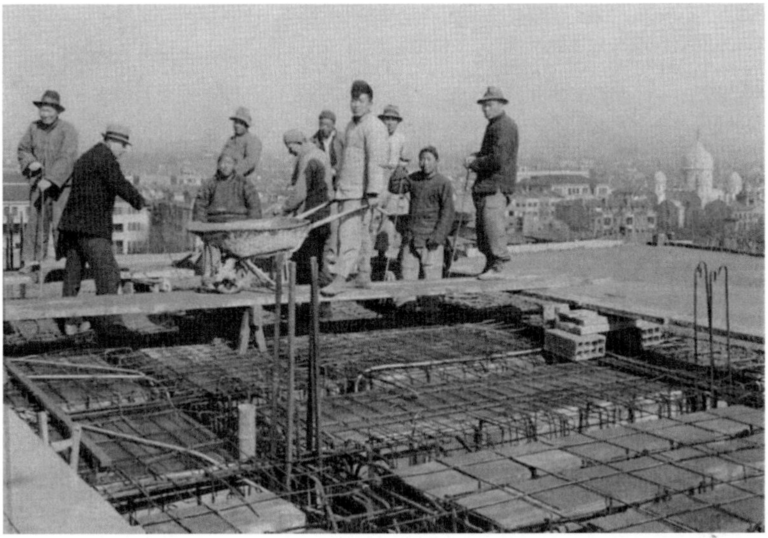

FIGURE 13.8: *Engineer and architect V.A. Kooklin (second from left) supervising the completion of the Hanray Mansions*, Shanghai, around 1939 (© Kooklin family).

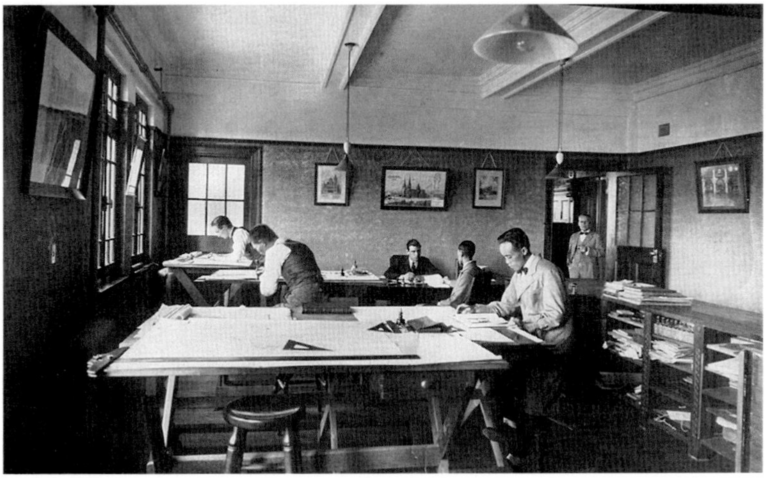

FIGURE 13.9: *Architecture studio of Lafuente & Yaron, 1926* (Leonardo Pérez 2019, p. 243).

Russian professionals in the construction industry capitalized on the knowledge and expertise they had acquired during their study in Imperial Russia. Among the earliest émigré architects was Alexander J. Yaron (1874–1935), who worked in tandem with the Spanish architect Abelardo Lafuente before embarking on a solo career (Leonardo Pérez 2019). Yaron's designs of a commercial warehouse, the mosque for the International Settlement and the cathedral for the Catholic mission

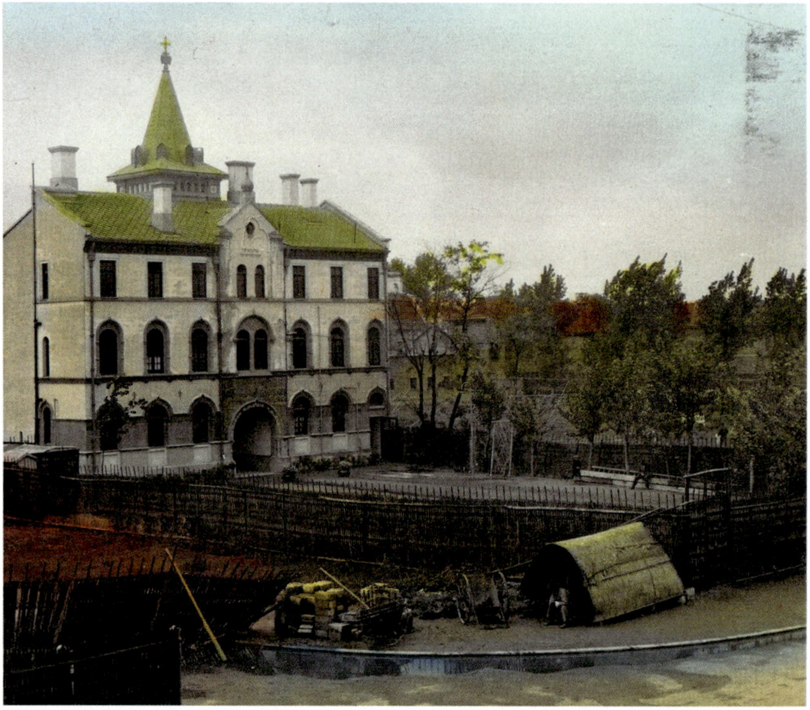

FIGURE 13.10: *Bishop Apartments*, designed by Alexander Yaron, and the site prepared for the construction of the Orthodox Cathedral, Shanghai, *c.*1933, Russian Spiritual Mission in Beijing.

in Fuzhou were displayed on the walls of Lafuente & Yaron studio on Bubbling Well Road. Yaron created his projects in a wide variety of international styles; only two of his known buildings, designed for the Russian Spiritual Mission, had a recognizable Slav appearance.

The Bishop Apartments (1932) and the two Orthodox churches – one designed by Yaron and another by his colleague Jacob Lehonos – are the only buildings in a distinctly Russian style that still survive in Shanghai. The Russian architects tended to embrace international trends and adapt to the demands of their Chinese and foreign clients. The majority of their creations were in the modernist (or Art Deco) style – the preferred aesthetic in Shanghai in the 1930s.

Having established themselves in the building industry during the construction boom of the early 1930s, the Russians readily filled the void left by the outflow of Western architecture studios at the precipitous onset of the Japanese occupation (1937–1945). Working individually and in partnerships, the Russians were instrumental in developing the Western French Concession, populating it with an innovative housing form – so called 'midget apartments' – which adhered to the irregular trajectories of the streets and small lot sizes. A typical midget apartment was a walk-up building not exceeding four stories in height, which employed 'economical, and in some cases ingenious planning', including

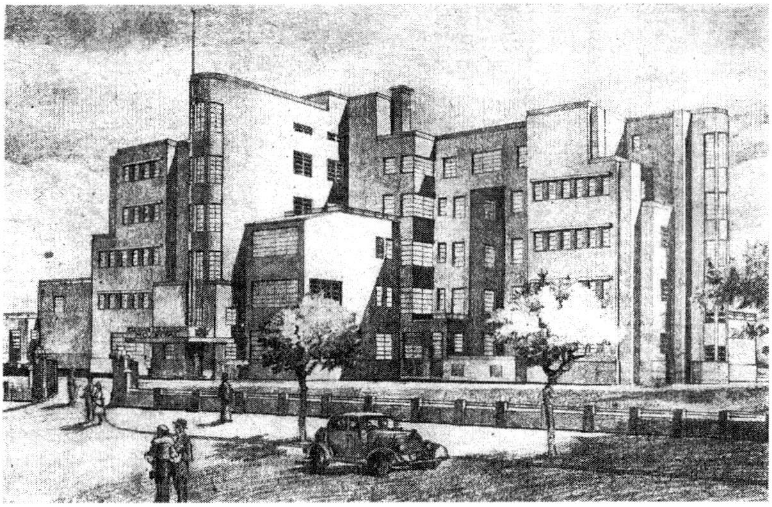

FIGURE 13.11: Vsevolod Kirkor, *Project of a hospital for the French Concession*, 1934, Drawing, in: *Shanghai Sunday Times Industrial Section, Supplement to Special Christmas Issue*, 15 December 1935, p. 28.

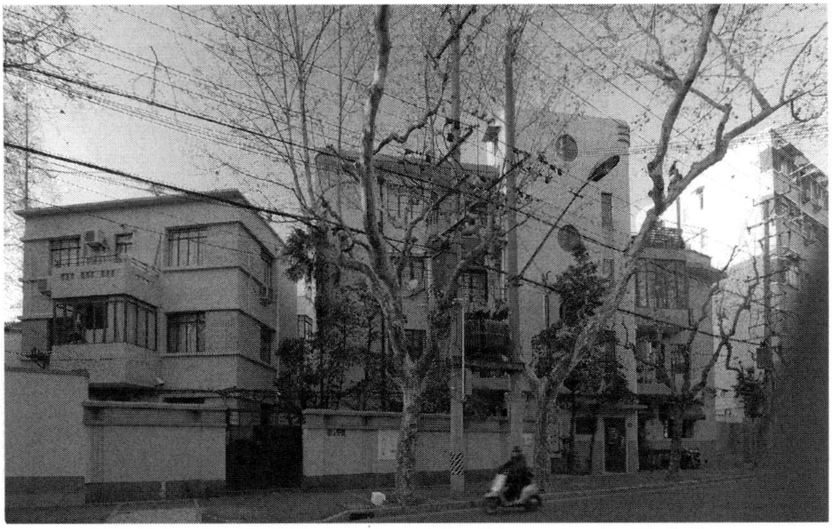

FIGURE 13.12: Katya Knyazeva, *Art Deco apartment buildings on Yongfu Road, designed by (left to right) I. Tomashevsky, V. Kooklin and N. Emanoff respectively*, Shanghai, 2018.

built-in furniture and roof gardens (Anonymous 1941, 19). Because thus far only a fraction of such apartment buildings in the French Concession have been identified and associated with their creators, visual analysis and research on location remain instrumental in the ongoing enquiry into these buildings' provenance and their architects' identity.

Conclusion

Clues taken from maps and photographs help enrich the methodology of the enquiry into Shanghai Russians and expose the vectors of their engagement with the city. Such a spatial approach helps dispel perceptions inherited from migration studies and national histories, with their emphasis on the loss of identity, the trauma of exile and cultural degradation. Instead, the rich geography of Russian entrepreneurship in Shanghai shows diaspora members in positions of authority and expertise, far from the image of a hermetic and nostalgic society at charity's receiving end. Russian women's agency and visibility in the labor market ensured their decisive role in shaping the global image of the city. The prolific and international style of the Russian architects testifies to their motivation to overcome the boundaries of ethnicity and faith. And despite the diaspora's dispersal to other countries, its built legacy in Shanghai serves as a tangible monument and an integral part of the urban environment.

NOTE

1. The term 'Russian' here includes all former subjects of the Russian Empire and their children, as well as all those identifying with Russia by birth, faith, language or self-description.

REFERENCES

Anonymous. "Russian Architect Helps to Alter City's Skyline." *Shanghai Times Industrial, Commercial and Engineering Supplement*, 1941, p. 19.

Ethington, Philip J. "Placing the Past: 'Groundwork' for a Spatial Theory of History." *Rethinking History: The Journal of Theory and Practice*, vol. 11, no. 4, 2007, pp. 465–493.

Fedoulenko, Valentin. *Russian Émigré Life in Shanghai*. University of California Bancroft Library, 1967.

Flamm, Christoph, et al., editors. *Transcending the Borders of Countries, Languages, and Disciplines in Russian Émigré Culture*. Cambridge Scholars Publishing, 2018.

Ilyina, Natalya. *Dorogy i sudby* [Roads and destiny]. Sovetskiy pisatel, 1985.

Jiganoff, Vladimir. *Russkie v Shanhae. Russians in Shanghai*. Slovo, 1936.

Knyazeva, Katya. "Building Russian Shanghai: the Architectural Legacy of the Diaspora." *The Journal of the Royal Asiatic Society China*, vol. 80, no. 1, 2020, pp. 165–196. *Academia*, www.academia.edu/45004587/Building_ Russian_ Shanghai_ the_ Architectural_ Legacy_ of_ the_ Diaspora. Accessed 1 July 2021.

Leonardo Pérez, Alvaro. *Abelardo Lafuente García-Rojo (1871–1931), A Spanish Architect in China*. Ph.D. dissertation, Alcala Henares University, 2019.

Paci Zaharoff, Floria. *The Daughter of the Maestro: Life in Surabaya, Shanghai, and Florence*. iUniverse, 2005.

Ristaino, Marcia. *Port of Last Resort: The Diaspora Communities of Shanghai*. Stanford University Press, 2003.

Smolnikov, Victor. *Zapiski shanhaiskogo vracha* [*Notes of a Shanghai Physician*]. Strategia, 2001.

The North-China Desk Hong List. North-China Daily News, Herald, 1925–1941.

14

Mapping Istanbul's Pera District between Arrivals and Departures

Merve Köksal and Seza Sinanlar Uslu

Introduction

As a uniquely situated city of crossroads linking Asia and Europe, Istanbul has always been a nexus of cultures that attracted travellers and migrants. Its cosmopolitan district of Pera, today's Beyoğlu, was a fascinating melting pot in which these travellers and migrants continuously intersected with one another and with city locals. In our study, on the Pera district, we render artists' studios and contact zones visible to reveal the multifaceted relations and networks cultivated by travelling, local (Muslim and non-Muslim) and migrant artists from the 1840s to the 1960s. Taking the relationship of art-making and urban experience as a starting point of our inquiry, we evaluate those artists as social actors and explore them not merely through their artworks but also with regards to their workspace, their inter-personal contacts and their cross-communal exchanges. It is only recently that Pera has received scholarly attention as an artistic milieu. Delving into the relationship of artistic production, urban space and networks, *Pera'da Resim Üretim Ortamı 1845–1916* (The Art Production Environment in Pera 1845–1916) (Sinanlar 2008) provides rich material to contextualize the district's cosmopolitan art scene and represents a basis for further exploration. In this respect, our study can be understood as the output of a learning process, as we strive to decode both the dynamics within this particular art-production space and the connections between travelling, local and migrant artists who were active in it.

We employ the mapping method to present a different story, and to bring into the picture the spatial practices and complexities of urban life that have been overlooked in canonical art-historical narratives of and in Turkey. Mapping makes tangible invisible interactions as well as social, spatial and artistic practices while also providing invaluable insights into the ways in which shops, cultural and entertainment venues, hotels, clubs and other institutions in Pera shaped the dynamics of the art world. A map lets us envision and grasp the city roads that the artists walked, the points at which they met, the social circles they were involved in, along with the venues they became regulars at and displayed their artwork at – all of which constitute an important element of the artistic process. Mapping adds new dimensions to our understanding of artistic connections and alliances by showing, for example, the proximity of individual artists' studios to each other. It also demonstrates unnoticed aspects of the district's art-exhibiting tradition by visualizing the distribution of exhibition spaces. Mapping ateliers, exhibition spaces and a wide range of contact zones allows us to observe those artists as real people forging ongoing relationships with each other and many other inhabitants of Pera. We seek to reveal these multi-layered stories as they are embedded in the urban fabric, and to decipher extant traces. In that vein, one of our objectives is to introduce Pera as the city's spatial nexus of art-making and to visualize its artistic prolificacy through our map in order to raise awareness of how important it is to maintain its cultural heritage.

To present an artistic and cultural mapping of Pera, we first explored the history of its urban development from maps of Cociffi (1854), Goad (1905) and Pervititch (1922–1945), in addition to current maps of Istanbul's Metropolitan Municipality. We then found and tracked the locations of studios, exhibition spaces and other artistic contact zones through the newspapers – including the *Journal de Constantinople, Stamboul*, and *The Orient News* – and the Oriental Directories' yearbook of commerce, the *Annuaire Oriental*, and integrated our findings into data obtained through the maps. Furthermore, a comparative analysis of life writing and literature about everyday life in Istanbul during the period covered by our research[1] also underlined the pivotal role Pera played in the city's cultural and artistic environment. After the proclamation of the Republic of Turkey in 1923 and the subsequent establishment of Ankara as its new capital, the contents of *Annuaire Oriental* became narrower and less inclusive. For this reason, tracing the artists was a challenge. Cities in Anatolia and important global commercial centres occupy a considerable part of the content from 1923, replacing Istanbul-focused indexing because of the political and cultural agenda of the newly founded state. Moreover, demographic shifts, such as the 1923 migrations between Greece and Turkey, inevitably affected the information given by this source. Turning to memoirs and literary outputs allows us to enter into cafés, taverns, nightspots, or artists' homes in the district during the Republican period.[2]

Old maps and newspapers tell us that there were streets, crossroads, buildings and venues shaping the urban development, social life and cultural fabric of Pera, an area surrounded from West to East by the districts of Kasımpaşa, Şişhane, Karaköy, Tophane, Cihangir, Taksim, Tarlabaşı and Tepebaşı. Its main artery Grande Rue de Péra (now İstiklal Caddesi), which stretches from Taksim Square to the street of Yüksek Kaldırım, creates a two-kilometre axis that is cut horizontally by three crossroads. The busy slope of Yüksek Kaldırım merged into Karaköy Port and led to Pera's hotels' area, which had emerged in the densely populated Asmalımescit neighbourhood. While the urban space surrounding the route to Taksim was less inhabited, Asmalımescit became the favoured residential area for foreigners and continuously developed over time due to its Dört Yol crossroads from Byzantium times and its cemeteries. Towards the 1850s, Galatasaray crossroads on Grande Rue de Péra appeared with an increase in habitations around Yeni Çarşı and Boğazkesen streets leading to Tophane. This second crossroads turned into a lively zone partly due to the Naum Theatre that entertained the Ottoman sultans in nightly programs; the police station, which existed until 1940, had been built for security measures. The location chosen for the police station was also related to the imperial schools built in the area: Galata Saray-ı Ocağı, Mekteb-i Tıbbiye, and Mekteb-i Sultani.[3] The residents of Pera intermixed with people coming from various parts of the Ottoman Empire to study at these boarding schools. The Sixth Department of Municipality of Beyoğlu and Galata, the first modern municipality of Constantinople, emerged in Pera in 1857, adopting the model of Paris' 6éme arrondissement. These urban transformations accelerated after the conflagration of 1870, which destroyed a considerable part of the district. After that, more ambitious structures appeared, habitations spread toward Taksim, and the third crossroads combining Taksim and Rum Kabristan streets gained importance. The Allied occupation (1918–1923) introduced another axis starting at Mac Mahon Barracks[4] and ending on Petits Champs' main street (today's Meşrutiyet Caddesi), which featured Kroecker's Hotel (the British headquarters) and the embassies of Great Britain and the United States. Aside from newly emerging nightspots, cultural and entertainment venues on Grande Rue de Péra, whose numbers had been increasing since the great fire, almost doubled, partly due to the loose regulations for obtaining liquor licences in place. After the emergence of the Republic of Turkey, the meanings attached to places on Grande Rue de Péra did not shift immediately. However, Taksim Square and its monumental statue of the Republic demarcated the urban space, and thus, physically and notionally delimited the flow of people passing through Pera. The expansion shifted from Taksim to Şişli; the Radio Building in construction in 1945 and the Hilton Hotel inaugurated in 1955 are two concrete examples of the growth that took place in this direction.

Taking into account these developments, we consider Pera as a cosmopolitan site of encounters where we can trace the cultural history of the late Ottoman Empire and modern Turkey. Our study comprises four parts, aiming to pinpoint the intersections of urban space and artistic production: the first part, beginning with the 1840s and ending in 1910, analyses the proliferation of travelling, local and migrant artists in ateliers and exhibitions. Focusing on the migrations that occurred throughout the wars and the occupation of Constantinople by the Allied Powers (Britain, France, and Italy), the second part investigates the impacts of shifting social and political circumstances on the art scene during 1910–1923. The third part discusses how Turkification policies after the proclamation of the Republic of Turkey – turning Constantinople into *Istanbul* and Pera into *Beyoğlu* – eradicated the multi-ethnic and multinational coexistence inherent to the district. Finally, we present on one single map artists' studios and exhibition spaces but also clubs, institutions and cultural and entertainment venues imbued with artistic encounters.

The city of arrivals

On the shore, there was a buzz rising from the streets of Pera!
No, such vitality has not been seen even in Naples!

(Hamsun/Andersen 2006, 141).

Tourism in Constantinople grew during the first half of the 19th century. When Hans Christian Andersen jotted down these first impressions in his diary, Pera had begun to turn into a cosmopolitan centre of commerce and leisure that offered European standards to travellers (Sinanlar 2008, 15). We can imagine a theatre company consisting of around twenty people from Italy getting off their ship in the boisterous port of Karaköy. There, the *hamals* (porters) would take trunks filled with costumes or sets and climb the steep slope of Yüksek Kaldırım leading to Pera's hotels. The group would leave their accommodation to rehearse in the famous Naum Theatre the next day, have lunch in a brasserie on Grande Rue de Péra and mingle with the locals of Constantinople as well as with an increasing number of foreigners. Among the motley crowds passing through this imperial capital were artists establishing ongoing relationships and ateliers in Pera. According to the data obtained from various newspapers and the *Annuaire Oriental*, there were around 63 artist studios in the district during 1840–1900, most of which existed in Asmalımescit and Tarlabaşı. The solidarity in the art world and the collective support of the residents, particularly the shopkeepers offering their shops as temporary exhibition spaces, were strong enough to unite people of different nations and religions in order to share their skills, resources and productivity.

The earliest Constantinople drawings of Maltese painter Amedeo Preziosi date back to 1842. He first lived at Hamalbaşı Sokak, no. 14, Pera, and then moved to Galatasaray crossroads on Grande Rue de Péra, where he became a neighbour to painter Giovanni Brindesi who lived at Yeni Çarşı Sokak, no. 60 (Sinanlar 2008, 27). Gérard de Nerval, a literary figure of French Romanticism who arrived in

Constantinople in 1843, re-encountered his close friend, the orientalist painter Camille Rogier, who had lived in Asmalımescit for three years (Nerval 1980, 159). In 1852, the Romantic writer Théophile Gautier stayed in Derviş Sokak, a street that featured the first masonry buildings of Pera, representing Westernization as opposed to traditionally wooden Ottoman houses which had been destroyed by fires (Gautier 1853, 78f.). The district already had a reputation for its dynamic European rhythm when the Crimean War (1853–1855) erupted, which brought painters and photographers monitoring the conflict; Naum Theatre's nightly programmes were replete with at least 60 opera performances during the turbulent years of war (Sinanlar 2008, 19, 26). Furthermore, the grand conflagration of 1870 paved the way for infrastructure projects aiming to renovate the district (Çelik 2017, 83–87). Having been built after the fire, the winter residence of Hagop Köçeoğlu, where Sultan Abdülaziz stayed when he came to Pera for watching the spectacles, was decorated with ceiling frescoes painted by Hippolyte Dominique Berteaux,[5] who had arrived in Constantinople in 1873 for this job (fig. 14.1; Sinanlar Uslu 2013, 701–708).

The inhabitants witnessed the rapid urban transformations Pera underwent while cabinetmakers, florists or artisans supported local and migrant artists by displaying artwork in their shops (Sinanlar 2008, 48–53). Around seventy painting exhibitions were held in various shops on Grande Rue de Péra from 1840

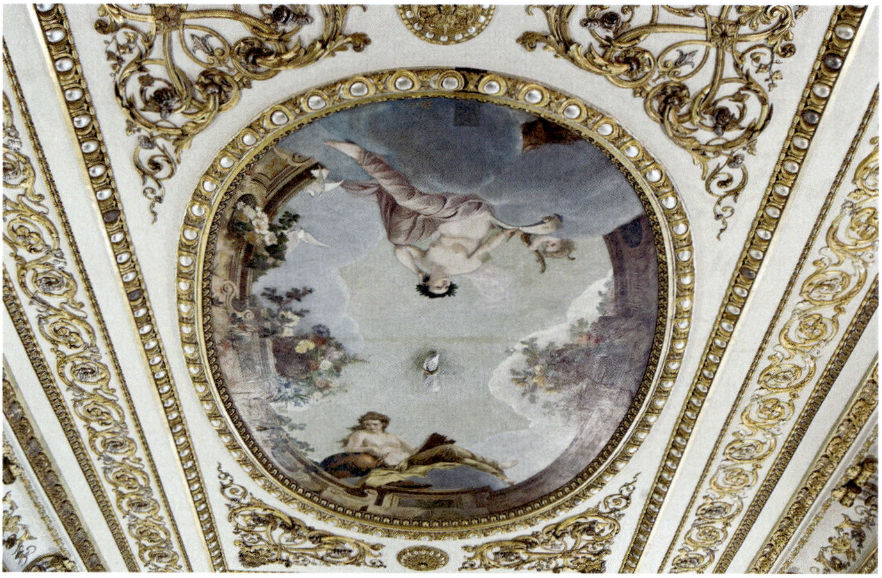

FIGURE 14.1: The ceiling fresco *Science and Literature* painted by Hippolyte Dominique Berteaux in 1873, Köçeoğlu Residence, Beyoğlu (Photo: Kayhan Kaygusuz, 2010).

to 1900 – among them was Zellich Papeterie[6] which hosted an exhibition of Adolphe Beaume's works in 1898 (*Stamboul*, 12 December 1898). These showcase exhibitions, which continued throughout the first half of the 12th century, brought into contact artists displaying their work at shops and the people strolling through Grande Rue de Péra. Social and cultural venues, hotels and institutions also hosted art events. In 1877, Şeker Ahmed Ali Pasha curated an exhibition of Constantinople artists in the Petits Champs Municipal Hall (Thalasso 1907, 367). Ten years later, the building hosted an intriguing collection of Baron A. De Fay Splenyi from the city of Buda. Containing works by Ruysdael and Corot, the exhibition was curated by the famous art dealer David Kleinberger, owner of Kleinberger Gallery in Paris, and was visited by the wealthy families of Constantinople, including Zarifi and Corpi. On behalf of Sultan Abdülhamid II, Şeker Ahmed Ali Pasha purchased Adolf Kauffmann's painting *Port of Istanbul*, which can now be found in the National Palaces Painting Collection (Sinanlar 2008, 65f.). Five years after the inauguration of Sirkeci Station in 1890, the Pera Palace Hotel – another significant contact zone – opened its doors under the influence of the legendary Orient Express tours. According to the ticket sale records of Şeker Ahmed Ali Pasha's exhibition in Pera Palace in 1897, the event welcomed two thousand visitors in two weeks (*Stamboul* 2, 3, 30, 31 Mai 1897).

In addition to selling their artwork, newly arrived artists could also earn a living by giving painting courses. Amadeo Preziosi, Pierre Guès and François Claude Hayette all offered their service to the prestigious imperial schools Mekteb-i Harbiye and Mekteb-i Sultani. Pierre Désiré Guillemet, on the other hand, played a pivotal role in the institutionalization of art education in Constantinople with his private school of painting founded in 1873, Academié de Dessin et de Peinture. He co-led this academy with his painter wife Hélène who educated female students on Hamalbaşı Street across the British Embassy, next to the Galatasaray crossroads. Sultan Abdülhamid II's palace painter Fausto Zonaro and teachers of the School of Fine Arts (Sanayi-i Nefise Mektebi), such as Leonardo de Mango, Joseph Warnia Zarzecki, Salvatore Valeri and Alexandre Vallauri, were artists of note living and teaching art in Pera. Numerous artists' studios in the district educated students interested in each other's art-making, which elevated the city's artistic prolificacy and raised the numbers of the exhibitions shown throughout the years. Based on contemporary art reviews and announcements issued in Constantinople newspapers, the number of exhibitions held during 1840–1880 is estimated to be above twenty. There had been a rapid rise reaching around fifteen from 1880 to 1890. Between 1890 and 1900, on the other hand, around 30 exhibitions were organized, including the annual School of Fine Arts exhibitions (Sinanlar, 2008, 48–53).

Until the Tripoli Conflict (1911–1912), this surge of productivity continued with the *Pera Salons* (1901–1903), the *Singer Exhibitions* (1904–1906) and the

Exhibitions of Sociéta Operaia (1906–1911). The annual *Pera Salons* were remarkable art events displaying student works alongside famous Constantinople artists while introducing new art movements to the public. Henri and Gabrielle Delavallée, two early representatives of Fauvism who participated in the *First Pera Salon* of 1901 organized in Passage Oriental on Dört Yol crossroads, made a profound impact on the artistic milieu. Since Louis Vauxcelles had not yet described the Fauvism movement, Régis Delbeuf, the editor-in-chief of *Stamboul* newspaper, used the phrase "yellows are too yellow, greens are too green" while commenting on paintings of the Delavallée couple (Sinanlar Uslu 2021, 343f.).

In 1908, the Turkist fraction of Young Turks, the Committee of Union and Progress (hereafter CUP), overthrew the absolutist regime of Abdülhamid II (Hanioğlu 2008, 147f.) and political exiles gravitated to the imperial capital under the influence of CUP's "Liberty, Equality, Fraternity and Justice" rhetoric. Armenian painter and political activist Panos Terlemezian, who returned from exile in 1910, shared an apartment with composer and musicologist Soghomon Soghomonian, known as Gomidas. Located in the district of Pangaltı and within a short walking distance from Pera, their apartment functioned as a studio until 1914, uniting intellectuals and artists of different nations (Tongo 2015, 126–128). However, soon after the revolution, Levantine art critic Adolphe Thalasso conveyed the anxieties stemming from xenophobia against Europeans living and painting in Pera: "Henceforth, they feel like outsiders" (Sinanlar Uslu 2014, 270f.). The Ottoman Empire was on the brink of perpetual wars that gave rise to mass migration and cataclysm.

The city of ambivalence

> *The street [Grande Rue de Péra] looked like a real apocalypse where everyone spoke every language.*
>
> (Averçenko 2019, 8)[7]

After a period of creative flourishing and artistic prolificacy as cultures intermingled freely, the Balkan Wars (1912–1913), the Great War (1914–1918) and the Turkish War of Independence (1919–1922) would bring great turmoil to Constantinople. The drastic impacts of nationalism exiled many non-Muslim residents from the city. But the occupation of Constantinople by Britain, France and Italy introduced new connectivities to the art world. The Allied occupation enabled the return of Ottoman-Armenian artists who aimed to revive Armenian intellectual life after the massacres of 1915–1916. Besides, the Allies opened the gates of the city to asylum seekers. There were vast numbers of Greek refugees, Poles, Finns, Letts, Lithuanians, Swedes, Germans and Italians, but migrants from the Russian Empire constituted the overwhelming majority (Davis 1922, 203f.). The influx of Russian-speaking émigrés, among them many artists, who fled from the civil war (1917–1922) after the Russian Revolution of 1917, expanded the city's cultural fabric, especially in Pera.

As a prelude, the Tripoli Conflict had drastic consequences for the Italian residents of Constantinople. Shortly before the battle, an anonymous collector put up for sale a collection containing the works of well-known artists including Tintoretto, Goya, El Greco and Courbet in the Petits Champs Municipal Hall and wanted to auction off unsold paintings; the exhibition lasted only eight days (Özyiğit 2012, 518–528). This collection might have been sold in haste by an Italian Levantine monitoring the territorial dispute and planning to leave Constantinople. When the war began, the CUP shut Italian institutions down and started to expel Italians. Painter Salvatore Valeri and architect Guilio Mongeri were suspended from the School of Fine Arts, where they would return to teach again in 1913. Many Italian citizens were deported and chose not to return in the aftermath (Ürekli 2018, 661–669). On the other hand, the Balkan Wars marked the beginning of a decade-long conflict of nation-state building. The overwhelming defeat deeply traumatized Ottoman society. The people of Constantinople witnessed destitute soldiers arriving from battlefields, and Muslim refugees living on the streets, in mosques and in train stations (Akın 2018, 20ff.).

The Ottoman Empire allied with Germany and entered the Great War against British, French and Russian forces with terrifyingly insufficient resources and many unhealed scars in November 1914. In order to mobilize the population, the warring governments aimed to invigorate the sentiments of nationalism. The CUP would follow an atrocious path to affect this. A correspondent of *Kölnische Zeitung*, Harry Stuermer (1917, 48, 197f.), who had lived in Pera between 1915 and 1916, was revolted by the CUP's antagonism toward Greeks, and particularly Armenians who were arrested, deported and ultimately killed. The non-Muslim population was fraught with panic and desperation. In 1915, the famous painter Salvatore Valeri left the imperial capital for good; it had been his home since the early 1880s (Germaner/İnankur 1989, 153). The replacement of various languages on street and shop signs with the Ottoman-Turkish script disrupted the daily life of polyglot Pera (Stuermer 1917, 165f.). Due to the entrance of German troops and decreasing influence of the French, Pera seemed unrecognizably strange to Émile Edwards (1915, 92). But eighteen-year-old German soldier Georg Steinbach (2017, 22–27) did not feel like an outsider in the district that he deemed almost identical to the modern cities of Germany. On 13 November 1918, immediately after the Ottoman Empire's defeat in the Great War, the Allied troops began landing in Constantinople. The Anatolian side went to Italy, Galata and Pera to the British, while the southwest was controlled by the French. The Allies would stay in Constantinople until 6 October 1923, making it the only capital occupied after the Great War (Criss 2015).

The Allied-controlled Constantinople welcomed Ottoman-Armenian intellectuals and artists who survived the 1915–1916 massacres. In 1920, reputed painter Panos Terlemezian and Levon Sevrope Kurkciyan held an exhibition in Pera (Anonymous 1920, 3; Tongo 2015, 138). A year later, the Society of the Artists of Armenia, founded in Tbilisi, organized its sixth exhibition in Pera and offered a visual response to the catastrophe while enabling Armenian visibility in Constantinople (Tongo 2021). On the other hand, the migration of Russians that occurred in waves with peaks in 1919 and 1920 brought almost 200,000 émigrés to Constantinople – this included ideologues, writers, performers, art critics, art dealers and artists who significantly contributed to Pera's cultural life (Dumont 1996, 177; Bakar 2015, 18, 43, 147–151). The Union of Russian Academicians, the Association of Russian Engineers and the *Presse du Soir/Vecherniaia Pressa* (1920–1925) newspaper,[8] all of which were founded in Pera, indicate the Russian émigré community's well-organized cooperation in exile (Deleon 1990, 39; Bakar 2015, 117, 122). Having started their operations in 1913 in Petits Champs, the Young Men's Christian Association (Y.M.C.A.) opened the Russian refugee club *Russky Mayak* (Russian Lighthouse) on 1 April 1920, at Rue Brousse, no. 40, Pera. With its library, gym, concert hall and exhibition space, this was a place where contacts could be established, particularly among artists, intellectuals and musicians (Bournakine et al. 1924, XLVI; Toprak 1994, 531; Harwood Philips 2019, 27). Mayak also sheltered an "Artists' Studio" for collaborations and hosted nine exhibitions of the Union of Russian Artists in Constantinople,[9] which was founded in 1921 and officially turned into an independent organization called the Union of Russian Artists in Constantinople by January 1922 (fig. 14.2). The union organized three more exhibitions in the Taksim Mac Mahon Barracks and the Y.M.C.A. building at Rue Kabristan, no. 40 (Anonymous 1922, 3; Anonymous 1923, 3; Bournakine et al. 1924, XLVI).

The occupation thus nourished cross-cultural collaborations and alliances within the Constantinople art world after the dormant years of the Great War. Dimitri Ismailovitch, a member of the Union of Russian Artists in Constantinople who lived in Pera, was the only non-Turkish painter displaying his artwork in the *Çemberlitaş Exhibition* of 1921 which was held in the Historic Peninsula (Anonymous 1921, 3; Gritchenko 2019, 213; Güler 2020, 172). The Turkish painter İbrahim Çallı tried to break with aesthetic traditions of the past by adopting a

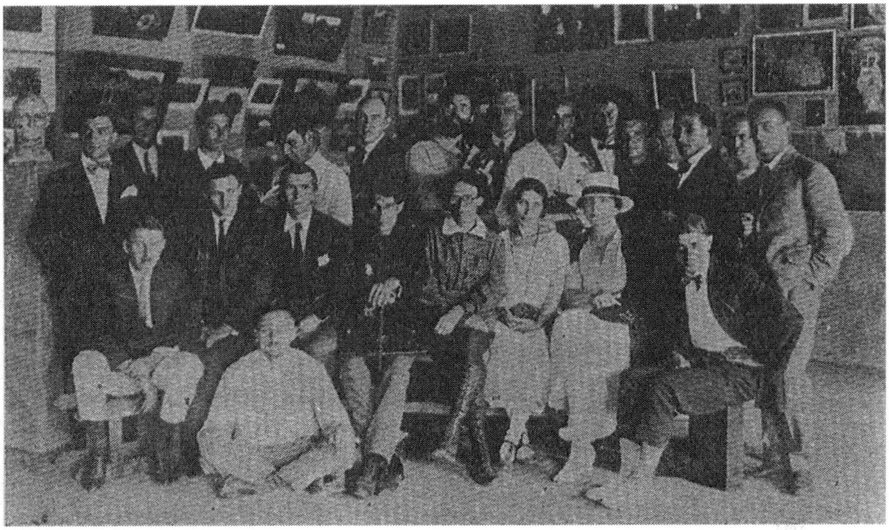

FIGURE 14.2: The group portrait of the Union of Russian Artists in Constantinople (Bournakine et al. 1924, XLVI).

modern approach to art under the stylistic influence of his friend, the Ukrainian émigré painter Alexis Gritchenko, who mingled with the Turkish artistic milieu (Gritchenko 2019, 147–157, 190ff.; see Güler 2020).

Russian émigrés transformed the cultural atmosphere of Grande Rue de Péra by operating numerous restaurants, patisseries, night-time establishments and shops. Nightspots such as Le Grand Cercle Moscovite, Rose Noire and Maxim eased the border-crossings between nations, religions and sexes (Üsdiken 1994, 20ff.; Alexandrov 2015, 191, 237). Russian patisseries and restaurants, too, hosted artistic gatherings in the early Republican period. Some of the most popular among those venues were Petrograd and Turquoise (Es 1978, 46ff.; Adil 1993, 45ff.). During the occupation, Rue Kabristan and Rue Mezarlık (today's Meşrutiyet Caddesi) became a noteworthy axis, home to the British headquarters at Kroecker's Hotel, the American Embassy, the Union Française, Pera Palace Hotel, Gardenbar and Petits Champs. Clubs, hotels and embassies played a significant role in vitalizing the art market since they acted as contact zones for art dealers, art buyers and artists passing through the city. Constantinople went through far-reaching transformations in an astonishingly short time, a metamorphosis owed to transnational flows of people as well as to political ambivalence. Nevertheless, the ongoing Turkish War of Independence in Anatolia would lead to the dissolution of this multinational atmosphere and the emergence of modern Turkey.

The city of departures

Istanbul, not Constantinople[10]

The victories scored by Turkish forces elevated the spirit of the Turkish national movement from the early months of 1921 onwards. The withdrawal of Italy and France from the lands of Anatolia affected the overall course of the Turkish War of Independence, which would evolve into a war fought between Greeks and Turks. The liberation of Izmir from Greek occupation in September 1922 heralded the end of the armed conflict and prompted the Greeks of Constantinople, especially those who were pro-Venizelos, to join the ongoing exodus of Armenians and Russians. On 29 October 1923, the Republic of Turkey was proclaimed, with Mustafa Kemal (later Atatürk) as its first president, and Ankara replaced Constantinople as its new capital. From then on, the revolutionaries aimed to secularize and modernize society.

Limiting social heterogeneity was neither a purpose nor a concern of the newly founded state, which instead took advantage of its cultural diversity to expand the scope of its transformation. From 1927, the Turkish government invited foreign specialists into the country in order to reach the standards of Western Europe, and from 1933 on those emigrants included German-speaking specialists such as architect Ernst Egli or art historian Ernst Diez (Dogramaci 2019, 112). Even so, intensifying Turkification policies had extreme consequences, including the campaign of 1927, "Citizen, speak Turkish!" For around 28 per cent of Istanbul's population, which had diminished to 794,000, Turkish was not the native language (Aslan 2007, 250). The year 1927 also saw the replacement of *Beyoğlu* with Pera and *İstiklal Caddesi* with its Grande Rue de Péra. Greeks, Armenians and Jews that once constituted the Ottoman Empire were now seen as minorities. Besides, the Russian émigré community had dwindled to only a few thousand by the 1930s, as Constantinople turned into transfer point for people fleeing the civil war (Bakar 2015, 294).

Turkish-nationalist enthusiasm gradually encouraged Turkish artists to incorporate local elements into their art-making, but a proper gallery was still absent in Istanbul. From the late 1920s, Turkish artists often held exhibitions in *Türk Ocakları* (Turkish Hearths) and later *Halk Evleri* (People's Houses). They also maintained the long-standing tradition of exhibiting artwork in various restaurants, theatres or bars in Beyoğlu. In 1931, the Union of Independent Painters and Sculptors, which consisted of local artists educated in Munich and Paris, held an exhibition at the Turquoise restaurant/bar at İstiklal Caddesi, no. 310 (fig. 14.3). Operated on the top floor of Karlmann Bon Marché by the Russian emigrant Mihail Mihailovitch, Turquoise was referred to as "Moscovite" in newspapers

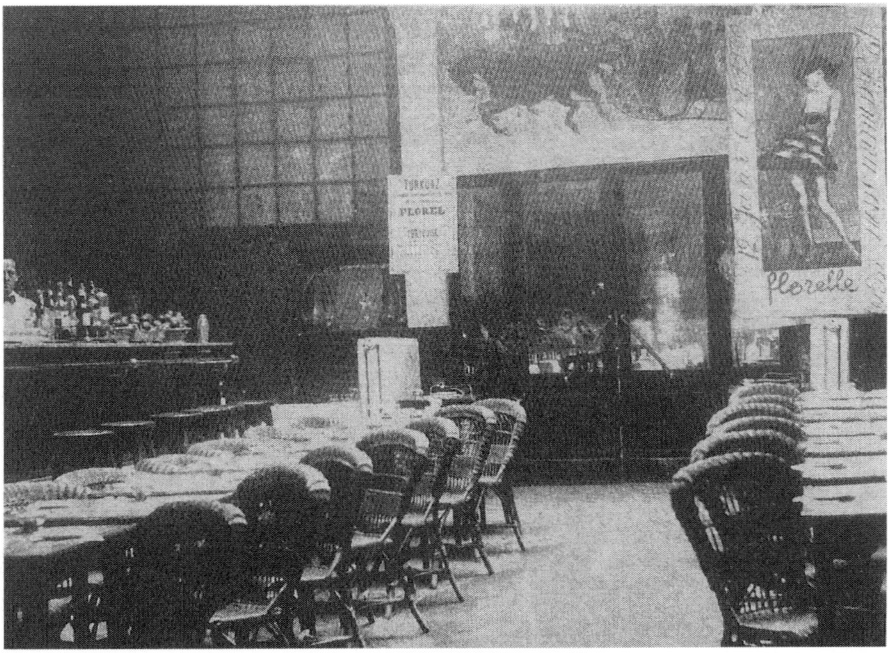

FIGURE 14.3: The interior of Turquoise bar/restaurant in Beyoğlu, the 1930s (Akıncı 2019b, 148).

(Pelvanoğlu 2007, 48–52). As one of the most celebrated nightspots of the occupation period, Le Grand Cercle Moscovite had changed its name to Turquoise after relocating to Karlmann Bon Marché in the mid 1920s (Üsdiken 1994, 21) but its legendary image persevered in public memory.

The years between the 1930s and the 1950s were a period marked by attempts to construct a national history of art (Dogramaci 2019, 119), defining new styles like 'Turkish Cubism', and exploring its 'roots' through *Yurt Gezileri* (Excursions to the Homeland). Inaugurated in 1950 at Kallavi Sokak, no. 20, Beyoğlu, the Maya Art Gallery hosted over seventy exhibitions in four years as it became one of the most influential contact zones for Istanbul's art world (see Smith 2020). In 1954, the AICA (L'Association Internationale des Critiques d'Art) held its sixth international congress in Istanbul under the title *The Effect of Eastern Art on Western Art* in conjunction with the painting competition *İş ve İhtihsal* (Work and Production), organized by Yapı ve Kredi Bank. Famous Turkish painters eagerly participated in the competition to prove how talented they were and how strictly they monitored the European art scene. However, the winner declared by Lionel Venturi, the head of the jury, was Aliye Berger, who did not receive her art education at the Istanbul Academy of Fine Arts (former Sanayi-i Nefise Mektebi).

Deeply shocked by this decision, the elites of the Academy started to question the very existence of the Turkish national art. From that moment on, Bedri Rahmi Eyüboğlu started to play a pioneering role, interpreting local elements to reconstruct a national art. The frustration in the Istanbul art world grew when Maya Art Gallery had to close due to financial difficulties. Fortunately, the patisseries, restaurants and cafés of Beyoğlu, such as Nisuaz, Markiz, Vienna Café House or Café Eptalofos, continued to host artists and intellectuals as they had always done (Akıncı 2019a, 130–137).

Until the violence committed against the Greeks on 6–7 September 1955, Beyoğlu had been a unique site of encounters that nourished Istanbul's artistic and cultural life. The organized attacks targeting the Greek community were gruesome, which inevitably affected everyday life, and deeply wounded not only Beyoğlu but also Istanbul. Nine years later, when the scars had not yet healed, a political crisis broke out between Greece and Turkey regarding the island of Cyprus; when it was Turkey's move, the presence of Greek citizens living in Turkey became the subject of dispute. More than twelve thousand Greek people were obliged to leave the country where their families' ancestors were born, with their residence and work permits revoked. Among them was the painter and illustrator Ivi Stangali, who was a member of the Onlar Group and one of Bedri Rahmi Eyüboğlu's students/assistants. Although a group of intellectuals, artists and writers of the time sent a letter saying that they had witnessed Ivi Stangali being a loyal artist to her country, the government's decision would not change. She eventually left Turkey and was never able to return after her expulsion (see Bozis/Sinanlar Uslu, 2019).

Conclusion: Pera as a site of artistic encounters

Our research seeks to understand broader political and social circumstances by focusing on artists' arrivals and departures from the 1840s to 1960 while mapping Istanbul's cosmopolitan district of Pera. Mapping our findings revealed the fertile potential hidden in unseen networks, relationships and possibilities, as we could make graspable a wealth of multidimensional connectivities (fig. 14.4).

The main difficulty in tracing Pera's residents, exhibition spaces and other contact zones lies in the scarcity of the material provided by the *Annuaire Oriental* during the Republican period. Additionally, such yearbooks were no longer available after the mid-1940s. Part of the buildings and venues marked on our map no longer exist today due to population shifts from rural to urban areas and ever-changing urban planning.

While working on our map, we took as our initial reference points the three crossroads of Grande Rue de Péra which irrevocably shaped urban development

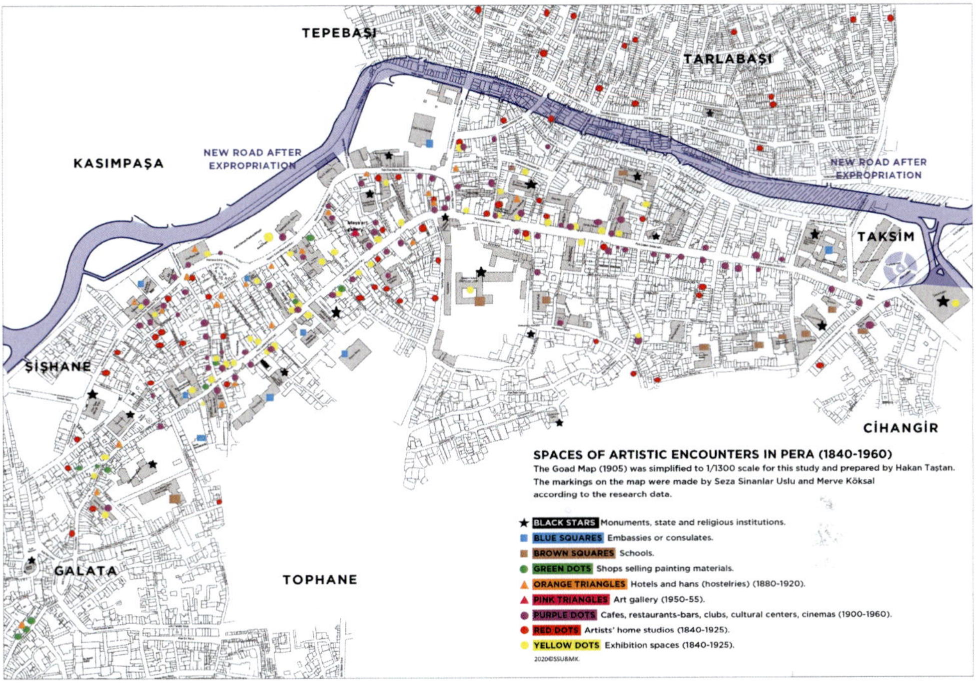

FIGURE 14.4: The markings on the map illustrating the 'spaces of artistic encounters in Pera (1840–1960)' were made by Seza Sinanlar Uslu and Merve Köksal according to research data. The Goad Map (1905) was simplified to a 1/1300 scale for this study and prepared by Hakan Taştan (2020©SSU&MK).

and cultural life. Dört Yol, the first and the oldest crossroads of the district, which exists since the Byzantium times, merges Asmalımescit and Kumbaracı streets; the second crossroad intersects with Galatasaray Square, a place that hosted important imperial schools, and the last one combines Taksim and Rum Kabristan streets. Additional significance is held by prominent tourist attractions that demarcated the urban space: Galata Tower (528 CE) and *Mevlevihane* (Whirling Dervish Lodge); the cemeteries of Petits Champs de Tepebaşı and Grands Champs de Taksim which were zones of encounter for Constantinople's Muslim[11] and non-Muslim[12] people; the embassies or consulates of Russia, France, Great Britain, Holland and Sweden.[13]

Having grown around Dört Yol and inhabited by Europeans – predominantly the French – Asmalımescit was one of the oldest quarters in the region after Genoese Galata. In addition, the nearby residential district of Tarlabaşı offered rental accommodation at relatively affordable prices. Our map accordingly shows that arriving artists usually chose to establish their home studios in Asmalımescit and

Tarlabaşı. Mapping also provided insights into potential artistic connections and collaborations; for instance, Giovanni Brindesi and Amedeo Preziosi, two émigré artists who happened to be neighbours in Yeni Çarşı Sokak near Galatasaray crossroads, might have already been acquainted before coming to Pera or met during their time at Yeni Çarşı, sharing ideas and skills. Another example would be Hippolyte Dominique Berteaux who presumably visited Pierre Désiré Guillemet's painting academy nearby the British Embassy while he was painting the ceiling frescos of Köçeoğlu Residence, located within a couple of minutes walking distance. The markings on the map do not merely represent urban locations but render visible a plethora of artistic connections and alliances.

We also notice that the showcase exhibitions we described earlier were held mainly on Grande Rue de Péra, especially in the shops between Dört Yol and Galatasaray crossroads. The influx of Allied soldiers and the takeover of the Taksim Military Barracks by occupying forces during 1918–1923 brought about the emergence of new music halls, bars, restaurants and similar venues on the Galatasaray-Taksim axis. Yet as the map also demonstrates, temporary exhibition spaces, the primary contact zones of artists, were not concentrated here and grow sparser around Mis Sokak without reaching the Taksim area, despite an increase in numbers of cultural and entertainment venues since the 1900s. Furthermore, our map indicates that the Asmalımescit neighbourhood – surrounded by Petits Champs' main street and Grande Rue de Péra – played a central role in establishing exhibition traditions and encouraging the district's cultural life.

Mapmaking adds a new and visual dimension to the story of art production in Pera, shedding light on the blind spots in our knowledge of the artistic process while also opening numerous possible paths to assess the cultural history of the late Ottoman Empire and modern Turkey. Strolling through İstiklal Caddesi means witnessing urban environments that have retained the air of past centuries, despite experiencing some losses. We are greatly indebted to those who inspired us by cultivating this fascinating example of coexistence unique to Pera.

NOTES

1. Examples of such works include Gérard de Nerval's *Voyage en Orient* (Charpentier 1851), Théophile Gautier's *Constantinople* (Michel Lévy Frères 1853), Alexis Gritchenko's *Deux ans à Constantinople* (Quatre Vents, 1930), Dorina Neave's *Twenty-six Years on the Bosphorus* (Grayson and Grayson 1933), Anna Grosser-Rilke's *Nie Verwehte Klänge: Lebenserinnerungen aus acht Jahrzehnten* (Verlag Otto Beyer 1937) and Said Naum-Duhanî's *Vieilles Gens, Vieilles Demeurres: Topographie Sociale de Beyoğlu au XIX ème Siecle* (Touring et Automobile Club de Turquie 1947).

2. For example, Fikret Adil's *Asmalımescit 74 (Bohem Hayatı)* (Sühulet Kütüphanesi 1933) and Salâh Birsel's *Ah Beyoğlu Vah Beyoğlu* (Sander Yayınları 1976).
3. Galata Saray-ı Ocağı was founded in 1481; Mekteb-i Tıbbiye (School of Medicine of Galatasaray) was founded in 1839; Mekteb-i Sultani (today's Galatasaray High School) was founded in 1868.
4. The Taksim Military Barracks were taken over by British forces and turned into Mac Mahon Barracks during the occupation.
5. The venue serves as Istanbul Cinema Museum at Atlas Pasajı, no: 131, Beyoğlu. The frescos of Hippolyte Dominique Berteaux are still extant.
6. Today, Panter Kırtasiye is selling art supplies at the same location.
7. *Zapiski Prostodushnogo* (Notes of the Innocent, 1921) by émigré satirist Arkady Averchenko (1881–1925) depicts the Russian daily life under occupation through the collection of stories set in Pera. It was first published by bookstore Kultura opened by Russian émigrés at Grande Rue de Péra, no. 385, in April 1921 (Deleon 1990, 39).
8. The printing house of *Presse du Soir/Vecherniaia Pressa* was at Asmalımescit Street, no. 35, Pera (Rizzo 1922, 906).
9. See Ekaterina Aygün's study: www.//metromod.net/publication/bogazin-ruslari-1920li-yillarda-beyoglundaki-rus-gocmen-sanatcilar. Accessed 19 July 2021.
10. Written by Jimmy Kennedy and composed by Nat Simon, "Istanbul (Not Constantinople)" is a song in swing style about Istanbul's name changes since the Ottoman conquest. Having been first performed by a Canadian music band, the original single of the piece was issued by Columbia (40082) by The Four Lads orchestra conducted by Norman Leyden, recorded on 12 August 1953.
11. Turks, Arabs, Kurds, etc.
12. Greeks, Armenians, Jews, etc.
13. Founded in turn in 1845, 1847, 1850, 1859, and 1870.

REFERENCES

Adil, Fikret. *Asmalımescit 74 (Bohem Hayatı)*. İletişim Yayınları, 1993.

Akın, Yiğit. *When the War Came Home: The Ottomans' Great War and the Devastation of an Empire*. Stanford University Press, 2018.

Akıncı, Turan. *Beyoğlu: Yapılar, Mekanlar, İnsanlar (1831–1923)*. Remzi Kitabevi, 2019a.

Akıncı, Turan. *Cumhuriyette Beyoğlu: Kültür, Sanat, Yaşam (1923–2003)*. Remzi Kitabevi, 2019b.

Alexandrov, Vladimir. *Siyah Rus*. Türkiye İş Bankası Kültür Yayınları, 2015.

Anonymous. "Armenian Paintings." *The Orient News*, 1 May 1920, p. 3.

Anonymous. "Ressamların Sergisi." *Vakit*, 14 May 1921, p. 3.

Anonymous. "Rus Ressamlar Sergisi." *Akşam*, 17 June 1922, p. 3.

Anonymous. "Rus Resim Meşheri." *Vatan*, 25 June 1923, p. 3.

Anonymous, [Exposition de peinture], np, Stamboul (Journal quotidien, politique et littéraire) 2–3 May 1897.

Anonymous, [L'Exposition Ahmed Ali Pacha], np, Stamboul (Journal quotidien, politique et littéraire) 30–31 May 1897.

Anonymous, [Exposition de tableaux], np, Stamboul (Journal quotidien, politique et littéraire) 12 December 1898.

Aslan, Senem. "Citizen, Speak Turkish!" A Nation in the Making, Nationalism and Ethnic Politics, vol. 13, no. 2, 2007, pp. 245–272. doi:10.1080/13537110701293500. Accessed 7 July 2021.

Averçenko, Arkadi. *Bir Safdilin Hatıra Defteri* (Modern Klasikler Dizisi, 117). Translated by Mustafa Kemal Yılmaz, Türkiye İş Bankası Kültür Yayınları, 2019.

Bakar, Bülent. *Esir Şehrin Misafirleri: Beyaz Ruslar*. Tarihçi Kitabevi, 2015.

Bournakine, A.A., et al., editors. *The Farewell Almanac*. Imprimerie L. Babok & Fils, 1924.

Bozis, Sula, and Seza Sinanlar Uslu. *İvi Stangali: Ressamı Hatırlamak*. Yapı Kredi Yayınları, 2019.

Çelik, Zeynep. *19. Yüzyılda Osmanlı Başkenti Değişen İstanbul*. Translated by Selim Deringil, Türkiye İş Bankası Kültür Yayınları, 2017.

Criss, Nur Bilge. "Istanbul Under Occupation (1918–1923)." *Constantinople 1918 / Konstantiniyye 1918*, edited by Ali Serim, Denizler Kitabevi, 2015, n.p.

Davis, C. Claflin. "Refugees." *Constantinople To-day or the Pathfinder Survey of Constantinople: A Study in Oriental Social Life*, edited by Clarence R. Johnson, The Macmillan Company, 1922, pp. 201–226.

Deleon, Jak. *Beyoğlu'nda Beyaz Ruslar (1920–1990)*. Çelik Gülersoy Vakfı İstanbul Kütüphanesi Yayınları, 1990.

Dogramaci, Burcu. "Strangers in a Foreign Language. Writings on Art and Architecture in Turkish Exile." *Migrating Histories of Art. Self-Translations of a Discipline*, edited by Maria Teresa Costa and Hans Christian Hönes, De Gruyter, 2019, pp. 111–124.

Dumont, Paul. "Beyaz Yıllar." *İstanbul 1914–1923*, edited by Stefanos Yerasimos and translated by Cüneyt Akalın, İletişim Yayınları, 1996, pp. 176–195.

Edwards, Émile. *Journal d'un Habitant de Constantinople (1914–1915)*. Librairie Plon, 1915.

Es, Hikmet Feridun. "Beyaz Ruslar İstanbul'da." *Yıllar Boyu Yakın Tarih Dergisi*, vol. 8, 1978, pp. 46–49.

Gautier, Théophile. *Constantinople*. Michel Lévy Frères, 1853.

Germaner, Semra, and Zeynep İnankur. *Oryantalizm ve Türkiye*. Türk Kültürüne Hizmet Vakfı, 1989.

Gritchenko, Alexis. *İstanbul'da İki Yıl 1919–1921: Bir Ressamın Günlüğü*. Translated by Ali Berktay, Yapı Kredi Yayınları, 2019.

Güler, Ayşegül. "In Pursuit of Alexis Gritchenko's Years in Istanbul." Ayşenur Güler and Vita Susak. *Alexis Gritchenko – The Constantinople Years*, edited by Nilüfer Şaşmazer, exh. cat. Vehbi Koç Vakfı / Meşher, Istanbul, 2020, pp. 131–207.

Hamsun, K., and H.C. Andersen. *İstanbul'da İki İskandinav Seyyah*. Translated by Banu Gürsaler-Syversten, Yapı Kredi Yayınları, 2006.

Hanioğlu, Şükrü. *A Brief History of the Late Ottoman Empire*. Princeton University Press, 2008.

Harwood Phillips, George. *Taking a Chance on Love: The Life and Music of Vernon Duke* (American Popular Music Series, vol. 5). University of Oklahoma Press, 2019.

Nerval, Gérard de. *Voyage en Orient*, vol. 1. GF-Flammarion, 1980.

Özyiğit, Halil. *1830–1920 Yılları Arasında Süreli Yayınlarda Türk Resim Sanatı Eleştirisi*. Ph.D. dissertation, Ankara Üniversitesi, Sosyal Bilimler Enstitüsü, Sanat Tarihi Anabilim Dalı, 2012.

Pelvanoğlu, Burcu. *Hale Asaf: Türk Resim Sanatında Bir Dönüm Noktası*. Yapı Kredi Yayınları, 2007.

Rizzo, Alfred, editor. *Annuaire Oriental, Oriental Directory. Commerce, industrie, administration, magisture*. Constantinople: Imprimerie de l'Annuaire Oriental, 1922. *SALT Araştırma*, www.archives.saltresearch.org/handle/123456789/2894. Accessed 7 July 2021.

Sinanlar, Seza. *Pera'da Resim Üretim Ortamı 1845–1916*. Ph.D. dissertation, İTÜ, Sosyal Bilimler Enstitüsü, Sanat Tarihi Anabilim Dalı, 2008.

Sinanlar Uslu, Seza. "Hippolyte Dominique Berteaux and His Journey to Istanbul in 1870s." *14th International Congress of Turkish Art (ICTA). Proceedings*, edited by Frédéric Hitzel, Collège de France, Paris, 2013, pp. 701–708. *Academia*, www.academia.edu/2557365/_ Hippolyte_ Dominique_ Berteaux_ and_ his_ journey_ in_ Istanbul _ in_ 1870_ s_ Paris_ 2011?auto=download. Accessed 7 July 2021.

Sinanlar Uslu, Seza. "Adolphe Thalasso'nun Gözünden Meşrutiyetin Osmanlı Sanat Ortamına Yansımaları 1908–1914." *Semra* Germaner Armağanı, edited by Banu Mahir, MSGSÜ Yayınları, 2014, pp. 261–272. *Academia*, www.academia.edu/7260911/Adolphe_ Thalassonun_ gözünden_ Mesrutiyetin_ Osmanli_ Sanat _ Ortamina_ Yansimalari_ 1908_ 1914_ Semra_ Germaner_ Armagani_ MSGSÜ_ Yayinlari_ Mart _ 2014_ s_ 261_ 272?auto=download. Accessed 7 July 2021.

Sinanlar Uslu, Seza. "Son Araştırmalar Işığında Pera Salon Sergileri." *Sanat Tarihi Dergisi*, vol. 30, no. 1, April 2021, pp. 337–367. *DergiPark*, doi: 10.29135/std.832675. Accessed 7 July 2021.

Smith, Sarah-Neel. "The Semiperipheral Art Gallery. A Case Study in 1950s Istanbul." *Third Text*, vol. 34, no. 2, 2020, pp. 271–290.

Steinbach, Georg. *Strolling Through Istanbul in 1918. The War Memoirs of the German Private Georg Steinbach* (Memoria: fontes minores ad historiam Imperii Ottomanici pertinentes, vol. 3), edited by Ruben Gallé, Max Weber Stiftung, Orient-Institut Istanbul, 2017, www.perspectivia.net/servlets/MCRFileNodeServlet/ ploneimport_ derivate_ 00011662/ galle_ istanbul. Accessed 7 July 2021.

Stuermer, Harry. *Two War Years in Constantinople*. Translated by E. Allen and Harry Stuermer, Hodder and Stoughton, 1917.

Thalasso, Adolphe. "Les Origines de la Peinture Turque."*L'Art et Les Artistes*, vol. 6, 1907, pp. 366f.

Tongo, Gizem. "Artist and Revolutionary: Panos Terlemezian as an Ottoman Armenian Painter." *Towards Inclusive Art Hsitories: Ottoman Armenian Voices Speack Back*, special issue of *Études Arméniennes Contemporaines*, vol. 6, 2015, pp. 111–238. *OpenEdition Journals*, doi: 10.4000/eac.893. Accessed 8 July 2021.

Tongo, Gizem. "'This Grand Slaughter': Art, Memory, and the First World War in Occupied Istanbul" (Conference Presentation at the Panel: From Empire to Nation-State | Rethinking Post-WWI and Armistice Through the Lens of Literature and Art), The University of Michigan's Center for Armenian Studies (CAS), 19 February 2021. *YouTube*, uploaded by Center for Armenian Studies, 24 February 2021, www.youtube.com/watch?v=XVt8WLVSN3w. Accessed 12 June 2021.

Toprak, Zafer. "YMCA." *Dünden Bugüne İstanbul Ansiklopledisi*, vol. 7, edited by İlhan Tekeli, Kültür Bakanlığı and Tarih Vakfı, 1994, pp. 531–532.

Ürekli, Fatma. "Tarblusgarp Savaşı'nın (1911–1912) Osmanlı Kurumlarında Çalışan İtalyan Sanatkârlara Etkisi ve İdarî Uygulamalar." *Tarihin* Peşinde Bir Ömür Abdülkadir Özcan'a Armağan, edited by Hayrunnisa Alan et. al., Kronik Kitap, 2018, pp. 647–678. *Academia*, www.academia.edu/47881640/_TRABLUSGARP_SAVASININ_1911_1912_OSMANLI_K URUMLARINDA_ÇALISAN_ITALYAN_SANATKARLARA_ETKISI_VE_IDARI_UYG ULAMALAR_Abdülkadir_Özcana_Armagan_Tarihin_Pesinde_Bir_Ömür_Tam_Metin_Full_Text_. Accessed 12 June 2021.

Üsdiken, Behzat. "Eski Beyoğlu'nda Restaurant, Birahane, Bar, Gazino ve Meyhaneler I." *Toplumsal Tarih*, vol. 3, 1994, pp. 20–25.

15

Russian Belgrade: In-between Alive and Dead

Marina Sorokina

Over the past decades, the humanities have focussed more and more on the complexity of collective historical memory. Numerous studies on how states, societies, communities and the public construct their past and what role "sites of memory" (following Pierre Nora's terminology) play in these narratives have been published in the last years (Nora 1989, 7–24). The accelerated development of migration studies has raised questions about the specifics of the formation and preservation of migrants' historical memory. In this sense, cemeteries are of particular interest since they, as specific 'sites of memory', can singularly reflect diasporic memory and capture the experience of trying to preserve national identity in a foreign environment: indeed, as I will show in this chapter, cemeteries create a particular embodied text as part of a migrant's historical narrative.

'Mortal' spaces are an important source for studying not only memory but 'life' itself – the practices, activities and interactions of migrants with their host society. The development of urban anthropology, as well as the rise of migration studies, has led to a shift in the understanding of migrant communities – from passive contemplators to self-determined agents who actively participate and often even significantly influence the development of many social and cultural institutions in their new host countries.

Although the Russian necropolis in foreign lands[1] has long been the focus of professional research and recent decades have seen more and more publications on Russian migrant cemeteries (such as Sainte-Geneviève-des-Bois and Caucade in France, Berlin-Tegel in Germany, and Olšany in Czech Republic) (see Видякина, Ковальчук 2004; Грезин 2009; Грезин 2012; Талалай 2014), the memorial practices of Russian emigrants in the urban space have never been the subject of study.

In this regard, the Serbian historian Milana Živanović's recently published monograph *И крст и петокрака. Руски гробни комплекси у Југославији у 20. веку* (I krst i petokraka: ruski grobni kompleksi u Jugoslaviji u 20. Veku)[2] deserves attention since it deals with the history of Russian migrants' grave complexes – cemeteries, plots, ossuaries, tombs, monuments, memorials and tombstones – located in former Yugoslavia in the context of both state and émigré policies and practices (Živanović 2020). However, even in this monograph, the question of how the professional/occupational skills of Russian migrants (especially architects) are reflected in memorial practices in the Serbian urban space is not considered.

That is why my chapter focuses on the New Cemetery (*Novo Groble*) in Belgrade – a place where collective historical memories and artistic practices of Russian migrants met with the challenges posed by a new environment and its urban agendas in the former Kingdom of Yugoslavia.

This research was conducted with the help of two interrelated methods. The first one, the archival method, deals with the history of the Russian émigré community and was implemented in Russian and Serbian archives – the Archives of Yugoslavia, the Historical Archive of the City of Belgrade and the State Archive of the Russian Federation, among others. This helped me locate the lives and work experiences of Russian exiles in both Russia and Yugoslavia. The second method consists of conducting relevant fieldwork: photographing the monuments, cleaning and reading the epitaphs, and attributing the tombs to Russian émigrés. I conducted this fieldwork during my research trips to the Belgrade New Cemetery over a period of seven years.[3] In this paper, I show how such an important local historic landmark as the cemetery can act as an entry point for the exploration of a significant but not well-researched topic, the interactive relationship between Russian émigrés and their host city Belgrade.

The role of Russian-speaking émigrés in Belgrade's urban transformations

The period after the First World War and the collapse of the great Austro-Hungarian, German, Ottoman and Russian Empires was followed by a stream of migrants and refugees on the one hand, and by the creation of a new geopolitical and sociocultural European space including new-born Slavic states (such as the Czechoslovak Republic, the Kingdom of Serbs, and Croats and Slovenes) on the other.

In the decade that followed the 1917 Russian Revolution, about a million Russian[4] refugees had settled in more than 60 countries in Europe, North and South America, China and Africa. They hoped to return to a 'Russia without Bolsheviks'[5] and founded 'Russia Abroad'[6] as an alternative to the Bolshevik world, with its own centres and capitals (Paris, Berlin, Prague) and a large number of artistic and intellectual institutions. 'Russia Abroad' was supposed to bolster the national and cultural identities of Russian migrants in exile. At the same time,

Russians actively participated and sometimes played a crucial role in the everyday life and urbanization of many European cities, especially in the so-called 'provinces of exile'.

The Kingdom of Serbs, Croats and Slovenes (KSCS), called the Kingdom of Yugoslavia from 1929, takes a special place in the history of the Russian diaspora in the interwar period of the 20th century. It was one of the main centres of the diaspora and consisted of more than forty thousand Russian migrants who had arrived after the Russian Revolution and the civil war (1917–1922).

As a new-born state, KSCS was undergoing a complex postimperial transformation itself, and struggled to construct a new national identity across a spectrum of international and domestic agendas. One of the consequences of this struggle was a certain loyalty to Russian refugees. Because the Royal Government was willing to assist Russian exiles, the entry and integration of the 'alien' (migrant) Russians into all spheres of interwar Yugoslavian life was relatively easy and effortless, in contrast to much harsher conditions in other countries.

Their high educational level helped many Russian refugees to integrate into their new environments quickly and successfully. Because they had a lot in common with the local people – similar language, religion and political regime[7] – many Russian intellectuals and professionals decided to stay in the Kingdom and to contribute to the development of the Yugoslav state and society: offering expertise that ranged from shipbuilding and science in general to architecture, ballet and opera (Јовановић 2006).

The new Balkan state – the Kingdom of Serbs, Croats and Slovenes – was founded on the unifying ideas of King Alexander I Karageorgevich (1888–1934) and had to demonstrate its new position in Europe. One of the most pressing problems for the KSCS was the urban identity of its political, economic, and cultural centre – the capital Belgrade. In contrast, for example, to Prague, whose urban face had preserved its historical past as a symbol of national and cultural continuity, Belgrade, which had been founded in Roman times, remained a patriarchate city in an agrarian country. It lacked the representative facilities necessary for state administration and the Court, and suffered from the absence of educated experts when it came to urban planning, architecture and construction. This opened up a significant space of possibility for Russian refugees equipped with appropriate qualifications and experience. To meet the new challenges of urban reconstruction, King Alexander[8] invited many Russian refugee architects and engineers – and they applied a Russian-imperial style to the postimperial urban space of Belgrade's city centre. Having received foundational education in the best academies and throughout their extensive professional careers, Russians now managed to occupy a relevant place in the most important state and municipal institutions within a short time; they often worked in private architectural companies, and ultimately reached a high position in the KSCS.

Like many others, the architect Nikolai Krasnov (1864–1939) did not accept the Soviet government and was forced to leave Russia in 1919. Krasnov served as the Chief Architect of the city of Yalta and headed the reconstruction of the Imperial Livadia Palace in the Crimea. Invited to Yugoslavia by King Alexander, he came to occupy a position as the head of the department in the Ministry of Constructing. By planning numerous monumental buildings and shaping Belgrade's urban architecture, he managed to embody the idea of strengthening the statehood of the young Yugoslavia. The renovations of the Royal residences in the Dedinje neighbourhood continued the architectural traditions of Crimean Imperial buildings, while also taking into account the peculiarities of local culture. To translate the idea of a 'unifying monarchy', a Russian migrant architect who dreamed of his homeland's imperial revival, developed a variety of attributes for Belgrade's urban architecture, ranging from customized designs and decorations to monuments and designs for state funerals (Ацовић 2017) (fig. 15.1).

The Russian migrants – architects, artists and engineers – cooperated with local professional communities and, in close collaboration, created a new Belgrade city space. They made a valuable contribution to different urban areas by designing

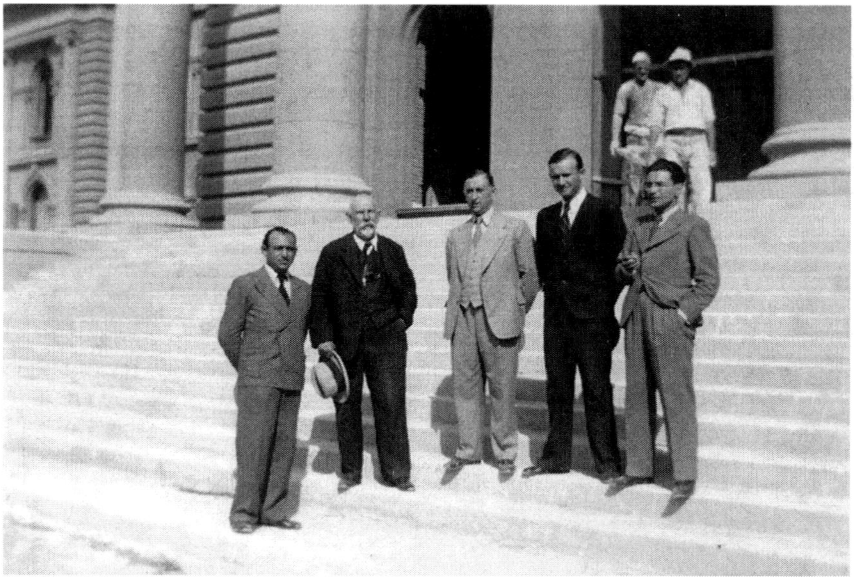

FIGURE 15.1: Architect Nikolai Krasnov (second on the left) with Serbian colleagues during the constructing of the *Narodnaia Skupshina* building (Parliament), Belgrade, 1936 (*Николай Краснов – русский зодчий Сербии: 1864–1939: Каталог выставки / Николај Краснов – руски неимар Сербије: 1864–1939: Каталог изложбе*, ред. Милан Медаковић, Дом русского зарубежья им. А. Солженицына, Москва, 2014).

and constructing government buildings, educational, commercial and industrial structures, hospitals, the Orthodox churches and monasteries, or military and civil memorials. They transferred the Russian imperial style to Belgrade's architecture and thus influenced the national Serbian-Byzantine style, too.

Russians proposed monumental solutions with richly decorated facades and defined the most important aspects of Belgrade's urban architectural identity: the Belgrade fortress, the pier of the Sava River, the promenade with the Great Staircase on Kalemegdan, the area around the Parliament, the main streets. They designed almost all of the most important state buildings of the capital: the Ministry of Finance, the Ministry of Forestry, Mining, Agriculture and Water Resources, the General Staff of the Army and the Navy, the State Archives, the Post and Telegraph building, as well as the Royal Palace in Dedinje and numerous other public buildings. These architects were Russian refugees who completely changed the official face of the capital and shaped the KSCS's modern 'Yugoslav Unitarianism' look (Боровняк 2017) (fig. 15.2).

Various Russian architects worked in Belgrade in very different directions and fields. George Kovalevsky (1888–1957) suggested a general urban plan for the city and designed the squares of Slavia and the Republic; Valery Stashevsky (1882–1945) developed residential buildings and designed the district Vozhdovats which

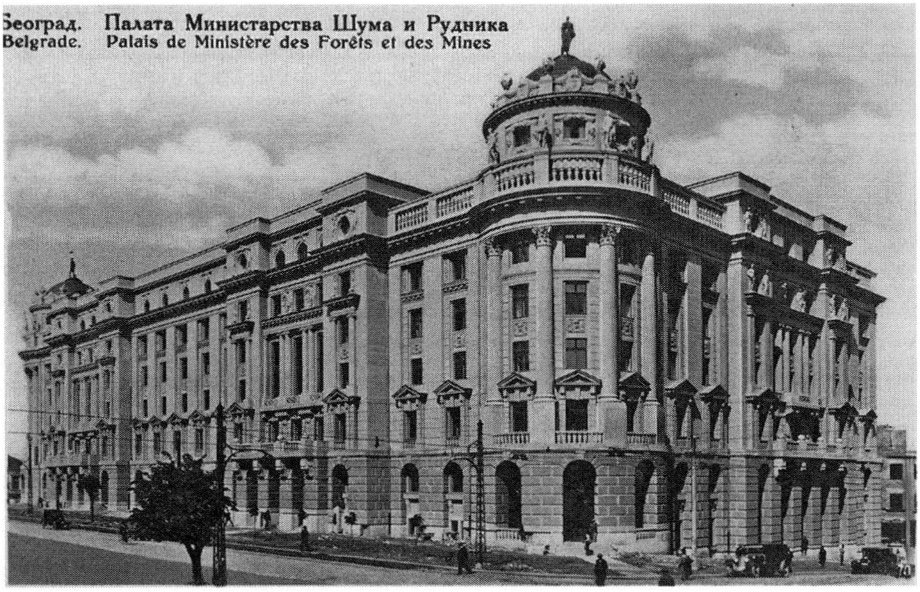

FIGURE 15.2: Nikolai Krasnov, *The Building of the Ministry for Forests and Mines*, Belgrade, 1930s, Postcard.

was mainly utilized by city officials. The architect Andrei Papkov (1890–1975) worked in the field of apartment buildings. Promoting the national style in Serbian architecture, King Alexander I Karageorgevich and the Serbian Orthodox Church invited Viktor Lukomsky (1884–1947) to manage the construction of the Patriarchate of the Serbian Orthodox Church, as well as a large number of other religious buildings (the Church of St. George in Čukarica, the Church of St. Sava on the Vračar plateau, the Church of St. Michael the Archangel on Khumskaya street, the Ružica Church located in the Belgrade Fortress and the Monastery of the Most Holy Theotokos in Senjak).

With the assistance of these Russian architects, Belgrade shed its provincialism and advanced to the level of Western Europe's capitals. Unique buildings designed by Russian migrants have shaped the urban look of Belgrade's centre, and even today their heritage is reflected in the urban texture of modern Belgrade. The Yugoslavian, now Serbian, capital became an eternal living monument to Russian migrant architects.

Russian-speaking émigrés and the New Cemetery (Novo Groble) *in Belgrade*

The Belgrade cemeteries – 'a kingdom of the dead' – were another space radically transformed by Russian migrants, among them many architects, and Belgrade's urban community.

Among the most important cemeteries counts the New Cemetery which is located not far from today's centre of the city. It was opened in 1886 and was called "new" (*Novo Groble*) because it inherited the old cemetery, which was located in the area of St. Mark's Cathedral and had been closed by the end of the 19th century. This new necropolis was the first in Belgrade to be painstakingly and systematically created as an architectural and memorial urban space for burials (Костић 1999; Брдар 2011).

The visual appearance of the New Cemetery reflects the dramatic history of the country in the 20th century – its wars and social changes, as well as the development of its artistic styles and cultural values. Today, this complex includes military cemeteries (graves from the times of the Serbian–Turkish Wars of 1876–1877, the Serbian–Bulgarian war of 1885, the Balkan Wars of 1912–1913 and the two world wars, 1914–1918 and 1939–1945), the cemetery of the liberators of Belgrade, the Jewish cemetery, the Alley of Honoured (Great) and Honorary Citizens. After the First World War, a number of foreign military cemeteries (French, Italian, Austro-Hungarian and Bulgarian) were added, as well as, after the Second World War, the Commonwealth cemetery.

Today the New Cemetery is a well-known and important 'site of memory'. It contains the burial places of some of the most famous and prominent citizens of former Yugoslavia and Serbia. It also features the graveyards of people known for their contribution to the social and cultural environments of the city, but also of those who remained unknown. These repositories of memories, united in one space, turn the New Cemetery into an 'open-air museum' (Брдар 2011) (fig. 15.3).

A great number of Russian migrants, ranging from ten to fourteen thousand at different times, found shelter in Belgrade. Initially, Russian refugees were buried in the KSCS near the main roads and in the front areas of municipal and local Orthodox cemeteries. Later, the city and local authorities allocated (both officially and unofficially) plots of land for deceased exiles on the periphery of the same cemeteries. Until the end of the 1920s, wooden crosses were installed on their graves, and then stone tombstones. They differed from the others with their eight-pointed crosses, epitaphs in Cyrillic and quotations from Holy Scripture (Арсењев 2011; Живанович 2017; Živanović 2020).

Like the other residents of Belgrade, Russian migrants were buried in free places on the New Cemetery. The first confirmed Russian burials date to February 1920, although Russians were already being buried in Belgrade in 1919, as well as before and during the First World War (Обреновић 2011).

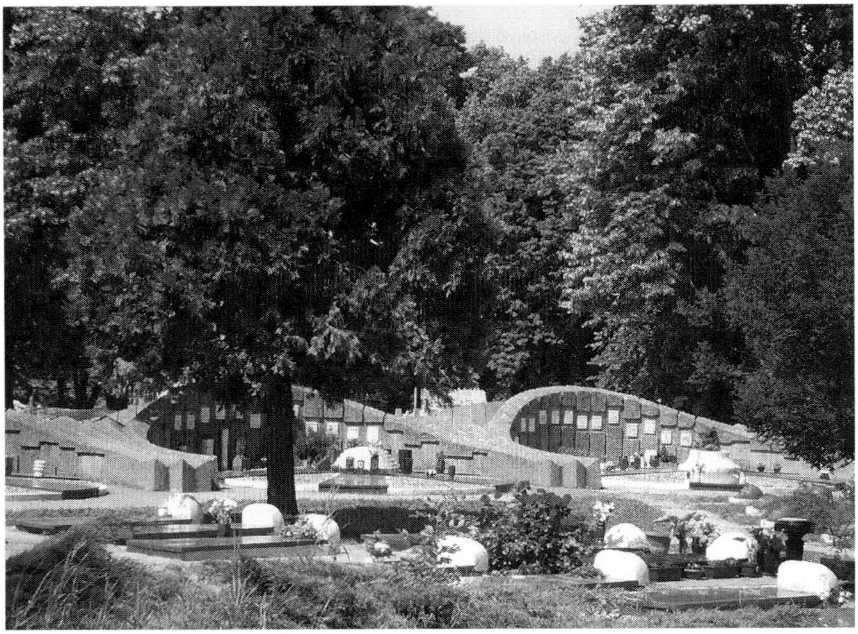

FIGURE 15.3: *Alley of Honored Citizens*, The New Cemetery, Belgrade (Photo: Marina Sorokina, 2019).

The desire to preserve Russian national and religious identity and the gradual steady increase of burials at the New Cemetery were the main reasons why separate Russian burial plots – the so-called 'Russian Necropolis' – were established in 1929. Within the contexts and conditions of migration, the cemetery as an urban public site could be singularly utilized to articulate a national identity. It is not surprising then that Russian plots were located inside the Serbian part of the cemetery: the gravestones in the form of a Russian Orthodox cross indeed gave the impression of a Russian 'island' right in the centre of the New Cemetery.

This 'island' was gifted to the Russian migrant community by King Alexander I Karageorgevich, chief patron of Russian immigrants. The Society for the Care of the Spiritual Needs of Orthodox Russians in Yugoslavia, headed by Princess Maria Svyatopolk-Mirskaya and Professor Alexei Shcherbakov, cared for this part of the cemetery. Today this memorial to 'Russia Abroad' is one of the largest compact burial sites of Russian migrants in the world and the biggest in Europe.

The Russian 'city of the dead' was one of the most important projects of the Russian migrant community in Belgrade. It differs very much from the Russian necropolises in other cities of the world because it displays and employs specific semiotic and symbolic systems[9] which can be read as meta-textual[10] references for the birth and death, the dawn and decline, of the Russian migrant community in former Yugoslavia, and the history of Russians in the Balkans more generally. On one hand, this meta-text includes and/or integrates the 'alien' (migrant) into the memorial culture and the afterlife of the local Serbian people, and on the other, it labels as well as constructs the collective identity of the Russian migrant community.

It is emblematic that the first building constructed and consecrated on the grounds of the Russian necropolis in 1931 was the Iverskaya chapel. This project, based on donations from Russian Belgrade migrants, was developed and implemented by the military engineer-refugee and architect Valery Stashevsky. The chapel is a one-to-one copy of the chapel situated at the entrance to Moscow's Red Square, demolished by the Soviets in 1929. The choice was not accidental – the news about the destruction of the Iverskaya chapel in Moscow reached Belgrade during the negotiations with the Belgrade city authorities, and engendered the idea of rebuilding the Iverskaya shrine on Serbian soil. The chapel became the resting place for many prominent ecclesiastical and secular Russian refugee-migrants. The crypt of the chapel contains the remains of Metropolitan Anthony (Khrapovitsky) of Kiev and Galicia and his cell attendant (later archimandrite of the Visoki Dečani Monastery in Serbia) Theodosius Melnik, the first rector of the Russian Church of the Holy Trinity in Belgrade, Protopriest Petr Belovidov, and others. Until the end of the 1960s, the Iverskaya chapel was in fact the second (after the Church of the Holy Trinity in Tašmajdan) Russian parish church built in Belgrade. Many prominent Russian migrants, including Countess Praskovya Uvarova (deceased in 1924), architect Nikolai Krasnov (deceased in 1939) and painter Stepan Kolesnikov (deceased in 1955), are buried on the chapel grounds.

The Belgrade municipality had provided New Cemetery land for the construction of another Russian War Memorial – a memorial to Russian soldiers of the Great War of 1914–1918. *The Monument to Russian Glory*, as it is commonly called, opened in 1935. The idea and initiative was implemented by Russian migrants, the colonel Mikhail Skorodumov and the architects Valery Stashevsky and Roman Verkhovsky (1881–1968) (fig. 15.4).

The top of the grey stone monument (= shell) is crowned by a huge angel whose wings point upwards. A Russian officer at the foot of the shell is reclining on a banner as if defending it. In the middle of the shell can be found a double-headed eagle and the date 1914. The sides of the monument have inscriptions in both

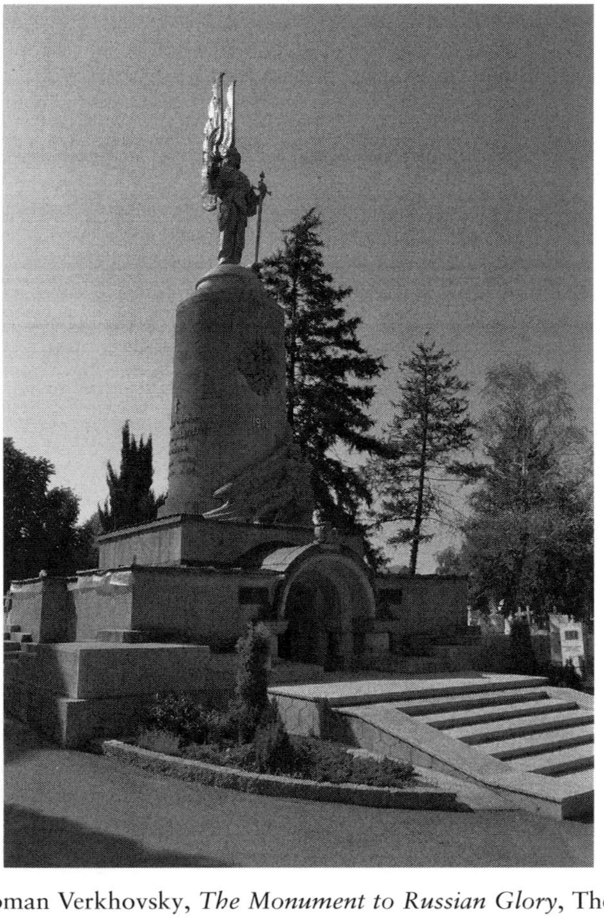

FIGURE 15.4: Roman Verkhovsky, *The Monument to Russian Glory*, The New Cemetery, Belgrade, 1935 (Photo: Marina Sorokina, 2019).

Russian and Serbian; a fact which can be considered as a token/symbol of friendship. But as Nora states, "the lieu de mémoire turns in on itself – an arabesque in the deforming mirror that is its truth" (Nora 1989, 20) – there is no doubt that this symbol of friendship can also be interpreted in different ways. The Russian text can be found engraved under the cross: "Eternal memory of Emperor Nicholas II and 2,000,000 Russian soldiers of the Great War". The Serbian phrase is located on the back of the monument: "Bravely to the fallen Russian brothers on the Salonica front in 1914–1918". A crypt-chapel located under the monument holds the remains of the Russian officers and soldiers who had died either at the Salonica front (also known as the Macedonian front) during the defence of Belgrade or from their wounds in hospitals in Serbia.

For decades, the *Monument to Russian Glory* was the only 'site of memory', both in Europe and in Russia, for Russians who gave their lives for the Fatherland during the First World War. It has thus always attracted huge attention all over the world.

Russian migrants have left their artistic marks on the New Cemetery, not only by constructing these Russian *lieux de mémoire* but also on the Serbian parts of the cemetery. Many important monuments of particular national importance for the Serbians and their history were designed by Russian émigré architects. This includes the Serbian crypt of the defenders of Belgrade in 1914–1918 and the Monument to those who died for the Fatherland, which still count as the most representative sights of the cemetery today.

The Serbian crypt of the defenders of Belgrade 1914–1918 was designed by the architect Roman Verkhovsky, who had made a similar crypt for the Russian soldiers of the First World War. He constructed it according to Serbian national style – with a Serbian two-headed white eagle, a Serbian soldier on top of the monument and a genuine Serbian cannon from the Great War. The whole complex was built from 1927 to 1931 by the Society of Military Officers and Reserve Soldiers with the support of the Belgrade Municipality. Once, it was the largest monument in the Kingdom of Yugoslavia, and the crypt under it, which holds the remains of more than four thousand Serbian soldiers who died during the Balkan Wars and the First World War, is one of the largest burial sites in the country.

Similar in size, and rising almost parallel to the Serbian crypt, one can find Russian and Serbian Great War Monuments which symbolically and ideologically represent the close link between the two nations. They were designed by Russian architects and engineers as symbols of Russian–Serbian friendship, support and cooperation, which, as conceived by the creators, had no limits either in time or space.

The architect Nikolai Krasnov designed another important monument for the Serbs – 'For Services to the Fatherland'. It was erected over the burial grounds of honoured citizens, statesmen and military leaders who died during the Great War at home or abroad. Moreover, the academic style chosen by Krasnov, emphasizing the stability and power of the country, pleased the local authorities so much that it became common-place and can still be found over the graves of honoured citizens and in other Serbian cemeteries.

Apart from official monuments, Russian architects designed and built a lot of private chapels – for the Serbian benefactor Velimir Teodorović, the merchant John Savic, the chapel of the academicians Vladimir and Ivan Spužić.

The architectural and artistic practices of Russian architects in the New Cemetery articulate their deep-reaching and permanent involvement in the development and maintenance of Belgrade's urban space – for both the dead and those still alive. The Russian pantheon in the New Cemetery was created as an object of great political, social and cultural importance for the Russian diaspora but at the same time, it was and still is an intrinsic part of Belgrade's urban spatial makeup. This ambivalence reflects the migrant community's persevering link to pre-revolutionary Russia, but also their desire to be accepted as an equal partner and friend in their new social environment (fig. 15.5).

As has become clear, famous Russian architects worked for both Russians and Serbians within the spaces of the New Cemetery. In comparison to other Russian cemeteries in the world (for example in Prague, Sofia or New York), this is unique.

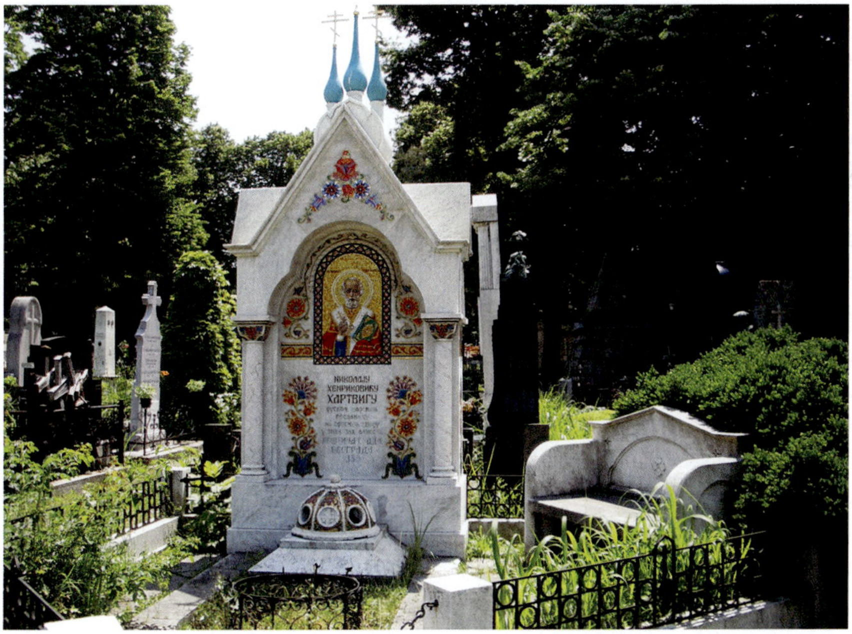

FIGURE 15.5: George Kovalevsky, *The Tomb of Nikolai von Hartwig (1857–1914),* Russian diplomat to Belgrade, The New Cemetery, Belgrade (Photo: Marina Sorokina, 2019).

As a collection of architectural and sculptural monuments and as an important memorial complex, the cemetery preserves the memory of Russian refugees of the 20th century. Finally, it is the New Cemetery that turned out to be the only 'location of dense residency' of Russians in Belgrade.

In lieu of a conclusion

The urbanization of the Yugoslavian capital in the interwar period entailed new architectural and urban planning policies, new urban programmes and many architectural models conceived and developed by Russian migrants. Three generations of Russian architects worked in Belgrade – the older generation arrived in the KSHS at the peak of their creative activity and consisted of several well-known and mature professionals with a richly implemented architectural practice (George Kovalevsky, Nikolai Krasnov and others); the middle generation grew professionally in Belgrade and has since firmly established itself in Yugoslavia (Viktor Lukomsky, Valery Stashevsky, etc.); the youngest generation completed their studies at the University of Belgrade (among this generation are Andrei Papkov, Grigory Samoilov and others). All of them worked to make the new urban space of Belgrade more modern and European-looking. The Russian architects impacted not only the city centre's architectural appearance, but also influenced many other districts of Belgrade. Guided by lofty ideals and a serious commitment to their profession, they made a significant contribution to strengthening Russian–Serbian relations, which are in turn embodied in the buildings and the urban atmosphere of the Yugoslavian/Serbian capital. In fact, King Alexander I Karageorgevich bestowed Yugoslav state awards to many Russian refugee-architects.

With the assistance of Russian migrants, the New Cemetery, an important urban site for both the dead and alive, has become an open-air historical monument that still magnetizes people.

Subsequent historical events – such as the Second World War, the German occupation of former Yugoslavia and the period after the liberation – forced many of the Russian migrants, including engineers and architects who had found a home in Belgrade, to travel new roads, this time to even more distant lands...

NOTES

1. As part of the activities of the Alexander Solzhenitsyn Centre for Studies of Russia Abroad in Moscow I conducted seminars on the topic of the 'Russian foreign necropolis' or, in other words, places in other countries where Russian emigrants are buried. One of these seminars was dedicated to the state of the Russian necropolis in Belgrade, Serbia.

2. Both the Cross and the Five-Pointed Star. Russian Burial Complexes in Yugoslavia in the 20th century (author's translation).
3. The results of this study are presented on two websites – *The Russian Scientific Necropolis* (www.russiangrave.ru) and *The Russian Serbia* (www.russianserbia.com).
4. The term 'Russian' is used in this text as a juridical definition – denoting citizens of the former Russian Empire/Russian Republic.
5. The title of the political party which had come to power in Russia in 1917.
6. The term 'Russia Abroad' was and is still widely used in academic literature. It covers a system of institutions that had been created by Russian refugees in the interwar period.
7. Before 1917, the Russian Empire was a monarchy; the Kingdom of Serbs, Croats and Slovenes was a monarchy in 1918–29.
8. He was educated in the former Russian Empire and spent a lot of time in Saint Petersburg.
9. According to Pierre Nora, "[c]ontrary to historical objects, however, lieux de mémoire have no referent in reality; or, rather, they are their own referent: pure, exclusively self-referential signs. This is not to say that they are without content, physical presence, or history; it is to suggest that what makes them lieux de mémoire is precisely that by which they escape from history. In this sense, the lieu de mémoire is double: a site of excess closed upon itself, concentrated in its own name, but also forever open to the full range of its possible significations" (Nora 1989, 23f., translated by Marc Roudebush).
10. In a sense that the cemetery here is an architectural 'text' that comments on the historical 'text'.

REFERENCES

Арсењев, Алексеј. *Самовари у равници: руска емиграција у Војводини*. Змај, 2011.

Ацовић, Драгомир. *Николај Краснов: албум сећања / Николай Краснов: альбом памяти*. Хералдички клуб / Геральдический клуб, 2017.

Боровняк, Джурджия. "Российские архитекторы и инженеры – эмигранты в Белграде между двумя мировыми войнами." *Ежегодник Дома русского зарубежья имени Александра Солженицына. 2017*, ред. Н.Ф. Гриценко, Дом русского зарубежья имени Александра Солженицына, 2017, *с*. 46–60.

Брдар, Милан, уредник. *Ново гробље у Београду. Отворено сведочанство историје. Поводом 125 година од оснивања*. ЈКП: Погребне услуги, 2011.

Грезин, Иван. *Алфавитный список русских захоронений на кладбище в Сент Женевьев де Буа* (Российский некрополь, вып. 9). Старая Басманная, 2009.

Грезин, Иван. *Русское кладбище Кокад в Ницце*. Старая Басманная, 2012.

Јовановић, Мирослав. *Руска емиграција на Балкану: 1920–1940*. Čigoja štampa, 2006.

Костић, Братислава. *Ново гробље у Београду*. ЈКП: Погребне услуги, 1999.

Nora, Pierre. "Between Memory and History: *Les Lieux de Mémoire*." *Memory and Counter-Memory*, special issue of *Representations*, no. 26, 1989, pp. 7–24. *JSTOR*, www.jstor.org/stable/2928520. Accessed 17 May 2021.

Обреновић, Виолета. “Руси на Новом гробљу у Београду.” *Ново гробље у Београду. Отворено сведочанство историје. Поводом 125 година од оснивања*, уредник Милан Брдар, ЈКП: Погребне услуги, 2011, *с*. 209–213.

Видякина, Светлана, и Светлана Ковальчук. *Покровское кладбище. Слава и забвение*. Multi-Centrs, 2004.

Талалай, Михаил. *Российский некрополь в Италии* (Российский некрополь, 21). Старая Басманная, 2014.

Živanović, Milana. *И крст и петокрака. Руски гробни комплекси у Југославији у 20. веку*. Institut za noviju istoriju Srbije, 2020.

Живанович, Милана. “Смерть на чужбине: Сербия как последний приют русских беженцев.” *1917 год в истории и судьбе российского зарубежья. Международная научно-просветительская конференция Москва, 26–28 октября 2017 года*, сост. М.Ю. Сорокина, Вифсаида, Русский путь, 2017, *с*. 643–665.

PART IV

SITUATING EXPERIENCE

16

Urban Exile: The Case of the Nazi Ghetto

Alexis Nouss

The ghetto this text revolves around is not a historical ghetto, such as the one in Venice, which has turned, not without irony, into a must-see on tourist circuits alongside the Doge's Palace or Saint Mark's Basilica; it is a concentration camp ghetto designed by the Nazis to confine Jews during the Second World War. Such a ghetto is part of an exilic spatiality in play during the Shoah. Preceding extermination camps, the concentration camp ghetto is a place where extermination is temporarily delayed. Testament to that is the Purim festival, which was celebrated in the Warsaw ghetto in 1941, commemorating the ancient story in which, under the Persians, the Hebrews were saved from extermination by Queen Esther:

> *Under conditions of this sort we celebrated Purim, 5701. The Book of Esther was not read in the darkened synagogues, because all public worship is prohibited; but we were happy about the defeat of the Persian Haman. We celebrated Purim in the Zionist soup kitchen at 13 Zamenhof Street, which is the centre of all Hebrew-Zionist social activity. [...] When we come here we forget our troubles and all the terrible events taking place outside.*
>
> (Kaplan 1973, 256)

Out of history while at the heart of history: this is the nature of urban exile provided by the ghetto.

Exilic spatiality

In the context of occupied Europe from 1940 to 1944, such ghettos exemplify forms of exilic spatiality which could be at work in a city. This is a spatiality alien to any territorial definition and the space of the exilic city – i.e. the city as it is structured by exilic experiences, or *exiliance* (see Nouss 2018) – turns provisional and fragile. This stands in stark contrast to the values of refuge and stability that any urban order is supposed to embody, which consequently leads to a deepening of the link between urban space and exilic space. Inevitably, this link disrupts the functions of the city, both in terms of the temporality that surrounds it and the topography that frames it. A paradoxical mixture of immobility and incessant movement defines exilic spatiality within the city. In this sense, the exilic city illustrates the "aesthetics of uprootedness" that Klaus Mann called for (Mann 1942, 117) in response to the torments and horrors of the Nazi period.

In a spatial and political sense, a ghetto occupies a city in a more effective way than any army could because it structurally modifies it. Nazified Warsaw was more Nazi because of its ghetto than because of the presence of the *Kommandantur*. Whether the Jews were regrouped in a ghetto in a city they had previously inhabited or whether they were transferred to a ghetto in a city they had not previously inhabited does not make much of a difference insofar as the modern urban reality remains wholly uniform: homogenous multistorey buildings, street networks and shops create an easily recognizable social as well as mental urban space. Moreover, the tragedy of the ghetto habitat is accentuated by the fact that it takes place in a familiar and non-frightening reality, unlike the camp (*shoah* or *gulag*). Known reality is erased and replaced by a terrifying reality or, rather, as is the case in a phenomenology of exile which compulsively combines past and present, the two realities are superimposed on each other, resulting in an *Unheimlichkeit* effect. In this respect, and without discussing the range of possible translations and etymologies of the Freudian concept, it can be noted that the German term connotes both *Heim* (house) and *Geheimnis* (secret), two words that resonate with the ghetto: a dwelling that remains hidden within the city insofar as its access is restricted. In this *heterotopia*, the Foucauldian notion to describe a place which disturbs the order of space, familiar images of the city mix with other images related to the concentration camp world: photos of the Warsaw ghetto show emaciated figures walking the streets, starving children begging at the foot of Haussmann buildings, corpses lying behind storefronts.

"People are trapped in history and history is trapped in them" (Baldwin 2017, 177). James Baldwin speaks of such a trapped, ghettoized history from his experience as a child of the black ghetto, concretely that of Harlem and, more globally, that of black existence in the United States. An individual ghetto, worn directly on the body, tailor-made to the size of each person, symbolizes the ostracized neighbourhoods of New York, Chicago and other cities and countries. Supported by brick walls or skin pigment, segregation – Jewish ghettos, Black ghettos – can have similar effects, with a noteworthy distinction. From the Jewish ghetto, one can potentially escape; regarding the black ghetto, escape is impossible or cruelly temporary: no social success, even up to a presidency, will erase a black skin. If Edgar Hilsenrath says of his 1941 Jewish character Ranek that "the ghetto life was stamped on his forehead" (Hilsenrath 2007, 169)[1] like Cain's sign of infamy, the inhabitants of the black American ghetto carry the stigma all over their body. Baldwin calls African Americans "Latter-day exiles" (Baldwin 2017, 69), stressing the identification of black Americans with the suffering of the Hebrews. But exile is not a state or a situation, it is a human condition – one of the human conditions – that circumstances can either activate or leave laying latent. To say that the ghetto turns its inhabitants into exiles says as much about their condition as about their being; without ever rooting them, it fixes their identity.

Exilic experience

An exilic experience as it is shaped by life in the ghetto exhibits three major aspects. The first concerns the question of the *outside*, which is illuminated by the experience of confinement in the ghetto and which is crucial for understanding the exilic experience. A ghetto dweller is, like an exile, cut off from their familiar space, although their experience is different: for them the *inside* does not exist in relation to an *outside* since their inside has closed in on itself as a condition of survival, existing intransitively. As for the exile, their fate is to be brutally exposed to the outside – an outside they will survive by creating an inside that in turn will become the true site of exile. This is an idea expressed by Saint-John Perse – who fled Nazi occupied Europe and chose to stay in his American exile after the war –, when he wrote of Dante that his banishment from Florence opened for him "the closed field of exile" (Saint-John Perse 1972, 455; my translation). Inside/outside, one cannot exist without the other: this dialectical game is well known. But if the outside is forbidden, if it is not possible to test it, then can it retain its authority or even its reality? What is more, the outside is by right shared and sharable, in opposition to an inside with a restricted communality. This is an opposition that overlaps with the divide between *public* and *private*. In the ghetto, such a logic is crushed: if the outside for the ghetto dweller may theoretically exist in a virtual exteriority demarcated by the ghetto walls, the inside is in no way private since it is totally shared. Because of overcrowding, any intimacy inside is denied and private lives are exposed, just as if in an outside context.

The *all-ghetto* factor characterizes the second aspect: in the ghetto, *everything is ghetto*. If diversity and openness have produced the city since modernity, the urbanity of the ghetto has lost any such qualities. A July 1942 dream by Mary Berg described in her memoirs of the Warsaw ghetto expresses this with cold precision:

> [July 10, 1942] During the last few nights I have had terrible nightmares. I saw Warsaw drowning in blood: together with my sisters and my parents, I walked over prostate corpses. I wanted to flee, but could not, and woke in a cold sweat, terrified and exhausted. The golden sun and the blue sky only irritate any shaken nerves.
>
> (Berg 2009, 231)

James Baldwin extends the metaphor and goes one step further: "All of Harlem is pervaded by a sense of congestion, rather like the insistent, maddening, claustrophobic pounding in the skull that comes from trying to breathe in a very small room with all the windows shut" (2017, 59). The confinement becomes internal, an *internment* in the proper sense of the word. It is written on every stone, every brick, every street. Like the law court in Kafka's *The Trial* or like the castle in the novel of the same name, the place merges with its function: the ghetto becomes the only place to live. As the Texan rapper Chamillionaire sang in his 2007 *Ultimate Victory* album: "Sometimes it seems like I'm stuck, I'm in the ghetto / But I've got love for the ghetto".[2] This homogenization of the city, here paroxysmal, is inscribed to the exilic ethos as it draws on the perception of the place of refuge as a heterotopic site. The urban refuge is unknown in its entirety and as such remains an object of distrust or rejection throughout. The only places where the one in exile can find solace are those occupied by other exiles, but these places do not belong to the city, as they constitute patches or reserved enclaves. In novels of exile under Nazism (such as written by Anna Seghers, Erich Maria Remarque, Lion Feuchtwanger or Klaus Mann), the characters cannot find rest anywhere, and the city is only a space to be traversed incessantly, on the run from the Nazis or in search of a visa, a passport, a boat ticket.

Of all the possible places of confinement, the ghetto is particular in the sense that it is not a space *for* confinement, its whole spatial function *is* confinement. The *all-ghetto* law dictates the rule of habitability: one does not dwell in a ghetto as one does in a city. Even if it is located within a city – that is, with the possibility of staying in one or another subspace of the city – in the ghetto, everything is ghetto. A city can have a ghetto as one of its functions, just as it can have gardens or hospitals, and the ghetto could become a segment in and of the urban system, but in itself the ghetto has only one function, which is to be a ghetto, and this function determines all other urban purposes the ghetto could encompass. The ghetto garden is not a space of escape since nobody could ever leave the ghetto; the ghetto hospital where the sick stay is not a space of healing since the inhabitants of the ghetto are all promised to death. The probability that a child can forget the walls and a sick person their suffering does not oppose the rule, it highlights its perversity. Opposing the *habitable* with the *uninhabitable* in the domus of the ghetto, Jean-François Lyotard takes up the example of the Warsaw ghetto which was dedicated to *Vernichtung* (annihilation) and posits: "It is necessary to erase it because it constitutes a useless opacity in the [Nazi] program of total transparency" (1988, 214; my translation). The ghetto is as dark and murky as the deepest night.

The third and final aspect under consideration here concerns the dimension of time which hosts a kind of parallel chronological structure, the representation of which goes back to Biblical narratives. Among the Jewish holidays, one holiday took on particular importance in the ghetto: Pesach, the Jewish Passover, the remembrance of the exit from Egypt and a celebration of the liberation from Pharaoh's tyranny. A short story from Adolf Rudnicki's collection *The Golden Windows* is titled "Passover", and it stresses the moment when the ghetto resistance embraces the opportunity to mix religious songs, popular songs and revolutionary songs. In this scenario, further developed from the biblical story and detailed in the reading for Pesach evening, the Haggada, one situation in particular applies to that of the ghetto, namely the episode of Passover night. Both scenes illustrate the idea of a divided but uninterrupted history: in order to be spared from the angel of death striking the Egyptians, the Hebrews must remain confined to their homes, but this does not remove them from history since it directly concerns their future liberation from slavery. It is because they stay confined to their houses that night that they will be free later.

Even if someone can be distant or separated from the course of history, no one can be really cut off from it. In the ghetto, the spatial exclusion is matched by temporal exclusion insofar as the ghetto dweller, being cut off from the world, is also cut out of the world's temporal fabric. But history moves forward and hovers over executioners as well as victims. When W.G. Sebald's character, Jacques Austerlitz, tries to come to terms with the memory of the Theresienstadt ghetto, he is unable to contain history in a narrative, and rather drowns in it (Sebald 2011).

The passivity that prevents intervention in the face of crime, whether singular or mass, often conveniently invokes the pretext of distance, although victims are not fooled:

> Of all this, of the children transformed alive into smoked meat, one used to say: "It's in the ghetto", which sounded like at an infinite distance. One would say, "This is the ghetto", and peace of mind would return. [...] A hundred meters away in space, fifteen months away in time – and that was enough.
>
> (Rudnicki 1979, 20f.; my translation)

The testimony of Marek Edelman, one of the leaders of the Warsaw ghetto uprising, echoes the novelist:

> The wall did not go beyond the second floor. From the second floor, we could see the other side, a merry-go-round, people… We heard music and we were terribly afraid of going unnoticed, afraid of disappearing behind it without anyone noticing our existence, our struggle, our death.
>
> (Edelman/Krall 1983, 71; my translation)

The ghetto does not belong to a distant reality, neutralized in tragic exoticism – it is part of the city: the Warsaw ghetto, the Lodz ghetto. It is the city transformed according to an operation that follows the law of exilic spatiality. The exilic space implies a displacement that cuts off a part of the planet from the rest – exilic space as exiled space. Inevitably, spatial as well as temporal rationality is henceforth ordered by an external principle: "'Today is Sunday', the Redhead grins / 'How do you know that?' / 'Can't you hear anything?' / Ranek pricks up his ears, motionless. 'Yes', he whispers… 'I hear them… in the distance… the bells. It's coming from the other side? From the Romanian shore?'" (Hilsenrath 2007, 210). In the Ukrainian ghetto of Prokov, only the Romanian side, the "other side", sets the pace.[3]

Exilic night

Marshal Antonescu ordered the systematic exile of Jewish people to the eastern regions of Romania, today's Ukraine, beyond the Dnjestr-Nistra river. The mass deportation of Jews from Romania began in July 1941 and few survived three freezing winters, typhus, cholera, hunger and violence. The writer Edgar Hilsenrath survived only to sink into a depression from which the writing of *Nacht* (Night), the major literary work about the ghetto, helped him to emerge after about a decade. Hilsenrath, disregarding the silence imposed on the survivors and their supposed vow of literary modesty, approaches the limits of what can be said. What was supposed to remain unspeakable separated the human being from what makes them human: language. Speaking out is an act that refuses to conceal the turpitude to which the inhabitants of the ghetto were subjected if they wanted to survive. In the ghetto, they live in an eternal night that seems to swallow up any salvation available for the human condition.

There is no need to stage a *journey to the end of the night*, the 'ghetto night' is never-ending, untouched from one end of the ghetto to the other. There is no need to invoke a violin above a roof (be it the Hollywood or the Chagall version) as music is liquidated, too. An old fiddler plays, holds his hat out to bystanders and receives only a spit:

> "What was he playing?" asked a woman in the crowd to her husband. [...] "I don't know what he was playing," the man said, "it wasn't a Romanian tune. Nor a Yiddish tune." / "Nor Ukrainian," said the woman, "nor Russian either. We would have recognized it." / "It was crap," the man said, "like any music"
>
> (Hilsenrath 2007, 99)

In the ghetto of Prokov, in the spring of 1942, in the bombed and burned city, the signs of everyday life are unclear and accentuate the contradictory superimposition of normality and urban exceptionality. In-between the The Grand Café and a brothel, a barber still cuts hair even though his main business connects to the black market; a shoemaker still practices his skill while the main protagonist, Ranek, steals shoes from the dying and trades them for a few onions; the same observes a desirable young girl to conclude that she is only "a garbage eater like him" (ibid., 261). Instead of bringing hope, the birth of a child becomes incongruous, useless, in this reign of death, this night of inhumanity. The ruined house where Ranek is staying is a dormitory without beds that provides night shelter for "the poorest of the poor in the ghetto" (400). The street has lost its name – could have been "Lenin" or "Gorky" – and most of the houses are destroyed. This ghetto within the ghetto becomes the central stage, rarely left, of the novel whose title in the first version was *The Night Asylum*. Survivors of all ages, many of them sick, pile up next to each other in horrible promiscuity and share what is not even fate anymore, without fraternity and solidarity. A nurse who came to deliver a baby remarks: "[...] the people here are different. [...] It's like they're not human beings anymore" (400). Further in the book, two orphaned children who also live in the asylum, a boy and his younger sister, observe Ranek and his companion Deborah: "Like us they have no one left. /– No one left? asked the child. /– They too are the last ones" (568).

This notion of the "last one" becomes even more terrifying as it is pronounced by a child to whom the burden of embodying the future falls: a child who should only ever be concerned with being the first one. A relevant variation on the theme is the idea of the 'last Jew', a concept meditated upon against the backdrop of the Shoah by Paul Celan and Jacques Derrida, among others. Could this last Jew be Ranek? The man is without morals and without feelings, it seems, a picaro of the abyss, half-Schweik half-Wozzek; a *shlemiel* if it were not for his resourcefulness and cynicism.[4] He is no more an anti-hero than Robert Musil's man-without-qualities would be, insofar as both characters evolve in certain environments – Ranek in the Prokov ghetto, Ulrich in 1900 Vienna – which, despite disparate historicities, dissolve the very notion of heroism by stifling the system of values indispensable to heroic functioning. "[He] looked like a scarecrow all slumped and silent in his rags, looking in the void. He wore a funny hat that was much too big, which clashed with his face" (Hilsenrath 2007, 462).

In its eccentricity, however, this hat which makes him recognized throughout the ghetto and the novel, illustrates a destiny other than that of the ghetto, a promise or an expectation, the proof that he can, without heroic exceptionality, not be the ghetto's last Jew, that he could get out from the ghetto – if only as the bearer of a narrative. This is a narrative of life or death, not in a clear-cut antagonism but in a diabolical intertwining, an infernal dialectic without resolution – at least from the survivor's viewpoint who is never sure of his survival.

Not-being-the-last-ones could sum up the resistance principle of the Polish ghettos of Warsaw, Wilno and Bialistock, which rose up under the action of Jewish fighters groups, and it should not be forgotten that "*Zog nit keyn mol*" (Never say), the "Song of the Jewish Partisans", was signed by Hirsch Glik, a member of the Wilno United Partisans Organization. Its second stanza refers to the world outside the ghetto as the battlefield for revolts: "From green lands of palm to lands with white snow / We come with our pain and our woes / And from where a spurt of our blood falls / Will sprout our strength and our courage."[5]

However, these movements of struggle and resistance are undertaken in the name of values external to their environment, values external to any environment, values from outside the ghetto. Emmanuel Ringelblum kept repeating the Warsaw resistance was primarily motivated by the willingness to remain human beings and to not be transformed into beasts as war usually does (see Ringleblum 1986). He was thus demanding for the ghetto the right to be a universal symbol, therefore transforming its spatiality: breaking down the ghetto walls, he was claiming an ethics for the world.

Ghetto ethics

Nacht encapsulates this humanism of the last Jew, the "hope for the hopeless" Walter Benjamin talked about in his 1922 essay on Goethe's *Elective Affinities* (Benjamin 1996, 356). In Hilsenrath's work, the representation of the ghetto reveals the darkest part of man, and how apparent normality is constantly being torn apart to give way to images that convey the unthinkable, the unbearable... sequence after sequence throughout the book. But the story ends with a *pietà-in-the ghetto*. "Deborah held the child closer to her, as if she feared losing him. '[...] They will not hunt us, as they hunted him [Ranek, dead]. I'll dig out something to eat, too'. Deborah smiled. 'Don't be afraid', she repeated. 'Mother is watching over you'" (Hilsenrath 2007, 632). These are last words of the book, uttered in the ghetto, yet heard by the reader, from outside.

For Hilsenrath, the ghetto remains forever nocturnal, a final night brought upon the city, the night of exile. And yet, he concludes on the *pietà* scene with a potential redemptive spark that, however, does not manage to tear the night apart. Such could be an ethics of the ghetto, as radical in its impossibility as that of Emmanuel Levinas – with one difference: it is not turned towards the other but towards the self, a kind of infra-ethics. It asks to act so that the self may live. The value of the ethical gesture toward the other stands in and for itself and not as any result for the other. This resembles Levinas' radical ethics insofar as it unfolds freely, outside of any moral code or contract, validated by its sole obligation: "One is going to too much trouble for this scum, he [Ranek] thought. Others are tougher, they would not have had as many scruples as you. One still tries to be decent [...] and then, what is in it for us?" (Hilsenrath 2007, 515). What's in it? Us. We gain by remaining human, by clinging to the human species, which, even if it becomes a species, is still human:

> But there is no ambiguity, we remain men, we will finish as men. The distance that separates us from another species remains intact, it is not historical. It is an SS dream to believe that we have a historical mission to transform our species, and as this mutation is done too slowly, they kill. [...] there are no human species, there is one human species.
>
> (Antelme 1978, 229; my translation)

NOTES

1. Excerpts from Edgar Hilsenrath's book are translated by Béatrice Gonzalés-Vangell and the author.
2. Chamillionaire. *Ultimate Victory* Chamillitary/Universal Motown, 2007.
3. The ghetto Hilsenrath was confined to from 1941 to 1944 was located in the city of Mogilev-Podolsk, renamed Prokov in the novel.
4. Jaroslav Hašek's Schweik and Georg Büchner's Wozzek are characters whose innocence and naivety are used to denounce the absurdity of war and of the modern world. In yiddish culture, a *shlemiel* is a clumsy and unlucky character.
5. "Zog Nit Keynmol." *Wikipedia*, www.//en.wikipedia.org/wiki/Zog_Nit_Keynmol. Accessed 10 May 2021. See also Kalisch/Meister (1985).

REFERENCES

Antelme, Robert. *L'espèce humaine*. Gallimard/TEL, 1978.

Baldwin, James. *Notes of a Native Son*. Penguin Classics, 2017.

Benjamin, Walter. "Goethe's Elective Affinities." Translated by S. Corngold. *Selected Writings Volume 1, 1913–1926*, Belknap Press, 1996.

Berg, Mary. *The Diary of Mary Berg: Growing up in the Warsaw Ghetto*. Translated and edited by S.L. Schneiderman, Oneworld Publications, 2009.

Edelman, Marek, and Hanna Krall. *Mémoires du ghetto de Varsovie. Un dirigeant de l'insurrection raconte*. Translated by Pierre Li and Maryna Ochab, Éditions du Scribe, 1983.

Hilsenrath, Edgar. *Nacht*, edited by Helmut Braun, Deutscher Taschenbuch Verlag, 2007.

Kalisch, Shoshana, and Barbara Meister. *Yes, We Sang! Songs of the Ghettos and Concentration Camps*. Harper & Row, 1985.

Kaplan, Chaim A. *The Warsaw Diary of Chaim A. Kaplan*. Translated and edited by Abraham I. Katsh, Collier Books, 1973.

Lyotard, Jean-François. *L'inhumain. Causeries sur le temps*. Galilée, 1988.

Mann, Klaus. Tagebuch. 5.6.1940–11.12.1942. Nachl. Klaus Mann/Biografische Dokumente (Münchner Stadtbibliothek/Monacensia, Munich, 22 March 1942), KM D 70. *Monacensia im Hildebrandhaus*, pp. 116–119. www.monacensia-digital.de/mann/content/titleinfo/30176. Accessed 25 June 2021.

Nouss, Alexis. *La condition de l'exilé. Penser les migrations contemporaines*. Éditions de la Maison des sciences de l'homme, 2018.

Ringelblum, Emmanuel. "To Live with Honor and Die with Honor." *To Live with Honor and Die with Honor! Selected Documents from the Warsaw Ghetto Underground Archives 'O.S.' ['Oneg Shabbath']*, edited by Joseph Kermish, Menachem Press, 1986, pp. 762–772.

Rudnicki, Adolf. *Les fenêtres d'or et autres récits*. Translated by Anna Posner, Folio, 1979.

Saint-John Perse. "Discours de Florence." Idem. *Œuvres complètes* (Bibliothèque de la Pléiade, no. 240), La Pléiade, 1972, pp. 449–459.

Sebald, W.G. *Austerlitz (Penguin Essentials)*. Translated by Anthea Bell, Penguin, 2011.

17

Booked for Exile: Leo Steinberg's Urban Passages and Textual Homelands

Louis Kaplan

> *The dwelling assigned, ascribed to Israel is the House of the Book. Heine's phrase is exactly right:* das aufgeschriebene Vaterland. *The 'land of his fathers', the* patrimoine, *is the script.*
>
> (Steiner 1985, 5)

Introduction

This chapter explores how thinking about books and about the relationship of a political refugee with his books – as valued possessions, as sacred objects, as sources of memories, etc. – can contribute to the growing field of Exile Studies. Specifically, I will explore what this relationship means in the biography of Leo Steinberg (1920–2011), a young Jewish refugee who was forced to leave his home in Berlin in the face of Nazi persecution in 1933. In applying the erudite literary critic George Steiner's theoretical framework as formulated in his essay "Our Homeland, the Text" (1985) to this individual life journey, my guiding assumption is that this exiled youth and Jewish diasporic subject replaced his lack of belonging to any nation-state or geo-territorial homeland with the 'textual homeland' of the book as a precious and even a sacred object. To offer a specific case history, I will focus on the meaning and the significance of the conscious decision that this boy made at the age of twelve to pack a particular art book as a valued treasure to accompany him into exile in England. This book stayed with him throughout his entire adult life foreshadowing and marking his own illustrious career as an exiled Jewish art historian.

These exilic themes resonate with an important book written by the Israeli-American literary historian and theorist Sidra DeKoven Ezrahi, but there is a different emphasis and disciplinary focus in her *Booking Passage: Exile and Homecoming in the Modern Jewish Imagination* (2000). Ezrahi explores the poetics of exile and return, and the first part is devoted to the travel fictions of well-known writers S.Y. Agnon, Sholem Aleichem and S.Y. Abramovitsh in what she refers to as "Jewish Journeys" (Ezrahi 2000, 52–140). While these trajectories dream of the return to Israel as an end of diaspora, the journey traced by Leo Steinberg runs along a westward path and moves further into exile until the United States offers him the opportunity to forge a new Jewish-American diasporic identity after the Second World War. Steinberg's immigrant persona as a suave and sophisticated art historian, however, certainly does not resemble the guise of the *schlemihl* character that Ezrahi identifies with other 'native' American writers (e.g., Philip Roth) in the second part of the book ("Jewish Geographies"). Furthermore, while Ezrahi writes about a group of authors whose reflections on the figure of Jewish exile and return are mostly mediated through their fictions, the methodological approach of "Booked for Exile" is rather the investigation of an individual author based on his autobiographical writings (particularly, memoirs and anecdotes recalled during the latter part of his life). These recollections focus on the memoirist's relationship to his books both as a child and a young man exploring how these textual homelands provided him with a way to ground his exilic experience as well as helping him to navigate his passage through major urban landscapes in four different countries speaking three different languages in what was an extremely turbulent historical period (1920–1945).

Moscow, Berlin, London, New York

These metropolitan centres map out the four stations in the transnational flight of the Jewish art historian and artist Leo Steinberg over the course of the first 25 years of his life. His early biography is a westward trajectory of urban passages and textual homelands that sketch out a life booked for exile. Born in Moscow on 9 July 1920 with the given Yiddish name of Zalman Lev, he was the only son and middle-born child of the Socialist Revolutionary political party leader Isaac Nachman (I. N.) Steinberg who once served as Vladimir Lenin's Minister of Justice in the Bolshevik coalition government in early 1918. With the rooting out of non-Bolshevik political differences by the end of Lenin's rule, I. N. Steinberg was forced out of Soviet Russia in November 1923. Thus, young Leo Steinberg would spend the next ten years of his childhood growing up in the Zehlendorf district of Berlin (Forststrasse 21) during the Weimar Republic until the rise of Hitler and the Nazis again forced his family into exile in late May 1933. This Jewish refugee family then fled to England and settled in metropolitan London where Leo would later enrol at the Slade School of Fine Art specializing in drawing and sculpture. After the Second World War and the Holocaust, Steinberg emigrated voluntarily to rejoin his family (who had arrived already in 1943) in another major urban centre, New York. He wrote art criticism and taught life drawing at the Parsons School of Design before taking up the rather urbane lifestyle of a Renaissance and Modern art historian with a successful academic career (affiliated with Hunter College in New York and the University of Pennsylvania in Philadelphia) that spanned nearly five decades and that made him an internationally renowned figure.

Given this diasporic narrative and its life writing, Leo Steinberg was booked for exile in terms of this unique journey through a series of urban passages and their dislocations. However, the phrase 'booked for exile' also brings us back to the material object of the book itself and to the crucial role that it played in grounding Leo Steinberg throughout his transnational sojourns. Steinberg relates this Jewish diasporic phenomenon of being at home in the "House of the Book" (to recall George Steiner's phrase) by means of both written and oral anecdotes during this formative period (Steiner 1985, 5). These stories articulate and enact the thesis formulated by Steiner that Jewish life in exile is founded on textuality (for the so-called "people of the book") (ibid.). In this way, Steinberg follows in the footsteps of the 19th-century German-Jewish poet Heinrich Heine who articulated this phenomenon as "*das aufgeschriebene Vaterland*" (which translates literally as "the written down Fatherland" but also "portable homeland") (Heine 1972, 40). But unlike traditional Jewish experience in the *shtetl* where the textual homeland was bound to orthodox religious beliefs and sacred texts (i.e., to the Hebrew Bible and its commentaries), the young Steinberg (like the literary convert Heine before him) transposed this passion for the book into predominately secular contexts and even assimilatory spaces. With its exacting bookkeeping and close reading, the present chapter offers an account of where and how the migrant Leo Steinberg as a modern secular Jewish intellectual and artist in urban exile repeatedly returns to the figure of the book as a mode of orientation and as a substitute (*Ersatz*) homeland. In each of the following scenes, we will see that several of Steinberg's crucial early memories detail decidedly urban encounters that are bookish and bibliophilic in nature.

An early vision

As fantastic as it sounds, Leo Steinberg is said to have articulated this 'textual homelands' position as his personal life philosophy at the ripe old age of 3½ while still in Moscow and speaking a child's Russian. While the veracity of the following anecdote is put into question by Steinberg himself who deems it to be a mythical "tale" (Steinberg 2006, n.p.), he nevertheless repeats his proud father Isaac's claim before providing a bit of ironic commentary laced with his self-deprecating Jewish wit. The primal scene for this "nomad of the word" (Steiner 1985, 24) takes place not in front of a mirror (as it might in Lacanian psychoanalysis) but rather in front of his father's bookshelves. It spells out a metaphorical chain that links the book to the human being, and it does this by evaluating its covers, its letters, its desires. Steinberg laments how it is most unfortunate that his father's diary (i.e., the textual home of this Russian tale) did not survive his family's diasporic journey:

> One other tale from this Russian phase I do not believe; at least not in the form my father claimed to have recorded in his diary – which has not survived. At age 3 and a half, looking at father's bookshelves, I'm supposed to have said:
>
> "Books are like people."
>
> "How so?"
>
> "Well, the covers are their clothes, and the letters are their teeth, and if you don't read them, they feel hungry."
>
> I discount this story because you hate to think that your imagination peaked at age three and the rest all downhill.
>
> (Steinberg 2006, n.p.)

In a fascinating act of psychoanalytic transference, the hunger for the book that the Jewish boy feels is transposed unto the book and its hunger to be read. The anecdote concludes with Steinberg's self-ironic and self-effacing refusal to give credence to his profound anthropomorphic illumination or to accept the possibility that the power of his imagination peaked at the age of three with such marvellous metaphors and fantastic insights into the nature of the book. But, as a matter of fact, they had only just begun.

A Chanukah present

December 1932 was an ominous time to be a Jewish boy living in Berlin with the Nazi Party on the rise and on the march. Notwithstanding this fact, Leo Steinberg self-ironically recalls a biographical incident and a minor 'miracle' that happened to his 12-year old self then and there when he accompanied his parents on a visit to the popular urban destination of a local bookshop owned by a Socialist acquaintance of his father. It was not on the order of the Maccabean miracle in Ancient Judaea that led to the lamps in the Holy Temple burning for eight nights when there was only enough oil for just one. The anecdote partakes of bitter irony as it illustrates that, however grim the circumstances, there was a silver lining to Hitler's imminent takeover that would benefit young Leo – enchanting his gaze and directing him towards his chosen discipline, vocation and passion. The story recounts a significant occasion and a memorable initiation rite because the presentation of this book sets him on the path of his life's work as an art historian, studio art teacher and artist. With a frustrated Austrian artist turned populist politician on the brink of assuming power in Germany and with the burning of the books (that he will witness) just over the horizon, a Jewish shopkeeper decides to present the young boy with a precious volume by the German art historian Richard Hamann entitled *The Early Renaissance of Italian Painting* (1909). It is quite a moving story that this greybeard tells as he looks back seventy years to an event that delivers a Christian art book to a future Jewish art historian in the final days of the Weimar Republic.

Our author sets up the anecdote by referencing his parents – his father I. N. Steinberg and his mother Nechama Esselson Steinberg – and their Socialist political views; this fact serves as a way for him to distinguish himself and his own budding aesthetic interests from his stern and moralizing father who did not value the visual arts. For the young Steinberg, his artistic predilections therefore become an act of rebellion against the Law of the Father. In walking into and browsing around this Socialist bookshop filled with socio-political subjects, Steinberg is pleasantly surprised to find Hamann's survey of Italian Renaissance painting. This is in itself already an aesthetic gift. While the father talks Socialist politics with the bookseller, the son projects his transfixed gaze on this art book and the masterpieces within its pages. In his recounting of the story, one also notes how Leo turns to his more aesthetically inclined and sympathetic mother with his plea to buy the book for him. Yes, he still belongs to the people of the book but his attachment to this Renaissance art treasure dominated by two hundred greyscale reproductions offers a transposition from the aniconic Jewish to the Christian icon and from the primacy of the textual to the primacy of the visual in what might be viewed as his art historical initiation rite (and Bar Mitzvah). Steinberg underscored this same point much later in his 1995 Norton Lectures at Harvard University that he titled "The Mute Image and the Meddling Text" and when he stressed the importance of recalling that "the work of art is the judge of the text" (Steinberg 2001, 171). Steinberg recounts this indelible memory involving the gift of a precious art book in the following manner:

> My parents were Socialists, and one day in December 1932 they took me along to visit a Socialist bookshop, whose owner my father wanted to speak to. While the grown-ups talked, I browsed along the shelves and soon pulled down one of the few books in the shop that had nothing to do with politics: Richard Hamann's *The Early Renaissance of Italian Painting*, Jena 1909, in its first printing of

> 30,000: 50 pages of text, plus notes at the back (none of which interested me); and 200 full-page gray-and-white reproductions of paintings by artists with sonorous names, the like of which I had never heard uttered – Pollaiuolo, Ghirlandaio, Piero di Cosimo.
>
> I was enchanted, and couldn't stop looking – from that day to this. And when, after too short an hour, I was told we were leaving, I would not re-shelve the book, but showed it to mother and asked timidly (for I knew we had little money) – could we buy it? Mother glanced at the price, shook her head, and looked quickly away; and all those images to vanish forever. And then a miracle happened: the bookseller turned to my father and said, "Look, any day now Hitler will be coming to power [as indeed Hitler did five weeks later, 30 January 1933], and the first thing the Nazis will do is close this shop. So why don't you just take the book for your boy."
>
> I have the book still, inscribed in pencil in a 12-year-old's hand, "1932, for Chanukah."
>
> (Steinberg 2006, n.p.)

This autobiographical account is also memorable because of the performative way in which it showcases the book as a survivor: this again foregrounds Steinberg's abiding passion for the book. Thus, Steinberg remembers the book that marks his career choice and that he carries with him as a "portable homeland" (in Heine's sense) as it is transported throughout the many stations of his life in exile over the course of seventy years. The story culminates with Steinberg offering up the living proof when he holds up the book for everyone in the audience to see in a most demonstrative manner. His long-time assistant Sheila Schwartz recalls: "When he said he still had the book & held it up, the audience burst into applause" (Schwartz 2012). The audience thus bears witness that this precious art book – this particular textual homeland – and its octogenarian owner have survived the Nazis, the Holocaust, and the treacherous urban passage from Berlin, to London, to New York. In this way, Steinberg's Chanukah miracle moves from the purchase of the book and its personal inscription in German ("*Zu Chanukka* 1932") to the witnessing and attestation of its survival in 2002.[1]

From book burning to bus swerving

There is only one passage in Leo Steinberg's voluminous writings where he mentions the fact that he was an eyewitness to the barbarous Nazi book burnings that took place in front of the State Opera House in Berlin on 10 May 1933. This 12 years old Jewish émigré boy (who was already being schooled in the refined ways of German *Bildung*) watched as the books of German-Jewish authors like

Walter Benjamin, Alfred Kerr and Siegfried Kracauer were consumed in flames. One can only imagine the shock and the horror of this traumatic experience and especially for this young bibliophile who believed from the age of three that "books are like people". (Of course, the young Steinberg's prescient analogy about books and people resonates with Heinrich Heine's eerie and prophetic warning in his tragic play *Almansor* when he wrote: "Where they burn books, they will in the end also burn people"[2]) (Heine 1920, 21). Steinberg does not make any mention in this passage of his being exposed to the inflammatory rhetoric of the Nazi propaganda minister Joseph Goebbels and his apocalyptic denunciation in his speech to the students that "the era of exaggerated Jewish intellectualism is now at an end" (Goebbels 1933).[3] This event signalled to both his father and uncle Aron that this also was the end of the Steinberg family's life in Berlin as they could read the writing on the wall (and in the flames). In response, they booked passage to England only a few weeks later where Steinberg would reside until the end of the Second World War. For someone already committed to George Steiner's cosmopolitan idea that being a diasporic Jew implied a connection to a textual rather than to a physical homeland – to an "unhousedness" and an "at-homeness in the word" (Steiner 1985, 24), the Nazi book burnings must be viewed as a profound act of expropriation given that they targeted these scripterly sites of Jewish belonging.

In Steinberg's memory, this horrific Berlin scene of the burning of the books is contrasted directly with the recounting of a personal anecdote of his own library books being saved from an oncoming bus in suburban London just one year later in 1934. At the age of 81, Steinberg looks back some 68 years and he recalls a bookish incident that leads to the setting up of a binary opposition in national characters, peoples and cultures. This draws a sharp distinction between Germans and the British as host nations from his Jewish diasporic perspective. While the Steinberg family's address was 245 Fordwych Road NW in Cricklewood at the time, we know that his destination in the following passage was the public library in Hendon and that his mode of conveyance was that very urban mode of transportation, the bicycle. (The exact distance is 3.3 miles or a bike ride of twenty minutes duration.) Steinberg hints at a massacre in the making – of a big bus running over and flattening his precious library books. He also notes that he "froze in horror" in a manner that echoes his sentiments in Berlin (Steinberg 2006, n.p.). But in contrast to the previous hellish scene of the book burnings, Steinberg observes here in the mundane streets something that he compares to "another miracle" (ibid.). This particular miracle consists of a Lucretian swerve on the part of the bus that saves the books from their impending doom. Steinberg recounts this biographical incident in great and vibrant detail:

> One day in 1934, I was on my bicycle with half a dozen library books strapped on behind, coasting downhill. You have to remember that in those days cars in

> suburban London were scarce, streets had maybe one or two cars parked, and little traffic. So, as I came speeding down, I suddenly saw people waving at me from the sidewalk. I stopped, turned around, and froze in horror. The strap had come loose, my books strewn across the roadway, a bus bearing down to ride over them, and me, condemned to stand by at their massacre, for I had a great sense that books, borrowed ones especially, must be treated with tenderness. They're like people, remember? But then – another miracle: the juggernaut slowed and made a careful detour around my books. I choked up – knew from this moment that I had passed into a different culture. Rightly or wrongly, I felt that this could not have happened in Germany, where, on May 10, 1933, my Uncle Aron had taken my older sister and me to watch the Nazi burning of books.
>
> (Steinberg 2006, n.p.)

One notes that this incident puts the young Steinberg at a loss for words and that he was overwhelmed with a sense of relief and a flood of emotion after escaping this close call with an imminent disaster. Of course, this loaded allegorical story offers a metonymic structure where the books stand in retrospectively for his and his family's own narrow escape from Nazi Germany. Even more precisely, the "choked up" feeling that Steinberg experiences must be read as a counterpoint to his earlier traumatic witnessing on the streets of Berlin just a year earlier. His tears of joy and his welling up of feeling only make sense in direct and stark contrast to the Nazi's brutal treatment and mishandling of the books and, by extension, of the Jews. In line with the thesis that the young Steinberg was driven by his Jewish diasporic identification with the book, the swerving London bus affirms for him the value and the sanctity of the textual homeland and its necessary defence. Indeed, the incident leads him to the forging of a libidinal attachment to this recently adopted nation-state that would protect his sacred books. In a nutshell, the barbarism of the Nazis is replaced by the humanism of the British. Steinberg also recalls the same incident with a few alterations in the Getty Art History Oral Documentation Project interview dated 17 February 1998: "The notion that a big bus would respect a few books scattered in the street accidentally by a thirteen-year-old gave me a new sense of humaneness, and I think from that moment I came to love England" (Steinberg 2001, 20).

Distinguishing father and son

But Steinberg's valorization of the book would not remain his sole and singular fetish object. When he enrolled as an art student at the Slade School in London, the passion for the book was supplemented by his love of sculpture, drawing and painting. Indeed, the visual arts would rise in his estimation and to such a degree that the shift to becoming an art student would provide Leo Steinberg with the opportunity to define himself in direct opposition to his father Isaac. Thus, the son's sensibility is set squarely against his father who remained an orthodox Jew for his entire life, who never wavered from valuing ethics over aesthetics, and who never had any interest in the visual arts. In contradistinction to the aniconic Jewish tradition, Leo Steinberg now finds himself at home in the world of images (many with Christian iconography), both as a practicing artist and as an art critic/historian – with the latter profession allowing for the return of the book and for textual homelands yet again. This move can be attributed to his assimilation of secular values with "the temple of art" (in the cultural historian Carl Schorske's sense) now replacing the Jewish synagogue as the place of worship (Schorske 1980, 264). This particular viewpoint has been articulated by Ruth Wisse (2019) with her coupling of Steinberg and the assimilated Jewish art historian, Angelica Zander Rudenstine.

Finally, one must remember that the Freeland League for Territorialist Colonization co-founded by I.N. Steinberg in the mid 1930s in response to rampant anti-Semitism and the rise of the Nazis was a political organization with a specific geo-territorial agenda that was quite at odds with the worldview of 'textual homelanders'. After all, the Freelanders wanted to find unsettled territory somewhere on the globe (favouring remote agrarian regions rather than urban centres) that the wandering Jews could inhabit and call a homeland whether it was located in the Kimberley region of Western Australia or the Saramacca district of Suriname (Rovner 2014). Young Leo was asked to be a dutiful son and to contribute his utmost to the organization and to his father's idealistic vision but he recalls that he was just going through the motions and that his heart was not really in it. As he reviews:

> He wanted me to work, and I did, in the youth movement of his organization, the Freeland League. In fact, I made speeches on its behalf, and wrote, but without real engagement. I was clever enough to do it well, but my father always knew that I was not committed.
>
> (Steinberg 2001, 24)

Instead, he thought that the Freeland League's vision was nothing more than "wishful thinking" – impractical, utopian and unworkable (Steinberg 2001, 12). As Steinberg recalls in his interview with Richard Cándida Smith: "My father was all his life one of these stargazing idealists" (ibid.). But the question to be posed to the elder Steinberg and the Freelanders and to their quest to forge Jewish cultural autonomy in rural settings is this: what would have happened to the urban passages and textual homelands that were championed by the younger Steinberg (and later by Steiner) if these so-called territorialist visions had succeeded? For these were calculated attempts in large-scale social engineering that were designed to house the Jews in a specific place rather than affirming their being at home in exile (Almagor 2018). The rebellion of the son against the father (and the desire to overcome the anxiety of his influence) was therefore also a rebellion of the aesthetic against the political and of the textual against the territorial.

NOTES

1. Steinberg tells this story during his acceptance speech of the Distinguished Scholar Award of his professional organization, the College Art Association, in February 2002. In another westward migration movement, the book is now housed in his archives at the Getty Research Institute in Los Angeles, California. We know this from Sheila Schwartz's own account that she signed and dated on 20 February 2012 in this book (now become relic) located in Box 31: "In 2005, Leo put a slip in the book, instructing me to give it to his good friend, the German art critic Renate Puvogel. She felt that it would be more appropriate in the Getty archives and asked me to include it with Leo's papers."
2. The haunting original German reads: "Dort wo man Bücher verbrennt, verbrennt man auch am Ende Menschen" (Heine 1920, 21).
3. Steinberg's pseudonymous "A Reply to Goebbels" (written by Vladimir Baranov) in 1941 and located in the "Music" folder of Box 25 in his Research Papers takes on new meaning in light of the fact that he witnessed the Berlin book burning eight years prior.

REFERENCES

Almagor, Laura. "Fitting the *Zeitgeist*: Jewish Territorialism and Geopolitics, 1934–1960." *Contemporary European History*, vol. 27, no. 3, 2018, pp. 351–369, doi: 10.1017/S0960777318000206. Accessed 17 June 2021.

Baranov, Vladimir. [Leo Steinberg]. A Reply to Goebbels. Leo Steinberg Research Papers 1945–1996 (Getty Research Institute, Los Angeles, California, 1 May 1941), 9300046: 23.

Ezrahi, Sidra DeKoven. *Booking Passage: Exile and Homecoming in the Modern Jewish Imagination* (Contraversions, 12). University of California Press, 2000.

Goebbels, Joseph. "Books Burn as Goebbels Speaks [Speech, Berlin, 10 May 1933, Historical Film Footage]." *United States Holocaust Memorial Museum. Holocaust Encyclopedia*, www.//usc.ushmm.org/wlc/en/media_fi.php?ModuleId=0&MediaId=158. Accessed 23 December 2020.

Hamann, Richard. *Die Früh-Renaissance der Italienischen Malerei: 200 Nachbildungen mit geschichtlicher Einführung und Erläuterungen* (Die Kunst in Bildern). Eugen Diederichs, 1909.

Heine, Heinrich. "Almansor: Eine Tragodie." 1821. Idem. *Heines Werke. Fünfter Teil: Almansor*, edited by Erwin Kalischer and Raimund Pissin, Deutsches Verlagshaus Bong & Co., 1920, pp. 14–62. *Project Gutenberg*, www.gutenberg.org/files/45600/45600-h/45600-h.htm. Accessed 23 December 2020.

Heine, Heinrich. *Aus den Memoiren des Herren von Schnabelewopski*. 1831. Idem. *Heinrich Heine: Werke und Briefe in zehn Bänden*, vol. 4., 2nd ed., edited by Hans Kaufmann, Aufbau, 1972, p. 40. *Zeno.org*, www.zeno.org/Literatur/M/Heine,+Heinrich/Erz%C3%A4hlprosa/Aus+den+Memoiren+des+Herren+von+Schnabelewopski/Kapitel+14. Accessed 7 May 2021.

Rovner, Adam. *In the Shadow of Zion: Promised Lands Before Israel*. New York University Press, 2014.

Schorske, Carl E. *Fin-de-Siècle Vienna: Politics and Culture*. Knopf Doubleday Publishing Group, 1980.

Schwartz, Sheila. Handwritten Note. Leo Steinberg Research Papers 1945–1996 (Getty Research Institute, Los Angeles, California, signed and dated 20 February 2012), 930046: 31.

Steinberg, Leo. *The Gestural Trace* (Art History Oral Documentation Project). Interview with Richard Cándida Smith. The J. Paul Getty Trust, 2001.

Steinberg, Leo. "False Starts, Loose Ends." (talk at the College Association Conference, Philadelphia, 21 February 2002). Revised and published in *The Brooklyn Rail*, June 2006, pp. 16–20, https://brooklynrail.org/2006/06/art/leo [unpaginated online publication]. Accessed 23 December 2020.

Steiner, George. "Our Homeland, the Text." *Salmagundi*, no. 66, 1985, pp. 4–25.

Wisse, Ruth R. "Arrival; or, Yiddish Makes Its Way to Harvard Yard." *Mosaic*, 29 May 2019, www.//mosaicmagazine.com/observation/history-ideas/2019/05/arrival-or-yiddish-makes-its-way-to-harvard-yard/. Accessed 23 December 2020.

18

Between Europe and America: Metropolitan Exchanges in the Context of International Antifascism

Diana Wechsler

Starting points to re-read the modern art process[1]

In the 1930s, the processes of the early interwar period (1918–1939), the rise of fascism and the effects of the global economic crisis of 1929 contributed to the tension and complexity of the international climate. The culture world was in turmoil as politics became the central catalyst for intellectual life. Cities were undoubtedly the arena of debates and symbolic struggles, a fact recognizable not only in the many networks and relationships established by artists and intellectuals but also in their imprints that have inscribed themselves into the memories of various metropolises.

Such accounts make it possible to engage in an exercise that places artists and intellectuals of different backgrounds in the same workshops, cafés and quarters – helping to shed light on other narratives whose reconstruction would not be possible without these articulations of geographical transit and the appropriation of spaces across the globe. These strategies enhance not only the history of modern art and its artists but also the history of the cities in which they worked and the synergy between cities, which makes it possible to identify active networks of exchanges.

Within the context of the interwar period, the need to take a stand vis-à-vis new conditions of existence prompted artists and intellectuals to devise different intervention strategies. In this environment, they contributed to the construction of new ways of seeing: art began to occupy new places, as it became necessary to experiment with other modes of representation and to create emergency images in response to a new problematic reality which was characterized by a re-elaboration of the modern project at different levels (Wechsler et al. 2005). The active exchanges between cultural metropolises such as Berlin, Paris, Madrid, Mexico, Buenos Aires and New York played a central role in this regard. In order to reconstruct these spaces of transit and exchange and to restore networks of relationships lost over time, I have outlined some routes between America and Europe laid out by artists, works of art, texts, images and ideas under the premise of travel, migration, exile and the varied flow of metropolitan exchanges. The urban experiences of artists, intellectuals and writers in transit in the interwar period – the time of the international anti-fascist movement and exile processes – afford the possibility to examine and compare the works of artists in depth with a view to recovering unknown aspects of the exchange, circulation and selection of aesthetic and artistic knowledge at a key moment of modernity.

The theoretical perspective of this paper seeks to delve into art history of the past, and to look beyond the glamourous aspects of avant-garde historical accounts in order to emphasize active processes of exchange. My aim is to provide the history of modern art with new shades of meaning, to establish networks that enhance our ways of seeing, and to challenge the historiography of modern art.

My research toolbox consists of art history, cultural sociology and visual and curatorial studies. The research conducted in collections, libraries and archives is put to the test in the curatorial field, which I conceive as the laboratory of my work. The encounter of works, different types of images, documents and memories in this unique curatorial laboratory allows me to examine working hypotheses and in turn presents, tests and creates tension in the images and their ways of activating different meanings, each one in its own right and with its own dialogue.

Travels, migrations and exiles

Migration of ideas: Books, magazines, images[2]

A regular image of neat rectangles, reminiscent of the Mondrian grid, can be seen in the wooden structure that gives shape to the bookcase of modern Argentine artist Raquel Forner (1902–1988). This unique collection – located in Buenos Aires – includes all kinds of books of diverse origins that show Forner's eager and inquisitive nature, as well as her wide range of interests. There are heavy volumes on the paintings of great masters of the past, such as Leonardo da Vinci, Michelangelo, Botticelli and El Greco, along with lighter, paperback editions that represent the voices of modern artistic and intellectual debate at a time when it was gaining prominence.

Among them is a key book in shaping the visual culture of the period: *Nach Realismus* (1925), the canonical essay by the German critic Franz Roh, translated into Spanish by *Revista de Occidente* in 1927, and edited by José Ortega y Gasset. Forner's had signed her copy with her own name (a usual practice at that times) before travelling to Europe in 1928. This book, one of the first essays on the contemporary plastic horizon, lent itself to the scrutiny of artists and critics. There, with precise delimitations of prewar art, we can read definitions of certain key notions for understanding early postwar figuration: objectivity, abstraction, sentimental projection and surrealism.[3]

Roh's book included an extensive series of images featuring Picasso's powerful, monumental figures (*Mother and Child by the Sea*), Funi (*Woman*), Metzinger (*Ecuyère*) and Togores (*Sleeping*) alongside uncanny landscapes by De Chirico (*Roman Landscape*) and Miró (*Posada*) as well as disturbing images such as De Chirico's *Self-Portrait* next to Max Ernst's *La belle jardinière* and *Les malheurs des immortels* (Roh 1927). These works, with their indisputably surrealist imprint, appeared together with metaphysical paintings, strong figurations in the classical tradition and some works that revealed a certain primitivism. All of them represented the whole body of contemporary figurations. Something similar can be observed with other books in this modern library, for example with the catalogue of the *Novecento Italiano* exhibition, which brought together more than two hundred images, accompanied by Margherita Sarfatti's 'curatorial' text on the show held in Buenos Aires in 1930 as part of a tour that began in 1926 (Chiarelli/Wechsler 2003).

Another section of this stimulating bookcase featured magazines. Among those published in Buenos Aires were *Sur*, the magazine launched by Victoria Ocampo in 1931, and *Conducta*, "*Al servicio del pueblo*", issued by the Teatro del Pueblo as of 1938 with anti-fascist activism as one of its distinctive features. Two sides of the same reality describe the wide range of interests that coexisted in that international cultural field. Two groups stand out among those published abroad, which show Forner alert and in tune with contemporary movements: among them *Cahiers d'Art*, Christian Zervos's magazine, first published in Paris in 1926, which the artist had bought in Buenos Aires before her trip to Europe in 1929 – and the entire collection of the surrealist magazine *Minotaure*, also published in Paris in 1933.

The former, *Cahiers d'Art*, recorded in each of its issues the latest developments in contemporary art, laying out and adjusting successive maps of figuration and other plastic alternatives in painting and sculpture during the interwar period. Its pages reveal the active presence of artists of different origins in Paris: Spaniards, Poles, Russians, Argentinians, French, Belgians, Italians; all of them took part in the developments of modern art, lending their voice to the debates around contemporary figuration.

As we know, the other magazine, *Minotaure*, took on a more modest role on the map of modern art. The editorial board members were André Breton, Maurice Heine and Pierre Mabille. Its pages merged surrealist images of Europe and America with anthropological experiences: the surrealist mingled with ethnography, psychoanalysis and the art of the past and the present. In the texts by André Breton, Paul Éluard, Salvador Dalí, Roger Caillois, Tériade and many others, surrealism and its lines of interpretation permeated aesthetic expressions of different periods and latitudes, thus becoming part of the Surrealist matrix, which also included the full report of the Dakar-Djibouti Mission, the results of ethnographic surrealism, as well as Breton's *Souvenir du Mexique*, in which Mexico was present in a surrealist dimension (Clifford 1995, 149–183).

In the 1930s, a number of magazines from other Latin American metropolises, such as the Mexican *Anthropos*, and publications on pre-Columbian art and Mexican mural painting, began to find a place in this library.

Being no isolated case, Forner's library is addressed here as evidence of the intense circulation of books, magazines, catalogues, photographs, news and – we might now add – correspondences between artists and intellectuals both in the metropolis and the peripheries. It is worth mentioning something, I have pointed out in previous works that reinforces this argument: among the publications of the time, magazines were preferential spaces for artists who wanted to stay up to date, participate in contemporary debates, and at the same time find signs of aesthetic identification. In fact, these publications served as identity markers for emerging groups of artists, while they also rapidly became cult objects for artists to obtain, keep and share, as they formed part of the imaginary network that linked artists and intellectuals on both sides of the Western world and beyond.

The material of this modern library allows the working hypothesis of this chapter to be based on an (extended) concept of migration. The starting point is to conceive modernity from the dynamic tension – both material and conceptual – between different spaces, people, times and borders. Modernity, then, must be defined on the basis of circulation, exchanges, networks, intense migratory flows – viewed as virtual or real movements as the case may be, of people, books, magazines, works, objects and ideas that circulate, are appropriated and re-appropriated in different ways and adopt a singular identity in each space. This process is then fed back into the dynamics of the productions and languages of modernity that were present, in different ways, in the cultural metropolises of the first decades of the 20th century.

With these issues in mind, this chapter will focus on the drifts of the figurative traditions of metaphysical painting, retour à l'ordre and surrealism between Paris, Buenos Aires and other modern metropolises on both sides of the Atlantic during the interwar period. These temporal markers also highlight the political tone that have inevitably permeated debates and aesthetic choices of the time.

The itineraries and processes identified and discussed in this chapter could only take place in metropolitan contexts (Williams 1989, 106). In this regard, it is impossible to dissociate the processes of modern art from urban logics, since it is in the cities – defined here as cultural metropolises – where the conditions unfold for the emergence, production and reproduction (with their constant disputes, tensions and negotiations) of the art system.

Between creativity and solidarity: travels, migrations and exiles

The works included in Forner's library were widely circulated among artists and intellectuals on both sides of the Atlantic, which in turn enables us to trace the presence of their works as evidence of a common action, a kind of co-production of the process of modern art. For example, a photograph of *Primary Form* by Argentine sculptor Pablo Curatella Manes appears in the dossier on modern art in the Parisian magazine *Cahier d'Art* in 1926 and *Figura de espaldas* by the Spaniard Salvador Dalí was first published in *La Prensa de Buenos Aires* in 1925.

While the magazines provide us with clues as to the dynamics of those years, the list of works in – for example – the back room of the Galerie Zak in Paris in the second half of the 1920s confirms and furthers the repertoire, with the inclusion of names of young French, Polish, Argentinean, Uruguayan, Brazilian and Mexican artists, among others. Just a few examples will illustrate the intense processes of exchange and mutuality herein described (Navarrete 2012).

In 1928, for example, the Italian-Argentine artist Juan Del Prete arrived in Paris, where he subsequently held his first solo show. He then took part in the first exhibition of the so-called *Première Exposition du Groupe Latino-Americain de Paris* along with Forner, Carlos Mérida, Agustín Lazo, Diego Rivera, Vicente do Rego Monteiro, Joaquín Torres García (who conceived the idea) and others. In 1932, Del Prete became a member of the Torres García Abstraction-Creation Group on the occasion of their first exhibition in that city.

Galerie Zak was located in Saint-Germain, close to Galerie Pierre and Galerie des editions Bonaparte, to mention just a few of those venues with exhibitions of Latin American artists. Numerous artists also moved to that area. This quarter and Montparnasse were home to possibly the greatest concentration of Latin American artists: the Argentine Antonio Berni, the Chileans Camilo Mori and Luis Vargas Rosas, the Uruguayans Pedro Figari and Carmelo de Arzadun, the Mexicans Àngel Zárraga and Julio Castellanos, and many more. These quarters also housed academies and workshops such as André Lhote's, Academie Julien's and Colarossi's, which were frequented by Latin American artists and others. There they made contact with young artists, such as Tamara de Lempicka and Henri Cartier-Bresson.

As further evidence of the frequent exchanges between artists in Paris, it is worth mentioning that the young Spanish painter Manuel Ángeles Ortiz recalled in his old age that it was the Argentinian painter Emilio Pettoruti who introduced him to Picasso (Carmona et al. 1996). This episode had particular significance in his life for two reasons: Manuel Ángeles was the only disciple acknowledged by Picasso and, what is even more remarkable for the hypothesis we are advancing: when the Spanish Civil War (1936–1939) ended and when he had to decide upon an exile destination (he was a militant republican), he chose Buenos Aires.

The cafés and, above all, the workshops and academies were the cradle of networks that were founded in the 1920s and which were later reactivated in the 1930s in an aesthetic-political key that offers today the possibility to identify ties, empaths, choices. Such solidarity networks would result in affiliation with the various regional sections of the international anti-fascist movement. Moreover, as a contribution to the debate of 'through' their works, declarations and manifestos, I have opted for the phrase: "between realism and surrealism" (Wechsler et al. 2006).

These are just a few examples of the approximately two hundred Latin American artists who resided in Paris in the 1920s, plus other foreign artists and intellectuals who lived in the city and added to its unique profile. All these considerations allow us to rethink the processes of modern art as part of a migratory scenario in which it is necessary to put to the test the knowledge and language of each individual, as well as the continuous negotiation and demarcation of identities involved in the definition of an 'us' and the 'others'.

The scope and activity of the artists' network over these decades is therefore indisputable and, as such, could be said to be at the root of processes of and debates on art and politics within the context of the international anti-fascist movement: this process as a whole encourages us to re-evaluate canonical narratives.[4]

Transits between metropolises and aesthetic-political itineraries: The case of Antonio Berni

Émigré artists gradually assimilated into the city of Paris and were instrumental in reconfiguring its vibrant urban fabric. A number of art galleries provided, together with workshops, academies and cafés, another meeting place and an alternative space in which to identify aesthetic debates embodied in the beacon artists of the time. As part of the dispute over the real, which in the 1930s would bring together aesthetic identities and political loyalties, Giorgio de Chirico (incidentally another émigré in Paris) appeared as primus inter pares on account of his incorporation into the Italian Novecento group, the identification of Breton as the mentor of surrealism and the admiration he aroused in authors such as Jean Cocteau, who also sought to lay out the map of modern art in the early post-war period.

In Dawn Ades' words, "De Chirico exerted a profound influence on Ernst, Tanguy and Magritte" (Ades 1975, 44). The same applies to the Italian painter's mark on numerous Latin American artists such as the Argentinians Raquel Forner, Antonio

Berni and Lino Spilimbergo, the Brazilians Cândido Portinari and Carlos Prado, and among the Mexicans, the works of Diego Rivera and Agustín Lazo, to name but a few. In short, his aesthetic perspective permeated much of the imagery of the 1930s.

Apart from the quality of his works, the singular nature of Paris undoubtedly acted a key factor in the enormous reach of his work. At different points, the presence of De Chirico's work drew a distinctive cartography in the city. In July 1925, De Chirico exhibited at the Galerie de Léonce Rosenberg in Paris and, despite Breton's criticism, a few months later he took part in the exhibition *La peinture surrealiste* at the Galerie Pierre in Paris, which featured works by Arp, Ernst, Klee, Masson, Miró, Picasso, Ray and Roy, and texts by Breton and Desnos. The following year Breton spoke of De Chirico as the "lost genius" in the 7th issue of *La Révolution Surreáliste* (Breton 1926, 5, translation by the author). However, his image continued to be present in Paris and beyond, with exhibitions in Berlin, Zurich, Amsterdam, Milan and other cities. In 1928, not only did he hold his first solo exhibition in New York and London but he also exhibited his latest works at Rosenberg's L'Effort Moderne Gallery in Paris. At the same time, the Surrealists organized an exhibition of "L'Œuvre Ancienne de Georges De Chirico" in their gallery. Both lines of his production were then accessible to the Parisian public, with the international resonance that such an intense presence implied. The young Argentine painter Antonio Berni was undoubtedly among the hundreds of spectators who devotedly visited the Italian artist's exhibitions.

In order to verify the vitality of these networks activated among artists and to connect different metropolises on the art map of high modernity, in the following I will focus on the case of Berni. He makes an early appearance among the Latin Americans who liaised not only with modern Italian painting but also with surrealism, and it was through this array of sources coming from metaphysical painting and ideas related to Breton's movement that he developed his work between 1928 and 1932. He undertook his nomadic travels to Europe in 1925, making a first stop in Madrid. This city brought him into the orbit of modern art and encouraged him to pursue his research. He then went to Paris, where he studied and conducted his explorations in two key workshops for the training of 'newcomers', namely André Lhote and Othon Friesz. Simultaneously, he witnessed the emergence of surrealism, participated in the movement and soon got in touch with several of its followers: Aragon, Dalí and Buñuel. He also became involved with the metaphysical figuration of De Chirico. In this connection, the atmosphere of eerie alienation that characterized Berni's surrealist works is anticipated in one of his first pieces influenced by the Italian artist: *Self-Portrait with Cactus* (1929). Berni depicts himself with an unsettling gaze in a relaxed yet tense position; this was produced by a strategic arrangement of the plastic elements and created an atmosphere of tragic serenity.

On the other hand, he also forged numerous relationships with other Argentine and Latin American artists with whom he shared experiences in workshops and cafés in Montparnasse and Saint Germain. One can imagine him not only with his fellow countrymen Spilimbergo, Forner, Aquiles Badi and Héctor Basaldúa but also with the Peruvians César Moro and César Vallejos, who were also in Paris at the time and involved with surrealism. As Berni recalls:

> Surrealism at that time embodied a whole vision of art and the world; it was the movement that represented youths, their state of mind, and their inner selves after the end of World War I. It was a dynamic and truly representative movement.
> (Berni, 1946, qtd. in Berni/Viñals 1976, 57)

Berni selected surrealist and metaphysical works for the 1932 exhibition in Buenos Aires, which might be considered the first surrealist exhibition in the region. These paintings share a common code that stems from a different way of grasping reality. This approach, inspired by his readings of Freud, Lautreamont and Rimbaud, made the painter state that to him "surrealism was a field for experimentation" (ibid.). The changes he introduced in his work took the spectator back to an oneiric image in which everything changed and at the same time remained in the memory with a strong imprint of reality: an insistent warning about impending authoritarianism and the crisis that was poisoning societies in Europe and America.

Amidst his readings of Freud and Marx, his artistic drift engages in a dialogue with texts by Breton and Aragon. Such a broad political dimension of artistic practice is conceived in terms of interventions in society that contribute to undermining the certainties of the bourgeois system and its ways of grasping reality. As we may well recall, this dimension was reflected in the *First Surrealist Manifesto*, as well as in the Declaration of 27 January 1925. Berni explores dreams as a different gate into the perception, construction and representation of the real, which provides another "density", another dimension of the world and enables the encounter in painting of objects from "two distant realities", as Breton put it. This affords the opportunity to envisage new, unforeseen articulations of the real, as can be seen in Berni's extensive series of paintings. These works also incorporate Aragon's perspective which, through a "surrealist image", anticipates the social conflict by stating that "slightly to the left, in my divine heaven, I perceive the unpainted glow of the perplexities of freedom, although it is undoubtedly but a mist of blood and murder" (Aragon 1930/1999, 439).

With the *Second Surrealist Manifesto* in mind and from a displaced position, Aragon fuelled the debate in *La pintura desafiada* – a text written in 1930 that accompanied an exhibition of collages in which Berni and Moro could well have participated. His argument focused on the tensions between the marvellous and the real as elements for the construction of a critical painting. Aragon claimed that "the conciliation of the real and the marvelous (is) [...] surreality, [...] it is this real line that brings together all the virtual images that surround us" (Aragon, 1930/1999, 440). Berni followed this critical view of Breton's surrealism and the anti-fascist movement. However, as of 1933, his surrealist affiliation shifted towards a figuration closer to a form of realism that prompted him to write the 1934 foundational proposal entitled *New Realism*.

Final considerations

In 1930s Europe and Latin America, surrealist metaphysical perspectives and political conflict were two sides of the same coin. Considering Berni's case as a model, the political situation, etched by the spread of authoritarianism in different parts of the world, along with his affiliation to the Communist Party undoubtedly made him, upon his return to an Argentina with its first de facto government, reconsider his artistic position and adopt a more realistic perspective. He nevertheless took a dissident stand against the socialist realism proclaimed by Moscow, as he expressed in his 1934 text *New Realism*. From then on, his aesthetic militancy remained inseparable from his political position. Major paintings such as *Manifestación*, *Desocupados* and *Chacareros* bear witness to this point.

Building further on Berni, in the certainty that he is one more artist in a vast network working on both sides of the Atlantic Ocean in the movement for 'the defence of culture' in this rich fabric of anti-fascist internationalism, we can affirm that the metropolitan exchanges on both sides of the Atlantic Ocean were decisive for the development of modern art – understood as a process of collective production and not as a mere irradiation from the centre to the peripheries. On the other hand, it is possible to argue that the migration of texts, works, ideas, artists and intellectuals contributed to the construction of international networks that were activated at different junctures, allowing a constant flow (from America to Europe and vice versa) that accounts for the international dimension – in its broadest sense – of the processes discussed during this stage of modernity.

This text summarizes the results of a wide-ranging investigation put to the test in curatorial essays that analyze the visions and convergences in the configuration of the realities produced by various artists active in singular cities across the globe. This curatorial exploration was twofold. One aspect focused on the archives and productions of artists such as Spilimbergo, Berni and Forner. The other, based on libraries, archives and artistic repertoires of artists from diverse cultural metropolises such as Paris, Berlin, Milan, Madrid, Mexico, Sao Paulo, Montevideo and Buenos Aires, allows for a comparative analysis that reveals the convergence of aesthetic perspectives, the political commitment, and powerfully unveils the "horizon of feelings" (Williams 1989) of the time.

For reasons of space, this text has focused on cases of Latin American artists. However, it is necessary to underline that, as previously noted, this chapter reconfirms the centrality of Paris – *primus inter pares* in the concert of modern metropolises – but at the same time seeks to demonstrate that (as they used to say) Paris – in the 1920s and 1930s – 'was a party' precisely because of the enormous presence of artists and intellectuals from different cultural horizons. Their diverse traditions, their experiences, the need to test their knowledge and the enriching encounter of one with the other are constitutive of the modern process.

Briefly, I will point out a few cases in point. For example, to recognize that Pablo Picasso and Juan Gris – two key figures for modern art – were also 'others' in Paris, helps to clarify the hypothesis underpinning my research. Recall that the fact that both were Spanish led early modern art historiography to think of Cubism as a 'Spanish style'. Similarly, within the Italian scene, the presence of the Argentinean artist Emilio Pettoruti, who was part of the 'artistic *famiglia*' of Futurism, led to his being labelled an 'Italian artist' in the publications of the time. Interestingly, during his stay in Paris, he had met the young Spanish artist Manuel Angeles Ortiz, whom he introduced to Picasso and, a few years later, during the exile of the Spanish Republicans due to the Civil War and the victory of Franco's regime, he was one of the references for Manuel Angeles Ortiz to choose Buenos Aires as a place of emigration. The reference to these ties of empathy, sometimes aesthetic, sometimes political, or both, could be followed by numerous examples.

In short, I have presented here only some clues of an intense and complex web of exchanges that are, in themselves, constitutive of the modern process thought of as a battlefield between ideas, aesthetic and political perspectives. In cafés, galleries, ateliers, newspapers and magazines, in works and manifestos, there was a struggle for the delimitation of ideas and language resources that would make it possible to provide answers to the complex reality of that period and to find ways of offering images capable of configuring aspects of the real. On these traces, I will continue working and I hope this text could stimulate other researchers to continue travelling this path.

Archives and reference libraries consulted

1. Archives: Spilimbergo (Buenos Aires), Berni (Madrid-Buenos Aires), Manuel de Falla (Granada), Novecento (Milano), Forner-Bigatti (Buenos Aires), Annemarie Heinrich (Buenos Aires), Getty Research Institute (Los Angeles, California), CEDINCI (Buenos Aires) and IIAC-UNTREF (Buenos Aires).
2. Libraries: Biblioteca Nacional de España (Madrid), Biblioteca y Hemeroteca Nacional (Buenos Aires), Getty Research Institute (Los Angeles, California), Centre Pompidou (París), MNCARS (Madrid) and IIE-UNAM (México).

NOTES

1. This chapter takes as its starting points the hypothesis and itineraries that were part of my research about the tensions between art and politics in the '30s and the curatorial narratives supported in the exhibitions I have curated, like *Novecento sudamericano. Relazioni artistiche tra Italia, Argentina, Brasile e Uruguay* (Milano/Sao Paulo, 2003), *Fuegos Cruzados* (Córdoba Spain, 2005), *Territories of dialogue, Madrid, México and Buenos Aires between the realism and the surreal* (México City/ Buenos Aires, 2006), and some publications, like *Los surrealistas, insurrectos y revolucionarios de Europa y América* (with M.T. Constantín, Longseller, 2005), "Disputas por lo real", in: *Arte moderno ideas y conceptos* (Fundación Mapfre, Madrid, 2009), *Imagenes e historias* (Fundación Mapfre, Buenos Aires, 2011), *Berni, la mirada intensa* (Fundación Picasso, Málaga, 2010), *Forner, una mirada moderna* (MUNTREF, Buenos Aires, 2015) and "Itinerarios latinoamericanos", in: *El cubismo y sus entornos* (Fundación Telefónica, Madrid, 2005), among others.
2. Cf. Diana Wechsler. "Mujeres del mundo." *Raquel Forner, en foco*, special issue of *Estudios curatoriales*, year 7, no. 10, 2020, pp. 46–60, www.//revistas.untref.edu.ar/index.php/rec/issue/view/57. Accessed 12 February 2021.
3. Franz Roh. "Nuevo realismo." *Revista de Occidente* [Madrid], 1927, pp. 121f.
4. The hypotheses and debates presented in this text show part of the itinerary of my theoretical–critical, historiographical and art-historical research. The international seminars "Narraciones de lo moderno" (the result of work carried out with Eugenio Carmona, Lola Jimenez Blanco and in which Raul Antelo, Maristella Margozzi and Jose Navarrete also participated, 2012) and "Pensar con imágenes" (carried out with Aurora Fernandez, Yayo Aznar and in which Georges Didi-Huberman among others also collaborated, 2014), both organized by the Instituto de Investigaciones en Arte y Cultura, UNTREF, were moments of intensity in the discussion and deepening of the work. Similarly, the opportunity to participate in the workshops of the Transregional academies project of the CAHA (Paris) and to present aspects of my work in that forum were also very enriching.

REFERENCES

Ades, Dawn. *Dada y el surrealismo*. Labor, 1975.

Adorno, Theodor W. *Ensayos sobre la propaganda fascista. Psicoanálisis del antisemitismo*. Paradiso, 2005.

Années *30 en Europe. Le temps menaçant 1929–1939*, edited by Suzanne Pagé and Aline Vidal, exh. cat. Musee d'Art Moderne de la Ville de París, Paris, 1997.

Aragon, Louis. "La pintura desafiada." 1930. Ángel González García, et al. *Escritos de Arte de vanguardia 1900/1945* (Colección Fundamentos, 147), Editorial Istmo, 1999, pp. 439f.

Berni, la mirada intensa, edited by Diana Wechsler, exh. cat. Fundación Picasso – Casa natal, Málaga, 2010.

Berni, Antonio, and José Viñals. *Berni: palabra e imagen*. Imagen Galería de Arte, 1976.

Breton, André. “Le surrealism et la peintrue.” *La Révolution Surreáliste*, no. 7, 1926, pp. 3–6. *Gallica*, https://gallica.bnf.fr/ark:/12148/bpt6k5845116s.image#. Accessed 18 July 2021.

Carmona, Eugenio, et al. *Manuel Ángeles Ortiz*, exh. cat. Museo Nacional Centro de Arte Reina Sofía, Madrid, 1996.

Carmona, Eugenio, et al. *El cubismo y sus entornos*, exh. cat. Fundación Telefónica, Madrid, 2005.

Clair, Jean. *Malinconia* (Balsa de la medusa, 90). Translated by Lydia Vásquez, Visor, 1999.

Clifford, James. *Dilemas de la cultura. Antropología, literatura y arte en la perspectiva posmoderna*. Translated by Carlos Reynoso, Gedisa, 1995.

Chiarelli, Tadeu, and Diana Wechsler. *Novecento sudamericano. Relazioni artistiche tra Italia, Argentina, Brasile e Uruguay*, exh. cat. Palazzo reale di Milano, Milan, 2003.

De Diego, Estrella, and Fernando Huici. *Fuera de orden, mujeres de la vanguardia española*, exh. cat. Fundación Cultural Mapfre Vida, Madrid, 1999.

Didi-Huberman, George. “La exposición como máquina de guerra.” Translated by Guadalupe González, *Minerva*, no. 16, 2011, pp. 24–28. www.circulobellasartes.com/revistaminerva/articulo.php?id=449. Accessed 3 March 2018

Encuentros *con los años '30*, edited by Jordana Mendelson et al., exh. cat. Museo Nacional Centro de Art Reina Sofía, Madrid, 2018.

Exilio, edited by Virgilo Zapatero, exh. cat. Fundación Pablo Iglesias, Madrid, 2002.

Fabris, Annateresa. *Portinari, pintor social*. EDUSP, 1990.

Il “Novecento” milanese: *da Sironi ad Arturo Martini*, edited by Elena Pontiggia et al., exh. cat. Spazio Oberdan, Milan, 2003.

Magalhães, Ana Gonçalves. “Modern Classicism: Margherita Sarfatti and Novecento Italiano, between Brazil and the United States.” *Selva: A Journal of the History*, no. 2, 2020, pp. 215–241, www.//selvajournal.org/article/modern-classicism-margherita-sarfatti/. Accessed 12 November 2020.

Memoria del futuro, *Arte Italiano desde las primeras vanguardias a la posguerra*, edited by Germano Celant and Ida Gianelli, exh. cat. Museo Nacional Centro de Arte Reina Sofía, Madrid, 1990.

Navarrete, Jose Antonio. “París 1930: Arte latino americano en la Galería Zak.” (inedit, presented in the “International Seminar Modern narratives”, UNTREF, Buenos Aires, 2012).

Pontiggia, Elena, editor. *Il novecento italiano* (Carte d'artisti, 33). Abscondita, 2003.

Wechsler, Diana. *Spilimbergo y el arte moderno en la argentina*. Fondo Nacional de las Artes, 1999.

Wechsler, Diana, et al. *Fuegos Cruzados*, exh. cat. Fundación Provincial de Artes Plásticas Rafael Botí, Córdoba, 2005.

Wechsler, Diana, et al. *Territorios de diálogo, España, México, Argentina, 1930–1945, entre los realismos y lo surreal*, exh. cat. Museo Nacional de Arte, México City/Centro Cultural Recoleta, Buenos Aires, 2006.

Williams, Raymond. *The Politics of Modernism: Against the New Conformists*. Verso, 1989.

19

Urban Exile: Bogotá in the First Half of the 20th Century

Claudia Cendales Paredes

Introduction

This paper centres a city not known for immigration, Bogotá, and focusses on some case studies and works of exiled and migrant artists who arrived there in the 1930s and 1940s.[1] In general, Colombia, unlike other South American countries, has not been the recipient of large migratory flows from Europa or other continents, due to different factors, including political, economic and social problems and geographical and climatic conditions (Aya Smitmans et al. 2010).[2] European migration after 1930, and directly resulting from the rise of National Socialism, did not occur with as much force as in other South American countries because of these factors and because the country did not have flexible immigration policies in place (Giraldo 2001).[3]

In 1938, Bogotá had a population of 330,312 according to the census, of which 6,396 were foreigners, corresponding to 1.9 per cent of the total population (Barón Leal/Zambrano Pantoja 2018, 64). There is no exact figure on how many artists arrived in Bogotá in the 1930s and 1940s and although research on some of these artists exists, their works have mainly been analyzed vis-à-vis their contribution, impact and influence in the Colombian context.[4] Aspects such as their migration stories, the conditions upon arriving to the country, their networks and the places where they socialized, pose questions which have not yet been answered and which provide fruitful ground for new research. This text focuses on the question: how can the works and experience of exiled artists in a city like Bogotá be interpreted? To answer this, an analysis of documents, works and the city plan of 1938 is carried out. In this context, the city of Bogotá is taken into account from two perspectives: the city will be considered, first, as characterized by certain geographic, administrative and topographical conditions, and second, following Manuel Castells' notions of space, as a material product in relation to other material products including people, who assign space a form, function and social meaning (Castells 2002, 444).

Urban interventions

Despite having been described as a small city at the height of the Andes, limited by the Eastern Hills,[5] Bogotá had seen a great increase in population since about the mid 19th century; this was related, among other factors, to internal immigrations, which, however, had not led to the expansion of the city but to its densification (fig. 19.1). There were issues related to overcrowding and hygiene that worsened due to the lack of urban planning, a problem addressed increasingly in the 1910s and 1920s. During his presidency Alfonso López (1934–1938) pushed for educational reform and urban modernization, contracting some foreign architects for projects, mainly for public works.[6] In addition to these architects, other artists arrived escaping National Socialism or seeking better opportunities, motivated by contacts and family members, while others arrived with the intention of leaving for other countries soon after, while yet others only arrived by chance because for many Colombia, and Bogotá, was not their first option as a destination.

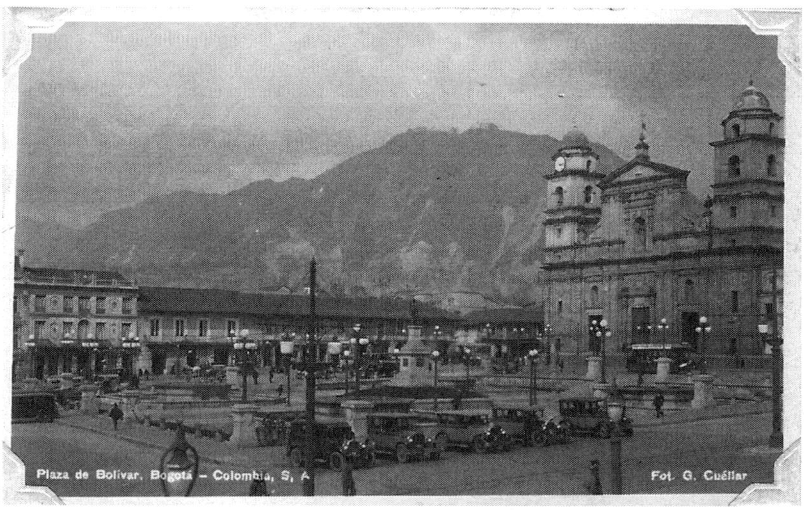

FIGURE 19.1: Gumersindo Cuéllar Jiménez, *Plaza de Bolívar, main square of Bogotá, with the Eastern Hills*, *c.*1930, photograph (Sociedad de Mejoras y Ornato de Bogotá, Archivo JVOR, No. registro IX-659c).

To carry out the much-needed urban planning of Bogotá, the Departamento de Urbanismo (Department of Urban Planning) was founded in 1933 and it was decided that a European city planner, someone who had at least some experience working in South American cities with more than 300,000 inhabitants, would be hired to lead it. The Austrian city planner Karl Brunner, who had worked in Santiago de Chile since 1929, was chosen for the project, and for carrying out the Plan Centenario, an urban project conceived to commemorate the 400th anniversary of the foundation of Bogotá in 1938.[7] Brunner was also the honorary consul of Austria from 1937 to 1948 when he returned to Vienna (Hofer 2003, 89–91).[8] Among his contributions in Bogotá, two aspects stand out that are related to the chequerboard inherited from the colonial past: the use of basic blocks that enhance some sectors, and the use of diagonal layouts through which the chequerboard layout is balanced out. This practice in Bogotá has been recognized as comprehensive urban planning (ibid., 182), which takes into account the city's specific location and topography.

Another important project for the expansion of the city towards the west was carried out by the German architect Leopoldo (or Leopold) Rother, who arrived in Colombia in 1936 following an announcement seeking experienced architects to work on state projects.[9] With a career as an architect in Germany but not very well known there, Rother had lost his job due to his Jewish background (Vendries Bray 2014, 142).[10] In Bogotá, he was given one of the most important state projects during that time: the university campus of the Universidad Nacional, which was based on a pedagogical reform designed by the German pedagogue Fritz Karsen (Cendales Paredes 2003, 20)[11] and which included an urban plan and several buildings considered among the first modern buildings in the city and in the country (fig. 19.2).

Brunner's and Rother's projects represented a break with urban space and are entangled with the modernization of the city (fig. 19.3). According to Jesús Martín-Barbero, in the 1930s and 1940s, the bourgeois sectors of most Latin American countries assumed that modernization necessarily meant incorporating the way of life of other, "modern countries" (Martín-Barbero 2006, 628). They thought that only one model of transformation could save their countries from an alleged "backwardness": the path to an urban Europeanized society (ibid., 628f.). The fact that specifically European architects and city planners were hired to 'bring' these models into the country, as was the case with Brunner and Rother, should be placed in this context.

In terms of interpreting architecture in exile in the context of Latin America, Jorge Liernur criticizes considering it a form of 'influence', because the old paradigm of the colonial times would continue to repeat itself. In his opinion, the only difference would be that this 'influence' would not come about willingly, as it would in the case of voluntary migration, but as the result of a tragedy. The colonialist mindset, however, would not change (Liernur 2003, 158f.). Partha Mitter also critiques what he calls the "pathology of influence" as a tool for the asymmetric assessment of cultural

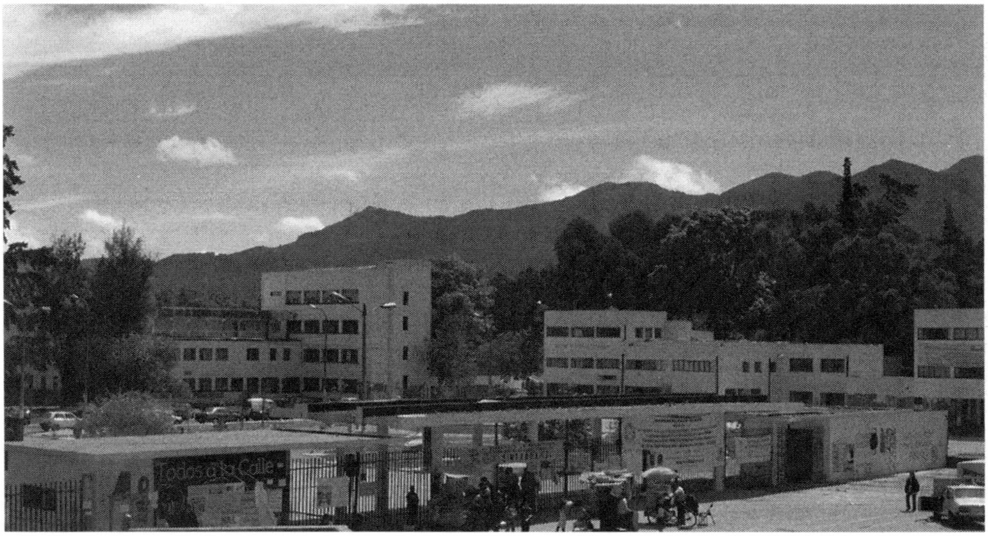

FIGURE 19.2: *Entrance and some buildings of the Universidad Nacional* (Photo: Claudia Cendales Paredes, 2015).

exchanges between Eastern and Western art (2008, 538). As Mitter affirms, *influence*, as seen from the point of view of art history, ignores aspects of cultural encounters, and it ignores especially how rewarding the cross-fertilization of cultures can be and how it should not be interpreted by way of notions of dominance or independence (ibid.). Although Mitter does not explicitly refer to exile here, such an approach can be fruitfully applied to our context in order to think in terms of a fertile and productive relationship for both sides, an exchange between city and artists. Examining the works of both Rother and Brunner thus promises valuable insights. Rother was able to apply a modern language he was familiar with but which he had not put to use in his works in Germany. In the long-term, in his new country, he adapted his work to relate to the country's specific climatic and topographic conditions (Vendries Bray 2014, 140–142). In the case of Brunner, his work also changed when he had to face the social conditions of South America and he became much more interested in new topics, such as public spaces and creating green spaces.

Urban experiences

One way of interpreting the experiences of artists in exile in Bogotá is analyzing where they lived (see fig. 19.3).[12] Several foreign artists who arrived in Bogotá in

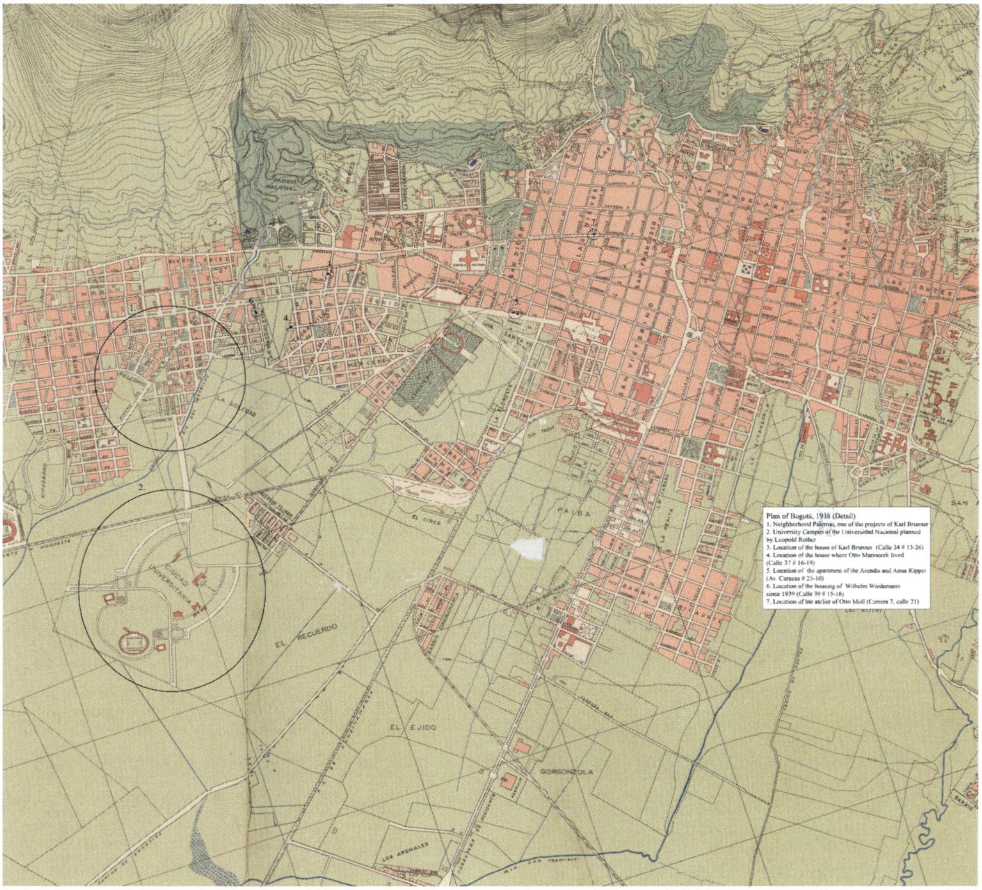

FIGURE 19.3: Secretaría de Obras Públicas Municipales, *Bogotá 1938*, 1938, 170 × 75 cm², ink on paper, Register P00386 (© Museo de Bogotá, Bogotá D.C.).

the 1930s and 1940s lived in apartments or houses in neighbourhoods that had been built recently and were associated with a sense of modernity, like Teusaquillo, Santa Teresita, Armenia and Las Nieves. In fact, Brunner lived in Teusaquillo, an exclusive neighbourhood that housed the elite and political leaders of Bogotá. Because there was no formal diplomatic office for Austria in the city, his home turned into an important space for socializing among the exiled community (Jursich Durán 2017, 14). The first house Rother lived in with his family in Bogotá was a rented house; one of the so-called MacAllister houses recently built and located on Calle 78 Carrera 11 (Devia de Jiménez 2006, 37; Mejía Pavony/Colón Llamas 2019, 220f.).[13] The house appears in a family photo of Rother and his children, Anna and Hans, taken in August 1937 (fig. 19.4). We do not know

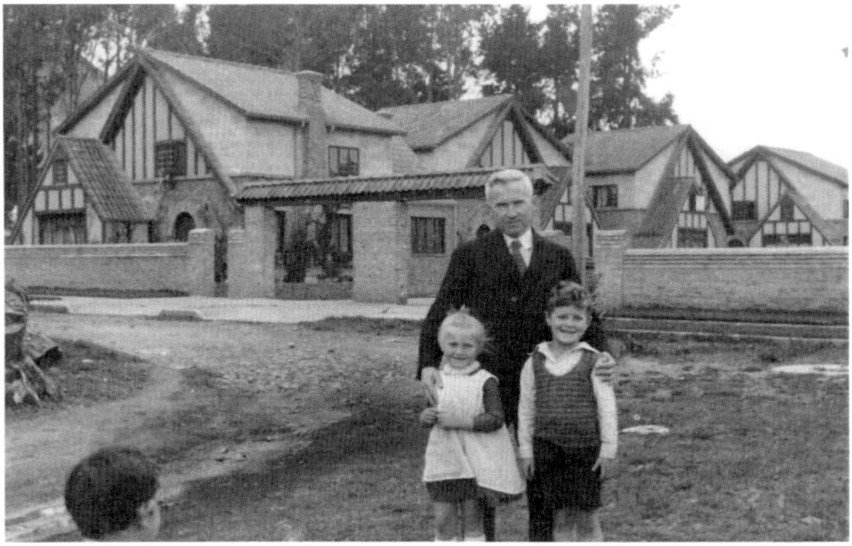

FIGURE 19.4: Unknown photographer, *Leopoldo Rother with his children Hans and Anna in front of one of the MacAllister houses*, 1937, photograph (Colección Leopoldo Rother, Museo de Arquitectura Leopoldo Rother, Bogotá D.C.).

why the Rothers chose to live there, but it is a house with Europeanized features, slightly resembling a *Fachwerkhaus* (a traditional half-timber house). One could imagine that they decided to live in this house because it reminded them of their country of origin in a place as far away as Bogotá, or that perhaps this similarity made it attractive enough to at least take a photo, which then could have served as proof of their new status, as a way of feeling they had ties to something or to show what their new home in exile looked like (Dogramaci/Lee 2019, 10).

Some artists, like the Austrian architect Otto Marmorek, lived on a temporary basis after their arrival in houses owned by families or in hostels (Marmorek 1938)[14] and found support in existing expatriate communities or Jewish associations (Toliver 1987, 161).[15] That was the case with German writer and translator, Erich Arendt, and his wife, German-Jewish philologist and translator, Katja Hayek-Arendt, who arrived in Bogotá in 1942 and who remained there until their return to the German Democratic Republic in 1950.[16] Upon their arrival, they were aided by support organizations until they moved into a small apartment in the neighbourhood of Las Nieves (ibid.), which had a large Jewish population (Martínez Ruiz 2010, 382). Erich had actively participated in the Asociación de Alemanes Libres (Komitee Freies Deutschland) since 1943 (Biermann Stolle 2001, 183), and to support themselves financially, the couple inaugurated a chocolate bonbon manufacturer called *Catherine* in their apartment (Toliver

1987, 178).[17] Their apartment turned into an important place for socializing for the exiled community and for Bogotá's intellectuals, with some of whom they stayed in contact with even after leaving Colombia (ibid., 166f.). During a dinner they hosted in their apartment on 18 February 1943, they presented a fictitious menu, written and drawn by them on a sheet of paper in two languages. Titled *10 Jahre camino*, because it commemorates the 10th anniversary of their exile, it emulates the menu designs of restaurants of the time. This work logs the stations they passed when fleeing Germany, and it reveals information about how artists perceived the city (fig. 19.5). The story begins in the middle upper part of the paper and goes from right to left, starting off with their expulsion by National Socialism

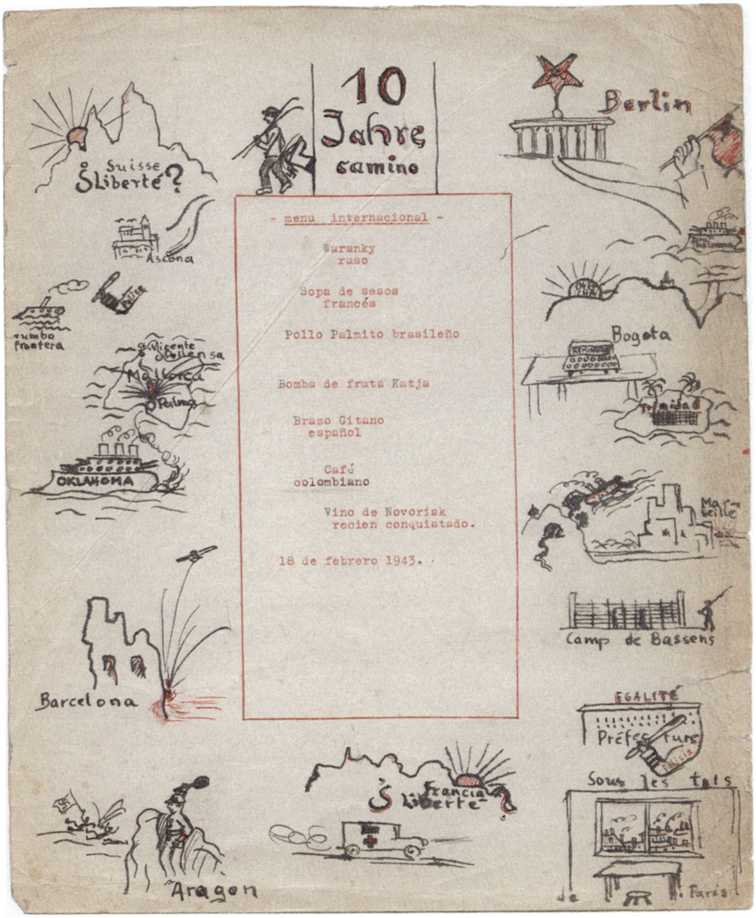

FIGURE 19.5: Erich Arendt and Katja Hayek-Arendt, *10 Jahre camino – menu internacional*, 18 February 1943, 31.5 × 25 cm², drawing (Akademie der Künste (AdK), Berlin, Erich-Arendt-Archiv, Nr. 1153).

illustrated, literally, by a kick. Every station of exile is shown as a distinctive place and outfitted with the means of transport they had used. Bogotá is depicted with the Eastern Hills and the rising sun called "CHIBCHA", which alludes to the former inhabitants of the city in pre-Hispanic times, the Muisca. This choice is not random, since both showed interest in those who had previously lived in the city. Katja criticized how they were exploited and segregated in the city while she was living there (Toliver 1987, 163f.) and Erich later described them as an advanced culture that lived in a city, namely Bogotá, that leaned against a wall of the mountain, that shone with golden palaces and precious stones, and where, according to legends, El Dorado was located (Arendt 1956, 8f.).

On the sheet of paper, and depicted near to Bogotá, they also included a Remington typewriter and, in the middle, surrounded by a red frame, they typed "*menu internacional*". This menu includes fake and real dishes, some alluding to places they encountered along their exile journey like "French brain soup" and "Colombian coffee". With some humour, the Arendts graphically reenacted their exile, covering stations and routes and creating a sort of subjective map (Dogramaci 2019, 24). Meanwhile, Katja narrated some aspects of their exile in her diaries, written between January 1944 and November 1945. She mainly referred to Bogotá as a grey city, a place of "intellectual bankruptcy", and as "rotten" (Toliver 1987, 168f.). She and Erich made trips to warmer and more tropical areas of the country with other artists, like the exiled German painter and photographer Guillermo (or Wilhelm) Wiedemann, and the Colombian-German photographer Otto Moll González, as a sort of community art practice[18] that helped Erich praise the purity of 'primitiveness'[19] in his later texts.

Essentially, the couples' urban experiences fluctuate between idealization and rejection. Despite the fact that they had to escape an incredibly dangerous situation, not all places in exile seemed to be the same. Due to their unfamiliarity with the country and the language, and due to their prejudices, many refugees that arrived in Colombia wanted to live in Bogotá and not in other cities (Kaiser-Bolbecher 2002, 5), even though some labelled the city as backward. Taking this into account, Liernur in his analyses of exile architecture suggests that from a dominant western perspective it was difficult to imagine Latin America as a site for modern exile. He refers to the uncomfortable role played by European exiles who conceived it not as a place of culture or civilization, but as a place of "primitiveness" (Liernur 2003, 167). Referring to Western observers analyzing 19th-century 'exotic' cultures, Marc Augé has similarly observed that these cultures did not seem "different" or exotic enough for Westerners to not first put them into their usual ethnocentric, stereotypical boxes (2013, 98). Something similar occurs in the case of prevailing architectural historiographies, as emphasized by Regina Göckede. If we take a look at historiographic narratives about modern architecture – one that triumphs over emigration and exile and is universalized in America –, architects of the European avant-garde seem to only achieve a synthesis of their efforts when in exile in the United States (Göckede 2007, 217). For the most part, these narratives revolve around the success stories of architects in the United States, including Mies van der Rohe and Walter Gropius, while the histories and stories of other architects who had emigrated to the Americas instead have remained largely unknown and incomplete. This standpoint, which can also be applied to other artists, explains why many exiled and immigrant artists in Colombia are unknown in their country of origin; inversely, one could think that, according to dominant historiographic accounts, they were not able to achieve 'success' (manifested in being part of an international canon), because the medium did not 'allow' them to. Exile in some regions like Africa and South America is not taken into account within those larger narratives because it is considered a "diverging phenomenon" (Göckede 2007, 217, 222f.).

Claude Lévi-Strauss suggests that it is not about whether a society can benefit from the lifestyle of a neighbouring society, but whether and to what extent it is able to understand it or at least become familiar with it. It is perhaps about understanding that other cultures are different to one's own in the most diverse ways, even if the true essence of these differences cannot be grasped or if, despite all their efforts, one can only comprehend them halfway (Lévi-Strauss 2013, 236f.). According to Augé, it is therefore about "decentering our view" (Augé 2013, 98) and in this case, it is not about belonging to a canon or validating it, but about giving space to other narratives.

Conclusions

This text focused on some case studies of artists and immigrants and their works in the 1930s and 1940s in Bogotá, a city not known for immigration or exile. As I have shown, foreign architects played a significant role in the modernization of the city. This was demonstrated by examining the works and lives of Brunner and Rother, two of the immigrant artists who have been studied the most within the Colombian context, and who were able to develop their craft during their stay in the city. In regard to specific urban exile experiences, some artists did not feel very comfortable in the city and oscillated between rejection for a city that did not or could not fulfil their expectations and their fascination for the tropics and the seeming 'primitiveness'. For many artists, Bogotá became a place where they could carry out their work, where they started a family, where they established themselves both temporarily and permanently, and where they finally even started to belong to an economic or intellectual elite: networks that can be made visible and graspable when we trace where these exile artists lived and with whom they interacted.

NOTES

1. Migration studies do not make a precise differentiation between the terms 'migration' and 'exile'. This paper uses these terms as synonyms and turns to Dogramaci to establish that "[o]ften, these conditions have fused into each other, in such a way that it is difficult to distinguish between those who are exiled and willing to return and those who have emigrated permanently" (Dogramaci 2011, 14). All quotations have been translated by Claudia Cendales Paredes.
2. In the context of the investigation into the causes of low immigration in Colombia, researchers have mentioned several factors such as the absence of public policies, restrictive public policies, low level of economic activity, geographic and climatic difficulties, lack of immigration flow that could initiate the process of immigration, civil wars and competition from more promising countries for immigrants, see Aya Smitmans et al. (2010).
3. To expand on this and on immigration in Colombia in general, see, among others: Aya Smitmans et al. (2010), Leal Villamizar (2011), Biermann Stolle (2001, 183) and Martínez Ruiz (2010, 436).
4. Research includes e.g. Inmigrantes (2013), Jursich Durán (2019), Hofer (2003), Vendries Bray (2014), Rother (1984).
5. The geographical location and height of Bogotá at 2,600 metres above sea level were often discussed among European travellers and immigrants during the 19th century, see Mejía Pavony (2000, 31).
6. These include architects Erich Lange, Ernst Blumenthal and Bruno Violi. See Schätzke (2015, 28) and Niño Murcia (2003, 108).
7. This date led to reflections about the city, and it was of symbolic significance to carry out urban projects, see Barón Leal/Zambrano Pantoja 2018.
8. Brunner (1887–1960) was hired in 1933 for three years, and later for twenty months until 1938. When his contract came to an end, he continued to serve as an advisor to the government and tried returning to Vienna, but the Nazi occupation of Austria impeded this. He remained in Colombia until the end of the war and, in 1941, he put together the Comité de Austriacos Libres along with other Austrians, see Kaiser-Bolbecher (2002, 2f.).
9. The first architecture faculty in Colombia had just been inaugurated in 1934 in Bogotá at the Universidad Nacional.
10. Leopoldo Rother (1894–1978) had completed his studies at the Technical College in Berlin-Charlottenburg in 1920 and had executed several projects in Germany, see Cendales Paredes (2003), Rother (1984), Vendries Bray (2014), Schätzke (2015).
11. After losing his job in February of 1933 due to his Jewish background, Fritz Karsen (1885–1951) had to flee Germany to Zurich and in 1936, he was invited to Colombia as an advisor for the educational reform designed by President López, see Radde (1999).
12. Based on personal documents, like letters and visiting cards, this paper examines the places where some of the artists lived in 1938.

13. The house is located in the El Nogal neighbourhood, which was urbanized in the 1930s with many houses considered as modern.
14. Letter written in German from Otto Marmorek (1917–1945) for his mother, 10 July 1938 (Archivo Adriana Marmorek, Bogotá).
15. To expand on immigration and restrictions for Jewish populations, and expatriate communities in Bogotá, see Martínez Ruiz (2010), Biermann Stolle (2001) and Leal Villamizar (2011).
16. Erich Arendt (1903–1984), member of the Communist party, had fled to Switzerland in 1933. In Ascona, he met up with Katja (1900–1979) and both fled to Mallorca in 1934. From 1936, he took part in the Spanish Civil War as a reporter. In March 1939, they fled to France, where he was detained in 1940 by German troops that had invaded the country. In 1942, he was able to obtain a visa to flee to Colombia with his wife, see Künste im Exil "Erich Arendt", n.d.
17. The address was Avenida Caracas #23-10, apartment 402. Katja describes how her Polish neighbour, Anna Kipper (1908–1989), a correspondent for the French news agency in Bogotá, motivated her in this idea, see Künste im Exil "Chocolates Catherine", n.d.
18. Wiedemann (1905–1969), Arendt and Moll (1904–1988) and their partners were close. Several photos of their relationship and trips exist, see Erich-Arendt-Archiv and Colección Guillermo Wiedemann. See Urrea Uyabán and Montaña Cuellar (2012).
19. After their return to the German Democratic Republic, Arendt published the books *Tropenland Kolumbien* in 1954 and *Tolú – Gedichte aus Kolumbien* in 1956, which condensed his experience in exile and his encounter with the Colombian tropics, see Böthig (1997, 46f.). According to Toliver, Katja participated in Erich's writings, but has not yet received individual acknowledgement, see Toliver (1987, 157).

REFERENCES

Archivo Adriana Marmorek, Bogotá.

Colección Guillermo Wiedemann, BADAC, Universidad de los Andes, Bogotá.

Colección Leopoldo Rother, Museo de Arquitectura Leopoldo Rother, Universidad Nacional de Colombia, Bogotá.

Erich-Arendt-Archiv, Akademie der Künste, Berlin.

Arendt, Erich. *Tolú – Gedichte aus Kolumbien*. Insel-Verlag, 1956.

Augé, Marc. "Nicht-Orte (1991)." *Texte zur Theorie des* Raums, edited by Stephan Günzel, Reclam, 2013, pp. 94–98.

Aya Smitmans, María Teresa, et al. "Indagación sobre las causas de la escasa inmigración en Colombia. ¿Ausencia de políticas públicas o políticas públicas restrictivas?" *Revista Opera*, no. 10, 2010, pp. 167–183, www.//revistas.uexternado.edu.co/index.php/opera/article/view/3105. Accessed 25 June 2021.

Barón Leal, Alfredo, and Fabio Zambrano Pantoja. *1938 El sueño de una capital moderna*, exh. cat. Museo de Bogotá, Bogotá, 2018.

Biermann Stolle, Enrique. *Distantes y distintos – Los emigrantes alemanes en Colombia 1939–1945*. Universidad Nacional de Colombia – División de Investigación Bogotá, 2001.

Böthig, Peter. *Grammatik einer Landschaft: Literatur aus der DDR in den 80er Jahren*. Lukas Verlag, 1997.

Castells, Manuel. *La era de la información – Economía, Sociedad y Cultura*, vol. 1: *La Sociedad Red*. Translated by Carmen Martínez Gimeno, Siglo XXI editores, 2002.

Cendales Paredes, Claudia. *Neubewertung der Universitätsstadt in Bogotá. Erste Bauphase 1935–1943*. Magisterarbeit [thesis], Ludwig-Maximilians-Universität München, 2003, doi: 10.5282/ubm/epub.4372. Accessed 25 June 2021.

Devia de Jiménez, Marta Inés. *Leopoldo Rother en la ciudad universitaria*. Universidad Nacional de Colombia, 2006.

Dogramaci, Burcu. "Netzwerke des künstlerischen Exils als Forschungsgegenstand – zur Einführung." *Netzwerke des Exils – Künstlerische Verflechtungen, Austausch und Patronage nach 1933*, edited by Burcu Dogramaci and Karin Wimmer, Gebr. Mann Verlag, 2011, pp. 13–28.

Dogramaci, Burcu. "Toward a *Migratory* Turn – Art History and the Meaning of Flight, Migration and Exile." *Handbook of Art and Global Migration – Theories, Practices, and Challenges*, edited by Burcu Dogramaci and Birgit Mersmann, De Gruyter, 2019, pp. 17–37.

Dogramaci, Burcu, and Rachel Lee. "Refugee Artists, Architects and Intellectuals Beyond Europe in the 1930s and 1940s: Experiences of Exile in Istanbul and Bombay." *ABE Journal*, nos. 14–15, 2019. *OpenEdition Journals*, doi: 10.4000/abe.5949. Accessed 20 August 2020.

Giraldo, Luz Mary. "Inmigrantes, desplazados y exiliados en la literatura colombiana." *Migrations en Colombie*, special issue of Les Cahiers ALHIM. Amérique Latine Histoire et Mémoire, no. 3, 2001. *OpenEdition Journals*, doi: 10.4000/alhim.540. Accessed 6 August 2020.

Göckede, Regina. "Weiße Götter und die Schatten ihrer Erfolgsgeschichten – Prätention und Selektion in der Historiographie des transatlantischen Architekten-Exils." *Building America*, vol. 2: *Migration der Bilder*, edited by Anke Köth et al., Thelem, 2007, pp. 217–233.

Hofer, Andreas. *Karl Brunner y el urbanismo europeo en América Latina*. El Áncora Editores / Corporación La Candelaria, 2003.

Inmigrantes: artistas, arquitectos, fotógrafos, críticos y galeristas en el Arte Colombiano 1930–1970, edited by Ruth Acuña et al., exh. cat. Fundación Gilberto Alzate Avendaño (FUGA), Bogotá, 2013.

Jursich Durán, Mario. "Crestomatía ungariana (Veintiocho notas sobre –y en torno a– la biblioteca de Hans Ungar)." *Boletín Cultural y Bibliográfico*, vol. 51, no. 92, 2017, pp. 4–45, www.//publicaciones.banrepcultural.org/index.php/boletin_cultural/article/view/7955. Accessed 25 June 2021.

Jursich Durán, Mario, editor. *Miradas cruzadas: las relaciones entre Austria y Colombia*. Amaral Editores, 2019.

Kaiser-Bolbecher, Siglinde. "Österreichische Emigration in Kolumbien." *Österreichische Literatur im Exil*, Universität Salzburg, 2002, www.sbg.ac.at/exil/l5040.pdf. Accessed 18 August 2020.

Künste im Exil. "Chocolates Catherine, Visitenkarte (um 1944)." *Künste im Exil – Objekte*, n.d., www.//kuenste-im-exil.de/KIE/Content/DE/Objekte/arendt-erich-chocolates-catherine.html?single=1. Accessed 18 August 2020.

Künste im Exil. "Erich Arendt." *Künste im Exil – Personen*, n.d., www.//kuenste-im-exil.de/KIE/Content/DE/Personen/arendt-erich.html. Accessed 18 August 2020.

Leal Villamizar, Lina María. *Colombia frente al antisemitismo y la inmigración de judíos polacos y alemanes 1933–1948*. MA thesis, Universidad Nacional de Colombia, 2011.

Lévi-Strauss, Claude. "Das räumliche Zusammenwirken der Kulturen (1952)." *Texte zur Theorie des* Raums, edited by Stephan Günzel, Reclam, 2013, pp. 233–238.

Liernur, Jorge Francisco. "The (Latin) American Friend: Architecture and European exile south of the Rio Bravo (1936–1948)." *Architektur und Exil – Kulturtransfer und architektonische Emigration 1930 bis 1950*, edited by Bernd Nicolai, Porta Alba Verlag Trier GmbH, 2003, pp. 157–167.

Martín-Barbero, Jesús. "The Processes: From Nationalism to Transnationalism." *Media and Cultural Studies: KeyWorks*, revised ed., edited by Meenakshi Gigi Durham and Douglas M. Kellner, Blackwell Publishing Ltd, 2006, pp. 626f.

Martínez Ruiz, Enrique. *Haciendo comunidad, haciendo ciudad. Los judíos y la conformación del espacio urbano de Bogotá*. MA thesis, Universidad Nacional de Colombia, 2010.

Mejía Pavony, Germán. *Los años del cambio: historia urbana de Bogotá 1820–1910*. Pontificia Universidad Javeriana, 2000.

Mejía Pavony, Germán, and Luis Carlos Colón Llamas. *Atlas histórico de barrios de Bogotá 1884–1954*. Instituto Distrital de Patrimonio Cultural, 2019.

Mitter, Partha. "Decentering Modernism: Art History and Avant-Garde Art from the Periphery." *The Art Bulletin*, vol. 90, no. 4, 2008, pp. 531–548.

Niño Murcia, Carlos. *Arquitectura y Estado: contexto y significado de las construcciones del Ministerio de Obras Públicas, Colombia, 1905–1960*. 2nd ed., Universidad Nacional de Colombia, 2003.

Radde, Gerd. *Fritz Karsen. Ein Berliner Schulreformer der Weimarer Zeit* (Studien zur Bildungsreform, 37). Peter Lang, 1999.

Rother, Hans. *Arquitecto Leopoldo Rother: vida y obra* (Colección Arquitectura, 9). Fondo Ed. Escala, 1984.

Schätzke, Andreas. *Transatlantische Moderne – Deutsche Architekten im lateinamerikanischen Exil*. MV-Verlag, 2015.

Toliver, Suzanne Shipley. "In Exile: The Latin American Diaries of Katja Hayek Arendt." *American Jewish Archives*, 29, no. 2, 1987, pp. 157–188.

Urrea Uyabán, Tatiana and Jimena Montaña Cuéllar. "A través de la lente: Otto Moll González." *Boletín Cultural y Bibliográfico*, vol. 46, no. 83, 2012, pp. 99–128, www.//publicaciones.banrepcultural.org/index.php/boletin_cultural/article/view/64. Accessed 25 June 2021.

Vendries Bray, Ernesto. *Leopold Rother und die moderne Bewegung in Kolumbien*. Ph.D. dissertation, Technische Universität Darmstadt, 2014.

20

(Re)routing and (Re)rooting in Urban Exile: Exploring Villa Ocampo in Buenos Aires and Jassim House in Bombay with Actor-Network-Theory[1]

Mareike Schwarz

> *[A] ser ya todo yo la total arboleda perdida de mi sangre. Y una larga memoria, de la que nunca nadie podrá tener noticia, errará escrita por los aires, definitivamente extraviada, definitivamente perdida.*
>
> (Rafael Alberti 1959/2003, 546)[2]

After 38 years in exile, the Spanish poet Rafael Alberti articulated his artistic development as a "lost grove" in his autobiography of the same name, *La arboleda perdida* (1959). For the anti-fascist intellectual, who fled to Argentina after the Spanish Civil War (1936–1939) and became a regular contributor to the Buenos Aires-based arts magazine *SUR*, this imaginary place is emblematic of the loss and uprooting he felt as a result of emigration (Sanz/Funes 2016). Such topoi of private and artistic rootlessness are often expressed in the context of modern exile (Fajardo 2010).[3] They raise the question of whether and how émigré artists could connect to cultural developments and actors in their respective exile cities: Could a 'third space' evolve between home and foreign, whose creative potential unfolds precisely through the experience of emigration and within new urban contexts? Along this metaphorical configuration of the third space in the sense of Homi K. Bhabha's postcolonial theory (Bhabha 1994), this chapter sets out to find the traces of artistic (re)rooting in exile.

At the centre of this search are two 'arrival cities' (Saunders 2010) studied in the METROMOD research project: Buenos Aires and Bombay, now Mumbai.[4] For it was there that displaced creatives from Europe contributed to the formation of "inspirational *and* conflict-laden" contact zones in the first half of the 20th century (Dogramaci et al. 2020, 11). Back then two private homes in Argentina and India became a nodal point for local and exiled artists resulting in significant cultural projects: Victoria Ocampo's Villa Ocampo in Buenos Aires, housing *SUR* magazine, and Jassim House in Bombay, a living and working space for the Modern Architectural Research Group (M.A.R.G.) and their periodical *Marg*.

This chapter uses Actor-Network-Theory (ANT), a theoretical and methodological approach to the social as a constantly shifting network of relationships, which has been developed since the 1980s by Bruno Latour and Madeleine Akrich, amongst others. The aim is to trace the human and non-human factors that made these dwellings a home for creative exchanges between exiles and locals. Starting from the respective arrival city, this methodological approach counter-acts exile studies' tendency to focus on biographical information.[5] As a result, the following questions are also addressed from an urbanistic, and less person-centred perspective: What kind of social and built environments enabled the formation of a third space resulting in significant transcultural mediators like *SUR* and *Marg*?[6] What personal dispositions let these networks grow? Which architectonic and interior design settings fostered creative dialogues? How are all these conditions connected to each city?

In a first step, I will reflect on the capacity of dwellings to emerge as third spaces under the premise of (e)migration. In the following, I will outline the methods of ANT in the expanded field of urban living and exile, which have yet to be sufficiently addressed in scholarship. Based on this, I will study and compare the actants of the transcultural encounters in Buenos Aires and Bombay, while differentiating these findings regionally and historically.

Exile dwelling as third space: "Too many houses for a home"[7]

In view of various cross-border migrations, which reached an immense scale in the 20th century due to colonialism, capitalism and the persecution caused by political systems, the traditional understanding of home and dwelling is put into question (Clifford 1997). The flows of information, people and things run counter to the well-received approaches of European philosophers like Martin Heidegger, whose conceptions of dwelling and home are rooted in a particular time and space. Home and roots for a mobile population may be inscribed not in a physical space but in words, opinions, gestures, styles of dress, (inter)actions and narrative forms (Berger 1984). The over-valuation of a single, fixed home and the over-proclamation of a somehow distorted rootlessness in modernity may have "as its necessary correlative the suspicion of mobility", as the cultural scientist David Morley (2008, 33) suggests.

'Being-at-home' has been so irrevocably re-interpreted by modern migration that it undoubtedly transcends the physical location of the 'house'. Therefore 'home' and 'dwelling' are introduced as plurilocal terms. This is in keeping with Bhabha, who pleads for a renewed understanding of home and the world in his book *The Location of Culture* (1994). In this study of cultural difference and the enunciation of minority identities the concept of the 'third space' is formulated, which is derived from hybridity theory (ibid., 217–229). With critical reference to the Marxist-oriented literary scholar Fredric Jameson, Bhabha defined the third space as a liminal space, where "difference is neither One or the Other but *something else besides, in-between*" (ibid., 219).

This conceptualization aims at overcoming binary divisions such as home/world or private/public through which social experiences are often presented as spatially opposed. "These spheres of life are linked through an 'in-between' temporality that takes the measure of dwelling at home, while producing an image of the world of history" (ibid., 13). Bhabha takes up the architectural metaphor of the stairwell, which "opens up the possibility of a cultural hybridity that entertains difference without an assumed or imposed hierarchy" (ibid., 4). Instead, it allows "to dwell 'in the beyond'" of race, class and gender, which can become a "space of intervention" (ibid., 7). According to Bhabha, such potentials are enacted by distinctive visual artworks as well as literary works of an intellectual community.[8] Bhabha's statement that such hybrid minority communities as a significant "antagonistic supplement" are formed in metropolises or imaginative geographies through gatherings of exiles and émigrés, is particularly noteworthy for the research thesis proposed here (ibid., 231–243).

But how is the artistic capacity of intervention located in arrival cities? This chapter suggests that third spaces emerge explicitly through liminal processes of (re)routing and (re)rooting of life and work in urban exile. Following the historian James Clifford (1997), the widely held notion that roots always precede routes is discarded. Instead, home (roots) and displacement (routes) are understood as co-existing shapers of cultural developments that, according to art historian Burcu Dogramaci (2013, 46), intertwine in "dwelling under the premise of (e)migration".[9] Thereby the root metaphor is not invoked without reservations. Maurizio Bettini (2018) has rightly criticized the identitarian implications of the notion of roots, which all too often negate cultural differences from the point of view of a putative guiding culture. In sharp contrast, the roots metaphor is drawn upon here in an

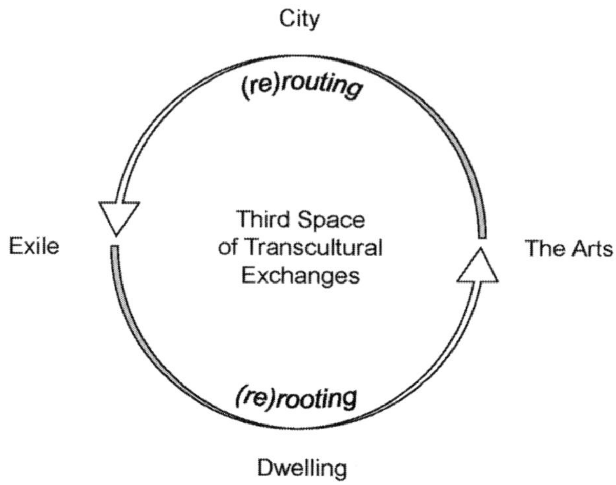

FIGURE 20.1: *The constitution of a third space along processes of (re)routing and (re)rooting* (model and illustration © Mareike Schwarz).

explicitly non-identitarian and plurilocal way.[10] (Re)rooting then means an ambivalent process within a metropolitan in-between-space, which grows out of transcultural exchanges. By situating emigrated artists in their urban communities as a place that simultaneously is and is not their home, third spaces emerge. This understanding of a (re)routing of feeling rooted in urban exile is outlined in fig. 20.1.

An ANT analysis of the urban sociotopology of exile

Dwelling, in the double sense of place and inhabiting that place (Dogramaci 2019), already terminologically eludes an assignment to the sphere of subjects or objects. Taking this hybrid character into account, ANT provides a productive methodology to explore dwelling in urban exile outside the conventional subject-object-dichotomy. Existing, person-centred exile studies are expanded by the biographies of non-humans.[11] This offers the possibility to not only examine entangled networks between exiles and locals but also to consider circulating ideas and things as equal parts (Hensel and Schröter 2012).

From the 1980s onwards, ANT has focused on reassembling the social (Latour 2005). The social, which is not to be confused with society, is understood as a temporary assembly of actors or actants in networks. An actant is considered to be an "entity that more or less successfully defines and builds a world filled by other entities with histories, identities, and interrelationships of their own" (Callon 1990, 140). This connecting process, which negotiates the characteristics and activities of any entity, is called 'translation'. In such networks of translations, all entities can obtain the potential for action: an "agency" (Hensel/Schröter 2012).

Reacting to the lack of a comprehensive ANT-application to dwelling, let alone in relation to exile, in the following I will draw on theorizations on architecture and design as actants. Following Albena Yaneva, I consider architectural outcomes as ever-changing rather than static projects. By exploring architecture in its historical entanglements with dwellers and immanent design challenges, the "social career of a building" is recollected (Yaneva 2009, 7). Regarding the interiority of these buildings, which encompasses the interior objects as well as their inhabitants' psychological inwardness, each object is seen as a vision of the world and programme of action for its users. Via these inherent 'scripts', the objects within a home afford certain activities and prevent others from being implemented. These 'affordances' act together with legal, technical, artistic and economic ties as one connector within networks manifesting the social (ibid., 285f.). According to this understanding, enlivened things act with people and vice versa (Belliger/Krieger 2006). Methodologically, these heterogeneous networks are approached through processual descriptions rather than periodizations or style analyses (Heß 2018).

Dwelling of exiles or locals conveys a tacit knowledge through its arrangements of human and non-human actants. These not only point to a person's present self-conception, but also their life routes in the past. As a kind of sign system, diverse memories and emotions are condensed within a home via assembled things (Dogramaci 2013). Particularly in consideration of the felt separation and foreignness inherent in exile, familiar objects may be loaded with great meaning. For displacement from the country of origin was usually accompanied by an enormous loss of acquainted places and things. In their book *Dinge des Exils* (Things of Exile) Doerte Bischoff and Joachim Schlör describe exile as a condition, in which "things often become central objects of reflection for the exiled person, who recognize and reflect their own being rejected and uncontrollably driven around in the existential mode of movable objects" (Bischoff/Schlör 2013, 15).[12] These actants in exile evoke embodied (hi)stories and life visions facilitating a kind of mobile home (Svašek 2014). These entangled networks affect their environment and vice versa. Places of encounters between exiles and locals can thus be studied by ANT beyond static essentializations (Latour/Yaneva 2008).

My analyses of relational contact zones in both Ocampo's and M.A.R.G.'s dwellings are based on descriptions of their thing constellations and architectural actings. Drawing on historical visuals and architectural layers persisting in the present, this chapter attempts to reconstruct the past lifeworld as precisely as possible. However, the processual, descriptive approach of ANT is limited by the fragmentary records of exilic life situations. In order to consolidate my analyses, I will consult (auto)biographical sources and scientific studies in a second step. As dwelling is "not *naturally* given, but always discursively mediated" (Nierhaus/Nierhaus 2014, 9), I will also draw on specialized and popular media which provide necessary background information regarding housing in Argentina and India.[13] Not only the distance in time but also the distance in place of the writer to the written place increases the risk of misinterpretations. I am aware of my culturally different perception in relation to the objects of study. In order to keep unconscious biases low, the ANT-based methodology requires the aforementioned contextualization.

Villa Ocampo: Exchanges of "the other" in Buenos Aires[14]

Arriving in Buenos Aires in the first half of the 20th century meant coming to a country that had incorporated immigration as one of the foundational myths in its national historiography (Bjerg 2016). Already in the 19th century, Argentina's capital featured an immensely diverse population since the city attracted foreigners with open immigration policies and promising economic prospects. Both colonialism and the continuous encounters of migrants with locals "allowed the city to open up towards plural forms" (Karp Lugo 2020, 49).

A multinational network existed in the 1930s and 1940s on an artistic level, too. Creative ideas, objects and people circulated especially through magazines, refuting the historiographic narrative of an isolated Latin American artistic community (Wechsler 2014). One of these transcultural networking hubs was the periodical *SUR*, which was founded by Victoria Ocampo in 1931 and which flourished under her direction for many decades (fig. 20.2). As the title and the cover with an arrow pointing downwards suggest, the starting point of this publishing work is situated in South America. The interdisciplinary editorial team consisted of both Latin American and European cultural figures, including the Argentine writer Jorge Luis Borges and the exiled Spanish philosopher José Ortega y Gasset (Karp Lugo 2020).

SUR offered plural perspectives on the political and aesthetic agenda of modern movements of the time; its writings often translated into Spanish for the first time (Majstorovic 2005). The first issue for instance contained both a literary contribution by Alfonso Reyes and an architectural treatise by Walter Gropius (SUR 1931). Its network soon crossed numerous national borders, which proved beneficial to European exiles in Argentina in the course of their forced displacements. According to Rosalie Sitman, *SUR*, unlike comparable magazines, took a clear stance

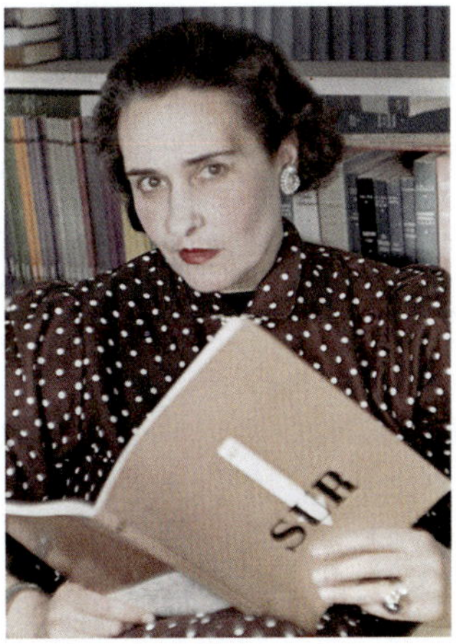

FIGURE 20.2: Gisèle Freund (émigré artist), *Photograph of Victoria Ocampo with SUR magazine*, Buenos Aires, 1944, diapositive, 24 × 36 mm (bpk | IMEC, Fonds MCC | Gisèle Freund).

against political extremes (Sitman 2008). It became an important press organ of the republican diaspora of Spanish writers such as Rafael Alberti or María Teresa León who opposed the dictatorship under Franco (Sanz/Funes 2016). At the same time, pro-Jewish articles contrasted with nationalistic groups, whose antisemitic propaganda continued to spread in Argentina. A month before the borders were to be tightened for Jewish exiles in Argentina, *SUR* advocated for the positive effects of immigration (Lombroso 1939).

Given Ocampo's intense involvement, *SUR*'s solidary position – strengthened by publicly known anti-fascists in *SUR*'s team, like Waldo Frank – connected to the editor herself.[15] Ocampo was the financial and administrative force behind various relief funds as well as the life-saving emigration of several artist friends (Thurn 2019): this ranged from her support of Jewish photographer Gisèle Freund to arranging a job for Odessa-born architect Vladimir Acosta (Karp Lugo 2020).

Among a selected circle, dialogues beyond national borders and resident status took place in Victoria Ocampo's privately owned houses, above all at Villa Ocampo, in the residential district of San Isidro. It was the setting for many *SUR* activities during the 1940s, which links it historically to the Bombay case study discussed later in this chapter. The house was designed by Victoria Ocampo's father, the engineer Manuel Ocampo, and built in 1891 (Bordelois/Grementieri 2006). It is a few minutes' walk from the historic centre of the suburb of San Isidro (fig. 20.3), which lies 25 kilometres outside the federal capital in the province of

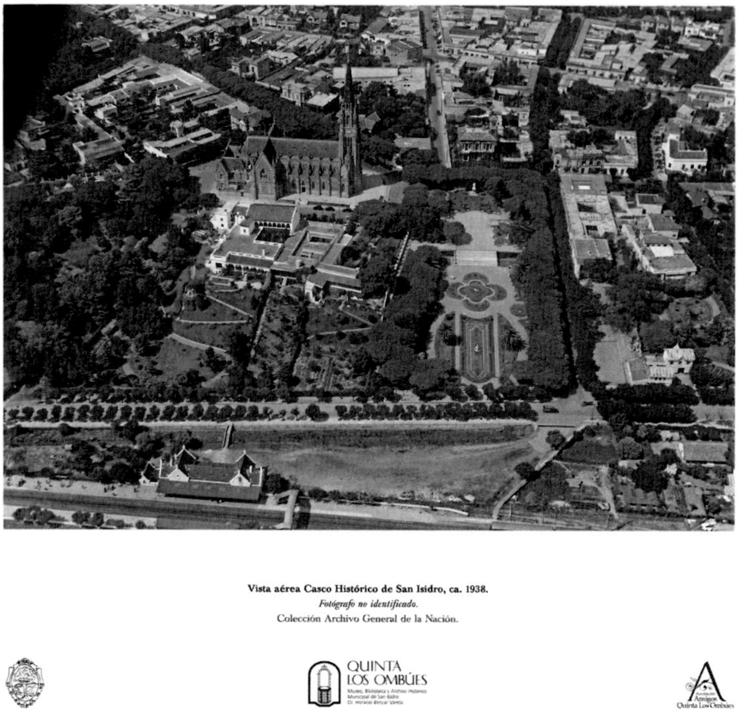

FIGURE 20.3: *Aerial view of the historic centre of San Isidro, Buenos Aires Province*, c.1938 (Argentina, Archivo General de la Nación, Departamento Documentos Fotográficos or AR_AGN_DDF/Consulta_INV: 185223_a.AGN. Caja 1651, courtesy of Museo, Biblioteca y Archivo histórico municipal de San Isidro "Dr. Horacio Beccar Varela").

Buenos Aires. A large gate leads from the street Elortondo 1837 into a garden overgrown with gnarled trees, cacti and palm trees. In its centre rises a stately house in warm ochre and sienna (fig. 20.4).[16] In a lighter earth tone, ornaments and fluted pilasters are set off on the facade, contrasting with the 'pietra serena' colored windows and roof. The architecture and luxurious furnishings may have evoked the feeling of "Old great splendour" that Walter Gropius described during his visit to San Isidro (Isaacs 1984, 1158).[17]

An external staircase flanked by balustraded railings opens the building to those coming from outside. It leads to an arcaded portico overgrown with bougainvillea. The large windows with light curtains give a first glimpse of the interior. At the carved wooden door, outside and inside, or to paraphrase the sociologist Georg Simmel, human "separateness and connectedness" (1984, 10), meet in a protective space.[18] Imposing and yet inviting, the view through the large portal is directed towards the entrance area. At the end of the vestibule, hangs a tapestry by

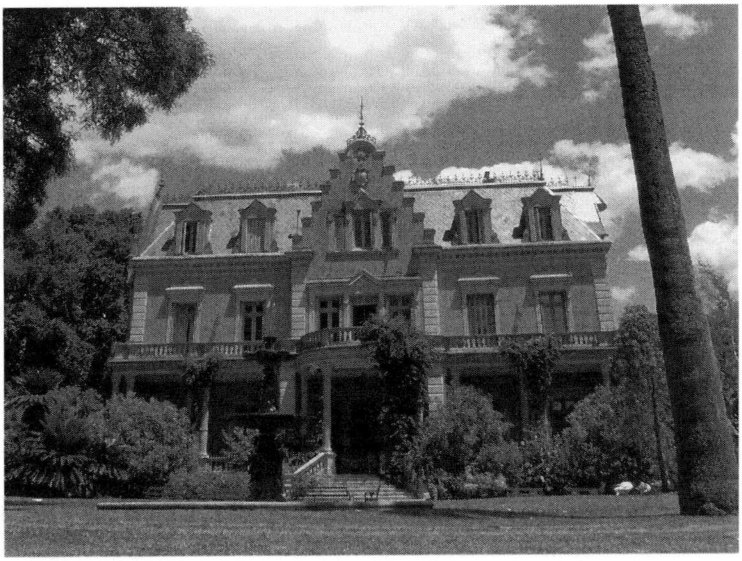

FIGURE 20.4: *Image of the renovated Villa Ocampo (built in 1891) in 2015* (Photo: Claudio Morales, 2015).

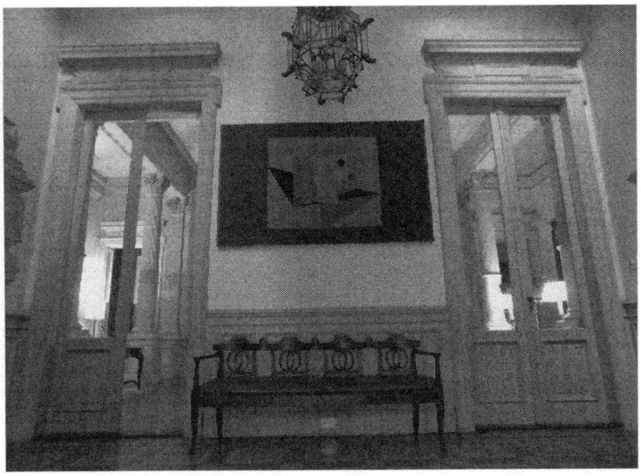

FIGURE 20.5: *Entry room in Villa Ocampo (as redecorated by Ocampo in the 1940s) in 2015* (Photo: Claudio Morales, 2015).

Pablo Picasso, marking a modern setting in neoclassical surroundings (fig. 20.5). On both sides of the modern work of art, white double doors with glass windows provide a view of a bright central hall supported by pedestalled columns, from which various lounges can be explored.

The architecture offers permeability so that sounds are transported across the individual levels. The open spatial structure delegates a distribution of individual conversations. If, in line with the sociologist and philosopher Michel de Certeau, the order of lived spaces relates to social structures, the result is a flexible configuration of contact possibilities (de Certeau 1988). The individual rooms have white walls, which Ocampo chose over the existing panelling and wallpaper. Due to the reduced ornamentation, the bookshelves, which reach up to the ceiling with deliberately selected painted portraits and photographs in their interstices, attract all the more attention. Just like Ocampo, who was socialized in French and English, the multinationally arranged libraries act as cultural mediators. A reach into the bookshelf could lead to a poem by Rabindranath Tagore dedicated to Ocampo: a materialized, transcontinental connection.[19] Other books, such as Borges' Ode to the German language "Al idioma alemán", refer to the multilingual *SUR* network (Borges 1994).

A mutual coexistence is manifested that takes place on a similar proverbial and literal eye level as the relations to exiles of other origins and languages. In the same environment, 19th-century family portraits by Prilidiano Pueyrredón meet an abstract carpet by Fernand Léger. In this way, the artworks act as a link between an avant-garde orientation towards the future and a traditional history of origin. Not far from each curated library is always soft seating furniture that affords the house's inhabitants and visitors a pleasant reading environment. In contrast to the material hardness of concrete and steel as in the rationalist Casa Ocampo, which Ocampo had built in the inner-city district of Palermo Chico with the architect Alejandro Bustillo, and which is generally considered one of the first modern buildings in Buenos Aires (Anonymous 1929), here the textiles of the furniture presuppose a sinking of the body: ideal for deepening the mind.

It is exactly this clear stance for ambivalence that set Ocampo's interiorities apart from contemporary comparative examples. The photograph of a living room in a nearby house from the Revista de Architectura of 1941 also shows a design hybrid of functional living and 19th-century borrowings. However, according to scholarly research on domestic architecture in Buenos Aires, these interiors are consciously oriented towards the idea of an Argentine homeland (Sánchez 2015). In contrast, Ocampo's home depicts a plurilocal understanding that translates non-verbally to visitors as glocal 'living knowledge' (Nierhaus and Nierhaus 2014, 11). Underlying the individual objects as well as the Argentinean interpretation of the Franco-Victorian architectural style is the vision of a cosmopolitan world as a 'script' for action.[20] This reflects Ocampo's self-image as a world citizen who always represented "the other" (Ocampo 1980, 61). She understood her role in Latin America as a writer in exile, which further affirms her solidarity with immigrants in Argentina (Cetraro Luna 2009).

Certainly, the exchange processes of local and exiled artists around Ocampo would not have been possible without her financial support. Coming from an aristocratic background, Ocampo and her choice of popular, often European protagonists for *SUR* were therefore criticized for being elitist (González 2018). Her personal patronage also led to some exclusion of artists such as the exiled author Paul Zech (Thurn 2019). Nonetheless, human and non-human actants of diverse, yet co-creative backgrounds gathered in San Isidro. According to her memoirs, Ocampo chose to renovate Villa Ocampo and its interior for the sake of a lively genius loci that would actively participate in the intellectual exchange of ideas (Ocampo 2000). In this international thought forum, encounter and retreat were just as possible as singularity and diversity.

Jassim House: Shared plans and dreams in Bombay[21]

Arriving in Bombay in the first half of the 20th century meant coming to a "secular, multicultural" city, whose urban imaginaries were, according to Arjun Appadurai (2000, 650), "modernist in their visions of equity, justice and cultural cosmopolitanism". Already during British colonial rule, which lasted from 1858 until the independence of India and Pakistan in 1947, the metropolis had become an economic hub used to foreign influx (Franz 2015). As a port city, Bombay was the principal entry point to India for Jewish refugees fleeing National Socialism, who were confronted with ambivalent social and political attitudes of the urban society, at least since if not preceding the beginning of the war (Singh 2017). For exiles associated with the arts, Bombay's broad entertainment and culture sector offered various income-generation opportunities (Franz 2020). The city was also an attractive arrival point due to its art and architecture schools (Dwivedi/Mehrotra 2001; Huppatz 2018). One specificity of the city's cultural field was its informal organization. Foreign entrants were welcomed into more or less private circles, which resulted in transcultural exchange processes (Dogramaci/Lee 2019).

An example of such an unofficial contact zone was Jassim House at 25 Cuffe Parade, later also known as Taraporewala Mansion. According to the autobiography of architect Minnette De Silva, who rented the lower floor of the villa in 1941, Jassim House became a space of debate and activity for several (trans)cultural projects whose participants were on the search for new aesthetics:

> As soon as I saw Jassim House and the ground floor flat, I knew I had found my corner of Bombay. [...] Sister Anil had joined me. So many seminal events happened there. The Indian Peoples' Theatre (IPTA), Kutub Publishers and MARG were all born there. Everything seemed to be happening. [...] It was such a mixed world of the

> political Left and Right: industrialists, army generals, executives, struggling artists, writers, film-makers, dancers, actors – a cosmopolitan world. After we had left, it continued to be an artistic hub of Bombay and India as Mulk Raj Anand stayed on.
> (De Silva 1998, 65)

In addition to IPTA and Kutub Popular Publishers, which were both co-founded by the art historian Anil (also Marcia) De Silva, the Modern Architectural Research Group (M.A.R.G) developed out of informal gatherings.[22] Besides intellectuals from Asia such as the Indian author Mulk Raj Anand and the De Silva Sisters from Ceylon (now Sri Lanka) , the total of 14 founding members also included a remarkably high number of German-speaking exiles (ibid.): the architect Otto Koenigsberger, who fled Germany in 1933 and later became India's Federal Director of Housing (Lee/James-Chakraborty 2012); the Berlin émigré art critic Rudolf von Leyden; and the art historian Hermann Goetz, who had completed his doctorate on Indian art at the University of Munich and was director of the Baroda Museum during the 1940s (Singh 2017). From 1946, the interdisciplinary team published the quarterly art and architecture magazine of the same name: *Marg*. Its title also means 'pathway' in Sanskrit (Anand 1946, 5). This resonated with the magazine's humanistic impetus in discussing the built, visual and performing arts of Asia, Europe and the United States. While it focused on modernist practices, it also aimed at re-contextualizing the region's cultural heritage in the process of nation building.

The place of *Marg*'s inception, Jassim House, is located on the sea-side promenade of Cuffe Parade where imposing villas are lined up one after the other in the wealthy Colaba precinct in South Mumbai (fig. 20.6). Recognizable from afar thanks to its dome and multifoil arches, the villa is simultaneously open and protected (fig. 20.7). The wall of ornamental stonework partially surrounding the site allows a frontal view of the building. Yet, the overall impression still signals privacy through its spatial demarcation and the portico in front of the entrance doors. The architecture is characterized by an eclectic architectural mix typical for Bombay during the British Raj. Often classified as 'Indo-saracenic', it combines contemporary colonial tropes with vernacular Indian building elements (Bryant 2020). The consistent patterning and symmetrical structure with large domes, arched doorways and delicate ornamentation are informed by Mughal and Sikh styles. The blending of the intricate facade design with more minimalist tilework in grey-blue anticipates later Bombay Deco architectures. According to sources, 'saracenic' embellishments, which seem initially in contrast to *Marg*'s anti-revivalist orientation, were added at the request of an Arab client (Mistri 1986, 226). However, compared to colonial representative buildings of this time, the ornamentation seems less like a pure transfer of supposedly local stylistic elements. This might be due to its Indian architect Jamshedji Mistri – father of the *Marg* co-founder Minocher J.P. Mistri.[23]

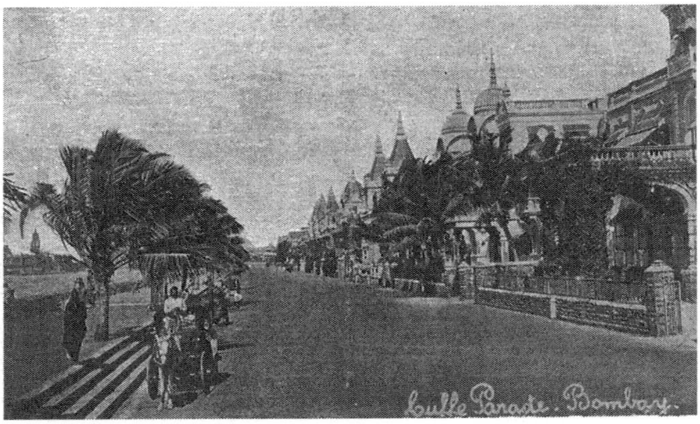

FIGURE 20.6: Postcard "Cuffe Parade. Bombay", n.d. (Private Collection Rachel Lee).

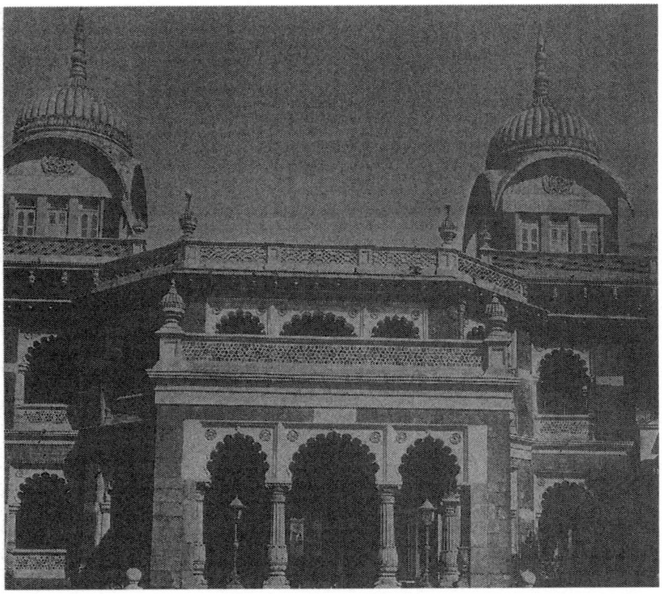

FIGURE 20.7: *Historic image of Jassim House, built around 1900* (Mistri 1986, 227).

The short walk from Cuffe Parade to the entrance is framed by tropical plants. Suited to the local climate, the house has embraced permeability, which is also the case with many buildings in this region and the architectural structures designed by Koenigsberger or Minnette De Silva. Taking in the view of the Arabian Sea, guests could step out onto the expansive open terraces, retreat to shady areas or enjoy the small backyard garden. In the covered portico, the corbelled pillars, which were probably made of poured concrete, stand out. Crafted, floral ornaments in the glazing immerse the entrance area, which was shared by all parties living in the house, in a diffuse light.

Upon entering through the three-door portal into the ground floor flat, spacious rooms with high ceilings open up. Anand described the specific spatial atmosphere of the living area as follows: "The people who built this room had an awareness – they left room for you to move and relax" (qtd. in Sales-Pontes 1985, 123). From the few published images of the historical interior, the only ornamental elements, such as pilasters or window shades, seem to be directly related to the outer skin of the building (fig. 20.8). In the otherwise reduced interior, the tiled floor with a graphic pattern is covered by a few bookshelves and low seats, similar to the low mattresses (*gaddi*) widely used in India (Chaudhuri 2012). Reflected in the piles of books on all shelves is an international interest ranging from Frank Lloyd Wright's architecture to "Soviet Ballet" and the "Battle for Asia". Several artisanal objects are placed in the immediate vicinity of artworks by Ceylonese painter George Keyt. The paintings tell a story about the quest for modern art in these very rooms, of Keyt's stay at Cuffe Parade initiated by Anil and thus of inter-Asian migratory routes.

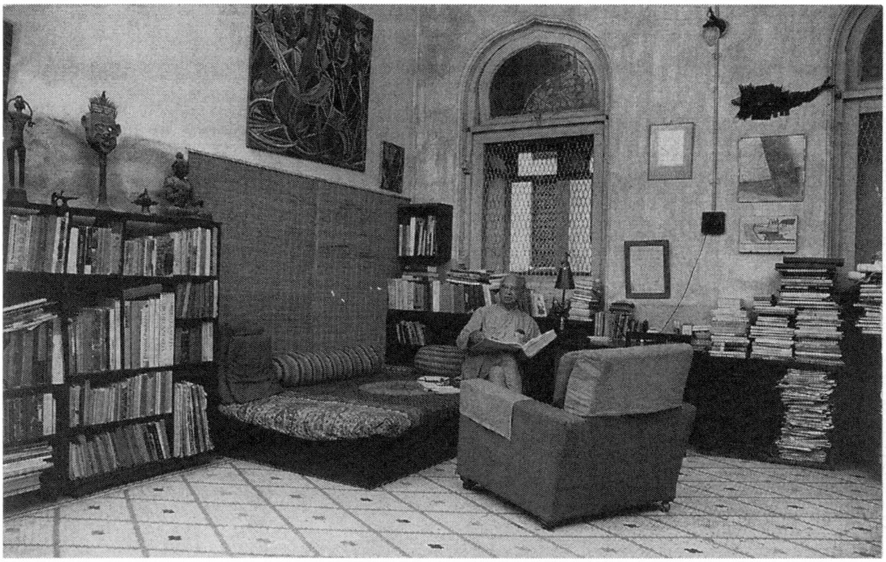

FIGURE 20.8: Dolly Sahiar, Photograph of Mulk Raj Anand in his late years at 25 Cuffe Parade, n.d. (Courtesy The Marg Foundation, Mumbai. Taken from: *Mulk Raj Anand: Shaping the Indian Modern*, edited by Annapurna Garimella, Marg Publications, 2005, p. 26).

In multiple ways, the material culture of Cuffe Parade's interior reflects the cultural politics verbalized in *Marg*. In a series of articles on interior design (fig. 20.9), the "impact of modern Europe [on India…], which have neither been synthesized with the surviving forms, nor been integrated into a new way of living"

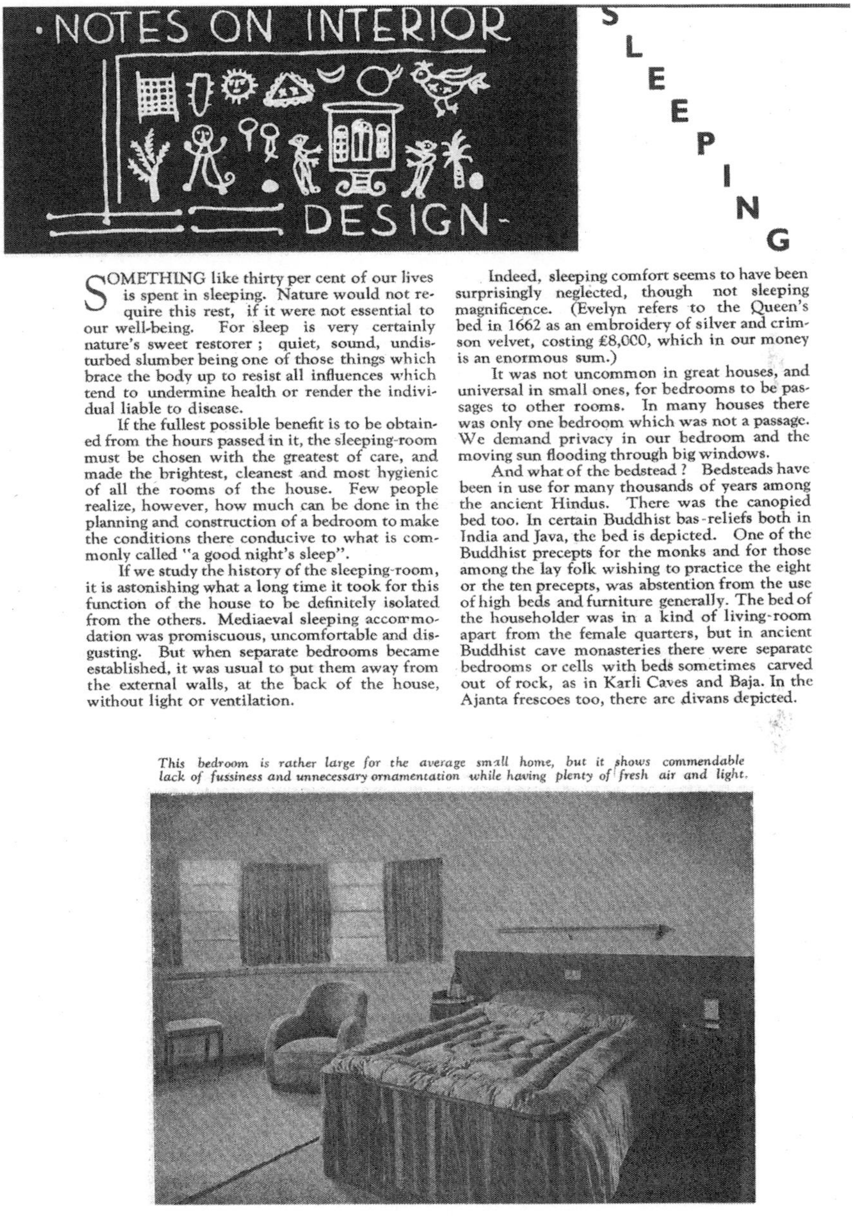

·NOTES ON INTERIOR DESIGN·

SLEEPING

SOMETHING like thirty per cent of our lives is spent in sleeping. Nature would not require this rest, if it were not essential to our well-being. For sleep is very certainly nature's sweet restorer ; quiet, sound, undisturbed slumber being one of those things which brace the body up to resist all influences which tend to undermine health or render the individual liable to disease.

If the fullest possible benefit is to be obtained from the hours passed in it, the sleeping-room must be chosen with the greatest of care, and made the brightest, cleanest and most hygienic of all the rooms of the house. Few people realize, however, how much can be done in the planning and construction of a bedroom to make the conditions there conducive to what is commonly called "a good night's sleep".

If we study the history of the sleeping-room, it is astonishing what a long time it took for this function of the house to be definitely isolated from the others. Mediaeval sleeping accommodation was promiscuous, uncomfortable and disgusting. But when separate bedrooms became established, it was usual to put them away from the external walls, at the back of the house, without light or ventilation.

Indeed, sleeping comfort seems to have been surprisingly neglected, though not sleeping magnificence. (Evelyn refers to the Queen's bed in 1662 as an embroidery of silver and crimson velvet, costing £8,000, which in our money is an enormous sum.)

It was not uncommon in great houses, and universal in small ones, for bedrooms to be passages to other rooms. In many houses there was only one bedroom which was not a passage. We demand privacy in our bedroom and the moving sun flooding through big windows.

And what of the bedstead ? Bedsteads have been in use for many thousands of years among the ancient Hindus. There was the canopied bed too. In certain Buddhist bas-reliefs both in India and Java, the bed is depicted. One of the Buddhist precepts for the monks and for those among the lay folk wishing to practice the eight or the ten precepts, was abstention from the use of high beds and furniture generally. The bed of the householder was in a kind of living-room apart from the female quarters, but in ancient Buddhist cave monasteries there were separate bedrooms or cells with beds sometimes carved out of rock, as in Karli Caves and Baja. In the Ajanta frescoes too, there are divans depicted.

This bedroom is rather large for the average small home, but it shows commendable lack of fussiness and unnecessary ornamentation while having plenty of fresh air and light.

FIGURE 20.9: Excerpt from "Notes on Interior Design" (Marg, vol. 1, no. 4, July 1947, p. 40 [image cropped as in the original]).

(M.A.R.G. January 1947, 42) is discussed.[24] Folk and tribal art forms are considered as equal shapers of the Indian modern aesthetic. Notwithstanding the sometimes superelevated internationalism of *Marg*, in particular in the field of architecture, Cuffe Parade showcases a balanced negotiation between Asian and European elements. Unlike the often lifeless transmission of the colonizer's design habits, as described by Rabindranath Tagore in his novel *Relationships* (*Jogajog*) of 1929, Jassim House energetically combined local with migrated habitational knowledge.

Similarly, the emancipated lives of the De Silva sisters did not follow traditional role assignments, cemented in 19th-century India by the architectural separation of women's household spaces inside and the male zone outside (Chaudhuri 2012). Even though historiography (Singh 2013; Deboo 2021) has mostly focused on Anand's role as *Marg*'s editor, Minnette was the first to rent the ground floor apartment and Anand was invited by Anil as a former London acquaintance. Apart from the fact that several sources suggest a love affair between Anil and Anand (Sales-Pontes 1985; De Mel 2001), egalitarian shared flats were not uncommon for the progressive left at the time (Loomba 2019). Furthermore, it was down to Anil's entrepreneurial spirit that Kutub, IPTA and maybe also *Marg* were finally put into practice.

The assumption that the 25 Cuffe Parade was already in itself an open-minded space is demonstrated not least by the other dwellers of the house who shared the same entry. From 1933 to 1970 the Jewish-Muslim Hamied family led a secular life there. With their legendary parties, Luba Derczanska and Khwaja Abdul Hamied, who met in Berlin, fostered exchange among Hindus, Muslims and Jews alike (Jonker 2020). Further evidence of the transculturality of this environment is the presence of exiles in *Marg* and its intellectual network. Although many articles are signed with the acronym M.A.R.G., the voices of exiled creatives resound. The founding manifesto "Architecture and you" echoes earlier lectures by Koenigsberger, promoting an understanding of architectural modernism as a site-specific method (Lee/James-Chakraborty 2012). Furthermore, the recurring support of the Bombay-based Progressive Artists' Group can be traced not only to Anand but also to von Leyden, who committedly featured young modern artists in his reviews for *The Times of India* (Franz 2015). His socialist perspective on art resonates with editorials like "Design and Patronage", which took a clear anti-fascist stance (M.A.R.G. July 1947).[25]

It can be argued that the transgressions of boundaries in the context of gender, origin and culture emerged from this specific constitution of Jassim House situated in the progressive milieu of 1940s Bombay. The cosmopolitan spirit seemed to have been manifested in both living and life in Cuffe Parade, where foreign input was to some extent welcomed. Even if the exiles' reputations were partly due to advantages gained through their racial, ethnic and cultural backgrounds in the segregated Indian society of the time, egalitarian reviews on Asian topics prove the spirit of openness permeating 25 Cuffe Parade.[26] Although these voices, due to the departure of the De Silva sisters and many exiles from Bombay, gradually decreased in the course of the 1950s, Jassim House as Anand's residence continued to be a transcultural contact zone (De Silva 1998).

Concluding remarks on the actants of urban exile

From these considerations, it can be concluded that in the specific urban contexts of Buenos Aires and Bombay in the 1930s and 1940s, a third space in Homi Bhabha's sense emerged through the interconnectedness of art and exile within both Villa Ocampo and Jassim House. Through the transcultural exchange processes circulating there, exiled creatives were able to (re)root themselves in personal networks and cultural projects such as *SUR* or *Marg* – at least for a time. This process was closely linked to the private homes and the cities they were embedded into, both of which had colonial pasts and relatively positive approaches to migrants. While in Bombay this could be explained by the lack of artistic infrastructure at the time, this argument is obsolete for Buenos Aires with its numerous art spaces. Rather, these domestic contact zones were made possible through certain socio-economic and cultural-political constitutions at work in both metropolises manifesting itself in a humane and design openness.

Analyzing these two dwellings' social and built environments as equal actants in diverse networks has enabled a new perspective on urban exile. My analyses combined architectural, urbanistic and biographical approaches based on historical text and imagery. Moreover, ANT proved to be a valid method to explore the complex historical entanglements of artistic exchanges between exiles and locals. Yet, the porous records in both contexts as well as the lack of field research on site made a holistic investigation difficult.[27] Therefore, additional secondary sources were taken into account to identify the human and non-human factors of transcultural encounters for the two cases.

Interconnectivity in urban exile is visible in the historical accounts of the setting within Villa Ocampo and Jassim House as well as within the pages of both magazines. This was of course closely linked to the editors. Both Ocampo and the group around Anand and the De Silva sisters belonged to an urban, multilingual elite. Their privileged living conditions enabled them to have more scope of action, which they in turn transformed and translated into collaborative creation. Due to previous stays in Europe, all of them were used to cultural differences and consciously wanted to surround themselves with European intellectuals. So, the resulting urban communities fulfil many of the characteristics that Bhabha describes as an "antagonistic supplement of modernity" (Bhabha 1994, 231).

Likewise, the architectural environments in Villa Ocampo with the mediating room structure and Jassim House with its flowing transitions between inside and outside were characterized by permeability. Books and artworks acted as mediators of global modernities, which co-existed with local heritage and handicraft. Multiple cultural references conveyed a living and lived plurality that interacted with progressive social agendas. There was a concern to join the international modernist movements, which offered decisive points of contact for exiles. In both cases, migrant-situated creativity, be it from Europe or the surrounding countries in South America or Asia, was largely perceived as stimulating, and materialized in everyday domestic dwelling.

The specific thing-human constellations opened up possibilities of arriving and settling far beyond the borders of one's own home. Considering the shattered lives of other exiles, (re)rooting in different spaces might have been easier for these artists, as they not only shared interests but also future visions with the locals. The bonding agency of common projects together with a lingual and cultural diversity that emerged from and was projected onto the private houses, fostered hybrid networks. The combination of economic means, cosmopolitan attitudes, the simultaneity of migrant and local forms of knowledge and representation, (interior) architectural structures of permeability and open cities led to the emergence of a transcultural third space for personal and artistic exchanges in modernity. In view of 21st-century migration routes, a (re)rooting of discussions about cultural difference just as much as a (re)routing of certain political actions appears desirable. What contemporary societies can learn from these specific case studies is that openness to plurality and tolerance of ambiguity can lead to outstanding creative results.

NOTES

1. I would like to thank Ania Loomba, Burcu Dogramaci, Claudio Morales, Hernán D. Caro, Laura Karp Lugo, Marg (Anjana Premchand, Mrinalini Vasudevan), Museo Beccar Varela/ Quinta Los Ombúes – San Isidro (Marcela Fugardo), Rachel Lee, Shiromi Pinto for their support of my research for this chapter.
2. In the edition translated into English by Gabriel Berns, the text passage reads: "[A] total grove that lives and pulsates inside of me. And a long memory of which no one will ever hear will be written fleetingly on the air; driven definitely off its course – definitely lost" (Alberti 1959/1981, 18).
3. In the following, the terms 'exile' and 'emigration' are used alternately, as both refer to a forced, indefinite stay outside the country of origin due to a political situation. In contrast, the term 'migration' also includes economically or socially enforced emigration (Dogramaci 2013, 19).
4. The research project "Relocating Modernism: Global Metropolises, Modern Art and Exile" (METROMOD) marks out a map of exiled artists' life and work in six global metropolises between 1900 and 1950, see www.//metromod.net/.

5. The focus on biographical details and approaches in exile studies partly prevents the analysis of wider intercultural dynamics (Gemünden/Kaes 2003).
6. The term 'transcultural' is preferrable to 'intercultural' or 'multicultural' because it indicates an ambivalent meaning (Marotta 2014). Following early conceptualizations by the anthropologist Fernando Ortiz, transculturalism not only acknowledges the potential of exchange between cultures, but also conveys the tensions within this process (Ortiz 1947).
7. The subheading is inspired by Jane M. Jacob's theorization of a 'sense of being at home' away from home in diaspora communities (Jacobs 2004).
8. Bhabha for instance refers to a museum installation by the contemporary artist Renée Green, see pp. 4–7.
9. In the original: "Wohnen unter der Prämisse der (Aus)wanderung". If not specified otherwise, all quotations have been translated by the author.
10. The use of the term is also explained by the self-statements and writings of exiles from the two networks discussed, as in Alberti (1959/2003).
11. Indeed, a full turning away from a biographical approach in studies on exile is proving difficult since the necessity of emigration was caused mostly by in- or externally ascribed identities.
12. In the original: "Dinge werden häufig zu zentralen Reflexionsobjekten des Exilierten, der sein eigenes Verworfensein und unkontrollierbares Umhergetriebenwerden im Existenzmodus der beweglichen Objekte wiedererkennt und reflektiert".
13. The German original phrase reads "nicht *natürlich* gegeben, sondern immer diskursiv vermittelt".
14. The subheading refers to Ocampo's self-description as "lo otro" (Ocampo 1980, 61) in her autobiography, which can be interpreted as a demarcation from a rather conservative upbringing and paternalistic milieu.
15. Sitman (2008, 144–147) gives a detailed account of Ocampo's anti-fascist engagement.
16. For a walk-through of Villa Ocampo see www.youtube.com/watch?v=5TxlpJBUmOU. Accessed 28 December 2020.
17. In a letter Le Corbusier attributed "Alter großartiger Glanz" to Villa Ocampo.
18. Simmel defines the metaphysical meaning of the door, in its "Getrenntheit und Verbundenheit", as an architectural element of human performance.
19. On the transcultural implications and misunderstandings of the relationship between Ocampo and Tagore, see Dyson (1988, 322–328), Klengel (2013).
20. According to Saito (2011), cosmopolitanism is understood as a sociological phenomenon defined by the three key elements: cultural omnivorousness, ethnic tolerance and cosmopolitics.
21. The subheading is inspired by *Marg*'s first editorial "Planning and Dreaming" (*Marg*, October 1946, 3–6).
22. According to the imprint, Cuffe Parade remained *Marg*'s headquarters until the summer of 1948, when the editorial staff moved to new offices in 3 Queens Road. See *Marg*, vol. 1–2, 1946–1948.

23. The author had access to undisclosed, historical material from private archives for her visual analysis. Further copyright-protected images of the renovated house can be found at sunilthakkar.in/portfolio/architecture/taraporewala-mansion-jones-lang-lasalle/. Accessed 01 April 2021.
24. See also *Marg* April 1947; *Marg* July 1947.
25. Even though *Marg*'s digital archive attributes this editorial to Mulk Raj Anand, the original magazine names M.A.R.G. as an author.
26. *Marg* dedicated entire issues to Ceylon, Buddhist and South Asian art; as outlined in detail in Garimella (2005, 102).
27. This was in part due to the impossibilities of research trips during the Covid-19 pandemic as well as the closure of archives.

REFERENCES

Alberti, Rafael. *The Lost Grove*. 1959. Translated and edited by Gabriel Berns, University of California Press, 1981.

Alberti, Rafael. *Con la luz primera: Antología de verso y prosa (obra de 1920 a 1996)*. 1959, edited by María Asunción Mateo, Edaf, 2003.

Anand, Mulk Raj. "Planning and Dreaming." *Marg*, vol. 1, no. 1, 1946, pp. 3–6.

Anonymous. "Mansión privada – Proyecto del Arq. Alejandro Bustillo." *Nuestra Architectura*, vol. 1, no. 3, 1929, pp. 92–109.

Appadurai, Arjun. "Spectral Housing and Urban Cleansing: Notes on Millennial Mumbai." *Public Culture*, vol. 12, no. 3, 2000, pp. 627–651.

Belliger, Andréa, and David Krieger. "Einführung in die Akteur-Netzwerk-Theorie." *ANThology. Ein einführendes Handbuch zur Akteur-Netzwerk-Theorie*, edited by Andrea Belliger and David Krieger, transcript, 2006, pp. 13–50.

Berger, John. *And Our Faces, My Heart, Brief as Photos*. Writers and Readers Press, 1984.

Bettini, Maurizio. Wurzeln. *Die trügerischen Mythen der Identität*. Translated by Rita Seuß, Verlag Antje Kunstmann, 2018.

Bhabha, Homi K. *The Location of Culture*. Routledge, 1994.

Bischoff, Doerte, and Joachim Schlör, editors. *Dinge des Exils* (Exilforschung, 31). edition text + kritik, 2013.

Bjerg, María. "La inmigración en la Argentina: un mito fundacional y un problema historiográfico." *Revista Electrónica de Fuentes y Archivos*, vol. 7, no. 7, 2016, pp. 322–329, www.//refa.org.ar/file.php?tipo=Contenido&id=165. Accessed 2 July 2021.

Bordelois, Yvonne, and Fabio Grementieri. *Villa Ocampo – Escenario de Cultura*. Editorial Sudamericana, 2006.

Borges, Jorge Luis. *Schatten und Tiger. Gedichte 1966–1972* (Werke: in 20 Bänden, 12). Translated by Gisbert Haefs, Fischer Taschenbuch-Verlag, 1994.

Bryant, Julius. "Colonial Architecture in Lahore: J.L. Kipling and the 'Indo-saracenic' Styles." *South Asian Studies*, vol. 36, no. 1, 2020, pp. 61–71. *Taylor & Francis Online*, doi: 10.1080/02666030.2020.1721111. Accessed 20 March 2021.

Callon, Michel. "Techno-economic Networks and Irreversibility." *Sociological Review*, vol. 38, no. 1, 1990, pp. 132–161.

Cetraro Luna, Elvira. *Los Testimonios de Victoria Ocampo Como Proyecto Cultural Argentino Moderno*. Doctoral thesis, Pontificia Universidad Católica del Perú, 2009, www.//tesis.pucp.edu.pe/repositorio/handle/20.500.12404/465. Accessed 20 March 2021.

Chaudhuri, Supriya. "Interiors and Interiority in Nineteenth-Century India." *The Domestic Space Reader*, edited by Chiara Briganti and Kathy Mezei, University of Toronto Press, 2012, pp. 351–358.

Clifford, James. *Routes. Travel and Translation in the Late Twentieth Century*. Harvard University Press, 1997.

de Certeau, Michel. *The Practice of Everyday Life*. University of California Press, 1988.

De Mel, Neloufer. *Women & the Nation's Narrative: Gender and Nationalism in Twentieth Century Sri Lanka*. Rowman & Littlefield, 2001.

De Silva, Minnette. *The Life & Work of an Asian Woman Architect*. Smart Media Productions, 1998.

Deboo, Khorshed. "Revisiting the Past, Reimagining a Future. How an Art Magazine Found a Place in India's Nation-Building Narratives." *Himal Southasian*, 16 February 2021, www.himalmag.com/revisiting-the-past-reimagining-a-future-2021/. Accessed 20 March 2021.

Dogramaci, Burcu. "Objekte der Migration. Zeitgenössische künstlerische Strategien und produktive Aneignungen." *Dinge des Exils* (Exilforschung, 31), edited by Doerte Bischoff and Joachim Schlör, edition text + kritik, 2013, pp. 35–54.

Dogramaci, Burcu. "The Migratory Living Room: Dwelling and Furnishing in a Foreign Land." *Handbook of Art and Global Migration. Theories, Practices, and Challenges*, edited by Burcu Dogramaci and Birgit Mersmann, De Gruyter, 2019, pp. 249–262.

Dogramaci, Burcu, and Rachel Lee. "Refugee Artists, Architects and Intellectuals Beyond Europe in the 1930s and 1940s: Experiences of Exile in Istanbul and Bombay." *ABE Journal*, no. 14–15, 2019, n.p., doi: 10.4000/abe.5949. Accessed 21 March 2021.

Dogramaci, Burcu, et al. "Arrival Cities: Migrating Artists and New Metropolitan Topographies in the 20th Century – An Introduction." *Arrival Cities: Migrating Artists and New Metropolitan Topographies in the 20th Century*, edited by Burcu Dogramaci et al., Leuven University Press, 2020, pp. 9–32, doi: 10.11116/9789461663245. Accessed 2 July 2021.

Dwivedi, Sharada, and Rahul Mehrotra. *Bombay: The Cities Within*. Eminence Designs, 2001.

Dyson, Ketaki Kushari. *In Your Blossoming Flower-Garden: Rabindranath Tagore and Victoria Ocampo*. Sahitya Akademi, 1988.

Fajardo, Salvador J. "Rafael Alberti's *La Arboleda Perdida*: Ethos in Time." *Anales de La Literatura Española Contemporánea*, vol. 35, no. 1, 2010, pp. 117–140.

Franz, Margit. *Gateway India. Deutschsprachiges Exil in Indien zwischen britischer Kolonialherrschaft, Maharadschas und Gandhi.* CLIO, 2015.

Franz, Margit. "From Dinner Parties to Galleries: The Langhammer-Leyden-Schlesinger Circle in Bombay – 1940s through the 1950s." *Arrival Cities: Migrating Artists and New Metropolitan Topographies in the 20th Century*, edited by Burcu Dogramaci et al., Leuven University Press, 2020, pp. 73–90, doi: 10.11116/9789461663245. Accessed 2 July 2021.

Garimella, Annapurna. "On Inheriting the Past." *Mulk Raj Anand: Shaping the Indian Modern*, edited by Annapurna Garimella, Marg Publications, 2005, pp. 88–105.

Gemünden, Gerd, and Anton Kaes. "Introduction." *Film and Exile*, special issue of *New German Critique*, no. 89, 2003, pp. 3–8. *JSTOR*, doi: 10.2307/3211142. Accessed 21 March 2021.

González, María Soledad. *Victoria Ocampo: escritura, poder y representaciones* (Colección historia & cultura, 12). Prohistoria Ediciones, 2018.

Hensel, Thomas, and Jens Schröter. "Die Akteur-Netzwerk-Theorie als Herausforderung der Kunstwissenschaft – Eine Einleitung." *Zeitschrift für Ästhetik und Allgemeine Kunstwissenschaft (ZÄK)*, vol. 57, no. 1, 2012, pp. 5–18.

Heß, Regine. "Vom Akteur im Singular zu den Akteuren im Plural. Neue Forschungsansätze aus Museum, Akteur-Netzwerk-Theorie und Architektursoziologie." *Architektur und Akteure: Praxis und Öffentlichkeit in der Nachkriegsgesellschaft*, edited by Regine Heß, transcript, 2018, pp. 231–248.

Huppatz, D.J. *Modern Asian Design* (Cultural histories of design). Bloomsbury Publishing, 2018.

Isaacs, Reginald R. *Walter Gropius. Der Mensch und sein Werk*, vol. 2. Translated by Georg G. Meerwein, Gebr. Mann Verlag, 1984.

Jacobs, Jane M. "Too Many Houses for a Home: Narrating the House in the Chinese Diaspora." *Drifting. Architecture and Migrancy*, edited by Stephen Cairns, Routledge, 2004, pp. 164–183.

Jonker, Gerdien. *On the Margins: Jews and Muslims in Interwar Berlin* (Muslim Minorities, vol. 34). Brill, 2020, www.//brill.com/view/title/56388. Accessed 21 March 2021.

Karp Lugo, Laura. "Alone Together: Exile Sociability and Artistic Networks in Buenos Aires at the Beginning of the 20th Century." *Arrival Cities: Migrating Artists and New Metropolitan Topographies in the 20th Century*, edited by Burcu Dogramaci et al., Leuven University Press, 2020, pp. 33–54, doi: 10.11116/9789461663245. Accessed 2 July 2021

Klengel, Susanne. "Victoria Ocampo und Tagore. Zur Problemlage transkultureller Biografik." *Anekdote – Biographie – Kanon: Zur Geschichtsschreibung in den schönen Künsten*, edited by Melanie Unseld and Christian Zimmermann, Böhlau, 2013, pp. 365–382. doi: 10.7788/boehlau.9783412211233. Accessed 2 July 2021.

Latour, Bruno. *Reassembling the Social: An Introduction to Actor-Network-Theory*. Oxford University Press, 2005.

Latour, Bruno, and Albena Yaneva. "'Give me a gun and I will make all buildings move': An ANT's view of architecture." *Explorations in Architecture: Teaching, Design, Research*, edited by Urs Staub et al., Birkhäuser, 2008, pp. 80–89.

Lee, Rachel, and Kathleen James-Chakraborty. "*Marg* Magazine: A Tryst with Architectural Modernity." *ABE Journal*, no. 1, 2012, n.p., doi: 10.4000/abe.623. Accessed 20 March 2021.

Lombroso, Gina. "El problema de los refugiados." *SUR*, no. 55, 1939, pp. 60–69.

Loomba, Ania. *Revolutionary Desires: Women, Communism, and Feminism in India*. Routledge, 2019.

Majstorovic, Gorica. "An American Place: Victoria Ocampo's Editorial Politics, the Foundation of 'Sur', and Hemispheric Alliances." *Arizona Journal of Hispanic Cultural Studies*, vol. 9, no. 1, 2005, pp. 171–180. *ResearchGate*, doi: 10.1353/hcs.2011.0193. Accessed 3 April 2021.

M.A.R.G. "Design and Patronage." *Marg*, vol. 1, no. 4, 1947, pp. 16–19.

M.A.R.G. "Notes on Interior Design." *Marg*, vol. 1, no. 2, 1947, pp. 41–46.

Marotta, Vince. "The Multicultural, Intercultural and the Transcultural Subject." *Global Perspectives on the Politics of Multiculturalism in the 21st Century: A Case Study Analysis*, edited by Fethi Mansouri and Boulou Ebanda de B'béri, Routledge, 2014, pp. 90–102.

Mistri, M.J.P. "M.J.P. Mistri – Descendant of Master Builders. An interview with Smita Gupta." *Vistāra – The Architecture of India*, edited by Carmen Kagal, exh. cat. The Festival of India in U.S.A., 1986, pp. 222–227. *Architexturez South Asia*, www.//architexturez.net/doc/az-cf-123816. Accessed 21 March 2021.

Morley, David. *Home Territories. Media, Mobility and Identity*. Routledge, 2008.

Nierhaus, Irene, and Andreas Nierhaus. "Wohnen Zeigen: Schau-Plätze des Wohnwissens." *Wohnen Zeigen: Modelle und Akteure des Wohnens in Architektur und visueller Kultur* (wohnen +/- ausstellen Schriftenreihe, vol. 1), edited by Irene Nierhaus et al., transcript, 2014, pp. 9–35.

Ocampo, Victoria. *Autobiografía 1. El archipiélago*. Sur, 1980.

Ocampo, Victoria. *Testimonios. Series Sexta a Décima*. 1977. Edited by Eduardo Paz Leston, Editorial Sudamericana, 2000.

Ortiz, Fernando. *Cuban Counterpoint: Tobacco and Sugar*. Alfred A. Knopf, 1947.

Saito, Hiro. "An Actor-Network Theory of Cosmopolitanism." *Sociological Theory*, vol. 29, no. 2, 2011, pp. 124–149.

Sales-Pontes, Alzira Hilda. *Dr. Mulk Raj Anand – A Critical Bibliography*. Doctoral thesis, Loughborough University of Technology, 1985, www.//hdl.handle.net/2134/10854. Accessed 27 April 2021.

Sánchez, Sandra Inés. "¿'Para Hoy' o 'Para Siempre'? Imágenes de Viviendas En Revistas En Las Décadas de 1930 y 1940." *Anales Del Instituto de Arte Americano e Investigaciones Estéticas "Mario J. Buschiazzo"*, vol. 45, no. 2, 2015, www.iaa.fadu.uba.ar/ojs/index.php/anales/article/view/177/html_130. Accessed 27 April 2021.

Sanz, Agustín, and Federico Funes. *El exilio intelectual republicano español en Argentina. La escritura como espacio imaginario de restauración y discurso en contra del olvido en Rafael Alberti y María Teresa León*. 2015. Universidad de Buenos Aires: Carrera Ciencias de la Comunicación, 2016, comunicacion.sociales.uba.ar/wp-content/uploads/sites/16/2013/02/Funes-Sanz-ok.pdf. Accessed 20 December 2020.

Saunders, Doug. *Arrival City: How the Largest Migration in History Is Reshaping Our World.* William Heinemann, 2010.

Simmel, Georg. "Brücke und Tür." Idem. *Das Individuum und die Freiheit: Essais*, Verlag Klaus Wagenbach, 1984, pp. 7–11.

Singh, Devika. "Approaching the Mughal Past in Indian Art Criticism: The Case of MARG (1946–1963)." *Modern Asian Studies*, vol. 47, no. 1, 2013, pp. 167–203, doi: 10.1017/S0026749X1200090X. Accessed 27 February 2021.

Singh, Devika. "German-Speaking Exiles and the Writing of Indian Art History." *Journal of Art Historiography*, no. 17, 2017, pp. 1–19. *DOAJ*, doaj.org/article/0971436ed0004ecfa1f89d7a6d9d0628. Accessed 28 April 2021.

Sitman, Rosalie. "Protest from Afar: The Jewish and Republican Presence in Victoria Ocampo's Revista SUR in the 1930s and 1940s." *Rethinking Jewish-Latin Americans*, edited by Jeff Lesser and Raanan Rein, University of New Mexico Press, 2008, pp. 132–51.

SUR, vol. 1, no. 1, 1931, www.//catalogo.bn.gov.ar/F/?func=direct&doc_number=001218322&local_base=GENER. Accessed 6 December 2020.

Svašek, Maruška. *Moving Subjects, Moving Objects: Transnationalism, Cultural Production and Emotions*. Berghahn Books, 2014.

Thurn, Hans Peter. *Persephone in Buenos Aires: Die argentinische Mäzenin Victoria Ocampo*. Ferdinand Schöningh, 2019.

Wechsler, Diana B. "París, Buenos Aires, México, Milán, Madrid...Migraciones, tránsitos y convergencias para un mapa del arte moderno." *Horizons et dispositifs des arts plastiques des pays du Río de la Plata (XXe sièle)*, special issue of *Artelogie. Recherche sur les arts, le patrimoine et la littérature de l'Amérique latine*, vol. 6, no. 6, Association ESCAL, June 2014, n.p., doi: 10.4000/artelogie.1228. Accessed 28 December 2020.

Yaneva, Albena. *The Making of a Building: A Pragmatist Approach to Architecture*. Peter Lang, 2009.

PART V

PLACE-MAKING/BELONGING

21

From Hamburg to Cape Town: The Denizen Photography of Else and Helmuth Hausmann

Jessica Williams Stark

On a Friday evening in early 1935, Else and Helmuth Hausmann were walking home after celebrating Shabbat with their family in Hamburg when they heard "noises of breaking glass and some faint shouting" (Hausmann n.d., 89).[1] Tightening their grip on one another, they quickened their pace through the darkening streets toward their apartment, the ground floor of which served as Else's photography studio. "Coming nearer to our place of residence", Helmuth later wrote, "we suddenly noticed a big crowd of mainly youngsters, teenagers", who were busy "throwing heavy stones at our place into our windows" (89). Terrified, they watched as young thugs shattered Else's display cases, destroyed her large studio camera and defaced their building with Nazi slogans. The following morning, while combing through "the broken shell of [their] once so lovely studio", the couple began making plans to leave Nazi Germany (90). After being refused asylum in Holland and Palestine, they managed to arrange passage on a ship bound for an "unknown continent which [they] had been told was still roaming with lions and hyenas" (124) and an equally unknown country – South Africa – whose population was also beginning to contend with the rise of white nationalism.

As Helmuth would recall roughly 30 years later, he and Else were shocked when they eventually set foot in Cape Town, a city that to them seemed impossibly cosmopolitan given its distance from Europe's metropoles. "We just could not believe all that we saw", he writes, "as we were told overseas that in all probability we [would have] to sleep in tents and close our doors at night for fear of wild animals roaming the streets" (132). However, as he continues, "all we saw and found [when we arrived] were cultured people, well laid out streets and gardens, [and] lovely and stately built homes" (132). Indeed, the Hausmanns were so "impressed by this growing Metropolis of the South" that they cancelled their plans to continue on to Johannesburg and decided to permanently settle in Cape Town (132). During the first few years in their new city, they sought to assimilate into colonial society as quickly as possible and worked to establish what would become one of South Africa's most successful commercial photography studios – Photo-Hausmann (fig. 21.1). Over the course of the next four decades, the Hausmanns produced work for the country's most widely-read newspapers and photographed South Africa's leading actors, actresses and politicians. They became photojournalists, wedding photographers and portraitists. Above all else, they became denizens.

Although now considered archaic, the term 'denizen' was once used in British law to refer to foreign nationals who were refused certain legal rights that had traditionally been reserved by the state for its native-born residents (Benton 2010, 12). Legally considered half or second-class citizens, denizens have long occupied what the 18th-century English judge and politician William Blackstone once described as a precarious "kind of middle state, between an alien and a natural-born subject" (qtd. in Benton 2010, 13). As resident non-citizens in their new countries, denizens are subject to laws they have no say over and subjected to systems they often have little, if any, recourse to. They are, as Meghan Benton has outlined in her theorization of denizenship, "both insiders (territorially) and outsiders (of membership)", defined as much by their inclusion in their new context as they are by their exclusion from the protection of its laws (2010, 11).

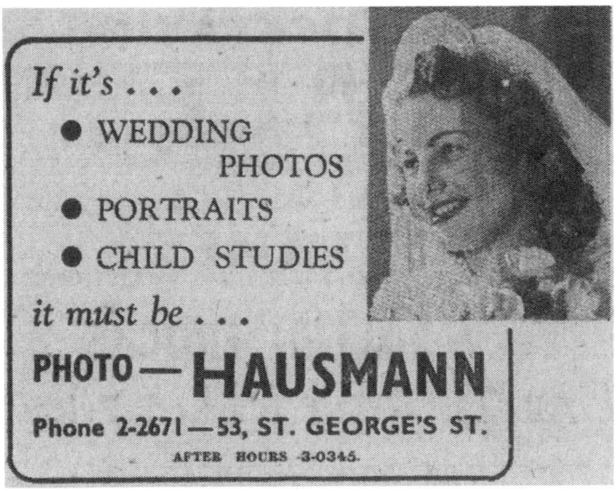

FIGURE 21.1: Photo-Hausmann Advertisement, *Cape Argus*, 11 June 1947, p. 4 (National Library of South Africa).

In recent years, political scientists have contributed to a growing literature on denizens and the challenges their existence poses to our understandings of liberal democracy.[2] While scholars outside of the humanities have begun to critically reexamine denizenship's legal valences, art historians have more recently claimed the figuration as a way to think through the work of exiled or foreign artists whose practices have contributed to more inclusionary and non-hierarchical forms of extra-national belonging. Marsha Meskimmon, for example, has developed in her work the notion of "worldmaking denizenship", describing it not as "a thing or quality [that] one has or attains" but as a process of becoming which "focusses on participation and the continual action of making oneself at home through different collectivities" (2017, 33). In theorizing denizenship as a practice through which "a vastly expanded concept of citizenship" can be created (32), Meskimmon has put forth an incredibly positive understanding of the denizen – one which, as we will see, arguably finds its antithesis in the Hausmanns.

Looking to Helmuth's unpublished memoir, as well as a number of his and Else's extant photographs, this chapter considers how the couple navigated, photographed and wrote their new city as anxious German Jewish refugees, determined parvenus and young denizen photographers.[3] While Else was rather quickly relegated to the feminine confines of their Cape Town photographic studio by a much more conservative society than they had known in Hamburg, Helmuth was almost immediately able to take to the city's streets with his Leica.[4] Shortly after they arrived in South Africa, he began wandering through his new urban context with his camera, frequenting white bourgeois nightclubs and restaurants and creating images which would help to conceptually establish a world that he and his wife hoped to be accepted into. While using the notion of the 'denizen' as an analytical tool affords an opportunity to consider the couple's particular experiences of exile, it also shows how their practice (and the work they produced) enabled them to secure a place in a society that was beginning to model itself after the one they had only recently escaped. In considering how the young couple sought to mitigate their belonging in Cape Town and disclosing how the sense of security they later won was paradoxically done so at the expense of others, this chapter ultimately reveals the need to more fully explore the ways in which exiles have used photography to mediate their relationship to their new homes – not only with critical eyes, as is more often discussed in the literature, but with assimilationist ones.

Figuring the Denizen

When the Hausmanns arrived in Cape Town in October 1936, they joined roughly 2,500 other German-Jewish refugees who had similarly sought asylum from

Hitler's Third Reich in South Africa that same year (Stone 2010, 44). Like many of their exiled contemporaries, their experiences of statelessness had led them to become determined parvenus eager to secure a sense of belonging in what they hoped would become their new homeland. Despite having learned about South Africa's growing Boer Nazi movement while en route from Europe, for example, the couple chose to remain optimistic and attempted to disregard the antisemitic sentiments they had heard were beginning to spread through the streets of their new city (Hausmann n.d., 127–131).[5] In their desire to put the trauma they had experienced in Nazi Germany behind them, they effectively turned a blind eye toward South Africa's burgeoning white nationalism and began working to assimilate as quickly and seamlessly as they could into their new context. In Cape Town, Helmuth writes, he and Else had finally found a place where they "could walk in the streets without fear of being molested for the only reason of being a Jew" (135). It was a city, they were allowing themselves to believe, in which members of all races and religions "lived next to each other in a voluntary segregation, but in the best of harmony" (134).[6]

When Else and Helmuth first arrived in South Africa, they settled into a kosher boarding house near Cape Town's Company Gardens and joined a community of similarly exiled Jewish refugees from Russia, Poland and Lithuania (Hausmann n.d., 132).[7] While Else was able to quickly secure a job retouching and developing prints in the studio of one of Cape Town's more established photographers, Helmuth (who lacked his wife's formal training in photography) set out into the city's streets with their Leica in the hopes of finding work as an itinerant street photographer (135).[8] Unable to afford tickets to ride the city's trolley, he slowly learned to navigate Cape Town on foot, exploring its various residential and urban areas from a ground level (136). Among the first photographs he took in South Africa were those of white children who were being looked after by their Black caretakers in De Waal park, a large public green space situated near the base of Table Mountain. Finding early commercial success in informal children's portraiture of this sort, Helmuth began frequenting Cape Town's affluent parks and gardens, photographing visitors and expanding his repertoire to include outdoor luncheons, wedding parties and other posh social functions. As the months progressed, he became a recurring presence not only on the city's streets, but among its white affluent social circles – a denizen who could always be found at important private and public events with his camera.

Between 1936 and 1939, while the Hausmanns were working to establish themselves in Cape Town and beginning to build up their own photographic studio, fascism continued to spread throughout Europe. As South Africa was drawn nearer to the brink of war, each passing day brought with it reminders of the couple's legal precarity and of how easily they could be expelled from the place they were trying to make their home. With the passing of the Aliens Act in early 1937, for example, the South African government legally deemed Jews unassimilable and threatened to revoke the residency permits of those whom it had earlier granted asylum.[9] When the country joined the war against Nazi Germany alongside Britain less than two years later, Helmuth writes that he looked up from his work only to learn that internment camps were being opened in South Africa for German nationals and that he and his wife had been declared "enemy aliens" (Hausmann n.d., 165).[10] Afraid that they would be interned because they were German-born and terrified that the South African government might repatriate them to a country that had only recently revoked their citizenship, the young couple grew increasingly uneasy.[11] "For many months we had nothing but worries over our heads", Helmuth recalled, and "the tempo of our integration into this country of our adoption became so much faster" (165f.).

Given the unstable position the Hausmanns occupied during these years as stateless refugees, the places Helmuth chose to visit in Cape Town and the people he opted to photograph carry a particular significance. Unlike his similarly exiled colleagues – such as Anne Fischer and Etel Mittag-Fodor, who had decided to establish themselves as photographers among the city's working classes – Helmuth had set his sights on becoming the go-to photographer for, what he refers to as, South Africa's "high society" (Hausmann n.d., 148). A true parvenu, his decision to spend time among the city's white bourgeois was not only financially motivated but also aspirational – the more he frequented Cape Town's elite venues and the more time he spent photographing and socializing with its wealthy white clientele, the stronger his position among their privileged cohort became. From the harrowing stories he relates in his memoir about his and Else's escape from Nazi Germany, it would seem that Helmuth had unfortunately learned what Hannah Arendt later argued all Jewish refugees eventually came to know, namely "that in this mad world it is much easier to be accepted as a 'great man' than as a human being" (Arendt 2007, 270). Until he could achieve the latter status in his new context, Helmuth sought security by surrounding himself with and photographing those who had achieved the former.

Among the innumerable images he took of Cape Town's white upper class during this period is a now-weathered picture of a man and woman who appear to be enjoying themselves over drinks at Del Monico's restaurant on Riebeeck Street (fig. 21.2). Leaning back in his chair with his elbows splayed, the now-anonymous man in this image wears a light suit and a dark tie which he has thoughtfully accented with a pocket square. Returning his gaze with a smile, the woman sitting next to him casually poses with two of her fingers set lightly against her temple. As her left hand hovers over the set of furs she has draped around her shoulders, her right rests on her handbag in such a way as to further display her

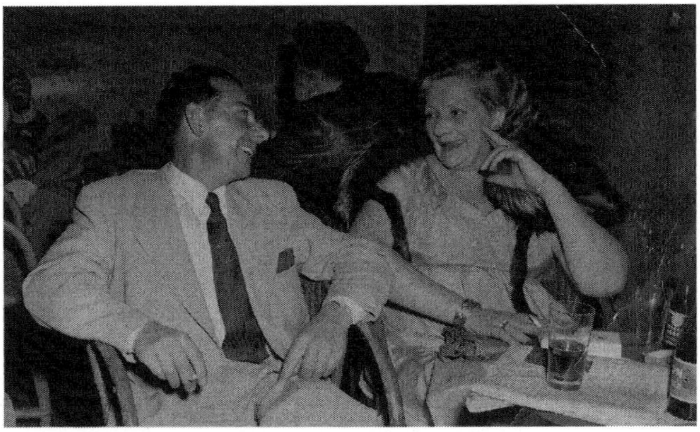

FIGURE 21.2: Photo-Hausmann, *Untitled (Del Monico's Restaurant, Cape Town)*, *c.*1936–1950, 13.8 × 8.8 cm^2, gelatin silver print (Collection of the Author).

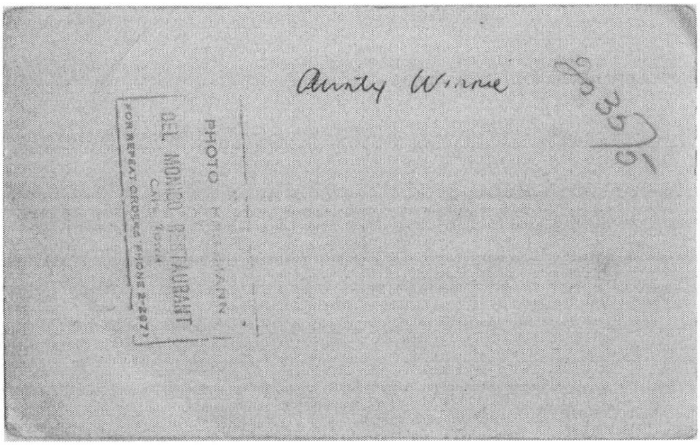

FIGURE 21.3: Photo-Hausmann, *Untitled (Del Monico's Restaurant, Cape Town)*, verso, *c.*1936–1950, 13.8 × 8.8 cm^2, gelatin silver print (Collection of the Author).

jewellery. On the print's verso, a cursive inscription in navy blue ink relates that she is someone's "Auntie Winnie" and a slightly faded indigo stamp directs viewers to the Hausmanns' studio on St. George's street where, at the time this picture was printed, additional copies of it and other photographs Helmuth had made could be ordered (fig. 21.3).

Taken during the war, Helmuth's snapshot of this well-dressed couple exemplifies the type of work he produced in South Africa as a young denizen photographer.[12] For years he visited Del Monico's and other posh venues in Cape Town where "night after night" he created what must have amounted to thousands of images of the city's white leisured bourgeois (Hausmann n.d., 149). Although novel, his business model was not necessarily new.[13] Upon arriving at one of Cape Town's upmarket restaurants, night clubs or hotels, Helmuth would move through its bustling social scene taking photographs of patrons as they drank, danced and dined. Bolstered by both the status of his clients and their seemingly insatiable desire to be seen, this venture into his new cosmopolitan city proved to be incredibly successful – so much so, he writes, that he "could hardly cope with the demand" and was forced to "work often right through the night to develop [his] films and to print the pictures" (149). Over the course of his first few years in South Africa, he boasts, "there was hardly anybody in town who not at one time or other went to [Del Monico's or the Blue Moon Hotel] and eventually was caught on my camera" (172). With each of his visits to these places, Helmuth either established a new relationship or strengthened an old one, his presence building up like a patina throughout the city and among the upper echelons of its white society.

As his connections with Cape Town's white elite grew, however, so, too, did his determination to differentiate between South Africa's increasingly racist policies and those he and his wife had only recently fallen victim to under Germany's National Socialism. Paradoxically, it would seem that the Hausmanns' own experiences of racial persecution and dislocation had not made them sympathetic to those in their new surroundings whom they knew were similarly being discriminated against on the basis of race. Indeed, as Lotta M. Stone has noted in her study on German-Jewish refugees and their early experiences of exile in South Africa, the "mixed feelings" of relief that many exiles felt upon learning where they stood in their new country's racial hierarchy did not often "extend to concern over the position and treatment of [its] non-white residents" (2010, 122). Rather than attempting to challenge South Africa's discriminatory status quo, she writes, "many of these refugees from persecution and intolerance rapidly adopted the local feelings of superiority over the 'inferior' races" (ibid.). As is evinced throughout his memoir, Helmuth was among those who readily welcomed the privileges his designation as 'European' afforded him in South Africa and expressed full-throated support for a racially segregated system which, he was beginning to see, could potentially benefit him.[14] Indeed, rather than allowing himself to acknowledge the parallels that existed between his new context and the one he had only recently escaped, the young photographer instead chose to adamantly maintain that "everybody was treated as an equal" in South Africa, despite being repeatedly presented with evidence to the contrary (Hausmann n.d., 133).[15]

In the decade leading up to apartheid, for example, many of the places that Helmuth chose to frequent upheld a social (although not yet legal) colour bar which, he was learning, was exclusionary of those who had been deemed 'non-white' and yet did not discriminate against Jews. Establishments like Del Monico's, for instance, readily welcomed German-Jewish émigrés who had been racialized in Europe, but from all accounts drew a line at admitting "dark-skinned" patrons whom the state had designated as "Non-European" (Stodel 1962, 48).[16] Located across the street from Cape Town's Alhambra Theatre, the restaurant was a place that boasted performances by Black artists and musicians but which refused to serve them, and whose predominately Coloured staff were nightly policed by a white "gatekeeper" whose job it was to search them for items it was assumed they had pilfered over the course of their shifts (ibid, 103).[17] With cigarettes poised leisurely between their fingers, the man and woman in Helmuth's image appear notably unconcerned with the structures of inequality that were enabling their evening and remarkably comfortable in a space that had been both created and reserved for them – one to which Helmuth had initially been permitted access to by means of his profession and which his photographic images would, over the years, help to reaffirm.

It is here that my interest in why Helmuth chose to image this particular world necessarily shifts to considering how, in doing so, he and Else also contributed to *producing* it. While many of the pictures the couple made during these years were purchased by their subjects – kept as mementos in private photo albums or passed along to friends and family – others were published and circulated en masse throughout South Africa's newspapers, magazines and illustrated weeklies.[18] Throughout the Second World War and in the years that followed, photographs by the Hausmanns of the city's wealthy socialites getting married, giving toasts at state dinners or posing in their studio could be found splayed across the pages of not only Cape Town's most read newspapers – such as the *Cape Times* and the *Cape Argus* – but the country's most widely circulated and sought-after pictorial magazines. Among the publications, their photographs appeared in most often was *The Outspan,* a richly illustrated South African weekly that boasted full-page pictorial instalments and frequent photographic competitions. Every week, for example, the magazine's editors printed spreads with pictures of white South Africans the reader was told he or she "may know", and almost every week these pages showcased one or more portraits by Photo-Hausmann (fig. 21.4).

In the years leading up to South Africa's 1948 elections, the Hausmanns' work not only depicted white members of South Africa's community but problematically contributed to a growing collective imagining *of this community as white.*[19] The innumerable photographs they produced, in other words, did indeed help to 'build a world', but one that was problematically predicated on shifting (and increasingly exclusionary) notions of whiteness. While it is unlikely that the couple could have foreseen the larger ideological role their work would play in helping to redefine what it meant to be South African under National Party rule, by 1948

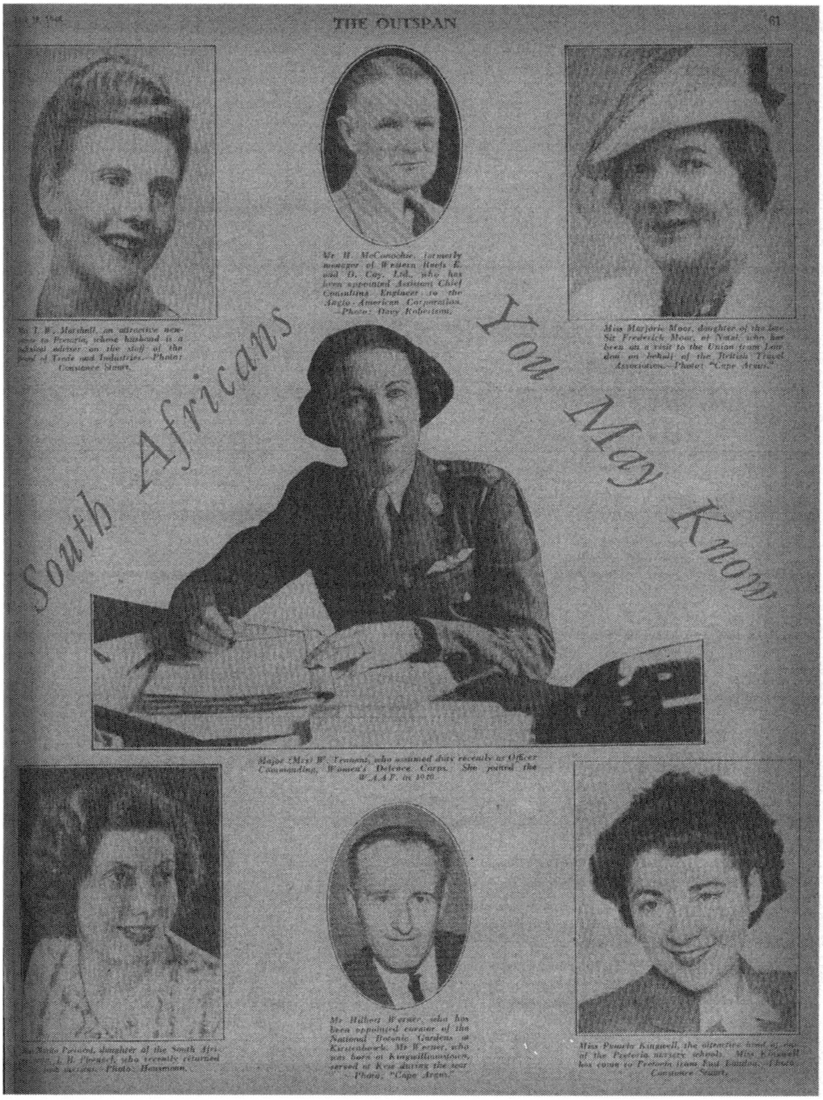

FIGURE 21.4: "South Africans You May Know." *The Outspan: South Africa's Weekly for Everybody*, 18 June 1948, p. 61 (New York Public Library).

they were more than well-versed in the nation's visual economy and fully aware of the power photographs could have in shaping notions of citizenship. Indeed, their understanding of the importance of images in this matter can perhaps best be seen in their decision to submit a portrait of themselves and their daughter to *The Outspan*'s newly launched "S.A. Family Competition" in what might have been a last bid for their own belonging in the months immediately leading up to the country's pivotal post-war elections (fig. 21.5). Published in early March 1948, the Hausmanns' appearance in the widely read weekly not only socially qualified their 'South Africanness', but visually signalled their right to be included in the consensus of the nation at this important moment in its history. Just as Helmuth's repeated presence in Cape Town's physical spaces had enabled him to build networks and to establish a sense of belonging in his and Else's new city, their frequent presence in the nation's mass circulated press (both in name and, in this instance, image) helped to affirm their position in its increasingly exclusionary – and notably white – imagined body politic.[20]

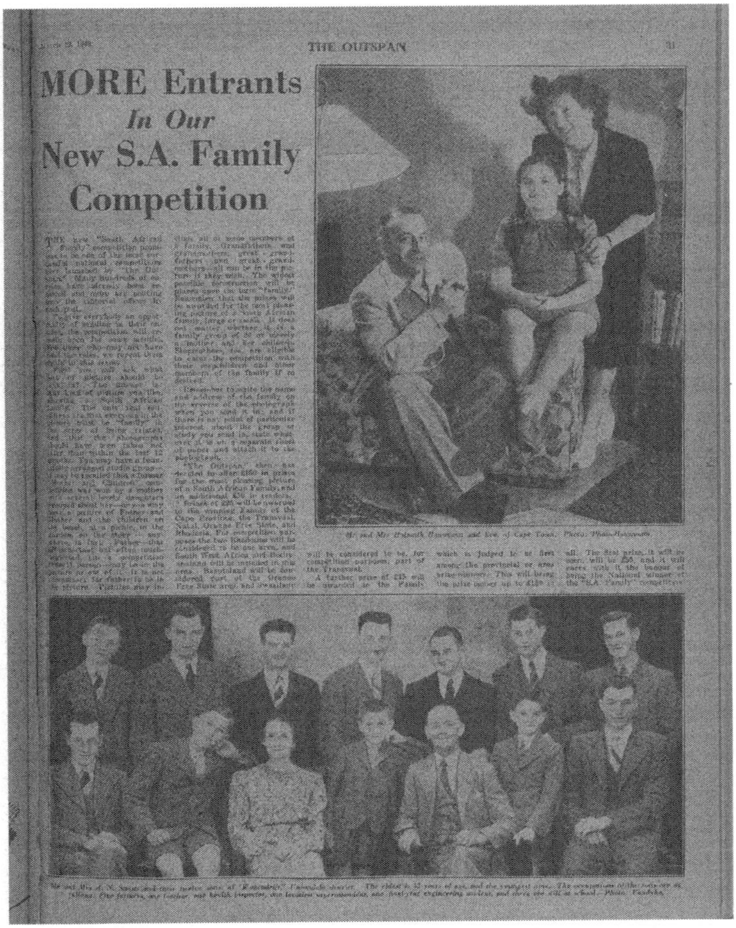
THE OUTSPAN

MORE Entrants *In Our* New S.A. Family Competition

FIGURE 21.5: "More Entrants in Our New S.A. Family Competition." *The Outspan: South Africa's Weekly for Everybody*, 12 March 1948, p. 31 (New York Public Library).

In a period in which millions of autochthonous South Africans were denied their rights based not on the place of their birth but on the colour of their skin, examining the conditions of Else and Helmuth's legal and social denizenship raises important questions about how they sought civic security in a new colonial context not with critical eyes, but with assimilationist ones. While the connections they forged and the work they produced over the course of their four-decade long career in Cape Town did ultimately enable them to secure a privileged place in this new city, it also secured their position on a side of history that, for many reasons, remains underexamined. While scholars across the humanities have begun to show how artists and their work can more positively reshape and reconfigure our world, their studies also point to the need to recover examples that can help lay bare its realities. Raised not as a challenge to these more positive figurations but as a provocation, my recovery of Else and Helmuth's archive is done so at a moment in which the world again stands on the precipice of needing to be remade. In the midst of recuperating more inspirational histories of resistance that can help motivate us in this work, the Hausmanns' commitment to their assimilation stands as reminder of not only how exceptional their more left-leaning colleagues' interventions were, but of how easily our own desires for belonging and stability can contribute to the exclusion and oppression of others.

NOTES

1. I would like to thank Jean Comaroff, Darren Newbury, Sarah Lewis, Mycah Braxton and the METROMOD team for their thoughtful feedback on earlier drafts of this material and for their help in bringing this chapter to its final form.
2. Outside of the humanities, the literature on denizenship, or 'alienage' as it is also called, is vast. Texts that have been key to my thinking on the subject include Hammar (1990), Benhabib (2004), Bosniak (2006), Cohen (2009) and Benton (2010).
3. A copy of Helmuth's unpublished memoir was generously provided to me by his grandson, Joseph Sanzul.
4. Because Else took on the more domestic role of managing their studio while Helmuth sought commissions on the city's streets, the first half of this chapter focusses more specifically on him. For more on Else and how her gendered experiences of exile inflected her photographic practice in Cape Town, see Williams 2020.
5. For a much more thorough discussion of antisemitism in South Africa than can be provided here, see Shain 2015.
6. To claim that Helmuth was simply naive about what was going on around him would be profoundly untrue. Begun in 1960, his memoir is laden with discussions about contemporary political events. In addition to addressing South Africa's role in the Second World War and the events that were unfolding in Europe, Helmuth also discusses the later "chaos"

that was caused by early decolonization efforts across the African continent, speaks to the world's growing criticism of South Africa's apartheid regime, and voices his concerns about the conflicts between Israel and Palestine (Hausmann n.d., 5f., 246f.).

7. The Hausmanns moved a number of times over the course of their first few years in Cape Town. After a short period in the kosher boarding house on Wesely Street where they had rented a single room, they moved into a small two-bedroom apartment of their own "near the city and center of town" (Hausmann n.d., 146). When Else fell pregnant in late 1937, however, they realized that they would need more space to accommodate their growing family and decided to move again, this time into a slightly larger two-roomed flat on Gordon's street in Gardens which also doubled as their photography studio (152). After being admonished by the Cape Town City Council for operating their business out of their home, the couple was forced to find a separate premise for their studio (153). In what was most likely early 1938, they began renting a shopfront on St. George's street where Photo-Hausmann would be based for the remainder of the war (198).
8. Helmuth writes that when he first began working as a photographer in Cape Town, he used the "little Leica" he had brought with him from Germany (Hausmann n.d., 135). Lacking any other photographic equipment during this early period, he also notes that he sought permission from Else's then-boss, Mr. Horwitz, to use his darkroom after hours in order to develop his prints (138).
9. For a much more detailed discussion of South Africa's policies toward German-Jewish refugees during the Second World War than can be given here (particularly with regard to the Quota Act of 1930 and the Aliens Act of 1937) see Cuthbertson (1981), Stone (2010) and Shain (2015).
10. Articles addressing the government's inability (or unwillingness) to discern between pro-Nazis, German Jews and others who had been deemed dangerous to the war effort in the early war years were particularly prominent in the leftist press. See, for example, "What is Behind Anti-Nazi Internments?" *The Guardian*, November 21, 1940, p. 1 and "Internments… Who's Next? Strong Deputation to Minister." *The Guardian*, December 5, 1940, p. 1.
11. Helmuth explicitly addresses these fears in his memoir, writing: "We had to ask in ever increasing anxiety what will happen to us? Will we be allowed to carry on, or would we, after all, be sent to the Internment Camps which were recently opened?" (Hausmann n.d., 166).
12. While this photograph's exact date is unknown, the stamp on its verso holds the phone number for the studio the Hausmanns first opened in 1939 (Hausmann n.d., 198).
13. In describing how he began this aspect of his work, Helmuth writes: "Then I had another idea, actually it was not new, but certainly new to South Africa, to take pictures with flashlight during the evenings. We had noticed", he continues, "that many South Africans were very fond of dining outside or having parties, *Braivleis* and other entertainments either at their own home or even at certain restaurants […] The Del Monico was just the place where, at that time, most of the High Society met for their social gatherings" (Hausmann n.d., 148). It is important to note that this style of itinerant 'event' photography was not, as

Helmuth claims, "new to South Africa". It had, in fact, been utilized for years by photographers of colour in Cape Town who were unable to afford the luxury of owning their own studios. What was novel about Helmuth's enterprise was his ability to access these spaces in the city based on his ability to be perceived as white. For more information about other itinerant photographers who worked in South Africa, see O'Connell (2018).

14. In writing about Helmuth's complicity in this racial system I am not the first to trouble the more well-established narratives about Jews and the complicated roles they played in South African politics during these years. For a more detailed discussion about these histories and what is at stake in not acknowledging them, see Frankental and Shain (1993), Adler (2000) and Braude (2009).
15. Although Helmuth's memoir cannot be given the full attention it deserves here, it is important to note how he later mobilized his experiences under National Socialism in order to downplay the National Party's racial policies. "As a member of the Jewish faith", he wrote shortly after the Sharpeville massacre in 1960, "[I] know what it means from many years of past experience to be called a second-class citizen, but I challenge the majority of the Europeans if they can compare the situation here in South Africa with any time during the Hitler regime" (Hausmann n.d., 6). Roughly three years later, he argued that South Africa was "the last bulwark of Western civilization" and declared that "it would be a tragic day for all of us, whatever race, color, or denomination we belong to should the government be forced to surrender to the pressure artificially created from a world of people who do not, and who do not want to know better. Let me tell the world at large", he asserted, "that right here in sunny South Africa we are still living in harmony. Nobody whatever race he or she belongs to is in danger of their lives and every one of us – be they black or be they of white skin – is able to find work and earn a decent living and of course is protected by the laws of the land, and so it shall be, forever" (250).
16. Discussions about racial categories in South Africa are complex and marked by apartheid-era classification systems which separated the nation's people into four main groups: Black, Coloured, Indian and White. As understanding the Hausmanns' position in South Africa is dependent on these categories and how they were understood at the time, I have used them here. For a brief introduction to this history, see Brown (2000).
17. Helmuth's own views on South Africa's Coloured population were similarly condescending and reflective of the National Party's later racial hierarchy. "I feel that there should be made a difference between [Black South Africans and] these human beings who are after all our own offsprings", he writes (Hausmann n.d., 6). "The Natives don't want them and they don't want the Natives. Most of them feel far more inclined to be absorbed with us Europeans whose obedient servants they have always been. The fact that quite a number of them are still very low grade should not distract any government from taking advantage of their capability to serve and their preparedness to serve under any European government" (6).
18. The Hausmanns also published photographs in the *South African Jewish Chronicle*, the *South African Jewish Times*, the *Zionist Record* and the *Lady's Pictorial*. In addition to

working as wedding and theatre photographers, they became the main photographers for African Consolidated Theatres, the Blue Moon Hotel, the Bohemian Club and Del Monico's, and would go on to photograph the nation's leading statesmen, including Jan Smuts, D.F. Malan and the so-called 'architect of apartheid', Hendrik Verwoerd.

19. For more on denizenship and Benedict Anderson's notion of "imagined communities," see Meskimmon (2016).
20. Shortly after the National Party was elected in May 1948, however, this once 'imagined' white body politic became very real. Denying that his party was antisemitic, South Africa's new Prime Minster D.F. Malan decided to count Jews who "had previously been seen as products of mixed race" among "whites who, he believed, would need to unite behind the Afrikaner nationalist banner to ensure the survival of the Afrikaner *volk*" (Braude 2009, 79). "Ironically, then", Claudia Braude writes, "Jewish 'whiteness' was guaranteed with the introduction of apartheid" (ibid.).

REFERENCES

Adler, Franklin. "South African Jews and Apartheid." *Macalester International*, vol. 9, article 12, 2000, pp. 185–197, https://digitalcommons.macalester.edu/macintl/vol9/iss1/12/. Accessed 21 April 2021.

Arendt, Hannah. "We Refugees." Idem. *The Jewish Writings*, edited by Jerome Kohn and Ron H. Feldman, Schocken Books, 2007, pp. 264–274.

Benhabib, Seyla. *The Rights of Others: Aliens, Residents, and Citizens* (The Seeley Lectures, 5). Cambridge University Press, 2004.

Benton, Meghan. *A Theory of Denizenship*. Ph.D. dissertation, University College London, 2010, www.//discovery.ucl.ac.uk/id/eprint/624490. Accessed 21 April 2021.

Bosniak, Linda. *The Citizen and the Alien: Dilemmas of Contemporary Membership*. Princeton University Press, 2006.

Braude, Claudia B. "Commissioning, Community, and Conscience." *Safundi: The Journal of South African and American Studies*, vol. 10, no. 1, 2009, pp. 77–90.

Brown, Kendrick. "Coloured and Black Relations in South Africa: The Burden of Racial Hierarchy," *Macalester International*, vol. 9, no.1, 2000, pp. 198–207.

Cohen, Elizabeth. *Semi-Citizenship in Democratic Politics*. Cambridge University Press, 2009.

Cuthbertson, G.C. "Jewish Immigration as an Issue in South African Politics, 1937–1939." *Historia*, vol. 26, no. 2, 981, pp. 119–133, www.//ojs.tetherprop.co.za/index.php/historia/article/view/3446. Accessed 21 April 2021.

Frankental, Sally, and Milton Shain. "Accommodation, Apathy, and Activism: Jewish Political Behavior in South Africa." *Jewish Quarterly*, vol. 40, no. 1, 1993, pp. 5–12.

Hammar, Tomas. *Democracy and the Nation State: Aliens, Denizens, and Citizens in a World of Global Migration*. Avebury, 1990.

Hausmann, Helmuth. "Child of the Twentieth Century." (unpublished manuscript, private collection, n.d.).

Meskimmon, Marsha. "As a Woman, My Country Is…: On Imag(in)ed Communities and the Heresy of Becoming-Denizen." *Home/Land: Women, Citizenship, Photographies*, edited by Marion Arnold and Marsha Meskimmon, Liverpool University Press, 2016, pp. 253–268. *Loughborough University*, www.//hdl.handle.net/2134/24000. Accessed 21 April 2021.

Meskimmon, Marsha. "From the Cosmos to the Polis: On Denizens, Art and Postmigration Worldmaking." *Journal of Aesthetics & Culture*, vol. 9, no. 2, 2017, pp. 25–35. *Taylor & Francis*, doi: 10.1080/20004214.2017.1343082. Accessed 21 April 2021.

O'Connell, Siona. "Archive, Injury, and Image: Imaging Freedom through the Photographic Archive of the Racially Oppressed." *Sources and Resources: Photography and Archives in Africa*, special issue of *Critical Interventions: Journal of African Art History and Visual Culture*, vol. 12, no. 2, 2018, pp. 184–196.

Shain, Milton. *A Perfect Storm: Antisemitism in South Africa, 1930–48*. Jonathan Ball Publishers, 2015.

Stodel, Jack. *The Audience is Waiting*. H. Timmins, 1962.

Stone, Lotta M. *Seeking Asylum: German Jewish Refugees in South Africa, 1933–1948*. Ph.D. dissertation, Clark University, 2010.

Williams, Jessica R. "A Working Woman's Eye: Anne Fischer and the South African Photography of Weimar Women in Exile." *Women and Photography in Africa: Creative Practices and Feminist Challenges*, edited by Darren Newbury et al., Routledge, 2020, pp. 23–44.

22

Suzhou River and Garden Bridge: Reading Images of Exile in Shanghai

Mareike Hetschold

The aim of this chapter is to reflect on the notion of exile in the context of historical urban art practices. This is followed by the question of whether a conceptual differentiation derived from art history and its pictorial evidence can inform a contemporary understanding of exile. This project advances current discussions surrounding the expansion of the concept of exile, which question its (historical) fields of meaning and (current) possibilities of application. (Dogramaci and Otto 2017; Dogramaci and Mersmann 2019; Hansen-Schaberg 2019, 16; Bischoff 2019, 18; Andress 2020).

This chapter, which is based on my research within the ERC Metromod project,[1] looks at urban exile experiences and art practices in Shanghai from the 1930s to the 1950s, specifically regarding émigrés fleeing from Europe (Germany and Austria) to China or Shanghai. Urban perspectives on artistic practice in exile, which conceive of the city itself as an actor, make this line of vision appear limited – in geographical and temporal terms. Shanghai has a complex history as an arrival city, as a place of refuge and as a place to flee from at the same time. It sheltered a wide range of émigré communities: 80 per cent of its Chinese population consisted of Chinese fugitives who had migrated from different provinces, mostly from Jiangsu and Zhejiang. The largest group of foreign émigrés were Japanese, followed by the British and by Russian speaking émigrés who fled their country in the wake of the Russian Revolution. At the end of the 1930s, between 1937 and 1939, around 21,000–22,000 European, mostly Jewish, refugees had arrived in Shanghai. (Shih 2001, 236; Aubrun et al. 2019, 39; Pan 2019, 12) They all contributed to its urban development which then in turn shaped not only their exile experience in Shanghai but also, in the context of the arts, their artistic practices and job opportunities. So while we should be careful to not essentialize exile artists, reading and interpreting art in exile helps us understand specific dynamics of creative production and, thus, the different conditions of exile themselves.

Within this complex understanding, we need to remain conscious of the questions surrounding the complicated, sometimes contentious relationship between the city, artistic practices and exile, as well as possible perspectivizations and contextualization's regarding notions of exile. Art practices in urban space are simultaneously involved in its production and conditioned by it: "Metropolitan art perceives urbanity not solely as a space that creates motifs, but [as] a complex web linking creativity and environment, art theory and metropolis" (Dogramaci 2010, 9, translated from German by the author).

Urban environments and their stories can be perceived and told in many ways. In the introduction to her book about life in Shanghai's alleyway homes, *Shanghai Homes. Palimpsests of Private Life,* the scholar Jie Li writes:

> This book is built on the concept that an old house, inhabited by various families over several decades, is a layered ruin of their private lives, woven into but not subsumed by larger historical events. [...] In such intimate spaces, history did not proceed cleanly, with each new era purging the bygone era, but rather accrued into rich sediments of personal memories. [...] Like a museum of history, it presents a selective assemblage of objects and narratives, but the selection process is seldom as deliberate and systematic as a curated exhibition. Instead, each house is a palimpsest of inhabited spaces, material artifacts, and personal narratives that evolved over time.
>
> (Li 2015, 2f.)

Jie Li addresses a specific urban setting: the lived space of Shanghai's alleyway houses and its transformations over time. She writes about spheres of the 'private', of 'everyday objects' or 'personal memories' interwoven with and part of urban processes, as well of as political events pointing beyond the city space. Individual, collective and (im)material (trans)formations of spatial practices overlap like geological sediments and emerge as palimpsests throughout her narrative.

In Cai Jun's short story "Suzhou River", the sediments of Shanghai's urban topographies act as the setting for an exploration of fantastic space–time loops on foot and in a bathtub: embedded in the diffuse dream and waking states, the first-person narrator wanders along shifting present, past, imagined and future cityscapes. When, during a flood, the water of the Suzhou River enters his flat and bathroom, his bathtub carries him out into the city.[2]

> I had always wanted to row on a boat by myself along the web of canals to the south of the Yangtze and listen to the sound of the women's singing through the mist as

> they picked water chestnuts. But I never wished to find myself navigating naked in a steel bathtub, wrapped only in a padded coat. Yet I had no choice.
>
> (Cai 2020, 141f.)

On the way he meets a Sikh, "probably still guarding the door at the bottom of the river" (ibid., 142), a European, "the one who's lost, forever repeating himself, going round and round in circles, on a never-ending loop" (ibid.), and a version of himself, "In the faint streetlight, I finally made it out. It was my face" (ibid., 146), before being carried out of the city by either the current of the river or his dreams:

> Wrapped in my cotton-padded coat, gently rocked by the ripples of the Suzhou River in the soft evening light, I finally slept. I dreamt that I floated out into the Huangpu River, then further out to the mouth of the Yangtze, and then out to the sea, until the ends of the earth.
>
> (ibid.)

Urban architectures, such as modern flat compounds with balconies and lifts and the Bund skyline, old alleyway house quarters that survived along the southern bank of the eastern Suzhou River, the bridges that span it, and the old Custom House on the Bund, structure the narrative into recurring spatial sections.

The titular Suzhou River becomes the real protagonist of the story and the city also takes on a life of its own:

> The day was drawing in and the busy city was acting like nothing happened. Neon lights flickered, emitting a dazzling brightness. Not a single trace was left of the devastating flood. I looked at the sleepless city, and then back at myself, pitiful, alone floating on the current in the middle of the Suzhou River.
>
> (ibid., 143)

These very different texts and readings, each in its own way, propose an understanding of urban practices, processes, events, perceptions, structures, spaces or topographies that allow for different levels of perspectivization and call upon different actors. Following on from Cai Jun's story, we can ask whether and how the Suzhou River as an 'urban actor' could be used to look at exile and art production in Shanghai in the first half of the 20th century. An approach via the motif of the Suzhou River is obvious: the teeming boats, the Garden Bridge and its Huangpu estuary have always been popular motifs, not only for commercial postcard production. My choice of images in this chapter is by no means meant to be exemplary. Rather, their differences create a space for reflecting on interwoven notions of exile. The images differ in terms of media and creation contexts, and thus negotiate exile-relevant questions in distinct ways: in this way, they allow for a considered and differentiated analysis of exile.

Urban topographies and exile experiences – Visual perspectivations of the Suzhou River

The mouth of the Suzhou River and the Garden Bridge was not only a popular motif for postcards but also became a neuralgic zone when the Sino-Japanese war broke out. As a 'natural' border, the river divided the Japanese occupied area in the north from the foreign territories in the south and witnessed massive interurban flight movements. With the proclamation of the designated area, established north of the river in Hongkou in 1943, the passage across the river into the 'city centre' became a rare occasion for its inhabitants, who depended on obtaining permits and on the arbitrariness of the Japanese authorities. Against this background, depictions of the Suzhou River appear significant to flight and exile experiences and help identify the varying positions of those exile artists creating them.

The artist and printmaker Emma Bormann's approaches the Suzhou River estuary in her print *Shanghai Garden Bridge* (fig. 22.1) from an elevated vantage point south of the river.[3] The former British Embassy is placed in the centre of the picture. Behind the mouth of the Suzhou River, we can see the Garden Bridge (now called Waibaidu Bridge) and the Broadway Mansion. The wide riverbed of

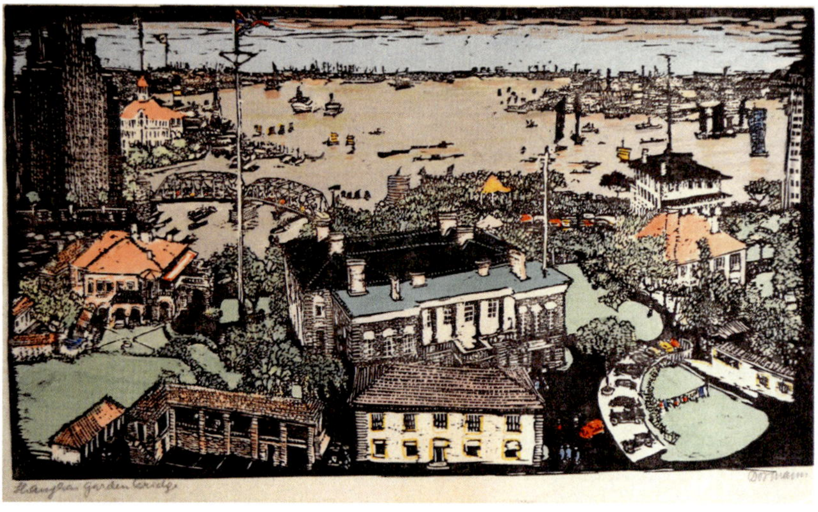

FIGUR 22.1: Emma Bormann, *Shanghai Garden Bridge*, woodcut, or linocut, around 1941 (© private collection).

the Huangpu opens out towards the horizon into the Yangtze estuary delta. The sky seems to merge with the sea behind. In the foreground, generously interspersed with green spaces and trees, the urban space grows denser towards the north, in the direction of Hongkou. The traffic on the Yangtze and the Suzhou River seems moderate, wide streets with dense traffic are not to be seen. Only small colourful spots indicate movement on the Garden Bridge, it is impossible to make out individual people. The colour scheme is strategic, not wasteful. The bright, loosely placed splashes of colour create an upbeat mood.

A few years earlier, another image of the same urban space was created. It is attributed to the businessman, founder and owner of the Sincere Department Store, Ma Yingbiao (Ma Ying-piu, 馬應彪), and was published without further details together with other photographs in *Life Magazine* on 13 September 1937 (fig. 22.2).[4] From the height of the Broadway Mansion, it captures the Garden Bridge looking north to south. The bridge turns into a wide road that winds along the Huangpu and the Bund into the International Settlements. The bridge and the street stretch from the lower right edge of the picture towards the upper left corner; their shape determines the photographed urban space. The free and empty green spaces south of the river mouth contrast with the dense crowds on the bridge and street. The photograph was taken in the summer of 1937 during the outbreak of the Sino-Japanese War. It shows people trying to escape from the Japanese military and the heavy warfare in the districts north of the Suzhou River to the relative safety of the foreign settlement areas. The short text accompanying the pictures reads: "Hundreds of Chinese Refugees, who had crossed the Garden Bridge were killed, when, on August 14 stray bombs landed on the Great World Amusement Park" (*Life* 1937, 25). Other pictures show the aftermath of the bombing of the Sincere Department and Wing One Store.

These disparate images and perspectives on the Suzhou River estuary and the Garden Bridge not only refer to their respective historical production contexts (when Ma Yingbiao took his photographs at the outbreak of the Sino-Japanese War, Bormann had not been in the city yet) and their creators' different artistic positions but also to the different roles Shanghai's urban and 'natural' topography (the Suzhou River and its bridges) played for the different experiences of flight and exile in Shanghai. While the photograph directly confronts the viewer with the ongoing flight of thousands of people across the neuralgic zone and over the bridge, the photographer's lense floats seemingly unaffected above the events.

Bormann's Shanghai prints address the (individual) experience of exile not always or directly, but often by referring to the invisible or the non-existent. Created after 1941 (no exact dating is given), the print's perspective on the Suzhou River estuary might not so easily have been replicated by other European artist colleagues who also lived in exile in Shanghai at the time.[5]

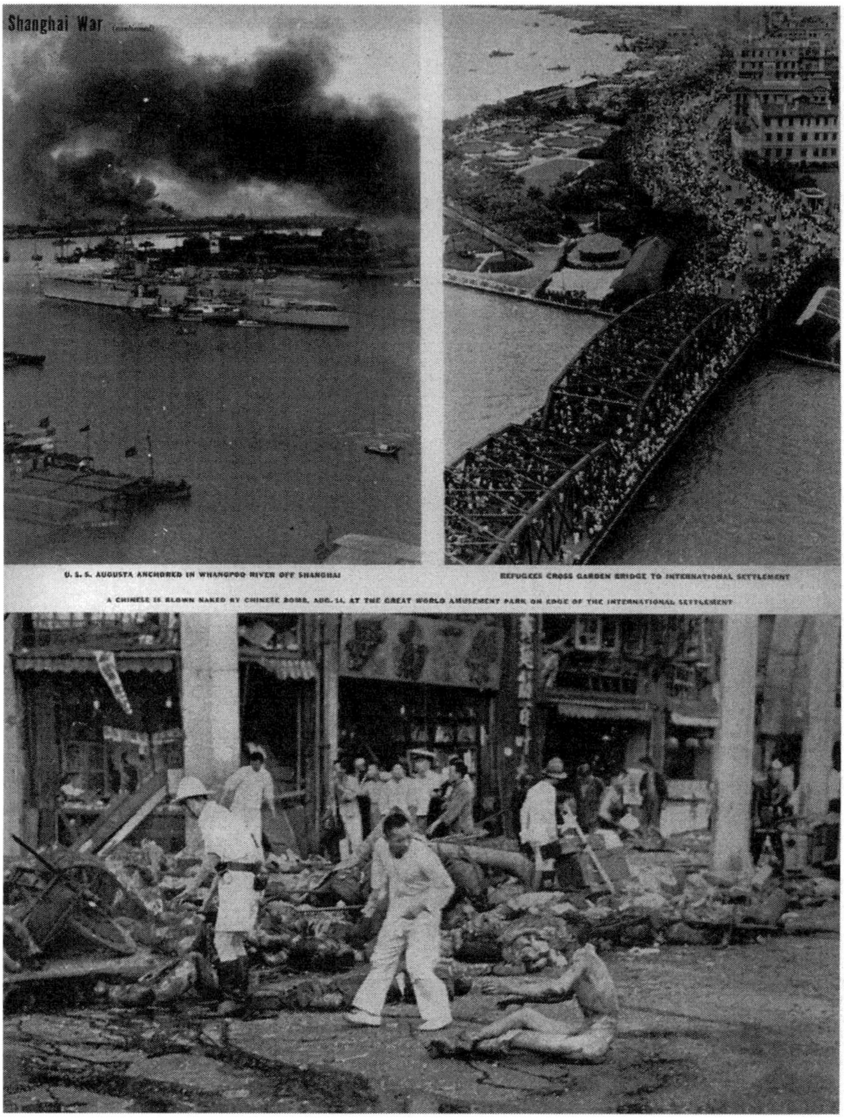

FIGURE 22.2: Ma Yingbiao (馬應彪), *Refugees crossing Garden Bridge*, 1937 (*Life*, vol. 3, no. 11, 13 September 1937, p. 25. Courtesy of the LIFE Picture Collection).

Bormann's lived urban space correlates with her artistic practice and the respective pictorial space. She was not forced to settle in the so-called Shanghai Ghetto, whose borders severely restricted the lived urban space for the artists enclosed there.

Reading these two images helps to understand the different roles Shanghai's urban topology played for its inhabitants, among them émigrés deeply affected by their various ethnical, socioeconomical, political or religious backgrounds.

It was not only the Sino-Japanese War in (modern) Chinese history that forced large parts of the Chinese population to flee. Shanghai's rapid increase in population in the second half of the 19th century during the Second Opium War (1856–1869) correlated with the Taiping Rebellion (1850–1864) and its lasting devastating demographic, socio-economic, political and environmental effects (Osterhammel 1998, 106–110; Aubrun et al. 2019, 13; Hsü 2000, 200–224).[6] Shanghai's population growth led to a successive densification of urban space (Aubrun et al. 2019, 13, 16). During the Sino-Japanese War, 60–95 million people were on the run at least once in their lifetime (Muscolino 2010, 453). Shanghai's population (density) increased enormously within a short period of time (Aubrun, et al. 2019, 13). The newcomers settled mainly in the districts north of the Suzhou River. On the outskirts of the city, shanty towns sprang up for those who came to Shanghai penniless (Henriot 2006, 217). Christian Henriot's study "Shanghai and the Experience of War: The Fate of Refugees" captures the fatal consequences of modern war for the heterogeneous population and refugee groups within the world's fifth largest metropolis at the time:

> Shanghai was probably the first large metropolis to experience large-scale modern warfare in its very midst. In 1937, bitter and brutal fighting raged for three months in and around the city, with intense bombardment from ships and planes. Within weeks, hundreds of thousands of residents were thrown on to the streets and turned into refugees. As war spread to the countryside, more people poured into the city.
>
> (Henriot 2006, 215)

The Suzhou River acted as a demarcation line, dividing the urban space into war zones, danger zones and zones of relative safety before the Japanese took control of all of Shanghai (1941 International Settlement, 1943 French Concession). In her book *Shanghai. China's Gateway to Modernity*, the scholar Marie-Claire Bergère describes the situation at the beginning of the war as follows:

> When fighting broke out, the inhabitants of Zhabei, Hongkou, and Yangshupu, fleeing the battlefield that their quarters had become, tried to take shelter in the international settlement by crossing the other side of the Suzhou River. The Garden Bridge, also known as "The Bridge of Life," now became a bridge of death. [...] For the residents of the concessions, the war was simply a spectacle to be watched from their rooftops and upper terraces [...]. However, the concessions were not completely spared. Their black Sunday came on August 14, when Chinese planes carrying bombs

> indented for Japanese ships at anchor on the Huangpu dropped them instead on the crowds throning the Bund and Edward VII Avenue. More than 3,000 corpses were found. [...] Soon the concessions had to cope with an influx of refugees that increased their population from 1.75 to 4.5 million within a few weeks.
>
> (Bergère 2009, 290)[7]

The Japanese set up checkpoints on Garden Bridge. Passage across the river between the occupied zones north of the Suzhou River and the concession areas to the south became a difficult, sometimes life-threatening undertaking (ibid., 291). Such massive inter-urban flight movements can be understood against the backdrop of Shanghai's semi-colonial structures of urban space. Passage from one part of the city to another also meant crossing different dominions that were subject to the jurisdiction and administration of different nations.

Interurban flight and exile – Crossing the Suzhou River and Garden Bridge

Another perspective on flight and exile experiences of the time can be addressed via another image dedicated to the fleeing people. Again, it references those for whom the Garden Bridge played a significant role in their flight and exile, as they were directly, materially confronted with it while attempting to cross it. Although the Chinese refugees did not technically leave the realms of their 'home country', the flight to a place of refuge *within* the country, and even within a city, meant the crossing of different national territories, due to the complex geopolitical power relations dividing Shanghai's urban dominions. While the last two images by Bormann and Ma I discussed helped address the issue of possible movement, for example, the positioning of oneself within disparate urban power realms at different times, the next image presented will help address the relations between different notions of exile, the city and exilic city dwellers.

In the early 1940s, the artist Jiang Zhaohe (蒋兆和) created a monumental work of art entitled *liumin tu* (流民图). The word *liumin* (流民) in the title is commonly translated as 'refugees', but also refers to 'exiles'. It is used to point to historical rather than contemporary political events. A more contemporary term for 'refugee' is *nanmin* (难民), directly translated as 'difficult people'.

An analysis of the term *liumin* or the usage and combination of the character *liu* in exile contexts is beyond the scope of my research. Nevertheless, the term in the title of Jiang's painting points to its diverse and dynamic fields of meaning and application. The *liumin* (directly translated as 'floating people') of Jiang's *liumin tu* designated a group of people who were forced to flee within the empire due to disasters, and social and political upheavals (Bianchi 2017; Huang 黄 2018; Huang 黄 2019; Lu 1999; Liu 2002; Theobald 2016; Theobald 2017; Waley-Cohen 1991). In his essay 红尘过客—明代艺术中的乞丐与市井 (Hongchen guoke – mingdai yishu zhong de qigai yu shijing), the art historian Huang Xiaofeng (黄小峰) elaborates on different yet interrelating Ming paintings which depict *liumin* in various urban and rural settings. The *liumin* figures seem to merge with those of the beggars, disabled and other displaced persons. The pictorial space of these figures is connected to discourses of artistic representations of the urban space, but not limited to it. According to Huang, the mobility of these figures who commute between rural and urban spaces can be understood as a representation of the urban itself (Huang 黄 2019, 4–15).

Jiang began to work on his project in Beijing in 1941. It resulted in an approximately 25–27 metres long and 2 metres higH picture scroll. Today, only a part of the scroll remains. It has been in the National Art Museum of China (NAMOC) in Beijing since 1998. The other parts have survived in black and white photographs (fig. 22.3). Originally from Luzhou, Sichuan, Jiang himself emigrated to Shanghai in 1920. There, he first worked as a commercial artist, among others for

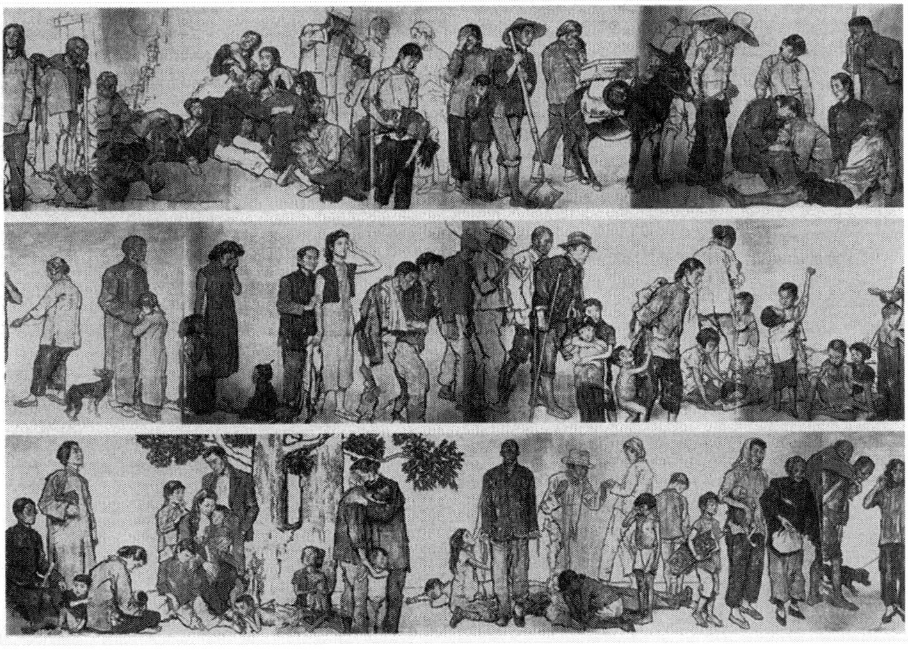

FIGURE 22.3: Photograph of 蒋兆和 《流民图》1943 中国美术馆 [Jiang Zhaohe, Liumin tu, 1943, Zhongguo meishuguan].

Ma Yingbiao's Sincere Department Store. The contact with the established artist Xu Beihong helped him pursue his artistic career. He taught at universities and art academies in Nanjing, Shanghai and Beijing. His work *liumin tu* depicts over 100 different figures. They refer to the many destitute people who were forced to flee the war.

The composition of the figures is diverse: peasants, citizens, workers, beggars and scholars, women, children and men of different ages, lifeless and emaciated bodies intertwine and line up. The story of this painting is as follows: To work on his figure-rich painting, Jiang travelled to Nanjing and Shanghai. He studied exiles who lived in precarious settlement areas at the time. He made numerous sketches and worked in secret with models in the studio in Beijing. After its completion in 1943, the painting was exhibited in Beijing as a 'group portrait'. Only a short time later, the exhibition was shut down by the Japanese military police. A second exhibition attempt was to take place in 1944 in Shanghai in the French Concession. There it was confiscated by the Japanese military and disappeared until 1953, when parts of it were found badly damaged in an old warehouse on the Suzhou River in Shanghai (Sullivan 1996, 108ff.; Liu 刘 1984).

Today, and after its rehabilitation in 1979, this ink figure painting is considered one of Jiang's most representative works. The black lines capture the figures in timeless gestures of sorrow, pain, grief and fear. Arranged in different groups, the figures' gazes correspond with each other and involve the viewer. Other figures gaze towards or avert their eyes from invisible sources of horror. Only a few hints in the background provide information about the spatial context. At the beginning, a few lines suggest the ruins of destroyed buildings. Towards the end, an old tree, a gnarled pine, gathers a group of figures around it.

Above all, the constellations of figures, their clothing, posture, gestures and facial expressions reveal the inhumane situation they have found themselves in and the horror they are facing. While most of the figures remain motionless, the picture's sheer dimension sets the viewer in motion. Only by walking along it is it possible to encounter the remaining figures and their "interlocking spatial units" (Wu 2018, 269). The motif of movement is inscribed in the painting on multiple levels – via the context of its creation, the title, the motif, the medium and the arrangement of its pictorial spaces, as well as via the process of viewing it as a whole.

Jiang's painting does not show a view of the Suzhou River or the Garden Bridge as the other visual representations, I have discussed throughout this chapter. But it evokes the massive movements of refugees and the people for whom the passage across the river and the bridge became a question of survival. In the preparation for his painting, Jiang studied the people of the shanty towns in Nanjing and Shanghai. Without being explicitly depicted, urban borders (such as the border of the Suzhou River) and their significance for those trying to cross them are deeply inscribed in Jiang's painting.

Conclusion

The fragmented, migratory and destructive histories of this art work and its artist are irrevocably interwoven with that of Shanghai. And while Emma Bormann's print *Shanghai Garden Bridge* could visually, materially and contextually not be farther from Jiang Zhaohe's *liumin tu*, it is similarly interwoven with Shanghai's history as a place of 'refuge'. These disparate visual worlds mediate the heterogeneous simultaneity of individual experiences of exile as they are situated in Shanghai's geography and urban topologies, and its semi-colonial and geopolitical structures. They enable us as viewers to trace and mine Shanghai's many layered sediments of flight and exile.

While my selection of images cannot be all-encompassing and should be perceived as experimental rather than representative, it has not only showcased how experiences of exile in Shanghai and their creative, artistic practices differ widely but also how the meaning and context of flight and exile constantly shift and evolve.

Jiang's painting inscribes itself in a painting tradition and calls up the (historical) rural and urban *liumin* while drawing a modern, urbanized version. The victory of the CPC (Communist Party of China) over the GMD (Guomindang) and the establishment of the PRC (Peoples Republic of China) then caused millions of people to emigrate and go into exile (liuwang 流亡) outside the borders of the new People's Republic of China. In the introduction to the *Chinese Reflections on the Exile Experience after 1949* issue of *Oriens Extremus: Kultur, Geschichte, Reflexion in Ostasien* (vol. 52, 2013), Thomas Fröhlich and Birgit Knüsel Adamec write:

> the different spheres of exilic experience and conceptual variety indicate the difficulty of arriving at a concept of exile: To what extent can we even refer to "exile" with regard to China in the 20th century?
>
> (Fröhlich/Knüsel Adamec 2013, 7)

They advocate for an understanding beyond "occidental ideas of exile" (ibid.) and suggest to listen to those "who define their own situation as being one of exile" (ibid.).

Around the same time during the first half of the 20th century, the definition of exile and its scholarly application underwent significant changes within different historical, cultural, political and linguistic contexts. Although these changes are triggered by interdependent larger historical events, including Western and Japanese Imperialism, German national socialism and WW II, these different contexts need to be taken into account when trying to sketch a general definition of 'being in a state of exile'. In addition to the reading of texts in order to understand specific local and historical exilic experiences, the 'reading of images' can enrich prevailing 'literary' perspectives on exile. As a visual practice rooted in complex compositional structures and media contexts, images can help us address the multitude of exilic experiences within a 'single urban frame', such as the frame of the Suzhou River for example. Besides providing a personal narrative of exile, these images and how they have been created refer to the respective urban conditions of exile and the possibilities of artistic practices in exile. As such, they call into question any notion of exile as definitive, finite or all-inclusive. Exile appears instead as a palimpsest-like, dynamic and lively complex that is continuously revised, renewed and reconfigured from past and present, private and public, individual and collective, homo- and heterogeneous texts and images.

NOTES

1. "Relocating Modernism: Global Metropolises, Modern Art and Exile (METROMOD)" is a 5-year project funded by an ERC Consolidator Grant and located at the Ludwig-Maximilians-Universität (LMU) Munich. For further information, see: www.//metromod.net.
2. Published in: Jin, Li and Dai Congron, editors. *The Book of Shanghai: A City in Short Fiction*. Comma Press, 2020, pp. 131–46. This anthology from the *A City in Short Fiction* series brings together ten stories by various contemporary authors. Jin Li writes in her introduction: "Airports, luxurious hotels, shopping malls, financial centres – these may be what most metropolises around the world have in common, what we expect to find, what we are thinking we're coming to look at, but what's unique about any destination is the particular outlook of the citizen living there, the intricate, varied and often hidden historical traditions each one carries with them. Even in the same city, the economic possibilities, lifestyles and living conditions of different groups of residents are multiple, complex, and widely disparate" (Jin, in Jin/Dai 2020, xiii).
3. Emma Bormann's oeuvre bears witness to her extensive travels around the globe and to the agility and versatility of her artistic rendering of the (urban) sites she encountered. Austrian born, married to a Jew and suspended from her teaching position at the University in Vienna, she followed her husband into exile to South China in 1938, from where she and her two daughters proceeded to Shanghai in 1941 in order to flee from the advancing Japanese military. For a comprehensive survey of her impressive artistic production and carrier see Johns, Andreas. *The Art of Emma Bormann*. Ariadne Press, 2016.
4. The title of the photo reportage is: "The Chinese Outfight the Japanese as Shanghai Blazes." *Life*, vol. 3, no. 11, 1937, pp. 23–26. On Ma Yingbiao as a photographer and his biography, see *Virtual Shanghai*, www.virtualshanghai.net/References/Biography?ID=173. Accessed 2 July 2021. On Sincere Department Stores, see *The China–Australia Heritage Corridor*, www.heritagecorridor.org.au/places/sincere-department-stores-hong-kong. Accessed 2 July 2021.

5. In 1943, declared 'stateless' by the Nazi regime, most Jewish European emigrants were forced into a small, designated area in Hongkou – the so-called Shanghai Ghetto – by the occupying Japanese authorities. Already facing harsh economic conditions, for many this meant the loss of previous income opportunities, as well as of their professional and social networks (Pan 2019, 11–28).
6. Shanghai is rooted in the complex geopolitical and cultural structures of a semi-colonial metropolis. After the First Opium War, the signing of the Treaty of Nanking in 1843 and the "most favoured nation" clause contained therein, Shanghai's territory as one of China's five port cities was split into British and American concessions (later known as the International Settlement) as well as French and informal Japanese concessions – each with its own jurisdiction. The term 'semi-colonial' can be traced back to the 1920s and was used, among other things, in Marxist criticism "as a way to describe the coexistence between the native feudal and the colonial." (Shih 2001, 31) Shih uses the term in order to describe the specific impacts of multilayered imperialist presence in China and their fragmentary colonial geography (largely confined to coastal cities) and control, as well as the resulting social and cultural formation (ibid.).
7. The administrative authorities were overwhelmed and initially tried to stop the refugees from entering the concession. Accommodating 250,000 refugees, the Jesuit father Jaquinot de Basenge created a safe zone located in the old Chinese town, which was respected by the Chinese and the Japanese military (Bergère 2009, 29; Kranzler 1974, pp. 40–60).

REFERENCES

Andress, Reinhard, editor. *Vorstufen des Exils / Early Stages of Exile*. Brill, 2020.

Aubrun, Charlotte, et al. *The Population of Shanghai (1865–1953): A Sourcebook* (Handbook of Oriental Studies. Section 4 China, vol. 35). Brill, 2019.

Bergère, Marie-Claire. *Shanghai. China's Gateway to Modernity*. Translated by Janet Lloyd, Stanford University Press, 2009.

Bianchi, Alice. "Ghost-Like Beggars in Chinese Painting: The Case of Zhou Chen." *Fantômes dans l'Extrême-Orient d'hier et d'aujourd'hui – Tome 1*, edited by Vincent Durand-Dastès and Marie Laureillard, Presses de l'Inalco, 2017. www.//books.openedition.org/pressesinalco/1484. Accessed 12 February 2021.

Bischoff, Doerte. "Globalisierung der Literatur." *Politik und Kultur. Zeitung des Deutschen Kulturrats*, vol. 6, no. 19, June 2019, p.18.

Chen, Janet. Y. *Guilty of Indigence: The Urban Poor in China, 1900–1953*. Princeton University Press, 2012.

Dogramaci, Burcu. "Die Stadt und die Künste – zur Einführung." *Großstadt: Motor der Künste in der Moderne*, edited by Burcu Dogramaci, Gebr. Mann, 2010, pp. 7–12.

Dogramaci, Burcu, and Elizabeth Otto, editors. *Passagen des Exils/Passages of Exile* (Exilforschung. Ein internationales Jahrbuch, vol. 35). edition text + kritik, 2017.

Dogramaci, Burcu, and Birgit Mersmann, editors. *Handbook of Art and Global Migration: Theories, Practices, and Challenge*. De Gruyter, 2019.

Fröhlich, Thomas, and Brigit Knüsel Adamec. "Introduction. Exilic Signifiers in 20th Century China: 1898, 1949, 1989." *Oriens Extremus: Kultur, Geschichte, Reflexion in Ostasien*, vol. 52, 2013, pp. 3–18, www.//oriens-extremus.org/wp-content/uploads/2016/07/OE-52-2.pdf. Accessed 12 July 2021.

Hansen-Schaberg, Inge. "Man geht nicht zum Vergnügen ins Exil." *Politik und Kultur. Zeitung des Deutschen Kulturrats*, vol. 6, no. 19, 2019, p. 16.

Henriot, Christian. "Shanghai and the Experience of War: The Fate of Refugees." *European Journal of East Asian Studies*, vol. 5, no. 2, 2006, pp. 215–245.

Hsü, Immanuel C. Y. *The Rise of Modern China*. Oxford University Press, 2000.

Wu, Hung. *Space in Art History*. Horizon Books, 2018.

黄小峰《底层的声音. 胡葭与《流民图》》《中央美术学院美术馆藏精品大系中国古代书画卷》《上海书画出版社》2018年5月版. [Huang Xiaofeng. Diceng de shengyin. Hu jia yu liumin tu. Zhongyang meishu xueyuan meishu guancang jingpin da xi zhongguo gudai shuhua juan. Shanghai shuhua chubanshe, 2018 nian 5 yue ban]. www.cafamuseum.org/exhibit/newsdetail/2651. Accessed 23 February 2021.

黄小峰《红尘过客—明代艺术中的乞丐与市井》《中国书画 杂志》2019年第11期. [Huang Xiaofeng. Hongchen guoke – mingdai yishu zhong de qigai yu shijing. Zhongguo shuhua zazhi, 2019 nian di 11 qi]. *Chinese Painting and Calligraphy*, vol. 11, 2019, pp. 4–15.

Kranzler, David. "Restrictions Against German-Jewish Refugee Immigration to Shanghai in 1939." *Jewish Social Studies*, vol. 36, no. 1, 1974, pp. 40–60.

Li, Jie. *Shanghai Homes. Palimpsests of Private Life*. Columbia University Press, 2015.

Jin, Li and Congrong Dai, editors. *The Book of Shanghai: A City in Short Fiction*. Comma Press, 2020.

Lu, Hanchao. "Becoming Urban. Mendicancy and Vagrants in Modern Shanghai." *Journal of Social History*, vol. 33, no. 1, 1999, pp. 7–36.

Liu, Lu. *A Whole Nation Walking: The "Great Retreat" in the War of Resistance, 1937–1945*. Ph.D. dissertation, University of California, San Diego, CA, 2002.

刘曦林.《藝海春秋. 蒋兆和传. 朵云现代国画家丛书》《上海書畫出版社》[Liu Xilin. Yi hai chunqiu. Jiang Zhaohe zhuan. Duo yun xiandai guo hua jia cong shu, Shanghai shuhua chubanshe] 1984.

Muscolino, Micah S. "Refugees, Land Reclamation, and Militarized Landscapes in Wartime China. Huanglongshan, Shaanxi, 1937–45." *The Journal of Asian Studies*, vol. 69, no. 2, 2010, pp. 453–478.

Osterhammel, Jürgen. "IV. China und der Westen im 19. Jahrhundert." *Länderbericht China: Politik, Wirtschaft und Gesellschaft im chinesischen Kulturraum*, edited by Carsten Hermann-Pillath et al., Bundeszentrale für politische Bildung, 1998, S. 102–117.

Pan, Guang. *A Study of Jewish Refugees in China (1933–1945). History, Theories and the Chinese Pattern*. Shanghai Jiao Tong University Press/Springer, 2019.

Shih, Shu-mei. *The Lure of the Modern: Writing Modernism in Semicolonial China, 1917–1937*. University of California Press, 2001.

Sullivan, Michael. *Art and Artists of Twentieth Century China*. University of California Press, 1996.

Theobald, Ulrich. "liu, 流, exile." *ChinaKnowledge.de*, 26 August 2016, www.chinaknowledge.de/History/Terms/liumin.html. Accessed 13 February 2021.

Theobald, Ulrich. "liumin, 流民, peasant refugees." *ChinaKnowledge.de*, 21 October 2017, www.chinaknowledge.de/History/Terms/liumin.html. Accessed 13 February 2021.

Waley-Cohen, Johanna. *Exile in Mid-Qing China: Banishment to Xinjiang, 1758–1820*. Yale University Press, 1991.

23

The Territorial Dimension of Spanish Republican Exile in the Cities of Argentina

Federico Martín Vitelli

Introduction

This article approaches the human dimensions of exile by focusing on the experience of a group of Spanish republican intellectuals who settled in the cities of Bahía Blanca and La Plata between 1936 and 1975. It will try to reconstruct, from a historical perspective, the territoriality of the collaborative, academic, cultural and political networks Spanish migrants integrated into. Taking into account the exiles' socio-demographic and political heterogeneity (regarding generation, ethnic group, gender, class belonging, escape context and ideological affiliation), this work traces their various social and civic contributions in a new country, while also acknowledging that what is local (territorial dynamics of centre/periphery) cannot be comprehended outside of transnational (expelling countries/receptive countries dynamic) and national (Buenos Aires/Province dynamic) dimensions.

Starting from a situated analysis and a number of case studies, this article aims to contribute – through the creation of comparative analysis categories, cartographical mappings concerning the territorialization of networks and interpretative models for their use as sources about exile – to the production of knowledge for approaching other similar processes in which the exiles appropriate their new environment as one of articulation between their memories (reconstruction of the past), their social and political praxis (intervention in the present) and their projects of returning (appropriation of the future). This investigation proposes to approach the resulting activation of new political and social spaces, established by the newly arrived with their host communities, in a context of immediacy, uncertainty and transiency.

The period opens with the arrival of the first exiled teachers to the aforementioned cities in 1936, among the outbreak of Spanish Civil War, and ends in 1975, when General Francisco Franco's death enables the beginning of Spain's transition to democracy, allowing for the exiles to return to their country if they so wished.

The case studies constitute "a profoundly empirical and multifaceted inquiry that explores a social phenomenon within its real context; it utilizes multiple sources of evidence or data; and it primordially (but not exclusively) uses qualitative research methods" (Yin 1984, 13). Case studies open an analytical space of growing complexity about relating the micro to the macro, the endogenous to the exogenous, and the individual to the collective.

Regarding this, I have chosen to privilege subnational case studies. This decision has the advantage, by allowing me to increment the focus of the analysis, of increasing the degree of precision to code the cases: it allows me to contemplate the territorial disparity that these processes of political and economic transformation have, and to contribute to the theorization and exploration of the dynamic link between different regions and political systems (Snyder 2001). In this sense, when approaching this type of case study, we need to remain aware that subnational autonomy is always limited within the structure of the Nation State. Keeping this in mind, my research is located at the intersection of inter-area and cross-area studies, as I contemplate the different spatial scales that intervene in the phenomena I examine.

Regarding the timescale, this is a synchronic study with an emphasis on analyzing two cases which overlap chronologically. This method is based on the intent of looking for underlying similarities in the same scenario and with common results, and then to infer the explanatory potential of the phenomenon to develop a general explanation (Lucca, Pinillos 2015).

I base my analysis on the study of a broad documentary corpus, composed of literary writings, autobiographical texts, transcribed lectures, interviews, different public interventions made by exiled teachers later edited and published in specialized magazines, local and Spanish press, letters, applications and bureaucratic procedures present in the archives of the Universidad Nacional del Sur (UNS) and in the Universidad Nacional de la Plata (UNLP), and existing migration documents in the Archivo General de la Guerra Civil Española of Salamanca.

This chapter is divided into two main sections. In the first, I will trace different forms of how exiled Spanish teachers and intellectuals related to cultural, political and associative networks in Bahía Blanca and La Plata. In the second, I will delve deeper into the study of the different spatial dimensions that link to this process of insertion, and the exiles' cultural and political urban activities during their stay in the two cities. By examining these elements, I aim to establish – in the closing section – some possible generalizations derived from the empirical research carried out.

The exiles' insertion in the cultural networks of Bahía Blanca and La Plata

The cases, which are based on the study of exiled republican teachers' entanglement with Bahía Blanca and La Plata, appertains to the importance of both cities in the provincial urban framework, to the magnitude of the exiles' arrival, and to their important contribution and public activities in both cities.

The cities' relevance corresponds with their population density,[1] the geographical space of privilege of their location, and the specific importance that they share in the strategic plan of national and provincial development. During that period, both cities featured national university institutions – UNS[2], UNLP[3] and Universidad Tecnológica Nacional (UTN)[4] – Spanish Consulate offices, subsidiaries of the Colegio Libre de Estudios Superiores (CLES)[5] and many Spanish and regionalist association centres, which constituted the central nodes in the formation of the cultural, ethnic and intellectual networks on a local, regional and national scale.

La Plata became an important node within the cultural and academic networks of the region, mainly because of its double role as the capital city of the province of Buenos Aires and its proximity to Capital Federal. This proximity allowed for the practice of the same profession in both locations, a fact from which different exiled teachers benefited. Among their institutions and cultural and academic entities, I chose to highlight the local leg of the CLES and the UNLP. It was in the latter and not in the Universidad de Buenos Aires – a space with little reception of Spanish exiles – where most of them were able to homologate their college degrees, a key requirement that enabled them to exercise their professions in Argentina (Schwartzstein 2001).

The UNLP gave shelter to a large group of exiled teachers, making it the Argentine university that housed the largest number of republicans in its body of teachers throughout its history, with a total of fifteen professionals that worked in areas such as mathematics, philology, history, law, medicine and psychology. Our period's list is composed of the following names: Pedro Pi Calleja, Luis Antonio Santaló Sors, Juan Cuatrecasas, Fernando Martínez Sanz, Pío del Río Hortega, Juan Rocamora, Ángel Garma, Niceto Alcalá Zamora, Luis Jiménez de Asúa, Américo Castro, Clemente Hernando Balmori, Claudio Sánchez-Albornoz, Nicolás Sánchez-Albornoz, Fernanda Monasterio Cobelo and Alberto Vilanova Rodríguez.

On the other hand, Bahía Blanca, located in the south of the province of Buenos Aires, 700 kilometres apart from the capital of Argentina, took a central role in the strategic plan of the nation, mainly because of its location on the shores of the deepest natural seaport in the country. From the 19th century, the perception of Bahía Blanca as a natural capital of Patagonia was wide spread. Because the city played a major role in the economic development of the region, something that was also reflected in its zonal prominence in cultural terms, it can be understood as a centre of artistic and intellectual irradiation. In this sense, the UNS as much as most of the local artistic and associative organisms, set out to achieve the crystallization of this idea by aiming to serve as an educational and artistic model for the vast territory's population.

As a way of reaching those goals, and due to the "insufficient number of teachers with a specific pedagogic and/or disciplinary formation available in the local medium and to the need of covering the newly opened teaching positions" (Cernadas 2006, 49), prestigious teachers and specialists exiled from Franco's Spain, with extensive experience in social and humanistic disciplines, arrived to work in the UNS. Among them, a total of seven republican exiles managed to take up a teaching position in the institution: Manuel Lamana, José Bernal Ulecia, Julio Hernández Ibáñez, Rafael Olivar Bertrand, Nicolás Sánchez-Albornoz, Fernanda Monasterio Cobelo and Alberto Vilanova Rodríguez.

Their designation – the same as for those working in the UNLP – under the category of republicans refers to their public positioning in defence of the democratic government embodied in the Second Spanish Republic, in clear opposition to Franco's regime. However, their political projects differed from one another: the 'republican' epithet referred to the communal sense of defeat, and to the context of the Spanish Civil War as a founding basis of a collective memory of the exile that linked different political cultures (Aguirre Herráinz 2017, 160). At the same time, when it came to local assimilation, the 'republican' label acted as an identity category that carried some advantages in a moment when public opinion associated the idea of the exile with the 'undesirable communist'. From the sense of brotherhood forged from the defeat that linked, with some nuances, their pasts and their presents, they were united by the common project of a possible, future return to Spain.

The professionals were contacted prior to their arrival by different means. Among them, we can highlight the intervention of international organizations such as the Organización Internacional para Refugiados (OIR),[6] national organizations like the Institución Cultural Española (ICE)[7] and the intervention of Argentine diplomatic authorities in Spain and France. Many of the exiles already knew their future residence destination because they had already worked there in the years prior. Regarding this, the institutional relationships developed in programmes that promoted the professional exchange between Spanish and Argentine teachers also played a relevant role. These programmes were executed by the Junta para de Ampliación de Estudios e Investigaciones Científicas (JAE),[8] by the ICE and by the immigrant centres that had been created to deal with the massive influx of Spanish populations to Argentina in the second half of the 19th century. This way, as part of this project, future exiles in Argentina like Pío del Río Hortega and Claudio Sánchez-Albornoz had already been working in the country during the decades of the twenties and the thirties (Diaz-R. Labajo 2010).

During the Civil War, Spanish associations and local institutions aligned on different sides of the conflict, with confrontations playing out in local disputes on Iberian soil. An example of this is Club Español, which adhered to Franco's regime in both cities, while most of the Regionalist and Republican Centres sided with the republicans. The latter served hosted exiled teachers who then quickly grew into the centres' intellectual elite, while simultaneously receiving material and social support from those same associations which would ultimately help them in their pursuit for job placement later. The spaces of association and relationality constituted a link to their past through shared language, customs, rituals and food. However, the deterritorialization of their trajectory as exiles, which left them devoid of their original spatial and geographical context, caused their conceptions of urban space to depend fundamentally on the future as their operating principle for the assertion of their identities, and not on their territorial past.

Depending on their ideological roots, the exiles merged with local intellectual networks of liberal and leftist persuasions. One of the main actors at a national level was the liberal group surrounding *Revista Sur*, directed by Victoria Ocampo[9], while on a local scale we can find the Asociación Bahiense Bernardino Rivadavia in Bahía Blanca[10] and most of the networks linked to the UNS and the UNLP as similar examples. Regarding leftist networks, which were consolidated as a response to the crisis of liberalism during the 1930s, there were those connected to the CLES, which in turn was linked to militants of the Communist and Socialist parties. These networks were articulated around the ideals of resolutely defending democracy and antifascism, merging stance sin favour of the republican with an opposition to Italian fascism, German Nazism and the persecution of Jews.

Theoretical notes for the analysis of the spatial dimension of the republican exile

The exiles' participation in the cultural and intellectual networks previously mentioned builds on three spatial dimensions. First, on a transnational scale, the exiled teachers found themselves at the intersection of being expelled from their country of origin and being received by their host countries. It is in this transnational dimension that we can locate the work of institutions such as the ICE and the JAE, whose relational capital's international scope, sustained in their institutional work prior to Franco's victory, allowed for many exiled teachers to arrive safely in Argentina where they then could start looking for local communities vital to finding a job.

This international dimension intersected with the scientific stances and contributions made by exiles in the field of urban planning projects. In Argentine educational institutions, the cultural view regarding what counted as European was raised in terms of dependency and asymmetry, articulating a centre-periphery antinomy within a transnational cultural framework that evolved during a period marked by North American hegemony and the emergence of the Third World. This traditional conception, based in viewing the symbolic national appropriations as part of an asymmetrical internationalization process, must be put in question, since it narrows Latin-American actions to passivity under the notion of 'influences', without highlighting existing appropriation and productivity modes that overlapped in multiple ways and from different geographical directions.

Second, on a national scope, an exile's engagement with space was influenced by tensions between Buenos Aires and the rest of the provinces. Argentine capital's centrality in cultural and labour terms made it a pole of attraction for exilic settlement, a situation which was compensated by the many teaching positions available in the recently opened universities in cities of the interior, such as the ones in Bahía Blanca and La Plata.

At the same time, exiles took the initial difficulties of entering the job market in the capital's environment and turned them instead into an opportunity to think anew.

Intellectual, cultural and political projects (among them many proposals of urban transformation), which had been cut short by the defeat they suffered and revive them in a context much more open to the contributions of exiles and immigrants.

Antoni Bonet, an exiled architect from Barcelona that shared his joint work with Pi Calleja in the Grupo de Artistas y Técnicos Catalanes para el Progreso de la Arquitectura Contemporánea (GATCPAC), and who introduced to the country many of Le Corbusier's proposals with whom he worked in Paris, said the following about the opportunities available in Argentina:

> Here in Paris, as you know, everything is provisory and theoretical. As an architect, I want to start building and, you know, there isn't much to do in here. Because of this and many other reasons I've decided to go to Argentina. I have friends and family living there and, above anything else, there's actual building taking place.
>
> (Di Bello 2014, 132)

Third, after their arrival the exiles witnessed and participated in tensions between centre and periphery on a local scale. On one hand, the ideological basis of their political and urban projects from the Spanish Second Republic, which included the planning of worker's homes, school buildings integrated with the exterior, and the so-called 'garden houses', positioned them as intervening agents in the cities' periphery. On the other hand, the spatiality of the networks and institutions in which they inserted themselves, added to the need of amplifying the scope of their protests and the chances of realizing their political and cultural projects, and caused the teachers to primarily intervene from the centre of the cities in which they had settled.

Such need for amplifying the complaints about what was happening in Spain made the exiles join forces with antifascist networks, such as the aforementioned CLES or the ABR, as a way of linking Franco's repressive regime to Italian fascism and Nazi Germany, thus making their political and cultural projects more understandable to the general public. Another method they chose was the use of local monuments in the republican public acts that linked the history and the memory of the host societies with exiled memories and with political projects cut short by exile. This way, the exiles' numerous interventions of and the regional ethnic associations they were involved in had their epicentre in monuments located in the centre of their respective cities, dedicated to Argentine patriotic heroes such as San Martín for example.[11] The symbolism carried by the use of the American liberator's image linked the host society's history with the exiles' own projects of liberating Spain from Franco's tyranny.

The public space was conceived as a significant place in which many discourses overlapped, and as a political space of representation and of society's collective expression. For its part, public space in its physical dimension is functionally multipurpose: it articulates and arranges the city, it facilitates meeting, exchange, mobility and the accessibility of urban resources, as well as people's permanence in it (Delgadillo 2014, 101).

The trajectory of these teachers and researchers was a successful example of the transactions that exiles can affect in transitional spaces: when their host country offered the necessary conditions to creatively overcome the state of crisis, rupture and mourning caused by the loss of their home, they created opportunities and innovation by further building on the educational, cultural and political backgrounds developed in their country of origin.

Final considerations

Exile dynamics are marked by an appropriation and reformulation of space, one that is driven forward by the productive intersection of three interconnected spheres: one, the revival of political and cultural projects that had seemed hopeless for exiles who had been defeated in their home countries in the past; two, their political praxis of the present, situated in the spatial and social context of the host cities; and third, future plans of return, as it would be in Spain where for many former exiles their projects previously cut short would finally materialize.

The key units of analysis for the theoretical studies about the processes of spatiality and territoriality of the networks of exile must contemplate that these are the result of the intersection of the working and material needs of exile; the ways of arrival and departure; the ideological formations of exiled people and networks; the institutional objectives of incorporating the labour forces and the intellectual prestige of the exiles, as well as their own goals of realizing their political and cultural projects cut short by defeat; the ever changing temporalities; the dispute for the memories and the past; the political conditioning of the host societies; the transfers of technical knowledge between agents and institutions; the centre-periphery dynamics in tension but also in complementarity; the local opening towards transnational elements; and the role of the exiles, the institutions and the cities inside the political and scientific projects of the nation. These units of analysis, reconstructed throughout this article regarding the cases of Bahía Blanca and La Plata, fashion, to our understanding, necessary axes for comparative scholarship that aims to study the urban dimension of the networks of exile.

It is noticeable that the contexts of immediacy and transience for exiles who have higher chances of returning to their homes, affect the degree of materialization of their cultural and urban projects. The more an exile is integrated into the host society, the more solid and durable are their projects – for those exiles who count on returning to their home countries soon, the projects remain more superficial and ephemeral. In this respect, not only the material recognition but also the cultural one, expressed by local institutions and networks, constitutes a symbolic compensation that is key to establishing and growing intellectual exchange between the local urban environment and the exiles. This recognition led many of them to leave behind an important legacy before, in all likelihood, dying far away from their home, which in turn reinforced the sense of gratitude and a commitment to the urban modernization of the host society. We must not forget that the urban projects that arose out of regional and republican academic and cultural fields were defended and exercised in the host cities with a militant sense of duty that would allow its ultimate realization after the defeat in the Peninsula.

The exiles' interaction with and insertion into local, national and transnational networks helped to avoid the fragmentation of their lives as they moved through equally fragmented, transitory spaces. These are local territories whose centres and peripheries, instead of relating to one another antithetically, showcased a considerable degree of dialogue, which in turn complemented the objectives of cultural action and political denouncement represented in exilic networks.

An anti-utopia – which consisted of the destruction of social relations, defeat and uncertainty through exile –, converged in space and time with the possibility of realizing a utopian space within which émigré Spanish republican intellectuals could imagine and materialize cultural projects that would otherwise have drowned in blood and repression in Spain.

NOTES

1. For the period I am working on, La Plata counted 338,772 inhabitants while Bahía Blanca had 150,400, which made them both the most populated cities in the Provincia de Buenos (Data supplied by the National Census of 1960).
2. The UNS was founded in 1956 on the foundations of the Instituto Tecnológico del Sur created ten years prior.
3. The UNLP, founded initially as a provincial university in 1897, was turned into the third national university of the country in 1905, utilizing the provincial university and other educational institutions as a basis.
4. The Universidad Tecnológica Nacional is a national public university of Argentina founded in 1959 as a continuation of the Universidad Obrera Nacional created in 1948. It has a federal organization, and it was conceived as a second cycle of technical formation, an academic structure that gives priority to different types of engineering.
5. The CLES (1931–1960) was an institution born in Capital Federal made up of intellectuals related to socialism and antifascism that spread throughout its years of existence to other cities, including Bahía Blanca and La Plata.
6. Created in 1947 as a non-permanent specialized organism of the UN, its work was limited to helping European refugees leave their countries of origin in the First World War and the Spanish Civil War. Its actions included different aspects like repatriation, legal and political protection, resettlement, and reinsertion of refugees.
7. Created in 1914 as a joint project between the universities of Buenos Aires and La Plata, it acted as intermediary in the cultural relations between the JAE and Latin America. The main objective of the ICE was to expose and disseminate research and literary studies from Spain in Argentina, by financing a chair in charge of Spanish intellectuals appointed by the JAE.
8. Created in 1907, it had a dual purpose: on one hand, it sent pensioners abroad as a mean of generating a current of scientific communication between Spain and outside countries, and on the other hand, it created work and research centres that served to group the cultural resources available in Spain, so that those who were sent abroad would be able to find an auspicious environment to continue their labour (Santamera Sánchez 1994).
9. *Sur* is the name of a literary magazine founded in 1931, based on the predominant liberal and antifascist orientation of the time.

10. It was founded in 1882 by the initiative of citizens with great influence in the cultural landscape of Bahía Blanca. It quickly became a central institution in the local cultural network, hosting lectures of many of the main thinkers of the region as well as Spanish exiles.
11. José de San Martín (1778–1850) was a member of the military and politician from Río de la Plata and one of the liberators of Argentina, Chile and Peru. In the canonical readings of the official national historiography, he occupies a central place in the pantheon of Argentine heroes.

REFERENCES

Aguirre Herráinz, Pablo. *¿Un regreso imposible? Expatriación y retorno desde el exilio republicano (1939–1975)*. Doctoral thesis, Universidad de Zaragoza, 2017.

Cernadas, Mabel. *Universidad Nacional del Sur 1956–2006*. EdiUNS, 2006. *Academia*, www.academia.edu/7907693/Historia_de_la_Universidad_Nacional_del_Sur_1956_2006_. Accessed 8 July 2021.

Delgadillo, Victor. "Urbanismo a la carta: teorías, políticas, programas y otras recetas urbanas para ciudades latinoamericanas / A la carte urbanism: theories, policies, programs and other urban recipes for Latin American cities." *Cad. Metrop*, vol. 16, no. 31, 2014, pp. 89–111. *Scielo Brazil*, doi: 10.1590/2236-9996.2014-3104. Accessed 8 July 2021.

Di Bello, Roxana. "El exilio catalán en la Argentina y su influencia en el campo disciplinar arquitectónico a través de un estudio de caso: Antonio Bonet." *Épocas*, no. 10, 2014, pp. 115–143, www.//p3.usal.edu.ar/index.php/epocas/article/view/3048. Accessed 8 July 2021.

Diaz-R. Labajo, Arantxa. "Redes y estrategias de migración exilio: el caso de los médicos republicanos exiliados en Argentina (1936–1961)." *200 años de Iberoamérica (1810–2010): Congreso Internacional: Actas del XIV Encuentro de Latinoamericanistas Españoles*, edited by Eduardo Rey Tristán and Patricia Calvo González, Universidade de Santiago de Compostela, 2010, pp. 1186–1205, www.//hdl.handle.net/10347/13419. Accessed 8 July 2021.

Lucca, Juan Bautista, and Cintia Pinillos. "Decisiones metodológicas en la comparación de fenómenos políticos iberoamericanos." *Documentos de Trabajo*, no. 25, 2015, pp. 5–37, www.//iberoame.usal.es/wp-content/uploads/2010/02/DocumentoTrabajo25_LuccaPinillos_final.doc.pdf. Accessed 9 July 2021.

Santamera Sánchez, Juan Antonio. *Reforma social y urbanismo en España de la Restauración a la Segunda República. (Institucionismo y urbanismo)*. Doctoral thesis, Universidad Politécnica de Madrid, 1994.

Schwartzstein, Dora. *Entre Franco y Perón: memoria e identidad del exilio republicano español en Argentina*. Critica, 2001.

Snyder, Richard. "Scaling Down: The Subnational Comparative Method." *Studies in Comparative International Development*, vol. 36, no. 1, 2001, pp. 93–110.

Yin, Robert. *Case Study Research: Design and Methods*. Sage Publications, 1984.

24

Calle de López or Spain in Mexico

Valeria Sánchez Michel

The Spanish Civil War (1936–1939) caused the exodus of hundreds of thousands of defeated Republicans to several countries across the globe. Mexico became the second largest host country for them.[1] Much has been said about the presence of the Spanish exiles in Mexico and scholars have pointed out how their arrival set in motion a cultural legacy without which the history of contemporary Mexico cannot be understood.[2] However, in this visual essay, I will focus on one specific locality in Mexico City, López Street (Calle de López), [3] in order to consider what an analysis from the perspective of visual culture might tell us about the Spanish in Mexico. Attentive to methodology, I will proceed step by step to show how the visual forms a substantial part of this research. What interests me is to recover the transformation of daily life in a part of Mexico City forever shaped by the arrival of the Spanish exiles.[4] My aim is to identify the social, economic and cultural changes and to recover through visuality how these dimensions materialized in the city, in its urbanization. Images take on a vital role because they contain information that does not necessarily make it into documents and allow us to rediscover the rhythm and daily practices of those who lived and walked in that space. At the same time, I will interweave historiography with visual sources, to track the traces of the historical relevance of both the Spanish exile in general and what this street meant at the time for those who lived there. This will help us to understand and analyze daily life from a micro perspective (building on individual testimonies) to a macro level (one that allows us to understand the social context). By placing visuality at the centre of my investigations – by considering photographs from family albums as well as from the press and from archives – I will be able to shed light on how visual imagery intersects in varied, complex ways with the histories of Spanish exile in Mexico.

López Street is a small street in downtown Mexico City where many families arrived, settled and left behind imprints of their presence. On this street, they not only opened shops and restaurants, they also lived and, in many ways, appropriated the space and built a community. To this day, despite the fact that the street has not been inhabited by Spaniards for several decades, the presence and memory of their exilic life still reverberates through the urban space.

Photo as a document

Nowadays, no one would dispute that photos are documents that can be read and analyzed. The photo helps us ensure that an image can be saved and that it has greater visibility and mobility. I took the photos featured in figs. 24.1 and 24.2

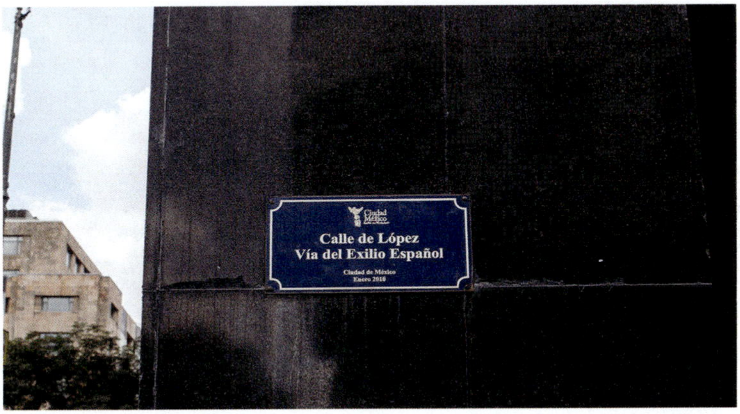

FIGURE 24.1: Lopéz Street nameplate which says "Vía del Exilio Español" (The Route of Spanish Exile) (Photo: Valeria Sánchez Michel, 2020).

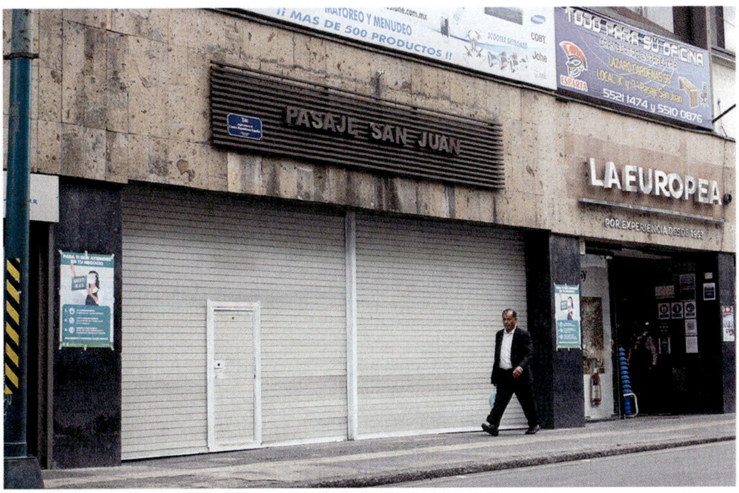

FIGURE 24.2: Pasaje San Juan, featuring a plate saying "Here was the Spanish Republican Centre" (Photo: Valeria Sánchez Michel, 2020).

as a record, to show the reader how the city has mounted plaques to indicate the history and memory of exile. It is advisable to keep an exhausting photographic record with photos (especially when working with space, as in this case) and then go back and look at the images. Thus, as I continued with my research, the "La Europea" shop in photograph number 2 acquired a different meaning thanks to the testimony of memories of the area. The liquor shop, now part of a chain that is found all over the city, was founded in 1953 by the Asturian Gumersindo Ruiz is an emblematic space that forms part of the memories of those who lived in López Street.

Mr Ruiz did not arrive with the first exiles in 1939 but in 1947. Yet, something that the written sources and testimonies highlight is that with the arrival of the Spaniards, the street began to have more cafés and businesses. The photos that I used as sources had other purposes and other uses at the time they were taken. For example, the Museo Archivo de la Fotografía (Museum Archive of Photography) keeps the photos that were taken as proof of the city's infrastructure projects. But it is by looking at them, by comparing photos from different periods, that one can see the transformation and the fact that each time there were more and more shops. Figs. 24.3 and 24.4 are useful for comparison: How has the street changed over time, which shops opened, which Spanish coffee shops are recognizable? At the time, the photos served to prove that the government was making improvements in the city, but now they allow us to look at and research these urban spaces.[5]

Analyzing the image

We live in a world surrounded by images. Often seeing them seems to be enough. However, we must not forget that images communicate information and that it might also be necessary to actively 'read' them. A first step is to describe the images, to go through them and learn to see composition, shapes, distribution of elements and details. We have to know how to interrogate the image and always keep in mind that even though it might not have been made with our research topic in mind (unlike the images I was talking about at the beginning), they are still important sources of information.

The Mexico City that welcomed Spanish Republican exiles did not have the spatial dimensions then as it has now. What we see today as downtown was practically the city itself. How do you choose the place where you come to live? Which factors influence that decision? Many Spanish migrant families came to live in López Street because they found cheap places there, or because other members of the family had

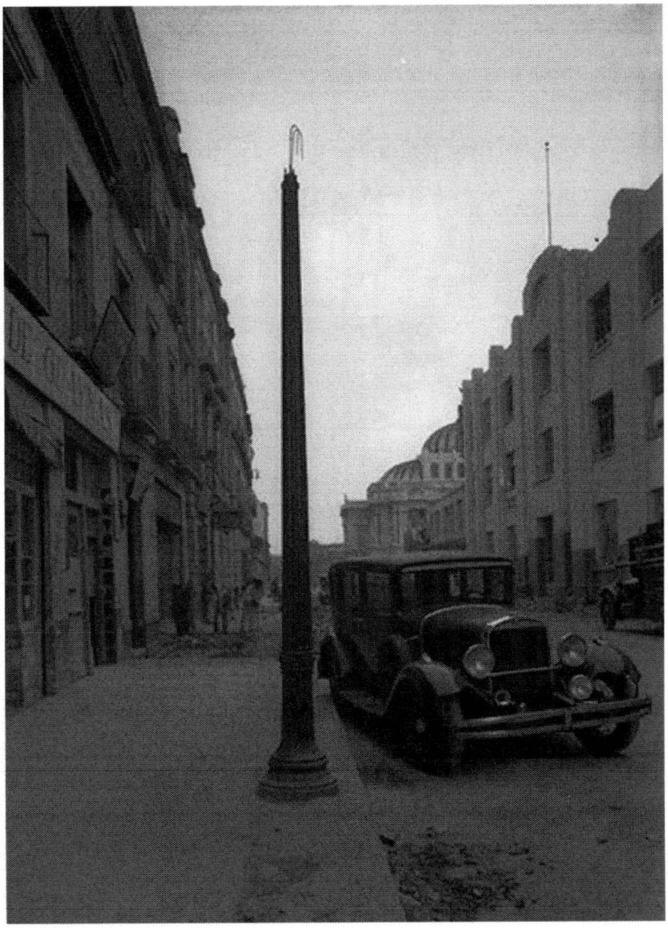

FIGURE 24.3: *Lighting up López and Independencia Street*, Mexico City, 2 February 1935 (Museum Archive of Photography, Mexico City, 001353-002).

first arrived there; little by little more exiles settled there, testifying to the importance of sociability. One seeks to live where there are others with whom you can identify. Specialist Jorge de Hoyos explains that the refugees were looking for something familiar, something that made them feel safe.[6] On López Street, there were several buildings housing exclusively exiles. This is the case for the building located at López St 82. The photograph in fig. 24.5 was taken inside the building. It is an image that makes us think of those photos taken to keep family memories alive but which, over time, become invaluable documents for retracing and salvaging the realities of past everyday life.[7]

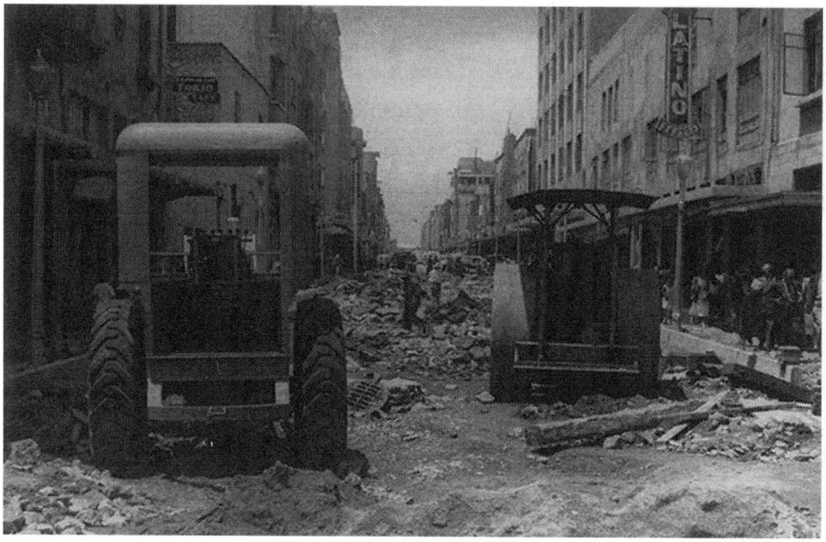

FIGURE 24.4: *Repaving López Street, Mexico City, 1950* (Museum Archive of Photography, Mexico City, 000376-002).

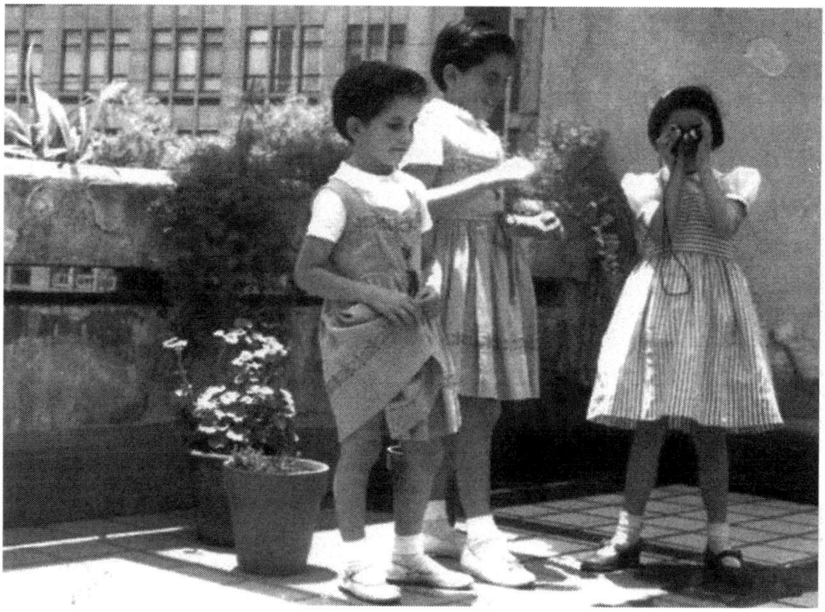

FIGURE 24.5: Family scene in López St 82, Mexico City, n.d. (Exilio Mexico, https://exiliomexico.cgeomap.eu/mapa/. Accessed 4 January 2021).

Visual culture

When we talk about visuality, we are not only referring to photos, but also to those other elements that form part of our visual experience such as cinema, press, advertising, etc. Considering this allows us to expand our sources of information. This is how, when looking through magazines, one can come across advertisements from the period which, in this case, provide us with valuable information. The photo in fig. 24.6 shows an advertisement in which a dentist who graduated from Madrid offers his services in the same building, number 2, that we have been talking about. This allows us to learn a little more about the life that must have been going on in that street, as it lets us see that there were professionals who sought to practice their occupation. López Street not only featured shops and restaurants but was also filled with people who sought to make a living by adapting their houses for that purpose.

Fig. 24.7 depicts an advertisement for Bar Manolo (Manolo bar) that covers an entire page of a magazine. Most of the advertisement consists of a photograph that shows the building in which the bar is located. The image displays the corner of a building, featuring modern architecture with a curved corner. Above the main door, you can read the name "Manolo", so it was probably the entrance to the bar. The photo allows us to see a busy corner, populated by both people and vehicles. The image transmits modernity, it lets us grasp a city in movement. The accompanying text mentions that the building is located on the

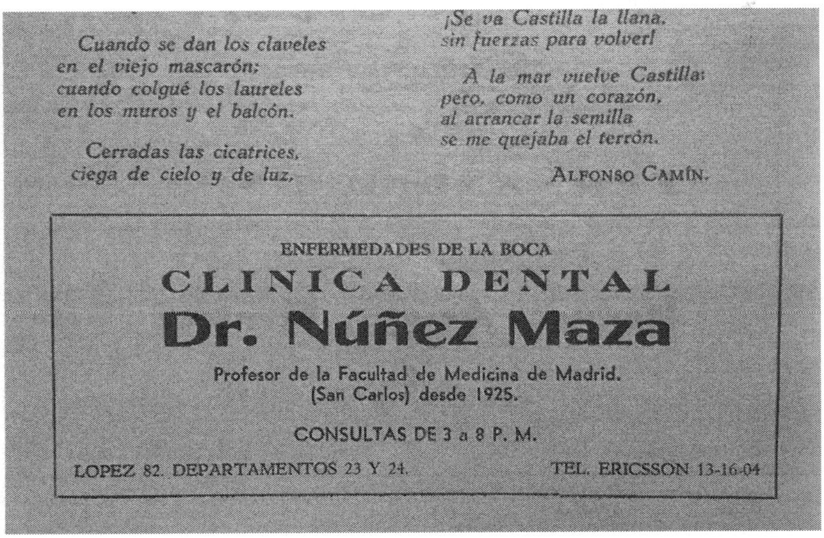
Cuando se dan los claveles
en el viejo mascarón;
cuando colgué los laureles
en los muros y el balcón.

Cerradas las cicatrices,
ciega de cielo y de luz,

¡Se va Castilla la llana,
sin fuerzas para volver!

A la mar vuelve Castilla:
pero, como un corazón,
al arrancar la semilla
se me quejaba el terrón.

ALFONSO CAMÍN.

ENFERMEDADES DE LA BOCA
CLINICA DENTAL
Dr. Núñez Maza
Profesor de la Facultad de Medicina de Madrid.
(San Carlos) desde 1925.
CONSULTAS DE 3 a 8 P. M.
LOPEZ 82. DEPARTAMENTOS 23 Y 24. TEL. ERICSSON 13-16-04

FIGURE 24.6: Commercial ads, in *Norte*, 1946, n.p. (Villasana Private Collection, Mexico City).

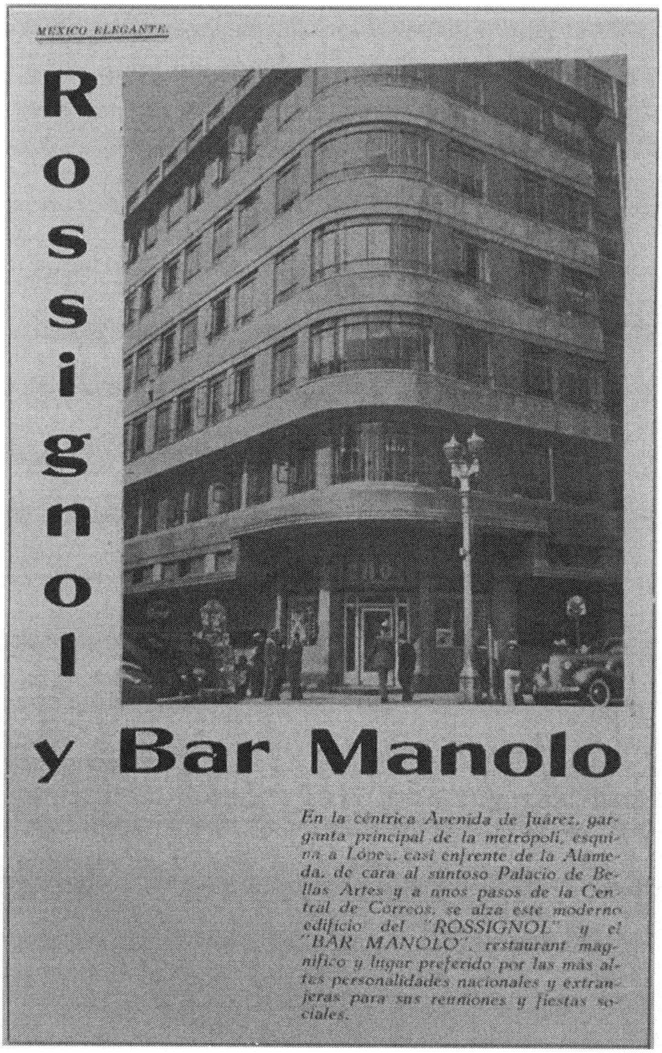

FIGURE 24.7: Commercial ads, in *Norte*, 1946, n.p. (Villasana Private Collection, Mexico City).

corner of Juarez Avenue and López Street, the 'main corridor of the metropolis'. It also describes Bar Manolo as the preferred place for the meetings of great national and foreign personalities. Text and photo highlight modernity and cosmopolitanism. From the visual clues we can see in the ad, we can go on to ask questions such as: What significance had bars such as this one at the time? How did López Street gain international status with the arrival of the Spanish exiles? How has "Manolo", the name of the bar, turned into something that, as Mexicans, we associate with Spain? How did the presence of the Spanish in Mexico's imaginary come about?

Images should not be analyzed in isolation. Historiographical research, the reading of sources and testimonies, allows us to more critically and productively interrogate visual sources. We should put them in dialog, compare them, build series and see how they complement each other. It is also necessary to cross-reference them and try to reconstruct the visual culture of the time in order to gain a deeper understanding of the subject we are studying. In doing so, our research benefits from a broader perspective in which the visual is understood as part of the world we want to analyze. At the same time, this process is also about us understanding what that image meant at the time of its creation, and understanding that there are scopic regimes regulating every-day life. The image is then no longer something that only illustrates, but something that provides information that must be carefully analyzed. The image acts as a representation that, in the words of Keith Moxey, "claims interpretations as sensitive to the effects of presence as they are to the effects of meaning" (2015, 99).

NOTES

1. To read about the Spanish Republic and its exiles in Mexico, you can consult the classic text published in 1973 *Exiles and citizens. Spanish Republicans in Mexico* de Patricia Fargen published by The University of Texas Press. A quantitative study that allows us to approach the dimension of the Spanish exile in Mexico is "Refugiados españoles en México: recuento y caracterización" (Pla Brugat, 1999).
2. Clara Lida has been reflecting on methodological issues in research on exile and migration. See Lida (1997). Dolores Pla Brugat has done seminal work on Spanish exiles and the intellectual, social and economic impact they had in Mexico. See Dolores Pla Brugat. "Un río español de sangre roja. Los refugiados republicanos en México." *Pan, trabajo y hogar. El exilio republicano español en América Latina*, coordinated by Dolores Pla Brugat, Instituto Nacional de Migración et al., 2007, pp. 35–128. Recent studies have focussed on exile and daily life, see for example Serrano Migallón 2021.
3. López Street is located in downtown Mexico City. It is made up of six blocks and joins two central avenues: Juarez Avenue and Chapultepec Avenue (both have played an important role in the urban history of the city). The street begins right in front of the Alameda Central, a public urban park in downtown Mexico City created in the 16th century and characterized by its vitality and its convergence of different social strata. When the Spanish exiles arrived, López Street was an integral part of the social and economic dynamics of the city. In the 1940s, the city issued a housing decree which fixed rents and made accommodation much cheaper (this also unfortunately caused the deterioration and abandonment of the buildings).

4. For example, the impact in intellectual and cultural terms can be found at Pérez Vejo (2017) y Yankelevich (2019).
5. For further analysis of the relationship between photography and urbanism, see: Nicholas Mirzoeff. "World Cities, City Worlds." Idem. *How to See the World: An Introduction to Images, from Self-Portraits to Selfies, Maps to Movies, and More*. Basic Books, 2016, pp. 159–208.
6. Jorge de Hoyos. Personal Interview by Valeria Sánchez Michel. 9 December 2020.
7. The analysis of the photos is further enriched when we relate them to the oral testimonies that tell us about daily life. Dolores Pla y Pilar Domínguez has bequeathed us testimonies in hers books, see Pla Brugat (2003) y Dominguez Prats (2009).

REFERENCES

Domínguez Prats, Pilar. *De ciudadanas a exiliadas: un estudio sobre las republicanas españolas en México*. Ediciones Cinca, 2009.

El exilio español en la Ciudad de México: legado cultural, exh. cat. Gobierno de la Ciudad de México / El Colegio de México, Mexico City, 2015.

Fagen, Patricia. *Exiles and Citizens: Spanish Republicans in Mexico* (Latin American Monographs, 29). Institute of Latin American Studies, University of Texas, 1973.

Lida, Clara. *Inmigración y exilio. Reflexiones sobre el caso español*. Siglo XXI Editores / El Colegio de México, 1997.

Moxey, Keith. *El tiempo de lo visual: la imagen en la historia*. Sans Soleil Ediciones, 2015.

Pérez Vejo, Tomás. "Intelectuales españoles en México: el exilio republicano desde la perspectiva de la larga duración histórica." *TSN*, vol. 2, no. 4, 2017, pp. 175–184. *Dialnet*, www.//dialnet.unirioja.es/servlet/articulo?codigo=6882129. Accessed 11 July 2021.

Pla Brugat, Dolores. "Refugiados españoles en México: recuento y caracterización." *Los refugiados españoles y la cultura mexicana: actas de las segundas jornadas, celebradas en El Colegio de México en noviembre de 1996*, El Colegio de Mexico, 1999, pp. 419–434. *JSTOR*, www.jstor.org/stable/j.ctv3dnq03.24. Accessed 11 July 2021.

Pla Brugat, Dolores. *El aroma del recuerdo: narraciones de españoles republicanos refugiados en México*. Plaza y Valdes / Instituto Nacional de Antropología e Historia, 2003.

Pla Brugat, Dolores, coordinator. *Pan, trabajo y hogar. El exilio republicano español en América Latina* (Colección Migración). Instituto Nacional de Migración et al., 2007.

Serrano Migallón, Fernando. *El exilio español y su vida cotidiana en México* (Pública histórica, 20). Bonilla Artigas Editores, 2021.

Yankelevich, Pablo. "Waves of Exile: The Reception of Émigrés in Mexico, 1920–1980." *European and Latin American Social Scientists as Refugees, Émigrés and Return-Migrants*, edited by Ludger Pries and Pablo Yankelevich, Palgrave Macmillan, Cham, 2019, pp. 151–179.

25

Reinhabiting the City as an Artistic Open Space: Urban Imprints of Exile Artists in Buenos Aires and Marseille in the 20th Century

Laura Karp Lugo and Marine Schütz

History and the uses of space

In 1935, the German artist Clément Moreau sailed from the port of Marseille to Buenos Aires. He had acquired a passport with the help of his future wife, Nelly Guggenbühl, whom he met at the Z-Haus in Zurich where he was hosted as an emigrant. Because of his political activism, he had to change his name, originally Carl Meffert, but retained the same initials with which he already signed his work (*Clément Moreau* 1994). As becomes clear when looking at figures such as Clément Moreau, the place-makings of exiled artists are multiple and make up a geography of "polycentric modern" art (Joyeux-Prunel 2018). The collaborative research presented in this chapter focuses on two different contexts inscribed into Moreau's exile journey – Buenos Aires and Marseille. These two cities are informed by the logics of circulation and forced mobility. While both were sites of great vitality due to the many creative endeavours of the exiled artists residing there, they were also port cities and as such have historically been places of departure and arrival. Port cities relate to space in very specific ways: their coastal location contributed to their importance for industry and trade, which in turn deeply affected the production of an urban space aimed at improving the speed of production (Hein 2011). The issues of speed and movement in port cities can also be connected to the many trauma-related displacements of the 20th century, caused for example by the rise of National socialism or by various postcolonial decolonization movements.

This chapter compares different imprints left by artists in urban space. As French historian Paul Veyne reminds us, the comparison is an "operator of individualization", aiming not to confuse historical situations, but enabling us to differentiate between them (Veyne 1976). It therefore directly engages with one of the central questions of historical research: the relationship between intellectual/artistic life and migration in mid-century societies. Throughout this chapter, we are applying the methodological frameworks of spatial history as they are uniquely positioned to mine and activate issues of artistic agency in and through cities. Refusing to posit space as a universal category, historians engaged in spatial methods promote a conception of space as contingent on political and economic conditions. This dimension is exemplified for instance by Lefebvre's famous dictum, "(social) space is a (social) product" (Lefebvre 1974). Born in the wake of the 1970s alongside developments in cultural history, the spatial turn in history offers a way to understand the past: it allows us to grasp the ways in which both built environment and mapping strategies serve as a context within which a range of political entities, from the body to the neighbourhood, can be reconsidered vis-à-vis a historical methodology.

This chapter casts new light on the relationship between exile, city and artistic creativity by mingling two spatial scales: in order to discern the cultures and mentalities of exile, we consider both material and imaginary spaces. A spatial method applied to the study of how art is created within the context of exile reveals itself to be particularly promising for overcoming the difficulty of locating artistic expression of/in exile, which can be difficult to grasp in its material forms (i.e. painting, photography, etc.). While they may be considered oppositional to the project of historiographical spatial history, material sites in cities and the imaginary projections attached to them can address one of the most important problems of historical research in art history, especially when it deals with exilic artistic production in the 20th century: that of sources.

These remarks intend to settle broader methodological and intellectual implications for historical research by facing the lack of archival traces of exile; these are implications that also resonate beyond the contexts of Buenos Aires and Marseille of course. One of the questions we need to ask is how we can preserve and understand the artistic expressions of émigrés today, especially considering their ever-changing status as citizens of different countries, so that our analytical and interpretive lens shifts from the material realm of artistic production to also include these artists' intellectual lives and communities. To address art in/off exile then also means to address a series of shifts: first, a shift in focus from the careers of individual artists to more collective artistic practices that emerge from migratory uprootings and re-routings. This is a question of mapping the global networks into which the local productions of artists are embedded, and the broader political contexts that lead artists to be exiled. Second, a shift concerning the scale of research: this means looking for archives rather than for single works, though the lack of material traces of art in exile does not mean that artistic life did not occur. A spatial methodology that focusses on both geographical sites and imaginary spaces allows us to overcome the paradox of exilic artistic production which leave sometimes ephemeral material traces that may be difficult to grasp today.

As Paul Stock posits, spatial methods can reveal issues that render the boundaries between material and representation more porous. Such methods allow us to address the relation between material environment and intellectual life (Stock 2015, 2). As such, this chapter draws on a historical approach that further develops the study of material space: buildings, hotels, cafés and publishing houses are considered as some of the most important 20th-century sites where intellectual life flourished – this allows us to analyze major artist networks and even some of the artworks that have survived from that time.

By drawing on different archives, we document domestic spaces (flats, studios) and public spaces (districts, hotels, streets, bars) that have been integral to both exilic artistic and social practices and exilic networks and interactions between émigrés. We also mine artworks and correspondences to delineate the importance of exiled artists of the cities they had to leave behind. A focus on spatiality thus allows us to foreground issues of representation, visualization and images, and to reconstruct visual processes even if usual sites of visual expression – the artistic work – remain largely inaccessible. This chapter constitutes a visual enquiry into the exilic city, supplementing a traditional art historian approach with cultural history as influenced by the spatial turn.

Indeed, the objects as well as the social relations produced in exile in the first half of the 20th century convoke material and methodological realities inscribed in profoundly spatial logics. Migration, poverty and untenable living conditions deeply affected artists, thereby bringing into light the fluctuation and uncertainties of artistic creation within exile, from its material forms to the sites where artists used to dwell and gather (café, hotels, etc.). Whether they concern the physical belongings of artists in the city or relate to purely imagined projections, the different forms of urban relations brought into play by exile seem to come under what Irit Rogoff has called a "general crisis of the capacity to represent any form of stable geographical knowledge as an orientation asset concerning identity" (2013, 3). Therefore, when art history rests on the assumption that geography is fixed, stable and determines identity, how can we apprehend exile when exile in and of itself denounces the principles on which art historical analysis is founded?

Adopting a method that reflects on the way in which exile links to the disruption of spatial knowledge can help to get around this very problem. This "emergent rhetoric of reterritorialized subject" (ibid.) that accompanies exile can be addressed by using approaches that (1) recognize that space is not an abstract category and (2) think about space beyond pre-existing conceptions which usually priorities hierarchies between centre and periphery and tend to nationalize artistic narratives. Finally, it is from the methodological perspective of decentering modernist narratives about art and places that this chapter wishes to make sense of the particularities that compose urban artistic traces in the two cities of Marseille and Buenos Aires. As they are based on conceptions of space as constructed, postcolonial studies prove to be a helpful tool to consider the spatial journeys of artists in unfamiliar places. Studying exile through a postcolonial lens forces us to reconsider traditional frameworks of cultural identity and to rework our relations to spatially-infused concepts such as cultural identity. Considering the latter, Edward Said explains for instance that exile means "acting as if one were at home where one happens to be" (2002, 55). In order to interrogate this argument, our study of exile urban traces, focused in particular on specific neighbourhoods, wishes to challenge methods of art history that hold on to ossified, old-fashioned understandings of space, art and materiality.

Marseille and Buenos Aires as exile metropolises

While Marseille was a city that for a long time relied on the mythic narrative of its foundation by "Others" (Péraldi/Samson 2006), this image was finally realized by early 20th-century economic migrations from Italy, Spain and Maghreb. During the Second World War, Marseille became a city of foreign refugees stranded in the southern zone. It was here, the only large French port still open after the defeat of 1940, where refugees were waiting for visas. After May and June 1940, the huge exodus was to push the banks of the Mediterranean a panic-stricken population who put under pressure Marseille's reputation as "welcoming city" (Hewitt 2019, 9). Marseille was the only possible place of departure to the arrival cities such as Buenos Aires for the Anti-Nazi Germans, foreigners, Jews, and subversive artists who hoped to leave a country where they were now undesirable (Yagil 2015). André Breton, his wife Jacqueline Lamba, Victor Serge, Óscar Domínguez, Victor Brauner, Wifredo Lam, Marcel Duchamp, André Masson, Jean Arp, Jacques Hérold, Hans Bellmer and Benjamin Perret were among the Surrealists established in Marseille (Bertrand Dorléac 1993; Guiraud 1999). Marseille was only one step on the path that led artists beyond metropolitan France towards the United States, Latin America, the Caribbean or North Africa. Some artists, however, stayed long enough to leave behind their exile imprints. It was in the district of Vieux-Port that many of these traces of mass migration and mass arrival can still be seen today. In Marseille, a city that had been largely provincial and focussed on regional themes (Guiraud 1999), the newly emerging modernist artistic geography marked one of the first and most visible effects of exile. Many surrealists had come to the region – some to flee the occupied zone, others waiting for a visa.[1] And while their artistic activities mainly focussed on the district of the Vieux-Port, this community of 'permanent travellers' soon infused the whole city, forever changing its socio-cultural structures.

On the other side of the globe, Buenos Aires can be regarded as Marseille's mirror: instead of hosting those who wanted to leave, it welcomed those who had come to stay. With a three centuries-long colonial history, the city was permeable to foreigners, be they exiles or migrants. Buenos Aires had been founded in 1580 and became the capital of the Virreinato del Río de la Plata in 1776.[2] Since then, it became a land of promises for generations and generations of Europeans, most of whom were Spanish at the time. The successive independence that Latin America has experienced since the beginning of the 19th century did not break this migratory inertia (Devoto 2003). Buenos Aires, and more generally Argentina, had a great reserve of natural resources and vast lands to attract Europeans in search of prosperity and fortune. Between 1878 and 1885, the military campaign that stripped the local populations of their land and their freedom left available land to be settled and worked. With the arrival of the new century, European migrations into the country intensified, also spurred by the improvement of the steam engine which allowed for faster transatlantic ship travel the 1860s on.[3] President Nicolás Avellaneda's law[4] in 1876 also fostered travel and settlement. Since then, and about roughly until the 1950s, Buenos Aires acted as an important arrival port for passengers from European ports, with a peak of foreign population in 1914 (Comisión Nacional del Censo/Martínez 1916, 203f.). During the 1930s and 1940s, due to the persecutions in Franco's Spain and Nazi Germany, the metropolis cemented its quality as a cosmopolitan city in which multiple customs and traditions coexisted and nourished each other.

Being and place-making in Buenos Aires and Marseille

Place-making in Buenos Aires and Marseille is closely linked to the artists who settled in these metropolises of exile. Whether exiles, expatriates, refugees or nomads, for those who experience distance from their homes and from their native languages, place- and home-making prove to be the most important aspect of migration (Suleiman 2012). Marseille's city centre became much more cosmopolitan, a fact which disrupted already-existing racial and social lines reflected in the city's geographical makeup. While many of the exile artists eventually found accommodation in Villa Air-Bel and Montredon, they initially stayed in cheap hotels beside Hotel Splendide near the Gare Saint-Charles (like Victor Serge and his wife and son, André Breton or Varian Fry) where they encountered areas which were predominantly Mediterranean and working-class (Dell'Umbria 2006; Breton/Maestraggi 2016). Jacques Hérold for example stayed in the Algerian district behind the Cours Belsunce and recalls: "My district in Marseilles was the rue Sainte-Barbe, the rue des Chapeliers [...] At night the corridor of the house where I lived was invaded by Arabs who slept there" (Hérold, qtd. in *La Planète affolée* 1986, 54). While the city centre was already inhabited by Algerian colonial workers, the additional settlement of exilic artists there upset traditional spatial orders (which allocated certain ethnic groups to certain spaces) and social borders.

As Surrealist artists migrated, they also brought their artistic activities and modalities to Marseille, enlivening the local coffee house culture which was usually found much more frequently in Europe's capitals. While cafés had been a space that served to ward off conservative forces since at least the 19th century, the new cultural geography developed in Marseille flourished in artistic innovation and frenzy. Surrealists gathered in the cafés of the Vieux-Port's like the Brûleurs de loups or Mont-Ventoux (*Le Jeu de Marseille* 2003), which were sites that both showcased avant-garde artistic expression and provided the concrete possibility of obtaining resources to survive exile and leave Marseille (Guillon 1999). There, exiles swapped stories and rumours of ship departures and plotted how to amass the tickets and the bewildering numbers of visas. As Anna Seghers writes in her novel *Transit:* "I even heard that there was mention of a certain boat to Oran. While next door, at Mont-Ventoux, the regulars would detail all the circumstances of a crossing, here people would discuss all the problems of a copper shipment" (Seghers 1995, 156).

Some 11,000 kilometres away, Buenos Aires had been a refuge not only for people fleeing Spanish fascism and German National-Socialism but also for communities from other European countries. The arrival of people from so many different contexts generated structural needs in a city open to urban transformations and to the development of new creative, collaborative networks. Buenos Aires thus saw the emergence of many different groups, communities and centres, some of which were motivated by common origin and language – the Circulo Italiano (Libertad Street 1264), the Centro Gallego (Belgrano Street 2199) and the Casal de Catalunya (Chacabuco Street 863), among others –, while others built on shared professional interests, such as the Agrupación de Intelectuales, Artistas, Periodistas y Escritores[5] (Belgrano Street 1732, meeting place; Perú Street 190, exhibition venue) and the Asociación Amigos del Arte[6] (Florida Street 950 and 659).[7]

As was the case with Marseille, the exiles' everyday habits were immediately transplanted and transfused into Buenos Aires' city life. In Argentina these early 1920s migratory waves were neither the first nor the only ones, although they were certainly among the most important. Buenos Aires' large scale offered many opportunities to settle and build a new life. The foreigners did not all stay in the same district, although many remained in the city centre and the neighbourhoods closest to the Río de la Plata, which opens onto the Atlantic Ocean and where the ships from Europe arrived. The city's main axis then was the famous Florida Street, still well-known today. Both foreign and local artists gravitated around it, attracted by the shops and galleries, many of them opened by first- or second-generation European exiles (Karp Lugo 2020, 35–38).

Gaining intimate knowledge about these local sites allows us to enter the daily lives of exiled artists, about whom historical sources are otherwise scarce. By tracking the streets and addresses where the artists socialized and created networks we can also re-trace the artistic trajectories of the European artists in exile in Buenos Aires. Of course, this strategy can also be extended to other communities and other geographies. In a previous article, we argued for Florida Street as the nodal centre of socialization in the artistic and cultural field of Buenos Aires (Karp Lugo 2020): galleries, bookshops, artistic and general shops and publishing houses lined the street every few metres, sometimes next to one another, facilitated artistic an economic circulation and dissemination. And when some of these places still exist today, as is the case with some of them, a stroll through the city is enough to grasp how close these places were to one another and how easy intellectual exchange must have been.[8] When they no longer exist, sources allow us to fill in the gaps. However, the sources in studies of exiled subjects are often deficient and fragmented. In our case, one of the most important sources are period guides as they provide the addresses of shops, doctors and artists. In this sense, guides such as the *Gran guía de la Ciudad de Buenos Aires*, edited by Edelmiro Mayer and published by Hugo Kunz & Cie from 1886 as well as the multiple editions of *Anuario Kraft* (Costa 2012) since 1885 are a valuable source for understanding the urban fabric of exiled artists' topographies. So are correspondences and business cards. The archive of French artist Henri Stein, first illustrator for and then editor and owner of the satirical newspaper *El Mosquito*, shows the wealth of resources that the careful preservation of business cards means for the researcher.[9] Addresses guides as much as business cards are valuable sources for exile/art historical research.

Thus, a topographical approach and a knowledge of the places that operated at the time provide interesting and rich alternatives to fill the gap left behind by fragmented sources. Having arrived in Buenos Aires in 1934, the Austrian artist Gertrudis Chale settled in the suburb of Quilmes, a neighbourhood in the south of the city, and quickly integrated into the metropolis' artistic and intellectual milieu, joining a group of artists and intellectuals made up of both Europeans and Argentinians. But why Quilmes, a neighbourhood that was twenty kilometres away from the city centre? An analysis of the existing historical structures in the city can help us to answer this question. Indeed, when Chale arrived in Quilmes, there was an important German community that had developed around the Cerveceria Quilmes (the Quilmes brewery), founded by German immigrant Otto Bemberg in 1888 (12 de Octubre Avenue y Gran Canaria Street, Quilmes). Very soon, facilities were developed to make daily life easier for the workers of the successful brewery, including a sports centre and a health service. Nearby, the German club of Quilmes (former Asociación alemana de cultura física de Quilmes – German Association of Physical Culture of Quilmes) was founded in 1923 (Hipólito Yrigoyen Street 1400, Quilmes). Many German-speaking immigrants (Germans, Austrians and Swiss) settled in Quilmes, attracted by the job opportunities offered by the Quilmes Brewery. There was also the Holmberg Deutsche Schule, known as the German School, which had opened in 1898 (Sarmiento 679, Quilmes). Undoubtedly, the German-speaking environment had attracted German, Swiss and Austrian exiles to the city of Quilmes, including Gertrudis Chale.

Artistic and literary presses as a nexus for exile networks

Magazines played a major role in the integration and gatherings of exile artists in both Buenos Aires and Marseille. The way exiled artists brought changes to the urban geographies of Marseille was also reflected in the transformation of cultural spheres, such as journalism, literature and publishing houses. The journal *Les Cahiers du Sud* helped make Marseille into a habitable, liveable place of possibility and futurity for refugees who could not imagine ever returning to their home countries. The journal was created by Jean Ballard whose offices were located in Quai du Canal and acted as an important *centre d'accueil*, sometimes even offering a physical place of asylum by accommodating intellectual refugees and artists who fled from the German invasion and the Vichy regime (Guiraud 1999; Hewitt 2019). While the journal functioned as a conceptual hub of connection, networking and solidarity in text form for a community of exiles, its offices in the city served as a concrete, material safe harbour for political refugees. As Nicholas Hewitt posits, under Ballard's leadership, *Les Cahiers du Sud* was committed "to a pan-European and pan-Mediterranean liberal humanism, a staunch supporter of the Front Populaire, the Spanish Republicans, Italian anti-fascists, and the opponents of Nazism it had given space to dissident writers throughout the 1930s" (2019, 76). Thus, from 1933, *Les Cahiers du Sud* became a shelter for exiled German writers and intellectuals, like Ernst Erich Noth, who was a regular member of the editorial team from 1935 onwards, and after the declaration of war for refugees such as Ernst Toler and Walter Benjamin (Breton/Maestraggi 2016; Hewitt 2019). The journal's hub-like character was sustained and underlined by Ballard's conception of the city as relating to long-distance geographical scales and scopes: and the journal was positioned within this global nexus. Opposed to provincialism, Ballard conceived the Vieux-Port as belonging to the Mediterranean, to trade networks and to travellers – and so did the journal. This sense of place directly contributed to the anchoring of his ideal of fraternity. As he wrote in 1927: "*Les Cahiers* is not the regional review of Provence. It is the review of Marseilles and it lives at the same rhythm as the city" (Hewitt 2019, 145). Ballard's publishing activities fostered a number of other charity organizations and aid platforms operating in Marseille from 1940 to 1942, most with religious affiliations. The most well-known among them is undoubtedly the American Emerging rescue committee established in 1938 by Thomas Mann, supported by Eleanor Roosevelt, and directed by the journalist Varian Fry from 1939 onwards.[10]

Published at about the same time as *Les Cahiers du Sud*, the magazine *Sur* similarly became a shelter for exiled German writers and intellectuals in Buenos Aires. The Argentine writer and intellectual Victoria Ocampo founded this literary magazine and the publishing house of the same name in 1931; both were aligned with the anti-fascist cause and should become a major hub for intellectual exchanges in Buenos Aires for the next two decades.[11] The close ties that Victoria Ocampo had with José Ortega y Gasset, a Spanish philosopher and writer, were decisive for the magazine's identity. Ortega y Gasset had first travelled to Argentina in 1916 to give a series of lectures. Very soon after his arrival, he met Ocampo, with whom he would maintain a lasting friendship. When Ocampo told Ortega y Gasset about her publication project, he was in Spain running the journal *Revista de Occidente*, which he had founded in 1923. The idea for the name for Ocampo's magazine arose out of their close friendship and the spirit of creative collaboration: "It was chosen over the phone, across the Ocean. It seems that the whole Atlantic was needed for this baptism" (Ocampo 1931, 14). *Sur* was published approximately every three months from January 1931 to July 1934. Monthly issues followed from July 1935 to January 1951.[12] Ocampo not only edited the magazine *Sur* but also founded a publishing house under the same name which, without a doubt, contributed to the dissemination of literary culture in Argentina. A large network of artists and writes surrounded her, including the exiles Gertrudis Chale, Grete Stern and Gisèle Freund.

Depicting the exilic city

While cafés constituted a landscape of refuge, the decoration of Marseille's Eden Bar by the exiled artists Zelman Otchakovsky and Bernard Zehrfuss allows us to highlight how the city was materially reshaped by a new and collective international artistic geography. Together with Alexey Brodovitch, Zehrfuss was the creator, after the armistice, of Le Groupe d'Oppède, a small group of students of architecture and painting from the Beaux-Arts, based in the oil mill buildings of the old village of Oppède of Provence located 88 kilometres from Marseille. The group organized a network of resistance while continuing to work on concrete architectural projects.[13]

In 1941, the architect Louis Olmeta commissioned Bernard Zehrfuss to decorate the Eden Bar, located at 2, rue Corneille, a street behind the Vieux-Port. He called upon several artists who were members of the Oppède group, such as Zelman Otchakovsky (who emigrated from Bessarabia to Paris in 1935) or Jacques Hérold and François Stahly (born in Germany, who emigrated to Paris in 1931). The decorations, now destroyed, were composed of heterogeneous parts forming an environment with a marine theme, at the heart of which was a monumental wooden mermaid sculpture by François Stahly featuring, in the upper part, "a sort of vault with dolphins" (Dubbeld 2010). This decoration was directly connected to the migratory experience of the artists. Evoking and echoing their coastal environments, these artworks trace the artists' mental and experiential maps, and the spatial political contexts they were surrounded by: tracing such processes allows us to understand the production of spatial imaginings within these cities of exile (Gilbert 2002). While possibly evoking longstanding ways to represent Marseille through maritime themes, the ocean (and its representations) gained new significance as a space of transit and travel inextricably linked to exilic identity. On their journeys towards the Americas, the Caribbean or North Africa, for exiled artists Marseille was only a transitory stop along the way. The surrealists for example explored the connective nature of this coastal space in graphic works in which they imagined Marseille as a physical door opening towards a journey or an imaginary landscape of exile, a site of anguish. In 1941, when exiled in Marseille, André Masson produced *La ville crânienne,* a drawing of the Vieux-Port which can be conceived of as a document of the exilic condition. Visualizing the local environment vis-à-vis his fear of death, he drew a ship and a seagull whose lines reconstruct a skull. While such figurative approaches encapsulate the city as a site of travelling connections and transit, global port cities also concretely materialize the 'urban imprints' of exile.

While Marseille is well known as a city that temporarily hosted a large part of the global intelligentsia, in Buenos Aires European artists and intellectuals arrived fleeing from war and dictatorial regimes and in most cases established themselves there permanently. They created new networks while also investing in already existing local networks; they portrayed the city and its surroundings. An analysis of such exilic artistic production reveals a deep fascination with the city and its urban fabric. The French painter Léonie Matthis, who had arrived in Argentina in 1912, worked on emblematic places in the city centre, contributing to shaping the historical imaginary of the city on the basis of events in Argentine history. She was interested in representative urban spaces such as the Plaza de Mayo, whose visual history she reconstructed from colonial to contemporary times.[14] The photographers Leonor Martínez Baroja and Grete Stern, Spanish and German respectively, depicted the everyday life of streets, wall posters and terraces. Stern left behind photographs of key buildings in the city of Buenos Aires, including the obelisk (fig. 25.1) and other main buildings in the city, such as the Edificio Kavanagh (fig. 25.2). The Argentine photographer Horacio Coppola, Grete's partner, left remarkable aerial views that show a particular interest in the river (where ships arrived from Marseille and other European ports), the Hotel of Immigrants built on its borders, the views of the city taken from the point of view of the passenger landing and aerial views where the city's grid pattern stands out. A similar interest in the city, but from a different perspective, led Gertrudis Chale to focus on representing the edges and limits of the city (fig. 25.3). Her exilic experiences motivated an interest in borders, belonging and displacement which infuse her creative endeavours (Karp Lugo et al. 2020). Her paintings and drawings explored the suburbs as a liminal space between two worlds: urbanity and nature. For Chale, Quilmes represented this ambiguous in-between space.

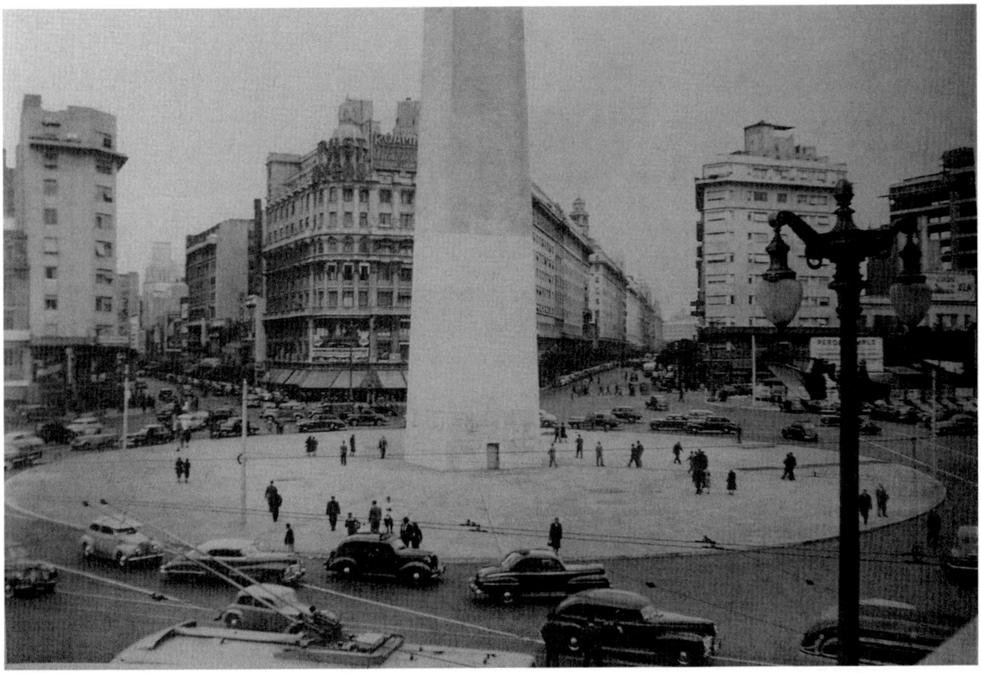

FIGURE 25.1: Grete Stern, *Obelisk*, Buenos Aires, 1951/1952 (Príamo 1995, 80).

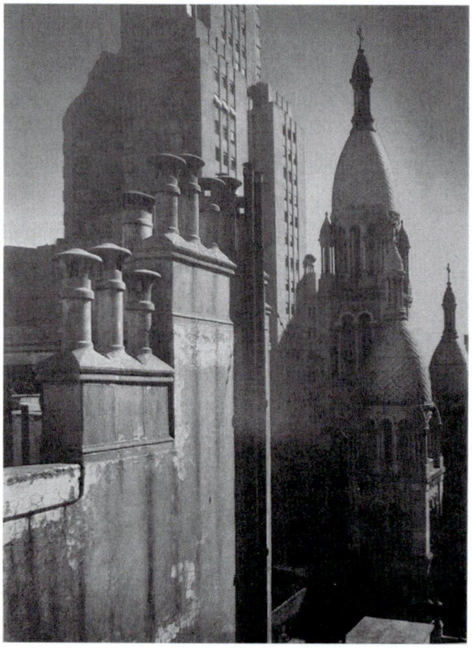

FIGURE 25.2: Grete Stern, *Holy Sacrament Church and Kavanagh Building*, Buenos Aires, 1951/52 (Príamo 1995, 80).

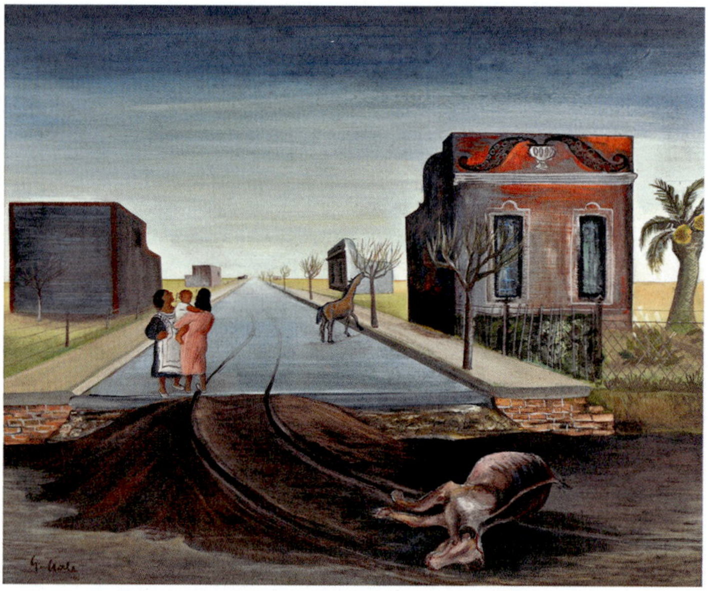

FIGURE 25.3: Gertrudis Chale, *Bocacalle de Sarandí*, 1940, tempera, 62 × 74.5 cm (© Museo Nacional de Bellas Artes, Buenos Aires).

Concluding remarks and open perspectives

This chapter played out as a game of mirrors between two port cities which, although distant, have a point in common in terms of the history of migration and exile. Marseille was, like Buenos Aires, a space of refuge for people fleeing the political regimes of their home countries. Entire neighbourhoods grew around this reality, this presence of foreigners. In the first half of the 20th century, Marseille hosted these exiles and gave them the opportunity to develop their networks and activities around the Vieux-Port, a geographical location which stood for the longing to board ships, to leave for less challenging living conditions or less dangerous regions (than Spain under Franco or Nazi Germany) where it was possible to continue their lives. As Anna Seghers has argued, the city forever remained linked to unresolved futures as exiles struggled to receive visas or obtain the permission to leave Europe (Seghers 1995). On the other side of the Atlantic, metropolises like Buenos Aires regularly welcomed ships loaded with passengers that Marseille and other European ports sent out to sea. While both were port cities, Marseille was one of the main cities of departure and Buenos Aires a major arrival city. Although the centre of Buenos Aires is located close to the port (thus giving the name "Porteños" to the inhabitants of the city) and even though the riverfront was a great source of inspiration for the artists (especially for photography), the new arrivals did not necessarily settle in the port area. The fact that many of the migrants who arrived in Buenos Aires were there to stay for good motivated them to settle in different parts of the gigantic metropolis, looking for more affordable areas or joining other exile communities from the same home country. This was the case for Quilmes which, as we have shown, had a substantial ties to the German-speaking community in Argentine.

Although this chapter focused on artists and cultural agents, its reflections on exile go beyond the discipline of art history insofar as our approaches and methods can be mobilized for the research of exile studies in general. When it comes to exiles, the sources scholarship depends upon – such as historical documents, letters, photographs, personal writings, etc. – remain particularly fragmentary, sometimes even wholly untraceable. There are many reasons for the dispersal or disappearance of such sources: quick and sometimes unexpected departures, the need to reduce luggage for the crossing, multiple changes of residence before finding a permanent accommodation. When the exiles had just arrived, they often did not know the city or did not have sufficient resources to choose a suitable place. It is exactly this moment in the lives of artists – when they arrive, when they leave, when they look for a network which they might fit into – which offers a rich source for understanding individual artists' strategies of enduring, even flourishing, in new environments. If personal sources are not preserved, an important part of the research is compromised. When these artists manage to settle down permanently and comfortably, the role of migrant/local networks tends to diminish. Although personal sources are usually best preserved at this stage of the exiles' lives, they are often of a different nature and do not reflect the key issues of the arrival and integration period. Faced with this paradox, this chapter, by reading the city as source for research on exile and art, has sought to propose a possible methodological approach to fill in as many gaps as possible left by incomplete or missing sources. Starting with addresses, maps and places, it is possible to follow the trail of artists in urban space: the encounters, the places they frequented, the neighbourhoods that were familiar to them and that marked their daily lives as much as their production.

NOTES

1. For accounts on Varian Fry's role in the process of helping exiles, see Fry (2008).
2. For a more extensive study of Argentine's history, see Fradkin/Garavaglia (2009), Yankelevich (2014).
3. See Thurston (2015).
4. "Ley de inmigración y colonización, n. 817" (Avellaneda law), article 12c, chapter V, enacted on 19 October 1867.
5. Agrupación de Intelectuales, Artistas, Periodistas y Escritores – AIAPE (Association of Intellectuals, Artists, Journalists and Writers).
6. Asociación Amigos del Arte – AAA (Friends of the Arts Association).
7. See the Buenos Aires Archive on METROMOD's website www.//metromod.net/.
8. See the Buenos Aires Walk on METROMOD's website www.//metromod.net/.
9. Fondo Enrique (Henri) Stein (Archivo General de la Nación, Buenos Aires).
10. Varian Fry is credited with saving between 2,000 and 4,000 anti-Nazi and Jewish refugees. Unlike other organizations, it focused predominantly on artists and intellectuals. For accounts on the Emergency Rescue committee, see Guillon 1999.
11. For a more extensive study of *Sur*, see King (1989), Pasternac (2002), Gramuglio (2010).
12. From then until 1970, the magazine was published every two months. In the last period, until 1980, special issues were published irregularly.
13. See Desmoulins (2008), Dubbeld (2010).
14. Her work can be seen in the Museo histórico de Buenos Aires Cornelio de Saavedra (Buenos Aires). See also Gutiérrez Zaldívar (1992).

REFERENCES

Art of Two Germanys: Cold War Cultures, edited by Stephanie Barron and Sabine Eckmann, exh. cat. Los Angeles County Museum of Art, Los Angeles, 2009.

Bertrand Dorléac, Laurence. *L'Art de la défaite : 1940–1944*. Seuil, 1993.

Breton, Christine, and Sylvain Maestraggi. *Mais de quoi ont-ils eu si peur?: Walter Benjamin, Ernst Bloch et Siegfried Kracauer à Marseille le 8 septembre 1926*. Éditions Commune, 2016.

Clément Moreau: con el lápiz contra el fascismo, edited by Beate Luca Engelbert et al., exh. cat. Instituto Goethe, Buenos Aires, 1994.

Comisión Nacional del Censo and Alberto B. Martínez, editors. *Tercer censo nacional levantado el 1 de junio de 1914: Ordenado por la ley 9108*. Talleres gráficos de L.J. Rosso y Cía, 1916.

Costa, María Eugenia. *Tradición e innovación en el programa gráfico de la editorial Guillermo Kraft: Colecciones de libros ilustrados (1940–59)*. Universidad Nacional de La Plata. Facultad de Humanidades y Ciencias de la Educación. Instituto de Investigaciones en Humanidades y Ciencias Sociales (UNLP-CONICET), 2012. *Memoria Académica*, www.memoria.fahce.unlp.edu.ar/trab_eventos/ev.1927/ev.1927.pdf. Accessed 15 March 2021.

Dell'Umbria, Alèssi. *Histoire universelle de Marseille. De l'an mil à l'an deux mille*. Agone, 2006.

Desmoulins, Christine. *Bernard Zehrfuss (Carnets d'architectes*, 2). Infolio, 2008.

Devoto, Fernando. *Historia de la Inmigración en la Argentina*. Editorial Sudamericana, 2003.

Dubbeld, Sabrina. "L'Eden Bar de Marseille ou la vie difficile d'artistes exilés en Provence sous l'Occupation." *Provence historique*, vol. 242, 2010, pp. 471–489.

Fradkin, Raúl, and Juan Carlos Garavaglia. *La Argentina colonial. El Río de la Plata entre los siglos XVI y XIX*. Siglo veintiuno editores, 2009.

Fry, Varian, *Livrer sur demande : quand les artistes, les dissidents et les Juifs fuyaient les Nazis (Marseille, 1940–1941)*. Translated by Edith Ochs, Agone, 2008.

Gilbert, Pamela K., editor. *Imagined Londons*. State University of New York Press, 2002.

Gramuglio, María Teresa. "*Sur*, una minoría cosmopolita en la periferia occidental." *Historia de los intelectuales en América Latina. II. Los avatares de la "ciudad letrada" en el siglo XX*, edited by Carlos Altamirano, Katz, 2010, pp. 192–210.

Guillon, Jean-Marie, editor. *Varian Fry : du refuge à l'exil*. Actes Sud, 1999.

Guiraud, Jean-Michel. *La Vie intellectuelle et artistique à Marseille à l'époque de Vichy et sous l'occupation, 1940–1944*. Jeanne Laffitte, 1999.

Gutiérrez Zaldívar, Ignacio. *Léonie Matthis*. Zurbarán, 1992.

Hein, Carola. *Port Cities, Dynamic Landscapes and Global Networks*. Routledge, 2011.

Hewitt, Nicholas. *Wicked City: The Many Cultures of Marseille*. Hurst & Company, 2019.

Joyeux-Prunel, Béatrice. "Jeux d'échelles (2) : histoire transnationale, histoire mondiale, transferts et jeux de miroirs." *Cahiers Jaurès*, vol. 229, no. 3, 2018, pp. 185–204.

Karp Lugo, Laura, et al. "Lebensrouten der Emigration. Abreise, Passage, (Zwischen-)Exil und Ankunft." *Leave, left, left. Migrationsphänomene in den Künsten in aktueller und historischer Perspektive*, edited by Burcu Dogramaci et al., Neofelis Verlag, 2020, pp. 105–126.

Karp Lugo, Laura. "Alone Together: Exile Sociability and Artistic Networks in Buenos Aires at the Beginning of the 20th Century." *Arrival Cities. Migrating Artists and New Metropolitan Topographies in the 20th Century*, edited by Burcu Dogramaci et al., Leuven University Press, 2020, pp. 33–54. *Open Access*, www.//library.oapen.org/handle/20.500.12657/41641. Accessed 17 July 2021.

King, John. *Sur: estudio de la revista argentina y de su papel en el desarrollo de una cultura 1931–1970*. Translated by Juan José Utrilla, Fondo de Cultura Económica, 1989.

La Planète affolée : surréalisme, dispersion et influences, 1938–1947, edited by Direction des Musées de Marseille, exh. cat. Centre de la Vieille charité, Marseille, 1986.

Le Jeu de Marseille autour d'André Breton et des surréalistes à Marseille en 1940–1941, edited by Danièle Giraudy, exh. cat. Musée Cantini, Marseille, 2003.

Lefebvre, Henri. "La production de l'espace." *Sociologie de la connaissance marxisme et anthropologie*, special issue of *L'Homme et la société*, no. 31–32, 1974, pp. 15–32. *Persée*, www.persee.fr/doc/homso_ 0018- 4306_ 1974_ num_ 31_ 1_ 1855. Accessed 17 July 2021.

Ocampo, Victoria. "Carta a Waldo Frank." *Sur*, year 1, no. 1, 1931, pp. 7–18. Biblioteca Virtual Miguel de Cervantes, www.cervantesvirtual.com/nd/ark:/59851/bmcf20x2. Accessed 15 April 2021.

Pasternac, Nora. *Sur, una revista en la tormenta: los años de formación, 1931–1944*. Paradiso, 2002.

Péraldi, Michel, and Michel Samson. *Gouverner Marseille : Enquête Sur Les Mondes Politiques Marseillais*. La Découverte, 2006.

Príamo, Luis. "La obra de Grete Stern en la Argentina." *Grete Stern: Obra fotográfica en la Argentina*, exh. cat. Museo de Arte Hispanoamericano Isaac Fernández Blanco, Buenos Aires, 1995, pp. 12–37.

Rogoff, Irit. *Terra Infirma: Geography's Visual Culture*. Taylor and Francis, 2013.

Said, Edward W. *Reflections on Exile and Other Essays*. Harvard University Press, 2002.

Seghers, Anna. *Transit*. Translated by Jeanne Stern, Autrement, 1995.

Stock, Paul, editor. *The Uses of Space in Early Modern History*. Palgrave Macmillan, 2015.

Suleiman, Susan Rubin, editor. *Exile and Creativity. Signposts, Travelers, Outsiders, Backward Glances*. Duke University Press, 2012.

Thurston, Robert Henry. *Histoire de la machine à vapeur*. Editions Decoopman, 2015.

Veyne, Paul. *L'Inventaire des différences*. Seuil, 1976.

Yankelevich, Pablo, editor. *Historia mínima de Argentina*. CDMX, El Colegio de México, 2014.

Contributors

Maddalena Alvi is currently Andrew W. Mellon Fellow at the Rijksmuseum in Amsterdam. In 2021, she completed her Ph.D. on the history of the European art market during the First World War at the University of Cambridge. She holds an MSc in economic and social history from the University of Oxford and an MLitt. in art history from the University of Glasgow. Her research was funded by the British Arts and Humanities Research Council, the German Studienstiftung and the Joint Center for History and Economics (University of Harvard & Cambridge). Before starting her Ph.D., she worked for a private foundation and managed a private art collection in London. Her latest publication is a peer-reviewed article on the German art market during the First World War.

*****

Ekaterina Aygün began her studies at the St Petersburg State University, Department of Oriental Studies (specialization – History of Turkey). In 2019, she was graduated from Istanbul Bilgi University with a master's degree in history. Her master's thesis explored the Ottoman Empire between 1908 and 1913, and Ottoman women through the eyes of two journalists: one from Russia, Ariadna Tyrkova and one from Great Britain, Grace Ellison. She currently works at the LMU Munich on the ERC-funded research project "Relocating Modernism: Global Metropolises, Modern Art and Exile (METROMOD)", and pursues her doctoral research project that deals with Russian-speaking artists in Istanbul at the beginning of the 20th century. In 2020, she was awarded a Travel Grant by the Istanbul Research Institute for her research on Istanbul as a city of 'First-wave emigration' and a place of creativity for Russian-speaking artists. Her most recent publication is "Boğaz'ın Rusları: 1920'li Yıllarda Beyoğlu'ndaki Rus Göçmen Sanatçılar", published in *Toplumsal Tarih* (June 2021), pp. 9–15. Research interests include late Ottoman history, Turkish–Russian relations, urban history, art history and the history of women and gender.

*****

Claudia Cendales Paredes studied art history, ethnology and sociology (minor) at the Ludwig-Maximilians-Universität (LMU) Munich. From 2003 to 2005, she completed a Master of Science in heritage conservation at the Technische Universität Berlin. In 2010, she was awarded her Ph.D. in art history at the Technische Universität Berlin (*Die Park-und Grünanlagen in Bogotá: Entstehung, Bedeutung und Entwicklung 1886–1938*. Imhof, 2013). From 2012, she has worked as a lecturer of art history at many universities in Bogotá, like the Universidad Jorge Tadeo Lozano, and as an independent researcher and curator. In 2016, she received the Herrenhausen-Research-Fellowship from the Leibniz Universität Hannover for a postdoctoral research stay related to international plant trade circuits in parks and gardens. Her research interests and publications focus on garden history, architectural history, heritage conservation and preservation and the intersection of exile and art from the late 19th to the middle of the 20th century. Her publications include: "Artistas migrantes alemanes y austriacos en Colombia: Rutas, redes y recuerdos." *Bauhaus 100+1: Reverberaciones Latinoamericanas* (ongoing); *La vida privada de los parques y jardines públicos – Bogotá 1886–1938*. IDPC Bogotá, 2020; "Die Reisenotizen aus Lateinamerika von zwei Pflanzensammlern des Herrenhäuser Berggartens in Hannover: Hermann Wendland und Clarence K. Horich." *Von Herrenhausen in die Welt. Gärten und Gartenkultur im Spiegel der Sommerakademie Herrenhausen 2015 und 2016*, edited by Sabine Albersmeier and Joachim Wolschke-Bulmahn, AVM Munich, 2018, pp. 313–337; since 2014 more than 100 articles about Latin American artists for the *Allgemeines Künstlerlexikon (AKL)*, edited by Bénédicte Savoy et al., De Gruyter.

* * * * *

Burcu Dogramaci is professor of art history at the Ludwig-Maximilians-Universität (LMU) Munich. She is the co-founder of the "Art Production and Art Theory in the Age of Global Migration" working group established in 2013. She leads the ERC Consolidator Project, "Relocating Modernism: Global Metropolises, Modern Art and Exile (METROMOD)" (2017–2023, www.metromod.net) at the LMU Munich. She is co-director of the Käte Hamburger Kolleg "Dis:connectivity in processes of globalization (global dis:connect)" established in 2021 at LMU Munich. Her research areas are exile, migration and flight, modern art, urbanity and architecture, photography, textile modernism, live art. Recent publications include *Arrival Cities: Migrating Artists and New Metropolitan Topographies in the 20th Century* (Leuven University Press, 2020, ed. with M. Hetschold et al., Open Access, www.library.oapen.org/handle/20.500.12657/41641): *Handbook of Art and Global Migration Theories, Practices, and Challenges*, De Gruyter, 2019 (co-edited with Birgit Mersmann); *Nomadic* Camera. *Fotografie, Exil und*

Migration, special issue of *Fotogeschichte. Beiträge zur Geschichte und Ästhetik der Fotografie*, no. 151, 2019 (co-edited with Helene Roth); *Design Dispersed. Forms of Migration and Flight* (Bielefeld: transcript 2019, ed. with K. Pinther), and *Fotografie der Performance: Live Art im Zeitalter ihrer Reproduzierbarkeit* (Fink, 2018).

* * * * *

JULIA EICHENBERG is a lecturer of modern European history at the universities of Bayreuth/Bamberg and principal investigator of the Freigeist research group "The London Moment", financed by VolkswagenStiftung (2014–2023). Before, she has held fellowships at Trinity College Dublin, University College Dublin and the Centre Marc Bloch, Berlin and has lectured at the universities of Tübingen and HU Berlin. She has widely published on paramilitary violence, pacifism, veterans' welfare, legal history and international collaboration. Her next book on 'The London Moment' explores the transnational collaboration of governments-in-exile in wartime London and its impact on European political communication in the 20th century. Selected recent publications: "Legal Legwork: How Exiled Jurists Negotiated Recognition and Legitimacy in Wartime London." In: *Crafting the International Order. Practitioners and Practices of International Law since* c.*1800* edited by M. Payk and K. Priemel, Oxford University Press 2021, pp. 162–190; *Zeitgeschichte des Rechts*, special issue of *Zeithistorische Forschungen/Studies in Contemporary History (ZHF)*, co-edited with M. Payk, K. Priemel, B. Lahusen, vol. 16, no. 2, 2019; "Macht auf der Flucht. Europäische Regierungen in London (1940–1944)." *Flucht als Handlungszusammenhang*, special issue of *ZHF*, vol. 15, no. 3, 2018, pp. 452–473; *Aftershocks. Violence in Dissolving Empires after the First World War*, special issue of *Journal of Contemporary European History*, vol. 19, no. 3, 2010), edited with J.P. Newman; *The Great War and Veterans' Internationalism* (Palgrave Macmillan, 2013), edited with J.P. Newman.

* * * * *

MARGIT FRANZ received her habilitation in contemporary history with *Gateway India: Deutschsprachiges Exil in Indien zwischen Kolonialherrschaft, Maharadschas und Gandhi* in 2019. Her recent research focuses on German-speaking actors in British India and their connected histories beyond national borders. Her present associations are with the Department of History at the University of Graz, CLIO-Verein für Geschichts- und Bildungsarbeit (Graz), METROMOD (Munich) and the Austrian Cultural Forum in New Delhi. Her recent publications include several entries in METROMOD's Bombay database and other articles related to artists' impact on the cultural life of Bombay, such as "Die multiplen Identitäten und Loyalitäten der Käthe Langhammer." *Das Exil von Frauen. Historische Perspektive und Gegenwart* (biografiA. Neue Ergebnisse der Frauenbiografieforschung, 26), edited by Ilse Korotin and Ursula Stern, Praesens Verlag, 2020, 148–167 or "From Dinner Parties to Galleries: The Langhammer-Leyden-Schlesinger Circle in Bombay – 1940s through the 1950s." *Arrival Cities: Migrating Artists and New Metropolitan Topographies in the 20th Century*, edited by Burcu Dogramaci et al., Leuven University Press, 2020, 73–90.

*****

NILS GROSCH holds the chair in musicology at the University of Salzburg/Austria where he is also Head of Department for art history, musicology and dance studies. He gained his doctorate at the University of Freiburg i. Br. with a dissertation about *Die Musik der Neuen Sachlichkeit*, and completed his habilitation at the University of Basel with a thesis on *Lied und Medienwechsel im 16. Jahrhundert*. His major research interests are music and media, music and migration and popular musical theatre. Nils Grosch co-heads research projects in the field of music, migration and mobility: "Music and Migration" (musik-und-migration.at) and "Music, Migration & Mobility" (musicmigrationmobility.com). Recent articles include "Exil und kulturelle Mobilität. Ernst Krenek und Kurt Weill." *Zeitgenossenschaft! Ernst Krenek und Kurt Weill im Netzwerk der Moderne* (Ernst-Krenek-Studien, vol. 8), edited by Matthias Henke, Argus, 2019, pp. 175–182; "Musik und Mobilität." *Musik und Migration: Ein Theorie- und Methodenhandbuch*, edited by Wolfgang Gratzer et al., Waxmann, 2021; "'Ev'ry hotsy totsy Nazi stand and cheer': Cultural Sensitivity to Musicals about the Third Reich." *The Oxford Handbook of the Global Musical*, edited by Olaf Jubin and Robert Gordon, Oxford University Press, 2021 (with Susanne Scheiblhofer); "Musical Comedy, Pastiche and the Challenge of 'Rewriting'." *Intertextuality in Music: Dialogic Composition*, edited by Violetta Kostka et al., Taylor & Francis/Routledge, 2021, pp. 156–166.

*****

MAREIKE HETSCHOLD has been a doctoral researcher with the ERC project "Relocating Modernism: Global Metropolises, Modern Art and Exile (METROMOD)" at the Ludwig-Maximilians-Universität (LMU) in Munich since 2018. Her doctoral research project deals with the visual culture in Shanghai between 1930 and 1950 and its diverse émigré communities. Her research interests include art and urbanity, architecture, migration and exile. Latest publication: *Arrival Cities: Migrating Artists and New Metropolitan Topographies in the 20th Century*, Leuven, 2020 (co-edited with Burcu Dogramaci et al.).

* * * * *

LOUIS KAPLAN is a professor of art history and visual studies at the University of Toronto where he is also an associate faculty member at the Anne Tannenbaum Centre for Jewish Studies and in the Department of Germanic Languages and Literatures. He is the author of several books including *The Strange Case of William Mumler, Spirit Photographer*, University of Minnesota Press, 2008; *Photography and Humour*, Reaktion Books, 2017; *At Wit's End: The Deadly Discourse on the Jewish Joke*, Fordham, 2020. He was awarded a Getty Library Research Grant in the summer of 2018 for a project exploring "Leo Steinberg's Jewish Questions". He has collaborated with the artist Melissa Shiff using augmented reality and virtual reality in pursuit of *Imaginary Jewish Homelands*.

* * * * *

LAURA KARP LUGO is an associate professor and researcher at the University of Lorraine (Nancy) in contemporary art history. She completed her Ph.D. at Panthéon-Sorbonne University and was awarded the Price of the Musée d'Orsay in 2015. Her research interest focuses on Latin America and on the intersection of exile and art from the late 19th to the middle of the 20th century. From 2007, she worked in several international research institutions, including the Institut national d'Histoire de l'art (INHA, Paris), the Universidad Nacional de Tres de Febrero (UNTREF, Buenos Aires), the Universitat Oberta de Catalunya (UOC-Barcelona) and the Deutsches Forum für Kunstgeschichte (DFK Paris). She is a researcher at the Ludwig-Maximilians-Universität (LMU) in Munich in the ERC project "Relocating Modernism: Global Metropolises, Modern Art and Exile (METROMOD)". Within this project, she works on Buenos Aires as an arrival city for exiled artists in the first half of the 20th century. Recent publications include "Exposer l'Amérique latine : d'une identité à l'autre." Online publication of the Deutsches Forum für Kunstgeschichte, Paris, arthistoricum.net – ART Books, 2022 (ongoing); "Lebensrouten der Emigration. Abreise, Passage, (Zwischen-)Exil und Ankunft." *Leave, left, left. Migrationsphänomene in den Künsten in aktueller und historischer Perspektive*, edited by Burcu Dogramaci et al., Neofelis Verlag, 2020, pp. 105–126 (with M. Hetschold, R. Lee and H. Roth); "Alone Together: Exile Sociability and Artistic Networks in Buenos Aires at the Beginning of the 20th Century." *Arrival Cities. Migrating Artists and New Metropolitan Topographies in the 20th Century*, edited by Burcu Dogramaci et al., Leuven University Press, 2020, pp. 33–54; "L'art espagnol de l'Europe à l'Argentine: mobilités Nord-Sud, transferts et réceptions (1890–1920)." *Artl@s Bulletin*, vol. 5, no. 1, 2016, article 4, pp. 38–49, www.docs.lib.purdue.edu/artlas/vol5/iss1/4.

* * * * *

KATYA KNYAZEVA, from Novosibirsk, Russia, is a historian and a journalist with a focus on urban form, heritage preservation and the Russian diaspora in Shanghai. She is the author of the two-volume history and photographic atlas *Shanghai Old Town: Topography of a Phantom City* (Suzhou Creek Press, 2015 and 2018). Her articles on history and architecture appear in international media and her blog www.avezink.livejournal.com. Her scholarly writing can be found in the Journal of the Royal Asiatic Society China, Global History and Built Heritage. Knyazeva received her second Master's degree from Bologna University and is presently a research fellow at the University of Eastern Piedmont, Italy.

* * * * *

MERVE KÖKSAL graduated in 2015 from the İzmir University of Economics with a first degree. As a graduate student, she studied at Yıldız Technical University (2016–2019) in the Department of Art and Design. Meanwhile, she started to work as a research assistant at Akdeniz University, Faculty of Fine Arts in 2017 and graduated from there in 2019. She was intrigued by the social history of the late Ottoman Empire, especially the artistic and intellectual milieu in 19th century Pera. She completed her master thesis titled *An Examination on the Formation of The Palace Painting Collection during the Abdülhamid II's Reign* under the supervision of Seza Sinanlar Uslu. She is currently pursuing her Ph.D. at the Akdeniz University in Art and Design. Her research interests include the social and cultural history of the late Ottoman Empire, with a particular focus on the occupation of Istanbul (1918–1923); underground culture, transnationalism, social life, cultural and artistic developments related to Pera.

* * * * *

RACHEL LEE is an assistant professor of the history of architecture and urban planning chair at the TU Delft, and an associated researcher with METROMOD. Her research explores the histories of colonial and postcolonial architecture and urbanism at their intersections with migration and exile, transnational practice, heritage, mobility and gender, particularly in South Asia and East Africa. She is currently also a Mellon Fellow with the Canadian Centre for Architecture's "Centring Africa" project. Recent publications include "Engaging the Archival Habitat: Architectural Knowledge and Otto Koenigsberger's Effects." *Comparative Studies of South Asia, Africa and the Middle East.* Special Section: *Architecture as a Form of Knowledge*, vol. 40, no. 3, December 2020, pp. 526–540, "Unlikely Collaborations? Planning Experts from Both Sides of the Iron Curtain and the Making of Abuja." *Transforming Cities: Urbanization and International Development in Africa and Latin America since 1945*, special issue of *Comparativ*, vol. 30, no. 1/2, 2020, pp. 38–59 (with Anne-Katrin Fenk and Monika Motylińska), and "Hospitable Environments: The Taj Mahal Palace Hotel and Green's Hotel as Sites of Cultural Production in Bombay." *Arrival Cities: Migrating Artists and New Metropolitan Topographies in the 20th Century*, edited by Burcu Dogramaci et al., University of Leuven, 2020, pp. 249–268.

* * * * *

Chris McConville holds degrees in history from Monash University and the University of Melbourne. He is currently teaching at Victoria University in Melbourne, Australia and at the University of Applied Sciences Tyrol in Kufstein, Austria. His major professional activities have been as a public historian engaged in landscape heritage, especially in the Victorian goldfields, and urban conservation in Melbourne. His recent publications include *Hanging Rock: A History* (Friends of Hanging Rock, 2018) and "A Five-Kilometre Economy." *Arena,* no. 4, Summer 2020, pp. 17–22 (with Phil Cleary).

* * * * *

Michaela Melián is an artist and musician renowned for her multimedia installations, audio dramas and sonic works. She is a professor for time-based media at the University of Fine Arts Hamburg. Her multimedia and audio-visual works have been shown internationally, most recently at Lenbachhaus Munich, Deichtorhallen Hamburg, Staatsgalerie Stuttgart in Germany, at the Fundació Juan Miró Barcelona in Spain and the Kunsthal Rotterdam in the Netherlands. In 2010, she created *Memory Loops*, an acoustic memorial to the victims of National Socialism, commissioned by the City of Munich. She lives in Munich and Hamburg.

* * * * *

ANNA SOPHIA MESSNER is a researcher at the Institute for Art History/Transcultural Studies at Heinrich-Heine University Düsseldorf. From 2019 to 2022 she was a scientific staff member at the Institute for Art History at the Ludwig-Maximilians-Universität (LMU) in Munich. From 2015 to 2018, she was a doctoral research fellow in the Max-Planck-Research Group "Objects in the Contact Zone – The Cross-Cultural Lives of Things" at the Kunsthistorisches Institut in Florenz – Max-Planck-Institut (KHI). In 2020, she earned her doctoral degree with a project on *Gazing at Palestine/Israel. Visual Geographies of German-Jewish Women Photographers after 1933* at the LMU. Her research focuses on Jewish art, historiography and culture with a special focus on migration and exile, visual culture of Israel and Palestine, transcultural art history as well as the history and theory of photography. Her publications include *Photography and Migration*, special issue of *International Journal for History, Culture and Modernity*, vol. 8, no. 1, 2020 (co-edited with Eva-Maria Troelenberg and Costanza Caraffa) and the volume *Reading Objects in the Contact Zone*, Heidelberg University Publishing, 2021 (co-edited with Eva-Maria Troelenberg and Kerstin Schwankweiler).

* * * * *

ALEXIS NUSELOVICI (NOUSS) is associate dean (Research) and professor of Comparative Literature, Aix-Marseille University. Chairholder, Chaire "Exil et migrations", Collège d'études mondiales, Paris. Research fields: European literature, exile literature, theory of translation. Publications: "Paul Celan. Les lieux d'un déplacement" (published in *Germanica*, no. 47, 2010, pp. 187–189, doi: 10.4000/germanica.1146); *La condition de l'exilé* (Éditions de la Maison des sciences de l'homme, 2015/2018); *Droit d'exil. Pour une politisation de la question migratoire: précédé de Covidexil* (Éditions MIX., 2021).

* * * * *

ROBERT PASCOE is dean laureate and a professor of history at Victoria University in Melbourne. He is the author, co-author or editor of three dozen books and research monographs. Pascoe's chapter is based on work undertaken with Dr Chris McConville on a book series entitled Streets Beneath Our Feet (ongoing). This book series uses theorists such as Kevin Lynch and Deleuze/Guattari to offer new perspectives on interesting and significant urban neighbourhoods worldwide, including Trastevere, Prenzlauer Berg, The Liberties and Boston's North End.

* * * * *

VALENTINA PINO REYES, born in 1987 in Santiago de Chile, has been living in Germany since 2006. After several internships, she trained as a theatre painter at the Konstanz Theater from 2011 to 2015, where she was permanently employed. Since 2015, she has been studying scenic and costume design with Professor Katrin Brack at the Academy of Fine Arts in Munich. She has designed several productions, including at the Residenztheater Marstall, the Münchner Kammerspiele, the Landestheater Coburg and the Landestheater Schwaben. Her artistic work has been supported since 2016 by the Hofbräu Brauerei Munich scholarship, among others. In 2017, she held a student scholarship from the Bavarian State Ministry of Education and Arts, in 2018 she was awarded scholarships from the Richard Stury Foundation and the Grübel Foundation of the Bavarian Academy of Fine Arts in cooperation with the Theater Akademie August Everding and the Goethe Institute Chile for her research work on abandoned theaters in Chile. She is also a fellow of the Studienstiftung des Deutschen Volkes.

*****

HELENE ROTH is a research assistant in art history at the Ludwig-Maximilians-Universität (LMU) in Munich and a member of the ERC Project "Relocating Modernism: Global Metropolises, Modern Art and Exile (METROMOD)" at the Ludwig-Maximilians-Universität Munich. Her Ph.D. project on German-speaking émigré photographers in New York is additionally funded by the Evangelisches Studienwerk Villigst e.V.. Her research interests include art and photography of the 20th and the 21st century with a focus on exile, migration, urbanity, architecture and fashion. Her publications include "'First Pictures': New York through the Lens of Emigrated European Photographers in the 1930s and 1940s", published in *Contact Zones: Photography, Migration and Cultural Encounters in the United States*, Leuven, 2021 (edited by Justin Carville and Sigrid Lien), pp. 111–132; *Arrival Cities: Migrating Artists and New Metropolitan Topographies in the 20th Century*, Leuven, 2020 (co-edited with Burcu Dogramaci et al.) and *Nomadic Camera: Fotografie, Exil und Migration*, special issue of *Zeitschrift für Fotogeschichte: Beiträge zur Geschichte und Ästhetik der Fotografie*, no. 151, 2019 (co-edited with Burcu Dogramaci).

*****

VALERIA SÁNCHEZ MICHEL holds a doctorate in history from El Colegio de México. She is a researcher at the Art Department of the Universidad Iberoamericana in Mexico City where she teaches the courses "Cultural Studies" and "History and Photography". She has undertaken historical research on the formation of institutions. She published a book on the history of the Teaching Center for Foreigners, where she analyzed the institutional development of the unit and its relationship with both the National Autonomous University of Mexico and the national context. She also has several publications on the political and architectural processes behind the construction of the Ciudad Universitaria (as a project that involved allocating an exclusive space for university students, which had repercussions on the University, its organization and its development).

*****

MARINE SCHÜTZ is from Marseille. She studied in a fine art school for five years before shifting to art history studies. In 2015, she submitted her Ph.D. on contemporary art history entitled *Between the Lines: Illustration, prints and Graphic Practices in Pop Art (1950–1975)* (Aix-Marseille University). From 2009 to 2013, she worked as a research officer at the Institut National d'Histoire de l'Art in Paris. From 2016 to 2017, she worked as a grant recipient for the Deutsches Forum für Kunstgeschichte (DFK Paris) where she studied the topic of postcolonial pop in French art in the 1960s. She has taught in several universities in Paris, Grenoble and Lyon. She has earned grants from the TERRA Foundation for American Art and the Getty Library. From 2018 to 2021, she was a postdoctoral researcher within the H2020 project "ECHOES" in which she addressed the relations between contemporary art and colonial histories in the cities of Bristol and Marseille. She is an associate professor in contemporary art at the Université de Picardie Jules Verne.

*****

MAREIKE SCHWARZ (MA art history) addresses questions of public art and public interest. She studied art history, economics and literature in Berlin, Cambridge, Hagen and Munich. Against this interdisciplinary background, her research ranges from social practices to the politics of memory and migration. Her master's thesis on commoning through public art and landscape design was awarded the University Prize of the City of Munich. In 2020, she conducted an oral history project on curating contemporary art in memorial places at the Universidad de Buenos Aires. At present, she holds a doctoral position in the ERC-funded research group "Relocating Modernism: Global Metropolises, Modern Art and Exile (METROMOD)" at LMU, where she focuses on transcultural movements and urban exile remembrance cultures. Her dissertation examines the effects of art in the public sphere. Current publications include:

"Political Agency of Sensory Actions. On Ambient Art Practice and its Atmospheric Effect." *Obscure Ambience*, edited by Kalas Liebfried, Edition Metzel, 2021, pp. 112–125; "Susanne Pittroff's public art: A plural semiosphere of connection", *Tuchfühlung. stay in touch*, edited by Susanne Pittroff, icon Verlag 2021, pp. 139–143. Recent exhibitions include *Global Design Politics* (Maximiliansforum, Munich, 2019).

* * * * *

SEZA SINANLAR USLU finished her studies at the Istanbul University, Department of History of Art in 1996. In 2001, she graduated from Boğaziçi University with a master's degree in History. In 2008, she was awarded her Ph.D. in art history at the Istanbul Technical University. Starting from 2015, she works as an associate professor at Yıldız Technical University, Faculty of Art and Design. Between 2007 and 2009, she was the Istanbul Coordinator of the EU project "MELT – Migration in Europe and Local Tradition". Since Istanbul was the European Capital of Culture in 2010, she undertook the role of assistant coordinator of the "Creative Cities and Creative Industries" Symposium which was supported by UNCTAD. While her academic studies are mostly focused on the cultural and artistic life that develops in the multicultural environment of the 19th–20th centuries in Istanbul, she has also curated various exhibitions such as *Painters of Pera* at Istanbul French Institute (2010) and *In Pursuit of an artist: Mario Prassinos* at Pera Museum (2016).

* * * * *

FELICITAS SÖHNER, D.Phil., historian, has held the position of scientific fellow at the Department of History, Philosophy and Ethics of Medicine at the University of Düsseldorf since 2016. Her research focus is in the medical and social history of the 20th and 21st centuries as well as on European memory culture and its biographical processing. Publications (selections): "Ethical Issues in Archiving and Reusing Interviewees Documents." *Bulletin de l'AFAS. Sonorités*, special issue: *law, ethics and fieldwork: how are research practices changing?* (2022); "Between participation in National Socialist Medicine and everyday administrative action – to the economic argument of the psychiatric 'planning commission' (1941–1945)." *Recognizing the Past in the Present: New Studies on Medicine Before, During and After the Holocaust*, edited by S. Hildebrandt et al., Berghahn Books 2020, pp. 72–190; *Psychiatrie-Enquete: mit Zeitzeugen verstehen. Eine Oral History der Psychiatriereform in der BRD*. Psychiatrie Verlag, 2020; "The impact of dealing with late effects of NS-terror to West-German psychiatric care." (with G. Baader) *Psychiatr Quarterly*, vol. 89, no. 2, 2017, pp. 475–487.

*****

MARINA SOROKINA is a leading research fellow in the Alexander Solzhenitsyn Centre for Studies of Russia Abroad (Moscow, Russia). She received her Ph.D. in historical archives and focuses on the personal, human and professional dimensions of the Russian émigré community in the context of global migrations of the 20th century. The author of many research papers and dictionaries of Russian scholars in exile, she has published a number of volumes of archival manuscripts dealing with Russian refugees. Her current project is "Big Politics and Big Slavistics". Research interests include the social history of science and scholarship, migrant and memory studies. Her recent publications include "Russian addresses of Belgrade: Professors of the Belgrade University" (Moscow, 2021, in the Russian language) and "Russians in Serbia. Pavel and Yurii Lobachev, Diplomat and Painter. Catalogue of the exhibition. Moscow, Belgrade, 2020" (together with Irina Antanasijevich, in Russian and Serbian languages).

*****

JESSICA WILLIAMS STARK is a historian of modern African art and photography. She received her doctorate in history of art and architecture from Harvard University in 2022 and is currently working on her first book project as the McCormick Postdoctoral Research Associate in the history of photography in Princeton's Department of Art and Archaeology. Her research engages the intersections of modernist, feminist and leftist histories and has been generously supported by the Peter E. Palmquist Memorial Fund, the Smithsonian Institution's National Museum of African Art, the Fulbright Program and Harvard University. Stark's work has appeared in *October* (Summer 2020) and in *Women and Photography in Africa: Creative Practices and Feminist Challenges* (2020). She is based in Cape Town.

*****

XIN TONG holds a doctorate in media studies from the University of Hamburg (2021) and has been working as a postdoctoral researcher at the Shanghai Academy of Global Governance & Area Studies, Shanghai International Studies University since 2021. Recent publications include *Transmedia Remembering: Eine Fallstudie des Shanghaier Exils in Deutschland und China seit 1990* (2022); "Around the

Alster, Around the World – The Wolf Brothers in Exile in Shanghai." *Key Documents of German-Jewish History: A Digital Source Edition* (2018); "The Art of Memory: 'Social Bookmarking Hamburg'." *Beyond Democracy: Innovation as Politics*, special issue of *Glocalism: Journal of Culture, Politics and Innovation*, no. 3 (2017, with Noga Stiassny).

*****

FEDERICO MARTÍN VITELLI teaches history at the Universidad Nacional del Sur, Bahía Blanca, Argentina. He is currently pursuing a Doctorate in History at the same institution, supported by an international doctoral scholarship granted by CONICET. His investigations have focused on the study of Spanish republican teachers exiled in different cities of Argentina. They have been published as a chapter in the book *Exilios: Un campo de estudios en expansion*, edited by Soledad Lastra, CLACSO, 2018 ("La inserción de los profesores exiliados republicanos en el medio universitario argentino [The insertion of the exiled republican teachers in the Argentine academic field]"), and as articles in specialized magazines: "La perspectiva comparada desde la historia de los exilios políticos: apuntes y aportes para el análisis (The comparative perspective from the history of political exiles: notes and contributions to the analysis)." *Cuadernos del Sur,* no. 46, vol. 1, 2017, pp. 79–98, and "Imaginar España, vivir en Argentina: la inserción de los profesores exiliados republicanos en las redes intelectuales y culturales en Bahía Blanca (1956–1966) (Imagining Spain, living in Argentina: the insertion of the exiled republican teachers in the intellectual and cultural networks of Bahía Blanca [1956–1966])." *Revista Intellèctus*, vol. 18, no. 2, 2019, pp. 92–123.

*****

DIANA WECHSLER holds a Ph.D. in art history, is a senior researcher at CONICET (National Council for Scientific and Technical Research) and a curator. She is Director of the Instituto de Investigación en Arte y Cultura "Dr. Norberto Griffa" and of the Master's Degree in Curatorial Studies of the Universidad Nacional de Tres de Febrero (UNTREF). She is the artistic director of the museums of this university (MUNTREF) and professor of Curatorial Narratives at UNTREF. She is the co-founder and artistic director of BIENALSUR. Her research work is based on curatorial activity, with exhibitions in different institutions in Berlin, Madrid, Paris, Rome, Milan, Mexico, São Paulo and Buenos Aires, among other cities. She integrates and directs research projects with national and international teams. She directs the research seminar: "Revisiting

Art History" through a Regional Network of University Museums and Archives project grant of the Getty Foundation in the program Connecting Art Histories. She has received grants and fellowships such as the Getty Foundation Postdoctoral Fellowship, and awards for art essays and curatorial studies from the International Association of Art Critics and for Scientific Production from the Argentine Senate. She has been distinguished by the French Republic with the honorary title of Chevalier des Palmes Academiques.

Index

Page numbers in italics refer to illustrations.